ACCOUNTING

A Management Approach

The Willard J. Graham Series in Accounting

ACCOUNTING

A Management Approach

GORDON SHILLINGLAW

Professor of Accounting
Graduate School of Business
Columbia University

PHILIP E. MEYER

Professor of Accounting
School of Management
Boston University

Seventh Edition

1983
RICHARD D. IRWIN, INC.
Homewood, Illinois   60430

ISBN 0-256-02801-X

Library of Congress Catalog Card No. 82–82696

Printed in the United States of America

1 2 3 4 5 6 7 8 9 0 K 0 9 8 7 6 5 4 3

This edition is dedicated
to

Myron J. Gordon

A wise and effective contributor
to five previous editions

Preface

Our title, *Accounting: A Management Approach,* expresses both the objective and the message of this book—to describe the nature, techniques, and uses of accounting from the perspective of people who manage businesses and investments in businesses.

Although our subject, accounting, has undergone an unending series of modifications and refinements over time, its essential character has remained intact. We think that *Accounting: A Management Approach* has had a parallel experience during its 32-year publishing history. While the book's tradition has been our guiding force, we've recognized the need for this seventh edition to update, refine, and improve upon the earlier editions.

EMPHASIS AND APPROACH

This book emphasizes conceptual understanding, but it is by no means all theory and no practice. We never lose sight of the fact that accounting exists because people need to use it. As a result, we concentrate on the significance, meaning, and implications of accounting concepts and practices, rather than on techniques and procedural rules. Although we examine the accounting model as it now exists, we don't hesitate to identify shortcomings and alternative approaches.

Despite the many significant changes in both structure and content in this edition, its objective is essentially the same as that of the previous six editions—to enable the reader to understand the concepts on which accounting information is based and the meaning of the amounts presented in both financial statements prepared for outside parties and accounting reports prepared for management's use. This approach enables us to describe the choices accountants and managers must make *and* to examine the reasons for choosing one measurement or presentation basis instead of others. While we do cover recordkeeping procedures and authoritative pronouncements, they are not emphasized.

ADAPTABILITY

One of this book's distinctive features is the *adaptability* of its 23 chapters to either one- or two-term courses which cover both financial and managerial accounting or financial accounting alone:

The comprehensive two-semester/two-quarter course can cover 10 to 13 chapters each term.

The comprehensive one-semester course can cover as few as 17 or as many as 20 chapters.

The one-term financial accounting course can cover as few as 12 of the 15 accounting and financial reporting chapters.

THE SEVENTH EDITION

Although this edition incorporates the strengths of previous editions, we've strived to introduce a fresh perspective. We've been mindful of the changes which have occurred in the business environment and of the accounting profession's responses. We've also recognized the need to relate accounting to the economic conditions of the 1980s. We have, for instance, adopted the corporate form of enterprise as our focal point from the very outset, and we give considerable attention to the importance of the after-tax perspective, the increasing emphasis on cash flow, and the problems created by persistent price-level inflation.

The financial coverage

In Part One, *Accounting Basics* (six chapters), the chapter on purchases, sales, and payroll accounting has been eliminated, and the chapter on financial statement preparation has been completely reorganized. Discussion of product costing techniques has been removed from the introductory chapter on manufacturing cost flows, and material on cash flow statements has been moved into the funds statement chapter.

In Part Two, *Financial Accounting* (six chapters), the inventory chapter has been simplified, and average costing has been reintroduced. The discussion of capitalization of costs and the depreciation of plant assets have been combined in a single, integrated chapter, and the accelerated cost recovery system (ACRS) is included in the discussion of income tax deferrals. The coverage of present-value techniques now provides a stronger conceptual foundation, and the chapter on business combinations has been completely rewritten.

In Part Three, *Financial Reporting* (three chapters), we've adopted a fresh approach to describe the significance of funds flows, including a no-worksheet method to prepare the statement of changes in financial position. Our coverage of measuring the effects of changing resource prices reflects the reporting requirements of FASB Statement No. 33.

The managerial coverage

Consistent with a decision-making perspective, Part Four, *Managerial Accounting* (eight chapters), begins with the fundamentals of incremental analysis. We introduce product costing—a new chapter on process costing covering both full costing and variable costing, and a completely reorganized chapter on job order costing which also includes a section on variable costing. We then proceed to discuss capital expenditure decisions, budgetary planning, and cost-volume-profit analysis.

The coverage then turns to control reporting to management, and here too we've adopted a novel approach. We first discuss profit reporting in a profit-center environment—and include basic coverage of transfer pricing. We have two reasons for beginning with internal profit reporting: Profit reporting is more comprehensive than departmental cost reporting (which is the conventional point of entry into control accounting), and profit reporting provides a substantive link between product costing/budgetary planning and the remaining chapters on control reporting.

We discuss cost control reporting primarily at the departmental and project level, beginning with basic concepts and reporting objectives, implemented by standard costing and flexible budgeting. After a brief look at project control reporting, the coverage concludes with a discussion of system design, analysis of overhead variances, and behavioral issues arising in the implementation of control systems. An important innovation is the expansion of the concept of flexible budgeting to resolve the long-standing question of how to integrate direct labor and direct materials usage and price variances into the analysis of overhead spending variances. Detailed journal entries and the use of accounts to derive cost variances have been omitted to make way for this integrative approach; since such material is essentially procedural, it can best be covered in second-level courses.

Overall teachability

Understandability of the text has been enhanced by the extensive use of numerical examples throughout the narrative, and numerous exhibits, tables, and diagrams. We continue to use a conversational writing style, highlight key technical terms, and provide study-reminders at appropriate points. Given the vital importance of having end-of-chapter material which reinforces understanding, addresses nuances and subtleties, and arouses interest in the subject, we offer a set of rich and varied exercises and problems which both challenge the student and provide the basis for wholesome classroom discussion. Each chapter's problems implement and complement its text, and each chapter has a series of independent study problems for which solutions are presented in Appendix B.

A WORD TO STUDENTS

Although we've made every effort to make this book clear and readable, it's still no novel. In our own teaching, we encourage our students to study the illustrations carefully, verify each amount, and even replicate the calculations. The next step is to work the independent study problems which are found at the end of each chapter. Once this has been done, the student should be in an excellent position to prepare solutions for the problems assigned by the instructor.

ACKNOWLEDGMENTS

We are grateful to our constituency for the success of the previous editions, and for the many helpful suggestions which have been offered over the years. A special note of appreciation goes to Myron J. Gordon, to whom this edition is dedicated. Despite the many changes we have made from edition to edition, the effects of his efforts on previous editions can be seen in every chapter. Our thanks also to Joshua Ronen, coauthor of the sixth edition, for his lasting contribution to this work. We regret that he had to limit his participation to that one edition only.

Kenneth Lambert, Melvin McClure, and James Sepe reviewed the sixth edition in great detail and offered many suggestions for improvements which we found invaluable. Charles Bastable, Joel Berk, and Carl Nelson reviewed drafts of several chapters in the present edition, and offered advice and counsel which led to major changes in content and presentation. We are grateful to them for giving so generously of their time and wisdom.

Many users of the sixth edition wrote to suggest changes in the text or problem material. Among these were William Baber, Dahsien Bao, Dan Givoly, David Gordon, Philip Meyers, Hugo Nurnberg, Pekin Ogan, Nancy Preis, William Ruland, Sharon Springer, and Victoria Rymer.

Material from the Uniform CPA Examinations (American Institute of Certified Public Accountants) and Certificate in Management Accounting Examinations (Institute of Management Accounting) has been adapted or reproduced with permission, for which we are most grateful. We express our appreciation to Charles Bastable, John Burton, and Carl Nelson for permission to use or adapt a number of their problems, and to the IMEDE management development institute in Lausanne, Switzerland, for permission to reproduce a number of cases from its collection. We also thank Janet Daniels for her painstaking review of the problem solutions in the *Instructor's Manual*, and Evelyn Felder for her patience, understanding, and willingness to type her way through draft after draft, and to keep the material flowing efficiently from author to author despite blizzards, postal delays, and ailing copying machines.

To our wives, Barbara and Ricki, we are grateful for their fortitude and good cheer.

GORDON SHILLINGLAW
PHILIP E. MEYER

Contents

PART TWO

FINANCIAL ACCOUNTING

PART THREE

FINANCIAL REPORTING

Part one

ACCOUNTING BASICS

1

The accounting environment

Accounting is the process of identifying and measuring economic variables in individual businesses and other organizations *and* communicating information based on these measurements to users who need to make informed judgments about the organization and its managers.[1] The purpose of this initial chapter is to identify the main branches of accounting and describe the environment in which accounting takes place. Here—and throughout the book—we'll concentrate on the private-sector business enterprise. The special problems of accounting in government bodies and private-sector, not-for-profit organizations require a detailed examination that is beyond our immediate objective.

MAJOR BRANCHES OF ACCOUNTING

One group of accounting measurements is designed to help *investors* evaluate the performance of an organization's managers and decide whether to let the organization use their goods or money, and on what terms. This is the focus of *financial accounting*. Reports based on accounting data for this purpose are known as *financial statements*.

A second type of accounting information is prepared to help managers decide how to use the resources entrusted to them and to monitor how effectively and efficiently those resources are being

---

[1] This definition is derived from the definition provided in *A Statement of Basic Accounting Theory* (Sarasota, Fla.: American Accounting Association, 1966), p. 1.

3

used. This is the focus of *managerial accounting*. Accounting data are also used to determine how much the business must pay in taxes, particularly income taxes (*tax accounting*), and in some situations to determine the amounts outsiders must pay the business for undertaking specific activities (*reimbursement accounting*).

Financial accounting is the primary topic of the first 15 chapters; managerial accounting is the subject of the final 8. Because tax accounting and reimbursement accounting are highly specialized topics, we'll devote little space to them.

THE ECONOMIC ROLE OF FINANCIAL ACCOUNTING

Accounting measurements are essential to the efficient allocation of resources in a market-based economic system. The prudent investor uses financial data to identify companies and industries in which future economic performance is likely to be strong. In general, companies with strong financial statements are usually far more successful in raising funds than companies with poor recent financial performance. In other words, financial statements have an effect on the allocation of available investment capital.

This claim may appear exaggerated. By the time companies publish the formal statements that summarize the financial effects of their operations and the other events of a period, the best-informed investors ordinarily will already have obtained most of the information the statements contain, at least in qualitative form. Only in unusual situations will the statements contain major surprises.

Even so, the published statements are both necessary and important. The first—and perhaps the most obvious—reason is that they provide quantitative confirmation of the judgments and estimates outside investors and analysts have made on the basis of previously available information. The variables investors try to forecast are either directly reported in financial statements (e.g., sales volume) or closely related to them (e.g., share of the market).

Second, the financial statements provide a great deal of detail, particularly in their footnotes, which investors can use in analyzing the company and preparing estimates of its future progress. Investors' estimates of key financial variables are likely to be considerably less accurate in the absence of credible financial statements.

Both these functions are important because most business activity in the United States and in other industrialized countries is conducted by large companies, directed by professional managers rather than by the investors who provide investment funds. Since they don't participate actively in management, most investors can't oversee the use of their money firsthand. Instead, they have to rely on reports based on accounting data to learn how effectively management has used the company's resources. Providing these reports is a price management has to pay for the privilege of managing the investors' capital.

ACCOUNTING: A MANAGEMENT APPROACH

The title of this book is *Accounting: A Management Approach.* How do we reconcile this with the fact that we'll spend about two thirds of our time on financial accounting and only one third on managerial accounting? The answer is simple. Managers approach accounting information as consumers rather than as producers of information; they aren't interested in generating accounting data. Instead, they want to interpret and use the data in performing various managerial processes, mainly in making decisions on how to use the resources of the business and in monitoring the effects of the actions they and their subordinates take.

The main difference between a *management* approach and most other approaches to the study of accounting is that it emphasizes the concepts accounting systems are based on *and* the meanings to be attached to accounting information. It ignores or touches only lightly on the procedures accountants use to process, accumulate, and summarize accounting data. For this reason we have no chapter on data processing, nor do we get very far into the details of such matters as who keeps track of what or who gets how many copies of what documents. Managers and managers-to-be who are studying accounting do need to work with numerical illustrations and exercises, but the purpose is to achieve a broad understanding of accounting information, not to attain proficiency in numerical manipulation.

A management approach includes a study of the fundamentals of financial accounting, mainly because managers' performance and the strength and performance of the businesses they manage are continuously being evaluated by the owners and other investors. Financial accounting information plays an important role in this process. The company's managers can't be indifferent to the messages the financial statements present to these evaluators.

Managers also need to understand financial accounting because they often have to negotiate with bankers, laywers, and others in connection with the issuance or redemption of corporate securities. They need to be able to discuss accounting issues with the company's accountants because some of the actions management takes may depend on how they will be accounted for. In addition, accountants' measurements often call for the use of professional judgment, and input from managers may be important—hence the need to understand the issues.

Underlying both these reasons is one that may be even more basic. A company's financial accounting system can be regarded as a model of the business as a whole. A manager who understands how various kinds of events affect this model is likely to understand how these events affect the business itself. Furthermore, many concepts in financial accounting apply to managerial accounting as well. Seeing their origins in financial accounting therefore is a useful way to understand their use in managerial accounting.

ACCOUNTANTS AND ACCOUNTING STANDARDS

Except in very small businesses, the people who prepare company financial statements and make other accounting measurements are employees of the company itself. Although these employees have a good deal of freedom to decide how to carry out their responsibilities, nonemployees have some influence, too. In this section, we'll describe the company's accounting staff and explain briefly how others are likely to affect accounting measurements.

The company's accounting staff

Most people who work in accounting are employed directly by businesses and other organizations. They prepare payrolls, record purchases and sales, and keep track of their employers' property. They prepare financial statements that summarize the effects on the organization of activities and events that have already taken place, and they help management develop budget plans for the future. They participate in the design of systems to do all this and help management understand the meaning of the figures that emerge from these systems.

Most activities of the accounting staff are routine clerical functions for which a college education is unnecessary. Superimposed on this routine procedural work are highly varied analytical tasks requiring a good deal of technical training and understanding of business operations. Most of the people who perform these tasks have college or graduate degrees. Overseeing and coordinating all these accountants is the chief accounting officer or *controller,* usually a person with many years of experience in subordinate positions. In a large company, the controller will have a number of immediate subordinates with titles such as assistant controller, plant controller, or divisional controller. We'll examine their duties in Part Four.

Many of the people now moving toward higher positions of this sort in the United States have *certificates in management account-*

ing (CMA). The CMA designation is granted to those who meet the experience, educational, and examination requirements of the Institute of Management Accounting, an offshoot of a professional society of managerial accountants, the National Association of Accountants. The Society of Management Accountants of Canada awards the Registered Industrial Accountant (RIA) certificate, and comparable certification arrangements exist in other countries as well. Possession of one of these certificates isn't an official requirement for advancement in controllership unless the company itself makes such a requirement, but it provides evidence of knowledge and skills that management may find useful in its employment and promotion decisions.

Setting financial accounting standards

In preparing company financial statements, the company's accountants must follow the measurement guidelines known collectively as *generally accepted accounting principles.* Generally accepted accounting principles evolved gradually and informally during several centuries, but further development is now entrusted in most countries to formal rule-making bodies. In the United States, for example, responsibility for specifying how accounting measurements are to be made is vested in the Financial Accounting Standards Board (FASB), created in 1973 with the support of the major professional associations of accountants and financial executives. The FASB's major pronouncements are called *statements of financial accounting standards.*

The FASB is a creature of the private sector, sponsored and financed primarily by corporations, accounting firms, and other nongovernment organizations. Governments also have an interest in private-sector accounting; the major federal government body with power to influence financial accounting standards in the United States is the Securities and Exchange Commission (SEC). The SEC has generally interpreted its role as deciding what must be disclosed and reported, usually allowing the FASB and its predecessors to determine how accounting variables are to be measured.

Financial accounting and reporting by nonbusiness organizations in the United States attracted little public interest until the 1970s, when the financial difficulties experienced by the city governments of New York and Cleveland renewed interest. Responsibility for measurement and reporting standards for private-sector, not-for-profit organizations has been assumed by the FASB, and a new Government Accounting Standards Board has been proposed to play a comparable role for public-sector organizations.

Auditing

Investors accept financial statements because they know they are based on generally accepted accounting principles. They know this because the statements have been reviewed by independent accountants known as *auditors*—trained professionals who are *not* employees of the company being audited. Auditing for this purpose can be defined as a systematic process of obtaining, evaluating, and reporting evidence on how well procedures or tested information satisfy previously established criteria (such as generally accepted accounting principles), or how valid a set of tested assertions appears to be.

To make the comparisons required by an audit, auditors must examine not only the statements themselves but also the records on which they have been based and the company's system of *internal controls,* including *internal audits.* Internal controls are procedures and rules the business managers establish to assure that the assets are protected from loss as a result of carelessness, dishonesty, or poor judgment. Internal audits, which are performed by specially trained company employees, test whether established procedures are being followed and controls are operating properly. The better the control system and the more thorough the internal audits, the less work independent auditors have to do to assure themselves that the financial statements conform to generally accepted accounting principles.

Internal controls are established because management is convinced they will produce benefits in excess of their costs. They became the subject of public concern in the United States in the 1970s in the aftermath of well-publicized illegal payments by business corporations to political candidates and foreign officials. As a result, the Foreign Corrupt Practices Act of 1977 established federal requirements for extensive internal controls. The scope of these requirements is likely to change from time to time, but the requirements themselves seem likely to remain.

We should emphasize that management, not auditors, prepares financial statements. The auditors examine the underlying accounting assumptions, principles, and procedures management has adopted, but the statements themselves are management's responsibility. This is made clear in the declaration in the upper part of Exhibit 1–1. This declaration was published by the management of Raytheon Company as part of its financial statements for 1981. The declaration in the lower part is the report (known as the *audit opinion*) the company's auditors prepared upon completion of their audit. It shows that they were satisfied that the statements conform to generally accepted accounting principles.

EXHIBIT 1–1.   Illustrative Management Declaration and Auditors' Opinion

Raytheon Company has prepared the financial statements and related data contained in this Annual Report. The company's financial statements have been prepared in conformity with generally accepted accounting principles and reflect judgments and estimates as to the expected effects of transactions and events currently being reported. Raytheon is responsible for the integrity and objectivity of the financial statements and other financial data included in this report. To meet this responsibility, the company maintains a system of internal accounting controls to provide reasonable assurance that assets are safeguarded and that transactions are properly executed and recorded. The system includes policies and procedures, internal audits and company officers' reviews.

The Audit Committee of the Board of Directors is composed solely of outside directors. The Committee meets periodically and, when appropriate, separately with representatives of the independent certified public accountants, company officers and the internal auditors to monitor the activities of each.

Upon recommendation of the Audit Committee, Coopers & Lybrand, independent certified public accountants, have been selected by the Board of Directors to examine the company's financial statements and their report follows.

Sheldon Rutstein   *D. Brainerd Holmes*   *Thomas L. Phillips*

We have examined the balance sheets of Raytheon Company and Subsidiaries Consolidated at December 31, 1981 and 1980, and the related statements of income, stockholders' equity and changes in financial position for each of the three years in the period ended December 31, 1981. Our examinations were made in accordance with generally accepted auditing standards and, accordingly, included such tests of the accounting records and such other auditing procedures as we considered necessary in the circumstances.

In our opinion, the financial statements referred to above present fairly the financial position of Raytheon Company and Subsidiaries Consolidated at December 31, 1981 and 1980, and the results of their operations and the changes in their financial position for each of the three years in the period ended December 31, 1981, in conformity with generally accepted accounting principles applied on a consistent basis.

Coopers & Lybrand

The audit opinion in Exhibit 1–1 is known as a "clean" opinion. If the auditors had been dissatisfied with some major aspect of the financial statements or the system used to generate the underlying data, they would have issued a "qualified" opinion, expressing their reservations on the amounts in question. Qualified opinions expressing major reservations as to the financial statements of large business enterprises in the United States are extremely rare: management will either make the changes the auditors call for or provide enough evidence to convince the auditors to withdraw their objections.

The audits of most published financial statements are performed by organizations known as public accounting firms. The firms with headquarters in the United States are organized as partnerships; each of the largest among them has more than 1,000 partners and operates in offices throughout the United States and in many other countries. As Exhibit 1–2 shows, each firm has three major divi-

EXHIBIT 1–2.   Divisions of Major Public Accounting Firms

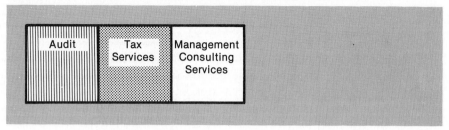

sions—audit, tax, and management consulting—but the audit division is the largest by far.

All the partners in the audit divisions of these large firms and most of the professional staff are professionally certified. Those with certificates issued in the United States are known as *certified public accountants* (CPAs); in Canada and the United Kingdom they are called *chartered accountants* (CAs). These people have satisfied the educational, experience, and examination requirements established by the states, provinces, or other jurisdictions in which they practice.

In performing the audit, the auditor of a U.S. business is guided by auditing standards and procedures based in part on long-standing practices and in part on pronouncements of the American Institute of Certified Public Accountants (AICPA), the professional organization of licensed CPAs in the United States.

Influences on managerial accounting

Management generally gets much more information from the company's accounting system than is prepared for external financial reporting. In general, outsiders have no authority to limit management's freedom to design the portion of its accounting system that provides this additional information. There is no Managerial Accounting Standards Board. The Management Accounting Practices Committee of the National Association of Accountants does issue guidelines on these matters from time to time, but it has no enforcement power. The Society of Management Accountants of Canada publishes monographs on managerial accounting topics periodically, but again their recommendations aren't binding.

Government has had a relatively minor influence on accounting for internal use. Statistical reporting requirements on such matters as employees' wages have undoubtedly affected the information base that is available to management, and income taxation also has affected the measurements of some variables, but the government's influence in a broad sense has been limited mainly to companies in regulated industries and to companies with substantial government contracts. Many of these contracts base the contract price on cost, and contractors have designed their systems to meet the government's demands for cost data. Such systems are often very different from those that otherwise might have been adopted. The Cost Accounting Standards Board, which was created by the U.S. Congress and operated from 1972 to 1980, established standards used for this purpose on cost-based negotiated defense contracts of the U.S. government.

The main constraint on management's freedom in system design is cost. Most accounting systems have to serve several purposes simultaneously, and clerical costs will skyrocket if every variable (for example, the cost of goods sold) has to be measured in several different ways, one for each purpose. Since externally oriented measurements have to be made anyway, the obvious solution is to use these for internal use as well, unless they are very badly suited to managerial needs. Management has to decide in each case whether the benefits of separate measurements for managerial uses exceed the costs of making them.

THE CONCEPTUAL FRAMEWORK OF ACCOUNTING

Although accounting has been practiced for centuries, it has only been since the 1970s that accountants have been definitively addressing the theory and principles of their discipline. The Financial Accounting Standards Board is currently engaged in a project to identify a conceptual framework for financial accounting. The framework is expected to be a coherent system of interrelated objectives and concepts that will prescribe the nature, function, and limits of accounting and financial reporting. The project has already reached the point of discussing specific financial reporting issues. We'll limit ourselves at this introductory stage, however, to summarizing the board's definition of the objectives of financial reporting and its identification of the qualitative characteristics of accounting information.[2]

---

[2] This entire section is a condensation of the first two statements emerging from the concepts project: Financial Accounting Standards Board, *Statement of Financial Accounting Concepts No. 1: Objectives of Financial Reporting by Business Enterprises* (November 1978), and *Statement of Financial Accounting Concepts No. 2: Qualitative Characteristics of Accounting Information* (May 1980). Condensed by permission.

Objectives of financial reporting

Financial reporting provides information that is useful to present and potential investors, creditors, and others in making rational investment, credit, and other decisions. Financial reporting enables these users to assess the amounts, timing, and uncertainty of prospective cash receipts from dividends or interest and the proceeds from the sale, redemption, or maturity of securities or loans. In addition, financial reporting provides information about an enterprise's economic resources, its obligations, and the effects of transactions, events, and circumstances on these resources and obligations.

Another important objective of financial reporting—which many people believe is the *most* important—is to provide information about financial performance during individual time periods. This is especially noteworthy because investors and creditors often use information about the past to assess the future prospects of an enterprise. Indeed, the contemporary expression *bottom line,* signifying a concise end result, has its origins in the reports of past financial performance.

In addition to measuring an enterprise's financial performance, financial reporting provides information about how funds are obtained and used, about borrowing and repaying cash, and about transactions between an enterprise and its investors. Another aspect of performance that is part of financial reporting is management stewardship. This means that besides the enterprise's managers being accountable to the owners for the custody and safekeeping of enterprise resources, managers are also accountable for their efficient and profitable use.

Qualitative characteristics

Accounting information has a number of characteristics that must be defined mainly in qualitative terms. These relate to the central accounting objective of *usefulness* to decision makers. To be useful, financial reporting information must be *understandable* to people who have reasonable familiarity with business activities and are willing to study the information with reasonable diligence. Decision usefulness also implies *relevance* and *reliability,* two characteristics inherent in the information itself. Two other characteristics, *costliness* and *materiality,* provide bases for judging whether the information is worth paying for. A few introductory words about each will be useful here.

Relevance.   For information to be relevant, it must be able to *make a difference.* Information can make a difference to decisions by improving decision makers' capacities to predict or to confirm or correct their earlier expectations. In this sense, the information has predictive value or feedback value, or both. For information to be relevant, it must also be *timely*. This means it should be available to decision makers before it loses its capacity to influence decisions. If information isn't available when needed or if it becomes available so long after the reported events that it has no value for future action, it lacks relevance and is of little or no use.

Reliability. For information to be reliable, it must faithfully represent the phenomena it purports to measure or describe. A second ingredient of reliability is that the information should be *neutral* in the sense that financial reporting doesn't color the image it communicates to influence behavior in some particular direction. A third aspect of reliability is that the information be *verifiable:* Since uncertainty affects accounting measures, verifiability means in effect that several accountants would likely arrive at the same accounting result.

Costliness. While the information provided by financial reporting benefits users, the enterprise itself incurs costs to produce the information. Although the monetary costs of keeping records and compensating accountants come to mind, other information costs also must be considered. One is the effect of any loss of competitive advantage that results from the disclosure of information. Disclosure of particular products' profit margins, for example, could have an adverse effect on a company's ability to price its output. Costliness in a financial reporting context therefore means that the benefits of information provided should equal or exceed the cost.

Materiality. Some accounting measurements must reflect the accountants' estimates of amounts no one can know with certainty. The independent auditors therefore may disagree with the estimates the company's accountants have made. Measurement errors can also occur, even in the most sophisticated accounting systems. Accountants use the concept of materiality to identify errors or disagreements that are large enough to affect investors' decisions. Errors or disagreements that are too small to be classified as material in amount need not be corrected before the financial statements are published.

The framework's contribution

The development of a conceptual framework offers several potential benefits to both preparers and users of accounting information. It will help the FASB to establish accounting standards, and it will provide accountants with a frame of reference within which to resolve accounting questions for which specific standards haven't been developed. It will also determine the bounds for judgment by accountants in preparing financial reports, and it may foster greater intercompany comparability in financial reporting. The conceptual framework may also turn out to be the vehicle through which users of financial statements obtain greater understanding of and confidence in financial reporting.

SUMMARY

Accounting is the primary means of organizing and reporting information, mostly in financial terms, for the use of an organization's management and outsiders. Accounting designed for outsiders is known as financial accounting; measurement and reporting for internal consumption are the domain of managerial accounting.

Accounting measurements for financial reporting to investors must follow the prescriptions laid down by financial accounting standards. Many of these standards provide only very broad guidelines, and accountants must use their judgment in applying them. Even so, the standards underlying published financial statements are intended to apply to all companies in like situations, and the certified public accountants who audit the statements attest that they have been followed.

The Financial Accounting Standards Board, which issues statements of financial accounting standards in the United States, is also carrying out a project to codify the concepts underlying these standards. The first statement of concepts identified decision usefulness as the primary objective of financial statements. The second statement identified relevance, reliability, costliness, and materiality as the main qualitative characteristics of financial information.

The company's accountants are subject to no such external constraints for internal managerial accounting. Accounting measurements for managerial use can take any form as long as they give management the information it wants at a price it is willing to pay.

KEY TERMS

Auditing

Certificate in management accounting

Certified public accountant

Controller

Financial accounting

Financial accounting standards

Financial statements

Generally accepted accounting
   principles

Internal controls

Managerial accounting

EXERCISES AND PROBLEMS

1. Distinguish between financial accounting and managerial accounting. How does managerial accounting differ from a "management approach" to accounting?

2. What are the reasons for the practice in the United States of having a private-sector body (the Financial Accounting Standards Board) rather than a government body codify accounting rules? What arguments can you advance against this practice?

3. What is the economic role of reports that attempt to tell investors what resources companies have and how effectively they have used these resources? What economic effects would you expect to result from a government ban on the publication of these reports?

4. What is the role of the external (independent) auditors who attest to the financial reports issued by investor-owned business corporations? Could these reports play the economic role you assigned to them in answer to question 3 if the external auditors' functions were abolished?

5. Why do companies have more flexibility in managerial accounting than in financial accounting? Is this flexibility desirable?

6. In what ways would you expect the qualitative characteristics of accounting information to differ when applied to managerial accounting rather than financial reporting?

7. Government bodies that levy taxes on businesses generally provide their own definitions of how pretax performance is to be measured. Some countries require companies to use these same definitions when they prepare their reports to investors; in other countries, including the United States, accountants insist on maintaining significant differences between tax reporting and investor reporting. What arguments can you think of to support each of these positions?

8. It has sometimes been argued that each business should be free to make accounting measurements in any way it chooses as long as it makes full accounting disclosure. Others have argued that all enterprises should make their accounting measurements in identical ways. What are the differences between accounting measurement and accounting disclosure? What are the relative advantages of the two positions?

9. To what extent should accountants consider the qualitative characteristic of costliness in their decisions on what and how to measure and report to managers and investors?

10. Prepare a brief list of the rights and responsibilities to the public you believe lawyers and physicans have. Should independent public accountants or managerial accountants have rights and public responsibilities similar to those you have listed? Why should they be alike or different?

11. What should be the professional qualifications of members of the Financial Accounting Standards Board? What criteria should they use in deciding the content of accounting rules?

12. Why is certification as a certified public accountant or chartered accountant required of those who issue opinions on the financial statements of investor-owned companies, while possession of the certificate in management accounting or certification as a registered industrial accountant isn't always required of those who prepare financial statements for use by management?

13. Think of an organization you have been closely associated with, such as a business, club, or religious group. Who used information on that organization's resources and economic performance? What information was provided? Why was this information considered necessary?

14. Data for owners' decisions. Angus MacTavish scratched his head in bewilderment. "I can't figure it out," he said. "I've been running this business for almost a year, and I have more customers by far than I had expected when I started. I have had to hire a new bookkeeper just to get out the bills to my customers and to record their payments when they come in. Yet here I am, just before Christmas, and I don't have enough cash in the bank to pay for that new coat I promised to buy my wife if the business did well. I wonder what has gone wrong."

MacTavish went into business for himself on January 1, 19x1. He took $30,000 from his savings, rented a store, bought a stock of merchandise from a wholesaler, hired a shop assistant, and opened his doors for business. The store proved to be in an excellent location, and MacTavish quickly earned a reputation of being an honest merchant with good-quality merchandise and favorable prices. As the year wore on, his store became more and more crowded with customers, and he had to add an extra clerk to handle the business.

During the year, he bought one additional display cabinet to display his stock of a new line of products that a manufacturer's representative offered to him. Other than this, he didn't recall any major purchases of furniture or equipment. It seemed to him, however, that the better his business became, the less cash he had in the bank.

MacTavish was confident that his December business would bring in enough cash so that he needn't worry about not being able to meet the payroll at the end of December, but, even so, he would have a good deal less cash in the bank at the end of the year than he had when he started in business. This disturbed him because, as he put it, "I have sunk everything I have into this business, given up a good steady job with a strong company, and have worked day and night to make a go of it. If it's not going to pay off, I'd like to know it soon so that I can sell out and go back to work with someone else. I've made a lot of sacrifices this past year to go into business for myself, and I'd like to know whether it was all worthwhile."

This statement was made by MacTavish to Thomas Carr, a local public accountant to whom he had turned for advice. Carr replied that the first thing that he would have to do would be to try to draw up a set of financial statements for the MacTavish store that would summarize the results of the first year's operations to date.

a. To what extent does the decline in MacTavish's cash balance indicate the success or failure of his business operations during this period? What other explanations can you offer for this change? How would you measure the degree of success achieved by the store during its first year?

b. If you were MacTavish, what kinds of information would you need before you could decide whether to stay in business or to sell out? How much of this information would you expect Carr to be able to supply?

c. Assuming that MacTavish decides to stay in business and decides that he needs a bank loan to provide him with additional cash, what kinds of information do you think the banker would have to have before approving the loan? Would this necessarily be the same as the information needed by Carr?

15. Data for owners' decisions. "We can't do business if you don't give me any more to go on than that," said Claude Montrone. After 15 years on the marketing staff of a large manufacturer of office supplies and equipment, Montrone was thinking of going into business for himself. A small inheritance, added to the accumulated savings of the past 15 years, gave him approximately $70,000 to invest. His older brother had indicated that he would be willing to invest up to $15,000 if he felt that the business venture was sound. Montrone also hoped to borrow from his bank additional amounts as needed. These amounts would be repaid during the first five years of the new venture. The manager of his bank had said that the bank would be happy to consider a loan application, but of course the actual granting of the loan would depend on the bank's appraisal of the ability of the business to generate enough funds to pay back the loan plus interest.

The statement quoted at the beginning of this case was directed to Paul Alain, owner of a store in Nutley, New Jersey. Alain owned several enterprises, and as he approached retirement age, he found it increasingly difficult to do an adequate management job in each one. Therefore, he had decided to sell his most important business, the Alain Stationery Store, and he was offering to sell the store's assets for $150,000. The buyer would also have to accept the obligation to pay the amounts owed to the store's suppliers (accounts payable), amounting to about $20,000.

Montrone thought he might be able to persuade Alain to spread some of the purchase price over a five-year period, but he doubted Alain would come down in his price as a result of bargaining. The purchaser would receive a five-year renewable lease on the store itself, the goods in inventory, and the amount owed to the store by some of its customers. If he bought the store, Montrone would have Alain's list of customers, and he saw no reason why he would not be able to keep the two store clerks who had been working in the store for more than five years.

Montrone had inspected the store and toured the area in and around

Nutley to get some idea of the location of his customers and potential customers and the quality of the competition. He was generally familiar with the competitive situation in the area and felt that he could develop considerable business with small and medium-sized commercial and industrial companies in the area. Alain gave him the names of several of his larger customers but was unwilling to show Montrone any details on his business with these customers.

The only data Montrone had were the following, all supplied to him by Alain:

Year	Sales to Customers	Salary and Dividends Paid to Alain
1973	$155,000	$17,000
1974	150,000	17,000
1975	165,000	17,000
1976	195,000	20,000
1977	190,000	20,000
1978	180,000	19,000
1979	195,000	22,000
1980	210,000	25,000
1981	220,000	27,000
1982	205,000	26,000

a. What additional information would Montrone want to have before deciding whether to buy this business? How much of this information would you expect to find in the accounting records of Alain Stationers, Inc.?

b. If you were Montrone's banker, what information would you want to have to assist you in evaluating a loan request from Montrone? Would this information be any different from the information Montrone would want for deciding whether to buy the business?

c. To what extent would you expect accounting data to have entered into Alain's decision to sell the store and to set the price at $150,000? What kind of data should be looked for in making these decisions?

d. If you were Montrone, what services would you expect an independent accountant—that is, an accountant not in Alain's employ—to render in connection with this acquisition?

2

Basic financial accounting concepts

Accountants think of a business as a set of resources gathered together under a common control and used to carry out interrelated functions to produce goods or services for outside customers and thereby generate profits for the owners. Our objective in this chapter is to set forth the basic concepts accountants use in financial accounting and apply these to a simple set of business activities.

BUSINESS OPERATIONS, RESOURCES, AND PERFORMANCE

Before a business can operate, it must have (1) one or more products or services to offer clients or customers, (2) a manager or managers, and (3) resources. Some businesses operate by buying goods ("merchandise") which they offer for sale to potential customers. Other businesses perform services for their customers (e.g., hair cutting or investment advice). Still others buy raw materials and process them into manufactured products which they offer to outside customers.

The business enterprise gets its first resources when the owners invest cash or other property in the business. They then appoint or elect managers. In some cases, the owners may be their own managers, but this is rare in large businesses. The managers then obtain the use of phsyical property, such as buildings and machinery, and hire any other people they need to get the business going.

The operating cycle

With these actions in the background, each business enterprise takes the first step in its *operating cycle.* For example, the operating cycle of a retail store begins when the managers buy merchandise from the company's suppliers. This has two consequences: (1) the store has something to offer its customers, and (2) the company has an obligation to pay its suppliers. These two effects are shown in the two rectangular blocks at the left of center in Exhibit 2–1.

EXHIBIT 2–1.   An Operating Cycle: A Retail Store

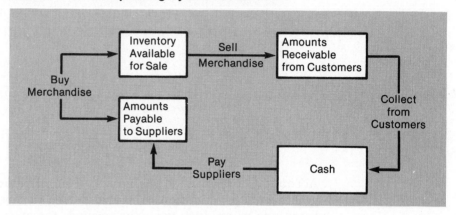

The operating cycle continues as the store sells merchandise to a customer. This reduces the amount of merchandise available for sale to other customers, but it does give the company the right to receive money from the customer who bought the merchandise. This change is indicated by the arrow at the top of the diagram. In the next stage the customer pays and the company receives cash. This cash can then be used to pay suppliers, and the operating cycle is complete. If the company is successful, the operating cycle will generate enough cash to pay the owners for the use of their money and allow the operating cycle to begin again.

Different companies, and even different parts of a single company, have operating cycles of different lengths. The cycle for a cheese store may be only a few weeks long because inventories are perishable and all sales are for cash, whereas a lumber dealer may have a six-month cycle due to the large inventories necessary in this kind of business. A whiskey distiller may have an operating cycle several years long because of the long aging process.

Assets of a business enterprise

Both the initial investment by the owners and subsequent actions taken by the managers provide the business with *assets,* which are objects, claims, and other rights owned by and having value to the organization. They have value either because they can be exchanged for cash or other goods or services in the future or because the company can use them to increase the amount of cash or other assets at its disposal in the future.

Some assets are *monetary assets,* representing enforceable claims on others for specified amounts of money. The first of these is *cash,* the money the company has in its cash registers ("cash on hand") and in its bank accounts ("cash in bank"). Another monetary asset, *accounts receivable,* consists of the claims the company has against its customers for goods or services provided to them.

Almost every business has at least some *nonmonetary assets* as well. Some of these are *tangible physical assets. Inventories,* for example, are physical items the company intends to sell to its customers (merchandise) or consume in operating the business (office supplies, raw materials, and so forth). *Plant assets* (known also by such names as fixed assets, long-lived assets, or property, plant, and equipment) consist of any land, buildings, and machinery the company owns and intends to use rather than sell.

Finally, many businesses have *intangible assets* which enable them to compete in the marketplace on favorable terms. The exclusive right to use a well-known trademark is an example of an intangible asset.

Sources of business assets

A business's assets are provided by its *owners* and by its *creditors,* who thereby become equityholders in the business. A creditor is someone from whom the company has acquired assets or services for which it becomes legally required to make payment or provide services in the future. A creditor who has provided cash to the enterprise is known as a *lender.* An owner, in contrast, is someone who has invested resources in the company—usually cash—in exchange for the rights and risks of ownership.

The main differences in the contractual relationships of creditors and owners are summarized in Exhibit 2–2. The general idea is that creditors accept limits on the rewards they will receive and, in return, assume relatively smaller risks than owners. In practice, both the legal and risk/reward relationships are less clear-cut than this discussion suggests, but these variations are insignificant for our purposes.

EXHIBIT 2–2.   Simplified Comparison of Owners and Creditors

Creditors	Owners
1. Make no decisions on how the company's resources are used.	1. Decide, either directly or through representatives they elect or appoint, how the company's resources are used.
2. Have a right to specified payments on specified dates and can bring legal action if a payment is not made when it is due.	2. Are entitled to receive payments only after the company has provided adequately for the amounts due its creditors.
3. Will receive no more than the specified amounts, no matter how prosperous the company becomes.	3. Can receive very large amounts if the company prospers.
4. Have the right to receive specified amounts, and no more, if the company is dissolved.	4. Have the right to receive whatever is left over after all creditors' claims have been met; will receive nothing if the creditors' claims are not met in full.

A creditor's equity in a business is a *liability* of that business. Four important kinds of liabilities are:

1. *Accounts payable,* measuring the amounts due to people or organizations for goods or services they have supplied to the company.
2. *Notes payable,* measuring the amounts lent to the company by banks and others, usually for short periods of time.
3. *Wages and salaries payable,* measuring the amounts due to employees for services rendered to the company.
4. *Bonds payable,* a form of *long-term debt,* the amounts lent to the company by outsiders for relatively long periods of time in exchange for the company's agreement to pay specified amounts at specified future dates.

The amounts the owners have provided to the business in exchange for their ownership rights constitute the *owners' equity.* In some cases, the original owners may transfer all or part of their ownership rights to others, who thereby become owners of the business. These transfers of ownership don't change the assets, liabilities, or owners' equity of the business. Not until the new owners either invest new resources in the business itself (as opposed to buying ownership rights from other owners) or withdraw resources already there, will the change of ownership have a direct effect on the company.

Business income

Owners invest in a business because they want the investment to increase their wealth. If the business does this, we say it has generated a *profit, income,* or *earnings* (the terms are used interchangeably). If the activities of the business reduce the owners' wealth, we say it has operated at a *loss.*

One of the accountant's most important tasks is to measure the amount of profit or loss the business generates each year or in any other relevant time period. The accounting measure of a company's profit during a particular time period is known as *net income* or *net loss.* This amount reflects the effects of *changes during a period of time.* A list of assets, liabilities, and owners' equity, in contrast, always refers to their *status on a particular date.*

Proprietorships, partnerships, and corporations

In setting up a business, the owners have to choose the legal form the business will take. Many small businesses and many professional firms, both large and small, are formed as *individual proprietorships* or as *partnerships* of two or more people. Businesses can be set up in either form very simply, with few formalities and little red tape. No permission needs to be obtained; from a legal point of view, the activities of the business are regarded as simply one portion of the activities of the individual owner or owners.

The other major form of business organization is the *corporation.* A corporation is established by the issuance of a corporate charter by a government body; in the United States, corporate charters are usually issued by state governments.

The property of the corporation is legally separate from that of its owner(s). If an owner dies, the corporation lives on because the ownership interest is simply transferred to a new owner or owners. Furthermore, the corporation, not its owner(s), is legally liable for the corporation's debts. This *limited liability* feature means that once the owners of the corporation have invested their funds in the corporation, they as individuals have no further obligation to the corporation's creditors. If the corporation fails to pay its bills, the creditors can't demand that the owners pay these bills with their personal assets.

Limited liability makes investment in a business feasible for many people who have confidence in its future but don't wish to be active in its management *and* do want to limit their risks. In fact, the development of large-scale industry in the Western world was made possible largely because of the corporate form of organization.

In exchange for their investment, the owners of a corporation receive shares of capital stock and are called stockholders, shareholders, or shareowners. Stock ownership entitles the shareholder to vote on such questions as the election of members of the board of directors and the appointment of the company's auditors. The board appoints the company's top managers, establishes the basic policies that management is expected to observe in operating the business, and reviews management's performance on the stockholders' behalf.

ACCOUNTING MEASUREMENT BY TRANSACTIONS ANALYSIS

Accounting measurements of assets, liabilities, owners' equity, and net income or loss are assembled from the accountants' analyses of the effects of the business's *transactions*—that is, the actions and events the business has a direct part in. We'll illustrate how this is done by examining the transactions that arise in the formation and operation of a small retail store.

Investment transactions

In June 19x1, the sales manager of Ajax Manufacturing Company offered Charles Erskine the exclusive dealership rights in his community for the Ajax line of refrigerators and other electrical appliances. Erskine, then a salesman for a wholesale distributorship of a competing line of appliances, decided that he had a good chance of succeeding. He obtained a corporate charter in the name of Erskine Appliances, Inc., gave up his old job, and began to devote himself full-time to the new business.

On June 30, 19x1, Erskine and two of his friends purchased all the shares (certificates of ownership) of the new corporation, paying a total of $30,000 in cash ($20,000 from Erskine and $5,000 from each of the others). Their purchase of these shares made the three friends shareowners or *stockholders* in the corporation. They had a stockholders' meeting and elected themselves members of the board of directors. The first acts of the Erskine Appliances board were to appoint Erskine president of the company and to authorize him to open a bank account in the company's name. Erskine then deposited the $30,000 in this account.

The exchange of shares of the company's stock for $30,000 provided the company with its first asset, $30,000 in cash. In return,

Erskine and his two friends received owners' equities in the new company. Accounting systems measure owners' equity by the amount the owners invest in the business. The full analysis of this first transaction therefore can be written as follows:

(1)

Asset Increase	Accompanied	Owners' Equity Increase
Cash $30,000	by	Capital Stock $30,000

This analysis shows what happened to the assets and equities of the *business,* as something separate and distinct from the owners' other interests and activities. For example, suppose Erskine bought his shares of stock in the new corporation by taking $20,000 from his personal bank account. From his point of view, he simply decreased one asset (cash in his personal bank account) and established another (investment in Erskine Appliances, Inc.). His total wealth didn't change.

This illustrates an important point. Financial statements always relate to a specific set of resources. The set of resources being reported on constitutes the *accounting entity.* To avoid confusion, therefore, accountants have to begin with a clear definition of the accounting entity they are working with. They can then exclude any transactions that don't affect this entity. For example, if Erskine were to take another $5,000 from his personal savings account to buy a new automobile for family use, this transaction wouldn't be reflected in the financial statements of Erskine Appliances, Inc.

The result of this investment transaction illustrates another point: *Every equity in one accounting entity is an asset in some other accounting entity.* This shows up clearly in Exhibit 2–3. A banker looking at Erskine as an accounting entity would regard his investment in the store as an asset. The same banker looking

EXHIBIT 2–3.   Relationship between Accounting Entities

Erskine Appliances, Inc.		Mr. Charles Erskine
Asset: Owners' Equity:	←→	Asset:
Cash Investment by		Investment
Mr. Erskine		in
		Erskine
		Appliances, Inc.

at the store as an accounting entity would see this same investment as an owners' equity.

A payment transaction

Immediately after opening the company's checking account, Erskine signed the Ajax franchise agreement and entered into a two-year lease (starting July 1) on a store containing ample office, storage, and display space. The rent on the store was $1,200 a month, and he paid the rent for three months in advance by writing a check for $3,600 against the company's balance in its checking account. A payment of cash is known as a *disbursement*.

How did the payment to the landlord affect the company's assets, liabilities, and owners' equity? First, we know that the amount in the checking account was $3,600 less than it had been. This means that the transaction reduced the size of the asset, cash, by $3,600. Second, by paying the landlord $3,600, the company acquired the exclusive right to use the store for three months. This right, which accountants call *prepaid rent,* was an asset—the company owned it and clearly expected to use it to carry out operations that would benefit the business (otherwise, the company wouldn't have paid $3,600 for it). In other words, the transaction was analyzed as follows:

	(2)	
Asset Increase	*Accompanied*	*Asset Decrease*
Prepaid Rent $3,600	*by*	Cash.................... $3,600

The accounting equation

Since one asset was exchanged for another with no change in the owners' equity, transaction (2) left *total* assets unchanged at $30,000—and owners' equity at $30,000 as well—producing the following equation:

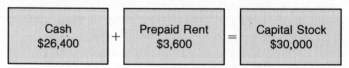

This equality is no coincidence. In the accounting systems used today, *the asset total must be identical to the total of the equities,* with equities being the sum of total liabilities and owners' equity. This identity is referred to as the *accounting equation:*

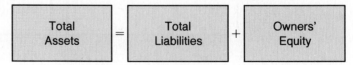

The accounting equation holds true for all organizations at all times. It holds true because the list of assets and the list of liabilities and owners' equity are merely two ways of looking at the same set of resources. The list of equities classifies the resources according to their source; that is, it answers the question: where did the resources come from? The list of assets, on the other hand, classifies the same set of resources according to their nature; that is, it answers the question; what form did the resources take?

Purchase transactions

Immediately after the lease was signed, Ajax Manufacturing Company delivered merchandise to Erskine Appliances, for which Erskine agreed to pay $13,000 during the next 30 days. By this transaction, the store acquired an asset, merchandise inventory, at a cost of $13,000. No asset was given up immediately, however, because Ajax agreed to wait 30 days for its money. In other words, Ajax in effect made a short-term investment in Erskine Appliances, and the company had its first creditor.

Once again we can see the two sides of an investment transaction. As a result of this transaction, Ajax had a claim against Erskine Appliances, and it regarded this claim as an asset. To Erskine Appliances, however, this same claim appeared as a liability because it would have to be settled by the payment of cash within 30 days. The store assumed this liability in exchange for the assets received from Ajax, and the transaction was viewed as follows:

(3)

Asset Increase	Accompanied	Liability Increase
Inventory $13,000	by	Accounts Payable $13,000

This increased the asset total to $43,000.

Next, Erskine bought secondhand equipment for the store, paying $9,000 in cash from the store's bank account. This transaction was just like the prepayment of rent: One asset, cash, was exchanged for another asset, equipment. The equipment was measured for accounting purposes just as the prepaid rent had been, at its cost— that is, by the amount of cash given up to acquire it. The transaction therefore was interpreted in the following way:

(4)

Asset Increase	Accompanied	Asset Decrease
Equipment $9,000	by	Cash $9,000

This left the total asset figure at $43,000, and the accounting equation remained in balance.

Erskine's final act on June 30 was to hire Karen Watson to work with him in the store at a salary of $1,400 a month. She was to start work the next morning. This had no effect on the June 30 assets and equities, however. Because Watson would be paid only if she actually showed up for work, the business owed her nothing on June 30. No asset was created because the company had no ownership right to Watson's future services.

Maintaining the accounting equation

Transactions analysis is governed by one restriction—the accounting equation must always remain balanced. This means the accounting analysis of *each* transaction must also be balanced; that is, a change in one item must be accompanied by a change in one or more other items so that the total of the assets remains equal to the total of the liabilities and owners' equity.

EXHIBIT 2–4

ERSKINE APPLIANCES, INC.
Assets, Liabilities, and Owners' Equity
June 30, 19x1

	Cash	+	Inventory	+	Prepaid Rent	+	Equipment	=	Accounts Payable	+	Capital Stock
(1)	+30,000										+30,000
(2)	− 3,600			+	3,600						
Bal.	26,400			+	3,600			=			30,000
(3)		+	13,000						+13,000		
Bal.	26,400	+	13,000	+	3,600			=	13,000	+	30,000
(4)	− 9,000					+	9,000				
Bal.	17,400	+	13,000	+	3,600	+	9,000	=	13,000	+	30,000

These specifications are met by the table in Exhibit 2–4, which shows the effects of Erskine Appliances' first four transactions. Notice particularly that the accounting equation remained balanced after each transaction was analyzed. The total of the amounts shown for the store's four assets at the end of June was $43,000, and the amounts shown for the liabilities and owners' equity added up to the same total. Of this, $30,000 had been supplied by the owners and $13,000 by a creditor, the supplier of merchandise.

Sale transactions: Revenues and expenses

Nothing the business did during June produced measurable income. When the store opened for business in July, however, Erskine hoped the events of that month would produce net income.

Accountants measure the net income of a specified time period by subtracting the expenses of the period from the revenues of that period. These terms can be defined as follows:

1. The *revenues* of a period are the resources received by the business as a result of providing products or services to outsiders during that period.
2. The *expenses* of a period are the resources consumed by the company to generate the revenues of that period.

For example, Erskine Appliances sold merchandise to its customers in July for $16,200. Of this, $2,800 was for cash, and the remaining $13,400 was sold on credit.[1] The merchandise covered by these sales had been part of the first shipment received from Ajax Manufacturing Company on June 30. The items sold had cost $10,600.

Notice what happened: The company exchanged one group of assets (merchandise) for another (cash and accounts receivable). As a result of these exchanges, total assets increased by $5,600, as follows:

```
Cash received ................................  +$  2,800
Receivables increased.........................  +  13,400
Inventory decreased ..........................  −  10,600
    Assets increased ..........................  +$  5,600
```

Since the liabilities went neither up nor down, the owners' equity increased by $5,600 as well.

We can see this more clearly if we restate the accounting equation in the following form:

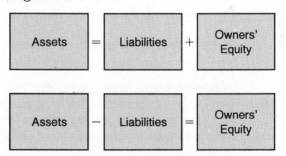

The quantity on the left side of this revised equation (assets minus liabilities) is sometimes called *net assets*. Obviously, anything that increases net assets also increases owners' equity, or vice versa. This is crucial. A business has net income only to the extent that it uses its resources to increase its net assets. If there is no increase

---

[1] The terms *on credit* and *on account* are used interchangeably to mean that payment for goods or services purchased or sold is to be made at some date later than the date of the delivery of the goods or the performance of the service.

in net assets, there is no income. And if the net assets increase, then the owners' equity also increases.

We are now able to summarize Erskine Appliances' July sale transactions in terms of the accounting equation:

		(5)		
Asset Increases		*Accompanied*	*Asset Decrease*	
Cash	$ 2,800	*by*	Inventory	$10,600
Accounts Receivable	13,400		*Owners' Equity Increase*	
			Income	5,600

This analysis measures the margin between sales revenue and the cost of the merchandise that was sold, usually referred to as the *gross margin*. It doesn't tell us, however, whether this was a large or a small percentage of revenue. Some companies, such as supermarket chains, deliberately keep their gross margin percentages low to penetrate mass markets; others, such as manufacturers of sophisticated medical equipment, need high unit margins to cover their marketing and administrative expenses and produce income. For example, the two companies represented by the bars in Exhibit 2–5 have identical gross margins but very different pricing policies. The one at the left operates in a very small market with high prices relative to the cost of the merchandise it sells. The company at the right is in a large market with a much narrower percentage spread between price and the cost of the merchandise sold.

The total revenue figure is also used as the numerator of other ratios and to measure the company's rate of growth, as we'll see in Chapter 16. To provide the basis for these calculations, accoun-

EXHIBIT 2–5.   Gross Margin Percentages

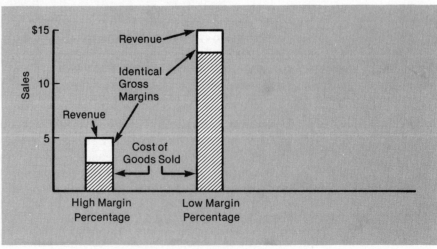

tants always divide the analysis of sale transactions into two parts, one dealing with the revenue and the other dealing with the expense (cost of goods sold). The analysis of Erskine Appliances' first set of sale transactions therefore showed the following:

(5a)

Asset Increases	Accompanied	Owners' Equity Increase
Cash .... $ 2,800	by	Revenues $16,200
Accounts Receivable 13,400		

The items on the left are the assets the store received from its customers during the month; the item on the right shows that assets worth $16,200 were provided for the owners' benefit. Taken by themselves, in other words, these sale transactions increased the owners' equity by $16,200.

We know, of course, that owners' equity didn't increase by the full $16,200. To earn this revenue, Erskine had to deliver merchandise which had cost the store $10,600. Since this removed merchandise from the company's inventory, that asset decreased in size and so did the owners' equity. This analysis can be summarized as follows:

(5b)

Owners' Equity Decrease	Accompanied	Asset Decrease
Expenses $10,600	by	Inventory $10,600

Taken together, these two analyses show the same changes in assets and owners' equity as analysis (5); the only difference is that two figures, +$16,200 and −$10,600, have been substituted for the one +$5,600 figure in analysis (5).

Terminology: Cost and expense

Two terms used in this illustration are often misused in practice, even by experienced analysts of financial statements. The terms are *cost* and *expense*. Cost is the broader term, and Exhibit 2–6 shows how costs flow through the company. First, resources are used to acquire assets (for example, inventories). These assets are measured by the amount of resources sacrificed to obtain them (their cost). When the assets are used to produce revenue, their costs are reclassified as expenses.

TERMINOLOGY REMINDER

Cost: the amount of resources sacrificed to obtain something or achieve some objective.

Expense: the cost of resources given up to obtain revenues of the current period; a cost subtracted from revenues on the income statement.

EXHIBIT 2–6. Distinction between Cost and Expense

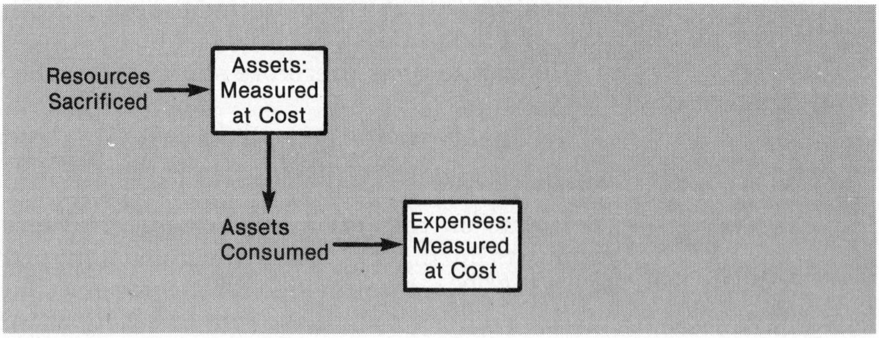

In other words, cost is the basis of measurement: Asset and expense are two stages in the life cycle of a cost. Nonmonetary assets are resources the company still has, measured at their cost; expenses are resources the company has used up in producing the revenues of a particular time period, measured at their cost.[2]

The term *expense* should also be distinguished from the terms *expenditure* and *loss.* An expenditure is any use of resources. Companies make expenditures when they acquire inventories, when they use inventories, or when they use their employees' services. Some expenditures lead to expenses of the current period; others do not. A loss is a reduction in an asset that does not have a related revenue benefit. Whereas use of office supplies is an expense, its uninsured destruction would appear as a loss in determining net income.

When a cost is incurred (that is, when resources are used for a purpose), the key question is: When is the company likely to reap the benefits resulting from the cost? If the benefits all materialize in the period in which the cost is incurred, the cost should be recognized as an expense immediately. If the benefits are expected to occur in the future, then the cost should be identified as an asset. The cost of merchandise purchased, for example, is treated as the cost of an asset until it generates revenue. At that time it becomes an expense because it will then have produced all the benefit management can reasonably expect from it.

Other operating transactions

Subtracting the cost of goods sold from sales revenues doesn't yield the net income figure. Many other goods and services are con-

---

[2] In contrast, monetary assets, which enable the company to buy assets and pay debts, are ordinarily measured at their value to the company.

sumed each period to create the period's revenues. This means that their costs are also expenses of the current period.

For example, Erskine Appliances used Watson's services during the month of July at a cost of $1,400. One clear effect of this transaction was to create a liability—by using Watson's services, the store acquired a legal obligation to pay her for those services.

What else did this transaction (use of Watson's services) do? Its purpose was to help the company create owners' equity by selling merchandise. Erskine saw no reason why Watson's work this month should benefit any period in the future. This means that the entire cost was a cost of generating revenues (increases in owners' equity) in July. Since revenues are increases in owners' equity, the costs incurred to produce them are reductions in owners' equity. In sum, using Watson's services therefore had the following effects:

	(6)	
Owners' Equity Decrease	*Accompanied*	*Liability Increase*
Expenses $1,400	by	Salary Payable $1,400

Another group of items had similar effects. Electricity, telephone, and other costs of operating the store and office during the month amounted to $700. Since these costs related to current operations, they were regarded as having been consumed in the creation of current revenues—in other words, treated as expense:

	(7)	
Owners' Equity Decrease	*Accompanied*	*Liability Increase*
Expenses $700	by	Accounts Payable $700

Once again, the use of these services reduced the owners' equity while increasing the company's liabilities.

CARDINAL RULES OF TRANSACTIONS ANALYSIS

1. The accounting equation must remain balanced at all times; the changes resulting from each transaction must also balance each other.
2. Expenses are recognized when resources are used up to create current revenues; *whether cash is paid for these resources at the time they are used, or earlier, or later has no bearing on the question of when the costs of the resources become expenses.*

Other transactions

A number of other transactions took place during July. First, additional merchandise was purchased on credit at a total cost of $6,400:

(8)

Asset Increase	Accompanied	Liability Increase
Inventory $6,400	by	Accounts Payable $6,400

The owners' equity was not affected by this set of transactions. Acquisition of the assets was financed temporarily by an increase in a liability.

Second, collections from customers on credit sales [see transaction (5a)] totaled $2,500. These were pure exchange-of-asset transactions and had no effect on the owners' equity. The analysis was:

(9)

Asset Increase	Accompanied	Asset Decrease
Cash $2,500	by	Accounts Receivable $2,500

Third, the company paid Ajax Manufacturing Company, the electric company, the telephone company, and other suppliers $12,500, part of the money they were entitled to as a result of transactions (3) and (7). This is known as paying money "on account." In other words, an asset (cash) was surrendered to reduce some of the company's liabilities (accounts payable). These transactions were analyzed in the following terms:

(10)

Liability Decrease	Accompanied	Asset Decrease
Accounts Payable $12,500	by	Cash $12,500

Fourth, the store paid Watson her salary. This had exactly the same effect as the payment to suppliers—an asset was used to cancel a liability:

(11)

Liability Decrease	Accompanied	Asset Decrease
Salary Payable $1,400	by	Cash $1,400

Payment of Watson's salary canceled the liability we identified in our analysis of transaction (6).

Finally, the company paid Erskine an $1,800 salary for July. This was the amount he would have earned if he had continued working for his former employer. Payment of the salary reduced both the assets and the owners' equity by $1,800:

(12)

Owners' Equity Decrease	Accompanied	Asset Decrease
Expenses $1,800	by	Cash $1,800

Rent expense

The data for each of the transaction analyses described above were found in documents that were prepared or received by Erskine Appliances as a matter of routine. Data for the analysis of merchandise purchases, for example, came from the bills or *invoices* received from the store's suppliers.

Not all the facts relevant to the preparation of periodic financial statements were in documents of this sort, however. For example, a portion of the asset *prepaid rent* was consumed during the month, but the landlord had no reason to send the company a document conveying that information. Erskine's accountant therefore had to be alert to make sure that the cost of the store rental for July wasn't overlooked.

Going back to the documents underlying transaction (2), the accountant found that the rental payment of $3,600 had covered a period of three months beginning July 1 at a cost of $1,200 a month. Since one month had gone by, one third of the total prepayment, or $1,200, had been consumed during July:

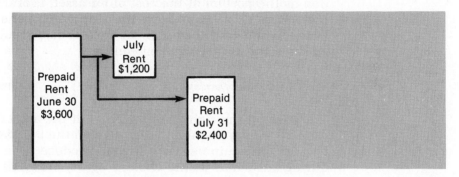

Here is about as clear an example of an expense as we're likely to find. Whatever benefits were to be obtained from use of the store in July *were* obtained in July. Management couldn't reasonably expect to gain any substantial benefit in future periods as a result of the July rental cost. The $1,200 therefore was an operating expense of the month; both the assets and the owners' equity had been reduced by $1,200. This analysis can be summarized as follows:

	(13)	
Owners' Equity Decrease	*Accompanied*	*Asset Decrease*
Expenses $1,200	by	Cash $1,200

Depreciation

One other resource was used in the business during July: the equipment the company had bought on June 30. The question was whether any of the $9,000 cost of this equipment had become an expense during the month.

This is a more complicated question than the one we answered in connection with the prepaid rent. As far as Erskine and Watson could see, the equipment was in just as good condition at the end of July as at the beginning. They knew it wouldn't last forever, however. It would have to be replaced sometime. Its benefits would be limited to the period between the date of purchase and the date of replacement. The costs, therefore, would be an expense of this long period. The problem was how much of this expense applied to the month of July and how much would apply to the other months that would benefit from the use of the equipment.

To resolve this issue, Erskine asked an equipment dealer how long he could expect to use the equipment in the store. They finally decided that five years (60 months) was a reasonable estimate and that $\frac{1}{60}$ of the $9,000 cost ($150) should be considered a cost of producing revenue each month for 60 months.

This cost is called *depreciation*. The accountant defines depreciation as the portion of the cost of an asset, useful for two or more periods, that is attributable to the operations of one of those periods. Depreciation of the equipment in July had the following effects on the company's assets and equities:

(14)

Owners' Equity Decrease	Accompanied	Asset Decrease
Expenses $150	by	Equipment $150

The item on the right says that part of the asset (equipment) was used up during the month; the item on the left says this happened because the equipment was used to produce revenues for the store during July; that is, the owners' equity was $150 less than if no equipment depreciation had taken place.

The process of transferring costs from asset to expense in this way is known as cost *amortization*. Amortization is necessary whenever an asset is expected to produce benefits in two or more periods and will be wholly or partially consumed as it does this. Under most circumstances, land doesn't depreciate because it makes its contribution without losing any of its power to contribute in the future. Equipment depreciates because it loses its usefulness sooner or later—usually due to physical deterioration and technological obsolescence. The cost of anything that depreciates must be amortized—that is, assigned in some way to the operations of the time between the date the asset is acquired and the date it is disposed of.

Cash dividends

When the owner of an individual proprietorship withdraws cash from the business for his or her own use, this action reduces both the company's assets and the owner's equity in the company. When the owners of a corporation withdraw cash for their own use, this withdrawal, called a *cash dividend*, reduces both the business's assets and the owners' equity.

Although all the data on the store's operations in July weren't yet available on the final day of the month, Erskine knew that sales volume in the first month had been far greater than he had expected. He was confident that the store had operated at a profit at this volume. Furthermore, the company had more than enough cash in the bank to meet the needs of the operating cycle in the next few months. To celebrate, the members of the board of directors declared a $300 cash dividend on July 31, payable on August 10, 19x1.[3] This transaction had the following effects:

(15)

Owners' Equity Decrease	*Accompanied*	*Liability Increase*
Dividend Declared $300	*by*	Dividend Payable $300

This analysis reveals a peculiarity of the corporate form of organization. The act of declaring a cash dividend makes it a legal obligation of the corporation. The stockholders of Erskine Appliances, Inc., therefore became creditors of the corporation to the tune of $300. At the same time, their owners' equity in the corporation dropped by $300.

THE FINANCIAL STATEMENTS

After these transactions were analyzed, the assets, liabilities, and owners' equity of Erskine Appliances appeared as in Exhibit 2–7. The numbers in parentheses refer to the transaction numbers in the preceding discussion. The plus and minus signs beside the various owners' equity elements identify them as positive or negative components of the total owners' equity.

The company's accountant prepared three financial statements based on the data in Exhibit 2–7:

1. An *income statement* (also known as an *earnings statement* or a *profit and loss statement*)—listing the revenues, expenses, and net income for the month of July.
2. A *statement of changes in retained earnings*—listing the changes in the owners' equity resulting from their ownership of this business during July.
3. A pair of *balance sheets (statements of financial position)*—listing the assets, liabilities, and owners' equity of Erskine Appliances, Inc., as of June 30, 19x1, and July 31, 19x1.

---

[3] In the United States, the power to declare dividends is vested in the board of directors. The directors of companies in which shares are owned by the general public ordinarily meet to declare dividends four times a year. In Europe and much of the rest of the world, dividends are declared once each year by a formal vote of the shareholders at the annual shareholders' meeting. The vote is usually on a dividend proposal formulated by the directors, however.

EXHIBIT 2–7

ERSKINE APPLIANCES, INC.
Assets, Liabilities, and Owners' Equity
For the Month Ended July 31, 19x1

Assets:

Cash

Bal. 7/1	17,400
(5a)	+ 2,800
(9)	+ 2,500
(10)	−12,500
(11)	− 1,400
(12)	− 1,800
Bal. 7/31	7,000

Accounts Receivable

Bal. 7/1	—
(5a)	13,400
(9)	− 2,500
Bal. 7/31	10,900

Inventory

Bal. 7/1	13,000
(5b)	−10,600
(8)	+ 6,400
Bal. 7/31	8,800

Prepaid Rent

Bal. 7/1	3,600
(13)	−1,200
Bal. 7/31	2,400

Equipment

Bal. 7/1	9,000
(14)	− 150
Bal. 7/31	8,850

Liabilities:

Accounts Payable

Ba. 7/1	13,000
(7)	+ 700
(8)	+ 6,400
(10)	−12,500
Bal. 7/31	7,600

Salary Payable

(6)	+1,400
(11)	−1,400
Bal. 7/31	—

Dividend Payable

Bal. 7/1	—
(15)	+300

Owners' Equity:

Capital Stock

Bal. 7/1	30,000

Income

Bal. 7/1		—
(5a)	Sales revenue	+16,200
(5b)	Cost of goods sold expense	−10,600
(6)	Salary expense	− 1,400
(7)	Misc. expense	− 700
(12)		− 1,800
(13)	Rent expense	− 1,200
(14)	Depreciation expense	− 150
Bal.	7/31	350

Dividends Declared

Bal. 7/1	—
(15)	−300

The income statement

The company's accountant arranged the month's revenues and expenses in the income statement shown in Exhibit 2–8. In this case, the revenues exceeded the expenses by $350, and this was the company's net income for the month. Net income is the accountant's estimate of the increase in the owners' equity as a result of their ownership of Erskine Appliances during July 19x1. Owners expect that increases in their equity in this business will result in increases in their *wealth*—through dividends or increases in the market value of their shares, or both.

Notice that the $300 dividend isn't shown as an expense. Net income measures the increase in the owners' equity resulting from revenue-producing activities. Dividends aren't contractual payments for revenue-producing services used. The declaration and distribution of a dividend merely reduce one of the owners' assets—their investment in the company—and increase another—first the amount receivable by the owners from the company and then cash in their possession when the dividend is actually paid.

We simplified this example slightly by assuming this company wasn't subject to income taxes on its first month's income. We need to emphasize at the outset, however, that income statements prepared as part of financial accounting *aren't* income tax returns. The purpose of an income tax return is to enable the government to determine the amount of income tax the company must pay; the final income figure on an income tax return is *taxable income,* the amount subject to income tax. In contrast, the final figure on an income statement is *net income,* the amount left after all losses and expenses, including income tax expense, have been deducted from the revenues of the period.

Taxable income in the United States and many other countries

EXHIBIT 2–8

ERSKINE APPLIANCES, INC.
Income Statement
For the Month Ended July 31, 19x1

Sales revenues		$16,200
Cost of goods sold		10,600
Gross margin		5,600
Operating expenses:		
Salaries	$3,200	
Rent	1,200	
Depreciation	150	
Other	700	
Total operating expenses		5,250
Net income		$ 350

often differs substantially from accounting income. The reason is that legislatures often use income taxation as a way of influencing the actions of managers and investors. For example, if the government wishes to encourage investments in oil exploration, it can rule that part of the spread between the revenues and the expenses of this kind of activity isn't "income" for tax purposes. Or, if the legislature wants to discourage political lobbying by business firms, it can rule that the costs of lobbying activities aren't deductible from revenues for tax purposes.

In both these situations, adoption of tax definitions of revenues and expenses for financial reporting might mislead investors. As a result, in measuring financial performance for reporting to investors, accountants try to estimate both the amount of resources earned during the period and the amount of resources sacrificed to obtain them, even if these amounts differ from those shown on the income tax return. Differences between the income statement and the tax return aren't necessarily fraudulent, either in intent or in result.

Statement of changes in retained earnings

The second financial statement Erskine Appliances' accountant prepared is the statement of changes in retained earnings, shown in Exhibit 2–9. *Retained earnings* is the accountants' name for the *cumulative* difference between net income and the amount of dividends declared. Because July 19x1 was Erskine Appliances' first month of operations, there were no retained earnings at the beginning of the month. Net income for the month was $350, dividends amounted to $300, and retained earnings at the end of the month amounted to $50.

The statement of changes in retained earnings is of relatively minor importance, calling for little explanation here. Its main purpose is to enable the reader of the financial statements to see the effect of the period's net income and dividends on the owners' equity reported on the balance sheet.

EXHIBIT 2–9

ERSKINE APPLIANCES, INC.
Statement of Changes in Retained Earnings
For the Month Ended July 31, 19x1

Retained earnings, July 1, 19x1	$ 0
Add: Net Income for the month	350
Less: Dividends declared during the month	(300)
Retained earnings, July 31, 19x1	$ 50

The balance sheet

A balance sheet consists of a list of the business's assets *as of a specific date,* together with a list of the liabilities and owners' equities in the company at that time. Exhibit 2–10 shows the balance sheets of Erskine Appliances, Inc., as of June 30 and July 31, 19x1. The June 30 figures come from the last line of Exhibit 2–4; the July 31 amounts come from Exhibit 2–7.

EXHIBIT 2–10

ERSKINE APPLIANCES, INC.
Comparative Balance Sheets
As of July 31 and June 30, 19x1

Assets

	July 31	June 30
Current assets:		
Cash	$ 7,000	$17,400
Accounts receivable	10,900	—
Inventory	8,800	13,000
Prepaid rent	2,400	3,600
Total current assets	29,100	34,000
Equipment	8,850	9,000
Total assets	$37,950	$43,000

Liabilities and Owners' Equity

	July 31	June 30
Current liabilities:		
Accounts payable	$ 7,600	$13,000
Dividend payable	300	—
Total current liabilities	7,900	13,000
Owners' equity:		
Capital stock	30,000	30,000
Retained earnings	50	—
Total owners' equity	30,050	30,000
Total liabilities and owners' equity	$37,950	$43,000

Working capital

Every business, like every person, needs to be able to meet its cash obligations when they come due; this is called being *liquid.* Most of us think of liquidity in terms of cash—in the pocket, in a checking account, in a cookie jar, and so forth. Businesses tend to take a longer view in deference to seasonal patterns and the length of their operating cycles. This means their notion of liquidity can include accounts receivable and other assets that will bring in cash in the near future.

One commonly used measure of business liquidity is the company's *working capital,* defined as the difference between *total current assets* and *total current liabilities.* In most cases, the assets classified as current assets are cash and all other assets management reasonably expects to convert into cash within one year. (If the operating cycle is longer than a year, assets convertible into cash during this longer period will also be classified as current assets, but these situations are rare.)

Erskine Appliances listed only four current assets in its first monthly balance sheet: cash, accounts receivable, inventory, and prepaid rent. The receivables are listed before the inventories in Exhibit 2–10 because they are one stage closer to cash in the operating cycle. Prepaid rent is classified as a current asset because it will be used up during the next year.

Current liabilities are expected to be eliminated by the use of assets that are classified as current in the same balance sheet. In any case, current liabilities include all liabilities that will become payable during the next 12 months, no matter how short the operating cycle may be. For example, if a company has a liability that will be paid off in installments spread over several years, the portion that will have to be paid during the next 12 months will be classified as a current liability. The classification of the accounts payable and the dividends payable as current liabilities in Exhibit 2–10 indicates that these amounts were to come due for payment within the next year.

Erskine Appliances had no noncurrent liabilities on July 31, 19x1, and only one noncurrent asset, the equipment in its store and office. Whereas particular accounts receivable and particular items of merchandise are expected to flow through the operating cycle fairly quickly, the equipment will be around for a long time. It will produce benefits not only in the next year but for many years to come. As a result, it is classified as a noncurrent asset.

Working capital is calculated partly in the belief that the current assets will be converted into cash soon enough to make them available to pay the current liabilities when they come due. It also measures the amounts of the current assets that must be financed from long-term sources. A large amount of working capital, in other words, is regarded as a useful safety device; that may be good, but it also increases the need for long-term capital, and that is likely to be less good.

OMISSIONS FROM FINANCIAL STATEMENTS

The amounts reported for *some* assets on a company's balance sheet are intended to approximate the *values* of those assets. Cash and accounts receivable, for example, are measured at the value of the company's claims against money-issuing authorities, banks, and customers. For other assets, however, the balance sheet lists *costs* rather than values. Merchandise, land, buildings, and equipment are measured on the basis of their historical costs. When the items in the two groups are added together, as they are on every balance sheet, the total represents neither the cost nor the value of the company's assets, but a mixture of the two.

Another shortcoming of the usual balance sheets is that they often omit assets that may have more to do with business success than many of the assets that are listed. Erskine became especially aware of some of these omissions when he planned to approach a local bank for a loan—because he was anxious that the balance sheet present every justifiable evidence of financial strength. He was concerned, for example, because the balance sheet failed to list the three resources he considered to be the company's most valuable assets: the dealership franchise, his customer following in the trade, and the lease on the store which he had obtained on very favorable terms.

The franchise and customer loyalty are our first examples of intangible assets, which enable the business to earn higher income than its investment in tangible assets would normally produce. There is no question that items such as these are important. Erskine certainly should have emphasized them in his discussions with the bank's lending officers. Accountants exclude them from the balance sheet, however, because they can't verify the evidence on which measurements of these quantities as assets would have to be based. This kind of asset appears on the balance sheet only if the company *buys* a franchise or access to a group of customers. In such cases the asset is measured at its cost because the purchase price can be verified fairly easily.

The financial statements also ignored the two-year lease on the store Erskine had signed. Signing this lease gave the company the right to use the store building for two years at a fixed rental; it also committed the company to a fixed series of payments to the landlord. This agreement was an important factor, one that would be favorable if property values went up and unfavorable if they went down. Even so, the accounting profession doesn't regard the signing of this sort of lease as an exchange of resources that should be recognized in the statements. The leased property enters the accounting system only as the property is used or as payments are made.

Since most assets in a conventional balance sheet are measured at their cost rather than at their value, it should be no surprise that the owners' equity reported doesn't measure the *value* of the owners' interest in the business. If unreported intangible assets are great, the value is likely to be greater than the reported owners' equity, and vice versa. *The amount shown as the owners' equity*

*in the usual balance sheet won't equal the value of the owners'
equity except by coincidence.*[4]

SUMMARY

From an accounting standpoint, a business can be viewed as a
set of resources assembled and used to carry out one or more activities with a profit objective. Accounting measures of a company's
financial position and performance are reported in the financial
statements. The balance sheet lists the company's assets and the
sources of those assets. These sources (equities) are divided into
two categories—liabilities and owners' equity. Since the list of assets
and the list of liabilities and owners' equity merely measure two
aspects of the same resources, the two lists have identical totals.
This equality is the basis of the accounting equation.

EXHIBIT 2–11. Balanced Transactions Analyses

An asset increases, another asset decreases.
An asset increases, a liability increases.
An asset increases, owners' equity increases.
An asset decreases, a liability decreases.
An asset decreases, owners' equity decreases.
A liability increases, another liability decreases.
A liability increases, owners' equity decreases.
A liability decreases, owners' equity increases.
One part of owners' equity increases, another part decreases.

Accountants also report on the economic performance of the resources used in the business. For a business enterprise, the accountant's measure of performance is known as net income. In general,
net income is the difference between the value of the resources
the business receives for its goods and services (its revenues) and
the costs of the resources it consumes in the process (its expenses).

Accounting measures of income and financial position are based
on summaries of the accountant's analyses of individual transactions. The analysis of a transaction consists of identifying its effects
on the company's assets, liabilities, and owners' equity. Each transaction affects at least two kinds of assets, liabilities, or owners'
equity. For each transaction, the sum of the asset changes must

---

[4] The concept of *value* is discussed at length in Chapter 6; lease accounting is
one of the topics covered in Chapter 10.

equal the sum of the changes in liabilities and owners' equity, as in the list in Exhibit 2–11. As a result, the accounting equation always remains balanced.

The income statement and balance sheet don't necessarily reflect all the available information about the financial status and performance of the business enterprise because accountants are generally unwilling to use estimates that can't be verified readily. This means that both management and outsiders must be alert, ready to recognize situations in which information on unmeasured quantities is vital to an understanding of the company and its operations.

APPENDIX: OWNERS' EQUITY IN THE INDIVIDUAL PROPRIETORSHIP OR PARTNERSHIP

The illustrative company in this chapter was a corporation. If Erskine Appliances had been an individual proprietorship or a partnership, the accounting would have been only slightly different. First, no shares of capital stock would have been issued. The balance sheet caption for the $30,000 initial capital investment therefore would have been something such as "Erskine, Capital," or "Partners' Investment." In fact, the entire amount of the owners' equity, including the retained earnings and the owners' original contribution, might have been shown as a single sum for an individual proprietorship, or as a set of sums in a partnership, one for each partner.

Second, proprietorships and partnerships don't declare dividends; the owners make *withdrawals*. These withdrawals aren't recognized until the owners actually take resources—usually cash—out of the business. There is no such thing as "withdrawals declared" or "withdrawals payable."

Third, individual proprietorships and partnerships don't pay salaries to their owners. Erskine's $1,800 salary therefore would have been treated as a withdrawal, not as an expense. Like a dividend, this withdrawal would have appeared on the statement of changes in owners' equity, not on the income statement.

The main reason for this third difference is that the owner or owners and the business aren't independent of each other. As an individual proprietor, for example, Erskine could have set his salary at zero or at $3,000 without getting approval from anyone else. In other words, he could have made the net income figure be as great as $2,150 or as little as he wished, simply by altering his salary. Although individual partners have less flexibility, the partners as a group have the same freedom to set their salaries at any level they choose. The corporation, in contrast, is viewed as a separate entity, independent of its owners. Any salary agreed to by the corporation becomes an obligation of this separate entity. In studying the profitability of unincorporated businesses, economists generally supply their own estimates of the fair amount of compensation for owners' services. They call these amounts "imputed wages" and base them on estimates of the going market prices for comparable services.[5]

For the closely held corporation (e.g., owned by Erskine and his two friends), the difference is largely metaphysical, of course, because the owners can still set their salaries at will. For this reason readers of the financial statements of these corporations may take the salary amounts with a grain of salt.

The fourth unique feature of the individual proprietorship or partnership from an accounting point of view is that it doesn't have income tax expense. (Neither did Erskine Appliances, Inc., but that was because we simplified the illustration; corporate income *is* subject to income taxation in the United States and in most other countries.) The main reason for this difference is that the business in an individual proprietorship or partnership is regarded as simply one of the activities each individual owner engages in. In other words, the taxable entity is the individual owner, not the business. In some cases, partnerships may elect to be taxed as if they were corporations, but in general income taxes are levied on the partners rather than on the partnership.

KEY TERMS

Accounting entity	Intangible asset
Asset	Liability
Balance sheet	Loss
Corporation	Monetary assets
Cost	Net assets
Current assets	Net income
Current liabilities	Operating cycle
Depreciation	Owners' equity
Disbursement	Retained earnings
Expenditure	Revenue
Expense	Transaction
Financial statement	Working capital
Income statement	

---

[5] Similar deductions are also made for "imputed rent" on owner-supplied business premises. And for corporations as well as for individual proprietorships and partnerships, economists often deduct "imputed interest" on the owners' investment in calculating the profitability of the business. We'll say something about this calculation in Part Four.

INDEPENDENT STUDY PROBLEMS (Solutions in Appendix B)

STUDY AID: THE TRANSACTIONS EQUATION

Solutions to many problems in transactions analysis require a thorough understanding of the relationship we refer to as the transactions equation:

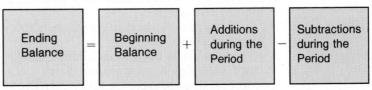

This equation applies to any statement component. Any of the four elements in this equation can be calculated if the other three are known.

1. **Organizing a balance sheet.** The following are all the assets, liabilities, and owners' equities of Bolter Company on December 31, 19x1:

Accounts payable	$13,300
Accounts receivable	8,120
Bonds payable	40,200
Buildings	65,760
Capital stock	35,000
Cash on hand and in bank	6,600
Equipment	4,450
Inventory of merchandise	11,200
Land	18,000
Notes payable (due in 19x2)	9,000
Retained earnings	To be derived
Wages payable	1,770

a. Calculate the amount of Bolter Company's retained earnings on December 31, 19x1.

b. Prepare a correctly structured balance sheet for Bolter Company as of December 31, 19x1.

2. **Income, dividends, and balance sheet changes.** Two sisters formed a corporation on January 1, 19x1, each of them investing $10,000 and receiving 1,000 shares of the corporation's capital stock in exchange. The corporation issued no more shares of capital stock during the next three years, and on January 1, 19x4, the company had total assets of $120,000 and total liabilities of $64,000.

During 19x4, the corporation issued 100 additional shares of its capital stock to a friend of the two sisters, receiving in exchange $6,000 in cash. Cash dividends amounting to $24,000 were declared and paid during the year. On December 31, 19x4, the company had assets amounting to $140,000 and liabilities of $68,000.

a. Calculate net income for 19x4.

b. Present the owners' equity section of the company's balance sheet on December 31, 19x4.

3. Transactions equation. Each of the following describes an asset or liability of Egbert Company, including certain transactions during a recent year:

1. Accounts receivable: beginning balance, $100; sales on account, $500; ending balance, $80.
2. Accounts payable: beginning balance, $50; payments to suppliers, $250; ending balance, $40.
3. Wages payable: beginning balance, $20; wages earned by employees, $300; wages paid to employees, $295.
4. Merchandise inventory: ending balance, $90; cost of goods purchased, $240; cost of goods sold, $265.
5. Prepaid rent: beginning balance, $45; ending balance, $60; rent paid, $130.

For each of these, use the transactions equation to calculate the missing amount. Explain in a word or brief phrase what each of these missing amounts represents.

4. Transactions analysis; income statement. A store had the following transactions in 19x1:

1. It bought merchandise on account for $1 million.
2. It sold merchandise on account for $1.5 million.
3. It used the services of its employees; these employees earned $300,000 by providing these services.
4. It received invoices totaling $100,000 from the electric company, the telephone company, and other outside firms for services used during 19x1.
5. It paid $1,050,000 to merchandise suppliers, utility companies, and other outside service companies.
6. It paid its employees $280,000.
7. It collected $1.6 million in cash from its customers.
8. It bought display cabinets and other store equipment for $40,000, paying $25,000 in cash and promising to pay the balance early in 19x2.
9. It determined that the cost of the merchandise sold (item 2) was $940,000.
10. It estimated that depreciation of store fixtures and equipment during the year amounted to $18,000.
11. It declared cash dividends to its stockholders amounting to $10,000.
12. It paid previously declared cash dividends of $7,500 to its stockholders.

a. Identify the effects of each of these transactions and other events on the company's assets, liabilities, and owners' equity. For each change, state both the amount in dollars and the direction of the change (+ or −).

b. Prepare an income statement for the year.

5. Analyzing transactions. A furniture store opened for business on January 1, 19x1. The store's transactions in 19x3, its third year of operations, included the following, among others:

1. The company purchased office furniture on July 1, 19x3, $4,200. The supplier was paid on October 1, 19x3. Office furniture in this company has a 12-year life.
2. Management hired a sales representative on October 1 at a salary of $1,500 a month. The representative started work immediately and remained in the company's employ until January 31, 19x4. Each sales representative's salary is paid on the 15th of each month, covering work done in the preceding month.
3. The company sold merchandise on account for $300,000. This merchandise had been placed in inventory in 19x2. It had cost $220,000 at that time.
4. The company paid a supplier $24,000 for merchandise received in 19x2.
5. The company paid $22,500 on November 1, 19x3, for store rental covering the period from October 1, 19x3, through March 31, 19x4.

a. Identify the effects of each of these transactions on the store's assets, liabilities, and owners' equity in 19x3.
b. How much expense should have been recognized in the store's 19x3 income statement as a result of each of these transactions in 19x3?

6. Transactions analysis; financial statements. The Handyman Tool Shop is an incorporated retailer of hardware supplies. Its balance sheet on December 31, 19x1, showed the following:

HANDYMAN TOOL SHOP, INC.
Balance Sheet
December 31, 19x1

Assets		Liabilities and Owners' Equity		
Current assets:		Current liabilities:		
Cash	$ 12,510	Accounts payable		$ 35,180
Accounts receivable	23,060	Salaries payable		1,400
Merchandise inventory	67,200	Total current		
Total current		liabilities		36,580
assets	102,770			
Equipment	19,020	Owners' equity:		
		Capital stock	$50,000	
		Retained earnings ...	35,210	
		Total owners'		
		equity		85,210
		Total liabilities and		
Total assets	$121,790	owners' equity		$121,790

The store's transactions for the year 19x2 are summarized in the following items:

1. Sold merchandise at a total price of $301,000. The cost of the merchandise was $181,000.
2. Collected $296,000 in cash from customers.
3. Purchased merchandise from suppliers on account at a cost of $246,300.

4. Bought a secondhand delivery truck on account, $3,800.
5. Occupied the store for the entire year at an agreed monthly rental of $1,250.
6. Used telephone, electricity, and other miscellaneous services costing $21,000.
7. Made cash salary payments to employees, $44,400. The company owed nothing to its employees at the end of 19x2.
8. Made other cash payments totaling $248,850, as follows:
   To suppliers of merchandise, $209,000.
   To seller of secondhand delivery truck, $3,800.
   To landlord for use of the store, $13,750.
   To suppliers of electricity and other miscellaneous services, $22,300.
9. Calculated the year's depreciation on the equipment, $4,800.
10. Issued 1,000 additional shares of capital stock to local investors in exchange for $60,000 in cash.
11. Declared a cash dividend of $25,000, to be paid to shareowners on January 20, 19x3.

a. Set up a table of the company's assets, liabilities, and owners' equities on January 1, 19x2, using the format of Exhibit 2–7.
b. Identify the effects of each of the year's transactions on the company's assets, liabilities, and owners' equities, and insert these in the table you set up in part a. Be sure to identify the direction of each change (+ or −).
c. Prepare an income statement for the year and a balance sheet as of December 31, 19x2.

EXERCISES AND PROBLEMS

7. Net assets and owners' equity. "Although the accountant chooses to derive the net income figure by measuring changes in the owners' equity, net income in reality consists of an increase in the firm's net assets (total assets minus total liabilities)."

Is this statement true? Describe a transaction that increases net assets without producing income. Does this disprove the statement?

8. Net income and cash on hand. "I don't get it! My company had record earnings this year, retained earnings grew, and total assets are at an all-time high. How is it possible that there's less cash on hand now than there was at the end of last year?

Is this a plausible scenario? Does it reflect a flaw in accounting techniques or a failure to understand accounting data? Reconcile the apparent anomaly for the perplexed entrepreneur.

9. Measuring expense. Andrew Jenkins worked 100 hours in the Acme Hardware Store during June. He was paid $450 during July for these services. How much of this amount was an expense of the store in June? How much was an expense in July? How much was income to Jenkins in June, and how much in July? Explain.

10. Concepts of wealth and income. Eugene and Janet Bronson own and operate a farm. Their title to the land includes the rights to any mineral wealth it contains. They have just discovered that a rich oil field recently found nearby extends far into their property. Drilling wells and selling the oil from these wells will be very worthwhile.

a. Did the discovery lead to an immediate increase in the known assets of this farm? Is it likely that the farm's market value increased as a result of the discovery? Did the discovery add to the Bronson's income of the period in which the discovery was made?

b. Would the accountant report an immediate increase in assets on the farm's balance sheet? On the income statement for the period in which the discovery was made?

11. True or false. State whether each of the following is true, false, or doubtful. Give reasons.

a. The total assets of a business are increased by the purchase of goods on credit.

b. Cash and owners' equity are the same.

c. The total of a company's assets occasionally may exceed the total of its liabilities and owners' equities.

d. Since long-term debt and owners' investments are both sources of assets, they may be considered as essentially identical.

e. Income is a source of assets.

f. When a company owes taxes to a government body, that government body is, in effect, providing some of the resources used by the company.

12. Analyzing a sales transaction. Merchandise costing $4,000 is sold for $5,200.

a. Analyze the effects of this transaction on the assets, liabilities, and owners' equity.

b. What expenses connected with this transaction are known at the time the sale takes place? What expenses are not known?

c. How and when will the profit or loss resulting from this transaction be determined?

13. Measuring and interpreting financial results. Stanley Throckmorton, who sells popcorn at public events, has no capital invested in his business other than the cash he keeps in his "business" wallet and a pushcart he bought five years ago for $200. This pushcart contains a corn-popping machine, storage space for materials (unpopped corn, butter, and salt), and a compartment in which the popped corn can be kept warm until a customer buys it.

One morning, Throckmorton left home with $100 in cash in his business wallet. Contemplating an unusually busy day, he bought materials (corn, butter, and salt) costing $120. Although he usually paid cash for his purchases, this was an exceptionally large one for him. Being a regular customer of his supplier, he was permitted to charge $50 of the total amount and pay cash for the rest.

He then attended a baseball game where he sold three quarters of his purchases for $135, all in cash. At the end of the day, he returned home with his unsold stock, planning to replenish his inventory, pay his bill, and obtain fuel for his corn popper on the following morning. (He normally bought fuel on alternate business days at a cost of about $4. A purchase of this size was enough for two days' operation of the corn popper.)

a.   How would you measure the results of Throckmorton's operations for this day? Quantify your answer as much as possible and list the items, if any, which you found difficult to quantify.

b.   Why should Throckmorton be interested in a measure of his operating results, defined as in *a*? How might knowledge c. operating results affect his business actions?

c.   What other information might Throckmorton want to be able to get from his accounting records?

14.   Calculating net income from balance sheet changes.   The XYZ Company balance sheet on January 1, 19x1, listed assets of $1.1 million, liabilities of $100,000, and capital stock for which the company had received $300,000.

During the year, $140,000 was received from the sale of additional capital stock, and dividends of $40,000 were declared and paid. The balance sheet on December 31, 19x1, showed assets of $1.5 million and liabilities of $350,000.

a.   Calculate retained earnings, January 1, 19x1.

b.   Calculate retained earnings, December 31, 19x1.

c.   Calculate net income for the year ended December 31, 19x1.

15.   Identifying income statement elements; balance sheets.   The following list includes all the items that should appear on the income statement for Omega Stores for the year 19x1, together with all necessary information to prepare balance sheets as of the beginning and the end of the year:

Accounts payable, beginning of year	70
Accounts payable, end of year	90
Accounts receivable, beginning of year	200
Accounts receivable, end of year	210
Cash on hand, beginning of year	70
Cash on hand, end of year	80
Cost of merchandise purchased during 19x1	630
Cost of merchandise sold during 19x1	600
Dividends declared and paid to owners in 19x1	20
Merchandise inventory, beginning of year	120
Merchandise inventory, end of year	?
Miscellaneous expenses during 19x1	60
Owners' equity, beginning of year	320
Owners' equity, end of year	?
Rent expense for 19x1	40
Salaries and wages expense for 19x1	110
Sales revenues for 19x1	1,000
Tax expense for 19x1	140

a.   Using the relevant data from this list, prepare an income statement for the year 19x1.

b.   Prepare balance sheets as of January 1 and December 31, 19x1.

16. Supplying missing information. From the following financial data for four businesses (I, II, III, and IV), determine the amount of each item missing:

	I	II	III	IV
Assets 1/1/x1	$ 60,000	$100,000	$ 80,000	$ J
Liabilities 1/1/x1	25,000	D	20,000	100,000
Assets 12/31/x1	70,000	E	G	600,000
Liabilities 12/31/x1	26,000	29,000	16,000	K
Owners' equity 1/1/x1	A	70,000	H	400,000
Owners' equity 12/31/x1	B	74,000	I	420,000
Revenues 19x1	350,000	500,000	400,000	L
Expenses 19x1	337,000	F	380,000	1,500,000
Dividends declared 19x1	C	5,000	8,000	15,000

17. Preparing financial statements from account balances. The financial records of Fox Automobile Repair Shop, Inc., showed the following amounts on December 31, 19x6:

Accounts payable	$ 22,100
Accounts receivable	41,000
Buildings	120,000
Capital stock	50,000
Cash	6,400
Dividends declared during 19x6	30,000
Equipment	121,300
General expenses	31,400
Inventory of repair parts	42,500
Repair parts used during 19x6	35,600
Retained earnings	?
Revenues	289,400
Wages expense	150,900
Wages payable	3,800

a. Prepare an income statement for 19x6 and a balance sheet as of December 31, 19x6.
b. Explain why the amounts shown for wages expense and wages payable aren't identical.
c. The stockholders invested no money in the business during 19x6. Calculate their equity in the business on January 1, 19x6 (the beginning of the year).

18. Transactions analysis. Listed here are Oliver Company's balance sheet amounts at seven successive times. Identify the reason for the change from each amount to its successor.

	A	B	C	D	E	F	G
Assets:							
Cash	$ 10	$ 10	$ 25	$ 25	$ 37	$ 37	$ 15
Receivables	20	20	43	43	31	31	31
Inventory	30	44	23	23	23	23	23
Machinery	40	40	40	45	45	42	42
Total	$100	$114	$131	$136	$136	$133	$111
Equities:							
Payables	$ 50	$ 64	$ 64	$ 64	$ 64	$ 75	$ 53
Capital stock	20	20	20	25	25	25	25
Retained earnings	30	30	47	47	47	33	33
Total	$100	$114	$131	$136	$136	$133	$111

19. Identifying transactions. McIntyre Company is engaged in wholesaling. The following are just a few of the many events that took place in 19x1:

1. A forklift truck was bought from Warehouse Machinery Company; payment was deferred until 19x2, but the truck was delivered and placed in service in one of McIntyre's warehouses in December 19x1.
2. A bookkeeper was hired, employment to begin on January 2, 19x2. One month's salary was paid in December 19x1 to help the bookkeeper pay off some outstanding personal debts before starting on the new job; this advance was to be deducted in installments from the bookkeeper's salary in 19x2.
3. The market value of the owners' equity in this company increased by 20 percent in 19x1.
4. Completion of a highway interchange in 19x1 doubled the market value of a parcel of land owned by the company.
5. A routine audit revealed that the company's cash balance at the end of 19x1 was $250,000 less than the amount shown in the company's records and that no insurance was carried against cash shortages of this kind.
6. An office machine was leased from Rothwell Service Company in December 19x1; payments were to be made annually for five years, and the first payment was made in January 19x2. At the end of the five-year lease period, the machine was to be returned to Rothwell.
7. One of McIntyre's research engineers was finally able to solve a difficult repackaging problem after several weeks of work in 19x1, paid for by McIntyre. McIntyre patented the solution in 19x1 and prepared to offer it commercially in exchange for annual royalty payments. A substantial number of royalty agreements were anticipated, but none was signed in 19x1.

Using what you have already learned about accounting, together with a dash of logic and a sprinkle of imagination, identify the immediate effect, if any, of each of these events on the accountant's measurements of the company's assets, liabilities, and owners' equity in 19x1. If the event had no effect, explain why.

20. Transactions analysis. The following events took place in an appliance repair business in August 19x1:

1. Performed services and billed the customer for $700.
2. Ordered an electric typewriter for the office, to be delivered in October 19x1, price $920 to be paid at delivery.
3. Purchased and paid for a two-year supply of office stationery, price $380.
4. Hired a new secretary on August 31 at a salary of $1,000 a month. The secretary started work on September 1, 19x1.
5. Paid a clerk a $750 salary for work performed in the company's office in July 19x1.
6. Paid the owner's salary for the month of August 19x1, $1,800. (The business operated as a corporation.)

7. Collected cash from a customer, $1,500, for services rendered in June 19x1.
8. Calculated the depreciation of store equipment in August 19x1, $360.

All transactions of previous months were analyzed correctly and recorded properly; no analyses of August 19x1 transactions have been made.

a. Indicate the effects, if any, of each of the foregoing events on the assets, liabilities, and owners' equity of this business. (Be sure to state whether the effect in each case was an increase or a decrease.)
b. How, if at all, would your accounting analysis of any of these events have differed if this business had been organized as an individual proprietorship? Explain why any such difference would have arisen.

21. Preparing a balance sheet. Although Robinson, Inc.'s $42,000 cash on hand as of December 31, 19x1, was far greater than the wages payable of $11,000, there was concern about the $56,000 accounts payable being twice the size of accounts receivable. Total liabilities were 80 percent of total assets, and retained earnings were three times as large as capital stock. Inventory on hand had cost $70,000, liabilities including a bank note due in July 19x3 totaled $192,000, and Robinson's assets also included machinery.

Prepare Robinson, Inc.'s December 31, 19x1, balance sheet.

22. Supplying missing data. You have the following balance sheets for last year for a small retail store:

	January 1	December 31
Cash	$ 10	$ 14
Accounts receivable from customers	20	25
Merchandise inventory	30	32
Current assets	60	71
Plant and equipment	50	52
Total assets	$110	$123
Accounts payable to suppliers of merchandise	$ 15	$ 22
Dividends payable	—	2
Current liabilities	15	24
Shareowners' equity:		
Capital stock	60	60
Retained earnings	35	39
Total liabilities and owners' equity	$110	$123

You are given the following additional data on the year's transactions:

1. Collections from customers, $145.
2. Payments to suppliers of merchandise, $95.
3. Purchases of equipment (all paid in cash), $6.
4. Dividends declared, $5.
5. Selling and administrative expenses, $37.
6. Plant and equipment retired or sold, none.
7. The only expenses last year were the cost of merchandise sold, depreciation, and selling and administrative expenses.

a. Calculate sales revenues for the year.
b. Calculate the cost of merchandise sold during the year.
c. Calculate depreciation for the year.
d. Calculate net income for the year.

23. Supplying missing information. The owners of the M Wholesale Company prepared the following table of their company's assets and liabilities:

	December 31	
	19x8	19x9
Cash	$ 2,000	$ 4,200
Merchandise inventory	12,300	15,000
Accounts receivable	7,000	5,000
Accounts payable for merchandise	8,000	10,100
Furniture and fixtures (net after deduction of accumulated depreciation)	3,000	2,600

Expenses for 19x9 consisted of the cost of goods sold, depreciation, and miscellaneous selling and administrative expenses. The goods and services classified as miscellaneous selling and administrative expenses were all bought and paid for in cash during 19x9.

A further analysis of the company's checkbook for 19x9 shows two more groups of transactions: (1) deposits of all amounts received from customers during the year, $50,000, and (2) payments to suppliers for merchandise amounting to $33,000. No other receipts or payments occurred during 19x9.

For 19x9, what were the:

a. Sales revenues?
b. Purchases of merchandise?
c. Cost of merchandise sold?
d. Other expenses?

e. Net income?
f. Owners' equity (12/31/x8)?
g. Owners' equity (12/31/x9)?

24. Transactions analysis. Grafton Company is organized as a corporation. The following transactions took place during 19x2. These transactions are completely independent and do not represent all the year's transactions of this company.

1. Purchase of merchandise on account, placed in inventory, $450.
2. Payment to supplier for merchandise received and placed in inventory in 19x1, $884. The purchase was recorded correctly in 19x1.
3. Issue of additional shares of capital stock to T. O. Pitt, principal stockholder, in exchange for $8,500 cash.
4. One month's salary earned by T. O. Pitt for his services as company president during December 19x2, $2,000, paid in cash on December 31.
5. Sale of merchandise from inventory on credit: sale price $1,200, cost $920.
6. Store clerks' wages earned during December 19x1, but not paid before the end of the month, $2,800.
7. Receipt of bill for electricity used in store and office during 19x1, $87.
8. Collection of $1,106 on accounts receivable.
9. Expiration of prepaid rent on store, $500.

Identify the effects of each of these transactions on the company's assets, liabilities, and owners' equity in 19x2. Be sure to indicate whether each effect is an increase or a decrease.

25. Transactions analysis. Gee Corporation operates a retail business. The company engaged in the following transactions, among others, in 19x2. Each transaction was completely independent of the others in this list.

1. Purchase of merchandise on an extended-payment contract, $2,100. The merchandise was placed in inventory, one third of the price was paid at the time of purchase, and the note for the remainder was to be paid in installments beginning in 19x3.
2. Payment of $15,000 to suppliers of merchandise on account.
3. Payment of $600 for insurance coverage for the year 19x2.
4. Sale of merchandise from inventory, $8,300 for cash and $13,700 on account; cost of merchandise sold, $16,400.
5. Purchase of land and building on December 31, 19x2, $22,000 for the land and $140,000 for the building; $80,000 was paid in cash and the remainder was financed by borrowing from a bank, giving in exchange a 20-year note payable.
6. Collection of $18,300 on customers' accounts.
7. Use of office supplies costing $800 from the office supplies inventory.
8. Depreciation of delivery equipment, $1,550.
9. Accountant's fee for services rendered in 19x2, $700, to be paid in 19x3.
10. Declaration and payment in cash of cash dividends to owners of the company's capital stock, $5,600.

Identify the effects of each of these transactions on the company's assets, liabilities, and owners' equity in 19x2. Be sure to indicate whether each effect was an increase or a decrease.

26. Transactions analysis; financial statements. The S&R Auto Parts Company operates an automobile supplies store. It had the following assets, liabilities, and owners' equity on January 1, 19x1:

Cash	$ 3,200	Accounts payable	$ 3,700
Accounts receivable	1,400	Bank loan payable	10,000
Inventory	22,000	Capital stock	11,000
Prepaid rent	800	Retained earnings	4,700
Equipment	2,000		
Total	$29,400	Total	$29,400

The company had the following transactions in January, 19x1:

1. Bought merchandise on account, $3,300, and placed it in inventory.
2. Sold merchandise from inventory: price to customers, $8,100 cash and $2,300 on account.
3. Collected $850 cash from customers, on account.
4. Used store clerks' services costing $1,840.
5. Made payments, as follows:
   To store clerks, $1,840.
   To merchandise suppliers, on account, $3,500.

To landlord, for rent for February, March, and April 19x1, $2,400.

To owner of a majority of the capital shares as a salary for services as president of the corporation, $1,500.

To electric and telephone companies for services in January, $200.

To local newspaper for advertising space used in January, $150.

6. Calculated the cost of the merchandise sold from inventory in January, $4,200.
7. Calculated the month's depreciation on the equipment, $50.
8. Paid the bank $100 for interest on the bank loan payable, covering the period from January 1 to January 31, 19x1.
9. Declared dividends of $1,000 to be paid in cash to stockholders on February 10, 19x1.

a. For each transaction or other event, identify the effects on the company's assets, liabilities, and owners' equity in January 19x1, using the format illustrated in Exhibit 2–4.
b. Prepare an income statement for the month of January 19x1 and a balance sheet as of January 31, 19x1, distinguishing between current and noncurrent items in the balance sheet. (The bank loan and prepayment should be classified as current items.)
c. C. Rowe, the company's president and majority stockholder, claims that the change in the cash balance each month is a better measure of the company's income or loss than the net income or loss you calculated as part of your answer to part b. Using numbers from this problem, prepare an analysis of this argument.

27. Transactions analysis; financial statements. Jane Doe formed a merchandising company on January 1. It had the following transactions during its first month:

1. Ms. Doe and a group of her friends made a cash investment of $90,000 in the business, receiving 10,000 shares of capital stock in exchange.
2. Land, $30,000, a building, $60,000, and equipment, $24,000, were purchased on January 1. Cash in the amount of $89,000 was paid for these items. The balance was owed on a five-year note payable.
3. Merchandise costing $40,000 was purchased on credit and placed in inventory.
4. Merchandise costing $30,000 was sold from inventory for $50,000. Of this latter amount, $21,000 was for cash and the balance was sold on credit.
5. Salaries and wages totaled $13,500 for the month. This entire amount was paid in cash.
6. Miscellaneous expenses amounted to $4,200. Of this amount, $3,300 was paid in cash; the rest will be paid in February.
7. The depreciation for the month was $150 on the building and $200 on the equipment.
8. The company paid $200, covering interest charges on the note payable for the month of January.

a. Analyze each of these transactions, identifying their effects on the following assets, liabilities, and owners' equities, using the format illustrated in Exhibit 2–4:

Cash   Equipment
Accounts receivable   Accounts payable
Inventory   Notes and interest payable
Land   Capital stock
Buildings   Retained earnings

Label each of these to identify it as an asset (*A*), a liability (*L*), or an owners' equity (*OE*).

b. Prepare an income statement for the month.
c. Prepare a balance sheet as of January 31.

28. Transactions and financial statements: individual proprietorship. On December 31, Grace Harvey completed her first year as proprietor of a sportswear store, which she operated as an individual proprietorship. The following data summarize the first year's transactions.

1. She invested $70,000 cash in the business.
2. In January she borrowed $30,000 cash from a bank and deposited it in the business's checking account. The loan was to be paid within 18 months.
3. In January she secured a five-year lease on shop space, with rental charges to be based on sales volume in the store. Rent for the 12 months that ended on December 31 amounted to $11,460, paid entirely in cash.
4. She bought furniture and store equipment for $37,500 cash.
5. She bought merchandise on credit for $142,925.
6. During the year she sold some of the merchandise described in 5. The cost of the merchandise sold was $108,450. She sold this merchandise for $161,000, of which $85,500 was cash and $75,500 was on credit.
7. She paid herself a salary of $30,000, paid $3,210 as wages to part-time employees, and paid $10,110 for other expenses, all in cash.
8. She returned defective merchandise to a supplier for full credit, $4,405.
9. She collected $22,130 of the amounts owed her by customers who had bought merchandise on credit.
10. She made payments to suppliers on account, totaling $107,600.
11. A shoplifter stole merchandise that had cost $410.
12. On December 31, Harvey repaid $1,500 of the amount she had borrowed from the bank (item 2), plus an additional $3,600 representing one year's interest on the amount borrowed.
13. She decided to depreciate the cost of the furniture and equipment evenly over a five-year period. She did not believe that any salvage value would be left at the end of that time.

a. Analyze the effects of the above transactions on the assets, liabilities, and owner's equity of Harvey's business, using the format illustrated in Exhibit 2–4.
b. Prepare an income statement for the year and a year-end balance sheet.
c. What further information would you want to have before you could tell Harvey whether her business venture was a success from a financial viewpoint?

29. Transactions analysis; financial statements. Westbridge, Inc., buys and sells iron pipe. On January 1, the business had the following assets, liabilities, and owners' equity:

Cash, $3,000; receivables, $50,000; inventories, $136,000; store equipment, $74,800; accounts payable, $33,800; wages payable, $0; taxes payable, $9,300; note payable, $0; capital stock, $150,000; retained earnings, $70,700.

The following transactions took place in January:

1. Merchandise costing $78,800 was purchased on account and placed in inventory.
2. Merchandise with a cost of $82,100 was taken from inventory and sold on account for $106,300.
3. The company's employees earned salaries totaling $5,000 by working for the company in January.
4. The costs of telephone service, electricity, and other supporting services provided by outside suppliers and bought on account amounted to $11,200.
5. Tax expense applicable to the month of January was estimated to be $2,000, but no taxes were paid during the month.
6. Customers paid bills amounting to $125,100.
7. Westbridge paid $5,000 to its employees, $109,700 to its suppliers of merchandise, and $9,700 to suppliers of supporting services.
8. Depreciation of store equipment amounted to $300.
9. Westbridge purchased and received new store equipment costing $20,000; payment for this equipment was to be made in March.
10. On January 31, Westbridge borrowed $6,500 from a bank and deposited this amount in the company's bank account. The company's president signed a note promising to repay this amount to the bank at the end of April.

a. List the January 1 assets, liabilities, and owners' equity, using the format illustrated in Exhibit 2–4. Then show the financial effects of the month's transactions, using only the 10 categories listed at the beginning of this problem.
b. Prepare an income statement for the month of January and a balance sheet as of January 31.

30. Transactions analysis; financial statements: individual proprietorship. In January, Alan Bucknell opened a retail grocery store to be operated as an individual proprietorship. The following list summarizes the transactions of his first year of business.

1. He invested $180,000 in cash, which he deposited in a bank account in the store's name.
2. He bought land and a store building for $80,000 and equipment for $10,000, paying $50,000 cash and borrowing the remaining $40,000 from the bank. Land accounted for $15,000 of the cost of land and building.
3. He bought on account merchandise costing $110,625 and placed it in inventory.
4. He sold merchandise from inventory. This merchandise had cost him

$94,550 and he sold it for $118,625, of which $62,750 was for cash and the balance was on credit.

5. He paid his employees' wages in cash, $21,225.
6. He paid $7,875 cash for other operating expenses.
7. He received $750 cash for rent of storage space in his store loft during the year.
8. He suffered an uninsured loss by fire of merchandise inventory that had cost $5,000 and equipment that had cost $2,600.
9. He paid $98,750 of his accounts payable, $86,250 with cash and $12,500 with notes payable.
10. His customers paid him $53,750 of the amounts they owed him.
11. During the year, he withdrew for his own use $12,000 in cash and merchandise that had cost $2,625. He calculated that if he hadn't gone into business for himself, he would have received a salary of $28,000 from his former employer.
12. Bills for expenses incurred in December but still unpaid on December 31 amounted to $550.
13. The depreciation of building and equipment during the year was estimated to be $2,000 for the building and $1,000 for the equipment.
14. On December 31, he paid the bank $4,800 interest on the bank loan, covering the period from the time of the loan to the end of the year.

a. Analyze the effects of the above transactions on these assets, liabilities, and owner's equity of Bucknell's business, using the format illustrated in Exhibit 2–4.
b. Prepare an income statement for the year and a balance sheet as of December 31.

3

The mechanics of transactions analysis

As we saw in Chapter 2, accountants base financial statements on the results of their analyses of individual transactions. Each analysis identifies the effects of a transaction on the company's assets, liabilities, and owners' equity. The purpose of this chapter is to describe the procedures accountants use to provide a cumulative record of their analyses of individual transactions.

THE BOOKKEEPING PROCESS

The means by which the accounting analyses of transactions are recorded in a formal way is known as *bookkeeping*. We'll discuss the following five aspects or components of bookkeeping systems:

1. Accounts.
2. Documents, journals, and ledgers.
3. Double-entry bookkeeping.
4. Debit/credit notation.
5. Closing entries.

Accounts

An account is simply a place in which to record the effects of a company's transactions on one of its assets, liabilities, or components of owners' equity. Each account must have some means of showing three kinds of facts: increases in the quantity represented by the account, decreases in the quantity represented by the account, and the *balance* in the account after all transactions have been recorded. The balance in an account on any date is the *cumulative* difference between the increases and the decreases that have been recorded in the account since it was created.

For example, suppose a new company has two transactions affecting cash on June 6, 19x1, its first day in business:

1. Issuance of capital stock for $100,000 in cash.
2. Payment of $25,000 for equipment.

The Cash account will show the following:

Cash

Date	Description	Amount
6/6	Issuance of capital stock	+$100,000
6/6	Payment for equipment	− 25,000
6/6	Balance	+$ 75,000

The chart of accounts

A list of the titles of a company's accounts is known as its *chart of accounts*. Exhibit 3–1 shows the chart of accounts Charles Erskine set up to record the transactions we analyzed in Chapter 2.

**EXHIBIT 3–1. Erskine Appliances, Inc.:
Initial Chart of Accounts**

Assets	Cash Accounts receivable Inventory Prepaid rent Equipment
Liabilities	Accounts payable Salary payable Dividend payable
Owners' Equity	Capital stock Retained earnings Sales revenue Cost of goods sold Salary expense Rent expense Depreciation expense Miscellaneous expense Dividends declared

Each company is free to decide which accounts it wants to use. These decisions depend on the information management wants to or must obtain from the accounting records for various purposes. For this reason, different companies in the same business are likely to have very different sets of accounts.

For example, suppose management wants to know the cost of telephone service each month. If telephone costs are included with the costs of water and electric power in an account titled "Utilities Expense," the accountant may have to review all the transactions affecting that account to isolate the telephone service component. To avoid that chore, the accountant will probably set up three separate accounts, one for each kind of utility service. The balances in these accounts can then be used to give management the information it wants. In another company, however, management may not need separate information on telephone costs and a single utilities expense account will be used.

The chart of accounts in Exhibit 3–1 is much shorter than even the smallest businesses are likely to use. We'll add account titles in this chapter as we need them, but even our finished list will be far from complete. The important point is to use titles that describe the asset, liability, or owners' equity item clearly, and then use these account titles consistently.

Documents, journals, and ledgers

Data usually enter the accounting system on documents that are prepared or received at the time the transactions take place. Most of these documents are prepared initially for some other purpose: The main purpose of a sales slip or invoice, for example, is to tell the customer how much to pay; similarly, the main purpose of a bill or invoice received from a supplier is to tell the company how much the supplier expects the company to pay, and for what. A company's accountants read these documents with something else in mind—namely, to decide which assets and equities have been affected and which accounts should be used to record these effects.

These analyses are typically assembled ("entered") first in a *journal,* a chronological record of the transactions represented by the documents. A journal is a book, file of papers, reel of magnetic tape, or other medium in which the accounting analysis of each transaction is recorded *in its entirety.* In some cases, a file of the documents themselves may serve as a journal. The record of a transaction in a journal is known as a *journal entry.*

A journal entry identifies the document from which the entry is prepared, lists the accounts affected and by what amounts, and explains the nature of the transaction. For example, the journal entry to record the analysis of the issuance of stock for $100,000 cash shows the following:

1. Cash account, increase by $100,000.
2. Capital Stock account, increase by $100,000.
3. Explanation: to record the issuance of capital stock for cash (reference: stock purchase ticket number 1).

Journals are ordinarily specialized. A *payroll journal,* for example, is used to record all the details of the amounts earned by each employee, together with the deductions from these amounts for taxes and other items. A separate line is provided for each employee each pay period. Similarly, a *sales journal* is used exclusively to record sales of merchandise. Some reasons for this specialization will become apparent in a moment, but now we'll ignore these special journals and assume that all transactions are recorded in a single journal, known as the *general journal.* In practice, this journal is used to record every transaction for which no special journal has been established. If a company has only one journal, it will be a general journal.

Documents and journal entries are the first two stages in the diagram in Exhibit 3–2. To complete the recording process, the amounts entered in the journals are transferred or *posted* to the individual accounts. The file of accounts is called the *ledger,* with each account appearing on a separate page or computer storage section. Since every transaction affects at least two categories of assets, liabilities, or owners' equity, each journal entry of necessity leads to two or more amounts posted to the ledger. In the ledger, the individual transaction no longer appears as a complete unit;

EXHIBIT 3–2. The Flow of Transactions Data

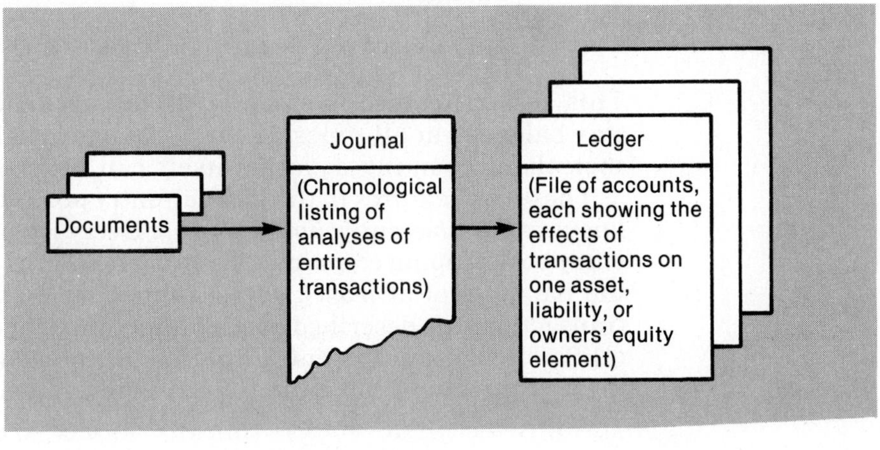

instead, its component parts are scattered in two or more accounts. For example, the issuance of stock for cash appears in two accounts:

Cash		Capital Stock	
6/6	+$100,000	6/6	+$100,000

Looking at only one ledger account will reveal only one aspect of this transaction, whereas in the general journal both aspects are visible together.

The main file of accounts is known as the *general ledger.* Many accounts in the general ledger are likely to be *control accounts,* however; that is, they represent a whole class of assets, liabilities, or owners' equity for which the detailed listing is in a separate file, known as a *subsidiary ledger.*

For example, if the general ledger has a single Accounts Receivable account, it will undoubtedly be supported by a subsidiary ledger showing the amounts owed by individual customers. A subsidiary ledger may take the form of a file of cards (one for each customer), a file of unpaid invoices (one for each purchase from a supplier), or perhaps a section of computer memory.

Double-entry bookkeeping

Each of our analyses of transactions in Chapter 2 had two essential characteristics: (1) Each transaction affected two or more assets, liabilities, or owners' equity components; and (2) the algebraic sum of the changes in the assets equaled the algebraic sum of the changes in the liabilities and owners' equity. We can express the second of these features mathematically, using the symbol Δ to denote a change:

$$\Delta \text{ Total assets} = \Delta \text{ Total liabilities} + \Delta \text{ Owners' equity}$$

This second feature is essential if the accounting equation is to stay balanced at all times. If every change is balanced in this way, then the accounting equation itself can never get out of balance.

These two features in the journal-entry process give us the system known as *double-entry bookkeeping.* Every journal entry in double-entry bookkeeping contains a symmetrical set of changes that affect the balances of at least two accounts. For example, the two cash transactions we described earlier affect three accounts: Cash, Capital Stock, and Equipment. Expressed in plus-and-minus notation, these transactions have the following effects on the accounts:

	Cash	+	Equipment	=	Capital Stock
(1)	+$100,000				+$100,000
(2)	− 25,000		+$25,000		
Balances	$ 75,000	+	$25,000	=	$100,000

In each of these two entries, the net change in the accounts on the left of the equals sign is the same as the net change in the account on the right.

Each of the accounts we've been using has had a single column of amounts, each accompanied by a plus or a minus sign. Although the form of the accounts may vary from company to company, each account can be visualized as the letter T. This schematic representation is known as a *T-account*. Additions and the account balance appear on one side of the T; subtractions appear on the other side. A T-account representing our Cash account and including the effects of the first day's cash transactions looks like this:

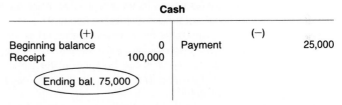

The balance in the account can be obtained at any time by subtracting the sum of the amounts on the right from the sum of the amounts on the left.

Putting the positive amount on the left side and the negative quantity on the right side of the Cash T-account follows a centuries-old tradition: Positive balances in asset accounts and amounts signifying increases in assets appear on the left in asset accounts, while amounts representing decreases in assets appear on the right side. In contrast, positive balances and increases in liability and owners' equity accounts appear on the right side; decreases appear on the left. The Capital Stock account therefore shows the following:

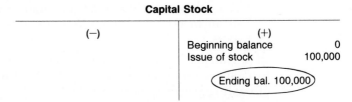

The main benefit of this *left/right* arrangement is that the nature of account balances and the effects of transactions are indicated clearly by the *positions* of the amounts, with no need for further verbal description. Furthermore, when we list the final account balances, we find that the total of the left-side balances equals the total of the right-side balances. In our example so far, we have:

	Left	Right
Cash	$ 75,000	
Equipment	25,000	
Capital Stock		$100,000
Total	$100,000	$100,000

This equality is simply another result of the accounting equation. Positive balances in liability and owners' equity accounts are on the right side; positive balances in asset accounts are on the left. Since total assets must equal the total of the liabilities and the owners' equity, the left-side total must equal the right-side total.

RULES GOVERNING THE USE OF T-ACCOUNTS

1. An *increase* in an *asset* is entered on the *left* side of the T, as is the balance in the asset account.
2. A *decrease* in an *asset* is entered on the *right* side of the T.
3. An *increase* in a liability or owners' *equity* is entered on the *right* side of the T, as is the balance in the liability or owners' equity account.
4. A *decrease* in a liability or owners' *equity* is entered on the *left* side of the T.

Debit and credit notation

Just as it is not precise to use the terms *plus* and *minus* without also specifying the kind of account, so is it also a bit cumbersome to use the terms *left side* and *right side* repeatedly. Accountants therefore have adopted a more concise notation:

> *Debit* (abbreviated as *Dr.*) is an amount on the *left* side, indicating a positive balance in an asset account, an increase in an asset, or a decrease in a liability or owners' equity. *Credit* (abbreviated as *Cr.*) is an amount on the *right* side, indicating either a positive balance or an increase in a liability or owners' equity, or a decrease in an asset.

In a transaction that brings cash into the company, the increase in cash is recorded by a debit to the Cash account; the payment of cash requires a credit to Cash.

All this is summarized in schematic terms as follows:

Asset		Liability		Owners' Equity	
+	−	−	+	−	+
Dr.	Cr.	Dr.	Cr.	Dr.	Cr.

The debit/credit notation gives us a more compact way to present the analyses of transactions than the increase/decrease notation we used in Chapter 2. For example, the analysis of a $10,000 purchase of merchandise on credit can be presented in the following way:

Accounts	Debit	Credit
Inventory	10,000	
Accounts Payable		10,000
To record the purchase of merchandise on credit.		

In this form, debits are written first; credits are written underneath, with both the account titles and amounts *indented to the right.* This is a journal entry, written in what is called *general journal form.*

The entry above is known as a *simple entry* because it contains only one debit and one credit. A *compound entry,* in contrast, contains more than two amounts. To keep the accounting equation in balance, the sum of the debit amounts must equal the sum of the credits. For example, if cash had been paid immediately for 40 percent of the $10,000 purchase of merchandise, the following compound entry would have been prepared:

Inventory	10,000	
Cash		4,000
Accounts Payable		6,000

The sum of the two credits is $10,000, just equal to the amount of the debit to Inventory.

Revenue and expense accounts

To prepare an income statement, the accountant has to separate the revenue amounts and expense amounts from other amounts that also affect the owners' equity. A separate account is therefore set up for each type of revenue and each kind of expense management wishes to identify.

To illustrate the use of revenue and expense accounts, let's assume a company sells merchandise from its inventory. The selling price is $6,000, the sale is for cash, and the merchandise was purchased earlier at a cost of $4,000. The company has one revenue account, Revenue from Sales. The journal entry recording the sale must reflect two basic facts: (1) The asset (cash) is increased by $6,000; and (2) the owners' equity (revenue) is increased by the same amount. The entry in general journal form is as follows:

```
Cash .............................................. 6,000
      Revenue from Sales ..........................        6,000
```

The first amount is a debit, denoting the increase in cash; the second amount, indented to the right, is a credit, identifying an increase in the owners' equity. (Since revenues are increases in owners' equity and increases in owners' equity appear on the right side of owners' equity accounts, it follows that increases in revenues should appear on the right side of revenue accounts.)

A second journal entry is necessary to record the company's $4,000 cost of the merchandise. This entry must show a $4,000 reduction in the company's inventory asset *and* a $4,000 reduction in the owners' equity. (Since revenues increase owners' equity and one of the costs incurred to generate these revenues is the cost of the mechandise delivered to the customer, it follows that the cost of the merchandise sold is a reduction in the owners' equity.)

The company in this illustration uses the expense account, Cost of Goods Sold, to record the costs of merchandise sold during a period. Because this is an owners' equity account and because reductions in owners' equity are shown on the left side of owners' equity accounts, the Cost of Goods Sold account has a left-side (debit) balance. The entry in general journal form is:

```
Cost of Goods Sold ............................... 4,000
      Inventory ......................................        4,000
```

The debit shows the expense (reduction in owners' equity); the credit shows the reduction in the asset.

We have now illustrated three owners' equity accounts; they can be grouped as follows:

Owners' Equity

(−) Cost of Goods Sold		(+) Capital Stock	
Dr.	Cr.	Dr.	Cr.
4,000			100,000

	Revenue from Sales	
	Dr.	Cr.
		6,000

These three accounts are shown as components of a giant T-account. Accounts that have positive balances (Capital Stock and Revenue from Sales) are shown on the positive (right-hand) side of the large

T. The account that has a negative owners' equity balance (Cost of Goods Sold) appears on the negative (left-hand) side.

Other owners' equity accounts

Some owners' equity accounts accumulate the amounts contributed to the corporation by investors who have purchased shares of stock from the corporation. These amounts are referred to as the corporation's *paid-in capital, contributed capital,* or *invested capital.* Although more than one account is likely to be used to accumulate these amounts, we'll use only one, the Capital Stock account. For example, if a company issues 10,000 shares of capital stock in exchange for $350,000 in cash, the entry is:

Cash 350,000
    Capital Stock   350,000

The debit records the increase in the corporation's assets; the credit to Capital Stock records the accompanying increase in the shareowners' equity.

A second type of owners' equity account measures the corporation's *earned* capital. This account is called Retained Earnings (or Reinvested Earnings) and it measures the amounts by which the company's net income has exceeded the amounts distributed to the stockholders since the company was formed. For example, suppose the company had a net income of $10,000 in its first year and $30,000 in its second year. It paid no dividends to its shareholders the first year but declared dividends of $5,000 in the second year. The balance in the Retained Earnings account at the end of the second year would be $35,000 ($10,000 + $30,000 − $5,000).

We know that income is calculated by analyzing revenue transactions and expense transactions. Since revenues have a favorable effect on owners' equity, they are a positive component of income; since expenses have an unfavorable effect on owners' equity, they are a negative component of income. Dividends also have an unfavorable effect on owners' equity, but they aren't an expense—because the asset consumption they require isn't for the purpose of generating revenue.

The journal entry to record the declaration of a $5,000 cash dividend is as follows:

Dividends Declared 5,000
    Dividends Payable   5,000

The debit to Dividends Declared records the reduction in owners' equity that takes place when the dividend is declared; the credit to Dividends Payable records the increase in the company's liabilities. The subsequent payment of the dividend has no additional effect on owners' equity since it reduces a liability (debit Dividends Payable) by reducing an asset (credit Cash).

Real accounts and nominal accounts

The following diagram shows the owners' equity T-accounts we've used so far:

Capital Stock		Retained Earnings	
(−)	(+)	(−)	(+)

	Dividends Declared		Income	
	(+)	(−)	(−)	(+)

		Expenses		Revenues	
		(+)	(−)	(−)	(+)

1. Capital Stock and Retained Earnings are the primary components of owners' equity and therefore are increased with credits and decreased with debits.
2. Retained Earnings *increases* as a result of profitable operations indicated by Income and *decreases* when dividends are declared, as indicated by the position of the Dividends Declared account.
3. Income, the positive component of Retained Earnings, increases with credits and decreases with debits. Dividends Declared, the negative component of Retained Earnings, increases with debits and decreases with credits.
4. Revenues, the positive component of Income, increase with credits and decrease with debits. Expenses, the negative component of Income, increase with debits and decrease with credits.

Although revenues, expenses, and dividends are components of owners' equity, their effect on owners' equity is merged with the effects of similar transactions in previous periods to constitute the end-of-period Retained Earnings balance.

All accounts with balances that appear in end-of-period balance sheets are called *real* accounts. Thus, all assets, all liabilities, and the Common Stock and Retained Earnings components of owners' equity are real accounts. By contrast, the revenue, expense, and dividend accounts are called *nominal* accounts, because at the end of each period these accounts' balances are merged and transferred to Retained Earnings. In the next section, we'll describe the process by which the nominal accounts' balances are transferred.

Closing entries

All nominal owners' equity accounts accumulate the effects of transactions during a single year. Before the journal entries reflecting next year's transactions can be posted, this year's balances in these nominal accounts must be removed. This is accomplished by *closing entries.* A closing entry is designed to transfer the balance in one account to another account:

1. If the account from which the transfer is made has a *credit* balance, that account is *debited* with an amount equal to the account balance; an identical amount is credited to the account to which the transfer is made.
2. If the account from which the transfer is made has a *debit* balance, that account is *credited* with an amount equal to the account balance; an identical amount is debited to the account to which the transfer is made.

For example, suppose our company has the following balances in its nominal accounts at the end of the year:

	Debit	Credit
Revenue from sales		$300,000
Cost of goods sold	$180,000	
Selling expenses	50,000	
Administrative expenses	40,000	
Dividends declared	5,000	

(In practice, and in the problems in this book, many more nominal accounts will be used; we've kept the number to five to avoid unnecessary complexity in this first illustration.)

The first closing entry removes the credit balance in the Revenue from Sales account by debiting that account by an amount equal to the account balance. The entry is:

Revenue from Sales 300,000
    Income Summary 300,000

The debit to Revenue from Sales reduces the balance in that account to zero; it is ready to receive the next year's entries:

Revenue from Sales

Closing entry	300,000	Revenue transactions	300,000

The Income Summary account is also a nominal account, used solely to assemble the revenues and expenses in one place at the end of the period. The $300,000 credit to this account indicates that sales revenues have increased the owners' equity.

Next, the debit balances in the three expense accounts are eliminated by crediting them with amounts equal to the account balances:

Income Summary	270,000	
Cost of Goods Sold		180,000
Selling Expenses		50,000
Administrative Expenses		40,000

This entry transfers the debit balances from three owners' equity accounts (Cost of Goods Sold, Selling Expenses, and Administrative Expenses) to the Income Summary. The credits to the expense accounts reduce the balances in those accounts to zero, so they are ready to receive next year's entries. The debit to Income Summary reduces the credit balance in that account to $30,000, the net income for the year.

The third closing entry transfers the net income to Retained Earnings:

Income Summary	30,000	
Retained Earnings		30,000

The debit to Income Summary reduces the balance in that account to zero:

Income Summary

Expenses	270,000	Revenues	300,000
Closing entry	30,000		

The credit to Retained Earnings shows that the company's activities this year have been profitable, increasing the owners' equity by $30,000.

The fourth and final closing entry removes the balance in the Dividends Declared account:

Retained Earnings	5,000	
Dividends Declared		5,000

The credit to Dividends Declared reduces the balance in that account to zero. The debit to Retained Earnings shows that the dividends reduced the owners' equity by $5,000. With income of $30,000 and dividends of $5,000, the company has increased its owners' equity this year, by retaining $25,000 of its net income in the business:

Retained Earnings

Dividends declared	5,000	Beginning balance	10,000
		Net income	30,000
		Ending bal. 35,000	

As long as the company's total net income to date exceeds the company's total dividends to date, the Retained Earnings account will have a credit balance, because credits represent increases (income) and debits represent decreases (dividends). Our $35,000 credit balance shows that this company's activities since its inception have had a positive effect on the owners' equity.

There is nothing sacred about the closing entries we've used in this illustration. For example, we could have omitted the Income Summary account, or we could have had a separate closing entry for each expense account instead of putting them together in a single entry. We could even have used one big closing entry to close all the nominal accounts at once:

Revenue from Sales	300,000	
Cost of Goods Sold		180,000
Selling Expenses		50,000
Administrative Expenses		40,000
Dividends Declared		5,000
Retained Earnings		25,000

To close all nominal accounts and bring
Retained Earnings to its correct balance.

Any combination of entries that reduces the nominal accounts to zero and adds $25,000 to Retained Earnings is acceptable.

ACCOUNTS FOR DEPRECIABLE ASSETS

Land, buildings, equipment, and other tangible assets provide operating capacity for several accounting periods into the future. Those that lose their usefulness due to physical deterioration or technological obsolescence are known as *depreciable assets.* We'll now see how the accountant uses accounts to record (1) property acquisition and depreciation and (2) sale of depreciable assets.

Property acquisition and depreciation

When a business buys equipment, it acquires an asset. Suppose, for example, a company paid $8,000 in cash for a large piece of office equipment it expected to use for eight years. This transaction increased one asset (equipment) and decreased another (cash). The entry to record the purchase was:

Equipment 8,000
　　　Cash . . . . 　　　8,000

The debit to the Equipment account recorded the increase in the asset; the credit to Cash recorded the decrease in that asset.

At the time of the purchase, the company estimated that depreciation on this equipment would amount to $1,000 a year. At the end of the first year, therefore, the company's accountants made the following analysis:

Decrease in owners' equity (Expense) $1,000	Accompanied by	Decrease in asset (Equipment) $1,000

This could be translated into an entry of the following form:

Depreciation Expense 1,000
　　　Equipment . . . . 　　　1,000
　　To record one year's depreciation on equipment.

If the entries recording depreciation were actually made this way, the accounts would show the following preclosing balances at the end of the third year:

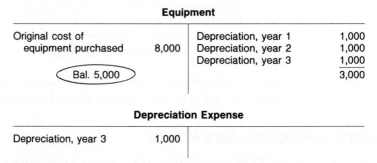

Equipment

Original cost of equipment purchased	8,000	Depreciation, year 1	1,000
		Depreciation, year 2	1,000
		Depreciation, year 3	1,000
Bal. 5,000			3,000

Depreciation Expense

Depreciation, year 3	1,000	

The $5,000 balance in the Equipment account shows the portion of the original cost that had not yet been charged to expense. The balance in the Depreciation Expense account for the third year would be the cost of only that portion of the asset's life that was consumed *during that year,* because expense accounts accumulate costs for one accounting period only and are closed out at the end of each period.

This method makes it impossible to identify the original cost of equipment without complete access to the company's records. Because this kind of information is generally thought to be useful (and is often required by law), the more common treatment is to use a separate account to accumulate the amounts reflecting the consumed portion of the original cost. This account is called *Accumulated Depreciation* or *Allowance for Depreciation;* the amounts on the right side of this account are those posted to the right side of the Equipment account earlier in this illustration. The two accounts now show the following:

Equipment		Accumulated Depreciation	
Original cost of equipment purchased	8,000	Depreciation, year 1	1,000
		Depreciation, year 2	1,000
		Depreciation, year 3	1,000
		Bal. 3,000	

The entry to record depreciation for the third year therefore is:

Depreciation Expense 1,000
        Accumulated Depreciation 1,000

As before, the debit records the reduction in the owners' equity, while the credit to Accumulated Depreciation records the consumption of the asset.

The Accumulated Depreciation account is our first example of a *contra account.* A contra account is always paired with some other account and serves to accumulate some or all of the negative effects of transactions on the asset, liability, or owners' equity to which it is coupled. For example, the Accumulated Depreciation account is a deduction-from-asset contra account, or *contra-asset* account. Since the parent asset account has a debit balance, the contra account has a credit balance. In financial reporting, the balance in the contra account should always be deducted from the balance in its parent account, as follows:

Equipment, at original cost $8,000
    Less: Accumulated depreciation 3,000
Equipment, net $5,000

The *net* figure is the asset's *unamortized cost*—that is, the amount that hasn't yet been amortized (i.e., depreciated). It is usually referred to as the asset's *book value.*

We should emphasize that although the Accumulated Depreciation account has a credit balance, it is neither a liability nor an owners' equity account. When the balance in this account is subtracted from the balance in the related plant asset account, the accounts show that some of the original cost of the plant asset has been consumed. The portion of the cost that is applicable to future periods is the difference between the balances in these two accounts. A credit to the Accumulated Depreciation account therefore records a decrease in the plant asset. It doesn't record an increase in a contra asset because there is no such thing as a contra asset. *Contra asset* is a term used to describe a certain kind of *account.* The balance in that account must be regarded as part of the description of the asset the contra account is attached to. It has no separate existence apart from that asset.

The amount in the Accumulated Depreciation account can be used as a rough index of the age of the company's equipment— the older the equipment, the higher is the ratio of accumulated depreciation to original cost. An increase in this ratio usually means that the company is riding on its past investments in facilities; a reduction in the ratio is likely to signal a modernization or expansion program.

Disposition of depreciable assets

From time to time companies dispose of depreciable assets by selling them, trading them for newer models, or losing them through involuntary destruction. The first step in recording a disposition is to recognize the depreciation between the beginning of the year in which the disposition was made and the disposition date. For example, suppose a machine costing $8,000 had accumulated depreciation of $3,000 in its first three years at the rate of $1,000 a year. The machine was sold for $2,300 in cash at the end of the first three months of year 4. This means that $250 (3/12 of the annual amount) should be recorded in year 4. The entry is:

```
Depreciation Expense ...............................   250
    Accumulated Depreciation ........................        250
```

(To reduce recordkeeping, the company might adopt a reasonable assumption about the length of the interval—such as that all retirements take place at midyear.)

The second step in recording a disposition is to remove both the asset's original cost and accumulated depreciation from the accounts. In our example, the original cost was $8,000 and the accumulated depreciation was $3,250. Before we can prepare the entry to remove these amounts from the accounts, however, we must find out whether the assets received for the sale of the machine were equal to, greater than, or less than the machine's undepreciated cost (book value). In this case, the amount received was $2,300 and the book value was $4,750 ($8,000 − $3,250). The difference between these two amounts is the *loss* on the sale, calculated as follows:

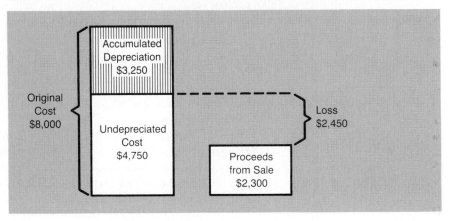

The entry to record the sale is:

Cash	2,300	
Accumulated Depreciation	3,250	
Loss on Sale of Equipment	2,450	
Equipment		8,000

In this entry, the credit of $8,000 removed the original cost of the machine from the accounts, while the debit of $3,250 did the same for the accumulated depreciation applicable to it. The debit to cash recorded the inflow of this asset, and the debit to the loss account recorded the decrease in the owners' equity that was recognized at the time of the sale.

If the machine had been sold for $6,300—instead of $2,300—the company would have recorded a $1,550 *gain*. Receiving cash of $6,300 in exchange for an asset with a book value of $4,750 means that *total* assets increased by $1,550, and that owners' equity increased by $1,550 as well.

The gain or loss on a disposition is recognized in the year the asset is disposed of, but it actually results from an incorrect estimate of either the asset's lifetime or its ultimate resale value. For our machine on which we recognized a $2,450 loss, if the lifetime and resale value had been forecasted correctly when the machine was acquired, a total of $5,700 would have been charged as depreciation during the first 3¼ years. As Exhibit 3–3 shows, this would have been just enough to bring the book value down to the ultimate $2,300 sale price in year 4.

It can be argued that the proper treatment of the loss would be

EXHIBIT 3–3. Lifetime Depreciation

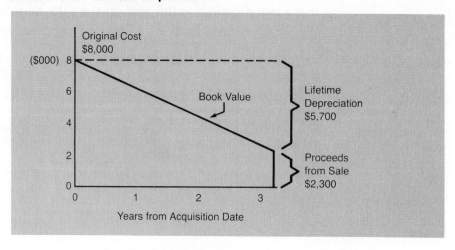

to go back and restate the company's earnings for the first three years. Unfortunately, the income statements of prior years are past history, and repeated correction of prior years' earnings can be very confusing. The company's accountants therefore reported the entire loss in the income statement for year 4, with no attempt to prorate any portion of it to earlier years.

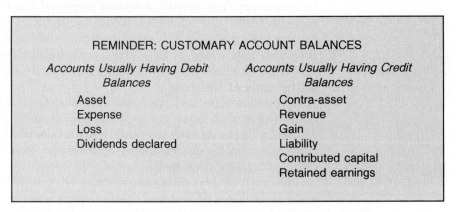

REMINDER: CUSTOMARY ACCOUNT BALANCES

Accounts Usually Having Debit Balances	Accounts Usually Having Credit Balances
Asset	Contra-asset
Expense	Revenue
Loss	Gain
Dividends declared	Liability
	Contributed capital
	Retained earnings

AN INTEGRATIVE ILLUSTRATION

To reinforce the message given earlier in this chapter, we'll apply our procedures to a set of transactions for Saturn Stores, Inc., for the year 19x1. Saturn Stores began the year with the following account balances:

	Debit	Credit
Cash	$ 100,000	
Accounts receivable........................	300,000	
Inventory	400,000	
Prepaid rent	50,000	
Equipment	800,000	
Accumulated depreciation		$ 350,000
Accounts payable...........................		200,000
Capital stock		850,000
Retained earnings		250,000
Total	$1,650,000	$1,650,000

For simplicity, we'll continue to ignore taxes. Notice that the sum of the debit balances at the beginning of the year equals the sum of the credit balances; this is necessary if the accounting equation is to balance.

The transactions

The company's transactions during the year can be summarized as follows:

1. Sales on account, $2,200,000.
2. Collections from customers, $2,150,000.
3. Purchases of merchandise on account, $1,300,000.
4. Payments to suppliers of merchandise, $1,375,000.
5. Cost of merchandise sold, $1,400,000.
6. Salaries earned by employees, $320,000.
7. Salaries paid to employees, $310,000.
8. Cost of other services purchased on account and used, $90,000.
9. Payments to suppliers of other services purchased on account, $85,000.
10. Rental payments for right to use store premises during the period from July 1, 19x1, to June 30, 19x2, $120,000.
11. Rental costs applicable to 19x1, $110,000 ($50,000 for the period from January 1 to June 30, 19x1, and $60,000 for the period from July 1 to December 31, 19x1).
12. Equipment purchased (paid for in cash), $100,000.
13. Depreciation on equipment, $82,000.
14. Proceeds from sale of equipment, $15,000 (original cost of equipment sold, $40,000; accumulated depreciation on equipment sold, $22,000).
15. Dividends declared, $60,000.
16. Dividends paid, $45,000.

Journal entries

The following journal entries identify and record the effects of these transactions on the company's assets, liabilities, and owners' equity. Each entry has an identifying number keyed to the list of transactions above and an explanation of the entry. In practice, each entry would also identify the document on which it is based, but we've omitted this because it would add nothing to our discussion.

1. Accounts Receivable 2,200,000
    Revenue from Sales   2,200,000
    To record increases in accounts receivable (asset) and in revenue (increase in owners' equity) resulting from sales.

2. Cash 2,150,000
    Accounts Receivable   2,150,000
    To record increase in cash (asset) and decrease in accounts receivable (asset) resulting from collections from customers.

3. Inventory 1,300,000
    Accounts Payable   1,300,000
    To record increases in inventory (asset) and in accounts payable (liability) resulting from purchases of merchandise.

4. Accounts Payable 1,375,000
    Cash   1,375,000
    To record decreases in accounts payable (liability) and in cash (asset) resulting from payments to suppliers of merchandise.

5. Cost of Goods Sold 1,400,000
    Inventory   1,400,000
    To record expense (decrease in owners' equity) and decrease in inventory (asset) resulting from sales of merchandise to customers.

6. Salaries Expense 320,000
    Salaries Payable   320,000
    To record expense (decrease in owners' equity) and increase in salaries payable (liability) resulting from use of employees' services.

7. Salaries Payable 310,000
    Cash   310,000
    To record decreases in salaries payable (liability) and in cash (asset) resulting from salary payments to employees.

8. Miscellaneous Expenses 90,000
        Accounts Payable 90,000
    To record expense (decrease in owners'
    equity) and increase in accounts payable
    (liability) resulting from purchase and
    use of miscellaneous services.

9. Accounts Payable 85,000
        Cash 85,000
    To record decreases in accounts payable
    (liability) and in cash (asset) resulting
    from payments to suppliers of miscella-
    neous services.

10. Prepaid Rent 120,000
        Cash 120,000
    To record increase in prepaid rent (as-
    set) and decrease in cash (asset) result-
    ing from rental payments covering the
    period from July 1, 19x1, to June 30,
    19x2.

11. Rent Expense 110,000
        Prepaid Rent 110,000
    To record expense (decrease in owners'
    equity) and decrease in prepaid rent (as-
    set) resulting from use of store premises.

12. Equipment 100,000
        Cash 100,000
    To record increase in equipment (asset)
    and decrease in cash (asset) resulting
    from purchase of store equipment and
    payment of cash.

13. Depreciation Expense 82,000
        Accumulated Depreciation 82,000
    To record expense (decrease in owners'
    equity) and decrease in equipment (as-
    set) resulting from depreciation of store
    equipment.

14. Cash 15,000
    Accumulated Depreciation 22,000
    Loss on Sale of Equipment 3,000
        Equipment 40,000
    To record increase in cash (asset), de-
    crease in equipment (asset), and loss (de-
    crease in owners' equity) resulting from
    sale of store equipment for $3,000 less
    than its book value.

15. Dividends Declared 60,000
    Dividends Payable   60,000
    To record increase in dividends declared (decrease in owners' equity) and increase in dividends payable (liability) resulting from declaration of dividends to stockholders.

16. Dividends Payable 45,000
    Cash   45,000
    To record decreases in dividends payable (liability) and in cash (asset) resulting from payment of cash dividends to stockholders.

Ledger posting

Each number in the journal entries must be posted to the appropriate ledger account. The accounts showing these postings, together with their opening balances, are presented in Exhibit 3–4. Notice that each debit and each credit is accompanied by a number identifying the transaction from which it arose. This is essential

EXHIBIT 3–4.   Saturn Stores, Inc.: Ledger Accounts

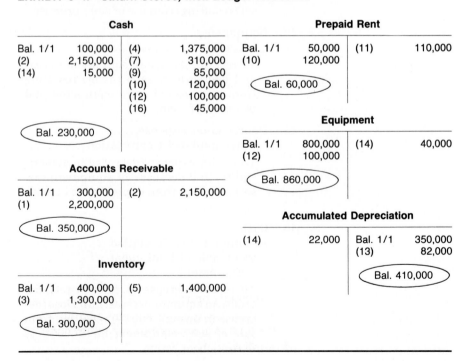

EXHIBIT 3–4 (*concluded*)

	Accounts Payable		
(4)	1,375,000	Bal. 1/1	200,000
(9)	85,000	(3)	1,300,000
		(8)	90,000
		Bal. 130,000	

	Salaries Payable		
(7)	310,000	(6)	320,000
		Bal. 10,000	

	Dividends Payable		
(16)	45,000	(15)	60,000
		Bal. 15,000	

	Capital Stock		
		Bal. 1/1	850,000

	Depreciation Expense	
(13)	82,000	

	Retained Earnings		
		Bal. 1/1	250,000

	Rent Expense	
(11)	110,000	

	Revenue from Sales		
		(1)	2,200,000

	Miscellaneous Expenses	
(8)	90,000	

	Cost of Goods Sold	
(5)	1,400,000	

	Loss on Sale of Equipment	
(14)	3,000	

	Salaries Expense	
(6)	320,000	

	Dividends Declared	
(15)	60,000	

because the accountant must leave a *trail* in case someone wants to verify an entry or trace an error to its source.

Closing entries

The nominal accounts can be returned to zero balances by a series of closing entries like those illustrated earlier in this chapter:

17. Revenue from Sales 2,200,000
      Income Summary 2,200,000
   To close the revenue account and transfer the balance to the Income Summary account.

18. Income Summary 2,005,000		
Cost of Goods Sold		1,400,000
Salary Expense		320,000
Depreciation Expense		82,000
Rent Expense		110,000
Miscellaneous Expenses		90,000
Loss on Sale of Equipment		3,000

To close expense and loss accounts and transfer balances to Income Summary account.

19. Income Summary 195,000		
Retained Earnings		195,000

To close Income Summary account and transfer the net income to Retained Earnings.

20. Retained Earnings 60,000		
Dividends Declared		60,000

To close the Dividends Declared account and transfer its balance to Retained Earnings.

After these closing entries have been posted, the following balances remain in the ledger accounts:

	Debit	Credit
Cash	$ 230,000	
Accounts receivable	350,000	
Inventory	300,000	
Prepaid rent	60,000	
Equipment	860,000	
Accumulated depreciation		$ 410,000
Accounts payable		130,000
Salaries payable		10,000
Dividends payable		15,000
Capital stock		850,000
Retained earnings		385,000
Total	$1,800,000	$1,800,000

Once again the total debit balance equals the total credit balance. This doesn't necessarily mean we've made no errors in analyzing the effects of transactions, but at least we haven't violated the accounting equation. Once the figures have been checked, however, a balance sheet can be prepared from these year-end balances, and the income statement for the year can be prepared from the preclosing balances in the revenue, expense, and loss accounts in Exhibit 3–4. We'll take a closer look at statement preparation in the next chapter.

SUMMARY

Accountants have developed a concise form of notation to identify the results of transactions analyses. The term *debit* is used to describe an increase in an asset or a decrease in a liability or in a component of owners' equity. The term *credit* describes a decrease in an asset or an increase in a liability or owners' equity. To summarize a transaction analysis in written form, the accountant merely has to write the names and amounts of the affected items in a journal, with the debits first and credits below and indented to the right.

Consistent with this notation, *accounts* are generally represented schematically by diagrams in the shape of the letter T. Debits are on the left side of the T, credits on the right. When the amounts credited to an account exceed the amounts debited to it, the account is said to have a credit balance; an excess of debits over credits produces a debit balance.

The debit/credit scheme affects all accounts. As a result, accountants strive to have all accounts *in balance* at all times. By seeing that the total of the debit balances equals the total of the credit balances, accountants know that the accounting equation—*assets equal equities*—is in balance.

This system provides a basis for subdividing some accounts into positive and negative components. If the account normally has a debit balance, then its companion, known as a contra account, will have a credit balance. The Accumulated Depreciation account, for example, is a contra-asset account with a credit balance, representing the portion of the cost of depreciable assets that has been charged to operations since the asset was originally acquired.

KEY TERMS

Account	Double-entry bookkeeping
Accumulated depreciation	Entry
Book value	Journal
Chart of accounts	Ledger
Closing entry	Paid-in capital
Contra account	T-account
Debit and credit	

INDEPENDENT STUDY PROBLEMS (Solutions in Appendix B)

1. Journal entries; ledger accounts. Kelly Company's ledger includes the following eight accounts, among others:

Account	Balance March 1, 19x1
Cash	$ 13,200
Accounts receivable	72,000
Merchandise inventory	92,000
Salaries and wages payable	450
Accounts payable	65,000
Sales revenues	130,000
Cost of goods sold	79,000
Salaries and wages expense	14,500

Kelly Company had the following transactions, among others, in March 19x1:

1. It bought merchandise costing $46,500 on account and placed this merchandise in inventory.
2. It sold merchandise from inventory for $57,000 on account; the cost of this merchandise was $36,000.
3. It collected $60,000 in cash on account from its customers.
4. It paid its merchandise suppliers $61,300 on account.
5. Its employees earned salaries and wages of $7,200 in March.
6. Store employees were paid $7,500; this included the March 1 liability.

a. Prepare T-accounts representing the eight ledger accounts listed and enter the March 1 balances. Be careful to place these balances in the correct columns.
b. Prepare entries in general journal form to record your analyses of the six transactions listed.
c. Post these entries to the T-accounts.
d. Calculate the March 31 balance in each of these accounts and state what each balance represents.

2. Depreciable assets; journal entries.   Alpha Company bought a truck on January 1, 19x6, for $10,000 in cash. Management decided to recognize depreciation of $2,000 each year for five years. The truck was placed in service immediately and was used until January 1, 19x9, when it was sold for $2,500 cash.

a. Prepare entries in general journal form to record the purchase of the truck and depreciation for 19x6.
b. Set up two T-accounts—*Truck* and *Accumulated Depreciation*—and enter the balances that should have appeared in these accounts on December 31, 19x8, just before the truck was sold.
c. Prepare an entry in general journal form to record the sale of the truck on January 1, 19x9.

3. Transactions analyses; journal entries.   The Harrel Corporation owns and operates a retail store. The following events took place last month:

1. The company purchased merchandise for $5,000; the supplier accepted, as payment for this purchase, the company's written promise (its *note*) to pay this amount next month.

2. The company received $4,000 from customers to pay for goods purchased by them in transactions recorded during the previous month.
3. The company paid previously recorded accounts payable of $6,000.
4. Store employees earned salaries of $1,000 during the month.
5. Store employees were paid $900 of the amounts they had earned.
6. The company borrowed $50,000 on a long-term note.
7. The company sold merchandise on account for $8,000; the cost of this merchandise, purchased in a previous period, was $6,000.
8. The company purchased a parcel of land at a cost of $7,000 cash.
9. The board of directors declared a dividend of $3,000, to be paid in cash to its shareholders next month. (The company uses a Dividends Declared account.)
10. Office stationery costing $60 was purchased on credit for current use.
11. Someone stole $100 in cash from the company. The loss is fully covered by insurance, but nothing has yet been received from the insurance company.

Prepare journal entries in conventional debit-and-credit notation, using account titles similar to those used in this chapter, including appropriately titled revenue and expense accounts. For each debit or credit, indicate whether it represented an increase ($+$) or a decrease ($-$) in an asset (A), a liability (L), or the owners' equity (OE). You may assume that all transactions of previous months were recorded correctly.

4. Journal entries; closing entries. The balance sheet of the Handyman Tool Shop and its transactions in the year 19x2 are listed in problem 6 at the end of Chapter 2. The company's chart of accounts include accounts with the titles listed in the December 31, 19x1, balance sheet, plus the following: Dividends Payable, Sales Revenues, Rental Expense, Salaries Expense, Depreciation Expense, Cost of Goods Sold, Miscellaneous Expenses, and Dividends Declared. The original cost of the equipment was $36,140 and the accumulated depreciation was $17,120 as of December 31, 19x1.

a. Establish T-accounts and enter the December 31, 19x1, balances.
b. Prepare entries in general journal form to record the company's transactions in 19x2, using only the accounts specified in this problem.
c. Post the amounts from the journal entries to the T-accounts and calculate the December 31, 19x2, account balances.
d. Prepare a closing entry or entries in general journal form.

EXERCISES AND PROBLEMS

5. Rental transactions. M. L., Inc., rents a warehouse at a cost of $900 a month for which several months' rent must be paid in advance. M. L. also leases office space from another landlord for $800 a month for which late payments are accepted without a penalty. M. L., Inc.'s balance sheets at December 31, 19x8 and 19x9 contained the following amounts:

	December 31	
	19x8	*19x9*
Prepaid rent	$2,700	$1,800
Rentals payable	1,600	2,000

a. What was the rent expense in 19x9?

b. How much cash was paid to landlords in 19x9?

6. Equipment retirement. A company uses an Accumulated Depreciation account. One of its machines was scrapped last month. This machine cost $1,000 initially and had a book value of $200 at the time it was scrapped. The company gave the machine to a scrap dealer, who paid the costs of removing it. Someone has suggested that the following entry be made to record the disposition of the machine:

Loss on Equipment Retirement 200
     Equipment 200

a. Why would this be wrong?

b. What entry would be correct?

7. Equipment accounts. The opening balance in an Equipment account was $300, with accumulated depreciation totaling $100 shown in a separate account.

Depreciation for the year is $50, equipment purchases during the year amount to $250, and items originally costing $75 are sold for $20, resulting in a retirement loss of $40.

a. What is the correct ending balance in the Accumulated Depreciation account?

b. Prepare journal entries to record the events described. You may assume that all purchases and sales of equipment were cash transactions.

8. Interpreting year-end owners' equity account balances. After all transactions for the year had been recorded, the following balances were found in the owners' equity accounts of a small corporation (the sequence of the accounts in the list is alphabetical and has no other significance):

	Debit	*Credit*
Capital stock		$ 20,000
Cost of goods sold	$70,000	
Dividends declared	6,000	
Other expenses	21,000	
Retained earnings		1,000
Sales revenue		100,000

a. What does the $6,000 opposite "Dividends declared" mean? Were these dividends paid in cash during the year?

b. What does the $1,000 opposite "Retained earnings" mean?

c. What balance would you show opposite "Retained earnings" on the year-end balance sheet?

9. Equipment accounts; journal entries. The balance sheet in a company's annual report for the year ended December 31, 19x1, showed the following amounts for plant and equipment:

	January 1	December 31
Plant and equipment	$400,000	$440,000
Less: Accumulated depreciation......	180,000	190,000
Plant and equipment (net)	$220,000	$250,000

The income statement for the year showed depreciation expenses of $30,000 and a gain of $10,000 on the sale of equipment. This equipment had a book value of $40,000, and it was sold for cash.

a. Calculate the cost of plant and equipment purchased during the year.
b. Prepare the appropriate journal entries to record the purchase of plant and equipment, the sale of equipment, and depreciation expense for the year. All plant and equipment purchases were cash transactions.

10. Equipment accounts. During 19x4, Ken Company bought equipment for cash of $95,000. During the year, Ken sold equipment that it had been using for several years; the cash proceeds of $17,000 resulted in Ken recording a $5,000 loss. Ken Company's balance sheets at December 31, 19x3 and 19x4, contained the following amounts:

	December 31	
	19x3	19x4
Equipment	$143,000	$192,000
Accumulated depreciation......	99,000	107,000

a. What was the depreciation expense in 19x4?
b. What was the original cost of the sold equipment?

11. Supplying missing amounts. Sardis Company's bookkeeper burned the company's journals and spilled acid on the ledger in a moment of pique. Fortunately, the acid destroyed only the amounts missing from the following table:

	Beginning Balance	Transactions Debits	Transactions Credits	Ending Balance
Accounts receivable	$35,000	$40,000	A	$36,000
Merchandise inventory	48,000	B	$26,000	42,000
Prepaid rent	3,000	1,000	2,000	C
Equipment	D	10,000	6,000	79,000
Accumulated depreciation	25,000	E	7,000	28,000
Wages payable................	100	7,700	F	400
Accounts payable	G	19,000	H	25,000

The Accounts Payable account is used only in connection with transactions between Sardis Company and its suppliers of merchandise inventory.

a. Make the necessary calculations to determine the amounts missing from the table.
b. After you have answered part a, the table has seven debits and seven credits arising from transactions of the current period. For each debit

and each credit, prepare an entry in general journal form that in your judgment was the entry in which the company originally recorded that debit or credit. If the debit or credit is to an account not included in the table, use any suitably descriptive account title.

12. Supplying missing amounts. Six accounts from Lea Corporation's ledger are presented in alphabetical order. All sales are on account, and all revenues and expenses are included in the transactions identified below.

	Beginning Balance	Transactions Debits	Transactions Credits	Ending Balance
Accounts receivable	$ 17,000	A	$140,000	$ 22,000
Dividends declared		B		
Merchandise inventory	40,000	$93,000	C	45,000
Prepaid rent	1,500	4,100	D	1,200
Retained earnings	114,500	E	F	126,700
Wages payable	1,900	28,100	G	2,200

Make the necessary calculations to determine the amounts missing from the table.

13. Journal entries; ledger accounts. Bellagio Company's ledger included the following eight accounts, among others, with these account balances at the beginning of April 19x1:

Cash.........................	$ 45,600
Accounts receivable	83,500
Merchandise inventory	93,400
Salaries and wages payable	800
Accounts payable	49,100
Sales revenues	213,900
Cost of goods sold	149,200
Salaries and wages expense......	19,700

Bellagio Company had the following transactions, among others, in April 19x1:

1. It bought merchandise costing $55,900 on account and placed this merchandise in inventory.
2. It sold merchandise from inventory for $53,400 on account; the cost of this merchandise was $33,300.
3. It collected cash amounting to $81,000 on account from its customers.
4. It paid its merchandise suppliers $46,200 on account.
5. Its employees earned salaries and wages amounting to $6,500 in April.
6. Store employees were paid $6,200; this included the liability as of April 1.

a. Prepare T-accounts representing the eight ledger accounts listed and enter the April 1 balances. Be careful to place the balances in the correct columns.
b. Prepare entries in general journal form to record your analyses of the six transactions listed.
c. Post these entries to the T-accounts.
d. Calculate the April 30 balance in each account and state what each balance represents.

14. Closing entries. The accounts of Wolf Repair Service, Inc., had the following balances on December 31, 19x1:

	Debit	Credit
Accounts payable		$ 11,050
Accounts receivable	$ 31,000	
Accumulated depreciation		40,000
Capital stock		60,000
Cash	7,050	
Depreciation expense	15,000	
Dividends declared	10,000	
Dividends payable		2,500
Miscellaneous expenses	5,000	
Parts expenses	25,000	
Parts inventory	5,250	
Plant assets	140,000	
Prepaid rent	3,000	
Rent expense	9,000	
Retained earnings		40,050
Salaries and wages expense	96,000	
Salaries and wages payable		2,700
Sales revenues		190,000
Total	$346,300	$346,300

Prepare entries in general journal form to close all nominal accounts in preparation for recording transactions in 19x2.

15. Interpreting entries in accounts. Explain the most probable meaning of each number in the following T-accounts (beginning balances, ending balances and other entries have been omitted):

	Accounts Receivable				Merchandise Inventory		
....	...	....	...	....	...	....	...
....	...	....	...	....	...	....	...
....	...	....	...	....	...	....	...
June 6	712	July 17	1,019	April 28	297	March 15	990

	Store Equipment				Accumulated Depreciation		
....	...	....	...	....	...	....	...
....	...	....	...	....	...	....	...
March 12	3,241	Nov. 29	2,062	Nov. 29	1,445	Dec. 31	865

16. Plant asset accounts; journal entries. On January 2, 19x1, Febrile Company bought an electric typewriter for office use, paying $540 in cash. Management decided to recognize depreciation of $90 each year for six years.

a. What was the correct preclosing balance in the Accumulated Depreciation account as of December 31, 19x3?

b. What was the correct preclosing balance in the Depreciation Expense account as of December 31, 19x3?

c. What was the "book value" of the typewriter on December 31, 19x3?

d. What entry would be required on December 31, 19x6, if the typewriter were sold on that date for $90 cash?

e. What entry would be required on December 31, 19x4, if the typewriter were sold on that date for $80 cash?

17. Identifying fixed-asset transactions from financial statement data. Two successive balance sheets showed the following amounts:

	End of Year 1	End of Year 2
Property, plant, and equipment (cost)......	$10,000	$11,200
Less: Accumulated depreciation	4,000	4,500
Property, plant, and equipment (net)	$ 6,000	$ 6,700

The income statements for the two years included the following items:

	Year 1	Year 2
Depreciation	$1,000	$ 900
Gain (loss) on the sale of property, plant, and equipment......	100	(200)

The notes to the financial statements reported that the original cost of property, plant, and equipment sold for cash amounted to $800 in year 1 and $700 in year 2.

a. Describe the transactions that led to changes in the Property, Plant, and Equipment and Accumulated Depreciation accounts *during year 2.* Quantify the effects of these transactions on the company's accounts. (If you decide to do this by means of journal entries, give a brief verbal explanation of the meaning of each entry line.)

b. Calculate the amounts in the balance sheet at the beginning of *year 1.* The proceeds from sales of property, plant, and equipment in year 1 totaled $300. No property, plant, or equipment was bought in year 1.

18. Transactions analysis; journal entries.   A number of transactions of an appliance repair business are described in problem 20 at the end of Chapter 2. Prepare entries in general journal form to record your analyses of these transactions.

19. Transactions analysis; journal entries.   A number of Grafton Corporation's transactions in 19x2 are described in problem 24 at the end of Chapter 2. Prepare entries in general journal form to record your analyses of these transactions.

20. Transactions analysis; journal entries.   A number of Gee Corporation's transactions in 19x2 are described in problem 25 at the end of Chapter 2. Prepare entries in general journal form to record your analyses of these transactions.

21. Transactions analysis; journal entries.   The Woods Company is organized as a corporation and is engaged in retail trade. The owners' equity section of the ledger contains one revenue account (Sales Revenue), a number of expense accounts, and two balance sheet accounts (Capital Stock and Retained Earnings).

The Woods Company had the following transactions, among others, this month (each transaction was independent of the others in this list):

1. Purchased office equipment on account, $4,700.
2. Received bill from plumbing contractor for repairs performed this month, $225.
3. Sold merchandise from inventory on account, $22,400; cost of merchandise was $16,700.
4. Issued 100 shares of the company's capital stock for $5,000 cash.
5. Hired clerk to start work the first of next month, salary $560 a month.
6. Collected $26,200 from customers on account.
7. Borrowed $1,000 cash from bank.
8. Ordered carload of bagged charcoal for sale to customers, $24,000.
9. Recorded $1,400 depreciation and $2,200 expiration of prepaid rent.
10. Recognized $1,500 salary earned this month by Mr. N. A. Woods, president of the company and owner of 75 percent of the corporation's capital stock.
11. Received bills, as follows:
   For new delivery truck, $2,600.
   For insurance policy to be effective the first of next month, $220.
   For this month's telephone service, $85.
   These bills will be paid next month. The dealer will not deliver the new delivery truck until it has been paid for:

a. Prepare a journal entry or entries in debit and credit form for each transaction reflected in the accounts.
b. For each debit and each credit, indicate (1) whether it represents an increase or a decrease in an asset, a liability, or the owners' equity, and (2) whether the amount would appear in full on the income statement for this month.

22. Erroneous journal entries. The Auld Sod Company sells seeds, garden tools and supplies, and outdoor furniture to retail customers. Four of the company's transactions during 19x5 were as follows:

1. It agreed to rent a warehouse from Park Enterprises for three years, effective January 1, 19x6. The monthly rental payment was $950, and the first month's and final two months' rent was paid immediately.
2. It bought office supplies for $99. Payment was made in cash and the supplies were distributed to the company's secretaries and other administrative personnel.
3. It paid cash, $167, for bunting, banners, displays, and refreshments purchased for use in a special sales promotion event taking place that same day.
4. It sold seeds, fertilizer, a garden tractor, and hand tools to Talbot Textile Company on account at a price of $850 for Talbot's use in landscaping its new office building. These products had cost Auld Sod $650.

The company's clerical personnel made one entry to record each of these transactions as it took place, as follows:

(1)	Rent Expense.....................................	2,850	
	Accounts Payable		2,850
(2)	Office Supplies Expense	99	
	Accounts Payable		99
(3)	Advertising Expense	167	
	Inventories		167
(4)	Accounts Receivable	850	
	Inventories		850

a. Disregarding the entries made by the company's clerical personnel, indicate how each of these four transactions affected the company's assets, liabilities, and owners' equity. You should use the words *increase* and *decrease* rather than *debit* and *credit*.

b. For each transaction, indicate whether the correct entry was made. If not, state why the entry was incorrect and construct the entry the company should have made, using suitable account titles similar to those used in this chapter.

23. T-accounts, journal entries, statements, closing entries. Freemont Hardware Store, Inc., had the following balance sheet on March 31, 19x1:

FREEMONT HARDWARE STORE, INC.
Balance Sheet
March 31, 19x1

Assets			Liabilities and Owners' Equity		
Current assets:			Current liabilities:		
Cash		$ 55,000	Notes payable		$ 15,000
Accounts receivable		120,500	Accounts payable		79,000
Merchandise inventory		108,500	Total current liabilities		94,000
Total current assets		284,000	Long-term debt		60,000
Plant assets:			Total liabilities		154,000
Land	$ 20,000		Owners' equity:		
Building	130,000		Capital stock	$200,000	
Equipment	54,000		Retained		
Total	204,000		earnings	89,000	
Accumulated			Total owners' equity		289,000
depreciation	45,000	159,000	Total liabilities and		
Total assets		$443,000	owners' equity		$443,000

The following items summarize the company's transactions for the month of April:

1. Purchased merchandise on account at a total cost of $67,500 and placed it in inventory.
2. Purchased an electric warehouse truck on account at a cost of $8,000.
3. Sold merchandise on account for $91,000; cost, $57,500.
4. Collected $75,000 on accounts receivable.
5. Received invoices covering telephone service, electricity, and other services bought and used during April, $5,700 (credit Accounts Payable).

6. Recorded employees' salaries for the month of April, $14,000.
7. Rented a small storeroom in a nearby building for 12 months, beginning April 1, 19x1, at a monthly rental of $550. Paid six months' rent in cash.
8. Paid $91,700 on accounts payable, $14,000 in salaries to employees, and $750 to holders of the company's notes payable and long-term debt, covering interest for the use of their money during April.
9. Calculated depreciation for the month of April: equipment, $800; building, $250.
10. The board of directors declared a dividend in the amount of $2,500 to be paid to shareholders in cash on May 15, 19x1.

a. Set up T-accounts for the items shown on the balance sheet and enter the March 31 balances.
b. Analyze each transaction and prepare journal entries in debit and credit form, using the account titles you adopted in part a plus any others required by your analyses.
c. Set up additional T-accounts, as required, and post your entries from part b.
d. Determine the April 30 balance in each account. Using these balances, prepare an income statement for the month of April and a balance sheet as of April 30. (Ignore income taxes.)
e. Prepare an appropriate closing entry or entries as of April 30.

24. Comprehensive problem. Wentworth Petroleum Company provides fuel oil and oil burner maintenance services to retail customers. Its fiscal year begins on July 1 each year, after the end of the heating season, and ends the following June 30. The company's account balances at the start of business on July 1, 19x1, were as follows:

	Debit	Credit
Cash	$250,000	
Accounts receivable	50,000	
Inventory	200,000	
Prepaid rent	60,000	
Equipment	300,000	
Accumulated depreciation		$125,000
Accounts payable		150,000
Salaries payable		25,000
Dividends payable		10,000
Capital stock		375,000
Retained earnings		175,000

The following information relates to the 12-month period that began on July 1, 19x1, and ended on June 30, 19x2:

1. Sales of fuel oil on account, $2,500,000.
2. Amount billed to customers for maintenance services provided on account, $250,000.
3. Salaries earned by employees, $500,000
4. Purchases on account: fuel oil, $2,000,000; repair parts for maintenance service work, $25,000; office supplies and postage, $12,500; maintenance of delivery vehicles, $20,000; gasoline and oil for delivery vehi-

cles, $75,000; new delivery truck, $50,000; telephone, electricity, and other miscellaneous services, $15,000.

5. Dividends declared, $100,000.
6. Cash collections from customers, $2,700,000.
7. Payments on account: to suppliers, $2,075,000; to employees for salaries, $515,000; to landlord for 12 months' rent from January 1 to December 31, 19x2, $135,000; to shareholders for dividends, $110,000.
8. Cash received from sale of old delivery truck, $5,000. This truck had been bought for $20,000 many years earlier and was fully depreciated at the time it was sold.
9. Cash received from the issuance of additional shares of capital stock, $90,000.
10. Depreciation for the year, $60,000.
11. The cost of the fuel oil in inventory on June 30, 19x2, was $450,000; the company maintained no inventories of office supplies or repair parts for maintenance services.

a. Draw a chart of accounts for Wentworth Petroleum Company, Inc., including appropriate revenue and expense accounts.
b. Set up T-accounts and enter the July 1, 19x1, balances.
c. Prepare journal entries to record your analyses of the information provided. For each debit and each credit, indicate whether it represents an increase or a decrease in an asset, liability, or owners' equity.
d. Post your entries to the T-accounts and calculate the June 30, 19x2, balances.
e. Prepare an income statement for the year ended June 30, 19x2, and a balance sheet as of June 30, 19x2.
f. Prepare a closing entry or entries to prepare the accounts to receive entries recording transactions in the 19x2–x3 fiscal year.

25. Comprehensive problem: incorporated school. The Greeley School, a private preparatory day school, accepted its first students and held its first classes in September 19x1. The school was founded by Jonathan Greeley, the former senior tutor of a large eastern preparatory school.

Greeley was anxious to try out a new system of instruction and had persuaded a group of wealthy businesspeople to supply most of the capital he needed to finance the new venture. He intended to operate the school for profit, partly to demonstrate that it could be done, and partly because this seemed to him the best basis on which to attract the required capital.

As expected, enrollment was below capacity during the first year, but by May 19x2, applications for September enrollment were so numerous that Greeley believed his classes would be filled during the second year.

His backers were impressed by the file of admission applications and pleased by the competence Greeley seemed to have shown in administering the school, but they were anxious to find out how much money the school had lost during its initial year of operations. As one of the shareholders said, "The enrollment figures are impressive, but so are those at the university, and they have to tap us alumni every year just to meet the payroll. I don't expect we'll show a profit at Greeley this year, but if the loss is much larger than we had expected we ought to think seriously of closing up shop or selling our shares for whatever we can get for them."

The school started its formal existence on July 1, 19x1, with the issuance of a corporate charter. The following transactions took place during its first 12 months:

1. Two hundred shares of capital stock were issued on July 1, 19x1, for $90,000 cash.

2. At the same time, the shareholders deposited an additional $30,000 in the corporation's bank account, receiving, in exchange, notes payable in this amount.

3. A two-year lease was signed, giving the school the right to use a large mansion and its grounds from July 1, 19x1, to June 30, 19x3. The monthly rental was $6,000. An initial cash payment of $18,000 was made on July 1, 19x1 covering the first month's rent and a two-month refundable security deposit, and cash payments of $6,000 each were made on the first of each succeeding month, through June 1, 19x2.

4. Classroom blackboards were purchased on credit for $10,800. Other private schools in the area estimated that, on the average, blackboards could be used for 12 years before replacement was necessary.

5. Classroom furniture costing $27,000 was purchased from the Tower Seating Company, which accepted a down payment of $12,000 in cash and a note payable for the balance. Classroom furniture was expected to have an eight-year life on the average.

6. Equipment of various kinds, with an expected average life of five years, was purchased for $21,000 cash.

7. Students' tuition and other fees amounted to $234,000. Of this amount, $18,000 had not yet been collected by June 30, 19x2, but Greeley was confident that this amount would be received before the new school year began in September.

8. Salaries were paid in cash:
   Teaching staff, $162,000.
   Office staff, $33,000.

9. On June 15, 19x2, two parents paid tuition for the 19x2–x3 school year, amounting to $10,200.

10. Various school supplies were bought on credit for $12,300. Of these, $600 were still in the school's storeroom unused on June 30, 19x2.

11. Utility bills and other miscellaneous operating costs applicable to the year ending June 30, 19x2, were paid in cash, $11,400.

12. Payments amounting to $13,500 were made on account to suppliers of items referred to in 4 and 10 above.

13. The holders of the school's notes were paid interest of $2,700. In addition, the Tower Seating Company was paid $4,500 of the amount borrowed (item 5).

a. Prepare a list of account titles you think would be useful for recording these transactions, including revenue and expense accounts and an accumulated depreciation account. Then analyze the transactions in debit and credit form. For each debit and each credit indicate (1) whether the effect is to increase or to decrease an asset (*A*), liability (*L*), or shareholders' equity (*OE*), and (2) whether the amount would appear in full on the income statement for the current year. For example:

Cash xxx
    Capital Stock xxx
Increase *A;* increase *OE;* no effect on current income.

Don't forget to record depreciation for the year.

b. Post these amounts to T-accounts.

c. Prepare an income statement for the year and a balance sheet as of June 30, 19x2.

d. Upon seeing your figures, Greeley objected to the depreciation charge. "We just can't afford to write off any of those costs this year," he said. "Next year our tuition will be up, and we can start recovering depreciation." Do you agree with Greeley, or do you have a different concept of depreciation? Defend your position.

e. If you were a shareholder, how would you use the financial statements in your evaluation of the financial success or failure of this new enterprise? Assuming your decision to retain your shares or sell them would be based on your forecast of future financial statements, would the financial statements of a period in the past be of any relevance to you?

4

Preparing financial statements

Perhaps the most fundamental aspect of the accounting process is the analysis and recording of transactions, which can be called the data-processing phase. Without the debit/credit mechanism and the journal entry/account medium, accountants would find it very difficult, if not impossible, to prepare financial statements.

In this chapter, we'll take a close look at the methods accountants use to transform ledger account data into intelligible financial statements. We'll begin with an overview of accrual accounting and then examine the end-of-year adjustments accountants must make. This will be followed by a discussion of how formal financial statements are prepared; it's not just a matter of arranging columns of numbers.

ACCRUAL ACCOUNTING

Just as Moliere's bourgeois gentleman was delighted to learn that he had been speaking prose all his life, it may be a pleasure to discover that while we have been learning the fundamentals of transactions analysis, we have been practicing accrual accounting. *Accrual accounting* is any system in which changes in assets, liabilities, and owners' equity are measured by flows of resources of all kinds rather than by flows of cash alone. The alternative to accrual accounting is cash-basis accounting.[1]

---

[1] The word *accrue* literally means to accumulate or to arise. Accountants use it to signify that an accountable event has occurred even though there has been no routinely recorded transaction.

For example, John Appleby operates a small management consulting business under the name of Appleby Associates. On January 25, he purchased and received materials costing $1,000 for use on an assignment. He paid for the materials on February 9 and started to work on an assignment on March 5. The project was completed on March 28, and the Jones Company was billed for the contract price of $12,000 on that date. Salaries of employees who worked on the assignment during March totaled $4,000, and this amount was paid on March 31.

This series of transactions is summarized in Exhibit 4–1. An expenditure in January was followed by a cash disbursement of $1,000 in February, another disbursement of $4,000 in March, and a cash receipt of $12,000 in April. Cash-basis accounting would indicate that the company lost $1,000 in February, lost $4,000 in March, and earned $12,000 in April, when cash was finally received from the client.

Anyone who has mastered the first three chapters of this book will recognize quickly that the cash basis ignores many significant resource flows. Accrual accounting would bring all the resource flows together in the income statement for March, when all the work was done. Income of $7,000 on this contract would be recognized in March, even though the company had a $5,000 cash deficiency at the end of the month.

While this example illustrates the basic nature of accrual accounting, implementing accrual accounting is more complicated.

EXHIBIT 4–1. Appleby Associates: Timing of Events

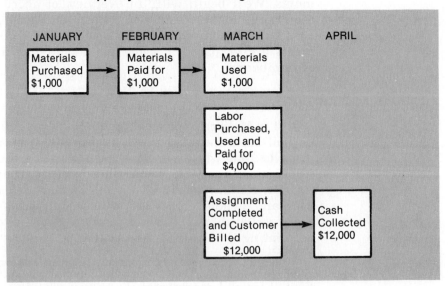

Certainly, whenever a transaction is recorded, the accountant must determine whether it affects the current period's income or creates an asset or liability that may affect future periods' income. There is another consideration, however. Even though proper accounting procedures are used during the year, there are always adjustments at the end of the period. These adjustments to revenues and expenses are necessitated by circumstances that either arise only at year-end or can be dealt with more efficiently once a year than on a continuing basis. (In practice, adjustments may also be made quarterly, or even monthly, if financial statements are prepared at these intervals. For simplicity, we'll assume that adjustments are made only once a year.)

REVENUE ADJUSTMENTS

Three year-end adjustments relate to revenues. Even though a company's accountants carefully record all revenue transactions during the year, special circumstances require that amounts be added to or subtracted from the revenue balances indicated by the ledger accounts. The three situations we'll discuss are:

1. Accrued revenues.
2. Unearned revenues.
3. Customer defaults.

Accrued revenues

Businesses occasionally accept promissory notes from customers if payment is to be deferred beyond the normal credit period. A *promissory note* is a promise to pay a set amount on a specified date known as the *maturity date.* The amount borrowed is termed the *proceeds,* the amount paid for the use of the proceeds is called *interest,* and the amount to be repaid to the lender on the maturity date is the *maturity value.*

For example, Baxter Stores supplied all the major appliances for a new block of apartments completed in 19x7. The price agreed upon was $110,000, but when the end of the normal credit period arrived on November 16, 19x7, the contractor was unable to pay the full amount in cash. Instead, the contractor offered to pay $15,000 in cash and give a 180-day promissory note with a maturity value of $100,000, including interest, to cover the $95,000 balance of the invoice price. Baxter's management agreed, and the note was signed.

Taking a note for a larger amount ($100,000) than the amount exchanged for it ($95,000) is known as *discounting* the note. In discounting a note, the lender calculates the amount due at the maturity date (including interest) and then deducts interest on this amount to determine the sum to be made available to the borrower.

In this case, Baxter Stores and the contractor agreed that $5,000 was an appropriate amount of interest on $95,000 for 180 days. This is roughly the same as interest of $10,000 for a full year, or about 10 percent. Baxter therefore said it was discounting the contractor's note at 10 percent.[2]

Baxter Stores made the following entry to record its acceptance of the note:[3]

Notes Receivable.	95,000	
Accounts Receivable		95,000

This entry shows that Baxter simply exchanged one asset (an account receivable) for another (a note receivable).

Baxter earned interest on this note for 45 days in 19x7 (14 days in November and 31 days in December). This was 45/180, or one fourth, of the full period before the note was to mature. Interest for the 45 days therefore was one fourth of the interest for 180 days:

$$\text{Interest revenue} = \tfrac{1}{4} \times \$5,000 = \$1,250$$

The adjusting entry to accrue this interest was as follows:

Notes Receivable.	1,250	
Interest Revenue		1,250

The debit in this case was made to Notes Receivable to emphasize that the amount lent to the contractor now included both the invoice price of the merchandise covered by the note ($95,000) and the interest due for the use of Baxter's money for 45 days ($1,250). If Baxter had had an Interest Receivable account in its chart of accounts, we could have debited that instead.

Interest Revenue is an owners' equity account. Interest revenue

---

[2] The contractor in this case actually paid interest at a rate slightly higher than 10 percent a year. In discounting transactions, the quoted interest rate is applied to the maturity value rather than to the amount actually borrowed. Since the contractor paid $5,000 for the use of $95,000 for approximately six months, the effective rate of interest was approximately $2 \times \$5,000/\$95,000$, or 10.5 percent a year.

[3] An equivalent alternative is to record the note at its face value, with an accompanying entry to a contra-asset account:

Notes Receivable	100,000	
Unearned Interest on Notes Receivable		5,000
Accounts Receivable.		95,000

is more commonly referred to as "interest income," but for the sake of clarity we prefer to reserve the word *income* for measures of differences between revenues and expenses for the company as a whole.

Unearned revenues

In December 19x7, Baxter Stores received a $10,000 payment in advance from a customer covering merchandise Baxter expected to deliver in early 19x8. By accepting the customer's money without providing goods or services in exchange, Baxter accepted a liability, measured by the amount of cash received. When the cash was received, however, a clerk in Baxter's accounting department recorded the transaction as an ordinary cash sale, as follows:

```
Cash ............................................  10,000
     Sales Revenue................................          10,000
```

The result was that the year-end balance in Sales Revenue was $10,000 too large, while the balance in the Advances from Customers liability was $10,000 too small. To avoid overstating sales revenues and understating liabilities, the following adjusting entry was made:

```
Sales Revenue ...................................  10,000
     Advances from Customers ....................          10,000
```

A liability for advances from customers is sometimes called *deferred revenue, unearned revenue,* or a *deferred credit.* No matter what it is called, however, it is a liability the company must meet, either by delivering goods as promised or by returning the customer's money.

Customer defaults

Most businesses recognize revenues at the time merchandise is shipped or delivered to customers and invoices are prepared. At that time, however, management isn't sure that every customer will actually pay the amount shown on the invoice. In fact, most businesses know that some of their customers won't pay for the goods or services they have received. These amounts that will never be collected are known as *bad debts, uncollectible amounts,* or *customer defaults.*

Correcting the overstatements of revenues and receivables. Because of customer defaults, both the sales revenues for the year and the year-end receivable asset will be overstated unless an appropriate adjustment is made at the end of the year. Unfortunately, companies can't wait to prepare financial statements until they know which customers will default. The year-end adjustment therefore has to reflect *estimates* of the amounts customers won't pay in the future. A common technique for estimating customer defaults is known as *aging the accounts.* This is based on the premise that the older the claim, the less likely it is to be collected. The analysis is performed as follows:

1. Customer account balances are classified by age—that is, by the length of time since the invoice date.
2. An estimated loss percentage is developed for each age group, partly from historical experience and partly from a qualitative examination of a sample of accounts in the group.
3. These loss percentages are multiplied by the amounts receivable in their respective age brackets.
4. The products of these calculations are added, and the total is used to adjust the appropriate account balances.

For example, Baxter Stores had gross sales revenues of $1 million in 19x7, including revenues from a large number of credit sales. It had $150,000 in outstanding accounts receivable at the end of the year. By aging the accounts, management determined that $12,200 of the year-end receivables would never be collected; this means that accounts receivable as of December 31 were overstated by $12,200. Sales revenues for the year were also overstated by $12,200 because all the year-end receivables arose from sales made on credit during 19x7. (Prior to 19x7, all Baxter's sales had been cash sales. We'll see in a moment how credit sales in previous periods affect the analysis.)

The adjustment at the end of 19x7 to correct the overstatements of revenues and receivables could have been made as follows:

```
Sales Revenues ...................................  12,200
    Accounts Receivable ..........................           12,200
```

This entry would have reduced the owners' equity and receivables asset totals to their correct levels. The entry wasn't made this way, however, for two reasons:

1. To provide a check on the accuracy of the ledger, the balance in the Accounts Receivable account should equal the total of the balances of the individual accounts outstanding.
2. Because many financial ratios are expressed as percentages of gross revenues (before deducting uncollectible amounts), most

companies want the balances in the Sales Revenues account to measure gross revenues.

To meet these needs, Baxter Stores set up two new accounts—*Estimated Customer Defaults* and *Allowance for Uncollectibles*—and made the following entry:

Estimated Customer Defaults 12,200
    Allowance for Uncollectibles   12,200

These two accounts were contra-accounts—to Sales Revenues and Accounts Receivable, respectively. Once this adjustment was made, the financial statements disclosed the following amounts:

Income statement:

Gross sales	$1,000,000
Less: Estimated customer defaults	12,200
Net sales	$ 987,800

Balance sheet:

Accounts receivable, gross	$ 150,000
Less: Allowance for uncollectibles	12,200
Accounts receivable, net	$ 137,800

TERMINOLOGY REMINDER: CONTRA-ACCOUNT

A contra-account is an account established to accumulate a specific class of deductions from the gross amount of some asset, liability, owners' equity, revenue, or expense. For presenting financial statements, the balance in the contra-account should always be deducted from the gross amount with which it is paired.

The $12,200 shown in the income statement as estimated customer defaults is a *sales deduction,* which must be subtracted from gross sales to reflect the fact that the amount to be collected from customers will be less than the gross sales amount. Sales deductions are like expenses in that both are subtracted from gross revenues in the determination of net income. Expenses, however, are *costs* of resources used to obtain revenues, while sales deductions are *corrections* of the gross revenue amounts. Therefore, although estimated customer defaults are often listed among expenses (and are called *bad debt expense* in those cases), they really belong in the revenue section of the income statement, as in the preceding table.

Write-offs of specific uncollectible accounts. At some point management will identify specific customers' receivables as being, in fact, uncollectible. Since the amounts were put in the Allowance for

Uncollectibles because some receivables eventually will prove un-collectible, the balance in this account is reduced whenever particu-lar receivables are written off.

In our example, the entry to record the write-off of a $1,000 ac-count would be as follows:

Allowance for Uncollectibles 1,000
    Accounts Receivable 1,000

The credit to Accounts Receivable reduces the balance in this ac-count, and the debit to the allowance reduces its balance by the same amount. The entry does not record a reduction in the asset, however, because the value of the receivables as a whole has not decreased. The only event is management's determination that an estimated uncollectible is now definitely uncollectible.

Receivables from previous years.   Baxter Stores' estimated customer defaults for 19x7 and the balance in the Allowance for Uncollect-ibles account at the end of 19x7 were identical—$12,200—because the company had no credit sales and therefore no uncollectible accounts before 19x7. Suppose we have the following facts for 19x8:

Credit sales $1,200,000
Collections on accounts receivable   1,150,000
Write-offs of specific uncollectible accounts   10,300
Estimated uncollectible amounts, December 31,19x8   14,700

Before adjusting entries were made at the end of 19x8, the receiv-ables accounts showed the following:

Accounts Receivable

Bal. 1/1	150,000	Collections	1,150,000
Sales	1,200,000	Write-offs	10,300
Bal. 12/31	189,700		

Allowance for Uncollectibles

Write-offs	10,300	Bal. 1/1	12,200
		Bal. 12/31	1,900

We know, however, that the correct balance in the Allowance for Uncollectibles account at the end of 19x8 was $14,700. The company had to add $12,800 to the $1,900 credit balance in this account to bring it to the correct level. The adjusting entry was:

Estimated Customer Defaults 12,800
    Allowance for Uncollectibles 12,800

Gross sales revenues were reduced by $12,800; net accounts receivable were reported to be $14,700 less than their gross amount.

This entry implies that $12,800 of the estimated uncollectibles arose from sales in 19x8; the other $1,900 arose from sales made in 19x7. In fact, the $12,800 is likely to be the sum of the estimated defaults on current sales and the correction of the estimate Baxter's management made at the end of the previous year. We don't usually try to separate these two components, however; it's usually accurate enough to refer to the combined total as the effect of the current year's sales.

EXPENSE ADJUSTMENTS

Adjustments are required to determine the correct measures of expenses incurred during each accounting period. This means that whether or not the related disbursement has already been made, the cost of services consumed is an expense in the period when the related revenue benefit occurs. We'll first consider three expense adjustments which arise from the need to recognize previously unrecorded liabilities. We'll then discuss three expense adjustments that arise from current-period consumption of previously recorded assets.

Accruing interest expense

For many businesses, an important source of funds, particularly to finance seasonal peaks of activity, is short-term borrowing from commercial banks. At the end of 19x7, Baxter Stores had notes payable amounting to $30,000. This amount came from a bank loan the company had taken out on December 1, 19x7, giving in exchange a 90-day, 12 percent promissory note. The period between the borrowing and maturity dates, in this case 90 days, is the life or term of the loan; 12 percent is the interest rate. Unless some other period is explicitly specified, interest is always stated in annual rates, regardless of the term of the loan.

It is accepted financial practice to compute interest on short-term loans on the basis of a 360-day year. Therefore, a 90-day note would require interest at 90/360, or one fourth, of the annual rate. Baxter Stores, in other words, agreed to pay the bank $30,000 plus interest of $900 (¼ × 12 percent × $30,000) on March 1, 19x8, exactly 90 days from the date of the loan.[4]

---

[4] The maturity date is computed on the basis of actual elapsed days, not on the basis of the 360-day year. In computing the maturity date, the day the loan is made is not counted. Thus, a loan made on November 15 gives rise to interest for 15

The next part of this transaction to be recorded in the normal bookkeeping routine would be the repayment of the loan plus interest on March 1, 19x8. No entry would be made until that date. The company used the bank's money for 30 days in 19x7, however, and the cost of using it for this period was a cost of doing business in 19x7:

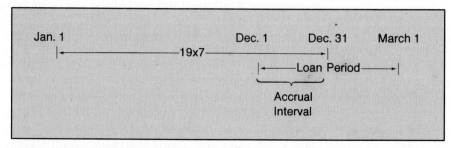

Recognizing the cost of the loan from December 1 through December 31 is an essential feature of accrual accounting. In this case, the company received services, use of the lender's money, without any current outlay of cash. The entry recognizing this is known as an *accrual.* An accrual is an entry made to recognize a revenue or expense, together with its related asset or liability, when the accounting period ends before the asset or liability is recorded as part of the ordinary recordkeeping routine.

In this case, 30/90 of the $900 total interest cost, or $300, was a 19x7 expense. The adjusting entry was:

Interest Expense	300	
Interest Payable		300

The debit to the expense account recorded the reduction in the owners' equity; the credit to Interest Payable recorded the liability for future payment of this amount.

When the note matured on March 1, 19x8, the entry to record the payment of principal and interest was:

Notes Payable..................................	30,000	
Interest Payable.................................	300	
Interest Expense	600	
Cash		30,900

The debit to Notes Payable recorded the reduction in the principal owed, and the debit to Interest Payable eliminated the liability that

---

days during November, starting with November 16. Debts maturing on a day on which banks are closed are payable on the next banking day. In this case, the term of the loan covered 30 days in December, 31 days in January, 28 days in February, and 1 day in March, for a maturity date of March 1.

had been recorded in the December 31, 19x7, adjustment. The $600 interest expense related to January and February 19x8, and the $30,900 reduction in cash was the sum of the $30,000 principal and the $900 interest cost for 90 days.

Accruing wages and salaries

Another kind of accrual, the accrual of payrolls, also arises because the regular bookkeeping cycle doesn't always end on the final day of the accounting period. Salaries and wages are often paid weekly, while the accounting period is a year or a month. The accounting period, in other words, doesn't necessarily end on the last day of a payroll period.

For example, Baxter Stores' last weekly payroll period of 19x7 ended on Saturday, December 28. Monday and Tuesday, December 30 and 31, were full working days, which means that some wages were earned by employees in 19x7 but were not recorded in the accounts as part of the normal bookkeeping process until the next year. These amounts were paid as part of the first weekly payroll of 19x8, but part of that payroll was really a cost applicable to 19x7.

Employees in the company's stores and offices earned $5,000 and $1,000, respectively, on the two working days between the end of the last weekly payroll period and the end of the year. The entry to accrue these costs was:

Salaries and Wages Expense 6,000
    Salaries and Wages Payable   6,000

The credit to Salaries and Wages Payable recognized the company's liability on December 31, 19x7, to pay its employees in 19x8 for work done in 19x7.

If the first payroll in 19x8 amounted to $16,000, Baxter would record the following entry at that time:

Salaries and Wages Payable 6,000
Salaries and Wages Expense 10,000
    Cash   16,000

This entry would recognize the payment of both the $6,000 end-of-19x7 liability and the $10,000 expense incurred in 19x8.

Providing for product warranties

Some costs arising from the sale of merchandise may not be incurred until after the merchandise is delivered to customers. A

EXHIBIT 4–2. Classifying Costs as Expenses: Revenues Recognized at Delivery

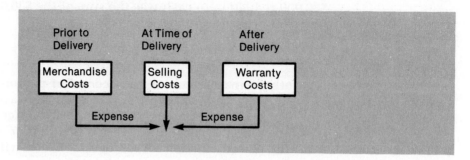

prime example is the cost of doing work under the terms of a product warranty. Since this is part of the cost of securing revenues, it should be recognized as an expense in the period in which revenues are recorded. Exhibit 4–2 shows how expense in the delivery period includes these costs as well as costs incurred both currently and in previous periods.

Suppose Baxter Stores decided in March 19x7 that, for all future sales, it would stand ready to repair or replace defective appliances, even after the manufacturers' warranty periods expired. The costs of providing these services enter the accounting system in two stages:

1. As an end-of-period adjustment, Baxter recognizes the future costs of service on these products as a current expense.
2. When warranty service is actually provided, the costs reduce the liability.

Baxter Stores estimated that its warranties in force at the end of 19x7 would lead to future costs of approximately $16,500. In other words, this was the company's warranty liability at that time. To get this amount into the financial statements, the company made the following adjusting entry:

Warranty Expense 16,500
    Liability for Service Warranty 16,500

After this entry was made, the liability account was ready for use in the next year (19x8). Warranty claims in 19x8 were satisfied by payment of $5,000 in cash and the use of merchandise from inventory, at a cost of $10,000. This required the following entry in 19x8:

Liability for Service Warranty	15,000	
Cash		5,000
Inventory		10,000

The liability account then showed the following:

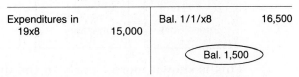

Liability for Service Warranty

Expenditures in 19x8	15,000	Bal. 1/1/x8	16,500
		Bal. 1,500	

Baxter then estimated that warranties in force at the end of 19x8 would lead to future costs of approximately $21,400. This required the following adjusting entry as of December 31, 19x8:

Warranty Expense	19,900	
Liability for Service Warranty		19,900

Since the liability had been reduced in 19x8 to $1,500, the amount needed to reach the desired $21,400 level was $19,900 ($21,400 − $1,500).

The liability for service warranty is a different kind of warranty from any we've seen up to now, for two reasons. First, this liability is often discharged by performing services or replacing parts or merchandise, not by paying cash to a creditor. Advances from customers was the closest to this among the liabilities we studied earlier. Second, the amount of the liability is uncertain. If the actual warranty claims turn out to be different from the estimated amounts, the expense that has been recorded will be corrected in a subsequent period—that is, when the claims are ascertained and discharged. For example, suppose the $21,400 estimated liability at the end of 19x8 included $2,400 in connection with merchandise the company sold in 19x7 and $19,000 in connection with 19x8 sales. This means that the $19,900 recognized as expense in 19x8 included $900 ($19,900 − $19,000) to correct the understatement of expense in 19x7.

Inventory adjustment

The sale of merchandise requires removing the cost of the goods sold from the Inventory account. The amount to be removed can be determined by either the *periodic inventory method* or the *perpetual inventory method.*

Periodic inventory method. Under the periodic inventory method, the cost of merchandise acquired is recorded in a Purchases account as transactions occur. At the end of the year, the remaining inventories are counted and their costs are determined. The cost of the goods sold is then determined by subtracting the cost of the ending inventory from the total cost of the beginning inventory and the goods purchased during the period:

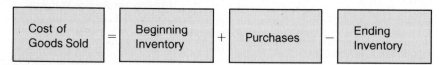

This is shown more clearly in the diagram on the left of Exhibit 4–3. The height of the large column represents the cost of all the goods available for sale during the period. After the ending inventory has been counted and subtracted from the total, what's left is the cost of goods sold. An adjusting entry brings the Purchases account to a zero balance and the Inventory account to its end-of-year level.

To illustrate, suppose the cost of Baxter's inventory on January 1, 19x7, was $82,000. Since one period's ending inventory is the following period's beginning inventory, this amount was based on the physical count at the end of 19x6. Purchases during 19x7 were $457,000, and the year-end count indicates that goods costing $89,000 were on hand.

The left side of Exhibit 4–4 demonstrates how these events were recorded. The $82,000 beginning balance in Inventory was unaffected by entries made during 19x7. The goods acquired were entered in the Purchases account, and no entry was made when merchandise was sold. In the end-of-year adjustment, the $7,000 debit to Inventory increased the year-end asset balance to $89,000, and the debit to Cost of Goods Sold established the $450,000 cost that appeared in the income statement. The $457,000 credit to Purchases reduced its balance to zero, thus enabling it to begin receiving debit

EXHIBIT 4–3. Calculating the Cost of Goods Sold

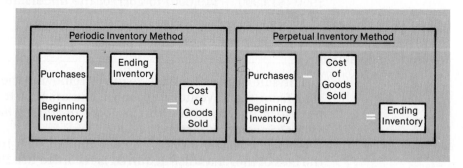

EXHIBIT 4–4. Periodic and Perpetual Inventory; Journal Entries

	Periodic			*Perpetual*		
Inventory, Jan. 1: $82,000						
Purchases: $457,000	Purchases ..... Cash	457,000	457,000	Inventory .... Cash	457,000	457,000
Cost of goods shipped: $449,000	No entry			Cost of Goods Sold .... Inventory	449,000	449,000
Inventory, Dec. 31: $89,000						
Adjustment, Dec. 31:	Inventory ...... Cost of Goods Sold .... Purchases .	7,000 450,000	457,000	Inventory Shrinkage Expense .... Inventory	1,000	1,000

amounts representing the following year's acquisition of merchandise.

Perpetual inventory method. The perpetual inventory method requires that the cost of purchased goods be added (debited) to the Inventory account at the time they are received. Each time an item is sold, an entry is made to transfer its cost from Inventory to the Cost of Goods Sold account. The right side of Exhibit 4–3 diagrams this sequence, and the right side of Exhibit 4–4 applies this method to Baxter Stores. When the purchases were made, their costs ($457,000 in our case) were entered in Inventory. When merchandise was sold, it was determined that its cost had been $449,000. As a result of these transactions, the Inventory account had a $90,000 balance as of December 31.

Inventory

Jan. 1	82,000	Cost of goods sold	449,000
Purchases	457,000		
	539,000		
Bal. 90,000			

Barring error, theft, or decay, the balance in the Inventory account should always equal the cost of the goods on hand. A physical count is taken periodically; the difference between the cost of the inventory actually on hand at that time and the amount shown in the

Inventory account is the cost of lost, stolen, or spoiled goods or the result of bookkeeping errors.

In our illustration, the tally on December 31 located merchandise with a total cost of only $89,000. The $1,000 difference between this and the $90,000 indicated by the inventory records became the basis for an inventory adjustment. Lacking any way of separating the amounts due to the various causes, Baxter's accountants charged off the entire amount with the following entry:

Inventory Shrinkage Expense	1,000	
Inventory		1,000

The credit to Inventory recognized the reduction in this asset that was revealed by the annual count; the debit to Inventory Shrinkage Expense recorded the accompanying reduction in owners' equity. If the count had exceeded the book value of the merchandise on hand, the account would have been credited. In published financial statements, the balance in this account is ordinarily reported as part of the cost of goods sold, leading to the same reported cost of goods sold as in the periodic method.

Depreciation of plant assets

A second type of expense-oriented adjustment which measures the consumption of an existing asset is *depreciation*. Recall from Chapter 3 that the objective of depreciation is to allocate the cost of plant assets systematically to the operations of the future periods that benefit from the assets' use. Even though depreciation occurs throughout the year, it is recorded at the end of each accounting period as part of the adjustment process.

Baxter Stores had furniture and equipment on hand at the end of 19x7 with a total original cost of $144,000, of which $39,000 had been depreciated in previous years. The company's property records showed the location and annual depreciation rate on each asset. From these records, the accountants found that depreciation amounted to $6,000 in 19x7 on the furniture and equipment in the stores, and $3,000 on office furniture and equipment, a total of $9,000. They made the following entry:

Depreciation Expense	9,000	
Accumulated Depreciation		9,000

The debit recognized the decrease in owners' equity resulting from the effect of the passage of time on the company's furniture and equipment. The credit to Accumulated Depreciation measured an asset reduction, reflecting the decline in the remaining usefulness of this group of assets.

Amortization of prepaid costs

Baxter's final adjustment is another instance of recognizing the consumption of an asset that the company had acquired previously. Although we saw a simplified prepaid-rent example of this kind in Chapter 3, we'll now consider *prepaid insurance* (sometimes called *unexpired insurance*).

The balance in Baxter Stores' Prepaid Insurance account was $6,000 at the end of 19x7. A review of the insurance file revealed that this amount could be traced back to five policies that had been in force for all or part of 19x7. This information is summarized in Exhibit 4–5.

The total at the bottom of column (4) is the balance in the Prepaid Insurance asset account. Column (5) shows the monthly premium for each of these policies, taken from information in the policies themselves. Column (6) shows how many months each policy was in force between January 1 and December 31, 19x7. The cost of insurance coverage for the year [column (7)] was then calculated by multiplying the monthly premium by the number of months. The total of these amounts, $2,925, had to be transferred from the Prepaid Insurance account to an expense account or accounts. The adjusting entry was:

Insurance Expense	2,925	
Prepaid Insurance		2,925

This entry reduced the balance in the Prepaid Insurance account to $3,075, the total at the bottom of column (8). This represented

EXHIBIT 4–5. Data for Insurance Expense Adjustment

(1) Policy No.	(2) Effective Date	(3) Expiration Date	(4) Un- adjusted Balance	(5) Monthly Premium Cost	(6) Months this Year	(7) Premiums Expired (5) × (6)	(8) Un- expired Premiums (4) − (7)
AB 406–721	1/1/x4	12/31/x7	$ 540	$ 45	12	$ 540	—
CD 492–881	4/1/x6	3/31/x7	60	20	3	60	—
XL 172–008	7/1/x5	12/31/x8	2,400	100	12	1,200	$1,200
CD 712–654	4/1/x7	3/31/x8	300	25	9	225	75
PL 202–903	1/1/x7	12/31/x9	2,700	75	12	900	1,800
Total			$6,000			$2,925	$3,075

the unexpired premiums on the three policies still in force on January 1, 19x8.

Applying the adjustments

Accrual accounting necessitates making revenue and expense adjustments at the end of every accounting period. Under accrual accounting, *income* is the net increase in net assets resulting from operations. Since *net assets* are the excess of assets over liabilities, accountants determine income by measuring the changes in *all* assets and liabilities resulting from operations—not just changes in Cash. End-of-period adjustments represent the culmination of that process. Despite accountants' adherence to the rules of accrual accounting throughout the year, year-end adjustments are always necessary. They are an integral part of accrual accounting, not a way to compensate for carelessness. If it is determined that substantive accounting errors or arithmetic mistakes have been made during the year, however, correcting entries are made at the time the recurring adjustments are recorded.

TRIAL BALANCE

The *accounting cycle* is the series of steps which lead from the initial recording of transactions through preparing a complete set of financial statements. In Chapter 3, we learned about the first two steps in this cycle—journalizing transactions in a debit/credit entry format and then posting the debits and credits to T-accounts comprising the general ledger. Before and after making the adjustments we've been discussing, accountants perform one other procedure—preparing a *trial balance.*

Unadjusted trial balance. As its name suggests, a trial balance is an effort to ascertain that the sum of all debit-balance accounts' balances is equal to the sum of all the credit-balance accounts' balances. The trial balance itself is a list of every account title *and* its balance. Exhibit 4–6 presents the *unadjusted* trial balance of Baxter Stores as of December 31, 19x7—unadjusted in that it does *not* include the effects of the nine adjustments discussed earlier in this chapter.

The account balances in the trial balance were taken from Baxter's ledger after all entries made as part of the normal bookkeeping routine had been posted. Notice that the trial balance shows both balance sheet and income statement accounts, with balance sheet items first. The only aspects of an account that have any relevance at this point are its balance and whether it is a debit or a credit balance.

Although the accounting cycle cannot be completed until a successful trial balance has been established, equality of the column totals doesn't necessarily mean that the accounting is free of errors. A balanced trial balance indicates only that the sum of posted debits equals the sum of posted credits. The trial balance may be balanced even though a correct debit in the journal was posted as a debit to the wrong ledger account, a balanced journal entry contained incorrect amounts, or even a transaction was not journalized. This means that even though being balanced is desirable, accountants must still be alert to substantive errors that would be undetected by a completed trial balance.

Adjusted trial balance. When Baxter Stores' initial trial balance was presented as Exhibit 4–6, it was identified as being an *unadjusted* trial balance. This meant that the account balances didn't

EXHIBIT 4–6

BAXTER STORES, INC.
Unadjusted Trial Balance
December 31, 19x7

Account	Debit	Credit
Cash	$ 64,000	
Notes receivable	95,000	
Accounts receivable	150,000	
Allowance for uncollectibles		—
Inventory	82,000	
Prepaid Insurance	6,000	
Furniture and equipment	144,000	
Accumulated depreciation		$ 39,000
Notes payable		30,000
Accounts payable		84,200
Salaries and wages payable		—
Taxes payable		19,625
Interest payable		—
Dividends payable		4,000
Advances from customers		12,000
Liability for service warranty		—
Capital stock		200,000
Retained earnings		44,150
Sales revenue		1,010,000
Interest revenue		—
Estimated customer defaults		—
Purchases	457,000	
Cost of goods sold	—	
Salaries and wages expense	274,000	
Depreciation expense	—	
Rent expense	80,000	
Utilities expense	23,000	
Warranty expense	—	
Insurance expense		
Interest expense	1,200	
Income tax expense	31,600	
Miscellaneous expense	19,175	
Dividends declared	16,000	
Totals	$1,442,975	$1,442,975

contain the debits and credits created by the end-of-year adjustments. Exhibit 4–7 presents Baxter's *adjusted* trial balance, based
on ledger account balances that include the nine year-end adjustments discussed earlier in this chapter. The adjusted trial balance
amounts that differ from those in the earlier trial balance appear
in boldface.

Baxter's nine adjusting entries are summarized in Exhibit 4–8.
Since Baxter Stores used the periodic inventory method, its trial
balance contained a Purchases account and the inventory adjustment was used to determine the cost of goods sold. Readers who
take a few minutes to return to the discussion of the adjustments
will be able to follow those amounts into the adjusted trial balance.

EXHIBIT 4–7

BAXTER STORES, INC.
Adjusted Trial Balance
December 31, 19x7

Account	Debit	Credit
Cash	$ 64,000	
Notes receivable	**96,250**	
Accounts receivable	150,000	
Allowance for uncollectibles		$ 12,200
Inventory	**89,000**	
Prepaid insurance	**3,075**	
Furniture and equipment	144,000	
Accumulated depreciation		**48,000**
Notes payable		30,000
Accounts payable		84,200
Salaries and wages payable		**6,000**
Taxes payable		19,625
Interest payable		**200**
Dividends payable		4,000
Advances from customers		**22,000**
Liability for service warranty		**16,500**
Capital stock		200,000
Retained earnings		44,150
Sales revenue		1,000,000
Interest revenue		**1,250**
Estimated customer defaults	**12,200**	
Purchases	**0**	
Cost of goods sold	**450,000**	
Salaries and wages expense	**280,000**	
Depreciation expense	**9,000**	
Rent expense	80,000	
Utilities expense	23,000	
Warranty expense	**16,500**	
Insurance expense	**2,925**	
Interest expense	**1,400**	
Income tax expense	31,600	
Miscellaneous expense	19,175	
Dividends declared	16,000	
Totals	$1,488,125	$1,488,125

EXHIBIT 4–8. Baxter Stores, Inc.: Adjusting Entries

Notes Receivable	1,250	
Interest Revenue		1,250
To record accrued interest revenue.		
Sales Revenue	10,000	
Advances from Customers..................		10,000
To reclassify revenue received in advance.		
Estimated Customer Defaults	12,200	
Allowance for Uncollectibles		12,200
To record estimated uncollectibles.		
Interest Expense	300	
Interest Payable		300
To record accrued interest expense.		
Salaries and Wages Expense	6,000	
Salaries and Wages Payable................		6,000
To record accrued payroll expense.		
Warranty Expense	16,500	
Liability for Service Warranty		16,500
To record estimated cost of servicing warranty claims.		
Inventory	7,000	
Cost of Goods Sold	450,000	
Purchases.................................		457,000
To record cost of goods sold and cost of goods on hand.		
Depreciation Expense	9,000	
Accumulated Depreciation		9,000
To record depreciation of plant assets.		
Insurance Expense.............................	2,925	
Prepaid Insurance		2,925
To record expiration of insurance coverage.		

FINANCIAL STATEMENTS

Successful preparation of an adjusted trial balance enables accountants to prepare the company's financial statements. While the function of financial statements is to list amounts that appear in the general ledger (as presented in the adjusted trial balance), however, we must keep in mind that even though accounting is basically a measurement process, financial reporting is essentially a communication process.

The difference between presenting accounting *data* and presenting accounting *information* lies in the means through which the accounting is transmitted. Whereas an adjusted trial balance presents accounting *data,* financial statements are constructed with the objective of communicating accounting-based *information.* In addition to accounting numbers being reliable and relevant, they must be understandable. Financial statements therefore contain amounts arranged in homogeneous categories, insignificant amounts are combined with others, and narrative disclosures are prepared to provide information not contained in the financial statements themselves.

Income statement

An income statement discloses the elements constituting net income for the period. These elements are revenues, expenses, gains, and losses. Revenues and expenses refer to transactions involving the company's main business activities such as selling goods or rendering services. Gains and losses represent the net result of transactions which are relatively incidental to the company's primary business activity. Although the gain on the sale of a used delivery truck and the loss on the accidental destruction of a warehouse are not transactions which represent the company's reason for being in business, they are still elements of the company's net income when they happen.

Baxter Stores prepared the income statement shown in Exhibit 4–9 to cover its operations for the year. This is known as a single-step statement in that all revenue items are grouped together at the top, and net income is determined by subtracting the expenses from this total in a single step.

Some companies use a different format, preferring to segment their income statements. A simple segmented structure would show the following (using hypothetical figures to illustrate the concept):

Sales revenue	$400
Less: Cost of goods sold	240
Gross margin	160
Less: Operating expenses	100
Income before income taxes	60
Less: Income taxes	26
Net income	$ 34

The purpose of segmentation is to highlight key relationships, such as the relationship between gross margin and sales revenue. We prefer the single-step statement because it is simpler to read. It allows readers to select the relationships they wish to emphasize and study. It is also the format used most frequently in published financial statements.

EXHIBIT 4–9

BAXTER STORES, INC.
Income Statement
For the Year Ended December 31, 19x7

Gross revenue from sales		$1,000,000
Less: Estimated customer defaults		12,200
Net revenue from sales		987,800
Interest revenue		1,250
Total revenue		989,050
Expenses:		
Cost of goods sold	$450,000	
Salaries and wages expense	280,000	
Depreciation expense	9,000	
Rent expense..	80,000	
Utilities expense	23,000	
Warranty expense	16,500	
Insurance expense	2,925	
Interest expense	1,400	
Miscellaneous expense	19,175	
Income tax expense	31,600	
Total expenses		913,600
Net income		$ 75,450

An important disclosure feature of the income statement is that special situations sometimes require a modification of the usual format. Since investors and other external users of accounting information analyze income statements to estimate future income levels, accountants identify and isolate those elements of income that suggest unique circumstances:

1. An *extraordinary item* is a gain or loss that both is unusual in nature and occurs infrequently—such as an earthquake, an expropriation, or a prohibition under a newly enacted law or regulation.[5]
2. *Discontinued operations* refer to a situation in which a company divests itself of a portion of its business. The income (or loss) resulting from its revenues and expenses is isolated and disclosed together with the gain or loss resulting from its sale or abandonment.
3. A *change in accounting principle* means that a company adopts a different accounting method to record transactions from the method that has been used previously. When this happens, the

---

[5] A loss sustained by a manufacturer upon selling a warehouse is not extraordinary: Even though it's infrequent for this company, in general it's not unusual for an owner to sell a warehouse. A weather-induced crop loss by a hurricane-belt farmer is not extraordinary: Despite its being unusual for farmers in general, hurricanes are not infrequent for this particular company.

cumulative effect of the change on income is included in the income statement in the period in which the change is first introduced.

The income statement of a company that experiences any of these special situations makes the disclosures in its lower portion. Exhibit 4–10 presents a segmented income statement, with hypothetical numbers inserted for illustration. (Baxter Stores encountered no unique circumstances in 19x7, so its income statement can't be used to illustrate this form of disclosure.)

EXHIBIT 4–10. Special Income Statement Disclosures

Income from continuing operations		$34
Discontinued operations:		
Income from discontinued operations		
(less applicable income taxes of $7)	$18	
Loss on disposal of discontinued operations		
(less applicable taxes of $3)	(11)	7
Income before extraordinary items		41
Loss from earthquake damage		
(less applicable taxes of $2)		(6)
Income before effect of accounting changes		35
Cumulative effect of changes in an accounting		
principle (less applicable taxes of $1)		(4)
Net income		$31

This form of segmentation helps readers of financial statements to predict future income and cash flows. The effects of extraordinary events and accounting changes, if unsegregated, would obscure period-to-period movements in income from recurring operations—and it is income from recurring operations that will be the principal source of cash flows in the future.

Segregation of the income contribution of discontinued operations is important for much the same reason. Since these operations have been discontinued, they will neither contribute to nor siphon off income and cash flows in the future. By reporting this component of net income separately, the company gives the statement reader a clearer picture both of the reason for discontinuing the operation and of the income and cash-flow stream that will remain in the future.

Statement of changes in retained earnings

The statement of changes in retained earnings ordinarily includes only the beginning and ending balances, net income, and the amount of dividends declared during the year, as in Exhibit

4–11. This may seem strange at first glance. As we have seen, many numbers in the income statement are estimates of amounts the company doesn't know with certainty. The amount of income tax is a good example because an income statement is usually prepared before the company has made an exact determination of its tax obligation. When the actual amount is determined, the financial statements for the period have already been issued and the net income of that period has been closed into retained earnings.

Although it may seem logical to add or subtract any differences between the actual and estimated amounts to or from retained earnings, accountants don't do this. They prefer to pass these corrections through the income statement of the period in which they are identified. By doing this, they hope to make the series of net income amounts a more complete history of the company's income. They fear that charges or credits to retained earnings may be overlooked;

EXHIBIT 4–11

BAXTER STORES, INC.
Statement of Changes in Retained Earnings
For the Year Ended December 31, 19x7

Retained earnings, beginning of year	$ 44,150
Add: Net income	75,450
Total	119,600
Less: Cash dividends declared	16,000
Retained earnings, end of year	$103,600

putting them in the income statement, as is done for a change in an accounting principle, makes them much more visible. Accountants adjust the retained earnings directly only to correct items such as errors from mathematical mistakes, mistakes in the application of accounting principles, or oversights or misuse of facts known at the time the financial statements were prepared.

Balance sheet

The third financial statement is the balance sheet; Baxter Stores' year-end balance sheet is shown in Exhibit 4–12. The asset and liability balances in this statement were copied from the adjusted trial balance in Exhibit 4–7. They are divided between current and noncurrent items, as defined in Chapter 2. Baxter had noncurrent assets in 19x7 but no noncurrent liabilities.

The retained earnings amount in this balance sheet differs from the balance in the Retained Earnings account in the adjusted trial balance. The latter figure, it will be remembered, was the balance

EXHIBIT 4–12

BAXTER STORES, INC.
Balance Sheet
December 31, 19x7

Assets

Current assets:
Cash		$ 64,000
Notes receivable		96,250
Accounts receivable	$150,000	
Less: Allowance for uncollectibles	(12,200)	137,800
Inventory		89,000
Prepaid insurance		3,075
Total current assets		390,125

Plant assets:
Furniture and equipment	144,000	
Less: Accumulated depreciation	(48,000)	96,000
Total assets		$486,125

Liabilities and Owners' Equity

Current liabilities:
Notes payable		$ 30,200
Accounts payable		84,200
Salaries and wages payable		6,000
Taxes payable		19,625
Dividends payable		4,000
Advances from customers		22,000
Liability for service warranty		16,500
Total current liabilities		182,525

Owners' equity:
Capital stock	$200,000	
Retained earnings	103,600	
Total owners' equity		303,600
Total liabilities and owners' equity		$486,125

in this account at the *beginning* of the year. The year-end balance was obtained by adding the net income for the year and subtracting the dividends—in other words, the amounts summarized in the statement of changes in retained earnings (see Exhibit 4–11).

The balance sheet includes two contra-account balances. As was the case in the income statement, each contra-account balance appears with the asset to which it relates. Accounts receivable appears as $150,000 gross and $137,800 net, "net" meaning net of the allowance for uncollectibles. Furniture and equipment are disclosed on a dual basis as well: Cost is $144,000 and book value is $96,000.

The first listed liability is notes and interest payable. In the adjusted trial balance, this sum appears as two separate amounts—notes payable of $30,000 and interest payable of $200. These amounts have been combined because the $200 amount of interest payable just isn't large enough to warrant separate disclosure. In fact, the next largest amount in the balance sheet (prepaid insurance, $3,075) is 15 times larger than this payable. Combining interest payable with notes payable is the logical solution since they relate to the same set of circumstances. In practice, however, it is not uncommon to see lump-sum amounts such as other assets, other liabilities, or as we saw in Baxter Stores' own income statement, miscellaneous expenses.

Funds-flow analysis

Whenever a U.S. company prepares an income statement and a balance sheet, it must also prepare a statement of changes in financial position. Although this is an activity-oriented statement, as is the income statement, it measures and discloses information relating to flows of funds—not elements of income. The techniques used to prepare this financial statement are complicated enough to require explanation in a separate chapter. We'll postpone that discussion to Chapter 13.

CLOSING ENTRIES

Once the adjusting entries have been posted to the ledger and the financial statements have been prepared, the only remaining step is to close the temporary owners' equity accounts and make sure the balance sheet accounts have the correct balances to begin

EXHIBIT 4–13. The Accounting Cycle

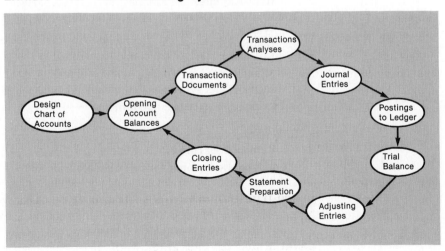

the next year. (The new year is well under way before this is done, but routine bookkeeping can proceed before the closing entries are made.) When these bookkeeping tasks are finished, the accounting cycle is completed. The accounting cycle is diagrammed in Exhibit 4–13.

Recall from Chapter 3 that closing entries are made to reduce to a zero balance each account that appears in the income statement as well as Dividends Declared. For Baxter Stores, closing entries were needed for Revenue, Expense, and Dividends Declared accounts. After these accounts were closed, Baxter's Retained Earnings account had an end-of-year balance of $103,600, the amount in the December 31 balance sheet.

Once the closing entries are posted, the accountant can prepare a postclosing trial balance. If the closing entries have been recorded properly, the only accounts with nonzero balances are the permanent balance sheet accounts. All the temporary accounts have zero

EXHIBIT 4–14.   Baxter Stores, Inc.: Closing Entries

Sales Revenue	1,000,000	
Interest Revenue	1,250	
Estimated Customer Defaults		12,200
Income Summary		989,050
To close the revenue-related accounts.		
Income Summary	913,600	
Cost of Goods Sold		450,000
Salaries and Wages Expense		280,000
Depreciation Expense		9,000
Rent Expense		80,000
Utilities Expense		23,000
Warranty Expense		16,500
Insurance Expense		2,925
Interest Expense		1,400
Miscellaneous Expense		19,175
Income Tax Expense		31,600
To close the expense accounts.		
Income Summary	75,450	
Retained Earnings		75,450
To close the Income Summary account.		
Retained Earnings	16,000	
Dividends Declared		16,000
To close the Dividends Declared account.		

EXHIBIT 4–15

BAXTER STORES, INC.
Postclosing Trial Balance
December 31, 19x7

Account	Debit	Credit
Cash	$ 64,000	
Notes receivable	96,250	
Accounts receivable	150,000	
Allowance for uncollectibles		$ 12,200
Inventory	89,000	
Prepaid insurance	3,075	
Furniture and equipment	144,000	
Accumulated depreciation		48,000
Notes payable		30,000
Accounts payable		84,200
Salaries and wages payable		6,000
Taxes payable		19,625
Interest payable		200
Dividends payable		4,000
Advances from customers		22,000
Liability for service warranty		16,500
Capital stock		200,000
Retained earnings		103,600
Totals	$546,325	$546,325

balances. Baxter Stores' closing entries and its postclosing trial balance are presented in Exhibits 4–14 and 4–15.

SUMMARY

Most bookkeeping is initiated by the need to prepare action documents such as payroll checks and customer invoices. Data for financial reporting are derived as a by-product of these important but routine activities.

It is probably not surprising, therefore, that the bookkeeping results fail to take account of all the factors that have a bearing on accrual-basis financial statements. These additional data must be processed in end-of-period adjusting entries, initiated by the accountant for the sole purpose of deriving financial statements. This chapter has illustrated nine common types of adjusting entries.

Once the adjusting entries have been made, accountants translate the adjusted account balances into an income statement, a balance sheet, and a statement of changes in retained earnings. After they have finished preparing these statements, they can close the temporary owners' equity accounts, thus setting the stage for the next accounting cycle.

KEY TERMS

Accounting cycle
Accrual
Adjusting entry
Allowance for uncollectibles
Customer defaults
Discontinued operations
Extraordinary item

Interest
Periodic inventory method
Perpetual inventory method
Promissory note
Shrinkage
Trial balance

INDEPENDENT STUDY PROBLEMS (Solutions in Appendix B)

1. Customer defaults. The Reilly Company recognizes revenues at the time it delivers products to its customers. You have the following information for the month of June:

1. Opening balances:
    Accounts Receivable, $950,000.
    Allowance for Uncollectibles, $25,000.
2. Gross sales, $500,000.
3. Collections from customers, $510,000.
4. Write-offs of specific uncollectibles, $8,000.
5. Estimated uncollectible amounts, June 30, $28,200.

a. Analyze the effects of items 2, 3, 4 and 5 on the company's assets, liabilities, and owners' equity. (Use +/− notation.)
b. Prepare journal entries to reflect your analyses in part a.
c. What amount should be reported to the shareholders for accounts receivable at the end of June?
d. What amount should be shown for customer defaults on the income statement for the month of June?

2. Interest accrual. On September 15, Calhoun Company borrowed $6,000 from the bank, promising to pay $6,000 plus accrued interest at 14 percent 60 days from the date of the note. On November 14, the company paid the accrued interest and renewed the note for an additional 30 days. At the second maturity, on December 14, Calhoun paid $4,000 in cash and gave a new 30-day, 14 percent note for the remaining amount due. This last note was paid in full when due.

a. Calculate Calhoun's interest expense for the year that ended December 31.
b. Prepare a journal entry to record the December 31 accrual.
c. Assuming that no additional entry was made between the accrual entry and the repayment date in January, prepare a journal entry to record the January payment.

3. Warranty accrual. For many years Philox Corporation has given each of its customers a two-year warranty on all purchases of Philox products. Management estimated that it would cost $55,000 to carry out its future obligations under the warranties in force on December 31, 19x1, and this amount was reflected in the company's ledger.

During 19x2, Philox paid $40,000 for warranty claims: three quarters in parts and complete units of merchandise, one quarter in cash. As of the end of 19x2, management estimated its warranty liability to be $83,500.

a. Calculate the amount of warranty expense to be shown on the company's income statement for 19x2.

b. Using whatever accounts are appropriate, prepare journal entries to record warranty expenses and other warranty-related transactions in 19x2.

4. Adjusting entries; financial statements. The December 31, 19x3, trial balance of the Guyton Company is as follows:

THE GUYTON COMPANY
Trial Balance
December 31, 19x3

Account	Debit	Credit
Cash	$ 30,900	
Notes receivable	17,700	
Accounts receivable	91,600	
Allowance for uncollectibles		$ 1,500
Inventory of merchandise, January 1, 19x3......	89,000	
Prepaid insurance	2,425	
Other prepayments	1,340	
Land	16,000	
Building and equipment......................	45,800	
Accumulated depreciation		8,100
Accounts payable...........................		18,800
Mortgage payable		45,000
Capital stock		150,000
Retained earnings		53,720
Sales revenues		400,000
Interest revenue		480
Purchases	344,500	
Advertising expense	1,200	
Salaries and wages expense	16,400	
Miscellaneous selling expense	5,800	
Property tax expense........................	3,300	
Miscellaneous general expenses	8,435	
Interest expense...........................	3,200	
Totals	$677,600	$677,600

The following information had not been recorded in the accounts when the trial balance was prepared:

1. A customer's account amounting to $165 was 18 months overdue, with little chance it would ever be collected; management decided to write it off.

2. Aging of the accounts receivable remaining on the books after the write-off in item 1 indicated that receivables amounting to $89,315, measured at gross invoice prices, probably were collectible.

3. The cost of the merchandise in the inventory on December 31, 19x3, was $86,440.

4. Merchandise costing $975 was received on December 31, 19x3, but was still in the receiving room and therefore wasn't included in the inventory count (item 3). The invoice covering this shipment wasn't reflected in the trial balance.
5. $1,725 of the insurance premiums paid before December 31, 19x3, were for insurance coverage in 19x4.
6. Depreciation for the year was $1,240.
7. Unrecorded interest accruing on the mortgage payable since the last interest payment amounted to $400.
8. Unrecorded wages earned by employees between the end of the last payroll period of 19x3 and the end of the year amounted to $240.

a. Prepare a journal entry for each year-end adjustment.
b. Prepare an adjusted trial balance.
c. Prepare an income statement for 19x3 and a year-end balance sheet.

EXERCISES AND PROBLEMS

5. Interest accrual. The Peterson Company borrowed $20,000 from a bank on January 21, giving in exchange a 90-day, 15 percent note.

a. Prepare an entry to record the borrowing.
b. Prepare whatever entry this transaction would make necessary on January 31 if the Peterson Company wished to prepare a set of accrual-basis financial statements as of the close of business on that date.
c. What entry would be necessary on January 31 if the Peterson Company prepared financial statements quarterly instead of monthly, the first quarter of the year ending on March 31? What entry would be made on February 28? On March 31?

6. Prepaid insurance and insurance expense. As of January 1, 19x4, Abigail Corporation's Prepaid Insurance account contained a $3,857 balance representing two policies: 3 months of fire and theft insurance and 14 months of motor vehicle insurance. The following insurance-related transactions occurred during 19x4.

February 20: Paid a $3,000 premium for one-year life insurance coverage for key company executives, effective March 1.

March 29: Paid $7,200 for three-year renewal of fire and theft coverage, effective upon March 31 expiration of the two-year policy that had cost $4,200.

August 24: Purchased business interruption insurance at a three-year cost of $4,860, effective September 1. Paid $1,620 immediately for the first year's coverage.

October 1: Paid $2,400 to increase the fire and theft coverage for the duration of the existing policy, effective October 1.

An entry debiting Prepaid Insurance was made for each of these transactions.

a. What was Abigail Corporation's insurance expense in 19x4?

b. What was Abigail Corporation's prepaid insurance as of January 1, 19x5?

c. What adjusting entry did Abigail make as of December 31, 19x4?

7. Interpreting account entries; adjusting entry. The following figures appeared in the Prepaid Rent account of a motion picture theater during 19x1:

Prepaid Rent

Bal. 1/1	10
Debits	75

Investigation shows that the balance in this account on December 31, 19x1, should have been $25.

a. How much money was paid to the landlord in 19x1?

b. What was the rent expense for 19x1?

c. What adjusting entry had to be made before the books could be closed at the end of 19x1?

8. Interest revenue; discounting a note. On November 6, 19x3, Sherburne Company sold merchandise to Bradley Corporation for $22,000. When Sherburne had bought the goods for $17,000 on October 5, 19x3, it had recorded the transaction as a direct debit to its inventory asset account. In exchange for the merchandise, Bradley gave Sherburne an 18 percent promissory note that would mature on January 5, 19x4. Sherburne instructed its accountant not to record the note at its $22,660 maturity value, however.

Prepare Sherburne Company's accounting entries of November 6 and December 31, 19x3, as well as the January 5, 19x4, entry or entries to record the receipt of cash.

9. Interest revenue, interest expense. McKay Company borrowed $40,000 from a bank on June 10, 19x2. The loan matured on February 5, 19x3, at which time McKay paid both the principal and 15 percent interest.

On September 27, 19x3, McKay lent $9,000 to Gardner, Ltd. Gardner paid the $9,000 note on February 24, 19x4, together with interest at an annual rate of 12 percent.

On December 11, 19x3, McKay accepted a customer's 60-day note to satisfy a past-due account. McKay recorded the note at the $62,000 amount of the unpaid balance even though its maturity value was $65,000. The customer paid the full amount on February 9, 19x4.

Prepare McKay Corporation's journal entries relating to these transactions.

10. Interpreting accounting entries; adjusting entry. The following amounts appeared in the Salaries Payable account of an advertising firm during 19x2:

Salaries Payable

(2)	1,360	Bal. 1/1	50
		(1)	1,400
		Bal. 12/31	90

The debit and credit shown here represent the many debits and credits that were actually entered in this account during the year.

All these figures were correct, and no further adjustments were necessary. Payroll taxes were zero, and all salary costs passed through this account.

a.   Calculate salary expense for the year.
b.   How much of the salaries earned by employees in 19x2 were paid in cash during the year?
c.   How much was paid to employees during 19x2 for work done in 19x1?
d.   How much will be paid to employees in 19x3 for work done in 19x2?

11.   Revenues and expenses. During 19x1, Arkin Company had sales of $450,000, its accounts receivable increased by $22,400, and its allowance for uncollectibles increased by $3,800. Its December 31 adjustments included recording cost of goods sold of $310,000 and its $14,700 estimate of customer defaults.

a.   How much cash did Arkin Company receive from its customers during 19x1?

During 19x2, Brockton Corporation had sales of $252,000, which represented a 50 percent markup over the goods' cost. Brockton's accounts payable to its merchandise suppliers increased by $18,700, while the cost of the year-end inventory was $16,500 less than it had been 12 months earlier.

b.   How much cash did Brockton Corporation pay to its suppliers during 19x2?

During 19x3, Carter, Inc., had a $5,000 increase in capital stock and a $14,700 decrease in total liabilities. Carter's directors declared and paid a $2,500 cash dividend, expenses were $97,300, and assets increased by $43,300.

c.   What was the amount of Carter, Inc.'s sales revenue in 19x3?

12.   Accruals and adjustments. During 19x3, Carlton, Ltd., paid cash of $24,000 for insurance, $82,500 for rent, $196,000 for salaries, and $17,100 for warranty claims. Carlton's end-of-year unadjusted trial balance included $58,000 of rent expense and $196,000 of salaries expense.

After all adjusting entries were made, Carlton's balance sheet showed changes from December 31, 19x2, in the following four accounts:

Prepaid rent, increase	$ 3,200
Prepaid insurance, decrease	12,200
Salaries payable, increase	6,300
Liability for warranty claims, decrease	3,300

You discover that when payment was made each month for that month's computer rental, the expense was recorded immediately. Rental payments for office space were made in advance and were recorded as prepaid rent.

a. What was Carlton's insurance expense for 19x3?
b. What was Carlton's rent expense for 19x3?
c. What was Carlton's warranty expense for 19x3?
d. What was Carlton's salaries expense for 19x3?

13. Revenues, expenses, and adjustments. Universal Corporation paid Dillon, Inc., $45,000 cash on August 1, 19x1, for the exclusive right to use Universal's computer from then until February 1, 19x3. Dillon recorded this transaction in a Revenue Received in Advance liability account.

About a year later, on August 4, 19x2, Universal bought merchandise for $13,000 cash, and it used the perpetual method of inventory recordkeeping to record the transaction. On September 14, 19x2, Universal sold the merchandise to Dillon; Dillon issued a 15 percent, 120-day note for the $18,000 invoice price, and it used the periodic method of inventory recordkeeping to record the transaction.

Dillon sold one third of the merchandise on December 10, 19x2, for $11,500 cash, and the remainder on March 2, 19x3, for $24,000 cash. On January 12, 19x3, Dillon paid Universal the principal and interest owed on the September 19x2 note.

Using parallel columns for Universal and Dillon, prepare the journal entries that each company recorded in 19x1, 19x2, and 19x3.

14. Effects of recordkeeping errors. Craft Company used the periodic method of inventory recordkeeping. An audit early in 19x5 established that the company had made the following eight recordkeeping errors in 19x3 and 19x4:

1. Failed to record accrued salaries in 19x3. These salaries were paid in 19x4.
2. Overstated cost of December 31, 19x3, inventory.
3. Forgot to record depreciation expense in 19x3.
4. Treated December 31, 19x3, prepaid rent as a 19x3 rent expense.
5. Recorded interest earned in 19x3 as revenue in 19x4.
6. Recorded January 19x4 advertising cost as expense when paid for in 19x3.
7. Recorded $9,280 estimated customer defaults as $19,280 on December 31, 19x4.
8. In 19x4, bought merchandise, recorded it as a machine, and recognized depreciation expense in 19x4; the goods were sold in 19x5.

Determine the effect of each error on the following financial statement elements:

a. 19x3 income.
b. December 31, 19x3, assets.
c. December 31, 19x3, liabilities.

d. 19x4 income.
e. December 31, 19x4, owners' equity.

To answer this, you should set up a five-column table and use O to signify overstatement, U for understatement, and X for no effect.

15. Revenues and receivables: missing data. You have the following partial data on two companies' revenues in a recent year and their receivables at the beginning and end of that year. All sales are on account. Supply the figures missing from this table.

	Company A	Company B
Allowance for uncollectibles:		
January 1	$ 4	$ 10
December 31	5	F
Collections from customers	A	545
Estimated customer defaults	B	6
Gross accounts receivable:		
January 1	50	G
December 31	C	90
Gross sales	370	H
Net accounts receivable:		
January 1	D	70
December 31	35	79
Net sales	E	I
Write-offs of specific uncollectibles	6	J

16. Recordkeeping errors. The Crown Company uses the periodic inventory method. The annual inventory count was made at the end of 19x1 and was reflected in the ledger at that time. Subsequently, the following recordkeeping errors were discovered:

1. A purchase of merchandise for $4,200 was incorrectly debited to Furniture and Fixtures.
2. Cash of $1,300 received from a customer on account was incorrectly credited to Sales.
3. A $400 payment to a vendor on account was incorrectly debited to Merchandise Inventories.
4. A sales invoice for $400 was not recorded; payment was not received from the customer before the end of the year, but Crown's management anticipated no difficulty in collecting it early in 19x2.
5. A $100 telephone bill was incorrectly charged to Entertainment Expense instead of to Telephone Expense.

a. For each of these, construct the adjusting entry that would have been made if the error had been discovered before the financial statements were prepared and before the year-end closing entries were made.
b. How would your answer to part a differ if these errors had been discovered after the closing entries had been made and the financial statements for the year had been published?

17. Revenues and receivables. Davis Company started operations early in 19x1. You have the following data for 19x1 and 19x2:

	19x1	*19x2*
Sales on credit	$320,000	$500,000
Collections from credit customers	260,000	480,000
Write-offs of specific accounts receivable	—	3,900
Amount of gross receivables at year-end management expects to be uncollectible (after specific write-offs)	5,000	6,000

a. Prepare entries in general journal form to reflect your analyses of this information, including closing entries for each year.

b. Calculate the company's net revenues as they should be shown on each year's income statement.

c. Show how accounts receivable should be reported on the year-end balance sheets for 19x1 and 19x2.

18. Preparing an income statement. Mountain Corporation was created in January 19x3. Its unconventional bookkeeping system produced the following data:

	Cash Exchanged	*No Cash Exchanged*
Rent of store location	$ 9,000	
Cost of merchandise purchased	83,500	$66,200
Salaries and wages	28,900	1,300
Sale of merchandise	98,800	83,100
Store fixtures acquired		14,000
Insurance cost	1,500	

Your investigation of 19x3's transactions reveals that rent has been paid covering the period from January 1, 19x3, through March 31, 19x4; the insurance policy covers the 12 months that began February 1, 19x3; the store fixtures are likely to last 10 years; and the year-end inventory cost $23,200.

Prepare Mountain Corporation's 19x3 income statement. Ignore income taxes.

19. Corrections; adjusting entries. The data that follow were collected by the companies' accountants before their companies' financial statements for the year 19x1 were prepared and before the closing entries for the year were made. Each company was engaged in wholesaling, with a fiscal year ending on December 31, 19x1.

For each company, prepare the journal entry necessary to adjust the accounts as of the end of the fiscal year. If no entry is necessary, write "no entry."

a. In Company A, local property taxes covering the period October 1, 19x1, through September 30, 19x2, were expected to amount to $30,000. These would be paid in July 19x2.

b. Company B received invoices on January 10, 19x2, covering telephone and electric service for the month of December 19x1, totaling $1,000.

c. Company C's perpetual inventory records and Inventory account balance indicated that the cost of merchandise on hand on December

31, 19x1, was $50,500. A physical count revealed that the amount actually on hand had cost $48,500.

d.   Company D's last weekly payroll period of 19x1 ended on December 26. The next weekly payroll covered the period December 27, 19x1, through January 2, 19x2. This included three working days in 19x1 and two working days in 19x2, holidays being counted as "working days" for this purpose. The total January 2 payroll was $25,000, of which $5,000 was for office employees and $20,000 was for store employees. The company uses a separate salary expense account for each department. Employer payroll taxes may be ignored.

e.   In 19x0, Company E bought merchandise for inventory amounting to $10,000, but at the time of acquisition the purchase was incorrectly debited to Office Supplies Expense. The merchandise itself was placed in the storeroom, however, and was counted properly in the annual physical inventory taken at the end of 19x0. In reviewing certain records now, just after the end of 19x1, the earlier error has been discovered.

f.   A machine that had cost Company F $11,000 when new was sold during 19x1 for $5,000. At the time of the sale, its book value was $3,000. To record the sale, an accounting clerk debited Cash and credited Other Income $5,000.

20. Supplying missing information.   The Tabor Supply Company sells scientific instruments to the trade. After all entries in the company's journals for 19x0 had been posted to the ledger accounts, the journals were destroyed by fire. The company's accountants have been able to reconstruct most of the journal entries from the basic documents, but in each of the following accounts *one* entry is still unexplained.

In each case, reconstruct the complete journal entry that was *most probably* made during the year and will account for the unexplained portion of the change in the account balance. Each problem is independent of the other problems. You should assume that the balances are correct and, therefore, that no correcting entries are required.

Example:

Given: Capital Stock account:

Beginning balance	$ 40,000
Ending balance	65,000

Answer:

Cash	25,000	
Capital Stock		25,000

a.   Retained Earnings account:

Beginning balance	$ 95,000
Ending balance	100,000
Net income for year, transferred by closing	12,000

b.   Prepaid Insurance account:

Beginning balance	$ 2,400
Expired during period	2,600
Ending balance	1,900

c. Wages Payable account:

Beginning balance	$ 1,100
Wages paid	10,500
Ending balance	1,400

d. Accounts Receivable account (at gross):

Beginning balance	$100,000
Written off as bad	2,000
Cash received	204,000
Ending balance	110,000

e. Prepaid Rent account:

Ending balance	$ 20,000
Rental payments	10,000
Beginning balance	14,500

f. Accounts Payable account:

Beginning balance	$ 50,000
Ending balance	70,000
Purchases	88,000

g. Machinery account:

Beginning balance	$200,000
New machine purchased	50,000
Ending balance	230,000

Machinery—Accumulated Depreciation account:

Net increase in account balance	$ 35,000
Depreciation expense	42,000

Note: There were no cash receipts from sale of machinery.

21. Revenues and expenses: missing amounts. The following table contains amounts relating to Dixon Company's 19x6 operations. Dixon sells tennis equipment on account. It also operates tennis courts for which it sells a 15-month membership plan: Cash is collected in advance, and members have unlimited access to tennis courts on a reservations basis.

	January 1	Debits	Credits	December 31
Wages payable	$14,900	$92,700	A	$ 12,600
Inventory	B	78,700	$ 75,200	13,400
Rentals received in advance	23,400	14,500	C	29,600
Interest revenue			D	36,900
Allowance for uncollectibles	14,200	E	26,600	34,400
Warranty expense....................		F		6,600
Interest payable	G	21,200	26,100	30,500
Liability for warranty claims	H	4,200	I	19,800
Accumulated depreciation	93,000	52,200	J	103,300
Interest receivable	14,500	K	L	16,100
Accounts receivable	35,400	M	306,500	38,900

a. Determine and label the missing amounts.

b. Using the amounts in the table, prepare Dixon Company's income statement for 19x6. Ignore income taxes.

22. Preparing financial statements. Listed below are account balances relating to Rogers Corporation's 19x3 financial statements.

Machinery	$ 20,000	Depreciation expense	$ 600
Prepaid insurance	400	Accounts payable	12,600
Notes payable (due 19x6)	12,400	Insurance expense	1,400
Estimated customer		Allowance for	
defaults	200	uncollectibles	300
Land	4,400	Retained earnings,	
Cash	4,600	Jan. 1, 19x3	18,000
Interest expense	1,300	Accumulated depreciation	5,400
Capital stock	1,500	Accounts receivable	14,000
Dividends declared	7,500	Merchandise inventory,	
Revenue from sales	141,500	Dec. 31, 19x3	4,300
Purchases of merchandise	22,900	Interest revenue	900
Wage and salaries		Income tax expense	1,800
expense	103,600	Notes receivable (due in 19x4)	5,000
Merchandise inventory,		Wages and salaries	
Jan. 1, 19x3	6,100	payable	1,200

a. Prepare the 19x3 income statement.
b. Prepare the 19x3 statement of changes in retained earnings.
c. Prepare the December 31, 19x3, balance sheet.

23. Misstated income, accounting errors. Arlington Company reported net income of $62,000 for 19x2 and $93,000 for 19x3. Based on the information that follows, determine the correct amount of income for each year.

a. The $15,000 wages paid on January 6, 19x3, were recorded as an expense even though 35 percent related to work performed in December 19x2.
b. On November 16, 19x2, Arlington lent $8,400 to a supplier for 60 days at 16 percent. Arlington recorded $224 interest revenue in 19x2.
c. Arlington paid $3,600 during March 19x2 for a life insurance policy that would be effective April 1, 19x2, and run for two years. Prepaid insurance was increased by $3,600 in 19x2 and reduced by $3,600 in 19x4.
d. In December 19x2, Arlington introduced a warranty reimbursement program. Since Arlington would honor claims relating to merchandise sold anytime in 19x2, it recognized $5,200 of warranty expense in 19x2. Warranties were also given on merchandise sold in 19x3. When warranty claims were presented in 19x3, the $4,300 paid in cash was recorded as an expense. At the end of 19x3, Arlington determined that future claims would likely be $5,900, and it therefore recorded additional warranty expense of $1,600 in 19x3 ($5,900 − $4,300).
e. As a friendly gesture to a landlord who was in dire financial straits, in December 19x2 Arlington prepaid rent for the first four months of 19x3 at the rate of $550 a month and recorded the payment as rent expense.
f. On April 1, 19x2, Arlington bought a delivery truck for $15,300, which it expected to use until the end of 19x5. Since all 12 months of 19x2 would not benefit from the truck, the bookkeeper decided to record depreciation so that 19x3, 19x4, and 19x5 would each be charged with one third of the vehicle's cost.

g. In 19x2, Arlington began making credit sales for the first time. The year-end aged accounts receivable indicated that $8,200 would probably never be collected. Since no accounts were written off during that year, the bookkeeper saw no sense in even recording the $8,200 estimate. When $5,600 of accounts were judged to be definitely worthless during 19x3, the following entry was recorded:

Loss   5,600

      Accounts Receivable   5,600

Although the end-of-19x3 aged receivables indicated that specific accounts totaling $9,700 would likely be written off as uncollectible in 19x4, the bookkeeper believed that consistency dictated that no entry be made to record this estimate.

24. Income statement disclosures. The year 19x3 was one that Troy Company had aptly characterized as a year of transition. Although Troy's $18,500,000 sales exceeded 19x2's sales, its net income was a disappointing $648,000. The company president was concerned that the earnings press release that would be issued in January 19x5 explain as succinctly as possible the seemingly dismal story of the poor 19x4 profit. He requested a summary report and was given the following condensed income statement.

TROY COMPANY
Income Statement
For the Year Ended December 31, 19x4

Revenue from sales		$18,500,000
Expenses and losses:		
Normal expenses	$12,910,000	
Pollution penalty	800,000	
Revenue-recognition switch	1,800,000	
Inventory write-down	550,000	
Business abandonment	1,360,000	17,420,000
Income before taxes		1,080,000
Income taxes		432,000
Net income		$ 648,000

The president was somewhat taken aback by what the report did not reveal. He discovered, for instance, that the business segment which had been sold represented $4,100,000 of Troy's sales and was responsible for $3,860,000 of the company's expenses. The pollution penalty related to fines and restitution costs resulting from a fluke case of water and air pollution of a variety that neither had happened previously nor was likely to ever happen again in an era of EPA and OSHA monitoring and enforcement.

The company's income had been adversely affected by two other matters whose timing was somewhat controllable by the management. Top management had decided that as of January 1, 19x4, all revenues would be recognized when merchandise was delivered. The cumulative accounting effect relates to those sales that had previously been recorded when production was completed that hadn't been delivered as of December 31, 19x3. The $550,000 inventory write-down pertains to an overstock of obsolete and spoiled raw materials and finished products that probably could have been written off a year or two earlier.

Prepare Troy Company's 19x4 income statement in accordance with the accounting profession's prescribed disclosure rules. The tax rate is 40 percent.

25. Adjusting entries and financial statements. Broden Company's unadjusted trial balance as of December 31, 19x4, is as follows:

BRODEN COMPANY
Unadjusted Trial Balance
December 31, 19x4

Cash	$ 46,200	Allowance for		
Accounts receivable	124,600	uncollectibles	$	1,300
Notes receivable	10,000	Accumulated		
Interest receivable	900	depreciation		39,900
Inventory	31,600	Accounts payable		42,400
Prepaid insurance	2,000	Liability for		
Land	60,000	warranty claims		1,100
Buildings	838,000	Notes payable		60,000
Machinery	86,700	Common stock		280,000
Cost of goods sold	219,800	Retained earnings		541,300
Salaries and		Sales		724,500
wages expense	188,400			
Utilities expense	40,300			
Dividends declared	42,000			
Total	$1,690,500	Total		$1,690,500

The following information became known shortly after year-end:

1. The company uses the perpetual method of inventory recordkeeping, and the year-end inventory count indicates that the cost of the goods on hand was $26,900.
2. The $10,000 note receivable is a 12 percent, two-year note which was received from a customer on April 1, 19x3. The customer will pay the amount due Broden Company, including interest for the full two years, when the note matures in 19x5. Interest in each of the two years is based on the $10,000 original amount of the note.
3. Management estimates that 7 percent of year-end accounts receivable will probably never be collected.
4. Salaries and wages of $2,700 were earned in 19x4 for which payment will be made on January 6, 19x5. No entry has been made to record these salaries and wages.
5. Depreciation for the year was calculated to be $31,778.
6. The company owes a bank $60,000. Although the principal is due in February 19x6, each year's interest must be paid within 15 days after the close of the calendar year. The $60,000 was borrowed on October 2, 19x4, and the interest rate is 14 percent.
7. The engineering department estimates that future warranty claims are likely to be $24,000.
8. A review of the insurance file indicates that as of January 1, 19x5, prepaid premiums total $200.

a. Prepare adjusting journal entries and an adjusted trial balance.
b. Prepare Broden Company's income statement and statement of changes in retained earnings for 19x4, and its balance sheet as of December 31, 19x4.
c. Prepare the year-end closing entries.

26. Adjusting entries, financial statements. Dover Corporation sells merchandise and publishes an industry newsletter. Its December 31, 19x5, trial balance is as follows:

DOVER CORPORATION
Trial Balance
December 31, 19x5

Account	Debit	Credit
Cash	$ 24,600	
Accounts receivable	51,300	
Allowance for uncollectibles		$ 1,800
Notes receivable	12,000	
Interest receivable	300	
Merchandise inventory	14,600	
Prepaid rent	3,500	
Prepaid insurance	1,700	
Machinery	16,600	
Accumulated depreciation		3,400
Accounts payable		7,700
Interest payable		200
Liability for warranty claims		900
Revenue received in advance		14,300
Notes payable		5,000
Capital stock		4,000
Retained earnings		32,600
Revenue from sales		176,400
Interest revenue		300
Purchases	73,400	
Salaries and wages expense	44,400	
Interest expense	200	
Dividends declared	4,000	
Totals	$246,600	$246,600

The following information had not yet been recorded when the trial balance was prepared:

1. Accrued interest on the notes receivable was $900 at year-end. The interest will be received when the notes mature in 19x6. Accrued interest on the notes payable was $400. Although the notes will mature in 19x7, Dover is required to pay the interest accrued in 19x5 in January 19x6. The trial balance interest amounts were errors.
2. Management's assessment of sales and year-end receivables determined that future warranty costs will probably amount to $2,500 and that $3,100 of the receivables will likely not be collectible.
3. Dover's rental cost was $250 a month, and its depreciation was $150 a month.
4. Based on newsletters Dover delivered during the year, $11,900 of amounts collected in advance was earned during 19x5.
5. Salaries and wages earned but unpaid as of December 31 totaled $900.
6. An examination of the insurance file indicates that Dover will begin 19x6 with $300 of prepaid coverage.
7. A physical count of the merchandise at year-end reveals that goods that had cost Dover $15,900 are on hand.

a. Prepare a journal entry for each year-end adjustment.
b. Prepare an adjusted trial balance.

c. Prepare Dover Corporation's 19x5 income statement, statement of changes in retained earnings, and the balance sheet as of December 31, 19x5.

d. Prepare the closing entries that assume the adjusting entries had already been posted to Dover's ledger accounts.

27. Adjustments and closing entries. Towle Company's December 31, 19x4, unadjusted trial balance is presented:

TOWLE COMPANY
Unadjusted Trial Balance
December 31, 19x4

Account	Debit	Credit
Cash	$ 14,400	
Accounts receivable	81,600	
Allowance for uncollectibles		$ 700
Merchandise inventory, January 1, 19x4	11,200	
Prepaid rent	1,300	
Machinery and equipment	9,500	
Accumulated depreciation		2,200
Accounts payable		41,800
Wages and salaries payable		1,900
Capital stock		5,000
Retained earnings, January 1, 19x4		49,600
Sales		216,600
Purchases	114,200	
Wages and salaries expense	59,900	
Rent expense	15,700	
Dividends declared	10,000	
Totals	$317,800	$317,800

Towle's accountants prepared a number of adjusting entries and posted them to the accounts. Once they had done this, they prepared and recorded the following closing entries as of December 31, 19x4:

Sales	216,600	
Estimated Customer Defaults		1,700
Income Summary		214,900
Income Summary...............................	195,000	
Cost of Goods Sold		116,300
Wages and Salaries Expense		61,300
Rent Expense		16,500
Depreciation Expense.......................		900
Income Summary.............................	19,900	
Retained Earnings		19,900
Retained Earnings	10,000	
Dividends Declared		10,000

Based on this information, prepare Towle Company's December 31, 19x4, balance sheet.

5

Manufacturing cost flows

Manufacturing companies face the same problems of measuring income and the cost of end-of-period inventories as the merchandising companies that have been our focus in the three preceding chapters. They also have other problems of their own. Our purpose in this chapter is to show how the principles of accrual accounting can be applied to the manufacturing operations of an income-seeking business.

THE MANUFACTURING CYCLE

Manufacturing is the process by which companies convert one set of goods (*materials*) into another set of goods (*finished products*). Manufacturing takes place in physical facilities, which are most commonly known as *factories*.

The sequence of events from the purchase of materials to the completion of finished products is known as the *manufacturing cycle,* illustrated in Exhibit 5–1. As this shows, the cycle begins with the purchase of materials. These are generally placed in storerooms or stockpiles when they are received. The quantities in these locations are known as *materials inventories*. When some of them are needed in production, they are transferred from the storeroom or stockpile to appropriate locations in the factory. When this happens, we say that materials have been *issued.* They then become part of the *work in process.*

Work in process is a form of inventory—an inventory of partly

EXHIBIT 5–1. The Manufacturing Cycle

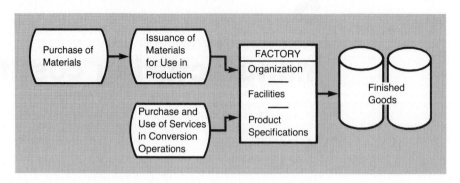

processed products. This inventory doesn't consist of materials alone, however. It also includes the other factory resources that have been used to convert the materials into their partly processed state. The most obvious other factory resource is *labor time*—the amount of time factory employees have spent working on the materials. Factory labor time and the other factory resources used in production are just as much a part of the work in process as the materials because they are just as necessary to bring the items in process to their present state.

The manufacturing cycle ends when the last operations have been performed on the product and it is placed in a warehouse or other location, ready for delivery to a customer. This product then becomes part of the *finished goods inventory*. Materials, work in process, and finished goods are all assets. Finished goods remain assets until they are shipped to customers, lost, or disposed of in some way.

MANUFACTURING COST FLOWS

Accountants see costs flowing through the accounting structure as resources flow through the manufacturing cycle. The left block in Exhibit 5–2 shows that when materials are purchased, their costs become the costs of the materials inventory. When some of these materials are placed in production, their costs are transferred to the work in process inventory, represented by the block in the middle of the exhibit. The costs of labor time (*labor cost*) and the costs of other factory resources consumed in manufacturing are included in the costs of the work in process inventory as they are incurred in production. When the manufacturing cycle ends, the costs of the completed products are transferred from the work in process

EXHIBIT 5–2. Costs of Factory Inventories

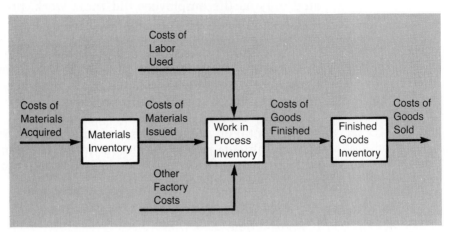

category to the finished goods category, as shown in the right of Exhibit 5–2.

In this section we'll use a simple example to show how a manufacturing company might use accounts to accumulate the costs of manufacturing operations and divide them between the costs of goods sold and the costs of the ending inventory for financial accounting purposes.

Preproduction transactions

Strong Cabinets, Inc., was founded by David Strong on July 1, 19x1, to manufacture bookshelves, cabinets, and other wooden furniture. Some of this furniture was made in standard designs to be sold to retail stores; the rest was of very high quality to fill the orders of specific customers.

Strong Cabinets began operations with $200,000 in cash, provided by Strong in exchange for shares of the company's capital stock. The entry was:

(1)

Cash	200,000	
Capital Stock		200,000

This showed the increase in the company's assets and the creation of owners' equity.

Strong hired skilled cabinetmakers, carpenters, and office workers as the company began operations. The company expended no resources in hiring these resources and acquired no property rights.

Nor did the company incur a liability—the liability would be created only as the employees did their work, providing services to the company. As a result, no entry was made in the accounts to record the hiring of these employees.

Three other transactions took place before manufacturing operations began: (1) prepayment of rent, (2) purchase of factory equipment, and (3) purchases of materials. The accounting treatment of these is familiar to us from previous chapters, so we'll describe them very briefly.

The rental on the factory space amounted to $84,000 a year, and Strong Cabinets paid a year's rent in advance on July 1, 19x1. The entry recording this transaction showed the acquisition of one asset in exchange for another:

(2)

Prepaid Rent	84,000	
Cash		84,000

Next, tools and equipment were bought on account for $100,000, and their cost was entered in a new asset account, Factory Equipment. The accompanying liability was also recognized at this time by an entry in the Accounts Payable account. The record of this transaction therefore showed the following changes:

(3)

Factory Equipment	100,000	
Accounts Payable		100,000

Third, the company bought lumber and other materials for use in the factory. These materials were bought on credit at a total cost of $220,000. The entries recording these purchases showed that both assets and liabilities increased:

(4)

Factory Materials Inventory	220,000	
Accounts Payable		220,000

The only difference between these purchases and the inventory purchases we discussed in previous chapters is that these are materials to be used in manufacturing processes, not merchandise ready for resale without further processing.

Recording the issuance of materials

When production materials are issued, they are merely transferred from one asset category to another. For example, Strong Cabinets issued materials from inventory with a total cost of $140,000 during the last six months of 19x1. In this company's highly simplified accounting system, a single account, Work in Process Inventory, is used to accumulate all the costs assignable to the in-process inventory assets. The entries that recorded the issuance of materials in 19x1 showed increases in the work in process inventory and decreases in the quantity of unissued materials on hand:

(5)

Work in Process Inventory	140,000	
Factory Materials Inventory		140,000

The costs of materials issued are still the costs of inventory assets. Issuance merely changes the physical location of these assets. Issuance creates no revenues, and the costs of materials issued therefore remain in inventory. Entry (5) recognized their change in status by transferring the costs from one inventory account to another.

Recording factory labor costs

Factory labor costs are incurred to produce assets—finished goods inventories—which have values in excess of the costs required to produce them. During the second half of 19x1 (the first six months of operations), wages and salaries in Strong Cabinets' factory amounted to $200,000. The entries recording these payrolls can be summarized as follows:

(6)

Work in Process Inventory	200,000	
Wages and Salaries Payable		200,000

The debit to the Work in Process Inventory account recorded an increase in the cost of this inventory asset. Factory labor costs add to the asset because they bring it closer to the form in which it will be useful to customers. They don't become expenses until revenues are earned and appear in an income statement, either later in the same period or in some subsequent period. Factory labor costs therefore differ from the costs of the wages and salaries of office and store employees, which are generally recognized as expenses immediately on the grounds that they are costs of generating the revenues of the current period.

Recording depreciation

A third element of factory cost is depreciation of factory facilities. Depreciation is ordinarily treated as a current expense when it relates to facilities used for administrative or marketing activities. When it relates to manufacturing facilities, however, it is a cost of producing inventory assets—work in process inventory in the first instance and finished goods later on.

This treatment again reflects the idea that the asset has merely been converted from one form to another; the services formerly embodied in a machine are now embodied in the goods produced during the period. Factory depreciation therefore doesn't become an expense until revenues from the sale of the resulting products are recognized in the income statement. Depreciation on Strong Cabinets' factory tools and equipment amounted to $8,000 in the second half of 19x1, and the entry was as follows:

(7)

Work in Process Inventory...................... 8,000
    Accumulated Depreciation 8,000

The credit to Accumulated Depreciation records the decrease in the company's equipment assets. This is a contra-asset account, as we explained in Chapter 3, and its end-of-period balance appears on the balance sheet as a deduction from the original cost of factory plant assets.

Other factory costs

Running a factory calls for the use of many more resources than materials, labor, and equipment. In the second half of 19x1, Strong Cabinets bought various services on account from outside suppliers—electric power and telephone service, for example—for immediate use in the factory's production operations. The total cost of these services was $70,000, and the entries to record these transactions can be summarized as follows:

(8)

Work in Process Inventory 70,000
    Accounts Payable 70,000

The debits to the inventory account showed that these costs were incurred to produce inventory assets: Costs of resources such as these are just as much part of the cost of production as materials, labor, and factory depreciation costs.

Strong Cabinets had one other factory cost in the first half of 19x1, the cost of the space the cabinet shop occupied. Rent of $84,000 had been paid on July 1, 19x1 [entry (2)], covering the ensuing 12 months. Six months of this period had elapsed by the end of the year, and six months' rent therefore had to be treated as a cost of factory operations in 19x1. The accountants' analysis showed the following asset changes:

(9)

Work in Process Inventory 42,000	
Prepaid Rent................................	42,000

This signifies that the prepaid rent asset decreased and that the rent cost became a cost of the work in process inventory asset.

Cost of goods finished

Entry (9) completed the recognition of the 19x1 costs of production. The Work in Process Inventory account then registered the following costs:

Work in Process Inventory

(5)	Materials	140,000	
(6)	Labor	200,000	
(7)	Depreciation	8,000	
(8)	Services	70,000	
(9)	Rent	42,000	
		460,000	

Some products Strong Cabinets' factory began working on in 19x1 were still unfinished at the end of the year. Work on other products was completed, however, and the finished units were placed in Strong Cabinets' shipping room. In examining the records, the accountants found that of the total cost incurred ($460,000), the portion associated with the finished units amounted to $350,000.[1] The entry to record the completion of these units was:

(10)

Finished Goods Inventory 350,000	
Work in Process Inventory	350,000

Both of these are asset accounts; the entry merely indicated the change in the inventory from an unfinished to a finished form.

The Work in Process Inventory account showed the following after this entry was made:

---

[1] We'll explain in Chapters 17 and 18 how accountants assign factory costs to individual units of product and thereby determine the total cost of all the products finished in a given period.

Work in Process Inventory

(5)	140,000	(10)	350,000
(6)	200,000		
(7)	8,000		
(8)	70,000		
(9)	42,000		
	460,000		
Bal. 110,000			

In other words, the cost of unfinished furniture still in process on December 31, 19x1, was $110,000.

Cost of goods sold

The Finished Goods Inventory account plays the same role in a manufacturing company as the Merchandise Inventory account plays in a retailing or wholesaling company. It keeps the costs of salable products in the balance sheet until revenues from the sale of the goods are reported in the income statement.

Strong Cabinets, Inc., has perpetual inventory records for its inventory of finished products. A separate record card is prepared for each kind of finished product. When units are finished, the costs assigned to them are entered on the card. When goods are sold and shipped to a customer, the costs assigned to the units shipped are subtracted from the balance on the card and identified as the cost of goods sold.

Using this system, Strong Cabinets determined that the sum of the factory costs of the items the company sold in 19x1 was $280,000. The delivery of these items to the company's customers constituted transfers of company-owned resources to these customers. The cost of these resources, the cost of goods sold, is shown in the income statement as an expense—in the same sense that the costs of advertising and sales salaries are classifed as expenses; that is, all were costs incurred to create the revenues recognized in this period. Strong Cabinets recorded this transfer of costs in 19x1 by the following entry:

(11)

Cost of Goods Sold	280,000	
Finished Goods Inventory		280,000

The debit to the Cost of Goods Sold account recorded a decrease in the company's owners' equity (an offset against the increase in owners' equity contributed by sales revenues). The credit to Finished Goods Inventory recorded the accompanying decrease in that asset.

Recognition of these transactions left a balance of $70,000 in the Finished Goods Inventory account, the cost of the finished furniture still on the storeroom shelves at the end of 19x1:

Finished Goods Inventory

(10)	350,000	(11)	280,000
Bal. 70,000			

Schedule of manufacturing costs

The flow of manufacturing costs through the accounts is diagrammed in Exhibit 5–3. Notice that inventories are found in three stages—unprocessed, partly processed, and finished. Each dollar amount identified with a cost flow in this diagram came from one of the entries in the illustration.

These cost flows are summarized in tabular form in the manufacturing cost schedule in Exhibit 5–4. This shows that of the $460,000 of total factory cost actually applicable to factory operations during 19x1, only $280,000 was transferred to expense in the income statement for the year. The remaining $180,000 was divided between

EXHIBIT 5–3. Manufacturing Cost Flows for Income Reporting

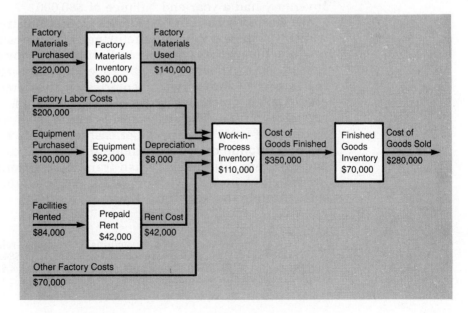

EXHIBIT 5–4

STRONG CABINETS, INC.
Schedule of Manufacturing Costs and Cost of Goods Sold
For the Six Months Ended December 31, 19x1

Factory costs:		
Materials costs:		
Materials on hand, July 1, 19x1	$ 0	
Materials purchased	220,000	
Cost of materials available for use	220,000	
Less: Materials on hand, December 31, 19x1	80,000	
Cost of materials used		$140,000
Factory labor cost		200,000
Other factory costs:		
Depreciation	8,000	
Rent	42,000	
Miscellaneous	70,000	120,000
Total factory cost		460,000
Add: Work in process, July 1, 19x1		0
Total cost in production		460,000
Less: Work in process, December 31, 19x1		110,000
Cost of goods finished		350,000
Add: Finished goods inventory, July 1, 19x1		0
Cost of goods available for sale		350,000
Less: Finished goods inventory, December 31, 19x1		70,000
Cost of goods sold		$280,000

the work in process inventory ($110,000) and the finished goods inventory ($70,000). The schedule also shows that the materials inventory had a year-end balance of $80,000.[2]

We started with zero inventories in this illustration because we wanted to show how manufacturing inventories are created. The manufacturing cost schedule in Exhibit 5–4 shows how beginning inventories can be inserted. The appendix to this chapter illustrates the impact of beginning inventories on the determination of the cost of goods finished and the cost of goods sold.

Notice that nowhere in this illustration have we referred to the payment of cash. The timing of cash payments has no bearing on the apportionment of costs among the various categories of assets and expenses. Eliminating cash transactions from the illustration interfered in no way with our ability to trace the manufacturing costs through the accounts.

---

[2] The year-end balance sheet also contains other factory-related costs not classified as *inventory:* (1) rent prepayments of $42,000 (6/12 of $84,000), and (2) factory equipment cost of $92,000 [because only $8,000 (entry 7) of its $100,000 original cost (entry 3) was used in the manufacturing process in 19x1].

NONMANUFACTURING COSTS AND THE INCOME STATEMENT

Every manufacturer incurs many costs for activities other than manufacturing. Advertising costs, the president's salary, and expenditures for research and development are only a few examples of costs that are incurred for purposes other than the conversion of raw materials into finished products.

All such costs are accounted for just as they would be in a retailing or wholesaling concern. Sales office rental costs and advertising costs are recognized as expense when the space and advertising services are provided, whether products have been sold or not. They aren't part of the cost of manufacturing products and therefore they don't enter the factory cost accounts in any way. They go directly to expense without passing through the Work in Process Inventory and the Finished Goods Inventory accounts along the way.

Strong's salary and the salaries of the rest of the selling and administrative work force in 19x1 amounted to $170,000. The entries to accrue these payrolls can be summarized as follows:

Selling and Administrative Salaries Expense   170,000
  Wages and Salaries Payable   170,000

The effect of these transactions, in other words, was to decrease the owners' equity and increase the company's liabilities.

Transactions giving rise to other selling and administrative costs had similar effects. They amounted to $31,000 and can be summarized as follows:

(13)
Other Selling and Administrative Expenses   31,000
  Accounts Payable   31,000

To complete the illustration of the operating cycle, we need to identify the revenues of the period and show what accounts they affected. Finished furniture was sold on account in 19x1 for a total of $500,000, thereby increasing the company's assets and its owners' equity:

(14)
Accounts Receivable   500,000
  Sales Revenue   500,000

Finally, the company made provision for income taxes attributable to the operation of the business in 19x1. The effective tax rate that year was 40 percent, and the income tax accrued at that rate was $7,600. The entry was:

(15)

Income Tax Expense 7,600
    Income Tax Payable   7,600

After all these entries were made, the company's accountants prepared the income statement shown in Exhibit 5–5.

EXHIBIT 5–5

STRONG CABINETS, INC.
Income Statement
For the Six Months Ended December 31, 19x1

Sales		$500,000
Operating expenses:		
Cost of goods sold (from Exhibit 5–4)..........	$280,000	
Selling and administrative salaries	170,000	
Other selling and administrative expenses	31,000	481,000
Income before income taxes		19,000
Income tax expense		7,600
Net income		$ 11,400

SUMMARY

Accounting treatment of manufacturing costs is an excellent illustration of the application of the accrual concept. Accounting views manufacturing as a process of adding the costs of manufacturing labor and other manufacturing services to the cost of purchased materials. The costs of manufacturing follow the flow of the goods themselves, from raw materials inventory to work in process to finished goods and finally to goods sold.

The costs of the goods at all these stages except the last are regarded as costs of assets and therefore are included in the inventory section of the balance sheet. Only when the goods are sold do these costs become expenses, identified in the income statement as the cost of goods sold. Costs of administering the company and of selling and distributing its products are recognized immediately as expenses, just as in a wholesaling or retailing business.

APPENDIX: ILLUSTRATION INCLUDING BEGINNING INVENTORIES

Strong Cabinets began the year 19x2 with the following balances in its manufacturing cost accounts (from Exhibit 5–4):

Factory materials inventory .... $ 80,000
Work in process inventory 110,000
Finished goods inventory 70,000

During the year 19x2, the factory had the transactions recorded in the following entries:

a. Factory Materials Inventory 400,000
        Accounts Payable 400,000
    To record the purchase of factory
    materials on credit.

b. Work in Process Inventory 390,000
        Factory Materials Inventory 390,000
    To record issuance of factory materials
    for use in production.

c. Work in Process Inventory 450,000
        Wages and Salaries Payable 450,000
    To record the use of factory labor.

d. Work in Process Inventory 16,000
        Accumulated Depreciation 16,000
    To record depreciation on factory
    equipment.

e. Prepaid rent 63,000
        Cash 63,000
    To record payment of nine months' rent
    on the factory building.

f. Work in Process Inventory 84,000
        Prepaid Rent 84,000
    To record use of the factory building.

g. Work in Process Inventory 130,000
        Accounts Payable 130,000
    To record other factory costs in 19x2.

h. Finished Goods Inventory 1,100,000
        Work in Process Inventory 1,100,000
    To record the completion of product
    units in 19x2.

i. Cost of Goods Sold 1,050,000
        Finished Goods Inventory 1,050,000
    To record the cost of the goods sold in
    19x2.

The flow of costs through the manufacturing cost accounts in 19x2 is shown in T-account form in Exhibit 5–6. Cash, Accounts Payable, and other accounts whose balances don't enter into the schedule of manufacturing costs are omitted from this exhibit. Notice that the balance in Factory Materials Inventory increased by $10,000 during the year, as the amount of materials issued was less than the amount purchased. The Work in Process balance decreased by $30,000, as the cost of the units completed exceeded the

EXHIBIT 5–6.   Strong Cabinets, Inc.: Factory Cost Accounts in 19x2

Factory Materials Inventory				Work in Process Inventory			
Bal.	80,000	(b)	390,000	Bal.	110,000	(h)	1,100,000
(a)	400,000			(b)	390,000		
				(c)	450,000		
Bal. 90,000				(d)	16,000		
				(f)	84,000		
				(g)	130,000		
				Bal. 80,000			
Finished Goods Inventory				**Cost of Goods Sold**			
Bal.	70,000	(i)	1,050,000	(i)	1,050,000		
(h)	1,100,000						
Bal. 120,000							

cost of the work done. The balance in the Finished Goods Inventory account increased, however, as the sales volume fell slightly short of the volume of goods finished during the year.

KEY TERMS

Factory labor	Manufacturing cycle
Factory materials	Work in process
Finished goods	

INDEPENDENT STUDY PROBLEMS (Solutions in Appendix B)

1. Manufacturing cost schedule.   Using the data in the appendix to this chapter, prepare a schedule of manufacturing costs and the cost of goods for the year 19x2.

2. Cost flow diagram.   Buildmore Manufacturing Company had the following inventories on September 1 and September 30, 19x1:

	September 1	September 30
Raw materials	$20,000	$25,000
Work in process	30,000	20,000
Finished goods	12,000	20,000

During the month of September the cost of raw materials purchased was $60,000, labor costs totaled $80,000, and other costs applicable to production amounted to $30,000.

Prepare a diagram showing the flow of costs through the inventories to the cost of goods sold.

3. T-accounts; journal entries. All Buildmore Manufacturing Company's purchases of factory materials in the month of September 19x1 (see problem 2) were purchases on account. Factory labor costs for the month were accrued, with payments to be made in October. All resources used in production in September, other than materials and labor, were purchased on credit during the month.

a. Set up inventory T-accounts similar to those used in this chapter and enter the opening balances.
b. Prepare a set of journal entries to record the factory's transactions in September, using account titles similar to those used in this chapter.
c. Post the amounts shown in the journal entries to T-accounts.

4. Manufacturing cost flows; income statement. King Appliance Company had the following inventories on October 1:

Materials	$11,650
Work in process	8,320
Finished goods	11,100

The following transactions took place in October:

1. Purchased factory materials on account at a cost of $4,500.
2. Issued factory materials to production departments, $7,250.
3. Accrued payrolls: factory labor, $5,100; selling and administrative salaries, $2,600.
4. Depreciation: on manufacturing facilities, $400; on administrative office equipment, $100.
5. Miscellaneous goods and services purchased on account for immediate use: in the factory, $1,820; by sales and administrative personnel, $1,735.
6. Completed all manufacturing operations on products costing $12,650 and transferred them to the finished goods storeroom.
7. Determined the cost of the finished goods inventory on hand on October 31, 19x1, $9,250.
8. Sales revenues from manufactured goods sold on credit, $19,350.

a. Account for these transactions using T-accounts, and establish the closing balances in the inventory accounts. Use a single account for selling and administrative expenses.
b. Prepare an income statement for the month. Ignore income taxes.

EXERCISES AND PROBLEMS

5. Supplying missing information. The following data were taken from the ledger accounts of Abcess Manufacturing Company for the most recent month:

Factory materials inventory, beginning of month .... $	0
Work in process inventory, beginning of month	0
Finished goods inventory, beginning of month	5,000

Purchases of factory materials	360,000
Depreciation on factory and factory equipment	15,000
Factory materials placed in production	290,000
Depreciation on office equipment	2,000
Sales and administrative salaries....................	59,000
Factory labor	140,000
Sundry selling and administrative expense	29,000
Sundry production costs for the month	135,000
Revenue from sales	525,000
Income taxes on taxable income for the month	24,000
Dividends declared during the month	35,000
Work in process inventory, end of month	115,000
Finished goods inventory, end of month	85,000
Retained earnings, beginning of month	40,000

Compute the following figures:

a. Total production costs for the month.
b. Total cost of goods finished during the month.
c. Cost of goods sold during the month.
d. Net income for the month.
e. Retained earnings, end of month.
f. Raw materials inventory, end of month.

6. Supplying missing information. The following data are available for a manufacturing operation:

Balance sheet data:

	December 31, 19x1	December 31, 19x2
Raw materials inventory	$240	$285
Work in process inventory	128	271
Finished goods inventory	87	172
Factory plant and equipment (net)	492	476

Totals for the year 19x2:

1. Purchases of raw materials, $1,250.
2. Purchases of factory plant and equipment, $23.
3. Wages earned by factory employees, $566.
4. Production costs other than raw materials, labor, and depreciation, $2,418.
5. Factory plant and equipment sold, none.

a. Calculate the cost of raw materials used during the year.
b. Calculate factory depreciation for the year.
c. Calculate the cost of goods finished during the year.
d. Calculate the cost of goods sold during the year.

(Prepared by Charles Boynton)

7. Statement of manufacturing costs. Albatross Corporation is engaged in the manufacture and sale of plastic water toys. Its inventories were as follows:

	January 1	June 30
Raw materials	$10,000	$16,000
Work in process	40,000	50,000
Finished goods	20,000	10,000

The following costs were incurred between these two dates:

Factory raw materials purchased	$90,000
Factory labor	40,000
Factory depreciation	7,000
Factory utilities and other costs.........	13,000
Sales salaries	5,000
Office salaries	8,000
Other selling and office costs	4,000

Prepare a schedule of manufacturing costs and cost of goods sold for the six months ended June 30.

8. Calculating the cost of goods finished. Manufacturing costs for a period totaled $300,000, the work in process inventory increased from $250,000 at the beginning of the period to $280,000 at the end, and the cost of goods sold during the period amounted to $310,000.

a. Calculate the cost of goods finished during the period.
b. By how much did the cost of finished goods on hand increase or decrease during the period?

9. Elements of cost of goods manufactured and sold. Scotch Company's inventories experienced the following changes during 19x3:

Materials	$14,300 increase
Work in process	2,900 decrease
Finished goods	11,800 increase

Factory costs other than materials and labor were $215,600, which was 140 percent of the labor cost. The cost of materials used was 20 percent of the total factory cost.

a. What was the total factory cost?
b. What was the cost of materials purchased?
c. What was the cost of goods finished?
d. What was the cost of goods sold?

10. Forecasting the cost of goods sold. The Velting Corporation manufactures and sells only one product. Management estimates that the company will sell 200,000 units of this product next year. You have been asked to estimate the cost of goods sold at this volume, based on the following information:

1. Each unit of the product requires approximately 4 pounds of material A and 0.1 pound of material B.
2. The company has no inventory of material A, which is highly perishable and is delivered to the factory daily in quantities sufficient for the day's production. Purchase prices during the coming year are expected to average 60 cents a pound.
3. The company will have 25,000 pounds of material B on hand at the beginning of the year and will buy no more until this stock has been exhausted. The material now in stock was purchased at a cost of $4 a pound. The market price of material B is now $4.50 a pound and is expected to hold constant at that level throughout the coming year.

4. It is estimated that two hours of labor at $8 an hour will be required to produce each finished unit.

5. Annual depreciation on factory buildings and equipment will be $136,000.

6. Other factory costs are expected to total $40,000 plus an additional $2,000 for every 10,000 units finished.

7. Production is of such a nature that there will be no beginning or ending inventories of goods in process.

8. The company will have 20,000 units of finished products in inventory at the beginning of the year, at a cost of $19 each.

9. A partially completed study by a research team leads you to feel that the final inventory at the close of the year should be 40,000 finished units.

10. Due to a design change, the units produced during the year will be slightly different from those in stock at the beginning of the year. For this reason, the units in the beginning inventory will be sold before any units produced during the coming year are placed on sale.

You have decided to perform the calculations in the sequence listed below. To help management understand these calculations, identify the steps you take and label each figure clearly.

a. Calculate the number of finished units to be produced next year.
b. Calculate the estimated cost of the raw materials to be used for the desired production.
c. Calculate the estimated cost of goods to be manufactured next year.
d. Calculate the estimated cost of goods to be sold next year.
e. Calculate the estimated cost of all materials and finished goods that will remain in inventory at the end of the coming year.

11. Journal entries; net income. Poirot Manufacturing Company has a very simple accounting system. It uses only 18 accounts, which had the following balances at the start of business on September 1, 19x1, the start of the company's fiscal year:

Cash	$ 20,000	
Accounts receivable	95,000	
Materials inventory	62,000	
Work in process	28,000	
Finished goods inventory	122,000	
Machinery and equipment	100,000	
Accumulated depreciation		$ 32,000
Accounts payable		38,000
Wages and salaries payable		—
Dividends payable		—
Notes payable		—
Capital stock		200,000
Retained earnings		157,000
Sales revenues		—
Cost of goods sold	—	
Selling and administrative expenses	—	
Nonoperating gains and losses	—	
Dividends declared	—	

The company completed the following transactions during the month of September:

1. Factory materials purchased on account and placed in the materials storeroom, $34,000.
2. Materials issued from materials storeroom to factory production departments, $35,000.
3. Wages and salaries accrued: factory labor, $20,000; selling and administrative salaries, $4,000.
4. Depreciation: factory machinery, $500; administrative office equipment, $300.
5. Costs of other goods and services acquired on account and used immediately: manufacturing, $8,000; selling and administrative, $3,800.
6. Products completed and transferred to finished goods inventories, $62,000.
7. Sales on account, $78,000.
8. The balance in the Finished Goods Inventory account was $1,000 more on September 30 than on September 1, after all appropriate entries for September were recorded.
9. Cash dividends declared, $20,000.
10. Collections from customers on account, $65,000.
11. Cash payments: to employees, $23,700; to suppliers on account, $69,600; to shareowners (dividends), $20,000.
12. Cash borrowed from the bank on September 30, $5,000.
13. Cost of factory equipment purchased on account and installed on September 30, $30,000.
14. Equipment sold for cash, $500. This equipment had an original cost of $9,000 and accumulated depreciation of $7,000.
15. Additional shares of capital stock issued in exchange for $50,000 cash.

a. Establish T-accounts to present the 18 accounts identified at the beginning of this problem, and enter the September 1 balances.
b. Prepare journal entries to record these transactions, using only the 18 account titles listed.
c. Post the amounts in your journal entries to the T-accounts.
d. Prepare a schedule of manufacturing costs and an income statement for September.

12. Supplying missing information; unit cost. Peerless Cloak Company manufactures silk-lined evening cloaks. The company filed a claim with its insurance company under its burglary insurance policy, stating that on the night of September 10 its workroom was burglarized. Compensation was claimed for the loss of 400 cloaks ($12,000) and 1,000 yards of silk ($3,500). An insurance claims adjuster analyzed the company's records and assembled the following information for the period from January 1 to September 10:

1. Inventories of cloaks, cloth, and silk had a cost of $211,200 on January 1.
2. Purchases were: cloth, 38,000 yards at $2 a yard; silk, 11,000 yards at $3.50 a yard.

3. 6,000 cloaks were manufactured, consuming 39,500 yards of cloth and 10,000 yards of silk.
4. 9,000 cloaks were sold.
5. Manufacturing costs for all elements other than materials totaled $42,000.
6. Materials and manufacturing costs per unit were approximately the same as during the preceding year.
7. A physical count of the inventories on September 11 yielded the following cost totals, approved by the adjuster: 13,000 yards of cloth, $26,000; and 6,000 yards of silk, $21,000. The inventory also contained 3,000 finished cloaks.
8. The insurance policy provided for compensation equal to the cost of any items stolen.

If you were the claims adjuster, how much of the company's claim would you approve for payment? (Suggestion: As one step in your analysis, you need to calculate the average unit cost of the cloaks manufactured.)

13. Transactions analysis; financial statements. On February 1, 19x1, Paltry Corporation's accounts showed the following balances (all accounts not shown had zero balances):

Cash	9,200	
Accounts receivable	13,000	
Raw materials	3,500	
Work in process	5,000	
Finished goods	6,200	
Prepaid insurance	1,000	
Plant and equipment	62,000	
Accumulated depreciation		22,000
Accounts payable		13,900
Capital stock		34,000
Retained earnings		30,000

The following transactions took place during February:

1. Purchased materials on account, $42,000.
2. Issued materials to factory for use on month's production, $38,500.
3. Sold merchandise: for cash, $10,000; on credit, $90,000.
4. Collected $93,000 on accounts receivable.
5. Paid rent on office equipment for February, March, and April, $900.
6. Purchased factory equipment on account, $9,000.
7. Purchased office furniture on account, $1,000.
8. Accrued employees' wages and salaries for the month: factory labor, $20,000; office and sales force, $8,000.
9. Received invoices for various goods and services bought on account and used during the month: factory, $25,200; office and sales departments, $15,000.
10. Recognized depreciation for February: factory, $300; office, $100.
11. Paid sales representatives and executives: for travel and entertainment expenses during month, $2,000; as advances against March expenses, $1,050.
12. Paid employees (for wages and salaries), $27,300.

13. Paid suppliers on account, $75,200.
14. Sold a piece of factory equipment for $500 cash; its original cost was $3,000, and it had accumulated depreciation of $2,100 at the date of sale.
15. Noted expiration of insurance premiums: on office, $50; on factory, $250.
16. Finished and transferred to warehouse goods costing $68,000.
17. Declared cash dividend to shareholders, $2,000, payable on March 15.
18. Counted inventories on February 28; cost of finished goods on hand was $5,800.

a. Prepare journal entries to record all this information. To accomplish this, you will need to use accounts other than those listed at the beginning of this problem.
b. Set up T-accounts, enter the February 1 balances, and post the journal entries to these T-accounts.
c. Using the balances in the T-accounts, prepare an income statement for the month of February and a balance sheet as of February 28.

14. Transactions analysis; financial statements. On May 1, 19x1, Deppe Company's accounts had the following balances (all accounts not listed had zero balances):

Cash	25,600	
Accounts receivable	11,800	
Materials and supplies	7,200	
Work in process	6,500	
Finished goods	12,900	
Prepaid insurance	1,200	
Plant and equipment	156,000	
Accumulated depreciation		76,000
Accounts payable		15,400
Capital stock		80,000
Retained earnings		49,800

The following transactions took place during May:

1. Materials and supplies purchased on account, $30,300.
2. Wages and salaries earned by employees during month: factory labor, $34,600; sales and office salaries, $23,400. (Note: Cash payments occasioned by employee payrolls are described in item 13 below.)
3. Materials issued for use in production, $18,800.
4. Equipment purchased on contract, $10,000, payments to be made in four quarterly installments of $2,500 each.
5. Goods sold on account for $110,000.
6. Supplies issued from storeroom and used: factory, $3,200; office, $2,700.
7. Costs of miscellaneous goods and services bought on account and used during May:
    Office rental, $2,300.
    Repairs of factory equipment, $600.
    Electricity and other utilities: factory, $3,600; office, $500.
    Newspaper advertising, $300.
    Other: factory, $11,860; office, $13,740.

8. Paid taxes on factory, May 1 through October 31, 19x1, $1,200.
9. Insurance premiums expired: factory, $200; office, $100.
10. Depreciation: factory, $800; office, $160.
11. Collections from customers, $106,000.
12. Sale of capital stock for cash, $10,000.
13. Payments made:

     To suppliers of materials and other goods and services, on account, $61,260.

     To equipment manufacturer, on contract (see 4 above), $2,500.

     To employees, $57,740.
14. Equipment sold, $300 cash (original cost, $5,000; book value $800).
15. Dividends declared, $3,000, to be paid on June 15.
16. Work in process, May 31, $16,160.
17. Finished goods on hand, May 31, $11,800.

a. Prepare journal entries to record all this information in accrual-basis accounts. You will need to open accounts in addition to those listed at the beginning of this problem.

b. Set up T-accounts, enter the May 1 account balances, and post your journal entries to these accounts.

c. Prepare an income statement for May and a balance sheet as of May 31. Ignore any income taxes that might be levied on Deppe Company's income for the month.

6

Cost and value

A business enterprise's balance sheet prepared in accordance with generally accepted accounting principles doesn't pretend to measure the *value* of the business, nor does an income statement pretend to measure all the changes in value arising during the period. The purposes of this chapter are to explain what value means and to call attention to the differences between values and the amounts that appear in company financial statements.

SOURCES OF ECONOMIC VALUE

The economic value of any asset to its individual or business owner is determined by its ability to benefit the owner. The benefit from a business asset may come from any of four sources:

1. The asset may give the business an immediate ability to pay for goods and services (cash).
2. The asset may be exchangeable for cash in the very near future (accounts receivable).
3. The business may be able to sell the asset and receive cash in the very near future (merchandise inventory).
4. The business may be able to use the asset to produce goods or services for which outsiders will pay more cash in one or more future periods than the business will have to pay to produce them (factory equipment, prepaid rent, etc.).

Value from any of these sources stems from the asset's ability to provide the enterprise with cash. The reason is that cash is the only universally useful asset, the only asset that can always be used to buy other assets or to pay creditors or owners. An oil well, for example, can be used to bring crude oil to the surface, but this oil has no value if the company has to pay more to extract it than customers will pay for it.

Assets other than cash itself derive their value from the cash that will be received in the future. These future amounts are known as *cash flows.* Some cash flows may be *negative;* that is, ownership of the asset may require cash payments or disbursements in one or more future periods—for example, cash paid to overhaul a machine midway through its lifetime. For the asset to have value, however, the sum of the *positive* cash flows (cash receipts) must exceed the sum of the negative cash flows.

The term *value* is often used to describe the amount of cash an independent outside buyer would be willing to pay for the asset. This amount is known as the asset's *market value.* For most assets, however, value stems from the cash flows that continued ownership and use will provide.

THE TIME VALUE OF MONEY

The future dates on which an asset's anticipated cash flows will take place affect the value the asset has now. To say why this is so, we need to study how the value of money is affected by the passage of time. To accomplish this, we'll use relatively simple mathematical notation and perform various calculations step by step. Following these steps is the best way to understand the concept of value and to learn how to apply it. Once we've gone through a set of calculations in this manner, we'll identify computational devices that can simplify the calculation procedure.

Future value

The future value of a sum of cash is the amount to which that sum will grow if it is invested at a specified interest rate for a specified period of time. Suppose, for example, that a bank will pay $1,150 one year from now in return for a $1,000 deposit today. We say that this bank is paying interest at the rate of 15 percent a year. This relationship can be expressed mathematically in the following expression:

$$F_1 = P(1 + r) \tag{1}$$

in which P = the present sum of money, r = the rate of interest, and F_1 = future value. If P = $1,000 and r = 0.15, then F_1 = $1,150.

Continuing the example, if the $1,150 is left in the bank for a second year, it will build up by the end of the two years to a balance of $1,150 + ($1,150 × 0.15) = $1,322.50. Interest in the second year amounts to $172.50 and is greater than the first year's interest because the bank is now paying interest not only on the original investment but also on the interest earned during the first year. The mathematical formula for computing the future value of a present sum two years later is:

$$F_2 = F_1(1 + r) = P(1 + r)(1 + r) = P(1 + r)^2 \qquad (2)$$

If $r = 0.15$, $(1 + r)^2$ will be 1.3225 and the future value of $1,000 now will be $1,322.50.

Extending these calculations beyond two years reveals the relationships shown graphically in Exhibit 6–1. Starting with $1,000, the depositor's account will build at 15 percent each year—to $1,150 in one year, $1,322.50 in two years, and so on, up to $16,366.54 at the end of 20 years.

This form of interest calculation, in which interest is earned on previously earned interest, is known as *compounding*. In this case interest has been compounded annually, meaning that interest is added to the bank balance only once a year. In general, it can

EXHIBIT 6–1. Future Values Equivalent to a Present Value of $1,000 (annual compounding at 15 percent a year)

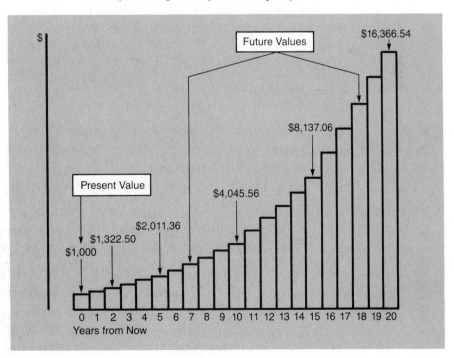

be shown that if an amount P is put out at interest of r percent a year, compounded annually, at the end of n years it will have grown to a future value (F_n) of the following amount:

$$F_n = P(1+r)^n \qquad (3)$$

Present value

This perspective can also be reversed—to focus attention on the *present value* of a future amount. The present value of a future sum of cash is the amount which, if invested now at compound interest at the specified rate, will grow to an amount equal to the future sum at the specified future date. Present value and future value, in other words, are just two ends of the same relationship. An investor who considers 15 percent annual compound interest a satisfactory reward will regard $1,322.50 two years from now as exactly equivalent to $1,000 now.

The formula for computing present value from known or estimated future values can be found by turning equation (3) around. Since $F_n = P(1+r)^n$, then

$$P = \frac{F_n}{(1+r)^n} = F_n(1+r)^{-n} \qquad (4)$$

This shows that the present value of any future sum can be determined by multiplying the latter by $(1+r)^{-n}$ or by dividing it by $(1+r)^n$.

For example, if r is 15 percent a year, and an asset is expected to yield a cash inflow of $1,000 one year from now, the present value of this cash inflow is:

$$P = \frac{\$1,000}{(1.15)^1} = \$869.57$$

This calculation shows us that $869.57 is the amount which will grow to $1,000 in one year if it is invested now at 15 percent interest compounded annually ($869.57 + 0.15 \times \$869.57 = \$1,000$). $869.57 therefore is the present value of $1,000 a year from now.

Similarly, if the cash flow is $1,000, n is two years, and r is 15 percent, equation (4) reveals that the present value of the cash inflow is:

$$P = \frac{\$1,000}{(1.15)^2} = \frac{\$1,000}{1.3225} = \$756.14$$

In other words, we'll have to invest only $756.14 instead of $869.57 if we're willing to wait two years instead of one for the promised $1,000 cash flow.

EXHIBIT 6–2.   Present Values of Future Cash Flows of $1,000 (annual compounding at 15 percent a year)

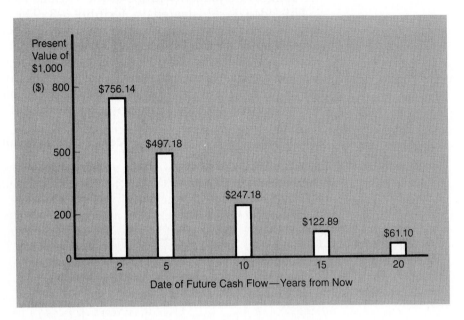

If we repeat our present value calculations for amounts to be received 5, 10, 15, and 20 years from now, we get the values shown in Exhibit 6–2, rounded to the nearest cent. The basic conclusion from this illustration is that cash available in the near future is worth more than the same amount of cash at a more distant date. The sooner the cash is available, the sooner it can be invested to earn more cash—this makes it more valuable.

The process of finding the present value of a future amount is known as *discounting.* In our illustration, we discounted $1,000 to be received two years from now by dividing it by the 1.3225 multiplier we derived from equation (2). The more common technique is to determine the *present value factor* or *discount factor*—the reciprocal of the future value multiplier—and multiply this by the amount of the future cash flow. For a cash flow two years from now to be discounted at a 15 percent annual rate of interest the present value factor is $1/1.3225 = 0.75614$. Using this factor to determine present value is equivalent to dividing the future cash flow by the future value multiplier.

The value of a series of cash flows

While some assets derive all their value from the expectation of a single cash receipt, the value of others is based on a series of future cash receipts. The present value of an asset of this kind is the sum of the present values of the various cash flows.

This idea is illustrated in Exhibit 6–3. The two blocks at the right represent two cash sums a company expects to receive from a creditor. The first of these, $5,000, will be received one year from now; the other, $10,000, will be received two years from now. The two blocks joined on the left side of the diagram are the present values of these two cash flows, calculated on the basis of a 15 percent interest rate. Since the company's ownership of this asset gives it

EXHIBIT 6–3. Value of a Series of Cash Flows Discounted at 15 Percent

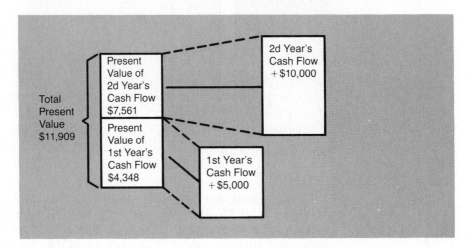

the right to receive both these future amounts, the present value of the asset must be the sum of the present values of the two amounts.

The calculations behind this exhibit are summarized in the accompanying table, using the present value factors we derived in the preceding section:

(1) Years from Now	(2) Cash Receipt	(3) Multiplier	(4) Present Value at 15% (2) × (3)
1	$ 5,000	0.8696	$ 4,348
2	10,000	0.7561	7,561
Total			$11,909

The present value factors are rounded off to four digits; further precision is seldom warranted.

Present value of an annuity

A *series* of equal annual cash flows is known as an *annuity*. The present value of a five-year annuity of $1,000 a year can be calculated by multiplying each of the five cash flows by the appropriate discount factor:

(1) Years from Now	(2) Cash Receipt	(3) Multiplier	(4) Present Value at 15% (2) × (3)
1	$1,000	1/1.15 = 0.8696	$ 869.60
2	1,000	1/(1.15)² = 0.7561	756.10
3	1,000	1/(1.15)³ = 0.6575	657.50
4	1,000	1/(1.15)⁴ = 0.5718	571.80
5	1,000	1/(1.15)⁵ = 0.4972	497.20
Total		3.3522	$3,352.20

A much simpler method is to add the annual discount factors and multiply this sum by the amount of the annuity. This sum can be expressed mathematically as follows:

$$P = A \times \left[\frac{1 - (1 + r)^{-n}}{r} \right] \tag{5}$$

in which A is the size of the annual cash flow. In this case the sum of the present value factors is 3.3522; multiplying this sum by the $1,000 annual cash flow gives us the same total present value, $3,352.20, we got by using the annual present value factors.

Annuity factors enter into a variety of calculations. For example, we might want to know how large a five-year annuity $10,000 can buy if interest is compounded annually at 15 percent. In other words, by investing $10,000 today, what constant amount would we receive at the end of each year for the next five years? The relationship is:

Present value = Annual cash flow × Present value factor

This is equivalent to:

$$\text{Annual cash flow} = \frac{\text{Present value}}{\text{Present value factor}}$$

Using the present value factor for a five-year annuity at 15 percent, we get:

$$\text{Annual cash flow} = \frac{\$10,000}{3.3522} = \$2,983.12 \text{ a year}$$

EXHIBIT 6–4.   Timetable of Cash Flows

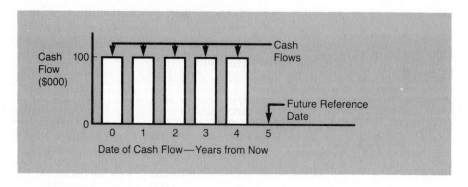

Future value of an annuity

Management may wish to know how much money it will have at the end of five years if it invests $100,000 at the beginning of each year for five years, compounded annually at 15 percent. Here the unknown amount is the *future value* of the annuity.

The best way to start is to diagram the timetable of cash flows. The diagram in Exhibit 6–4 reflects the assumption that the company will make the first payment immediately. This means it will have five years to accumulate interest, and the future value of this payment will be $100,000 × (1.15)^5 = $201,140. The second payment will accumulate interest for four years, and so on. The future value of this annuity is as follows:

Years from Now	Cash Payment	Multiplier at 15%	Future Value at 15%
0	$100,000	$(1.15)^5 = 2.0114$	$201,140
1	100,000	$(1.15)^4 = 1.7490$	174,900
2	100,000	$(1.15)^3 = 1.5209$	152,090
3	100,000	$(1.15)^2 = 1.3225$	132,250
4	100,000	$(1.15)^1 = 1.1500$	115,000
Total		7.7538	$775,380

In other situations, future value may be known and the purpose of the calculation is to determine the amount of the equivalent annual cash flow. For example, suppose management wants to accumulate a fund of $1 million five years from now by investing a fixed amount (A) each year for five years, interest to be compounded annually at 15 percent. This time management plans to make the first payment a full year from now. This cash flow timetable is diagrammed in Exhibit 6–5. Notice that the first payment will grow for only *four* years (from one year from now to five years from

EXHIBIT 6–5. Timetable of Cash Flows

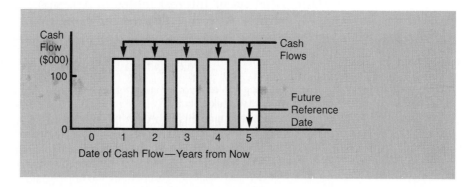

now) and the final payment won't grow at all. The calculation at a 15 percent interest rate is:

Years from Now	Cash Payment	Multiplier at 15%	Future Value at 15%
1	A	$(1.15)^4 = 1.7490$	$1.7490A$
2	A	$(1.15)^3 = 1.5209$	$1.5209A$
3	A	$(1.15)^2 = 1.3225$	$1.3225A$
4	A	$(1.15)^1 = 1.1500$	$1.1500A$
5	A	$(1.15)^0 = 1.0000$	$1.0000A$
Total		6.7424	6.7424A

Since future value is determined by multiplying the annual cash flow by a future value factor (in this case 6.7424), the amount of the annual cash flow can be determined by dividing the future value by the factor. In this case the equivalent annual cash flow is $1,000,000/6.7424 = $148,315 a year.

Interest tables

The calculation of discount factors [for example, $1/(1.15)^5 = 0.4972$] is time-consuming. Fortunately, we don't have to make these calculations by hand. We can use an electronic computer, if we have one, or a calculator containing a present value program. If we don't have ready access to either of these, we can consult published interest tables which contain the values of $(1 + r)^{-n}$ for many values of r and n.

Although the remainder of this chapter can be read and understood without the aid of calculators or interest tables, few of the problems and exercises at the end of this chapter can be solved efficiently unless a calculator or a set of interest tables is used.

To meet the need for computational aids, we have provided an abbreviated set of interest tables in Appendix A at the end of the book, together with instructions for using them.

CALCULATING PRESENT VALUE

1. Estimate the amount of each future cash flow and the date or period when it will take place.
2. Enter these amounts in a cash-flow timetable.
3. Choose an appropriate interest rate.
4. Identify the present value factor at this rate for each amount in the timetable and enter these factors in the next column of the timetable.
5. Multiply each cash-flow amount by the appropriate discount factor and enter these amounts in the last column of the timetable.
6. Add the amounts in the last column to obtain the asset's total present value.

DETERMINANTS OF PRESENT VALUE

The value of an asset depends on four factors: the amounts of future cash flows, their timing, the interest rate used to discount them, and the length of the compounding interval.

Amount and timing of future cash flows

The significance of amounts and timing can be summarized in two observations. First, the greater the cash flow in any future period, the greater is its present value at a specified interest rate. Second, the closer a given cash flow is to the present, the greater is its present value at a specified interest rate.

For example, suppose the interest rate is 15 percent and we have four assets, with the following streams of future cash flows:

Years from Now	Asset A	Asset B	Asset C	Asset D
1	+$24,000	+$30,000	+$10,000	−$10,000
2	+ 16,000	+ 20,000	+ 20,000	0
3	+ 8,000	+ 10,000	+ 30,000	+ 70,000
Total	+$48,000	+$60,000	+$60,000	+$60,000

Asset B has the same time pattern of cash flows as asset A, but each cash receipt is 25 percent greater. Assets B, C, and D have identical net lifetime cash-flow totals (+$60,000), but they differ in the timing of the cash flows. Asset D even requires us to pay

EXHIBIT 6–6.   Present Values of Four Assets

Years from Now	Interest Factor at 15% $[1/(1.15)^n]$	Present Value at 15%			
		Asset A	Asset B	Asset C	Asset D
1	0.8696	+$20,870	+$26,088	+$ 8,696	−$ 8,696
2	0.7561	+ 12,098	+ 15,122	+ 15,122	0
3	0.6575	+ 5,260	+ 6,575	+ 19,725	+ 46,025
Net present value		+$38,228	+$47,785	+$43,543	+$37,329

an additional $10,000 a year from now to obtain an even greater cash inflow in the third year.

The present values of these four assets are shown in Exhibit 6–6. The interest factors are multiplied by each asset's future cash flows to derive the present value amounts in the last four columns. The present value of asset B is exactly 25 percent greater than the present value of asset A because each of its cash flows is 25 percent greater. Asset B is more valuable than either asset C or asset D because its positive cash flows will occur sooner than those of either of the other two.

Interest rate

An important aspect of the time value of money is that the higher the interest rate at which future cash flows are discounted, the smaller is the present value of a given stream of cash flows. For example, the asset shown in Exhibit 6–3 is expected to produce one cash receipt of $5,000 one year from now and another of $10,000 one year after that. If the interest rate is 10 percent, the present value of these cash flows is $12,809, the amount shown at the bottom of the 10 percent column in Exhibit 6–7. If the interest rate is 15 percent, the present value is $11,909 (taken from the middle column). And if the interest rate is 20 percent, the present value is the $11,111, shown at the bottom of the right-hand column.

EXHIBIT 6–7.   Present Values at Three Different Rates

Years from Now	Cash Receipt	10%		15%		20%	
		Multiplier	Present Value	Multiplier	Present Value	Multiplier	Present Value
1	$ 5,000	1/1.10 = 0.9091	$ 4,545	1/1.15 = 0.8696	$ 4,348	1/1.20 = 0.8333	$ 4,167
2	10,000	1/(1.10)² = 0.8264	8,264	1/(1.15)² = 0.7561	7,561	1/(1.20)² = 0.6944	6,944
Total			$12,809		$11,909		$11,111

In other words, if the interest rate is 10 percent compounded annually, the company will be willing to pay $12,809 for this asset. If the interest rate is 20 percent, the maximum it will be willing to pay for the asset is $11,111. At a 20 percent rate, the two cash flows will be exactly large enough to pay the company $11,111 plus interest.

The reason for this relationship is that as the rate of interest increases, more of each cash flow will go to pay interest on the amount invested, leaving less to repay the investment itself. If $11,909 is paid for the asset and the interest rate is 10 percent, then $0.10 \times \$11,909 = \$1,191$ is interest in the first year. This leaves $3,809 of the first year's $5,000 cash receipt to provide a partial recovery of the initial investment. If $11,909 is paid and the interest rate is 15 percent, then $0.15 \times \$11,909 = \$1,786$ of the first year's $5,000 cash receipt will go to pay interest; $3,214 is a partial recovery of the initial investment. On the other hand, if the interest rate is 20 percent, the first year's interest will be $0.20 \times \$11,909 = \$2,382$, leaving only $2,618 to apply toward the recovery of the investment.

The effect of these differences in the amount of capital recovery is shown in Exhibit 6–8. The first two rows show what will happen if the interest rate is 15 percent and the amount invested in the asset at the beginning of year 1 is $11,909. As we saw in the preceding paragraph, $3,214 of the first year's cash flow is available for recovery of the investment, leaving $8,695 unrecovered at the end of year 1. This is the amount shown in the right column of the table. In the next year, the 15 percent interest rate yields $1,304, with the result that the $10,000 cash receipt is the sum of the $1,304 interest and the $8,695 investment balance (with a $1 rounding discrepancy). We thus see that $11,909 was the correct present value of the two future cash flows. Investing this amount enabled the

EXHIBIT 6–8.   Investment Recovery at Various Interest Rates

Year	(1) Beginning Investment	(2) Interest Rate	(3) Interest (1) × (2)	(4) Cash Receipt	(5) Available for Recovery of Investment (4) − (3)	(6) Ending Investment (1) − (5)
1	$11,909	0.15	$1,786	$ 5,000	$3,214	$8,695
2	8,695	0.15	1,304	10,000	8,696	(1)
1	11,909	0.10	1,191	5,000	3,809	8,100
2	8,100	0.10	810	10,000	9,190	(1,090)
1	11,909	0.20	2,382	5,000	2,618	9,291
2	9,291	0.20	1,858	10,000	8,142	1,149

investor to earn interest at 15 percent and recover the entire investment.

To consider this result from another perspective, suppose the same $11,909 was invested but that the interest rate was either more or less than 15 percent. We should begin to sense that in one case the investor will benefit and in the other case the result will be unfavorable. The second pair of rows in Exhibit 6–8 shows the amounts available for recovery of the investment if the interest rate is 10 percent. Since interest now takes a smaller portion of each cash flow, the company will have $1,090 more than enough to recover the initial investment. If the interest rate is 20 percent, however, the calculations in the third pair of rows are valid. Interest now takes a much larger share of each cash flow, with the result that the company still hasn't recovered $1,149 of the original investment at the end of the asset's two-year life.

Compounding interval

The length of the compounding interval is the third factor affecting an asset's value. Interest may be compounded once a year, once every six months, quarterly, monthly, daily, or even instantaneously. The more frequently interest must be compounded, the less a given stream of future cash flows is worth today.

Let's approach this by means of an example. Suppose we want to know the present value of an asset that is expected to generate a single cash inflow of $10,000 two years from now. If the interest rate is 10 percent a year and interest is compounded once a year, the present value of the asset will be $10,000/(1.10)^2 = $8,264$. The interest earned in the two-year period will be $10,000 - $8,264 = $1,736$. If the compounding interval is cut in half (to six months) and the interest rate per period is also cut in half (to 5 percent each six-month period), the present value of this asset will be $10,000/(1.05)^4 = $8,227$. Now interest earned will be $10,000 - $8,277 = $1,773$. The present value is $37 less now because the investors demand that interest be compounded twice a year—therefore, $37 more of the future cash flow must be given to them as interest.

Most of us are familiar with a calculation that is closely related to the one summarized in the preceding paragraph: the compounding of interest on certain kinds of bank deposits. If one bank compounds interest daily at a chosen nominal annual rate (e.g., 10 percent), a given deposit will earn more interest and grow faster than the same deposit in another bank that compounds interest quarterly at the same nominal annual rate.

Notice the difference between these two examples. In the first example, the future value was known; the length of the compounding interval affected the *present value*. In the bank example, the present value was known (the initial deposit), and the compounding interval affected the *future value*.

In all our illustrations so far, we have assumed a one-year compounding interval. Cash flows may take place at any time, however, and may be reinvested immediately, without waiting until the end of the year. When this is true we should shorten the compounding interval accordingly if precision is important. In most money market operations today, daily compounding is commonplace because money can be invested or borrowed for a period as short as a single day. To avoid unnecessary confusion, we'll stick to annual compounding in this chapter.

APPLICATIONS OF THE TIME-VALUE-OF-MONEY CONCEPT

The time-value-of-money concept pervades all facets of economic life. For example, an individual may wish to compare various means of financing a major vacation trip several years in the future. The proprietor of a relatively small business contemplating a purchase of machinery may need to select from alternatives that have different projected cash-flow patterns, and officers of a large diversified corporation may need to measure the cash-flow consequences that would result from entering or leaving different markets. Individuals and businesses alike often need to decide which investment instruments are most attractive—money market funds, certificates of deposit, corporate bonds, government bonds, common stocks, etc.

Calculating equivalent annuities

Many of these situations require the calculation of future amounts or annuities that are equivalent to other future amounts or annuities. The methods described in this chapter can be used to solve problems of this sort.

For example, suppose we'll need $10,000 each year for five years, with the first receipt to be six years from now. An insurance company will compound interest annually at 15 percent. The question is: How much will we have to pay the insurance company each year for five years, with the first payment to be due one year from now, to entitle us to receive the annuity we need?

The cash-flow schedule in this problem is diagrammed in Exhibit 6–9. The analysis itself is based on the proposition that two annuities that are equivalent to each other must have the same present value. From our earlier calculation, we know that the present value of each dollar in each annual payment in the payments series is

EXHIBIT 6–9. Cash Flows in Two Annuities

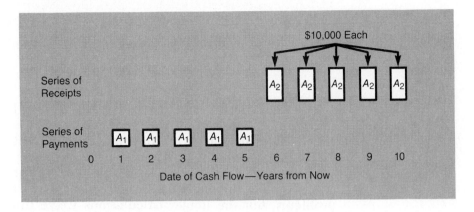

$3.3522 (from Table 4 in Appendix A, 15% column, 5-year row). We don't know the size of the annual payment, but we can represent it by the symbol A_1. The present value (P_1) of this annuity therefore is $3.3522 \times A_1$.

The present value of the other annuity (A_2) is also $3.3522 for each dollar of annual cash flow, but it has this value at a time one year before the first receipt—that is, five years from now. (The 3.3522 present value multiplier applies to cash flows one, two, three, four, and five years after the "now" date. If the first payment in the annuity is six years from now, then the "now" date for this calculation must be one year before that.) Fortunately, we know that the present value of a dollar of cash flow five years from now is $1/(1.15)^5 = 0.4972$. We can link these factors together—$3.3522 \times 0.4972 = 1.6667$—to determine the present value (P_2) of the later annuity at the zero date (i.e., $P_2 = 1.6667 \times \$10,000$).

Setting the two present value figures equal to each other, we get the following:

$$P_1 = P_2$$
$$3.3552 \times A_1 = 1.6667 \times \$10,000$$
$$A_1 = \$4,972$$

In other words, we'll have to pay $4,972 at the end of each of the next five years if we want to receive $10,000 at the end of each of the following five years. Interest provided by the insurance company will take care of the rest of the cash flows in the receipts series.

Alternatively, we can calculate the value of each series at a time five years from now:

Payment series: Future value$_5 = 6.7424 \times A_1$ (from Table 2, Appendix A)

Receipts series: Present value$_5 = 3.3522 \times \$10,000$

Setting these two expressions equal to each other, we have:

$$6.7424 \times A_1 = \$33,522$$
$$A_1 = \$4,972$$

The \$4,972 figure shouldn't surprise us. If we look at the blocks in Exhibit 6–9 we can see that *each* payment buys a \$10,000 receipt exactly five years after the payment is made. All we have to do is calculate the present value at 15 percent of *one* cash receipt five years in the future; we can do this by multiplying \$10,000 by 0.4972 (from Table 3, Appendix A). Similar shortcuts are available in many problems, but the longer calculations we've illustrated here can be used if shortcuts can't be found.

Application to large-scale decisions

The time-value-of-money concept is as applicable to large-scale decisions as it is to narrowly defined choices. The broader the scope of the endeavor, the greater are the uncertainties and thus the greater is the need for caution. From the vantage point of a business organization and of investors interested in its value, perhaps the ultimate role to be filled by the time-value-of-money concept is measuring the present value of the enterprise itself. This role is the focus of the remainder of this chapter.

PRESENT VALUE OF A GOING CONCERN

Most individual assets are likely to generate cash flows for a few years at most. The company as a whole—that is, the company as a "going concern"—is likely to have a much longer life, replacing assets with other assets to maintain its overall cash-flow stream. We therefore introduce the concept of *net cash flow*, which in any year consists of the following:

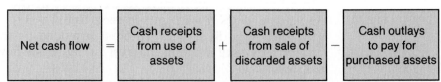

The question is how to calculate the present value of a series of company-wide cash flows defined in this way.

Present value of a perpetual annuity

To begin with, let's assume that the cash flow will be $1 million each year for 20 years, after which the company will be worthless. Let's also assume that the appropriate interest rate for this company is 15 percent, compounded annually.[1] From Table 4 in Appendix A, we find that the present value of a 20-year annuity at 15 percent is $6.2593 \times A$. The present value of the company under these assumptions therefore is $1,000,000 \times 6.2593 = $6,259,300.

In a sense, the $1 million annual net cash inflow is the reward the company gets for keeping its resources invested in their present uses, much as a bank pays interest to its depositors to reward them for letting the bank use their money for a time. With no new deposits or withdrawals, we can calculate the bank's effective annual interest rate by dividing the amount of interest added to our account balance in a year by the amount we have on deposit at the beginning of the year.

We can make the same calculation for an assumed investment of $6,259,300, invested to obtain $1 million a year for 20 years:

$$\frac{A}{P} = \frac{\$1,000,000}{\$6,259,300} = 16 \text{ percent}$$

This doesn't mean that the business is earning 16 percent on the present value of its investments, however. Unlike our savings bank deposit, the investment here will be worthless at the end of 20 years, when the cash-flow stream finally dries up. Part of each annual cash flow therefore can be regarded as recovery of part of the initial present value. The part that's left after we deduct this recovered amount is the amount we can call interest. The *real* interest therefore must be less than 16 percent. In fact, the interest rate is 15 percent, because the denominator of our fraction is $6,259,300, the present value of the future cash flows, discounted at 15 percent. *By definition,* this is the amount someone could spend to obtain the rights to the future net cash inflow of $1 million a year and earn a full 15 percent interest each year on the amount invested.

If we add more years to the cash-flow stream, we'll increase the present value—but we'll also decrease the amount of the initial present value we have to deduct from each year's cash flow to determine the amount available for interest. This will bring the ratio of annual cash flow to present value closer to the interest rate used in the present value calculation.

---

[1] We determine this by estimating the interest rate the company has to pay to obtain funds from investors. This rate is determined primarily by forces outside the company, in the financial markets. We'll explore the meaning of this rate more thoroughly in Chapter 19.

EXHIBIT 6–10.   Relationship between Life of the Business and Present Value (based on cash flows of $1 million a year and a 15 percent interest rate)

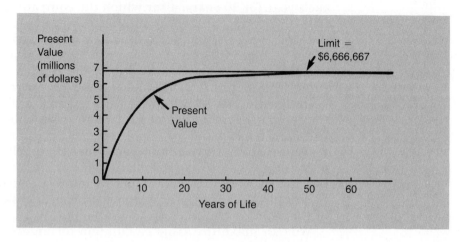

For example, using the factor for a 30-year annuity in Table 4 of Appendix A, we find that the present value of a 30-year annuity of $1 million a year is $6,566,000. The ratio of the annual net cash flow to the present value is now only 15.23 percent:

$$\frac{A}{P} = \frac{\$1,000,000}{\$6,566,000} = 15.23 \text{ percent}$$

This is much closer to 15 percent than the ratio at a 20-year life because the initial value can be spread over an extra 10 years. If the life of the annuity is 50 years, the present value is $6,660,500, and the A/P ratio is 15.01 percent—virtually identical to the 15 percent interest rate on which the present value figure is based. Since the recovery of the initial value can be spread over 50 years, it has only an insignificant effect on the A/P ratio.

The relationship between the life of the business and its value if cash flows are steady is diagrammed in Exhibit 6–10. Value reaches its limit at $1,000,000/0.15 = $6,666,667. This limit is the present value of a *perpetual annuity,* an annuity that goes on forever. It can be calculated by multiplying the annual net cash flow by the reciprocal of the interest rate. This reciprocal is known as the *capitalization ratio:*

$$P = \frac{1}{r} \times A$$

A business that produces a steady flow of cash in perpetuity will have an A/P ratio equal to the interest rate:

$$r = \frac{A}{P}$$

In the present case, r equals 15 percent, meaning that an investment of $6,666,667 in this business will earn 15 percent interest if the cash flow goes on forever. This happens because none of the annuity has to be used to pay off any of the original investment.

Present value of rising and declining cash-flow streams

The capitalization formula can be used to estimate the present value of a going concern only if the cash flows are expected to remain at a relatively steady level for a very long time. If the annual net cash inflows are expected to grow from year to year, present value will be higher than if they are expected to remain level. And if the annual net cash inflows are expected to shrink or to have only a short life, present value will be lower than the value indicated by the capitalization formula.

We've seen that the present value of an infinitely long series of net cash inflows of $1 million a year, discounted at an annual rate of 15 percent, is $6,666,667. Now suppose that the first year's net cash flow is expected to amount to $1 million but that the net cash flow in each subsequent year is expected to be $100,000 more than the preceding year's net cash flow. The present value of each of the cash flows in this new series will be greater than the present value of the comparable cash flow in the steady series, except for the first year's net cash receipts, which are identical. The present values of the first three years' cash flows in these two series are as follows:

Years from Now	Steady Series		Rising Series		Difference	
	Net Cash Flow	Present Value at 15 Percent	Net Cash Flow	Present Value at 15 Percent	Net Cash Flow	Present Value at 15 Percent
1	$1,000,000	$ 869,600	$1,000,000	$ 869,600	—	—
2	1,000,000	756,100	1,100,000	831,710	$100,000	$ 75,610
3	1,000,000	657,500	1,200,000	789,000	200,000	131,500
Total		$2,283,200		$2,490,310		$207,110

The rising stream of cash flows has a $207,110 larger present value for this three-year period than the steady stream. Since no year's net cash flow in the rising series will ever be as small as the net cash flow in the steady series, this difference can only get larger as we extend the two series further and further into the future.

A similar comparison can be made for declining cash-flow streams. The present value of a declining cash-flow stream will always be less than the present value of an infinitely long, level stream if both start at the same level and are subject to the same interest rate.

INCOME MEASURED ON A PRESENT VALUE BASIS

If we take a value approach to the measurement of business income, we can define income as the increase in the value of the owners' personal assets resulting from their ownership of the business during a specified period of time.[2] The owners' equity in the business is one of their personal assets; cash in their possession is another. Income measured on this basis therefore has two components: (1) the amounts distributed to the owners during the period, thereby increasing their cash assets; and (2) the difference between the present value of their equity in the business at the beginning of the period and the present value at the end of the period.

For example, suppose Star Company begins the year 19x1 with an expectation of a 20-year annuity of cash flows amounting to $1 million a year. The interest rate is 15 percent. During the year, the net cash inflow amounts to $1 million, as anticipated, of which $800,000 is distributed to the owners as cash dividends. The other $200,000 is reinvested by the company in plant assets and working capital to provide for future growth. At the end of the year, the expectation is that the future cash flow will be $1,050,000 a year for 25 years; the interest rate is now 14 percent. (A possible explanation is that the company is in the oil-producing business and operations this year reveal a richer and longer-lasting underground oil deposit in the company's drilling area; a reduction in the rate of inflation has been accompanied by a reduction in the interest rate.)

The income calculated under these circumstances is diagrammed in Exhibit 6–11. The block at the left shows the present value of the 20-year annuity at the beginning of the year, $6,259,300, as calculated earlier in this chapter. The second block shows the present value of the $1,050,000 25-year annuity at the end of the year: $1,050,000 × 6.8729 = $7,216,545. (The 6.8729 interest factor comes from the 25-year row of the 14 percent column in Table 4 of Appendix A.) The difference between these two present value figures is $957,245 and is shown in the lower portion of the block toward the right in the exhibit. Income for the period is the sum of this increase in value and the dividends of $800,000 that are distributed during the year, a total of $1,757,245.

---

[2] The underlying definition can be found in J. R. Hicks, *Value and Capital* (London: Oxford University Press, 1939), p. 172. Further examination of this concept can be found in Robert K. Jaedicke and Robert T. Sprouse, *Accounting Flows: Income, Funds, and Cash* (Englewood Cliffs, N.J.: Prentice-Hall, 1965), chap. ii.

EXHIBIT 6–11. Income on a Present Value Basis

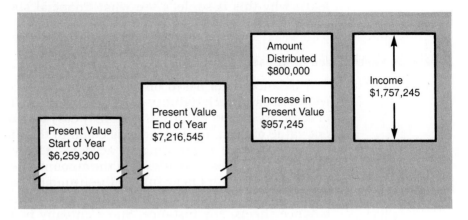

This income is the result of three factors: (1) the size of the expected annual cash flow has increased from $1 million to $1,050,000, (2) the length of the annuity has been extended from 20 to 25 years, and (3) the interest rate has decreased from 15 percent to 14 percent. Notice what would have happened if the original expectations had remained constant, and if the business had distributed the entire $1 million cash flow as dividends. The business would have had a 19-year annuity remaining at the end of the year, and the change in present value would have been a $61,100 decrease:

Present value, January 1, 19x1: $1,000,000 × 6.2593	$6,259,300
Present value, December 31, 19x1: $1,000,000 × 6.1982	6,198,200
Decrease in present value	$ 61,100

Net income for the year on a present value basis therefore would have been $1,000,000 − $61,100 = $938,900. Not surprisingly, this is 15 percent of the initial present value, $6,259,300, showing that the owners did earn exactly the rate of interest specified at the beginning of the year.

FINANCIAL STATEMENTS BASED ON PRESENT VALUE

We've been exploring the concept of present value mainly for two reasons. First, value is much more relevant to the decisions management and investors must make than are the historical costs of the company's assets. Second, value-based measurements enter into some conventional accounting calculations, as we'll see in later chapters. In general, however, the balance sheets and income statements prepared in accordance with the accounting methods described in earlier chapters don't show how much the business is worth or how much its value has changed during the period. To learn why this is so, let's see what financial statements based on present value would require.

A balance sheet based on present value

A balance sheet based on the present value concept should list each asset and each liability at its present value. The present values of some assets and liabilities are fairly easy to determine. The present value of cash, for example, is equal to the amount of cash the company has on hand. Current accounts receivable are reported on conventional balance sheets at the amounts the company expects to collect in the very near future; these amounts are generally close enough to the receivables' present value to be used in value-based balance sheets. For instance, Star Company had cash of $350,000 and accounts receivable of $1,500,000 on January 1, 19x1. These amounts would appear in its value-based balance sheet without change.

Similarly, current accounts payable and other short-term, noninterest-bearing liabilities are listed in conventional balance sheets at the amounts to be paid to creditors in the very near future; again, these amounts are generally close enough to the payables' present value to be used in value-based balance sheets. Star Company had $300,000 in current taxes payable and $750,000 in current accounts payable on January 1, 19x1. These amounts also appeared in its value-based balance sheet.

Unfortunately, the amounts shown in conventional balance sheets for inventories and plant assets are much less likely to approximate their present values. For one thing, their conventional measurement reflects costs incurred at various times in the past, and these are unlikely to approximate current values. Just as important, the future cash flows associated with individual plant assets are ordinarily inseparable from the present value of the business as a whole. As a result, to prepare a balance sheet on a present value basis we must find some other measure that will approximate the present value of the inventories and plant assets.

Appraised value.   The method we use is to measure each identifiable asset at its *appraised value,* if a good approximation to present value isn't available from another source. The appraised value of an asset is an expert's informed estimate of the amount the company would have to pay to acquire a comparable asset in an arm's-length market transaction under current conditions.[3] Star Compa-

---

[3] Appraisals can also measure the estimated *selling* prices of the company's assets. We don't use appraisals of this sort in these calculations because our calculations assume that the company is a *going concern,* one that will continue to use its assets rather than sell them.

ny's inventories on January 1, 19x1, for example, had a cost of $1,600,000, while their appraised value amounted to $2,100,000. The company's plant assets had unamortized costs of $2,900,000, but the appraised value totaled $3,800,000.

The amounts shown in conventional balance sheets for long-term liabilities, such as bonds payable, are also unlikely to measure their present values. Star Company's long-term bonds payable, for example, amounted to $800,000 on January 1, 19x1, but they entered the value-based balance sheet at only $650,000. The reason for this $150,000 difference is that bonds are fixed-dollar obligations, with fixed interest payments due each year for a number of years. Star Company's bonds were issued when interest rates were 6 percent, but the market rate of interest for comparable securities was 15 percent on January 1, 19x1. Since investors could get 15 percent interest on their money elsewhere, they were unwilling to pay as much for these bonds ($800,000) as they had been willing to pay when the bonds were first issued. Instead, they forced the market price of the bonds down until it equaled the present value of the company's future payments to the bondholders, discounted at 15 percent. In other words, long-term bonds appear in a value-based balance sheet at the amount the company could obtain from a creditor in the current market for the cash payments the company is now obligated to make, and this amount depends on current interest rates, not the rates that prevailed when the bonds were issued.[4]

Intangible assets. Exhibit 6–12 shows two balance sheets for the Star Company as of January 1, 19x1. The first column shows the amounts appearing in a conventional cost-based balance sheet; the second column shows the amounts that appeared in a balance sheet based on the present value concept. Only one asset appears in this second column but not in the first. This is the asset identified as *goodwill,* and it represents the value of the company's *intangible assets.* An intangible asset is any attribute that enables a business to generate more net income than the business's tangible assets would normally be expected to generate.

A company's intangible assets sometimes have specific names. For example, the company's high earning power may be clearly ascribable to the ownership of a well-known trademark or a particularly valuable patent. In such cases, it may be possible to estimate the present value of one or more specific intangible assets; any such amounts can be listed separately on a value-based balance sheet.

Most of the time, however, high earning power is the *joint* result of many factors, such as superior product design, marketing and

---

[4] The application of the present value concept in the measurement of corporate bond liabilities is discussed in detail in Chapter 10.

EXHIBIT 6–12

STAR COMPANY
Balance Sheets on Conventional and Present Value Bases
As of January 1, 19x1

	Conventional Basis	Present Value Basis
Assets		
Current assets:		
Cash	$ 350,000	$ 350,000
Receivables	1,500,000	1,500,000
Inventories	1,600,000	2,100,000
Total current assets	3,450,000	3,950,000
Plant and equipment	2,900,000	3,800,000
Total tangible assets	6,350,000	7,750,000
Goodwill	—	209,000
Total assets	$6,350,000	$7,959,000
Liabilities and Owners' Equity		
Current liabilities:		
Taxes payable	$ 300,000	$ 300,000
Accounts payable	750,000	750,000
Current assets	1,050,000	1,050,000
Bonds payable	800,000	650,000
Total current liabilities	1,850,000	1,700,000
Owners' equity:		
Capital stock	2,000,000	2,000,000
Retained earnings	2,500,000	4,259,000
Total owners' equity	4,500,000	6,259,000
Total liabilities and owners' equity	$6,350,000	$7,959,000

managerial skills, and a reputation for providing prompt, careful attention to customers' needs. In these cases, we generally use a single term, *goodwill,* to describe the entire package of intangible assets. Goodwill is the set of attributes that gives an ongoing business enterprise a total value in excess of the amounts ascribed specifically to other assets.

Conceptually, the way to measure goodwill is to estimate the present value of the company as a going concern and then subtract the present value of the cash flows the company would have if it had no intangible assets:

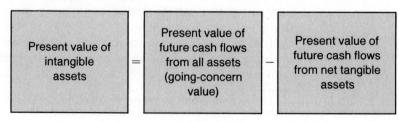

| Present value of intangible assets | = | Present value of future cash flows from all assets (going-concern value) | − | Present value of future cash flows from net tangible assets |

As a practical matter, the values used in this calculation will be a mixture of present values and appraised values, as we explained earlier.

Star Company had no specific intangible assets for which separate estimates of present value could be derived. Instead, its January 1, 19x1, value-based balance sheet listed a single intangible asset, goodwill, in the amount of $209,000. This was derived from the values we calculated for Star's individual tangible assets and liabilities as follows (to the nearest thousand dollars):

Present value of the going concern		$6,259,000
Value of the net tangible assets (from Exhibit 6–12):		
Total tangible assets	$7,750,000	
Total liabilities	1,700,000	6,050,000
Value of the intangible assets		$ 209,000

The owners' equity in a balance sheet based on the concept of present value is the company's going-concern value. For Star Company, this was $6,259,000 on January 1, 19x1. This differed from the $4,500,000 book value of the owners' equity by $1,759,000; all but $209,000 of this difference was accounted for by differences in the measures of the inventories, plant assets, and bonds payable. The division of the owners' equity into two components is arbitrary; we have chosen to concentrate all the adjustments in the retained earnings amount.

Notice that we haven't calculated goodwill by comparing the company's total present value with the total *book value* of its tangible assets. Book values of tangible assets reflect transactions that took place in the past, when conditions were very different from those of today. The fact that a company bought land 50 years ago for $1 an acre is irrelevant; if it buys the land as part of a package today, it is paying current prices for the land, not the prices of 50 years ago.

Companies list intangible assets in their cost-based balance sheets only if they bought them from outsiders. A company that buys a patent, trademark, or copyright, for example, would list it as an asset, measured at its cost. Even goodwill may be listed if the company has bought it—that is, if it has bought an ongoing business at a price greater than the current appraised value of its net tangible assets.

Most intangible assets are developed internally, not bought. The typical company builds goodwill gradually by patient and skillful development of its organization, product lines, and markets. The accountants classify the costs of the activities that produce this result as expenses as they take place. No portion of the current marketing cost, for example, is treated as the cost of acquiring an intangible asset. As a result, intangible assets acquired in this way don't appear in conventional balance sheets.

An income statement based on present value

Income statements also can be constructed on a present value basis. The right-hand column of Exhibit 6–13 shows how an income statement based on present value might look. The $1,757,245 net income is the amount we derived in Exhibit 6–11; the depreciation and cost of goods sold amounts are based on appraised values. The final item in the income statement, "Value adjustment," is a residual, reflecting changes in value not reflected in the revenues and expenses. It is determined by subtracting the income before

EXHIBIT 6–13

STAR COMPANY
Income Statements on Conventional and Present Value Bases
For the Year Ended December 31, 19x1

	Conventional Basis	Present Value Basis
Sales revenues	$10,000,000	$10,000,000
Cost of goods sold	6,000,000	6,300,000
Gross margin	4,000,000	3,700,000
Operating expenses	(1,900,000)	(2,100,000)
Income tax expense	(900,000)	(900,000)
Income before value adjustment	1,200,000	700,000
Value adjustment	—	1,057,245
Net income	$ 1,200,000	$ 1,757,245

the value adjustment from the estimated net income on a present value basis.

The conventional net income in the first column of Exhibit 6–13 is $1,200,000, not the $1 million net cash inflow on which Exhibit 6–11 was based. The reason is that during the year the company paid more cash to purchase inventories, plant, and equipment than it expensed for the use of these kinds of assets. As we pointed out earlier, the annual cash flow used in present value calculations includes *both* the proceeds from discarded plant assets *and* the cash paid to acquire new plant assets during the year. During and after an inflationary period and during periods of growth, cash flow calculated on this basis is likely to be less than net income. During and after inflation, replacement prices generally exceed the original costs of the equipment on which current depreciation charges are based. And in a period of growth, purchases of plant assets ordinarily include both purchases for replacement and purchases for expansion.

Inapplicability of present value for periodic financial reporting _____

In light of the relevance of present value to managerial and investor decisions, why isn't it the primary basis of routine financial reporting on the position and performance of business enterprises? Two major objections may have become apparent in our explanation of how the concept might be applied:

1. The cash-flow estimates in most situations can't be verified satisfactorily.
2. The appropriate discounting rate isn't known with certainty.

The amount, timing, and duration of the future cash flows of a business are highly uncertain, to say the least. Accountants can verify management's past estimates of future cash flows to some extent, but their ability to verify current estimates is much more limited. Present value-based financial statements therefore would summarize management's estimates, relatively unrestrained by objective tests applied by outsiders. The most the accountants could do would be to review the assumptions on which management based its estimates, using available information on economic conditions and the political climate. The credibility of statements prepared on a present value basis probably would be quite low.

The second obstacle to financial reporting on a present value basis is that estimates of the appropriate rate at which to discount the estimated future cash flows are far from precise. Errors in the rate can have significant effects on estimates of present value and on income amounts based on these estimates. For example, we found that the present value of a 20-year, $1 million annuity at 15 percent interest is $6,259,300. If we vary the interest rate just one percentage point, to 14 percent or 16 percent, we change the present value by more than $300,000—to $6,623,100 or $5,928,800 (based on the present value factors in Table 4 of Appendix A). Reducing the interest rate to 10 percent increases the present value to $8,513,600; increasing the rate to 20 percent reduces the present value to $4,870,000.

The choice of the interest rate would also affect the relevance of the statements to individual investors. Some investors may wish to capitalize future cash flows at 15 percent, some may wish to use 12 percent, and others may prefer to adjust for perceived differences in future cash flows by discounting different portions of the cash-flow stream at different interest rates. No matter which rate or set of rates is chosen, it won't meet everyone's needs.

As a result of these difficulties, present value has been ruled out as the basis for routine financial reporting. It is a powerful and useful concept, however, and we'll return to it time and again as we expand our understanding of accounting measurements in later chapters.

SUMMARY

The value of a business asset depends on the amount and timing of the cash flows it can produce in the future *and* on the rate of interest the owners expect to earn from these future cash flows. Distant cash flows are less valuable than those expected to take place in the near future; these differences in timing require that all cash flows be discounted to their present values at a single point in time. The present value of a cash flow is the amount which, if invested at the specified interest rate for the specified period of time, will grow to equal the cash flow when it occurs. The present value factors in Appendix A make the calculation of present values easier.

A conventional business balance sheet doesn't pretend to measure the value of the business, nor does a conventional income statement measure all the changes in value arising during the period. A balance sheet reflecting values would require accountants to approximate the present value of each company's assets and liabilities, including any intangible assets the company may have. An income statement based on present value would show the change in the company's present value from the beginning of the period to the end, plus the amount of dividends distributed during the period.

Some of these present values can be estimated directly, such as those for receivables and payables; for others, such as inventories and plant assets, present values would have to be approximated by appraisals. Accountants don't develop these estimates for their regular financial statements because they would require the use of judgment that couldn't be verified satisfactorily by objective tests.

KEY TERMS

Annuity	Goodwill
Appraised value	Intangible asset
Capitalization ratio	Interest factor
Cash flow	Interest tables
Cash flow timetable	Net cash flow
Compound interest	Present value
Future value	Present value factor

INDEPENDENT STUDY PROBLEMS (Solutions in Appendix B)

1. Present value exercises. Calculate the value on January 1, 1985, of assets that have the following cash flows, with interest at 12 percent compounded annually:

a. Outlay: $35,000 on January 1, 1985.
   Receipt: $100,000 on January 1, 1995.
b. Outlays: $80,000 on January 1, 1985; $20,000 on January 1, 1990.
   Receipts: $10,000 on each January 1, 1986 through 1991; $20,000 on
    each January 1, 1992 through 2001.
c. Outlays: $20,000 on each January 1, 1985 through 1995.
   Receipt: $250,000 on January 1, 1997.

2. Future value exercises. For each of the three assets in Problem 1, calculate the future value at 12 percent, compounded annually, as of the date of the final cash receipt. In each case make a calculation to verify that your answer is consistent with your answer to Problem 1.

3. Calculating an equivalent annuity. Future Company has just borrowed $1 million. Interest on this amount will be paid to the lender each year for 10 years. In addition, the $1 million will have to be repaid to the lender at the end of 10 years.

a. How much will Future Company have to deposit in the bank at the end of each of the next 10 years to enable it to repay the $1 million at the end of the 10 years if the bank compounds interest annually at a rate of 8 percent? An identical amount is to be deposited each year.
b. How much will Future Company have to deposit at the end of each year if the bank compounds interest annually at 12 percent?
c. How much will Future Company have to deposit at the end of each six-month period for 10 years if the bank compounds interest semiannually at a nominal rate of 12 percent a year (6 percent every six months)?

4. Calculating the annuity equivalent to a different annuity. You will need $4,000 a year for five years, starting exactly four years from today. You wish to purchase this annuity by making a series of seven annual payments of equal size. The first of these payments will be made immediately. Interest will accrue at a rate of 8 percent, compounded annually. Calculate the size of the annual payment.

5. Calculating income on a present value basis. William Appersham operates a ferry service across Deepwater Bay. A bridge is now being built across the bay. When it is completed two years from now, Appersham will close the ferry service and retire to his plantation in the Virgin Islands. He expects the following cash flows from the ferry operation:

Year	Cash Receipts	Cash Disbursements	Net Cash Receipts
1	$350,000	$200,000	$150,000
2	400,000	220,000	180,000

At the end of each year he will withdraw the year's net cash receipts and invest them in highway bonds where they will earn interest at an annual rate of 12 percent, compounded annually. In addition, at the end of year 2, he will be able to withdraw the $50,000 he must now maintain as a working cash fund to keep his ferry service going.

The sale value of his ferry boats two years from now will be virtually zero.

a. What is the present value of the ferry service to Appersham now?
b. Assuming that all forecasts are correct, what will be the present value of the assets of the ferry service a year from now, before Appersham withdraws the net cash receipts of the first year's operations?
c. Compute the net income of the ferry service for the first year on a present value basis, assuming that all forecasts are correct.
d. Compute the ferry service's income for the second year on a present value basis, again assuming that all forecasts are correct.
e. Appersham has just discovered that he can invest his available cash at 15 percent, compounded annually, instead of at 12 percent. How would this affect your analysis?

EXERCISES AND PROBLEMS

6. Valuation differences. The management of the Gupta Corporation has recently been cited by a national society of industrial engineers for its efficiency in organizing and controlling the company's affairs. The aggregate market value of the company's stock, based on the current market price per share, is $10 million; book value is only $4 million. Management's own forecast of future cash flows, discounted at an interest rate that seems appropriate for a company of its size and class, is $9 million.

The board of directors of the Marshall Company has just made a cash offer of $12 million for the outstanding stock in the Gupta Corporation. What might account for the premium valuation placed by Marshall on the Gupta Corporation?

7. Calculating present value without interest tables. Without using the interest tables, calculate the present value at 10 percent of a single sum of $100 to be received six years from now. Then verify your answer by using the appropriate table in Appendix A.

8. Present value exercise. Using Table 4 in Appendix A, determine the present value of a series of payments of $100 a year for each of the next six years. Assume that the first payment is received one year from now and the interest rate is 12 percent, compounded annually.

9. Present value exercise. Check your answer to Problem 8 by using Table 3.

10. Calculating present value. You are considering the purchase of six promissory notes. The issuers of these notes will pay you nothing until the notes mature, at which time they will pay the face value of the notes. Three of the notes have face values of $100 and will come due one each at the end of years 3, 4, and 5. The others three have face values of $150 and come due one each at the end of years 6, 7, and 8. If your interest rate is 15 percent, what will you be willing to pay for the full set of six notes at the beginning of year 1? (Use Table 3 in Appendix A.)

11. Verifying present value calculation. Use Table 4 to solve Problem 10.

12. Determinants of present value. Dolly Company has an asset that is expected to generate future net cash receipts of $100,000 during its lifetime. Calculate the present value of this asset under each of the following assumptions:

a. Receipts of $10,000 a year, beginning one year from today; interest rate 10 percent, compounded annually.
b. Receipts of $10,000 a year, beginning five years from today; interest rate 10 percent, compounded annually.
c. Receipts of $20,000 a year, beginning today; interest rate 10 percent, compounded annually.
d. Additional outlay of $50,000 one year from today; receipts of $25,000 a year, beginning one year from today; interest rate 10 percent, compounded annually.
e. Receipts of $10,000 a year, beginning one year from today; interest rate 20 percent, compounded annually.
f. Receipts of $5,000 every six months, beginning six months from today; nominal interest rate 20 percent a year, compounded semiannually.
g. Receipts of $2,500 every three months, beginning three months from today; nominal interest rate 20 percent a year, compounded quarterly.

13. Present value exercises. Calculate the present value of each of the following at 10 percent, using the interest tables in Appendix A:

a. $100,000 to be received 10 years from now; interest compounded annually.
b. $10,000 to be received at the end of each of the next 10 years; interest compounded annually.
c. $5,000 to be received at the end of each of the next five years, plus $15,000 to be received at the end of each of the five years after that; interest compounded annually.
d. $15,000 to be received at the end of each of the next five years, plus $5,000 to be received at the end of each of the five years after that; interest compounded annually.
e. $5,000 to be received at the end of each of the next 20 six-month periods; interest compounded semiannually at 5 percent each six-month period.

14. Future value exercises. For each of the cash-flow streams described in Problem 13, calculate the net future value 10 years from now at an interest rate of 10 percent. In each case, check to make sure your answer is consistent with your answer to Problem 13.

15. Calculating annuity equivalent to present value. A pension fund not subject to income taxes plans to buy a piece of equipment for $10,000 and lease it to a manufacturer. The equipment has an estimated useful life of 10 years and is to be leased to the manufacturer for that time. It will have no salvage value at the end of its ten-year life. The pension fund's management wishes to charge the manufacturer an annual rental that will enable the fund to recover the purchase price of the equipment during the ten years and earn 8 percent a year on its investment.

a. What is the lowest annual rental the pension fund should accept if the rental is received at the end of each year for ten years?
b. What is the lowest annual rental the pension fund should accept if the rental is received at the beginning of each year for ten years?

(Prepared by Professor Carl L. Nelson)

16.   Value of asset to buyer and seller.   A boat can be bought for $21,000, payable in cash immediately. Alternatively, the seller will accept a series of cash payments, starting with $10,000 immediately and then $2,000 at the end of each of the next eight years.

a. If buyers can always invest their money at 10 percent, compounded annually, which of these alternatives should they prefer?
b. Assuming that sellers can invest their money at 8 percent, what is the series of payments worth to them?

17.   Comparability of values at different times.   You have three assets for which you forecast the following cash flows:

Years from Now	Asset A	Asset B	Asset C
1	+$1,000		
2	+ 1,000		
3	+ 1,000	+$1,700	
4	+ 1,000	+ 1,700	
5	+ 1,000	+ 1,700	+$2,000
6			+ 2,000
7			+ 2,000

Each of these assets is being managed by one of your company's trainees. You have asked them to calculate the values of these assets, assuming that money is worth 10 percent. They have given you the following figures:

Asset A: present value today, $3,791.

Asset B: present value three years from now, $4,650.

Asset C: future value seven years from now, $6,620.

Which of these assets is the most valuable? Which is the least valuable? Show your calculations.

18.   Comparing two short-term investments.   A bank offers a $20 immediate cash bonus to anyone who deposits $1,000 in the bank today and leaves it on deposit for a year. The bank will add interest to this deposit at the end of each three-month period at a nominal annual rate of 11 percent, compounded quarterly.

If you don't accept the bank's offer, you will invest $1,000 in a money market fund which will add interest to your investment monthly, at a nominal annual rate of 12 percent, compounded monthly.

If you accept the bank's offer, you will invest the $20 cash bonus in the money market fund described in the preceding paragraph.

Which of these opportunities should you accept? Quantify the advantage this opportunity has over the other. (Note: you will not be able to use the interest tables in Appendix A to solve this problem. You can solve it either by performing a sequence of operations or by using one or more of the mathematical formulas that accompany the tables in Appendix A.)

19. Annuity equivalent to future value. A company that owns a gravel pit is obligated to pay the cost of leveling the terrain at the time the gravel deposit is exhausted. It is estimated that this payment will be made seven years from now and that the amount will be $20,000. The company wishes to build up a fund to be used to meet this obligation at the end of seven years. It will make seven equal annual payments into the fund, one at the end of each year; the seventh payment is to be made at the time the gravel deposit is exhausted.

If the fund earns interest at the rate of 12 percent, compounded annually, how much must each annual payment be?

(Prepared by Professor Carl L. Nelson)

20. Annuity equivalent to an annuity. On January 1, 1983, Meridian Products entered into an employment agreement with its president. As part of that agreement, the firm agreed to pay the president $20,000 each year for 10 years after his retirement. The payments were scheduled to start on July 1, 1993, and to terminate on July 1, 2002.

The company wished to make these payments out of a fund. This fund was to be built up by equal annual payments starting July 1, 1983, and ending July 1, 1993. It was anticipated that the fund would earn 12 percent a year, compounded annually. How much was each payment?

(Prepared by Professor Carl L. Nelson)

21. Calculating residual amount. A company borrowed $100,000 on October 1, 1975. The interest rate was 8 percent. The company agreed to pay $15,000 a year for 10 years, starting October 1, 1978, to cover interest and a portion of the principal each year. No amounts were to be paid on October 1, 1976, or October 1, 1977.

A "balloon" payment to repay the indebtedness remaining on October 1, 1988, was to be made on that date. How large a payment should the company have planned to make on that date?

(Prepared by Professor Carl L. Nelson)

22. Calculating the value of an asset. Thomas Peterson is an investor who expects to earn at least 8 percent a year on his investment. He estimates that an investment in a new mine will bring him $10,000 in cash at the end of each of the next 15 years. At the end of that time, the mine will be worthless.

a.   How much is the mine worth to Peterson?
b.   How much would the mine be worth to Peterson today if it were expected to produce $10,000 a year for 25 years? For 40 years? For 50 years?

c. Prepare a diagram with "values" on the vertical scale and the number of years on the horizontal scale. Enter your answers to parts a and b on this diagram. From the diagram, try to estimate how much the mine would be worth if it were to be productive at the present rate for 100 years. What other method or methods could you have used to calculate this amount?

23. Goodwill. The book value of Company A's net tangible assets is $100,000. The current appraised value is $125,000.

Net income before extraordinary items has averaged $15,000 a year for the last five years, and capital expenditures each year have equaled the annual depreciation of $15,000. Present forecasts are that net income and capital expenditures will continue at this level indefinitely.

a. Calculate the amount of goodwill, assuming the normal rate of return in this industry is 10 percent.
b. Company B has just bought Company A's net assets for $145,000. How much goodwill should it recognize in its balance sheet?

24. Discussion question: Effects of purchase and sale on income. On July 1, 19x1, Ruth Norris bought 500 shares of stock in the Parkway Corporation at a price of $20 a share. She estimated that the present value of these shares to her was $22 a share at that time.

Norris received cash dividends of 50 cents a share on December 30, 19x1. On December 31, 19x1, she estimated the present value of these shares at $24 a share. She sold the shares on that date at a price of $25 a share.

a. If Norris were to measure her income on a present value basis and ignore income taxes, how much income would she say she had earned from this investment (1) on July 1, 19x1, and (2) between July 1, 19x1, and January 1, 19x2?
b. How, if at all, would your answer to part a change if Norris hadn't sold her stock on December 31, 19x1? Discuss the differences between this situation and the situation addressed in part a and the arguments for and against treating the two situations differently.

25. Effect of timing of cash flows on asset value. Cole Hammerlowe, the famous author-composer of Broadway musicals in the 1940s, bequeathed the rights to all his literary and musical works to the Hammerlowe Foundation, a newly established charitable organization. Some of these rights were due to expire in a few years, but others would be valid for 30 years.

Hammerlowe's work had a small but loyal band of admirers, and a steady stream of royalty payments could be counted on for a number of years. In addition, the trustees of the foundation expected that Hammerlowe's works would have several years of renewed popularity as a new generation of theater critics rediscovered them, a phenomenon that had been observed for every other author-composer of Hammerlowe's stature in the past. Accordingly, the trustees prepared the following estimates of the cash flows the foundation would be likely to receive:

Year	Annual Cash Receipts
1–5	$ 50,000
6–10	200,000
11–15	100,000
16–20	50,000
21–30	20,000

The trustees expect to be able to invest any funds that become available to them to yield an annual rate of return of 10 percent. The foundation is not subject to income taxes.

a. Compute the value of Hammerlowe's gift to the foundation.
b. The anticipated cash flows in this case average $70,000 a year for 30 years. Suppose that a long-established, respectable commercial publisher were to offer to pay the foundation $70,000 a year *forever* in exchange for the rights to Hammerlowe's works. Should the trustees accept this offer? Explain briefly.

26. Calculating equivalent annuity; effect of interest rate. William Lazere wished to provide for the college education of his three children. He estimated that he would need the following amounts:

August 31, 1990	$10,000
August 31, 1991	20,000
August 31, 1992	30,000
August 31, 1993	30,000
August 31, 1994	20,000
August 31, 1995	10,000

On September 1, 1983, Lazere asked the representative of an insurance company to draw up an endowment policy that would provide these amounts. The insurance company compounded interest annually at 12 percent.

a. What is the amount Lazere had to pay each September 1 from 1983 to 1994, inclusive, to obtain the funds needed for his children's education? Show your calculations.
b. Recompute your answer to part *a* on the basis of a 15 percent interest rate, compounded annually.

27. Goodwill; appraised values. The book value of Company Y's tangible assets is $750,000, and its liabilities amount to $250,000. The tangible assets have a total appraised value of $800,000; the liabilities are appraised at $250,000. The historical-cost balance sheet shows no intangible assets.

Company Y's net income has been $72,000 a year for the last five years. Annual expenditures on plant and equipment have equaled the depreciation each year, $20,000.

a. Calculate the present value of the shareholders' equity in Company Y, on the assumption that shareholders expect to receive a rate of return of 12 percent on investments in this industry and that income and expenditures for plant and equipment will continue at their current levels forever.

b. Calculate the value of Company Y's goodwill.

c. Company X has offered to buy Company Y's assets, giving in exchange $650,000 in cash and also accepting responsibility for Company Y's liabilities. How much has Company X offered to pay for Company Y's goodwill?

d. If Company Y rejects Company X's offer, how much goodwill will appear on Company Y's balance sheet immediately after the rejection? Explain.

28.   Value of shares of stock.   Carrington Corporation has been in operation for three years. It markets a new kind of plastic foam for sale to industrial customers. The company has reported a net loss each year since it was founded, but sales are now increasing, and management expects to report a small net income this year.

To finance the company's growth and broaden its ownership base, the owner-managers have decided to "go public" and have offered to sell shares of the company's common stock at $10 a share. Book value per share is now $4.

You have $25,000 you wish to invest in a growth situation of this sort, and you are willing to buy this stock if you think it will yield an annual return of 12 percent before taxes.

You forecast that Carrington Corporation will report earnings and pay dividends as follows:

Years from Now	Earnings per Share	Dividends per Share
1	$0.10	—
2	0.75	$0.50
3	1.00	0.50
4	1.25	0.50
5	1.50	0.50
6	1.75	0.50
7	2.00	1.00
8	2.00	1.00
9	2.00	1.00
10	2.00	1.00

(For simplicity, you should assume that dividends will be paid once each year, at the end of the year.)

You believe that the market price of this stock 10 years from now will probably be about $16 a share.

What is this stock worth to you? Show the calculations that support your answer. Ignore income taxes.

29.   Calculating income on a present value basis.   The city of El Dorado has decided to sponsor an international exposition promoting the values of rural living. The exposition will operate for four years. The city will provide a site for the exposition in Bucolic Park, rent free.

Turning to experts, the city has asked the International Corporation for Expositions (ICE) to construct the buildings and operate the exposition. ICE has prepared the following estimates of operating cash receipts and cash disbursements:

Year	Receipts	Disbursements
1	$2,000,000	$1,300,000
2	3,000,000	1,500,000
3	2,000,000	800,000
4	1,350,000	350,000

Construction costs, all to be paid at the beginning of year 1, are estimated to be $4 million. An additional investment of $300,000 will be necessary at that time to provide a working cash fund; the need for this will continue throughout the four-year period. The exposition buildings will be sold to the city at the end of year 4 for $1 million.

ICE has enough confidence in the predictions to participate in the venture if it will earn a return of 10 percent before income taxes. If it decides to do so, it will form a subsidiary, the El Dorado Exposition Corporation. This subsidiary will issue common stock to ICE for $1,000 and will borrow the remaining $4,299,000 from ICE, giving noninterest-bearing notes as evidence of its indebtedness. The subsidiary will repay the notes as rapidly as possible, keeping only a cash balance of $300,000. ICE assumes in all its calculations that all cash receipts and disbursements take place at the end of the year.

The subsidiary will be liquidated at the end of year 4, and its remaining cash assets will be paid back to ICE at that time.

a. Assuming that ICE agrees to undertake this project and that all the forecasts are correct, compute the subsidiary's income for each year if assets are measured by the present value approach. Ignore income taxes.
b. If the historical-cost approach is used instead of present value, what will be the income for each year? Historical-cost depreciation will be the same for each of the four years. Ignore income taxes.

30. Financial statements on a present value basis. Vista Realty Company raised $25 million by issuing shares of its capital stock to a small group of wealthy investors. It then built the Vista Hotel at a cost of $16 million on land acquired at a cost of $9 million. Construction was completed on January 1, 19x1, and the company leased the hotel on that date to an operator who agreed to pay Vista 40 percent of the hotel's revenues, with payment to be made in cash at the end of each year for 25 years. The operator also agreed to pay all the hotel's operating expenses, including property taxes. Vista Realty had no other assets and no liabilities on January 1, 19x1.

Vista Realty's management estimated that the hotel would gross an annual revenue of $10 million. The hotel would probably close its doors at the end of 25 years, and the land and building would be sold at that time for an estimated $9 million.

In its conventional income statements, Vista Realty depreciated the cost of the building by $640,000 a year.

Because the Vista Hotel was built under a special economic incentive program, Vista Realty was exempt from income taxes for 25 years on its income from ownership of the hotel. One provision of this arrangement was that the company would obtain an appraisal of the land and building each year. No appraisal was necessary on January 1, 19x1, because both the land and building had been obtained in recent market transactions.

The Vista Hotel had revenues of $8 million in its first year, and the operator made the first year's rental payment on schedule. Vista Realty had no expenses other than depreciation and paid no dividends to its shareholders in 19x1.

Toward the end of 19x1, the local government began building a domed stadium and related facilities for conventions, professional sports, and so forth. Vista Realty's management believed this would increase annual hotel revenue to about $12 million a year, starting in 19x3. The revenue projection for 19x2 remained at $10 million.

The annual appraisal of the land and building on December 31, 19x1, gave the land an appraised value of $11 million and the building an appraised value of $15,800,000, after deducting accumulated depreciation.

a. Calculate the present value of Vista Realty Company as of January 1, 19x1, at an interest rate of 15 percent, compounded annually.
b. Prepare a value-based balance sheet as of January 1, 19x1, reflecting your answer to part *a*.
c. Calculate the present value of Vista Realty Company as of December 31, 19x1, at an interest rate of 15 percent, compounded annually.
d. Calculate Vista Realty's 19x1 income on a present value basis. Did the company earn 15 percent on its owners' investment in 19x1?
e. Prepare a balance sheet as of December 31, 19x1, reflecting your answers to parts *c* and *d*. Explain the meaning of any change in goodwill.
f. Amanda Jones, a wealthy investor, had an opportunity to buy a 10 percent interest in Vista Realty Company on December 31, 19x1. Assuming she accepted management's estimates, calculate the maximum price she should have been willing to pay for this stock if she required a 12 percent return on her investment.

Part two

FINANCIAL ACCOUNTING

7

The timing of revenue and expense recognition

Accountants recognize changes in the value of a business, for the most part, only as revenues are recognized. The income statement reports the difference between the sum of a set of current values (revenues) and the sum of another set of past values and current values (expenses). For example Exhibit 7–1 shows the amount invested in an asset (inventory) increasing gradually as costs are incurred to bring it to the point of revenue recognition. At that point the accounting measurement increases because the value of the asset—that is, the inventory or the cash or receivable exchanged for it—exceeds the cost that has been incurred up to that point.

This chapter has two goals: (1) to explain the criteria accountants use in deciding when the value of marketable goods and services is measurable enough to justify the recognition of revenue, and (2) to see how the choice of a revenue-recognition point will affect the figures shown in the financial statements.

CRITERIA FOR REVENUE RECOGNITION

At least six distinct events can be found in the operating cycle of a manufacturing company:

1. Acquisition of resources.
2. Receipt of customer orders.
3. Production.
4. Delivery of goods or performance of services.
5. Collection of cash.
6. Completion of all contractual obligations.

EXHIBIT 7–1. Accounting Measurement of Value Changes

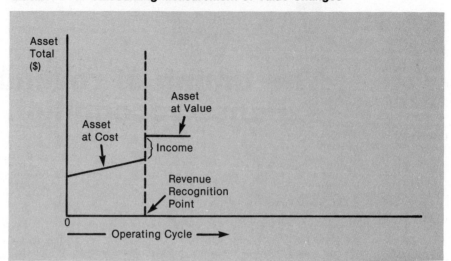

In the illustrations we used in earlier chapters, revenues were always recognized at the time of delivery, and our task was to decide which costs were to be reported as expenses of generating those revenues. The time of delivery isn't the only possible choice, however. Any of the six events in our list might conceivably be taken as the signal that revenues have been earned; that is, it is conceivable that each might be adopted under certain circumstances as *the revenue-recognition basis.* Our first problem, therefore, is to see what criteria accountants use in choosing among these six possibilities.

We should point out at the outset that *each* of these is a productive activity which adds value in some measure to the goods or merchandise purchased. On these grounds, a portion of the ultimate sale price ought to be recognized as revenue as each activity is performed. The difficulty is that the ultimate sale price is the *joint* product of *all* activities and it is impossible to say with certainty how much is attributable to any one of them. *For this reason, accountants select one event as the signal for revenue recognition and ignore the others.*

In choosing a basis for revenue recognition, accountants follow a basic rule: The investor's interests call for recognizing revenue just as soon as the value change it represents can be measured reliably. Investors' decisions presumably are influenced by the *rate* at which value changes take place; the sooner they learn about *changes in this rate,* the sooner they can act on this information.

Given this rule, accountants generally recognize revenue for public financial reporting at the *first* point in the operating cycle at which *all* the following conditions are satisfied:

1. The principal revenue-producing service has been performed.
2. All costs that are necessary to create the revenue but have not yet been incurred either are negligible or can be predicted with reasonable accuracy.
3. The amount ultimately collectible in cash or its equivalent can be estimated with reasonable accuracy.

Revenues and their related expenses aren't recognized before these conditions are met because, before this time, no one can be sure that the value change has actually taken place in the amount indicated. The accountant wants to notify the public promptly, but only if the amounts reported can be counted on as a reasonable measure of what has actually happened. In other words, there is a trade-off between promptness and reliability—the accountant's job is to locate the point beyond which more promptness can be had only by too great a sacrifice in reliability.

THE DELIVERY BASIS

We'll look at the delivery basis first because it is used most frequently in practice. Specifically, we'll try to answer four questions:

1. What is the delivery basis?
2. Why is the delivery basis used so widely?
3. What estimates have to be made if this basis is used?
4. How will assets, income, and expenses be measured?

The nature of the delivery basis

The delivery basis probably should be called the *shipment basis.* When the delivery basis is used, revenues and their associated expenses are usually recognized at the time merchandise is shipped to customers and invoices are prepared, even though delivery takes place a few days or weeks later. The time lag is usually short, however, and the distinction between shipment time and delivery usually has no practical significance.

We might also have referred to this as the *sale basis* of revenue recognition, the term most accountants use. We don't use this term because we find it ambiguous. The sales force "makes a sale" when it persuades a customer to place a purchase order. This may be days, weeks, or even months before delivery takes place. Since accountants identify the time of delivery as the time of sale, we find it simpler to refer to this revenue-recognition basis as the delivery basis.

Reasons for the use of the delivery basis

The delivery basis is widely used because, in most cases, it's the first point in the operating cycle at which all three revenue-recognition criteria are met:

1. The seller's economic role has been performed, for the most part, when the goods are delivered or the services are performed.
2. Few, if any, costs remain to be incurred in the future, and those that remain can be predicted accurately—e.g., warranty costs.
3. While the amount that eventually will be collected from customers is unknown, it is usually predictable. Defaults, customer discounts, and other future leakages from the stated price of the goods delivered are generally small and predictable.

A second reason for the prevalence of the delivery basis is that it permits the company to reduce its recordkeeping costs. Invoices have to be prepared to notify customers that payments are due. These invoices are usually prepared when the merchandise is shipped or when services are performed for customers. Using these invoices as the source to recognize revenues avoids the need to perform these same calculations at some other time. Although recognition of revenue at some other time might provide better information, the added cost of providing that information may outweigh the added benefits.

Estimates required: Cash collections

In any basis of revenue recognition, the key amounts to estimate are (1) the sum to be collected from the customer and the date it will be collected and (2) the costs still to be incurred after the recognition point. As to the first of these, the total amount of cash collected from customers is almost always less than the total invoice price, for one or more of the following reasons:

1. The company grants *cash discounts* to its customers for prompt payment.
2. The company grants *sales allowances* (price reductions) to customers who agree to accept merchandise not meeting their specifications.
3. The company cancels all or part of the invoice price of merchandise returned by customers (*sales returns*).
4. Customers fail to pay the full amounts they owe the company (*customer defaults*).

5. The company accepts an *asset other than cash or a short-term receivable* in exchange for the merchandise.

Acceptance of assets other than cash or short-term receivables is a way of giving a customer a concealed discount, a way of settling an account that otherwise would be uncollectible, or sometimes a way of making a sale to a customer who is short of cash but rich in longer-term assets.

Regardless of the reason, the company's problem is to determine the amount at which to record the asset it receives in exchange for its goods and services and the gain or loss on the exchange. Sometimes the asset is a long-term receivable, meaning that the company is lending money to the customer. Part of the face value of the receivable, therefore, is interest on this loan. For example, an exchange of merchandise for a $10,000, one-year promissory note when the appropriate lending rate is 10 percent, compounded annually, should lead to the recognition of $9,091 in revenues, the present value of the $10,000 future amount. The remaining $909 represents a year's interest on the $9,091 loan. (The $9,091 would appear on the balance sheet as a note receivable, or at the $10,000 face value of the note less $909 in unearned interest.)

In other cases, the company may exchange goods or services for some asset the customer owns, not for cash or the customer's promise to pay. The customer, for example, may transfer shares of stock in other companies, corporate bonds, equipment, or real estate; the problem is to determine the current value of the asset received. Value in such cases is measured either by the estimated market value of the asset given up or by the estimated market value of the asset received, whichever is more clearly evident. For example, if the company accepts 100 shares of actively traded stock in exchange for merchandise with a list price of $10,000, the revenue is measured by the market value of the stock at the time of the settlement, whether this is $11,000 or $9,000. The stock's market value is likely to be more readily determinable than the market value of unsold inventories.

Establishing value in this way has two effects. First, if revenues have already been recognized in the usual way, the subsequent acceptance of a new asset in exchange for the previously recognized receivable is likely to result in a gain or a loss. If our company accepts stock worth $9,000 to settle a $10,000 account, the loss is $1,000.

Second, this estimate of *value* is accounted for as the *cost* of the asset received when it is used or sold later. Suppose the stock is worth $9,000 at the exchange but is sold later for $7,000. The $2,000 difference is a loss resulting from management's decision to hold onto the stock instead of selling it right away. After all, a decision not to sell an asset is economically equivalent to a decision to buy it. Any change in the value of an asset held for investment is a gain or loss on the act of investment—it doesn't matter how the asset was acquired in the first place.

Delivery basis: Measuring inventories, receivables, and income

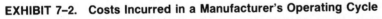

When revenues are recognized at the time of delivery, the past, present, and future costs associated with those revenues should be recognized as expenses at the same time. For example, suppose Castle Company sells merchandise at an invoice price of $100. It offers no sales discounts, expects to receive payment promptly (within 30 days), has negligible sales returns and allowances, and expects customer defaults to average 2 percent of the average invoice price. The net revenue from an average shipment of merchandise with an invoice price of $100, therefore, is $100 − $2 = $98.

The diagram in Exhibit 7–2 shows the costs Castle Company incurs at each state in its operating cycle. It spends $20 to buy the materials for a unit of product, $10 a unit to a sales representative to secure an order from a customer, $40 to process the materials into a unit of finished product, $6 to deliver it to the customer, $4 a unit to collect the amount due from the customer, and $5 to provide service under the terms of the warranty attached to the product. These costs add up to $85.

The heights of the solid blocks in Exhibit 7–3 show the cumulative total cost assignable to an average $100 customer order if the sequence in Exhibit 7–2 is followed. The vertical distances in the shaded areas at the top of the three right-hand bars represent the $13 income which is added to the balance sheet when the goods are delivered and revenues are recorded. If the accounting is consistent with this diagram, none of the costs incurred prior to delivery—for materials, order getting, and production—will be expensed before delivery takes place. And there will be no effect on income later, when collection and warranty service costs are incurred. In

EXHIBIT 7–2. Costs Incurred in a Manufacturer's Operating Cycle

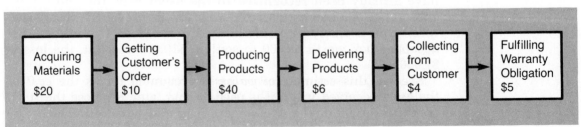

EXHIBIT 7–3. Delivery Basis: Cumulative Total Cost and Income

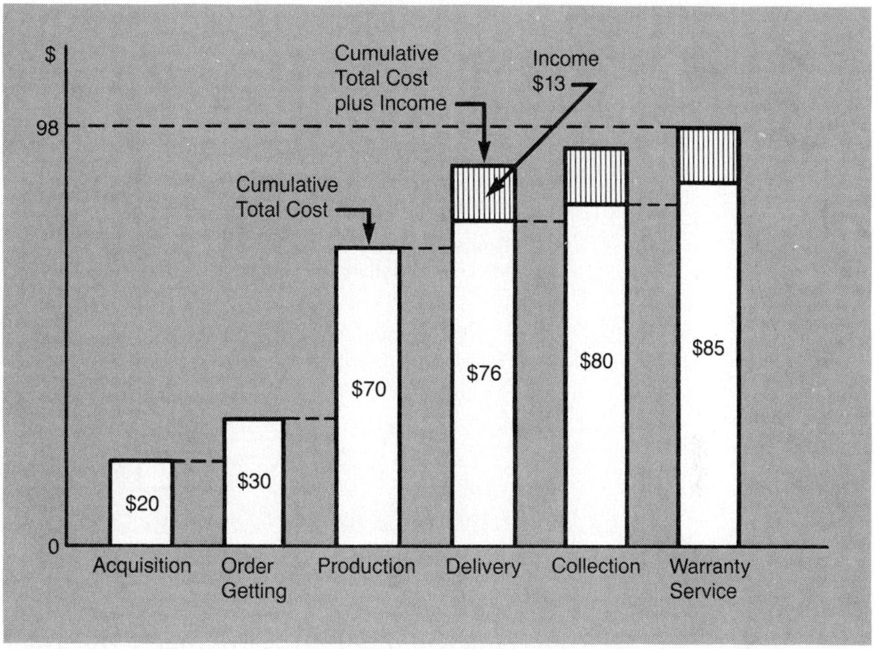

other words, the expenses in the period of delivery will be those shown in Exhibit 7–4. The costs of the first four elements are known at the time of delivery; the costs of the other two are estimated.

Under this approach, an *undelivered* inventory of the finished goods associated with a $100 customer order would appear in the balance sheet at a cost of $70 ($20 in materials costs, $10 in order-getting costs, and $40 in production costs). The $10 in order-getting costs might be capitalized separately from the costs of the physical inventory as a "deferred charge" against future revenues, similar in effect to prepaid expenses such as rent or insurance.

Delivery of an average $100 order would then have the following effects:

Increase in receivables		$94
Gross amount	$100	
Less: Anticipated customer defaults	2	
Net amount collectible	98	
Less: Anticipated collection costs	4	
Net value of the receivable	94	
Decrease in inventory and capitalized order-getting costs		(70)
Decrease in cash (delivery costs)		(6)
Increase in liability for warranty service		(5)
Increase in owners' equity		$13

EXHIBIT 7–4.   Expenses Associated with a $100 Order from an Average Customer

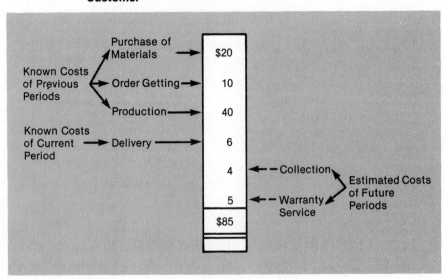

To be consistent with this approach, the amount receivable after the delivery is made should appear in the balance sheet at $94, the net amount the company expects to realize at the time of collection. This could be recorded in a single account or the gross amount could be recorded in one account, with the anticipated discounts and collection costs entered in appropriately titled contra-asset accounts. The estimated warranty liability would be entered in a separate liability account.

Delivery basis: Pragmatic criteria

Actual practice may depart from the income and asset measurement principles described in the preceding paragraph. For example, accountants usually recognize order-getting costs and collection costs as expenses when they are incurred, not when delivery is made. Warranty costs, too, are sometimes expensed as they are incurred rather than when goods are delivered. Three factors account for these practices:

1. The amounts may be small enough to be classified as immaterial.
2. The amounts may be very difficult to attribute to individual customer orders or groups of orders.
3. Companies can reduce their clerical costs by adopting income

tax definitions for financial reporting, and income tax regulations encourage or require expensing these items at the time of expenditure.

Materiality is an important accounting concept that refers to whether the difference between two alternative accounting treatments or modes of presentation will affect the meaning readers of financial statements attribute to the figures in the statements. A difference is immaterial if it is highly unlikely to change the interpretation of the statements. Immateriality is probably the main reason collection costs are expensed when they are incurred. It may also explain the failure to accrue warranty service liabilities in many cases.

The *difficulty of attributing costs* to individual orders applies particularly to order-getting costs. Management incurs costs, such as advertising and sales salaries, not to obtain a specific order, but in the hope and expectation of securing many orders. The company may spend millions of dollars and never receive an order from a customer. And when the orders do come in, management seldom knows whether they resulted from the current period's order-getting activities or from those of one or more previous periods. Lacking any clear basis for associating the current period's costs of order getting with specific present or future orders, accountants ordinarily treat them as expenses as they occur.

In the United States, *tax considerations* merely reinforce the first two reasons for expensing the costs of order getting, collection, and warranty fulfillment as they are incurred. If the costs are material in amount and readily identifiable with specific revenues, generally accepted accounting principles require that they be recognized as expenses when the related revenues are recognized, no matter what the tax regulations require or allow. Tax considerations, therefore, affect the financial accounting treatment only in borderline cases, when materiality or ease of association is in doubt.

ACQUISITION BASIS

We'll point out in Part Four that management should base its decisions to acquire inventories and equipment on estimates of the difference between the present values of the cash flows they will generate and their present cost. For decision purposes, in other words, management should recognize revenues at the time resources are acquired.

The acquisition basis is never used for public financial reporting, however, because some (usually all) of the three revenue-recognition criteria haven't been met at that time. The company hasn't performed all its major value-creating functions, costs subsequent to acquisition are large and uncertain, and the amounts of cash to be received from customers are usually even more uncertain. This means that the income numbers measured under this basis would be too unreliable for use by outsiders.

SALES ORDER BASIS

Another possible point for revenue recognition is the point at which the sales order is received. The order is a significant event in the operating cycle. Most companies that experience significant lags between the date of the order and the date of the shipment will keep track of the orders received so that the amount of orders on hand for future delivery (the backlog) can be reported periodically to management. In these circumstances, the performance of the sales force probably should be judged more on the basis of orders received than on goods shipped.

Order and backlog information may also be reported to creditors and stockholders to guide the appraisals of the company's future prospects, but revenues and receivables are never recognized in externally published reports on the basis of orders received during the period. The reason is simply that the criteria for revenue recognition are not met at the time the order is received—the goods have not yet been produced, the costs of producing them are not adequately predictable, or order cancellations are frequent and variable.

PRODUCTION BASIS

The third potential alternative to recognizing revenue at the time of delivery is the *production basis*. Under this method, revenue is recognized during or at the end of the production process, even though title to the goods still belongs to the seller. The production basis may be used only when the following conditions exist:

1. The costs to be incurred subsequent to production are either immaterial or highly predictable.
2. The amount of ultimate collection is reasonably certain, and collection costs are immaterial.
3. The timing of deliveries is more volatile than the timing of production.

As the method that views completion of production as tantamount to a sale, its application is most common in shipbuilding and other industries in which the production cycle is very long and production is initiated only on receipt of firm orders.

Measuring inventories, receivables, and expenses

Applying the production basis strictly to our previous example, Castle Company would recognize income of $13 at the time of production. Exhibit 7–5 identifies the bases on which the various components of expense would be recognized. This exhibit is like Exhibit 7–4, except that delivery costs have been moved from the *known* costs to the *estimated* costs associated with the order.

When the production basis is used, the net realizable value of the goods is recognized as revenue. *Net realizable value* is the amount the company expects to collect less the estimated costs of future periods; for Castle Company, $98 − $15 ($6 + $4 + $5), or $83. In terms of journal entries, Castle might record the following:

Finished Goods Inventory 83
    Sales Revenue 83
  To record production-basis revenues ($98 − $15).

Cost of Goods Sold 70
    Cash (and other accounts) 70
  To record known costs of the current period ($20 + $10 + $40).

EXHIBIT 7-5. Expenses Associated with a $100 Order from an Average Customer: Production Basis

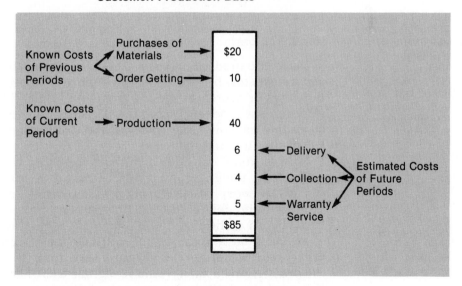

Because the inventory of undelivered goods appears in the year-end balance sheet at its net realizable value, it can also be viewed as being in effect an unbilled receivable.

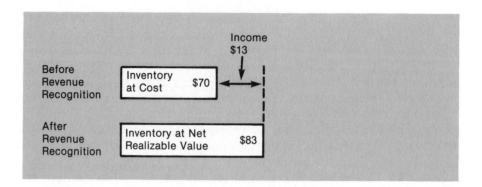

When the production basis is used in practice, provisions for delivery and collection costs are seldom made. Furthermore, order-getting costs may not be capitalized, and provisions for warranty liabilities may not be accrued. The reasons are the same as those we listed in discussing departures from the strict application of the delivery basis: (1) future costs are immaterial in amount, or (2) no clear basis can be found for attributing costs to individual production orders. The second of these reasons is particularly applicable to order-getting and collection costs, but it may apply to the others as well.

Advantages of the production basis

Using the production basis when the recognition criteria are met serves investors by informing them more promptly of owners' equity increases or decreases arising from operations. This is particularly important whenever production precedes delivery by a substantial or widely varying time interval and production is the last major value-creating activity.

For example, consider a mining company which produces ore and sells it under a long-term contract at $12 a ton, the buyer to pay all delivery costs. During the first three quarters of 19x1, it produced and delivered 600,000 tons at a total cost of $6.3 million. It mined an additional 180,000 tons of ore during the final quarter of the year at a cost of $1.8 million, but a transportation strike prevented the delivery of this ore until 19x2. If the company used the production basis, it would recognize $360,000 more income than if it used the delivery basis, as the following table shows:

	Delivery Basis	Production Basis
Revenues:		
First three quarters (600,000 tons × $12)	$7,200,000	$7,200,000
Fourth quarter (180,000 tons × $12)	—	2,160,000
Total revenues	7,200,000	9,360,000
Expenses	6,300,000	8,100,000
Income before taxes	$ 900,000	$1,260,000

The production basis in this case is clearly more informative than the delivery basis. With a contract under which the customer takes all the company's production at an agreed-upon price, and with all costs known when production is completed, the act of production really completes the earning process, and investors should be informed of its success or failure at that time rather than later, when delivery takes place.

Percentage-of-completion accounting

The most widely used version of the production basis is the percentage-of-completion method of revenue recognition. Percentage-of-completion accounting has four main features:

1. Costs are accumulated separately for each distinct work project, contract, or job order. For simplicity, we'll refer to each of these as a *job*.
2. The ratio of the amount of work done on each job to the total amount of work required by that job is estimated at the end of each period.
3. Revenue from each job is recognized in proportion to progress on the job, as measured by the ratio of work done to total work required.
4. Job costs are classified as expenses as revenues are recognized.

For example, Marsden-Brown, Inc., decided to adopt the production basis for recognizing revenues. Marsden-Brown is an engineering firm specializing in the design and installation of lighting systems. In mid-19x1 the firm obtained a contract to install the lighting for the Arkwright County Sports Arena, a job that was to take six months. The contract price was $200,000, and the estimated total cost was $160,000. Marsden-Brown was to bill the customer at the end of each quarter for 80 percent of the sales value of the work done to date.

Work began on October 18, 19x1, and the actual costs charged to the job prior to December 31, 19x1, amounted to $80,000. Progress on the contract was reviewed at the end of the year, and the job was estimated to be 45 percent completed. Production-basis accounting therefore required recognition of revenue of $90,000 for 19x1 (45 percent of the $200,000 contract price). The customer was billed for *progress payments* of $72,000 (80 percent of $90,000).

In practice, the account structure to record this information would be relatively complex. In essence, however, Marsden-Brown's income statement showed a gross margin of $10,000:

Contract revenue	$90,000
Less: Cost of work performed	80,000
Gross margin on contract work performed	$10,000

The balance sheet showed:

Accounts receivable		$72,000
Inventory (market value of contract work performed to date)	$90,000	
Less: Progress billings	72,000	
Inventory (net)		18,000

The only novel element here is the method used to measure the inventory. The inventory is measured not at cost, but at the value of the work done. Furthermore, since a portion of this value has already been billed to customers, only the unbilled portion is shown as an inventory amount. The inventory, in other words, can be viewed as being tantamount to an unbilled receivable, not unlike the undelivered goods in the previous example.

We should also emphasize that the $72,000 amount *billed* in 19x1 had no effect on the amount of revenue recognized during the period. When the job was completed in 19x2, the revenue for that year was $110,000—that is, the full contract price ($200,000) minus the $90,000 that was recognized in 19x1.

The percentage-of-completion method is most often used when the production cycle is long, the work is done under contracts with specific clients or customers, and adequate data on progress are available. The contracts provide a basis on which to estimate the amount of cash to be collected after all production work has been completed; if the progress percentage data are valid, they provide assurance that the work done to date will ultimately lead to the collection of cash. Since the cost of the work done to date is readily measurable, the three revenue-recognition criteria are satisfied at the time of production as long as valid progress percentage data are available.

Use of the percentage-of-completion method when the production cycle is long has two effects. First, it leads to an earlier recognition of revenue and expense than the delivery basis would yield. Investors, therefore, will be informed more promptly of changes in the volume of activity or in the profit rate.

Second, this method is likely to report a smoother income stream in long-cycle operations than delivery-basis accounting would report. Suppose Marsden-Brown completed four contracts in 19x1, eight contracts in 19x2, and two contracts in 19x3. Its reported income on a delivery basis might follow the path traced by the solid line in Exhibit 7–6. The work done was approximately constant over the three years, however, and revenue recognition on a production (percentage-of-completion) basis might lead to the income pattern traced by the dashed line in the exhibit. Although the number of deliveries declined drastically in 19x3, production-basis income rose because the company was able to work more efficiently in 19x3 than in 19x2.

EXHIBIT 7–6. Income Smoothing Effect of Production Basis

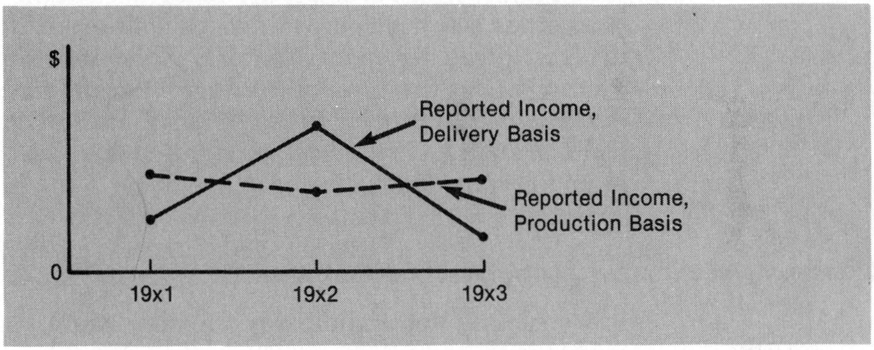

In addition to considering the effect of the percentage-of-completion method on reported earnings, justification for its use ultimately lies in the nature of the company's operations. For situations in which the method is appropriate, its use better reflects each period's actual activity. It would be wrong not to apply the percentage-of-completion method when in fact the circumstances warrant its use.

Estimating the percentage of completion

Estimating the percentage of completion isn't easy. Most authorities agree that it should be based on the amount of progress achieved rather than the amount of cost actually incurred, but how to measure progress is not at all clear. For example, should the purchase of materials to be used on the job be regarded as progress?

Probably the best solution is to decide in advance how much of the contract price is to be assigned to each phase of the contract, with most if not all of the weight assigned to labor and other services that are intended to add value to purchased materials. If the available evidence points to the probability of substantial cost overruns on remaining portions of the contract, however, the profit margin on the contract as a whole should be reestimated and a new allocation prepared. In practice, if the anticipated overrun is large enough to produce a loss on the contract, the entire amount of the anticipated loss will be reported immediately.

COLLECTION BASIS

In most situations, as we have already said, revenue is recognized at the time products or services are delivered to customers. We have also pointed out that the revenue-recognition criteria are sometimes met earlier, when goods are produced or work is done. When this is true, revenues are recognized at the time of production.

Another set of circumstances is that either the amount of cash to be collected or the amount of cost yet to be incurred isn't readily predictable at the time of production or delivery. In this situation, revenue recognition is deferred until cash or its equivalent is collected from the customer; this is called the *collection basis* of recognizing revenue.

Measuring inventories, receivables, and expenses

A strict application of the collection basis would require the accountant to capitalize all the costs related to particular products and customer orders until the customers have actually paid for the goods. At the time of delivery, the inventory asset would become a receivable, but it would continue to be measured at cost until the time of collection. No allowance for customer defaults would be made; instead, the costs of goods delivered to defaulting customers would be written off when the defaults were recognized.

On 100 orders like those described in our previous example, the company would capitalize $7,600 in costs prior to the collection point:

Materials	$20
Order getting	10
Production	40
Delivery	6
Total	$76 × 100 = $7,600

At the time of collection the company would:

Collect and recognize revenue	98 × $100 = $9,800 in cash

Recognize as expense	$100 \times \$5 = \$$	500 in warranty liability[1]
Spend and expense	$100 \times \$4 =$	400 in collection costs
Expense	$98 \times \$76 =$	7,448 in previously capitalized costs
Expense	$2 \times \$76 =$	152 as the cost of defaulted accounts
Total		$\overline{\$8,500}$

Recognize income	$= \$1,300$

In other words, the collection of cash would be the signal to the accountant to remove costs of $\$7,448 + \$152 = \$7,600$ from the receivables and recognize income of $1,300 ($9,800 − $8,500).

In practice, the order-getting and delivery costs might not be capitalized, for the reasons we cited earlier.

Use of the collection basis[2]

The collection basis is used very sparingly. Very few types of receivables are so uncertain of collection that customer defaults can't be forecasted accurately enough to satisfy the revenue criteria earlier than the time of collection. The collection basis is now encountered mainly in small businesses which sell services rather than goods.

The best-known application of the collection basis is in the *installment method,* used to account for certain types of installment sales. Under the installment method, revenues and expenses are recognized when customers make their installment payments, not before. Land development companies, for example, use the installment method because they can't predict collections and future costs reliably enough at the time of delivery or production. This method shouldn't be used for most installment sales of merchandise, how-

---

[1] We assume, for simplicity, that deliveries are made to dealers, some of whom default, but warranty service is provided to ultimate consumers who don't lose their warranty rights because the dealers default.

[2] The collection basis of revenue and expense recognition should not be confused with the so-called *cash basis* of accounting, the alternative to the accrual-basis system we are describing in this book. In cash-basis accounting, the expenses of a period are measured by the cash disbursements of that period; under the collection basis of revenue and expense recognition in accrual accounting, expenses may be recognized either before or after cash disbursements are made.

ever, because customer defaults ordinarily can be predicted quite accurately.

Before leaving this topic, we should point out that collection doesn't always *follow* the delivery of goods and services. In many cases the two events coincide, and sometimes customers even pay cash *before* delivery is made. Magazine subscribers, for example, usually pay cash before the publisher begins producing and delivering the magazines covered by the subscriptions. In such cases, revenues are recognized as magazines are published and mailed to the subscribers. Revenues aren't recognized when cash is received, because the first criterion of revenue recognition—completion of all significant revenue-producing activities—hasn't been met at that time. Instead, the receipt of cash gives rise to a liability.

COMPLETED OBLIGATIONS BASIS

In most cases, the final stage in the operating cycle is the completion of all obligations to the purchasers of the company's products or services. For companies with warranty obligations that hadn't existed in earlier years, this stage is being reached later than it used to be, and the revenue-recognition criteria are becoming harder to meet before the obligations have been completed than they used to be. Consumer groups and government agencies in the United States are more active in demanding product reliability, and individual consumers are more preconditioned to demand service, even beyond the end of formal warranty periods. This means that income measured at earlier stages is somewhat less predictable than it used to be in like circumstances.

Even so, accountants never use the completed obligations basis. The main reason is that waiting for the last obligation to be liquidated would deprive investors of timely information and thereby presumably reduce the quality of their decisions. Fortunately, the costs of warranty service are seldom a large percentage of the selling price, and the inaccuracies in estimates of warranty liabilities are relatively small. In other words, we can still use other methods even though product warranty costs are larger than they used to be.

IMPACT ON THE FINANCIAL STATEMENTS

Only one revenue-recognition basis is appropriate in any given situation. The three recognition criteria we discussed earlier—performance of service, determination of costs, and probability of collection—must be used, and they will point to only one method in each situation. The financial statements of a production-basis company don't have quite the same meaning as the statements of a collection-basis business, however, and the reader should be aware of these differences.

We have already seen that one effect of the production basis may be to reduce or "smooth" the fluctuations in reported income because the rate of production is likely to be more stable than the rate of delivery or the collection rate. The basis selected has other effects, however, even if the delivery pattern is stable. These effects depend on four factors:

1. The volume of business done.
2. The size of the profit margin.
3. The length of the operating cycle.
4. The rate of growth.

The no-growth case

To illustrate the effects of these factors, we'll use the amounts of net revenue and manufacturing cost we've been using right along, $98 and $60 a unit. To simplify the discussion, we'll assume that the $25 costs of order getting, delivery, collection, and warranty service are expensed as the expenditures for these purposes are made. We'll also assume a stable volume of production, deliveries, and collections of 160 units a year. The interval from production to delivery is three months; delivery and collection are separated by the same interval.

Income statement effects. At a zero growth rate, the number of units sold in an average period equals the number of units delivered and also the number of units on which collections are made. In other words, each of the three revenue-recognition bases—production, delivery, and collection—will lead to the same total revenue and, therefore, the same net income. In this case, net revenue will be $160 \times \$98 = \$15,680$ a year, no matter which revenue-recognition basis is used. The gross margin will be $160 \times (\$98 - \$60) = \$6,080$.

Balance sheet effects. The choice of the revenue-recognition basis will affect the balance sheet, even if business volume remains steady from period to period. Given our assumptions of three-month intervals between production and delivery and between delivery and collection, the company will always have three months of produced but undelivered production and three months of receivables from products already delivered to customers. The inventory at any time, therefore, will be 3/12 of 160, or 40 units. The receivables will represent another 40 units. At a cost of $60 a unit, the inventory or receivable will amount to $40 \times \$60 = \$2,400$; at $98, the net realizable value of 40 units will add up to $40 \times \$98 = \$3,920$.

If these assumptions hold, the following amounts will appear in the balance sheets of production-basis, delivery-basis, and collection-basis companies:

	Production Basis	Delivery Basis	Collection Basis
Accounts receivable	$3,920	$3,920	$2,400
Inventory	3,920	2,400	2,400
Total	$7,840	$6,320	$4,800
Percentage of delivery-basis total	124.1%	100.0%	75.9%

Since income is the same in all three cases, the apparent rate of return on investment for the collection-basis company is higher than for the other two companies—because of its smaller investment base.

Changing the assumptions.   What happens if we change the assumptions on which these calculations were based? The first three factors—profit margin, volume, and cycle length—will determine the relative size of the differences between revenue-recognition bases:

1. Increasing the profit margin from $38 a unit ($98 − $60) to some larger amount will increase the balance sheet differences.
2. Increasing the physical volume of business done from 160 units to some larger quantity will increase the balance sheet differences.
3. Lengthening the interval between production and delivery will increase the balance sheet differences between the production and delivery basis; lengthening the interval between delivery and collection will increase the balance sheet differences between the delivery and collection bases.

Conversely, decreasing the size of any one of these three variables—profit margin, volume, or interval—will decrease the balance sheet differences between bases.

Changes in the profit margin or volume of business, incidentally, will change the amount of income reported each year. Because there is no growth from year to year, however, the sale value of the goods delivered each year will be identical to the sale value of the goods produced and to the amount collected. The amount of income therefore will be identical for all three bases of revenue recognition.

The impact of growth

The illustration so far has reflected a no-growth assumption in which production, deliveries, and collections are all at the same level. Suppose, however, the business is growing by 32 units a year. Now we'll see differences in reported income as well as differences in balance sheet totals. The reason: Collections in one period arise from deliveries in an earlier period, when volume was lower, and from production in a still earlier period, when volume was lower yet.

The 32-unit annual growth in our revised example is achieved by increasing production by two units each quarter. While the production of 160 units represented quarterly volumes of 37, 39, 41, and 43 units in 19x1, the quarterly production in the next year was 45, 47, 49, and 51 units. This means that production each quarter was eight units larger than production in the comparable period a year earlier. Production figures for two years are shown in the upper panel of Exhibit 7–7. If revenues are recognized at the time of production, revenues and gross margins for 19x2 will reflect the production of the four quarters of 19x2—the top bar in the lower panel of the exhibit. If the delivery basis is used, however, revenues and gross margins will be recognized with a one-quarter lag.

EXHIBIT 7–7. Revenue Recognized on Different Bases in 19x2

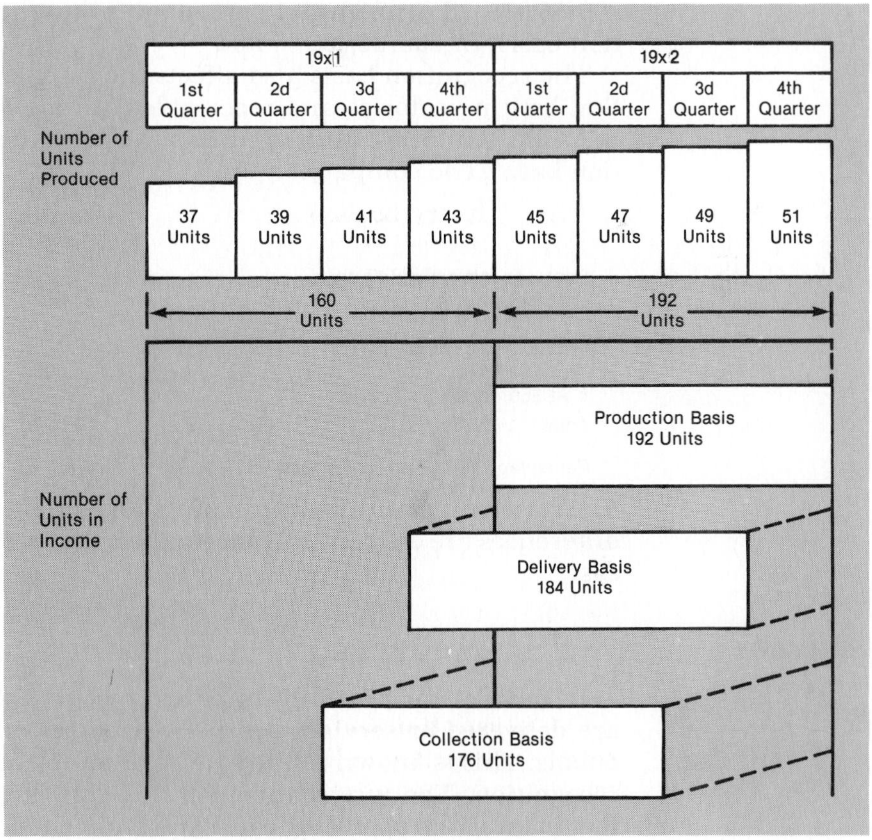

The second bar in this panel is slightly smaller. Since production in the fourth quarter of 19x1 was eight units less than production in the fourth quarter of 19x2, delivery-basis revenues are eight units less than production-basis revenues in this growth situation. The bar at the bottom of the lower panel is the smallest of all because the collection basis takes units into revenue with a two-quarter lag; that is, it brings in two quarters of 19x1 production instead of only one.

These amounts translate into the following gross margin results for 19x2:

	Production Basis	Delivery Basis	Collection Basis
Revenues (at $98)	$18,816	$18,032	$17,248
Directly related expenses (at $60)	11,520	11,040	10,560
Gross margin (at $38)	$ 7,296	$ 6,992	$ 6,688
Percentage of delivery-basis margin	104.3%	100.0%	95.7%

Using the production basis increases both revenues and gross margins by 4.3 percent over those yielded by the delivery basis ($7,-296/$6,992 − 1.0) and by 9.1 percent over those yielded by the collection basis ($7,296/$6,688 − 1.0).

The recognition basis also affects the asset amounts. Remember that both inventories and receivables are measured at cost under the collection basis; both are measured at value under the production basis. The comparison is:

	Production Basis	Delivery Basis	Collection Basis
Accounts receivable (49 units):			
At $98 value	$4,802	$4,802	
At $60 cost			$2,940
Inventory (51 units):			
At $98 value	4,998		
At $60 cost		3,060	3,060
Total	$9,800	$7,862	$6,000
Percentage of delivery basis total	124.7%	100.0%	76.3%

The basis-to-basis differences are substantial, but the percentage differences are only slightly larger than they were in the no-growth case.

SUMMARY

In most companies, revenues are recognized at the time goods are delivered or services are performed for outside customers or clients. This is known as the sale basis or delivery basis of revenue recognition. The justification for this rule is that delivery is the first point in the operating cycle at which the income is both earned and quantifiable with sufficient accuracy. Earlier revenue recognition would delay the transmission of information unnecessarily.

Under the delivery basis, the reported revenue is the selling price of the goods or services delivered, less discounts, returns, allowances, and any anticipated customer defaults arising from these transactions. If the goods or services are exchanged for an asset other than a short-term receivable, the revenue is measured by the current market value of the goods and services delivered or by the market value of the asset received from the customer, whichever is more clearly evident.

The costs of producing the delivered goods or services are subtracted, when the delivery basis is used, as expenses of the period in which delivery is made, along with the order-getting costs, delivery costs, and collection costs actually incurred during that period. If the costs of fulfilling the company's warranty obligations to its customers are likely to be substantial, estimates of these amounts are recognized as expenses when delivery is made; if the amounts are small, they will be expensed as they are incurred.

In delivery-basis companies, then, inventories are measured at the cost of production (including the costs of raw materials). Receivables are measured at the amount billed less the estimated customer defaults included in these amounts. A liability for warranty service is recognized if the future cost of discharging present warranty obligations is substantial.

The delivery basis is not always used. Revenues should be and are recognized prior to delivery if their contribution to income is both earned and accurately determinable earlier. They should be and are deferred to a later point if quantification is subject to too much uncertainty at the time of delivery. On these grounds, revenues are sometimes recognized as production takes place (production basis) or as cash is collected (collection basis). In each case, the expenses deducted from the revenues of a given period are the costs attributable to those revenues, to the extent that a ready basis can be found for linking costs with specific revenues. Until the point of revenue recognition, the inventory or account receivable is measured at cost.

KEY TERMS

Cash discount	Percentage-of-completion accounting
Collection basis	Production basis
Delivery basis	Revenue-recognition criteria
Income smoothing	Revenue-recognition basis
Installment method	Sales allowance
Materiality	Sales return
Net realizable value	

INDEPENDENT STUDY PROBLEMS (Solutions in Appendix B) _____

1. Effect of recognition basis on assets and owners' equity.   The Burfran Manufacturing Company has just been formed to produce a new product at a cost of $12 a unit, which will be paid in cash at the time of production. It will cost $6 a unit to sell the product, and this amount will be paid at the time of shipment. The sale price is to be $25 a unit; all sales will be on credit. No collection costs are incurred.

The following results are expected during the first two years of the company's operations:

	Units Produced	Units Shipped	Cash Collected from Customers
First year	100,000	70,000	$1,500,000
Second year	80,000	90,000	1,875,000

a. State the effect on the various assets and owners' equity of producing one unit, shipping one unit, and collecting $25, if revenue is recognized at the time of production.

b. What total income would the company report in each year if revenue were recognized at the time cash is collected from the customer? (For this purpose, assume that general administrative expenses amount to $200,000 a year and that income taxes are zero.)

2. Production basis versus delivery basis.   The Gilbert Company recognizes revenue at the time of production and classifies selling costs as expenses as they are incurred. You have the following information about Gilbert Company's operations for 19x1:

1. The company produced 100,000 units of product in 19x1 at a total production cost of $350,000. It sold and delivered 90,000 units at a price of $5 a unit.
2. Payments to factory employees and suppliers of raw materials and other goods and services for use in the factory (as described in item 1) totaled $330,000.
3. Factory depreciation (included in the production costs listed in item 1) amounted to $10,000.
4. Customer defaults were estimated to be $10,000.
5. Selling costs for the year, all paid in cash, totaled $80,000.
6. Administrative costs for the year, including collection costs, amounted to $50,000, all paid in cash.
7. Collections from customers totaled $420,000; write-offs of specific accounts as uncollectible totaled $8,500.
8. The company's liability under its product warranties was negligible.

a. Prepare an income statement for the Gilbert Company for the year 19x1. (Ignore income taxes.)

b. The company had no inventories at the beginning of 19x1. At what amount was the finished goods inventory reported on the company's December 31, 19x1, balance sheet?

    c. Recompute net income on the assumption that the company recognizes revenue at the time of delivery.

    d. What effect, if any, would changing to a delivery basis of revenue recognition have on the reported finished goods inventory figure?

EXERCISES AND PROBLEMS

    3. Cash-basis accounting versus collection basis of revenue recognition. Joan and Samuel Marx, doing business as Marx Enterprises, design and make fine wooden furniture. They have always kept their records on a cash basis, meaning that they have recognized revenues when customers have paid their bills, and have measured the expenses each year by the amounts of cash paid to employees, suppliers, and government agencies in that year.

    The business has grown, and the Marx family has been advised to move from the cash basis to accrual accounting. Because the company sells mainly to persons whose credit ratings are difficult to establish, they have decided to recognize revenues on the collection basis once the changeover to accrual accounting is made.

    a. What changes will have to be made immediately in the balance sheet of Marx Enterprises to reflect the changeover to accrual accounting?

    b. In what respects will the income statement on the collection basis differ from a cash-basis income statement?

    4. Measuring revenue. On January 1, 19x1, Arleigh Equipment Company sold and delivered 10 earth movers to Denby Contractors, Inc., at a list price of $20,000 each. To secure this order, Arleigh agreed to let Denby pay for this equipment on the following schedule:

Immediately	$ 50,000
One year later	50,000
Two years later	100,000

Arleigh recognizes revenues at the time of delivery. Denby made its payments on schedule. The applicable interest rate was 8 percent, compounded annually.

    a. How much revenue did Arleigh Equipment Company report at the time of delivery?

    b. How much revenue originating in the transaction with Denby did Arleigh include in income for the year 19x1? What caption would you assign to the number representing the difference between this amount and your answer to part *a*?

    5. Effects of transactions; different recognition bases. Quantify the effects on the assets, liabilities, and owners' equity of the events described in each of the following:

    a. The firm recognizes revenue at the time of production. *Events:* The firm produced goods at a cost of $10,000 and paid cash in this amount. The estimated selling price was $16,000, estimated selling costs were

$4,000, and collection costs and uncollectible accounts were insignificant.

b. The firm recognizes revenue at the time of delivery. *Events:* Goods which had cost $10,000 in a previous period were sold on account for $16,000. Selling costs, paid in cash, were $4,000. Estimated collection costs were $500. Of the $16,000, $300 was expected to be uncollectible.

c. The firm recognizes revenue at the time of collection. *Events:* Goods which had cost $12,000 in a previous period were sold on account for $19,000. Selling costs, paid in cash, were $3,500. Estimated collection costs were $200. Of the $19,000, $1,500 was expected to be uncollectible.

6. Measuring revenue.   The Herklion Company purchased a large quantity of used industrial equipment and shipped it to a foreign country for use in the government's industrialization program. Herklion paid $800,000 for the equipment and an additional $30,000 to transport it to the foreign country.

By the time the equipment arrived at its destination, the customer government had no foreign exchange to pay for it. Instead, it offered to give Herklion $100 of its own 15 percent bonds for every $95 due on the shipment of equipment. At that time, these bonds had a market value in the United States of $91 for every $100 of bonds.

Herklion accepted the offer and received $1 million in bonds which it kept for two years and then sold at a price of $90 for every $100 of bonds. During this two-year period, the foreign government paid interest promptly and regularly on these bonds at the prescribed interest rate of 15 percent a year.

a. Did the contractor make a profit or a loss on the equipment transaction? When and how much?

b. How, if at all, would your answer to part *a* have differed if the bonds had been sold immediately at the $91 market price?

c. How, if at all, would your answer have differed if the bonds had been held until their maturity date and then collected in full?

7. Delivery basis.   A company recognizes revenue at the time it ships merchandise to its customers. The beginning-of-year balance sheet showed gross accounts receivable of $20,000 and an allowance for uncollectibles of $1,000.

During the year, goods which cost $100,000 were shipped to customers on account for $160,000. Selling and administrative costs amounting to $40,000 were paid in cash.

Collections on accounts receivable amounted to $155,000 during the year. A bill-collecting agency was paid $5,000 for its services in helping the company collect a portion of this, representing part of the beginning-of-year balance in accounts receivable. Collection costs of this kind ordinarily amount to 3 percent of credit sales, but collection costs are expensed only when they are incurred.

Accounts with a face value of $1,200 were recognized as uncollectible during the year.

The company expects that 1 percent of its credit sales will eventually prove uncollectible and a year-end aging of accounts has confirmed that estimate for this year.

a. Prepare an income statement for the year, ignoring income taxes.
b. Show how the accounts receivable would be presented on the year-end balance sheet.
c. Is the company's method of accounting for collection costs consistent with the delivery basis of revenue recognition? Explain.

8. Choosing a recognition basis. Sam Stephens operates a pig farm. Each year his sows give birth to piglets, which he raises for eventual sale to meat packers. Each year he buys feed for the pigs and pays a hired man to feed them. Some years when pig prices are high, he sells more pigs than are born; in other years, he sells fewer pigs than are born, resulting in an increase in the total number and weight of his herd. Sales are always for cash, and quotations of prices from hog auctions are published daily in the newspapers.

a. What basis of revenue and expense recognition would be most meaningful to Stephens in this case? Explain your reasoning.
b. Assume that feed and labor costs average $2 per pig per month. A pig born on July 1 weighs 80 pounds in December when hog prices are 30 cents a pound. It is sold the following March for $40. Using the method of revenue recognition you selected in part *a,* compute the cumulative effect of these transactions on the figures shown as total assets and total owners' equity on the December 31 and March 31 balance sheets.

9. Comparing recognition bases. The Saranac Company produces a single product at a cost of $6 each, all of which is paid in cash when the unit is produced. Selling expenses of $3 a unit are paid at the time of shipment. The sale price is $10 a unit; all sales are on account. No customer defaults are expected, and no costs are incurred at the time of collection.

During 19x1, the company produced 100,000 units, shipped 76,000 units, and collected $600,000 from customers. During 19x2, it produced 80,000 units, shipped 90,000 units, and collected $950,000 from customers.

a. Determine the net income that would be reported for each of these two years:
    1. If revenue and expense are recognized at the time of shipment.
    2. If revenue and expense are recognized at the time of production.
    3. If revenue and expense are recognized at the time of collection.
b. Would the asset total shown on the December 31, 19x2, balance sheet be affected by the choice among the three recognition bases used in part *a*? What would be the amount of any such difference?

10. Delivery method and production method. Discovery of a precious metal called *Mep* has far-reaching ramifications for strategic military purposes. As a result, legislation has been enacted that makes it illegal for any person or business entity to possess even the slightest amount of Mep. However, rather than merely confiscate any Mep that might be extracted from underground reserves, the federal government is required to purchase the commodity for $3 a gram.

Stanley Corporation extracted 40,000 grams of Mep during 19x1, of which 25,000 grams were delivered to the government and for which cash was received. The cost of extraction was $2 a gram and administrative expenses were $12,000 for the year as a whole.

Stanley's year-end balance sheet contained the following six items:

Accounts payable ..	$187,000	Inventory	?
Capital stock	100,000	Plant assets	$180,000
Cash	90,000	Retained earnings ..	?

Prepare Stanley Corporation's 19x1 income statement and December 31, 19x1, balance sheet, using first the delivery method and then the production method. Explain your treatment of administrative expenses.

11. Percentage-of-completion accounting. Lark Construction Company was hired to build a stadium for $32 million. Work began late in 19x1 and the stadium was completed in 19x3. Lark had expected to earn $7 million in income before taxes on this project and did in fact earn this amount. Relevant data are:

Year	Amounts Billed	Cash Collected	Costs Incurred	Estimated Remaining Cost to Complete
19x1	$ 3,000,000	$ 1,900,000	$ 2,500,000	$22,500,000
19x2	22,500,000	14,100,000	17,500,000	5,000,000
19x3	6,500,000	14,400,000	5,000,000	—

Since most of Lark's previous construction jobs had been started and completed in the same calendar year, it had consistently recognized revenues and expenses when the jobs were completed. In light of the company's experience with the stadium project, however, Lark's management decided to investigate the desirability of adopting the percentage-of-completion method.

a. Calculate the percentage of completion each year. Explain the basis for your calculation and the reason you chose it.
b. Calculate each year's income under both methods.
c. What were the amounts of Lark's (1) receivables and (2) inventories at the end of each year under each method?

12. Different revenue-recognition bases. Swazy Company secured a contract with the state of Iowa for the construction of 15 miles of highway at a contract price of $1 million a mile. Payments were to be made as follows for each mile of construction:

1. 40 percent when concrete was poured.
2. 50 percent when all work on that mile was completed.
3. 10 percent when all 15 miles of highway were completed, inspected, and approved.

At the end of the first period of operation, five miles have been entirely completed and approved, concrete has been poured and approved on a second five-mile stretch, and preliminary grading has been done on the third five-mile stretch.

The job was originally estimated to cost $800,000 a mile. Costs to date have coincided with these original estimates and have totaled the following amounts: (1) $800,000 a mile on the completed stretch; (2) $640,000 a mile on the second stretch; and (3) $100,000 a mile on the third stretch. It is now estimated that each unfinished stretch will be completed at the costs originally estimated.

a. Determine revenue, expense, and income for the period to date if revenue is recognized at the time of production (percentage of completion).
b. Determine revenue, expense, and income if revenue is recognized at the time of shipment (completion).
c. Determine revenue, expense, and income if revenue is recognized at the time of delivery (completion).

13. Different revenue-recognition bases. The Aim Company, a farm corporation, produced the following in 19x1, its first year of operations:

	Selling Price per Bushel
9,000 bushels of wheat	$2.40
6,000 bushels of oats	1.40

During the year it sold two thirds of the grain produced and collected three fourths of the selling price on the grain sold; the balance of the selling price is to be collected in equal amounts during each of the two following years. You also have the following additional data for 19x1:

Depreciation on productive plant and equipment	$3,000
Other production costs (cash)	4,500
Administrative costs (cash)	3,600
Selling and delivery costs (incurred and paid at the time of sale) per bushel	0.10

Aim Company's administrative costs are incurred exclusively to support its production activities.

a. What is income before taxes in 19x1 if revenues are recognized when production is completed?
b. What is income before taxes in 19x1 if revenues are recognized when goods are delivered?
c. What is income before taxes in 19x1 if revenues are recognized when cash is collected from customers?

(AIPCA adapted)

14. Effect of recognition basis on income; managerial aspects. The XYZ Manufacturing Company was in a declining industry. Each year its sales decreased; each year it reduced its inventories; each year the accounts receivable balance decreased. Uncollectibles, fortunately, were insignificant.

In 19x1 the company delivered products to its customers with a total sales value of $1,050,000. It manufactured 10,000 units of product at a total manufacturing cost of $700,000, an average of $70 a unit. Its inventories of manufactured products, measured at their manufacturing cost, decreased in 19x1 by $35,000, to $210,000. The amounts due from customers decreased by $15,000, to $150,000. Selling and administrative costs totaled $200,000, none of them readily attributable to specific deliveries or collections.

Management expected deliveries to fall by 10 percent in 19x2. Selling and administrative costs would amount to $190,000; increasing them wouldn't increase deliveries enough to justify the expenditure. Production volume would also be reduced by 10 percent, but average manufacturing cost would remain at $70 a unit. The amount due from customers would be $15,000 less at the end of 19x2 than at the beginning. Selling prices were the same in 19x2 as in 19x1.

a. Calculate total revenue, gross margin, and income before taxes for 19x1: (1) on a production basis, (2) on a delivery basis, and (3) on a collection basis. You should assume that the ratio of manufacturing cost applicable to revenue was the same for all three bases. (Suggestion: Start with the delivery basis and then redo the calculation on the other two bases.)

b. Make the same calculations for 19x2.

c. In these circumstances, would you suggest that reports to management reflect the production basis for revenue recognition even though the company uses the delivery basis for public financial reporting? Why might management even consider doing this; that is, what purpose would it be intended to serve? In particular, consider whether this practice would be likely to do a better job than other methods of achieving the purpose you have ascribed to it.

15. Effect of recognition basis. The Naive Manufacturing Company produces a product at a cost of $7.50 a unit, all of which is paid at the time of production. It costs $2 a unit to sell the product, all of which is paid at the time the product is shipped to the customer. The sale price is $10 a unit. All sales are on account. Collection costs are 2 percent of the amount collected, all paid during the period of collection. No customer defaults are expected, and the income tax rate is zero.

During the first year of operation, the company expects to produce 20,000 units, to ship 18,000 units, and to collect $170,000 from its customers.

During the second year it expects to produce 30,000 units, to ship 29,000 units, and collect $280,000 from its customers.

a. Suppose the company recognizes revenue and all related expenses at the time of production:
  1. State the effect on the various assets and owners' equity of producing one unit and incurring the related production costs.
  2. State the effect on the various assets and owners' equity of shipping one unit and incurring the related selling costs.
  3. State the effect on the various assets and owners' equity of collecting $10 and incurring the related collection costs.
  4. What net income will be reported for the first year?
  5. What net income will be reported for the second year?

b. Repeat the calculations called for in part a, but on the assumption that the company recognizes revenue and all related expenses at the time of shipment.

c. Repeat the calculations called for in part *a*, but on the assumption that the company recognizes revenue and all related expenses at the time of collection.

d. Companies that recognize revenue at the time of shipment ordinarily treat collection costs as an expense of the period of collection. Using this procedure, what is the net income for each year?

e. Companies that recognize revenue at the time of collection ordinarily treat selling costs as an expense of the period in which they are incurred. Using this procedure, what is the net income for each year?

(Prepared by Professor Carl L. Nelson)

16. Usefulness as a criterion in choosing a recognition basis.[3]

Smith & Wells, Ltd., manufactures a variety of machined parts which it sells to customers in the automotive and transportation industries. About half the company's sales are of products listed in the company's regular catalog. The remainder of the annual sales is in custom items. Sales revenues for both types of products are recognized at the time the goods are shipped to the customers.

Deliveries of catalog items, except for very large orders, are made from warehouse inventories, which are allowed to fluctuate from month to month to help stabilize production levels.

Custom items, often designed to the customer's own specifications, are manufactured only upon receipt of a firm order. Cancellations of orders on which production operations have commenced are extremely rare, and Smith & Wells, Ltd., can always recover its costs on any such cancelled orders.

During 1981 the company's sales force turned in a gratifying 20 percent increase in new orders over their 1980 level, almost all the increase being for custom products. To meet this increased demand, the rate of production in the company's factory was increased twice during the year, once in July and once again in October. Because the production cycle for custom items averages four to six months, however, the increase in the rate of production did not lead to any marked rise in revenue.

In mid-January 1982, T. E. S. Evans, the managing director of Smith & Wells, Ltd., received a preliminary set of financial statements for 1981 from his chief accountant, J. B. Burke. Excerpts from these statements are shown in the exhibit on the next page.

Evans understood that income was recognized at the time of delivery, but asked Burke whether something could be done to reflect the increase in customer orders in the income figures. Burke replied that the company's auditors would never accept customer orders as evidence that revenue had been earned.

a. Could the revenue-recognition criteria be met for either product line under an order basis for revenue recognition? Under a production basis?

---

[3] Copyright 1967, 1982 by l'Institut pour l'Etude des Méthodes de Direction de l'Entreprise, (IMEDE), Lausanne, Switzerland. Reproduced by permission.

b. Reconstruct the income statements for 1980 and 1981 with revenues from custom products recognized at the time of production.
c. Do the income figures you derived in answer to part *b* provide a better measure of management's operating performance than those stated at the top of Exhibit 1? Would they meet Evans's objections to the existing reporting basis? Would you recommend a shift to the production basis?

EXHIBIT 1

SMITH & WELLS, LTD.
Selected Financial Data for 1979–81
(in 000s)

	1979	1980	1981
Net revenue from goods shipped:			
Catalog items	£xxx	£ 960	£ 970
Custom products	xxx	990	1,030
Total	xxx	1,950	2,000
Cost of goods shipped	xxx	1,170	1,240
Selling and administrative expenses	xxx	600	620
Net operating income before taxes and special charges	£xxx	£ 180	£ 140
New orders received, net of cancellations (at sale prices):			
Catalog items	£xxx	£ 980	£1,000
Custom products	xxx	1,020	1,400
Total	£xxx	£2,000	£2,400
Inventories on December 31 (at cost):			
Materials	£100	£ 100	£ 150
Work in process:			
Catalog items	45	50	50
Custom products	148	155	230
Finished goods (catalog items only)	470	500	480
Details of custom products work in process on December 31:			
Total contract sale prices	£480	£ 500	£ 625
Estimated total production cost	290	300	375
Production costs incurred to date	148	155	230
Percentage of work completed to date	50%	50%	60%
Orders on hand but not yet put into production on December 31, custom products (at contract sale prices)	£790	£ 800	£1,045

xxx—Data not available.

8

Inventory costing

Companies that recognize revenue on a production basis measure their inventories at the value of the net cash flows they will generate in the future, as we noted in Chapter 7. All other companies measure their inventories at their historical cost or at their market value, whichever is lower. The main purpose of this chapter is to explain how these companies determine the historical cost of their inventories and the cost of goods sold. We'll also explain how the market value of the inventories affects accountants' measurements.

HISTORICAL-COSTING METHODS

When each item passing through a company's inventory is unique, cost measurement is simple. As each item is received, its cost is identified as the cost of inventory. When it is sold, this cost becomes the cost of goods sold. Interchangeable items can't be accounted for this easily, however. In this section we'll identify the components of the costs of interchangeable items to be distributed in any period (the cost of goods available) and describe three commonly used methods of distributing these costs:

1. First-in, first-out (FIFO) costing.
2. Last-in, first-out, (LIFO) costing.
3. Average costing.

The cost of goods available

The total number of physical units sold or otherwise disposed of during a period and the number of units in the ending inventory must equal the total number of units available for sale during the period. By the same token, the total of the costs of the goods sold and the costs of the ending inventory must equal the total costs of the goods available for sale during the period.

For example, suppose a company had two units in inventory at the beginning of 19x1, bought ten units and sold eight units during the year, and had four units in inventory at the end of the year. Each of these units was acquired at a historical cost of $50. These amounts are shown in Exhibit 8–1. The numbers in the upper diagram refer to physical quantities; the amounts in the lower diagram

EXHIBIT 8–1.   Goods Acquired, Available, and Sold during a Period

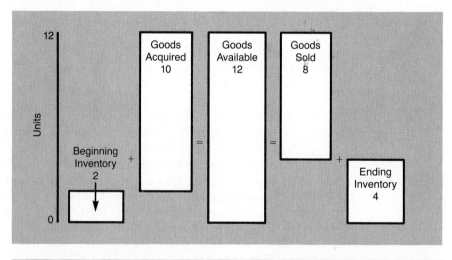

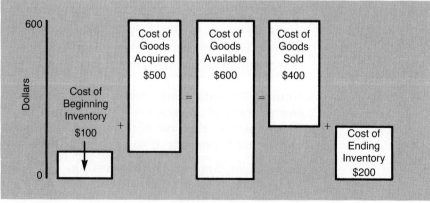

refer to dollars of cost. Goods available for sale in any period come from two sources: inventory at the beginning of the period and the quantity acquired during the period—represented by the two blocks at the left of each diagram. The total of these two sources is the goods available, represented by the large block at the center: the quantity available in the upper diagram, the cost of the goods available in the lower diagram.

Two things can happen to the goods available for sale in any period: They will either be sold (or stolen, damaged, evaporated, or lost in other ways) or remain in inventory at the end of the period.[1] If an item isn't sold or lost, it will be in inventory at the end of the period. These two outcomes are represented by the two blocks at the right in each diagram of Exhibit 8–1. In the upper diagram, the two blocks represent the number of units sold and the number of units still on hand. In the lower diagram, these two blocks represent the *cost* of goods sold and the *cost* of the ending inventory. The cost of the goods available thus becomes the cost of goods sold *and* the cost of the goods that remain in inventory at the end of the period.

From Exhibit 8–1 we see that the cost of goods sold in 19x1 was $400. If these goods were sold for $90 a unit, or a total of $720, the income statement would show the following:

Revenue from sale of goods	$720
Cost of goods sold	400
Gross margin	$320

The $200 cost assigned to the ending inventory will become the cost of the beginning inventory in the next period, and the cycle will be repeated.

First-in, first-out (FIFO) costing

The FIFO method assigns the oldest unit costs in the total cost of goods available to the items that are transferred out of the stockroom first. The ending inventory is therefore measured at the unit cost(s) of the purchase or purchases that were made closest to the end of the period.

For example, suppose a company started operating in 19x1. All the goods acquired during 19x1 cost $50 each, and at year-end four units remained in inventory. The company's beginning inventory in *19x2* therefore had a cost of $200 (4 × $50). The company bought seven units in April 19x2 at a price of $60 each, and eight units in July at $75 each. It sold 12 units during the year, leaving seven units in inventory at the end of the year.

---

[1] For inventories of materials destined for use in manufacturing, the words "goods issued" should be used in place of "goods sold."

EXHIBIT 8–2.   First-in, First-out (FIFO) Costing

19x2

Cost of goods available		*Cost distributed*	
Beginning inventory: 4 × $50	$ 200	Cost of goods sold:	
Purchases:		4 × $50	$ 200
7 × $60	420	7 × $60	420
8 × $75	600	1 × $75	75
Total purchases	1,020	Total cost of goods sold ..	695
		Ending inventory: 7 × $75	525
Total cost available	$1,220	Total cost distributed	$1,220

19x3

Cost of goods available		*Cost distributed*	
Beginning inventory: 7 × $75	$ 525	Cost of goods sold:	
Purchases: 13 × $85	1,105	7 × $75	$ 525
		7 × $85	595
		Total cost of goods sold ..	1,120
		Ending inventory: 6 × $85	510
Total cost available	$1,630	Total cost distributed	$1,630

The FIFO costing method divides the cost of the goods available in 19x2 as shown in the upper panel of Exhibit 8–2. The first four units sold are assigned a unit cost of $50, the cost of the *first* units that were available during the year ($200). The next seven units sold are assigned a cost of $60 each, the cost of the *next* units to become available during the year ($420). The twelfth unit sold is assigned a cost of $75 since that was the unit cost of the next batch of goods to be acquired. The FIFO cost of goods sold is the sum of these three amounts ($200 + $420 + $75 = $695).

The seven units in inventory at the end of the year are assigned the costs of the *last* seven units to enter the inventory during the year: 7 × $75 = $525. (The first-in, first-out method may also be viewed as the "last-in, still-here" method.) In fact, we could have started by determining the cost of the ending inventory, subtracting this from the total cost of goods available to determine the FIFO cost of goods sold:

Beginning inventory	$ 200
Goods acquired ($420 + $600)	1,020
Cost of goods available	1,220
Less: Ending inventory	525
Cost of goods sold	$ 695

The $525 FIFO cost of the December 31, 19x2, inventory is also the FIFO cost of the January 1, 19x3, inventory. The company bought 13 additional units in 19x3 at a cost of $85 each. It sold 14 units during the year and had six units in the inventory on December 31, 19x3. FIFO costing in 19x3 would produce the results shown in the lower half of Exhibit 8–2. The cost of goods sold consists of the cost of the seven units in the beginning inventory ($525), plus the cost of the first seven units purchased during 19x3 (7 × $85 = $595). The six units in the ending inventory are assigned the costs of the last six units bought during 19x3 ($85 each).

We should emphasize that FIFO costing—as well as the other two methods we'll describe shortly—is applied to groups of items that are identical and interchangeable. They are identical physically because they have the same physical properties (size, weight, etc.); they are identical economically because they will be used identically by those who buy them. In other words, the user will obtain the same satisfaction (or utility) from identical goods no matter which units are used. As a result, the current market prices of all the units will be identical at any given time, even if they have been acquired at different unit costs. Any units that aren't identical to the others should be treated separately, as a separate group or groups of products.

When the units available for sale are identical, as in our illustration, any division of costs between the goods that are sold and the goods that remain in inventory is arbitrary. This arbitrariness can't be avoided by choosing one method rather than another, because all methods produce arbitrary distributions of the cost of goods available. The real question is which method provides the most useful information. We'll return to this question after we've described the other available methods.

Last-in, first-out (LIFO) costing

The second method of dividing the total cost of goods available between the income statement (cost of goods sold) and the balance sheet (inventory on hand) is the last-in, first-out method, or LIFO. Under LIFO, unit costs enter the cost of goods sold in the reverse of the order in which they enter the cost of goods available; that is, the costs of the last purchase during the year are the first to be assigned to the cost of goods sold, the costs of the next to last purchase are the next to be assigned to the cost of goods sold, and so on. The costs in the ending inventory are determined by starting with the earliest costs in the cost of goods available ("first-in, still-here") and moving to later and later costs until the inventory quantity has been fully accounted for.

For example, our illustrative company was founded in 19x1. All its purchases in 19x1 were at a unit cost of $50, meaning that its December 31, 19x1, inventory of four units had a cost of $200, no matter what inventory method was used. The company bought 15 units in 19x2, seven of them on April 3 at $60 each and the other eight on July 17 at $75 each. The cost of goods available therefore was $1,220, as shown in the upper panel of Exhibit 8–3.

The LIFO distribution of these costs is shown in the right-hand section of the upper panel. As this shows, the company sold 12 units in 19x2. The *first* eight units sold are assigned the unit costs of the *last* eight units bought during the year (8 × $75 = $600). The cost of the other four units sold is measured at the unit cost of the *next most recent* purchase (4 × $60 = $240). The total of these two amounts is $840.

The LIFO cost of the ending inventory is measured by starting with the *oldest* unit cost and working forward. The cost assigned to the first four units in the ending inventory therefore is the cost

EXHIBIT 8–3. Last-in, First-out (LIFO) Costing

	19x2	
Cost of goods available		*Costs distributed*
Beginning inventory: 4 × $50 .... $ 200		Cost of goods sold:
Purchases:		First eight units: 8 × $75 ...... $ 600
7 × $60 420		Next four units: 4 × $60 240
8 × $75 600		Total cost of goods sold .. 840
		Ending inventory:
		19x1 layer: 4 × $50 200
		19x2 layer: 3 × $60 180
		Total inventory 380
Total cost of goods available $1,220		Total cost distributed $1,220

	19x3	
Cost of goods available		*Costs distributed*
Beginning inventory:		Cost of goods sold:
19x1 layer: 4 × $50 .... $ 200		First 13 units: 13 × $85 .... $1,105
19x2 layer: 3 × $60 180		Next unit: 1 × $60 60
Total inventory 380		Total cost of goods sold .. 1,165
Purchases: 13 × $85 1,105		Ending inventory:
		19x1 layer: 4 × $50 200
		19x2 layer: 2 × $60 120
		Total inventory 320
Total cost of goods available $1,485		Total cost distributed $1,485

of the four units in the beginning inventory, $50 each. This is known as the LIFO *base quantity,* or *initial layer.* The next oldest unit cost is the cost of the first lot purchased during the year, $60 a unit, and this is the cost assigned to the other three units in the ending inventory.[2] The $180 cost of these three units ($3 \times \$60$) constitutes the *19x2 layer* in the inventory. The total LIFO inventory therefore consists of two layers: the 19x1 layer of $200 and the 19x2 layer of $180, a total of $380. Once again, the total of the cost of goods sold and the cost of the ending inventory equals the cost of goods available, $1,220.

This illustration reflects the method known as *LIFO periodic,* in that variations in inventory levels during the year are ignored. Thus, none of the costs of the beginning inventory appear in the cost of goods sold as long as the number of units in the year-end inventory is at least as large as the number of units on hand at the beginning of the year. Even if the company was completely out of stock on March 31, 19x2, before the first new purchase was made, the entire cost of goods sold would still reflect 19x2 purchase prices.

The company entered the next year (19x3) with the same inventory (seven units at a total LIFO cost of $380) it had at the end of 19x2. It bought 13 units in 19x3 at a cost of $85 a unit. The cost of goods available in 19x3 therefore was $1,485, as shown on the left of the lower panel of Exhibit 8–3. This differs from the total cost of goods available in 19x3 under FIFO because the LIFO cost of the beginning inventory was only $380 instead of the FIFO cost of $525.

The company sold 14 units in 19x3, leaving six units in inventory at year-end. The LIFO cost of goods sold is once again determined by working backward, starting with the most recent purchase. The cost assigned to the first 13 units sold in 19x3 is therefore $13 \times \$85 = \$1,105$. The cost of the other unit sold comes from the beginning inventory. Since under LIFO the first costs to leave the inventory are the most recent costs to go into it, they must come first from the last-in layer, in this case the 19x2 layer: $1 \times \$60$. This transfer from the beginning inventory is known as a *LIFO liquidation.*

The six units in the ending inventory are measured at the six oldest unit costs in the beginning inventory. The oldest costs are those in the 19x1 layer (four units at $50); the remaining two units are measured at the unit costs of the 19x2 layer ($2 \times \$60$).

---

[2] In practice, a company may elect to distribute the cost of the current year's purchases in other ways—for example, at the average of all the current year's purchase prices. We'll ignore these alternatives in this chapter.

STUDY REMINDER

FIFO (first-in, first-out) is an inventory costing method which lists the units available for sale in any year and their unit costs in the order in which these units become available. The cost of goods sold is determined by starting with the oldest unit cost on the list and working forward until the requisite number of units has been included. The cost of the ending inventory is determined by starting with the most recent unit costs and working backward

LIFO (last-in, first-out) is an inventory costing method which lists the units available for sale in any year and their unit costs in the order in which these units become available. The cost of goods sold is determined by starting with the most recent unit cost and working backward until the requisite number of units has been included. The cost of the ending inventory is determined by starting with the oldest unit costs and working forward.

Average costing

The third major method of determining the cost of goods sold and the cost of the ending inventory is known as *average costing*. Under average costing, a single average cost per unit is used to determine both the cost of goods sold during a period of time and the cost of the inventory on hand at the end of that time. This average may be recalculated every time a new purchase is made, or once a month, or once a year.

Exhibit 8–4 illustrates the application of average costing, using a full year as the averaging period. This exhibit is based on the

EXHIBIT 8–4. Average Costing

	Units	Unit Cost	Total Cost	
Inventory, January 1, 19x2	4	$50	$ 200	
19x2 purchases:				
April 3	7	60	420	
July 17	8	75	600	
Available in 19x2	19		1,220 →	New average: $1,220/19 = $64.21
Goods sold in 19x2	12	64.21	771	
Inventory, December 31, 19x2	7	64.21	449	
19x3 purchases	13	85	1,105	
Available in 19x3	20		1,554 →	New average: $1,554/20 = $77.70
Goods sold in 19x3	14	77.70	1,088	
Inventory, December 31, 19x3	6	77.70	$ 466	

same data we used in illustrating the FIFO and LIFO methods. The calculation consists of dividing the total cost of the goods available for sale by the number of units available. During 19x2, 19 units were available for sale at a total cost of $1,220. Dividing $1,220 by 19 units gives an average cost of about $64.21 a unit. The 12 units that were sold in 19x2 therefore have an average cost of $771 (12 × $64.21, rounded to the nearest dollar), and the seven units in the ending inventory appear in the balance sheet at $449 (7 × $64.21).

These amounts appear in the middle of the right-hand column in Exhibit 8–4. The remainder of the exhibit shows what happens when the procedure is repeated in 19x3. Notice that each unit in the beginning inventory brings with it a cost of $64.21. Since these units are available in 19x3, their cost is included in the determination of 19x3's average unit cost. As the exhibit indicates, 19x3's average unit cost turns out to be $77.70—heavily influenced by the $85 unit cost incurred during the year but also by the $64.21 unit cost of the beginning inventory. Using $77.70, we can distribute the $1,554 cost of the goods available—$1,088 (14 × $77.70) to the goods sold and $466 (6 × $77.70) to the ending inventory.

CONSEQUENCES OF THE CHOICE OF COSTING METHOD

Although LIFO isn't an acceptable costing method in some countries, all three inventory costing methods described in the preceding section are equally acceptable for U.S. companies. Management is therefore free to choose among them, subject to the requirement that the method selected be used consistently, year after year. This being the case, we need to answer four questions:

1. Which method is most likely to maximize the company's net income?
2. Which method is most likely to minimize the company's income taxes and therefore maximize its net cash flow?
3. Which method is most likely to have the greatest information value?
4. Which method is least subject to abuse?

Because average costing and FIFO costing produce virtually identical income and cash-flow amounts in most practical situations, we'll limit our analysis to a comparison of FIFO and LIFO.

Income effects

Other things being equal, management would rather report higher income to the company's shareholders than smaller income.

This preference may be due in part to executive compensation agreements that tie managerial bonuses and other rewards to the company's reported income. Another reason that higher income is more attractive than low income may be that the company's creditors have imposed restrictions on managerial actions if reported income (or retained earnings) falls below a specified level.

A third possible explanation of managers' preference for high rather than low income is that they may assume that large reported earnings can induce higher market prices for the company's shares. Although research in the past two decades suggests that this result is likely to occur only if larger positive cash flows will follow as well,[3] many managers apparently believe that the market accepts earnings numbers at face value.

Management's decision on which method to adopt should be based on its estimate of the impact of this decision in most future periods rather than in one year only. Whether FIFO or LIFO is likely to maximize net income in most years depends mainly on whether acquisition prices are rising or falling. In general, FIFO leads to a higher net income than LIFO if prices are rising. The cost of goods sold amounts in our illustration in the preceding section were as follows:

	FIFO Cost of Goods Sold	LIFO Cost of Goods Sold	Difference
19x2	$ 695	$ 840	$155
19x3	1,120	1,165	45

With a smaller cost of goods sold in periods of rising prices, FIFO produces a larger gross margin and a greater net income.

Income considerations therefore favor the use of FIFO costing for any item that is subject to a generally rising price trend. But how does the choice affect income in any one year? The answer depends on a number of factors, mainly the following:

1. Whether prices this year are higher or lower than the FIFO unit cost of the beginning inventory.
2. Whether the physical inventory quantity at the end of the year is greater than, equal to, or less than the inventory on hand at the beginning of the year.
3. If a liquidation takes place, the size of the liquidation relative to the quantity of goods sold.
4. If a liquidation takes place, whether the spread between current

---

[3] For a summary of evidence on this point, see Nicholas J. Gonedes and Nicholas Dopuch, "Capital Market Equilibrium, Information Production, and Selecting Accounting Techniques: Theoretical Framework and Review of Empirical Work," *Studies in Financial Accounting Objectives: Supplement to the Journal of Accounting Research,* 1974, pp. 48–169.

acquisition prices and the average price of the liquidated LIFO layers is greater than the increase in price from the preceding year.[4]

If the inventory quantity increases or remains constant, FIFO income will exceed LIFO income when acquisition prices are increasing, will equal LIFO income when prices are steady, and will be less than LIFO income when prices are falling. The reason is that LIFO never brings prior-year prices into the income statement if inventories increase or remain constant, whereas FIFO always brings these old prices into the cost of goods sold. If prices are rising, these old prices will be lower than LIFO costs; if prices are falling, the old prices will be higher than current LIFO costs.

The comparison is more complex for a year in which an inventory reduction takes place. Whether FIFO cost of goods sold will exceed the LIFO cost of goods sold in that year depends on the relative size of two amounts:

Expression 1	Decrement quantity	$\times$	Current price − Average price of liquidated LIFO layers
Expression 2	Beginning inventory quantity	$\times$	Current price − Price of beginning FIFO inventory

If the first of these amounts is greater than the second, then the LIFO cost of goods sold will be less than the FIFO cost of goods sold. If the second expression is greater, then the LIFO cost of goods sold will be greater than the FIFO cost of goods sold. And if the two expressions are equal, LIFO and FIFO incomes will be identical.

The price difference in the first of these expressions is a *cumulative* difference and thus ordinarily will be greater than the price difference in the second expression if the secular trend of prices is upward. The decrement quantity is likely to be a small percentage of the beginning inventory quantity, however, and this means that unless current prices are stable, falling, or rising very slowly, the LIFO cost of goods sold ordinarily will exceed the FIFO cost of goods sold, even in a year in which an inventory liquidation takes place.

---

[4] This analysis applies to a single type of inventory and to situations in which all inventory classes are subject to the same price and quantity changes. The effects of the choice are more difficult to categorize when the inventory includes a mixture of items, some with rising prices and some with falling prices, some with increasing quantities and some with decreasing quantities.

Our earlier illustration can be used to show how this analysis works. We had a one-unit LIFO liquidation, bringing $60 out of the inventory in a year in which the current price was $85. The beginning inventory consisted of seven units at a FIFO unit cost of $75. Our two expressions are:

1. $1 \times (\$85 - \$60) = \$25$
2. $7 \times (\$85 - \$75) = \$70$

The first expression tells us that the LIFO gross margin would be $25 greater than it would have been if the company had bought another unit at $85, thereby avoiding the liquidation. The second expression tells us that the FIFO gross margin would be $70 greater than it would have been if the entire cost of goods sold had been measured at the current $85 price. The decrement wasn't large enough to offset this, and the FIFO gross margin therefore was larger than the LIFO gross margin.

Suppose a three-unit liquidation had taken place in 19x3, however. The most recent LIFO layer consisted of three units at $60 each. The first of our two expressions therefore would have been:

Expression 1: $3 \times (\$85 - \$60) = \$75$

This exceeds the value of the second expression by $5, showing that the LIFO cost of goods sold would have been $5 less than the FIFO cost of goods sold that year—assuming, of course, that the adoption date for LIFO was no later than the beginning of 19x2.

Exhibit 8–5 summarizes the income effects of the choice between FIFO and LIFO under different conditions.

Income tax effects

If cash flow were the only variable, management would be expected to choose the method that would maximize the company's cash flows. A large net cash flow gives management the ability to make the company grow, to pay its employees competitive salaries and wages, to declare cash dividends, and to reward the managers themselves. The more cash that can be generated, the faster the company can grow and the greater the prestige and monetary rewards the managers can reap for themselves.

The only direct effect of the choice of inventory method on cash flow is on the company's income taxes. A peculiarity of income taxation in the United States is that a company that elects to use LIFO for tax determination can't use FIFO or average costing for financial reporting. Although our concern, as always, is with the measurement of results and position for financial reporting, we must consider the tax effects because these are likely to have a strong influence on management's choice of inventory methods.

The impact of the FIFO/LIFO choice on taxable income is the same as its impact on the income before income taxes that is reported in the company's financial statements. If FIFO income is greater than LIFO, therefore, FIFO income taxes will be greater than LIFO's—and FIFO net cash flow therefore will be smaller than LIFO's. Conversely, in a year in which LIFO income is greater than FIFO income would be, LIFO's net cash flow will be less than FIFO's net cash flow. We could construct another exhibit identical to Exhibit 8–5 to show the effects of the FIFO/LIFO choice on the company's net cash flow in any subsequent year; the only difference is that the cash flow would be shown to be smaller in any period in which income was larger, and vice versa.

LIFO generally meets the cash-flow criterion better than FIFO

EXHIBIT 8–5. FIFO versus LIFO: Impact on Income in a Given Year

If Current Unit Price Is: And Ending Inventory Is:	Higher than in the preceding year	The same as in the preceding year	Lower than in the preceding year
Greater than the beginning inventory	LIFO income will be smaller than FIFO income	LIFO and FIFO income will be the same	LIFO income will be larger than FIFO income
The same as the beginning inventory	LIFO income will be smaller than FIFO income	LIFO and FIFO income will be the same	LIFO income will be larger than FIFO income
Smaller than the beginning inventory	LIFO income will be greater than FIFO income if the value of expression 1 exceeds the value of expression 2, and vice versa; FIFO and LIFO income will be the same if the values of the two expressions are equal	LIFO income will be larger than FIFO income if liquidated LIFO layers have unit costs lower than current unit cost	LIFO income will be larger than FIFO income if liquidated LIFO layers have unit costs lower than current unit cost

because the prices of most products and commodities have been and continue to be on long-term upward trends. In addition, since most businesses are usually growing, the quantity of inventory that is bought and sold tends to be increasing as well. With a combination of rising prices and generally rising or steady inventory levels, LIFO produces a greater cost of goods sold, lower income taxes, and a greater net cash flow than FIFO.

Notice that the tax advantage of LIFO in a period of rising prices is cumulative—and it isn't cancelled out when prices eventually stabilize. By placing more costs on the income statement and therefore on the income tax return, the company places fewer costs on the balance sheet. The difference in inventory cost therefore is the cumulative difference in taxable income. For example, the costs of the December 31, 19x3, inventory in our previous illustration were as follows:

FIFO inventory cost (Exhibit 8–2)	$510
LIFO inventory cost (Exhibit 8–3)	320
Difference	$190

In other words, the use of LIFO in the illustrative solution would shield $190 of the company's cash flow from taxation in 19x2 and 19x3. And because the LIFO cost of the first two inventory layers would remain constant forever as long as the inventory never fell to a lower level, this tax advantage would persist as long as current prices remained above the 19x2 level.

In practice, management's inventory method decision is usually whether to switch to LIFO from FIFO or average costing, effective in the fiscal year that has just ended. The reason is that FIFO and average costing have been in use much longer than LIFO and one of them is likely to have been adopted long ago in the company's history. Whenever prices move upward sharply and appear likely to continue rising for a number of years, the tax advantages of LIFO are likely to seem more important to management than its unfavorable income effects. In 1974 alone, a year of great price changes, 153 of a sample of 600 of the largest U.S. corporations changed the bulk of their inventories to LIFO. By 1981, 66 percent of the companies in this group had all or part of their inventories on LIFO.[5]

The decision to adopt LIFO shouldn't be based on the situation in a single year, of course; the switch, however, should be made in a year in which LIFO will reduce taxable income. This means that the LIFO base quantity will be at a low unit cost relative to the year-end FIFO cost, and this low cost will carry forward into

---

[5] See *Accounting Trends and Techniques,* 31st and 35th editions [New York: American Institute of Certified Public Accountants, 1977 (p. 111) and 1981 (p. 136)].

the future. Since inventory method decisions are made after the end of the year but before the tax returns and financial statements for the year have been prepared, management has the data necessary to make the LIFO/FIFO comparison for the year. If the long-term price trend is upward but prices fell during the year just ended, the switch to LIFO can be postponed.

Information effects

Outsiders are expected to use the data in company financial statements to predict the amount and timing of the company's future cash flows *and* the uncertainty surrounding them. The inventory costing method with the greatest information value therefore is the method that is the most likely to be useful to those who make these predictions.

Although it isn't entirely clear how this requirement can be implemented, we suggest it might mean that the preferable method is the one that comes closest to providing investors and other outsiders with the following:

1. The dollar cost assigned to the goods sold should help the investor identify the *sustainable gross margin*—that is, the profit the company can sustain on a continuing basis.
2. The dollar cost of the inventory on hand should bear a normal relationship to the amount to be realized from a future sale of that inventory.

Sustainable gross margin. Sustainable gross margin is the spread between products' selling prices and replacement costs. As the cost of buying goods increases, the selling price is likely to rise as well. If the selling price doesn't increase as fast as the unit cost rises, the company's ability to generate cash and pay dividends will be reduced. The company will also find it difficult to continue to replace the sold goods and to maintain its operating capacity at the previous level, let alone expand it. Investors in turn might reasonably conclude that the company is stagnating and losing its competitive edge.

Insights such as these can be obtained by examining income amounts that reflect a company's sustainable gross margin. Measures of net income that don't reflect the spread between selling price and replacement cost may convey erroneous and misleading impressions if they are used in these kinds of analyses. For example, suppose a retailer buys 10 units of merchandise from a wholesaler at $10 a unit and sells them to retail customers at a price of $15, a margin of $5 a unit. If the replacement cost has risen to $12 at the time of the sale, the sustainable gross margin will be only $3 a unit. Unless conditions change, the gross margin on the *next* sale of 10 units will be only $3 a unit, because the cost of goods sold will be $12, not $10, a unit.

Given this argument, the best inventory method is the method which produces a gross margin that best approximates the margin between the current selling price and the current acquisition cost of the items sold. In a period of stable or increasing inventory levels, the LIFO cost of goods sold is likely to be closer than FIFO to the current acquisition price.

The main disadvantage of LIFO is that the direction and size of the gap between LIFO gross margin and sustainable gross margin are difficult to determine when inventory liquidation takes place. The FIFO cost of goods sold can be closer to current acquisition cost than LIFO if a substantial inventory reduction takes place, bringing lower prior-year prices into the cost of goods sold. FIFO may also produce better approximations of sustainable gross margin if purchases are made during the year at prices that reflect unusual conditions. For example, if most purchases during the year are made at penalty prices during a strike in suppliers' plants, these will be reflected in their entirety in the LIFO cost of goods sold if the year-end inventory is at or below the beginning-of-year level. The FIFO cost of goods sold in that year may be closer to the normal replacement cost.

In short, LIFO may approximate the current replacement cost of goods sold better than FIFO, but not always. Furthermore, the amount and direction of the error are difficult to estimate without supplemental information.

Inventory measurement.   In a strict sense, inventories are measured at their historical cost because this shows the amount of resources that have been used to acquire them. Many readers of balance sheets, however, interpret *cost* to be a surrogate for the *value* of companies' inventories. Although accountants disclaim any responsibility for this interpretation, many readers of financial statements would like to use the cost of companies' inventories as the basis for imputing the value of the merchandise on hand. This value, in turn, becomes an important number for investors seeking to predict the company's future cash flows. They reason that cost is a reasonable approximation of the amount that will remain from the ultimate selling price after deducting such factors as selling costs, interest on investment, customer defaults, and normal merchandising profit.

This assumption, if it is valid at all, is valid only if the unit costs in the end-of-period inventory reflect current or near-current prices. Prices paid for inventory in the distant past have no relevance to how much can be recovered from their sale today. The only prices that come close to answering this question are those that could be obtained for the inventory sold in an orderly manner, less selling costs, customer defaults, and interest on the investment in the inventory in the interim. Alternatively, under certain conditions, current replacement costs could serve as surrogates for the recoverable amounts.

FIFO does a better job of approximating the current replacement cost of inventories than LIFO does. The unit costs in a FIFO inventory are seldom more than a few months old; LIFO inventories, by contrast, may be measured at the unit costs of 10, 20, or even more years in the past.

Susceptibility to abuse

Outside readers of financial statements need assurance that management has few opportunities to affect net income by taking actions that don't affect the company's wealth. FIFO passes this test better than LIFO.

For example, suppose a company is approaching the end of its fiscal year with fewer items in inventory than it had at the beginning of the year. If it takes no action, and if LIFO is used, some of the current year's cost of goods sold will be measured at prior-year prices. Management can prevent this by buying enough before the end of the year to bring the inventory up to the beginning-of-year level. Management therefore is in a position to affect net income by its year-end purchasing decisions. Under FIFO, these purchasing decisions will merely affect the cost of the ending inventory.

REPORTING REPLACEMENT COST DATA

The comparisons in the preceding paragraphs demonstrate that no one method is the answer to all the questions we raised at the beginning of this section. We'll examine the implications of these differences in Chapter 14, but before leaving the subject we should mention that almost 1,500 of the largest U.S. companies have been required since 1980 to supplement their conventional financial statements with estimates of current replacement costs. This requirement is a response to recognition of the need for information for use in judging the information value of reported gross margins and inventory costs and in judging the effects of LIFO inventory liquidations.

Exhibit 8–6 presents data which appeared in the 1980 annual reports of two large U.S. corporations: Monsanto Company, which used LIFO, and Dart & Kraft, Inc., which used FIFO costing. The

EXHIBIT 8–6.   Current-Cost Disclosures: Two Corporations ($ millions)

	Monsanto Company (LIFO)	Dart & Kraft, Inc. (FIFO)
Cost of goods sold, 1980:		
Current cost	$5,161.5	$7,122.1
Historical cost	5,149.0	7,032.8
Excess	$ 12.5	$ 89.3
Inventory, December 31, 1980:		
Current cost	$1,340.3	$1,700.6
Historical cost	832.3	1,646.9
Excess	$ 508.0	$ 53.7

current cost of Monsanto's goods sold was $12.5 million greater than its LIFO-based cost of goods sold—less than one quarter of 1 percent. By contrast, the current cost of Dart & Kraft's goods sold was $89.3 million greater than its FIFO-based cost of goods sold. The difference at Dart & Kraft was relatively small because the company had a relatively high inventory turnover (i.e., its opening inventory was a very small percentage of the total cost of goods sold)—but in percentage terms it was still five times as large a difference as at Monsanto. The significant differences were in the ending inventory measurements: The current cost of Monsanto's ending inventory was 61 percent greater than its LIFO cost, while the current cost of Dart & Kraft's inventory assets was only 3 percent greater than the FIFO cost.

What needs to be emphasized is that when current-cost disclosures accompany financial statements, readers are better able to estimate companies' sustainable profit margins—as well as the current value of the inventory on hand—than with historical-cost data alone.

THE LOWER-OF-COST-OR-MARKET RULE

Conventional financial statements measure nonmonetary assets on the basis of their historical cost. If the market value of the ending inventory is lower than its recorded cost, however, the asset is written down to market value. The write-down results in income statement recognition of a loss: A loss is any reduction in an asset for which there is no compensating benefit. The procedure through which the asset basis is reduced and the loss is recognized is called the *lower-of-cost-or-market* rule.

To illustrate, suppose a company has an ending inventory of 10 units at a FIFO cost of $25 each. Just prior to year-end, the market value of this merchandise falls to $18 a unit. The inventory will be written down by $7 a unit ($25 − $18), a total of $70. Let's now assume that the income statement contains sales revenues of $800, cost of goods sold of $450, and other expenses of $220. The $70 write-down loss this year is recognized as a determinant of this year's income, with alternative disclosure formats as follows:

	Format A	Format B
Sales revenues	$800	$800
Cost of goods sold	450	520
Gross margin	350	280
Operating expenses	220	220
Inventory loss	70	—
Total	290	220
Income before income taxes	$ 60	$ 60

Notice that the ending inventory will be reported as $180 (10 × $18). This is the amount of the asset's historical cost that the company will carry forward into the next year. Under FIFO, it will be the cost of the first 10 units sold in the next year. In other words, *the year-end inventory is still measured on a cost basis, even under the lower-of-cost-or-market rule;* current market value measures the proportion of the historical cost the company normally can expect to recover in the future—and the written-down amount is treated as a cost amount in all subsequent accounting.

Pros and cons

The argument in favor of the lower-of-cost-or-market rule is that no asset should appear on a company's balance sheet in an amount greater than is likely to be recovered from the use or sale of that asset in the normal course of events. Unrecoverable amounts have no value and therefore aren't assets. The main objection to this rule is that it treats value increases and value decreases differently. If the market value of merchandise is greater than its cost, there is no recognition of the increased value on the balance sheet.

What we have, then, is an adjustment that is used in only one direction. This inconsistent approach is defended by accountants on the grounds of "conservatism." Even though the market-value data are as reliable and as relevant whether they are greater or less than cost-based amounts, accounting doesn't recognize value increases until they are realized in arm's-length transactions. The nature of decreases in value, on the other hand, demands measurement and disclosure as soon as the marketplace indicates the likelihood of an adverse outcome.

Generally accepted accounting principles in the United States require the use of the lower-of-cost-or-market rule, no matter which method is used to establish the cost of the ending inventory. LIFO-basis companies can't use the lower-of-cost-or-market rule for tax purposes in the U.S., however. If market value drops below year-end LIFO cost, the inventory must continue to be measured at LIFO cost for tax purposes. This seldom affects a company's cash flows, because LIFO unit costs are almost always much lower than current market values.

Definition of market value

Determining the market value of the inventory is a judgmental process for which the accounting profession has developed technical guidelines. We needn't concern ourselves with the details of these guidelines, except to say that market value is usually determined either by net realizable value or by current replacement cost. *Net realizable value* is the amount of cash an outside buyer will pay in an orderly transaction (i.e., not a forced sale), reduced by any costs that must still be incurred to make the inventory ready for sale, sell it, and collect the proceeds.

Current replacement cost is likely to be used if it is easier to determine than net realizable value and if there is no reason to suspect that net realizable value is lower than replacement cost. Net realizable value is the *maximum* amount accountants will use to measure an inventory's market value. It will be used when it is more readily measurable than current replacement cost.

Inventory pooling

An important issue in the application of the lower-of-cost-or-market rule is whether inventory write-downs should be calculated for individual products or for groups of related products.

For example, suppose a company has two items in inventory—a unit of product X with a cost of $30 and a market value of $35, and a unit of product Y with a cost of $50 and a market value of $48. If the rule is applied product by product, product Y will be written down to $48, a $2 write-down. If the rule is applied to the two products as a group, however, no write-down will be made—because total market value ($35 + $48) exceeds total cost ($30 + $50).

As this illustration shows, product-by-product application of the rule will lead to more write-downs and lower reported inventories than application of the rule to pools. The main purpose of the lower-of-cost-or-market rule is to insure that reported inventory doesn't exceed its recoverable value, however; pooling is likely to achieve that.

SUMMARY

When revenues are recognized at the time of delivery, inventories are measured for financial reporting purposes at their historical costs. When different units of product are interchangeable, the costs of the goods available in any year are distributed between the cost of goods sold and the cost of the ending inventory on the basis of a preselected sequence. The main inventory costing sequences are first-in, first-out (FIFO), last-in, first-out (LIFO), and average costing. Each method is equally acceptable in financial reporting by U.S. businesses.

In periods of rising prices, LIFO tends to produce a higher cost of goods sold and lower net income in most periods than either FIFO or average costing, because current acquisition costs constitute more of the LIFO cost of goods sold than of the FIFO or average-costing cost of goods sold. For the same reason, LIFO is likely to produce income statements that reflect the concept of the sustainable gross margin better than FIFO-based statements in most periods, but the closeness of fit varies and is difficult to determine without supplemental information.

Because LIFO produces a higher cost of goods sold in most periods when prices are rising, it also produces lower income taxes if it is used for income tax determination. LIFO inventory costs are usually a much poorer approximation than FIFO costs to the current acquisition costs of the goods in inventory. Finally, LIFO is more subject to abuse than FIFO because inventory reduction will bring prior years' purchase prices into the LIFO cost of goods sold, and management can control whether this reduction will take place and how large it will be.

In addition to using an inventory costing method consistently each year, accountants compare the derived cost of the period's ending inventory with its market value. When the indicated value is less than the recorded cost, the asset is written down and a loss is recorded, resulting in reduced income for the period. Such adjustments are made only when value is less than cost, not when value exceeds cost. In practice, because the LIFO cost of the inventory almost never exceeds market value, this lower-of-cost-or-market adjustment ordinarily comes into play only in connection with inventories measured on a FIFO or average-costing basis.

KEY TERMS

Average costing
Current cost
First-in, first-out (FIFO)
Last-in, last-out (LIFO)
LIFO inventory layer
LIFO liquidation

Lower-of-cost-or-market rule
Market value
Net realizable value
Replacement cost
Sustainable gross margin

INDEPENDENT STUDY PROBLEMS (Solutions in Appendix B)

1. FIFO cost; LIFO cost. The Higby Company had 10,000 pounds of product in inventory on January 1, 19x1, at a FIFO cost of $30,000. Management decided to switch to the LIFO method beginning in 19x1. Purchases and sales for the next eight years were as follows:

Year	Purchases	Sales (pounds)
19x1	60,000 × $3.10 = $186,000	55,000
19x2	70,000 × $3.50 = 245,000	68,000
19x3	90,000 × $3.75 = 337,500	80,000
19x4	70,000 × $3.80 = 266,000	72,000
19x5	80,000 × $4.00 = 320,000	75,000
19x6	70,000 × $4.25 = 297,500	80,000
19x7	100,000 × $4.40 = 440,000	85,000
19x8	95,000 × $4.50 = 427,500	95,000

a. Calculate the LIFO cost of goods sold for each year and the LIFO cost of the inventory at the end of each year.
b. Calculate the FIFO cost of goods sold for each year and the FIFO cost of the inventory at the end of each year.

2. FIFO and LIFO exercise. New York Corporation made the following purchases during its first year of operation:

January 10, 19x7	1,000 units @ $3.00
March 20, 19x7	2,000 units @ 3.25
May 12, 19x7	2,500 units @ 3.30
November 10, 19x7	1,200 units @ 4.00
December 20, 19x7	1,800 units @ 4.05

The company sold 6,000 units during 19x7 at a price of $5 a unit. It had pretax operating expenses of $5,000 and was subject to income taxes at a rate of 25 percent.

a. Calculate the cost of goods sold, the cost of the ending inventory, and the gross margin, all on a FIFO basis.
b. Perform the same calculations, using LIFO costing.
c. Discuss the impact of the choice between the two inventory costing methods on the company's income and cash flows.

3. Lower-of-cost-or-market rule. Apex Corporation has four products in inventory at year-end:

Product	No. of Units	Cost/Unit	Market Price/Unit
A	10,000	$10	$ 8
B	20,000	15	16
C	30,000	20	23
D	40,000	10	8

a. Calculate the ending inventory by applying the lower-of-cost-or-market rule (1) item by item and (2) to the inventory as a whole.

b. Calculate the effect on the net income of using one version of the lower-of-cost-or-market rule instead of the other.

c. Which way of applying the lower-of-cost-or-market rule do you prefer? State your arguments.

4. LIFO: effect of inventory liquidation and replenishment. The Franklin Steel Warehouse Company adopted LIFO on January 1, 19x2, and its 15,000-ton inventory was costed at its FIFO cost of $125 a ton on that date, a total of $1,875,000.

During 19x2, the company purchased 100,000 tons at an average price of $130 a ton, and sold 95,000 tons. The last 20,000 tons purchased during December 19x2 cost $135 a ton.

Sales in 19x3 amounted to 105,000 tons, but purchases totaled only 90,000 tons at an average cost of $140 a ton. (The last 5,000 tons purchased during 19x3 also cost $140 a ton). The inventory was down to 5,000 tons at the end of 19x3 because a steel strike had cut off supplies. The company expected to rebuild its inventories to 15,000 tons as soon as steel became available again in 19x4.

The Franklin Steel Warehouse Company measures the annual increments to its LIFO inventory at the average of all purchase prices paid during the year.

a. Provide the figures necessary to complete the following table, showing inventories and cost of goods sold on both a FIFO and a LIFO basis:

	Inventory Cost		Cost of Goods Sold	
	FIFO	LIFO	FIFO	LIFO
January 1, 19x2	$1,875,000	$1,875,000		
			19x2 _____	_____
December 31, 19x2	_____	_____		
			19x3 _____	_____
December 31, 19x3	_____	_____		

b. Assuming that 15,000 tons is the normal inventory quantity and that the company intended to rebuild its inventories to this level as soon as possible, what was the effect of the "involuntary liquidation" of inventory on income before taxes for 19x3?

c. Assuming that inventories were increased to 15,000 tons by the end of 19x4, with 19x4 purchases at a cost of $145 a ton, what was the net effect of the 19x3 involuntary liquidation on LIFO inventory cost as of December 31, 19x4?

d. Assuming an income tax rate of 50 percent, calculate the effect of the choice between FIFO and LIFO on the company's cash flows in 19x2, 19x3, and 19x4. The company purchased 100,000 tons of steel in 19x4.

EXERCISES AND PROBLEMS

5. LIFO costing exercise.   A company had 60,000 units in inventory on January 1, 19x8, at the following LIFO cost:

	No. of Units	Unit Cost	Total Cost
Base quantity	30,000	$ 5	$150,000
19x1 layer	15,000	6	90,000
19x4 layer	10,000	8	80,000
19x6 layer	5,000	10	50,000
Total	60,000		$370,000

It made the following purchases and sales during 19x8 and 19x9:

January 1–June 30, 19x8	Sales, 40,000 units
July 1, 19x8	Purchase, 100,000 units @ $12
July 1–December 31, 19x8	Sales, 50,000 units
January 1–June 30, 19x9	Sales, 60,000 units
July 1, 19x9	Purchase, 100,000 units @ $13
July 1–December 31, 19x9	Sales, 70,000 units

Calculate the LIFO cost of goods sold and the LIFO cost of the ending inventory for each year.

6. FIFO costing exercise.   A company had 60,000 units in inventory on January 1, 19x8, at a FIFO cost of $11 a unit. It made the purchases and sales in 19x8 and 19x9 described in Problem 5. The market value of the company's inventories was determined to be $11.50 a unit at the beginning of 19x8, $12.50 at the end of 19x8, and $12.40 at the end of 19x9.

a. Calculate the FIFO cost of goods sold and the FIFO cost of the ending inventory for each year.

b. Apply the lower-of-cost-or-market rule to determine the inventory and the cost of goods sold for each year.

7. Average costing exercise.   A company had 60,000 units in inventory on January 1, 19x8, at an average cost of $10.90 a unit. It made the purchases and sales in 19x8 and 19x9 described in Problem 5.

a. Calculate the cost of goods sold and the cost of the ending inventory for each year on an average costing basis.

b. Comment on the numerical differences between your answer to part a and the answers to Problems 5 and 6.

8. Meaning of published replacement cost data. The balance sheet in a company's annual report described the company's inventories as follows:

Inventories—substantially all stated at cost on "last-in, first-out" basis with current replacement cost approximately $28,100,000 in excess of stated cost $53,334,933

A year earlier, the corresponding inventory figure was $56,047,919, and the current replacement cost was approximately $24,200,000 in excess of stated cost.

What information about the financial position and operations of the company do the figures on excess of replacement cost over stated cost provide?

9. FIFO cost and lower-of-cost-or-market. Percy, Inc.'s inventory purchases in 19x2 were as follows:

Date	Quantity	Unit Cost
January 18	3,500	$14
May 12	4,200	28
October 3	2,700	37
December 20	1,100	34

Percy uses the FIFO cost method and applies the lower-of-cost-or-market rule each year-end.

The merchandise on hand on January 1 had been written down to $15 a unit. During the year, 10,900 units were sold at an average selling price of $41. At year-end, Percy's inventory consisted of 1,400 units whose market value was $32 a unit. Operating expenses (other than the cost of goods sold and write-down loss) were $114,900.

a. What was the amount of the loss from writing down the year-end inventory to its market value?

b. Prepare Percy, Inc.'s income statement for 19x2. Ignore income taxes.

10. FIFO cost and lower-of-cost-or-market. Riley Corporation had 850 units of merchandise on hand on December 31, 19x3; all were reflected in inventory at that date's $22 market value. During 19x4, Riley had the following transactions:

March 18	Bought	1,750	@	?
July 9	Sold	1,630	@	$56
August 3	Bought	?	@	$31
October 5	Sold	1,510	@	$58
November 30	Bought	300	@	$34

Riley used the perpetual system of inventory recordkeeping and recorded FIFO-based cost of goods sold of $38,200 on July 9 and $41,710 on October 5. When Riley discovered that the market value of all 1,200 units on hand at December 31 was less than their recorded costs, it recorded a $3,300 write-down loss. Operating expenses (other than the cost of goods sold and write-down loss) were $74,230.

a. At what amount should inventory be recorded in Riley Corporation's December 31, 19x4 balance sheet?

b. Prepare Riley Corporation's 19x4 income statement. Ignore income taxes.

11. LIFO liquidation. Cox Associates accounts for its inventories on a LIFO basis. It experienced LIFO liquidations in two recent years, as shown in the following table:

	Units	Unit Cost	Ending Inventory	Replacement Cost at End of Year
December 31, 19x1 ..	400 ×	$ 8 =	$ 3,200	$ 9.50
December 31, 19x2 ..	400 ×	8 = 3,200		
Purchase, 19x3	300 ×	10 = 3,000	6,200	12.00
December 31, 19x3 ..	400 ×	8 = 3,200		
Purchase, 19x4	300 ×	10 = 3,000		
Purchase, 19x4	200 ×	13 = 2,600	8,800	14.50
December 31, 19x4 ..	675 ×	? =	?	16.00
December 31, 19x5 ..	400 ×	8 = 3,200		
Purchase, 19x6	275 ×	10 = 2,750		
Purchase, 19x6	320 ×	15 = 4,800	10,750	19.00
December 31, 19x6 ..	350 ×	? =	?	20.00

The company could have avoided these liquidations by making the necessary purchases at the prices prevailing in December of those years. These were equal in each case to the replacement cost at year-end, shown in the right-hand column of the table.

a. What was the effect of each year's LIFO liquidation on Cox Associates' income before taxes?
b. What was the effect of the spread between the LIFO cost and the current cost of the inventory on each year's financial statements?

12. Change from FIFO to LIFO; recommendation to management. The Weeks Woolen Company had always used the FIFO method of inventory costing. For the years 19x7 and 19x8, its reported income or loss before deducting income taxes was as follows:

19x7 .... $234,690 profit
19x8 ....   60,140 loss

Early in 19x9, the company's management was considering shifting to a last-in, first-out basis. Investigation revealed that the inventory amounts for the three years were or would have been as follows:

	Pounds	FIFO Amount	LIFO Amount
December 31, 19x6	500,000	$225,000	$225,000
December 31, 19x7	475,000	403,000	210,000
December 31, 19x8	513,000	338,000	235,000

The cost of goods purchased amounted to $400,000 in 19x7 and $350,000 in 19x8. The inventory had a market value of 90 cents a pound on December 31, 19x7, and 66 cents a pound on December 31, 19x8.

a. Compute the income before income taxes that the company would have reported each year if it had adopted the LIFO method of inventory costing as of January 1, 19x7.
b. Would adoption of LIFO as of that date have led to more informative income statements for the two years? Explain your reasoning.
c. By the beginning of 19x9, management no longer had the option of adopting LIFO as of January 1, 19x7, but it could adopt it as of January 1, 19x8. Write a brief report to management, recommending for or against adoption of LIFO as of that date, giving reasons for your recommendation.

13. LIFO costing; inventory recordkeeping. The XYZ Company uses FIFO for inventory recordkeeping in its perpetual inventory system and LIFO for external financial reporting. The inventory accounts showed the following balances on January 1, 19x1:

Inventories (50,000 units) .... $50,000 dr.
LIFO Inventory Adjustment .... 20,000 cr.

The balance in the LIFO Inventory Adjustment account measured the difference between LIFO and FIFO inventory costs on that date. In other words, the LIFO cost of the January 1 inventory was $30,000.

Purchases and sales during the year were as follows:

Quarter	Purchases	Sales
1	50,000 units × $1.10	45,000 units
2	40,000 × 1.15	50,000
3	60,000 × 1.12	55,000
4	70,000 × 1.25	60,000

Annual increments to the LIFO inventory were measured at the prices paid for the first units purchased during the year.

a. Calculate the FIFO cost of goods sold for each quarter and for the year as a whole.
b. Calculate the LIFO cost of goods sold for the year.
c. Set up a T-account to represent the Inventories account, enter the opening balance, record the purchases and cost of goods sold as the company would record them each quarter on a FIFO basis, and calculate the ending balance in this account.
d. Prepare the entry that should be made to adjust the balance in the LIFO Inventory Adjustment account at the end of the year.
e. Management told the shareholders that "inventory losses" in the fourth quarter erased most of the net income reported on the interim financial statements for the first three quarters of the year, despite record fourth-quarter sales. Explain what happened.

14. Effect of inventory method on income. Barrow Company uses FIFO for inventory recordkeeping in its perpetual inventory system and periodic LIFO for external financial reporting. The company had an inventory of 15,000 pounds of product on January 1, 19x9. This was shown on the balance sheet in the following way:

Inventory, at FIFO cost	$30,000
Less: Adjustment to reduce inventory to a LIFO basis	15,200
Inventory, at LIFO cost	$14,800

The supporting data showed the following:

Base quantity	8,000 lbs. × $0.80	$ 6,400
19x0 layer	4,000 lbs. × $1.00	4,000
19x3 layer	2,000 lbs. × $1.40	2,800
19x6 layer	1,000 lbs. × $1.60	1,600
Total inventory, at LIFO cost		$14,800

The company bought 25,000 pounds of material during 19x9 and sold 29,000 pounds. Each unit purchased cost $2.50, and the purchase price remained constant at this level throughout the year. On December 31, 19x9, however, the company's supplier announced that the price of the material had been raised to $3, effective immediately.

a. Compute the December 31, 19x9, inventory on a LIFO basis.
b. Suppose this company had always used FIFO instead of LIFO. By what amount would FIFO income before taxes in 19x9 have differed from LIFO income in that year?
c. What was the total effect of the company's shift to LIFO on income before taxes in all years since the adoption of LIFO, taken together?

15. Relationship of inventory growth to effects of inventory method. A company started in business on January 1, 19x0, by purchasing 10,000 units of merchandise at a cost of $10 each. Sales amounted to 50,000 units in 19x0, and the company had 10,000 units in inventory at the end of 19x0.

The purchase price of the merchandise increased by $1 a unit on January 1 of each year for the next four years. For example, all purchases in 19x0 were made at a price of $10, all purchases in 19x1 cost $11, and all purchases in 19x4 cost $14. The income tax rate was 40 percent for the entire five-year period, and the company had taxable income each year.

a. Calculate the cost of the ending inventory for each of the five years on the assumption that the inventory quantity remained at its 19x0 level: (1) on a FIFO basis, and (2) on a LIFO basis.
b. Repeat the calculations called for in part a on the assumption that year-end inventory quantities increased by 2,000 units each year, beginning in 19x1.
c. Repeat the calculations for the situation described in part b, except that the year-end inventory quantity fell to 4,000 units in 19x3 and then returned to 18,000 units at the end of 19x4.
d. Given these calculations, describe briefly how growth influences the effects of the inventory costing method choice on income and cash flow.

16. Effect of inventory method on managerial decision. "We'd be foolish to buy now," Helen Hunt, the Carthage Company's purchasing agent said. "The price can't be any higher next spring than it is now, and I expect

it to be much lower. We can make $7,000 by keeping our inventory down to 80,000 pounds until the new crop comes in next year."

"You forget," replied Dave Jones, the company's controller, "that if we don't replace these inventories before the end of the year, we'll lose our favorable LIFO base. Not only that, but if you aim at an 80,000-pound inventory, you'll be buying in uneconomically small lots. You'll probably have to pay premiums on rush orders, too."

The Carthage Company is a large wholesale distributor of food products. One product is made from citrus fruits. The annual price is determined largely by the size of the winter crop in Florida. A very severe winter in 1981–82 caused heavy damage to the Florida citrus crop. The purchase price went up to 32 cents a pound in January 1982 and remained at this level throughout the year.

In 1976, the company had adopted the LIFO method of inventory costing for all its products, both for tax purposes and for financial reporting. The balances in the company's inventory accounts on January 1, 1976, became the costs of the LIFO base quantities.

Separate accounts were established at that time for the materials cost and processing cost components of the LIFO inventories. The company's inventories of its citrus-based product on January 1, 1976, contained materials with a purchase weight of 100,000 pounds, at an inventory cost of 20 cents a pound, a total of $20,000. Increments to inventories in subsequent years were at the prices paid for the first purchases during the year cumulating to the incremental quantity.

The following table shows purchases and inventory data for the materials content of this product for the years 1976 through 1982:

Year	Beginning-of-Year Inventory (pounds)	Price Paid for First Purchases (per pound)	Total Cost of Materials Purchased
1976	100,000	$0.20	$ 60,000
1977	100,000	0.22	74,000
1978	110,000	0.23	92,000
1979	150,000	0.24	96,000
1980	180,000	0.30	88,000
1981	130,000	0.26	112,000
1982	200,000	0.32	?

Because of the high purchase prices, Hunt deliberately bought less citrus fruit in 1982 than the company was using. As a result, the inventory had dropped to 80,000 pounds by the end of October 1982, the quantity referred to in the conversation quoted earlier. Her recommendation was to maintain inventories of this product at this level until the new crop was processed in the spring of 1983.

Jones opposed this and recommended that inventories be rebuilt to 200,000 pounds by the end of 1982, at a purchase price of about 32 cents a pound. He estimated that if this were not done, the lower inventory levels would increase purchasing and handling costs by $2,000 in 1982 and $400 in 1983.

Both executives agreed that an inventory of 200,000 pounds of this product was an optimum inventory level. If her proposal was accepted, Hunt planned to rebuild inventories to this level as soon as the 1983 crop was processed. An average crop in 1983 would lead to a price of about 26 cents a pound.

The income tax in both years was 40 percent of taxable income.

a. Calculate the materials cost component of the cost of goods sold and the materials cost component of the end-of-year inventory of this product for each year, 1976–81.

b. By how much would 1982 reported income before taxes have been increased or decreased if the purchasing agent's proposal had been accepted?

c. Assuming that all purchases are paid for immediately in cash, would the purchasing agent's proposal or the controller's alternative have led to a larger cash balance after inventories were replenished in 1983? What would have been the amount of the difference? Ignore interest costs.

d. Should the purchasing agent's proposal have been accepted? Would your conclusion be different if the company's inventory had been on FIFO? How, if at all, does the inventory costing method influence decisions of this kind?

9

Plant assets

A business enterprise incurs costs to create income—either by generating revenues in excess of cost or by reducing other costs. These income effects may be expected to occur either in the current period or in one or more future periods. The cost of any resource that has been consumed to obtain the *current* period's revenues is an *expense.* By contrast, the cost of any resource that will be used to obtain revenues or reduce operating costs in *future* accounting periods is an *asset.* When an expenditure qualifies to be recorded as an asset, it is said to be *capitalized.*

These distinctions are not always easy to apply in practice, and accountants therefore have to exercise judgment. Our objective in this chapter is to examine the factors that affect capitalization decisions and to learn how accountants then determine how capitalized costs become expenses in future periods.

CAPITALIZABLE COSTS

An expenditure to acquire an asset is often accompanied by one or more ancillary expenditures, more or less related to the acquisition. Additional expenditures are likely to occur during the years an asset is being used and already generating revenue benefits. Some costs incurred at acquisition and some post-acquisition costs are capitalizable; we'll consider these two cases in turn.

Acquisition costs

The basic principle is that the cost of an asset consists of all outlays necessary to render the asset suitable for its intended use. In the acquisition of a machine, for example, capitalizable costs include the price charged by the vendor, freight charges, installation expenditures, and start-up costs. (By start-up costs, we're referring to costs incurred during the few days or weeks that it takes to get the machine in proper working condition, such as to achieve harmony and consistency with the company's operating procedures.)

The price charged by a seller is the net-of-discount price, and it includes the applicable excise or sales tax. Freight and installation charges are included whether the service is provided by an outside party or by the buyer's own personnel. If part of the installation procedure necessitates constructing a foundation to support the machine, this cost is capitalized.

The same principle applies to real property—land and buildings. The cost of land therefore includes not only the contract price but also brokers' commissions and legal fees. The cost of a building includes the contract price or construction costs, architects' charges, building permit fees, and costs incurred in the preparation of plans, specifications, blueprints, etc.

Interest cost. If time is required to construct a plant asset and bring it to the condition necessary for its intended use, the related interest cost incurred during that period is treated by U.S. companies as a cost of the asset.[1] The amount of interest that is capitalized is the sum that would have been avoided if expenditures for the asset hadn't been made.

Interest capitalization raises a number of issues which can be dealt with effectively only in an advanced text. The basic principle, however, is that interest on interest-bearing debt outstanding during the period of construction is just as much a cost of bringing a plant asset to the condition necessary for its intended use as are the costs of bricks and bricklayers' services.

Joint acquisition cost. Two or more assets are sometimes acquired at a single purchase price, known as their *joint cost.* The joint cost is usually allocated on the basis of the relative *market values* of the purchased assets. For example, Dixon Company bought a

---

[1] The same capitalization treatment also applies in the United States to assets produced for lease or sale in lengthy production processes—such as ships or real estate developments. Interest arising during the process of maturing inventories intended for lease or sale (e.g., timber or whiskey) isn't capitalized as part of the cost of these inventories, even though the economic causes of interest are essentially the same.

building and the land on which it sits for a lump sum of $8 million. Consultation with an independent appraiser provided the following estimated market values: land $3 million, and building $9 million. Since the sum ($12 million) exceeds the cost actually incurred ($8 million), allocation is effected on the basis of the assets' relative market values:

	Market Value	Percentage	Allocated Cost
Land	$ 3 million	25%	$2 million
Building	9 million	75%	6 million
Total	$12 million		$8 million

Since the relative values are 25 percent land and 75 percent building, 25 percent of the $8 million cost is allocated to the land ($2 million) and 75 percent is assigned to the building ($6 million). This approach is based on the assumption that separate prices of the individual assets would have borne the same relationship to market value as in the joint acquisition.

Cost of unwanted assets. A company may sometimes buy a group of assets to obtain one of them. For example, Eagle, Inc., bought land for $5 million *and* an old loft building on the land for $2 million, intending to raze the building and erect a new one. In this case the entire purchase price ($7 million) clearly relates to the land. What distinguishes this situation from the previous case is that we don't have two joint products, because the land is the only desired asset purchased. Were Eagle then to expend $200,000 to demolish the old building, this too would be treated as a cost of the land because it's a cost incurred to place the land in a condition to be used as the site of the new structure.

Noncash acquisitions. When companies acquire assets for consideration other than cash or the promise of cash, this is called a *nonmonetary transaction.* The basic rule in such cases is to record the acquired asset at the fair value of the asset(s) exchanged for it. For example, if a company acquires a machine in exchange for government bonds which had cost $4,000 and whose current market value is $5,000, it will record the machine's cost as $5,000 and recognize a $1,000 gain.

When *similar* assets are exchanged, however, the asset acquired is usually recorded at the same amount as the asset given up. For example, Garden Company exchanges land in a distant location that had cost $80,000 for property adjacent to one of its factories, with both parties agreeing that each tract is worth $95,000. Because the assets are similar, the new property is recorded at $80,000, the cost basis of the land given up. The accounting rationale is that because trading similar assets does not signify culmination of the earning process, a ($15,000) gain shouldn't be recorded. The earning process is concluded only when dissimilar assets are traded.

The accounting treatment is different if the fair value of each property is less than its cost basis. If the market value of each property in Garden Company's exchange is $70,000 (rather than the earlier $95,000), trading land that had cost $80,000 indicates that a $10,000 loss has already occurred. In the light of accountants' desire to report losses sooner rather than later, the $10,000 indicated loss is recognized and the newly acquired land is recorded at its $70,000 market value. These two cases are summarized in the upper portion of Exhibit 9–1.

These rules for the exchange of similar assets apply even when some cash is included in the exchange. For instance, if Circle Corporation acquires a new delivery truck by giving up an old truck and cash, this is also treated as an exchange of similar assets. Let's assume the book value of the old truck (cost less accumulated depreciation) was $6,000, its market value was $7,000, and cash paid was $2,500. The new truck is recorded at $8,500, the sum of the cash ($2,500) and the book value of the old truck ($6,000). If, on the other hand, the market value of the old truck had been $5,700, the indicated loss of $300 ($6,000 − $5,700) would be recorded and the new truck would be recorded at $8,200 ($2,500 + $5,700). These two exchange transactions are summarized in the lower portion of Exhibit 9–1.

EXHIBIT 9–1.   Exchanging Similar Assets

	Old Basis of Old Asset	Fair Value	Indicated Gain (Loss)	Reported Gain (Loss)	Basis for New Asset
Garden Company					
Case 1	$80,000	$95,000	$ 15,000	—	$80,000
Case 2	$80,000	$70,000	$(10,000)	$(10,000)	$70,000
Circle Corporation					
Case 1					
Truck	$ 6,000	$ 7,000	$ 1,000		
Cash	2,500	2,500			
Total	$ 8,500	$ 9,500		—	$ 8,500
Case 2					
Truck	$ 6,000	$ 5,700	$ (300)		
Cash	2,500	2,500			
Total	$ 8,500	$ 8,200		$ (300)	$ 8,200

Post-acquisition expenditures

Although a company may spend a significant amount of money to buy a plant asset, it frequently expends additional funds to preserve and improve the asset during its operating life. This raises the question of whether such expenditures should be capitalized (i.e., added to the asset) or treated as expenses of the period in which the costs are incurred.

Betterments versus maintenance. When a plant asset is acquired, the criterion is whether the expenditure is necessary to render the asset suitable for its intended use, the ultimate purpose being to generate revenues in the future. When dealing with a post-acquisition expenditure, however, the question is: Did the expenditure *expand* or *maintain* the previously anticipated service capacity of the asset? Accountants treat this as a problem of distinguishing between *betterments,* some form of progressive change, and *maintenance,* the prevention or retardation of retrogressive change. Costs of betterments are capitalized; maintenance costs are charged to current operations.

At the time of acquisition, each asset has an expected lifetime capacity reflecting an intended maintenance policy. Any cost incurred to obtain the service initially expected of an asset is a maintenance cost. Any cost incurred to increase the lifetime productive capacity by increasing the output rate, extending the economic life past the length that was estimated at the time of acquisition or reducing operating costs to less than their originally anticipated level, is a capitalizable betterment.

Maintenance versus replacement. A second important distinction is between maintenance expenditures and replacement expenditures. The question is whether an expenditure that is made to replace one or more components of a plant asset should be treated as maintenance (a current expense) or as replacement cost (capitalized as an asset cost). The answer depends on whether the plant asset was originally identified as a single asset or as a set of related assets. Replacement of an *entire* asset requires removing that asset from the accounting records and capitalizing the cost of the replacement. The cost of replacing *part* of an asset, however, is usually treated as a maintenance cost, unless it is expected to increase the asset's service potential or extend its useful life beyond the amounts anticipated at the time the asset was acquired.

For example, although most people would regard an entire airplane as a single asset, an airline may capitalize the costs of the airframe, engines, and interior fittings as three separate assets. As a second example, suppose a company has installed a conveyor system to transport materials, work in process, and finished products between work stations in its two-story factory. Every five years the company has to replace the treads which form the load-carrying surface of the conveyor system. If the conveyor is the unit of account and its estimated useful life is based on the assumption that the treads will be replaced periodically, then subsequent expenditures for replacement treads will be treated as maintenance costs and will be expensed immediately. If the treads are capitalized separately at the outset, however, then the cost of the original treads must be removed from the accounting records when they're replaced. The cost of the replacement treads then must be capitalized in their place.

Let's suppose the conveyor is expected to last for 20 years, with treads costing $8,000 to be replaced every five years. If the cost of the first set of treads is capitalized as part of the cost of the conveyor, it will be depreciated over 20 years at an average of $400 a year. The sum of depreciation and maintenance expenses therefore will be $400 each year, except in years 6, 11, and 16, when replacements take place. In those three years, the depreciation and maintenance expenses will total $8,400. This cost pattern is indicated by the solid line in Exhibit 9-2. The dashed line in the exhibit depicts the annual cost if the treads are capitalized separately. In that case, the cost of each set of treads will be depreciated over five years at an average of $1,600 a year ($8,000/5), thereby smoothing the annual cost.

EXHIBIT 9-2.   Effect of Separate Capitalization on Reported Annual Cost

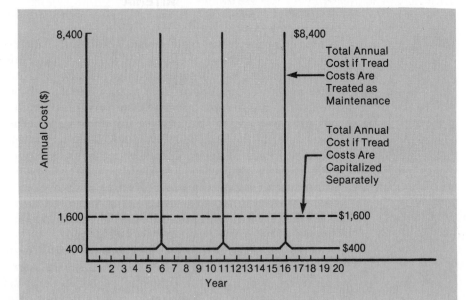

If the unit of account is made small enough, even a routine lubrication can be treated as a replacement with no room left for the concept of maintenance. Although this conclusion would appear to be extreme, it does point out that separate capitalization is likely to have a slight smoothing effect on year-to-year movements in operating costs.

Major overhauls. A similar question arises in connection with expenditures made for major overhauls of existing assets. If the overhaul is made to *restore* the service potential that was anticipated at acquisition, the cost of the overhaul is treated as maintenance expense. If the overhaul *extends* an asset's remaining lifetime service potential beyond the amount originally anticipated, the cost to achieve this extension is capitalized.

To illustrate, suppose Elastic, Inc., bought a tractor trailer for $90,000 with the expectation that it would provide five years of service. The company planned to record depreciation expense of $18,000 ($90,000/5) each year for five years. At the beginning of the fourth year, a new transmission had to be installed at a cost of $5,000. If, as a result of this development, Elastic expects the useful life of the truck now to be seven years, the cost of the new transmission will be capitalized.[2] If the truck is still expected to last only five years, the expenditure will be treated as an immediate expense.

ANCILLARY EXPENDITURES: PRAGMATIC CRITERIA

In practice, the facts are often less clear-cut than a textbook description may make them appear. Although the Financial Accounting Standards Board is making an effort to reduce freedom of choice on accounting questions, companies still have a good deal of latitude in applying the general measurement principles stated above. In exercising their judgment, companies' managers and accountants are influenced by pragmatic considerations, most of which generally lead to *earlier* expense recognition than the principles themselves would suggest.

Recordkeeping convenience

Among the least impressive but by no means least important of these influences is recordkeeping convenience. Work in connection with an asset already in place frequently has a mixture of

---

[2] The $5,000 would probably be recorded as a reduction of Accumulated Depreciation rather than as an addition to the asset's original cost. In other words, rather than have the asset's $41,000 book value be based on $95,000 − $54,000, Elastic's balance sheet would reflect the amounts as $90,000 − $49,000.

objectives: making improvements in the asset, extending its useful life, and doing normal maintenance. Separating the costs of achieving each of these objectives from the costs of achieving the others is difficult and often requires decisions that can only be characterized as arbitrary. Treating all such expenditures as expenses makes life a good deal simpler.

Much the same reasoning is often used to justify expensing the cost of hand tools and other high-volume, low-unit-cost items that will be used for more than a year. Although the total cost of these items may be millions of dollars a year in large corporations, they are usually expensed to avoid the cost of maintaining detailed property records. This also relieves accountants of the need to make a large number of accounting judgments. A limit of, say, $500 is established; the costs of all items costing less than this are expensed automatically, no matter how long they are expected to last.

Tax advantage

Another reason to expense costs that might otherwise be capitalized is the tax advantage to be gained thereby. So long as a company has current taxable income, increasing the amount of current expense will reduce current tax payments. Although treating a cost as an immediate expense rather than deferring it to future periods generally will inflate future taxable income, this is a deterrent only when the tax rate is expected to increase. Dollars saved this year are unquestionably worth more than dollars that may be saved in some future year, both because money has a time value and because the purchasing power of dollars is likely to be less in the future than it is today.

Since taxable income is not necessarily the same as accounting income, a cost may be capitalized for financial reporting while being expensed for tax purposes. The taxpayer may be better able to make a case for current tax deductibility of borderline items, however, by expensing them for both purposes.

Accounting conservatism

When a legitimate question exists as to whether to capitalize or expense a cost, and the decision will have no impact on tax treatment, accountants tend to expense the cost because it is the conservative thing to do. Although the cost of training cashiers to operate sophisticated cash registers could justifiably be capitalized and expensed over several future periods, accountants are likely to treat the training cost as an expense as soon as it is incurred.

Income control

All three factors just discussed introduce a bias toward expensing costs that might, on theoretical grounds, be capitalized. The fourth factor, income control, can work in either direction.

Managers of companies have an understandable interest in "controlling" the amount that is reported as net income. Net income, often expressed in terms of earnings per share, is widely regarded as a primary index of corporate performance. If earnings exceed the level anticipated by the securities market, the price per share is likely to increase; if income turns out to be disappointing, the market price is likely to decrease.

Reported income is also widely regarded as a measure of managerial skill. Even if managers' compensation isn't tied directly to the company's earnings, managers who are able to generate income levels that in turn cause the market price of the stock to rise are likely to be rewarded. Management might be expected, therefore, to select a capitalize-or-expense strategy—for costs on the borderline between asset and expense—that will most likely help achieve a specified bias in the pattern of reported income. This strategy may be to maximize net income (by capitalizing all borderline costs) or to smooth net income (by expensing more in high-income years than in low-income years).

Consistency and disclosure

Probably the most serious problem posed by the application of these pragmatic criteria is that they give management a great deal of power to affect reported income. To limit management's ability to distort net income, the accounting profession requires companies to be *consistent* from year to year in their treatment of specific types of cost. This requirement is based on the belief that a bias consistently followed impairs the usefulness of information less seriously than a bias that depends on what management wants investors to believe.

A company is said to be consistent if it adopts a set of accounting policies and applies them each year. For example, if a company's policy is to expense employee training costs as they occur, it must expense them every year, not just in years in which expensing meets management's income objectives.

Assuring total consistency in practice is very difficult, probably impossible, to achieve. Management can alter the way it views transactions from year to year even without deliberately attempting to do so. The costs of materials processed in test runs of new equipment may be classified as production costs in some years and as training costs in others.

The consistency doctrine doesn't lock a company into a single set of accounting practices forever. Conditions change, and companies change the ways they account for some of their assets, liabilities, and owners' equity from time to time. As accounting changes are made, however, the company must provide full explanations of their nature and dollar-amount effects on the financial statements.

As one might imagine, consistency is not an unmixed blessing. For example, partly because a particular amount is not *material* (that is, not large enough to be significant), a company may decide to expense the cost of alterations to equipment and find this accounting practice to be satisfactory for a number of years. Sooner or later, however, it may come to a year in which the cost is large because of a large-scale plant modernization effort. Under these circumstances, the company's accountants may well insist that this cost should be capitalized and expensed over the expected remaining life of the equipment. This departure from consistent reporting is justified by the materiality of the amount. The company, however, must disclose in its financial statements the nature and dollar-amount effect of this change.

ACCOUNTING FOR DEPRECIATION

Capitalization occurs only for expenditures that are expected to provide future benefits. Annual charges for depreciation represent the accountants' effort to assign capitalized costs to the periods in which the anticipated benefits are expected to materialize. In this section we'll see how accountants approach this task.

Depreciation and economic value

The use of an asset's services is expected to result in future net cash flows to the company in excess of the net cash flows that would have been generated in the absence of that asset. These excess cash flows are known as the *incremental cash flows* attributable to the asset. As we saw in Chapter 6, the present value of these incremental cash flows measures the value of the asset to the company. Since management won't buy an asset that isn't expected to be worth its cost, we can assume that the present value of these cash flows is expected to be at least equal to the asset's cost at the time it is acquired.

This means that two amounts can be identified or estimated for every asset starting its life in a company: (1) its economic value, based on its estimated incremental cash flows, and (2) its acquisition cost. Each of these could be a a starting point to calculate depreciation.

One possibility is to base depreciation on the change in value that occurs each year. As the asset's services are used during a given year, the incremental cash flows attributable to it and arising in that year are realized. This leaves fewer services available for the future and fewer cash flows; the asset's value therefore will be less at the end of the year than it was at the beginning (unless some of the estimates change). An economist would use *this* decline as the estimated depreciation for the year—that is, "economic" depreciation.

Accountants don't record economic depreciation, at least partly because they start with a different total amount to be depreciated. They base annual depreciation charges on the asset's original cost instead of on its value. In other words, they use *cost* to represent the asset's total lifetime service potential; depreciation in any year is the cost of the asset's services used up during the year.

Depreciable cost

In a conventional accounting system in which expenses are measured by the historical cost of the resources used to generate current revenue, the total cost applicable to a depreciable asset's usable service potential is the difference between the asset's original cost and its end-of-life resale or salvage value. This difference is known as the *depreciable cost:*

$$\text{Depreciable Cost} = \text{Original Cost} - \text{Estimated End-of-Life Salvage Value}$$

An asset's anticipated salvage value is treated as the cost of services the company doesn't expect to use but plans to sell to someone else. In practice, salvage is often assumed to be zero, in which case the original cost becomes the depreciable cost. By contrast, *book value* is the term accountants use to refer to an asset's cost less its accumulated depreciation.

Useful life

Having decided to base depreciation charges on *cost,* management estimates the period during which the asset is likely to be used. This estimate reflects that each asset's useful life is affected by physical deterioration and functional obsolescence. Physical deterioration arises through asset use, the passage of time, and accidental damage, the result being a decline in the quantity of the asset's output or a rise in its unit cost. Obsolescence results from shifts in market demand (e.g., the shift from cloth diapers to throwaways) or to changes in technology which cause an existing asset to be less efficient than a newer unit. At some point, it pays to abandon the existing asset to be able to reap the benefits of a successor model.

Depreciation time patterns

In our illustrations in Part One, we assigned the same amount of depreciation to each year of an asset's useful life. Depreciation isn't always calculated that way in practice, nor should it be. In principle, each year's depreciation should be proportional to the year's anticipated percentage of the amount of benefit the company expects to reap from the asset during its useful life. (To eliminate the possibility of year-by-year manipulation of the depreciation charge, the formula governing the amount of depreciation to be recognized each year is established when the asset is first placed in service.) In the next few pages we'll describe four different depreciation methods or formulas, each of which will approximate some assets' lifetime benefit patterns:

1. Straight-line depreciation.
2. Sum-of-the-years'-digits depreciation.
3. Double-rate, declining-balance depreciation.
4. Production-unit depreciation.

Straight-line depreciation. In straight-line depreciation, the depreciation amount is the same each year, no matter how lightly or heavily the asset is used. If a new machine costing $36,000 is expected to last 12 years with an estimated $1,500 end-of-life salvage value, the amount of straight-line depreciation each year will be:

$$\frac{\$36,000 - \$1,500}{12} = \$2,875$$

For convenience, the straight-line method is usually expressed as a *depreciation rate,* equal to the reciprocal of the expected years of useful life—in our example, $\frac{1}{12} = 8.33$ percent. This rate is then multiplied each year by the depreciable cost (original cost less estimated end-of-life salvage value). In practice, a salvage value of zero is almost always used except for assets with well-established resale markets, such as automobiles and trucks.

Accelerated depreciation. As the term implies, the accelerated-depreciation approach produces annual depreciation amounts that are larger than the straight-line result in the earlier years and smaller in the later years. This approach therefore may also be called a *diminishing-charge* approach. Two formulas that may be used to implement this approach are the *sum-of-the-years'-digits* and the *double-rate, declining-balance* methods.

Sum-of-the-years'-digits depreciation. The first step in the sum-of-the-years'-digits method is to number each year of the asset's estimated useful life, starting with 1 for the first year, 2 for the second, and so on. The next step is to add these digits to get their sum. In our example, where the asset is expected to last 12 years, the sum of the digits $1 + 2 + \cdots + 12 = 78$. Using n to signify the number of years, the formula to derive this sum is as follows:

$$\frac{n(n + 1)}{2}$$

In this case, since $n = 12$, the sum is $(12 \times 13)/2 = 78$.

The third step is to assign the 12 numbers to the years in reverse order. Thus, the number 12 is assigned to year 1, the number 11 to year 2, and so on. The fourth step is to calculate a *separate* depreciation rate for each year. This is done by dividing each year's assigned number (12, 11, . . .) by the sum of the digits (78). The depreciation rates are 12/78 for the first year, 11/78 for the second, and so on, down to 1/78 for the 12th year.

The final step is to multiply these rates by the depreciable cost to determine the annual depreciation amounts. The sum of these amounts will reduce the asset's book value to its expected salvage value at the end of its estimated life. In our example, depreciable cost is $36,000 - $1,500 = $34,500 and the first year's depreciation is 12/78 × $34,500 = $5,308. This amount appears on the first line in the second column of Exhibit 9–3. The rest of this column lists the depreciation amounts for the subsequent years, computed in this way. Book value at the end of 12 years is $1,500, the amount that had been estimated at the outset to be the expected salvage value.

Double-rate, declining-balance depreciation. Double-rate declining-balance depreciation is calculated by using a *fixed rate* to determine each period's depreciation. The fixed rate is applied to the asset's book value, which declines each year. The amount of depreciation recorded each period therefore is smaller than that of the previous period.

The fixed depreciation rate in this formula is twice the straight-line rate, and salvage value is ignored in calculating the rate. Since the straight-line rate for an asset with an estimated 12-year life

EXHIBIT 9–3. Comparison of Depreciation Schedules

Year	Sum of the Years' Digits Beginning Book Value	Sum of the Years' Digits Annual Charge	Double Rate, Declining Balance Beginning Book Value	Double Rate, Declining Balance Annual Charge	Straight Line Beginning Book Value	Straight Line Annual Charge
1	$36,000	$ 5,308	$36,000	$ 6,000	$36,000	$ 2,875
2	30,692	4,865	30,000	5,000	33,125	2,875
3	25,827	4,423	25,000	4,167	30,250	2,875
4	21,404	3,981	20,833	3,472	27,375	2,875
5	17,423	3,538	17,361	2,894	24,500	2,875
6	13,885	3,096	14,467	2,411	21,625	2,875
7	10,789	2,654	12,056	2,009	18,750	2,875
8	8,135	2,212	10,047	1,674	15,875	2,875
9	5,924	1,769	8,373	1,395	13,000	2,875
10	4,155	1,327	6,978	1,163	2,875	2,875
11	2,828	885	5,815	969	7,250	2,875
12	1,943	442	4,846	807	4,375	2,875
13	1,500	—	4,039	2,539	1,500	—
Total		$34,500		$34,500		$34,500

is 8.33 percent a year, the double rate is 16.67 percent a year. The depreciation amounts generated by this method are shown in the fourth column of Exhibit 9–3. For year 1, depreciation is 0.167 × $36,000, or $6,000; depreciation in year 2 is 0.167 × $30,000, or $5,000.

As we consider the depreciation amounts for the last years of the machine's useful life, we observe that the asset's book value is *not* reduced to the amount of the estimated salvage value by the end of year 12. Instead, the book value stands at $4,039, or $2,539 more than the estimated salvage value. If the asset were in fact sold in year 13 for the $1,500 that had been estimated, a $2,539 loss would be recorded in year 13. Because this outcome results in an income statement charge that would not have occurred under the two other popular methods, it is common for companies that use this method to modify its application by switching to straight-line depreciation in the last years of the asset's life.[3]

---

[3] The switchover occurs in the year in which the depreciation is less than it would be if the remaining depreciable cost had been subjected to straight-line depreciation thenceforth. In our illustration, this happens in year 8, when the remaining depreciable cost is $10,047 − $1,500 = $8,547 and the asset still has five years of life left. The comparison for that year is:

Straight-line depreciation of remaining depreciable cost: $8,547/5 = $1,709.

Double-rate, declining-balance depreciation: 0.167 × $10,047 = $1,674.

Depreciation for years 8 through 12 would be $1,709. This would bring the book value down to $1,500 at the end of year 12.

EXHIBIT 9–4. Graphic Comparisons of Annual Depreciation and Book Value

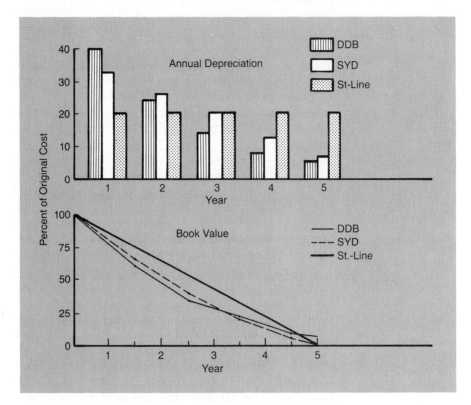

Comparing the results. Both the sum-of-the-years'-digits and the double-rate, declining-balance methods produce depreciation amounts greater in the early years of an asset's life and smaller in the later years than straight-line depreciation.

To make these relationships stand out as clearly as possible, study the diagrams in Exhibit 9–4. The upper graph depicts annual depreciation amounts for an asset which costs $100,000 and for which management expects no salvage value at the end of its five-year useful life. The lower graph presents the book-value amounts that would appear in the company's balance sheet each year under each depreciation method. The link between the two graphs is: The higher the annual depreciation charges, the lower the end-of-period book value.

Production-unit depreciation. Whereas all three depreciation methods discussed so far are based on the passage of time, some companies calculate depreciation on the basis of production units. The production-unit depreciation approach uses the following formula:

$$\text{Depreciation per Unit} = \frac{\text{Original Cost} - \text{Estimated Salvage Value}}{\text{Units of Lifetime Production Capacity}}$$

Each year's depreciation is then equal to the number of units of output (e.g., pounds, liters, miles, or usage hours) multiplied by the unit production rate. For a machine which costs $36,000, has a $1,500 estimated salvage value, and is expected to provide 20,000 hours of service in its lifetime, the production-unit depreciation rate is:

$$\frac{\$36,000 - \$1,500}{20,000 \text{ hours}} = \$1.725 \text{ an hour}$$

If the machine is used for 4,200 hours during the first year, production-unit depreciation for that year will be $7,245.

Production-unit depreciation is rarely used for ordinary commercial or industrial assets because useful life is more likely to be determined by rising costs or obsolescence—due to the passage of time—than by the number of units produced or hours of use. The method is used widely, however, to account for the *depletion* of such natural resources as oil and gas reserves and mineral deposits and the depreciation of the costs of the wells, mines, and other assets necessary to extract these resources. For example, if a company buys an oil field for $25 million with an estimated reserve of 20 million barrels, the depletion cost per barrel is $1.25 ($25 million/20 million). If 4 million barrels of oil are removed during the first year, a depletion expense of $5 million (4 million barrels × $1.25) will be recorded in that year.

Implicit-interest depreciation

None of the four depreciation methods we described recognizes explicitly the reasons why companies acquire plant assets. Companies buy assets because they expect them to generate net cash inflows at various times in the future. For an acquisition to be profitable, these future cash flows must be large enough to pay back the cost of the asset *and* to provide an adequate rate of return each year on the amount the company invested in the asset.

A fifth method, implicit-interest depreciation, produces a cost-based depreciation schedule that reflects the relationship between the original cost of the asset and the future cash flows it is expected to generate. This schedule may show level annual charges, decreasing charges, or even increasing charges, depending on the anticipated time pattern of the cash flows.

An implicit-interest depreciation schedule is based on the assumption that the income component of each year's cash flow should be calculated in such a way that the rate of return on the company's investment in the asset will be the same every year if the initial forecasts of cash flows are accurate. In other words, if the lifetime rate of return is 15 percent and the asset costs $36,000, income in the first year should be $5,400 (15 percent of $36,000). If the first year's net cash flow is $8,275, only $2,875 of this is available to cover depreciation of the asset's cost.

The book value of this asset is $33,125 at the end of the first year ($36,000 − $2,875). Income in the second year therefore must be $4,969 (15 percent of $33,125) if the 15 percent rate of return is to be maintained. Depreciation in the second year is the difference between $4,969 and the anticipated cash flow that year.

If the anticipated cash flow is *constant* from year to year, implicit-interest depreciation will be small at first and then rise more and more rapidly as the asset ages. This outcome arises because a smaller percentage of each succeeding year's cash flow will represent income. The reason is that the book value on which the fixed rate of return is calculated gets smaller and smaller as the asset ages.

If the anticipated cash flow decreases slowly enough each year, the annual depreciation charge may still increase from year to year. The charge may be constant from year to year if the decrease in cash flow is sharper—because the decrease in the annual income requirement will be offset by the decrease in the annual cash flow. How much sharper the cash flow must decline to achieve this result depends on the starting level, the length of life, and the rate of return or interest rate. And at some faster rate of decline in the cash flows, the implicit-interest method will produce depreciation amounts that resemble those generated by one of the diminishing-charge methods.

The appendix at the end of this chapter illustrates the implicit-interest method with numerical examples. Based on this introductory discussion alone, however, we can make one important observation: Even though the implicit-interest method isn't used explicitly in practice, each method used in practice is consistent with a particular pattern of future cash flows. Use of an accelerated method implies the most sharply decreasing set of cash flows, and straight-line depreciation implies gradually decreasing cash flows.

Choosing a depreciation method: Pragmatic criterion

From the standpoint of investors and other external users of a company's financial statements, the best accounting method is the one that best helps them predict the company's cash flows, the timing of these flows, and the uncertainty surrounding them. Implicit-interest depreciation (or another method which produces roughly similar depreciation schedules) probably meets this criterion better than other methods because it produces income numbers closer to the sustainable rate of return on the company's assets.

In practice, the anticipated time patterns of the future cash flows are ordinarily difficult to verify. In most cases, therefore, the company's independent public accountants have little basis for disputing management's choice of a depreciation method. The result is that management may choose some other depreciation method to achieve a desired pattern of year-to-year movements in net income.

The income effect of the choice of depreciation method depends on the rate of growth. If a company isn't growing but has a stable mix of assets of different ages, the total depreciation will be the same, no matter which method is selected. Some assets will be in their early years, others in the middle, and some in their final years. Book value amounts, however, will be smaller when an accelerated method is used than under straight-line depreciation, thus yielding a higher reported rate of return because of the smaller asset denominator of the rate-of-return fraction.

A growing company, in contrast, will have proportionally more young assets which will be generating depreciation amounts that are higher under accelerated methods than under straight-line depreciation. Book value amounts will be smaller, as in the no-growth company. The effect of the choice on the rate of return will depend on the relationship between the percentage difference in income and the percentage difference in the investment denominator.

Most large, publicly owned corporations in the United States use straight-line depreciation for investor reporting. This may reflect management's judgment that benefits are associated with greater reported income. Alternatively, it may mean that management's choice is based on information considerations, and management believes that straight-line depreciation approximates the anticipated time pattern of future cash flows better than accelerated methods.

Tax depreciation versus financial depreciation

The depreciation method chosen for use in public financial reporting in the United States has no bearing on how a company reports depreciation expense on its federal income tax returns. Tax considerations therefore don't affect the choice of depreciation methods. Large, publicly owned corporations in the United States had generally used some form of accelerated depreciation in determining taxable income since accelerated methods became permissible in 1954. Accelerated depreciation was more attractive than straight-line depreciation for income tax purposes because it shifted tax deductions to earlier years, thereby reducing taxable income and income taxes in those years. Reducing income taxes increased the company's cash flows in the early years of assets' lives, thereby giving these cash flows greater present values than if they came later.

The separation of tax depreciation from depreciation for financial reporting was made virtually absolute in 1981, when the U.S. Congress adopted for tax purposes a new system known as the *accelerated cost recovery system* (ACRS) for assets placed in service after 1980. In fact, the break with financial accounting was so great that the law establishing this system didn't use the term *depreciation* to describe the annual tax deductions—the term *cost recovery* was used throughout the law. Useful life is ordinarily so much longer than the amortization periods prescribed by the ACRS that the ACRS life can't be used for financial reporting.

The law establishing the accelerated cost recovery system classified depreciable property into four classes and prescribed an abnormally short tax life for assets in each class—3 years for assets such as automobiles, 5 years for most industrial machinery, 10 years for assets such as public utility property, and 15 years for most buildings. The law also prescribed the annual "cost recovery" percentages for assets in each class. For example, the percentages for assets in the three-year class acquired in 1981 and later are 25 percent the first year, 38 percent the second year, and 37 percent the third year. Schedules such as these have no usefulness for financial reporting.

Revisions of depreciation schedules

Depreciation schedules adopted at the time assets are acquired may turn out to be incorrect. Two situations require changes in depreciation schedules. In the first, it becomes inescapably clear that the economic value of the asset's remaining service potential has fallen materially below its book value. This requires a *write-down* of the asset.

For example, suppose an asset costing $10,000 has been depreciated on a straight-line basis for three years at $1,000 a year. It has been used mainly to manufacture a product the company has withdrawn from the market, and it will be used only intermittently in the future, probably for another seven years. Suppose in this use it is worth $2,800 or 40 percent of its present book value. The entry to recognize this fact is:

```
Loss from Write-down of Equipment ................  4,200
    Accumulated Depreciation .....................         4,200
```

The write-down debit has an immediate, one-time effect on income; the increase in Accumulated Depreciation reduces the amount of the asset's cost that has yet to be depreciated.

Once a write-down has taken place, the remaining portion of the depreciation schedule has to be redrawn to amortize the remaining depreciable cost over the remaining life. With seven years to go, an adjusted book value of $2,800, and zero estimated salvage value, this machine would have annual depreciation charges of $2,800/7 = $400 for the remaining seven years of its life.

A second situation in which a revision in the original depreciation schedule is necessary arises when evidence is found that a life estimate is seriously wrong. An error in an estimate of useful life results in an overstatement or understatement of depreciation during the years before the error is discovered.

In the interests of greater accounting accuracy, the accountant ought to correct the depreciation charges for prior years and calculate future depreciation as it would have been calculated originally if the estimates had been made accurately. Current practice in the United States, however, is to make no corrections of prior-year depreciation, mainly on the grounds that these changes would reduce public confidence in the statements and might confuse readers. Instead, the remaining depreciation amount is spread over the remaining years of useful life reflected in the new estimate.

For example, suppose an asset's book value is $150,000 and the remaining life estimate has been shortened from five years to three, with no salvage value. Under straight-line depreciation, the annual depreciation charge would be raised from $30,000 to $50,000 a year. The accumulated depreciation from prior years would not be changed to reflect the new estimate.

Intangible assets

Companies sometimes buy *intangible assets,* consisting of valuable rights such as patents, trademarks, copyrights, and franchises. The costs of intangible assets must be *amortized* systematically— that is, recognized as expenses—during their anticipated useful lives. When the period of usefulness can be predicted easily, the cost is amortized during this period. When no such basis can be found, current practice in the United States is to amortize the cost over an arbitrarily chosen period, not to exceed 40 years. The argument for setting an upper limit of this sort is that all intangibles lose their value at some time, meaning that their cost should be deducted from the revenues of the years in which the assets are expected to be productive.

Expenditures for sales promotion and for the research and development of new products are expensed immediately by U.S. companies and therefore aren't subject to amortization. Even though they are usually incurred to generate benefits in future periods, the amounts and duration of these benefits are so difficult to estimate that no attempt is made to recognize the creation and use of the intangible assets arising from these expenditures.

Since amortization of the costs of intangibles takes the same form as depreciation of plant assets, we won't illustrate it separately here other than to observe that instead of using a contra-asset account, the credit entry is a direct reduction of the intangible asset.

CURRENT-COST DISCLOSURES

Throughout our discussion of accounting for plant assets, the focal point has been the historical-cost basis of accounting. We have pointed out that an economic value orientation might enable investors to discern more effectively the potential cash-flow impact of plant assets, but we've noted that practical difficulties preclude any widespread adoption of this approach.

Large corporations in the United States are required, however, to provide supplemental disclosures relating to the effects of inflation and changes in replacement costs, as they relate to selected financial statement items. Among the designated items, two disclosures deal specifically with plant assets: The current cost of plant, property, and equipment must be disclosed as well as depreciation expense based on the assets' current costs. The nature and significance of these disclosures will be examined in depth in Chapter 14.

SUMMARY

The use of historical cost to measure assets when they're acquired raises a number of difficult questions. Some result from uncertainty—for example, will the expenditures lead to a commensurate future benefit? Others are definitional—for example, did the expenditure increase the company's total productive capacity or merely prevent it from deteriorating? All such questions require the exercise of accounting judgment. The basic accounting approach calls for capitalizing all costs that are incurred in anticipation of benefits beyond the current accounting period. An apparent exception is maintenance costs, but here the future benefit was already assumed in the decision to capitalize the costs of the asset to which the maintenance relates.

The measurement of depreciation expense is intended to allocate the original cost of assets to the future period which will benefit from them. Accountants measure depreciation by estimating the amount of each asset's service potential that is consumed each period. This means that there be a determination of both the asset's useful lifetime and the salvage value once its life has ended. In addition, it is necessary to identify the time pattern of depreciation; the most popular approaches are straight-line (uniform annual amounts) and accelerated methods (smaller amounts in each succeeding year).

The criteria for determining the amount of cost to be capitalized and the ensuing depreciation schedule are difficult to apply precisely. As a result, management has some discretion over the amounts to capitalize and the time pattern of depreciation charges. Once an accounting policy on these matters has been adopted, however, it must be implemented consistently each period.

APPENDIX: IMPLICIT-INTEREST DEPRECIATION

Implicit-interest depreciation is calculated in such a way that the income attributable to an asset each year will be a constant percentage of the beginning-of-year book value, if all cash-flow forecasts turn out to be correct. For example, suppose Bolton Company buys a machine for $6,000. Management expects the machine to generate incremental cash flows of $1,503 at the end of each of the next five years. The machine is expected to come to the end of its life five years from now, at which time it will have no salvage value. These cash flows are equivalent to an annual rate of return of 8 percent during the asset's life.[4]

Column (5) in Exhibit 9–5 shows a depreciation schedule calculated to enable the company to report an 8 percent rate of return on the asset's book value each year, if the cash flows are as predicted. For example, income for the first year must be $6,000 × 0.08 = $480 if the asset is to earn 8 percent on the asset's $6,000 beginning book value. This $480, referred to as *implicit interest,* is the first amount in column (4) of the exhibit. This leaves $1,023 of the $1,503 cash flow to cover amortization of the asset's cost, and this amount is entered in the first line of column (5).

Depreciation of $1,023 in the first year reduces the asset's book value from $6,000 to $4,977 at the beginning of the second year. An 8 percent return on this amount would be $398, the amount shown in the second line of column (4). If Bolton Company reports

---

[4] We'll explain this calculation in Chapter 19, but what we've done is find the rate of interest at which the present value of the future cash flows is equal to the machine's $6,000 cost. The present value multiplier for five periods at 8 percent is 3.9927; except for a rounding error, $1,503 × 3.9927 = $6,000.

EXHIBIT 9–5. Implicit-Interest Depreciation: Level Cash-Flow Stream

(1) Year	(2) Book Value (= Present Value), Beginning of Year [line above: (2) − (5)]	(3) Anticipated Cash Flow	(4) Income (2) × 8%	(5) Implicit-Interest Depreciation ("economic depreciation") (3) − (4)
1	$6,000	$1,503	$480	$1,023
2	4,977	1,503	398	1,105
3	3,872	1,503	310	1,193
4	2,679	1,503	214	1,289
5	1,390	1,503	111	1,392

this income in the second year, its reported rate of return on book value will be just 8 percent:

$$\text{Rate of Return} \quad = \quad \$398/\$4{,}977 \quad = \quad 8 \text{ percent}$$

Depreciation for the second year, therefore, must be $1,503 − $398 = $1,105, the amount shown in the second line of column (5). Repeating this process for the other three years produces the figures shown in the last three lines of column (5). The $2 difference between the depreciation charge for the fifth year and the asset's book value at the beginning of the year is a rounding error and has no significance.

Each book value amount in column (2) equals the present value of the machine's anticipated future cash flows, discounted at 8 percent. For example, the book value at the beginning of the second year is the present value of four annual receipts of $1,503 each. [$1,503 times 3.3121, the four-year factor in Table 4 of Appendix A, equals $4,978, which differs from the amount in column (2) by a $1 rounding error only.] Similarly, the present value of three annual $1,503 receipts is $3,875, the book value at the beginning of the third year, and so on.

Alternatively, we could have derived the depreciation schedule in column (5) by computing the present values of the machine in succeeding years [as in column (2)] and subtracting. Depreciation for the first year thus is $6,000 − $4,977 = $1,023.

To summarize, if Bolton Company calculates present value at the interest rate that is implicit in the acquisition decision—that is, if acquisition cost equals present value at the time of acquisition—then the periodic cash flows produced by an asset are exactly equal to economic depreciation plus interest.

KEY TERMS

Accelerated (diminishing-charge)
  depreciation
Ancillary expenditure
Betterment
Depletion
Depreciable cost
Double rate, declining balance
  depreciation

Implicit-interest depreciation
Maintenance
Obsolescence
Production-unit depreciation
Straight-line depreciation
Sum-of-the-years'-digits
  depreciation
Write-downs

INDEPENDENT STUDY PROBLEMS (Solutions in Appendix B)

1. Depreciation methods exercises. Fast Buck, Inc., has just bought a sophisticated copying machine for $30,000. It is expected to last five years and has an estimated salvage value of $1,500. The annual cash flow from ownership and use of this machine is expected to be $7,668, and this will produce a rate of return on investment of 10 percent. Calculate depreciation for each of the five years by:

a. The straight-line method.
b. The double-rate, declining-balance method.
c. The sum-of-the-years'-digits method.
d. The implicit-interest method.

2. Ancillary expenditures. An automobile manufacturer bought six heavy stamping machines at a price of $16,250 each. When they were delivered, the purchaser paid freight charges of $4,200 and handling fees of $1,200. Four employees, each earning $10 an hour, worked three 40-hour weeks setting up and testing the machines. Special wiring and other materials applicable to the new machines cost $600.

How much of these costs should be capitalized as costs of these machines?

3. Major overhaul. In January 1964, Abercrombie Mills, Inc., bought and placed in service a new paper machine costing $50,000. Its estimated useful life was 20 years, with no major overhauls planned for that period. Depreciation was to be calculated on a straight-line basis, with a zero estimated salvage value.

In December 1967, certain improvements were added to this machine at a cost of $6,000. Twelve years later, in the fall of 1979, the machine was thoroughly overhauled and rebuilt at a cost of $12,000. It was estimated that the overhaul would extend the machine's useful life by five years, or until the end of 1988. Depreciation charges for 1979 were unaffected by the overhaul.

a. Calculate the machine's book value at the end of 1967, after depreciation for the year was recorded but before the improvements were accounted for.
b. Show the journal entry required to record the improvements added in December 1967.

c. Compute depreciation for 1968 on a straight-line basis.

d. Compute depreciation for 1980 on a straight-line basis.

4. Choosing a depreciation method. Book publishers spend substantial sums to edit textbook manuscripts and to prepare the photographic plates from which the books themselves are printed. Textbook A is expected to remain in print for about five years. Up-to-date competing textbooks will be published each year by other publishing companies. The longer a textbook has been in print, the more out of date it is likely to be, making it more and more difficult to compete with the newer textbooks on the market.

a. What depreciation method should be adopted for textbook A?

b. What effects would your choice have on the publisher's financial statements?

EXERCISES AND PROBLEMS

5. Consistency versus uniformity. A financial executive recently stated that the only important requirement for a capitalization policy is consistency; in other words, the details of the policy are unimportant so long as it is applied consistently from year to year. Can you identify any possible adverse effects of allowing management to choose its own capitalization policy and apply it consistently? If so, are they likely to be important?

6. Joint acquisition costs. The Coyle Construction Company paid $61,000 for a house and lot. The house was then torn down at an additional cost of $2,000 so that Coyle could begin to construct a gasoline service station on the site. At the time of the acquisition, an appraisal of the property placed the value of the land at $48,000 and the value of the house at $19,000.

What asset(s) did the company acquire? Calculate the cost of each asset you identified.

7. Betterment or maintenance. The Bay Shore Company built an office building 10 years ago. It rented space to several tenants, but its major tenant, Gallagher Coal Company, gradually took more and more space so that, by last year, it occupied the entire 10-story building.

A year ago Gallagher notified Bay Shore that it would not renew its lease on the building unless Bay Shore made extensive alterations to the building to make it suitable for use as the company's headquarters. Since other tenants were unlikely to use as much space as Gallagher or to pay the rentals Gallagher was paying, Bay Shore decided to make the changes.

The alterations cost $1.4 million. Bay Shore's management estimated the present value of the future cash flows from the renovated building to be $3.2 million.

Before the renovation took place, the building was listed at its original cost of $2.4 million, less accumulated depreciation of $800,000. The land on which the building was located had cost $400,000. An appraiser estimated that the land and the renovated building had a market value of $3 million but that finding a buyer might take a year or more.

How should the renovation expenditure be accounted for? List the alter-

natives you considered and your reasons for choosing the one you are recommending.

8. Noncash acquisition. The Griffin Company bought a 10-acre plot of
land from Gargoyles, Ltd., issuing 20,000 shares of its own capital stock
in exchange for this land. The land was to be the site of Griffin's new
corporate headquarters.

Gargoyles had bought this land 15 years earlier for $20,000 and had
used it as the site of a drive-in theater. The land was near the intersection
of an interstate highway and the local arterial highway, making it very
attractive for potential users.

Gargoyles' balance sheet listed the land at $20,000; the theater installa-
tions had been destroyed in a storm six months earlier and the company
had written the costs off completely. Although the assessed valuation for
tax purposes was $100,000, an appraiser estimated that the land was worth
twice that amount.

Griffin's stock was traded actively on the New York Stock Exchange
at prices ranging from $24 to $26 at the time of the acquisition.

List the alternative bases on which Griffin might have capitalized this
property, choose the basis you would have recommended, calculate the
capitalized amount, and state the reasons for your choice.

9. Exchange of assets. The Park Wells Company has just purchased
all the tangible and intangible assets of the Crawford Corporation, giving
in exchange government bonds which were purchased two years ago for
$1 million. The market price of these bonds was $960,000 on the day Park
Wells purchased the Crawford assets.

On the date of the purchase by Park Wells, Crawford's books showed
current assets of $300,000 and plant and equipment with a book value of
$200,000. No other assets were listed on Crawford Corporation's books.

An appraiser hired by Park Wells estimated that the replacement cost
of the current assets on the purchase date was $360,000. The replacement
cost of the plant and equipment, less an allowance for depreciation, was
$540,000.

a. Should the Park Wells Company have recognized $1 million, $960,000,
or some other amount as the total cost of the Crawford assets?

b. How should this total amount have been allocated among the various
assets acquired? Prepare a journal entry reflecting your allocation and
give reasons for your choice.

10. Ancillary expenditures; joint costs. To obtain a new factory site,
the Mosk Manufacturing Company purchased a 12-acre tract of wasteland,
paying $13,000 to the former owners. Costs of searching titles and draw-
ing and recording deeds amounted to $300. Grading cost $2,800. As only
six acres were required for its own factory, it considered two offers for
six acres: (1) $12,000 for the north half and (2) $8,000 for the south half.
It accepted the offer of $8,000 for the south half and received a certified
check in payment.

a. At what amount should the remaining land be carried on the next
balance sheet?

b. What gain or loss, if any, should be reported on the income statement for the current period?

11. Capitalization: one asset or two? A machine has cost $21,000 and is expected to be useful for 12 years, with no end-of-life salvage.

A major component of this machine is a heavy-duty air compressor that must be replaced every four years. Replacement compressors cost $6,000 each.

Straight-line depreciation is appropriate both for the machine and for the compressor.

a. Determine for each of the next 12 years the effect on net income of capitalizing the compressor and the other components of the machine in separate accounts instead of in one single account.
b. Which of these two alternatives do you prefer? Give your reasons.

12. Exercise: different depreciation methods. Shakey Corporation bought a building on January 1, 19x1, together with title to the land on which the building was located. The building and land cost $1 million, and the land was appraised at $300,000. The building was assumed to have a 35-year useful life, with zero net salvage value.

Calculate depreciation for the second year (19x2) appropriate to:

a. Straight-line depreciation.
b. Sum-of-the-years'-digits depreciation.

13. Exercise: different depreciation methods. A company has just bought four assets for which you have the following data:

Asset	Cost	Life	Salvage	Method
Truck	$ 11,000	200,000 miles	$ 1,000	Production unit
Machine	300,000	12 years	25,000	Double rate, declining balance
Typewriter	660	3 years	—	Sum-of-the-years'-digits
Furniture	3,500	8 years	500	Straight line

The truck was driven 50,000 miles the first year and 40,000 miles the second year.

Calculate the depreciation for each asset for each of the first two years.

14. Calculating depreciation schedules; justifying the choice. F. Coons, Inc., bought a dump truck for $10,450. This truck was delivered on January 2, 19x1, and was placed in service immediately hauling salt for the local highway department. The company's past experience led management to believe the costs of maintaining and operating the truck would increase as it grew older, but the truck would be used about the same number of weeks each year and carry about the same number of loads.

Management decided to depreciate this truck by the sum-of-the-years'-digits method, based on a six-year life and a $1,000 estimated end-of-life salvage value.

a. Prepare a depreciation schedule for this truck.
b. Recompute depreciation by the double-rate, declining-balance method.

c. Do the company's estimates justify the use of one of these accelerated methods instead of straight-line depreciation?

15.   Choosing a depreciation method.   A company has just bought a new electric typewriter for $750. The manufacturer of the typewriter will provide service on this typewriter for eight years at an annual cost of $100. With this service contract, the typewriter will be inoperative, awaiting service, for approximately five days each year.

After eight years, the manufacturer will provide service only on a time-and-parts basis. This arrangement is likely to be so expensive that the company will sell the typewriter at the end of eight years. In the past, used electric typewriters have been sold to employees for about 20 percent of their original cost.

a. Which depreciation method would you recommend for this typewriter? Give your reasons.
b. Calculate the annual depreciation charge for each of the next eight years.

16.   Implicit-interest depreciation.   On January 1, 19x1, the Lubberdink Company purchased a machine for $56,910. The machine was expected to produce cash savings at the rate of $15,000 a year for five years and to have a salvage value of $5,000 at the end of that time.

a. Calculate annual depreciation by the straight-line method. For each year, compute the ratio of the machine's earnings after depreciation to its book value as of January 1 of that year.
b. Recompute annual depreciation by the implicit-interest method such that the annual rate of return on the machine's January 1 book value is 12 percent each year.
c. Is the rate of 12 percent appropriate to use in this case? Could the implicit-interest method have been applied with a rate such as 15 percent? Support your conclusion with appropriate calculations.
d. Calculate economic depreciation as the difference between successive present values, using the same discount rate (12 percent).

17.   Depreciable assets; missing amounts.   For each of the six independent cases (I–VI) in the accompanying table, determine the missing amounts.

	I	II	III	IV	V	VI
			Sum-of-the-		Double Rate,	
	Straight Line		Years'-Digits		Declining Bal-	
					ance	
Year number	4	5	3	3	2	3
Original cost	$14,000	$17,300	G	$39,000	$50,000	P
Estimated salvage value	2,000	D	$ 1,400	I	4,000	5,000
Book value, Jan. 1	A	E	9,400	J	L	33,750
Depreciable life (years)	B	7	5	4	10	8
Depreciation expense	C	2,200	H	6,000	M	Q
Accumulated depreciation, Jan. 1 ...	4,500	F	12,000	K	N	26,250

18. Plant asset transactions. Barkley, Ltd., engaged in the following transactions in 19x8:

1. On January 3, it traded a used delivery truck for a new vehicle that had a list price of $12,000. The used truck had cost $9,000 and had a book value of $3,200 on January 3. Barkley received a $4,000 trade-in allowance and therefore paid $8,000 cash. Barkley expected to use the new truck for four years.
2. On January 4, it sold for $16,500 office equipment that had cost $72,000, 75 percent of which had been depreciated.
3. On March 1, the company bought a parcel of land and the building on that land. Barkley paid $600,000 cash. The appraised value of the land at that time was three times the appraised value of the building. On March 10, the structure was razed at a cost of $5,000, paid in cash. By the end of November, a new building had been constructed at a cost of $720,000 cash; it began functioning as a warehouse on December 2, and it had an expected useful life of 30 years.
4. The company paid $24,000 cash on April 1 to buy the exclusive right to use the trademark of a defunct business. Management believed the value of this trademark would last forever and that it was likely to increase in value by $5,000 each year under Barkley's management.
5. It paid $45,000 cash at a bankruptcy auction on May 1 for a "package" consisting of a factory machine, a photocopier, and a delivery truck. An appraiser was engaged to estimate their market values and expected remaining useful lives, and this was the result:

Machinery	$37,500	5 years
Office equipment	30,000	8 years
Delivery truck	7,500	2 years

a. Prepare entries in general-journal form to record the transactions. The company uses a separate account for each class of plant asset.
b. Record the necessary year-end adjusting entry or entries. Barkley uses straight-line depreciation on a monthly basis and assumes zero salvage value.

19. Ancillary expenditures; trade-in value. In January 19x1, a storekeeper bought a used delivery truck for $2,000. Before putting the vehicle into service, $280 was spent for painting and decorating the body and $520 for a complete engine overhaul. Four new tires were bought and mounted for $200. The storekeeper expected to keep the truck in service for three years, at the end of which time it would have a trade-in value of $600.

Gasoline, oil, and similar items were charged to expense as procured. In January 19x2, a new battery ($40) and miscellaneous repairs ($180) were purchased. Straight-line depreciation was used.

Four new tires were bought for $220 in January 19x3, and the body was repainted at a cost of $350. Miscellaneous repairs were made at a cost of $300. Management still expected to trade in the truck at the end of 19x3.

In January 19x4, the storekeeper traded the old truck for a new truck with a list price of $6,800, giving the dealer $5,940 in cash and receiving an $860 trade-in allowance on the old truck.

a. Which of the outlays made in 19x1 should be capitalized?
b. Which of the outlays made in 19x2 and 19x3 should be capitalized?
c. Calculate depreciation on a straight-line basis for each year, 19x1 through 19x3. (A full year's depreciation should be taken in each year.)
d. Indicate how the replacement of the old truck by a new one would be accounted for in 19x4.

20. Betterment, overhaul, and retirement. A barge with an estimated life of 20 years and no end-of-life salvage value was bought in January 19x1 for $200,000. Straight-line depreciation was used.

The barge proved too small to be profitable, and five years after it was bought the company lengthened it at a cost of $30,000, paid in cash.

At the end of 15 years, the barge was thoroughly overhauled and reconditioned at a cost of $40,000, paid in cash. This action was expected to extend the life of the barge to 10 years from the date of the reconditioning (that is, to 25 years from the original acquisition date).

Early in its 22d year, the barge struck a rock and sank in a heavy storm. The company collected $15,000 from the insurance company.

a. Determine the book value of the barge at the end of five years.
b. Should the cost of lengthening the barge have been capitalized or expensed? State your reasons.
c. Calculate depreciation for the sixth year.
d. Should the cost of reconditioning the barge have been capitalized or expensed? State your reasons.
e. Calculate depreciation for the 16th year.
f. Determine the book value of the barge at the end of 21 years.
g. Calculate the gain or loss resulting from the sinking of the barge and the collection of the insurance.

21. Discussion question: stating and applying an accounting principle. The general ledger of Enter-tane, Inc., a corporation engaged in the development and production of television programs for commercial sponsorship, contains the following accounts before amortization at the end of the current year:

Account	Balance (debit)
Sealing Wax and Kings	$51,000
The Messenger	36,000
The Desperado	17,500
Shin Bone	8,000
Studio Rearrangement	5,000

An examination of contracts and records has revealed the following information:

1. The balances in the first two accounts represent the total cost of completed programs that were televised during the accounting period just ended. Under the terms of an existing contract, Sealing Wax and Kings will be rerun during the next accounting period at a fee equal to 50 percent of the fee for the first televising of the program. The contract

for the first run produced $300,000 of revenue. The contract with the sponsors of The Messenger provides that they may, at their option, rerun the program during the next season at a fee of 75 percent of the fee on the first televising of the program.

2. The balance in The Desperado account is the cost of a new program which has just been completed and is being considered by several companies for commercial sponsorship.
3. The balance in the Shin Bone account represents the cost of a partially completed program for a projected series that has been abandoned.
4. The balance of the Studio Rearrangement account consists of payments made to a firm of engineers which prepared a report recommending a more efficient utilization of existing studio space and equipment.

a. State the general principle or principles by which accountants are guided in deciding how much of the balances in the first four accounts should be shown as assets on the company's year-end balance sheet.
b. Applying this principle or principles, how would you report each of these first four accounts in the year-end financial statements? Explain.
c. In what way, if at all, does the Studio Rearrangement account differ from the first four? How would you report this account in the company's financial statements for the period?

22. Small tools; effect of capitalization policy. Asobat, Inc., commenced business operations at the beginning of year 1. At that time its accountants decided, with the approval of management and the company's independent auditors, to expense immediately the costs of all small tools and other long-life items which cost less than $50 apiece. The company's purchases of these items during the first 11 years of operations, together with its reported net income, were as follows:

Year	Purchases	Net Income (Loss) before Taxes
1	$20,000	$(21,000)
2	2,000	400
3	0	5,400
4	6,000	6,600
5	4,000	6,600
6	10,400	1,800
7	11,200	4,200
8	5,600	16,600
9	4,400	21,800
10	7,680	20,920
11	11,280	21,720

Having noticed how large these purchases have been in comparison with net income, the controller asked an assistant to look into the matter. The assistant's inquiry has turned up the following additional information:

1. Purchases seem to have been amply justified by legitimate operating needs.
2. Twenty percent of the items purchased were discarded after four years'

use, another 60 percent were discarded after five years' use, and the remaining 20 percent were disposed of at the end of six years.
3. The scrap value of the discarded items was negligible.
4. The company's new computer could be used to calculate annual depreciation charges on these items at a very low cost.

a. Calculate straight-line depreciation, year by year, on the items purchased in the first 11 years of Asobat's existence. Assume that all purchases were made at the beginning of the year and all retirements took place at the end of the year, after the annual depreciation charge was calculated. Depreciation on all items should be based on a five-year life.

b. Restate income before taxes for each of these years as it would have been reported if these expenditures had been capitalized and depreciated on the basis described in part a.

c. What conclusions, if any, about the firm's capitalization policy do these calculations seem to point to?

23. Self-manufactured equipment: determining the capitalizable amount.

The Beckman Company late in 19x1 requested bids from several equipment manufacturers on the construction of a unique piece of special-purpose equipment to be used in the Beckman factory to replace an outmoded piece of equipment then in use. Several bids were received, the lowest in the amount of $55,000. The management of the Beckman Company felt that this was excessive. Instead, the machine was manufactured in the company's own machine shop which was then operating at substantially less than full capacity.

The machine was built during the early months of 19x2 and was placed in service on July 1, 19x2. The machine was capitalized at $55,000, comprising the following elements:

Raw materials used in construction of new machine	$ 8,000
Direct labor used in construction of new machine	20,000
Amount paid to Ace Machinery Service Company for installation of new machine	1,000
Cost of dismantling old machine	800
Cost of direct labor for trial runs	1,500
Cost of materials for trial runs	500
Costs of special tooling for use in operating the machine	6,000
Savings in construction costs	17,700
Less: Cash proceeds from sale of old machine	(500)
Total cost of machine	$55,000

The following additional information is available:

1. Factory costs other than labor and materials averaged 80 percent of direct labor cost. This percentage was used to assign these other costs to products made in the factory for sale to outside customers.
2. Freight charges on the materials used in construction of the machine amounted to $250. This amount was debited to an expense account.
3. The replaced equipment had an original cost of $25,000 and accumulated depreciation of $21,000 at the time it was dismantled and sold.

4. The new machine had an anticipated useful life of 15 years; the special tooling would be useful for three years.
5. Savings in construction costs were computed on the basis of the difference between the lowest outside bid and the net costs charged to the job during construction. These savings were credited to the account Gain on Construction of Equipment.
6. Products produced during the trial runs were scrapped; scrap value was negligible.

a. At what amount should the new machine have been capitalized in the equipment account on July 1, 19x2? Show the details.
b. Explain how you would have accounted for each of the cost elements in the above list that you would not have capitalized as part of the cost of this piece of equipment.

24. Ancillary expenditures. The Realty Corporation owns a large number of buildings which it rents to commercial and residential tenants. In January 19x1, it bought a building for conversion into quarters suitable for use by a trade association. The building was in an advanced state of disrepair but was structurally sound except for the top (fourth) floor. This floor had been vacated two years earlier on the order of a city building inspector.

The purchase price of this property was $300,000 for the building and $500,000 for the land. Extensive remodeling and interior decorating were begun immediately to adapt the building to its intended use. The following outlays were made during the period January through June, 19x1:

1.	Interior painting and decorating	$ 40,000
2.	Structural alterations including replacement of plumbing fixtures at a cost of $50,000 and landscaping at $20,000	130,000
3.	Replacement and renewal of electrical wiring	20,000
4.	Removal of fourth story	50,000
5.	Payment of hospital and medical expenses of passerby injured by falling brick	5,000
6.	Architect's fees, building permits, and so forth	30,000
	Total	$275,000

In addition, property taxes accrued for the period January 1 through June 30 amounted to $15,000.

Late in June, the company was notified that it was being sued for $1 million for the personal injuries and mental anguish suffered by the passerby who was hit by the falling brick (item 5 above). The suit was scheduled for trial in February 19x2. At the time the remodeling work was done, the Realty Corporation had elected to be its own insurer in matters pertaining to public liability, and therefore it was not insured for either the medical expenses or the amount of any payment that might result from the lawsuit. The premium that an insurance company would have charged for liability coverage during the period of remodeling was $3,200.

The building was ready for occupancy on July 1, 19x1, and a 10-year lease, running from July 1, 19x1, was signed with the tenant.

Indicate how these facts should have been reflected in the company's accounts as of July 1, 19x1. How much should have been capitalized and under what account titles? How much should have been charged to expense for the first half of 19x1? Give reasons for your treatment of each item.

25.   Choosing a depreciation method.[5]   The Alexander Cargo Service was started in 1967 to carry freight from a coastal seaport in the United States to several inland locations. By the beginning of 1982, the company had three small cargo vessels capable of operating in the small river which flowed into the port.

A fourth ship was purchased for $550,000 and placed in service on July 1, 1982. The public accountant who audited the company's financial statements pointed out that the company's first three ships were being depreciated on a straight-line basis over a 20-year period. Although a shorter life was prescribed by the taxing authorities in 1982, the auditor argued that this wasn't a relevant consideration in choosing a depreciation rate for financial reporting.

Mr. Alexander couldn't agree that the estimated life of this new vessel would be as long as 20 years. He had seen so many changes in the transportation pattern in his area just since he started in business that he felt a 10-year life would be much more likely. From experience that he had had in buying and selling secondhand ships, he also concluded that he could sell the ship for at least $50,000 at the end of 10 years even if economic conditions did not permit its use for containerized service locally after that time.

By the time the ship went into service on July 1, 1982, it was clear to Alexander that his original estimates were sound, at least for the first few years of the new ship's life. Contracts had been signed with several shippers. Bookings for space on the new vessel continued near capacity throughout the first six months of its operation. Alexander felt that he might gradually lose some of this business from year to year as the pattern of local cargo operation changed, but he saw no reason why he could not continue to operate the vessel for at least 10 years before the volume of business declined so far that he would find it necessary to take the new vessel out of service and sell it.

Sales revenues of the Alexander Cargo Service amounted to $5 million in 1982 and were expected to reach $6 million in 1983. Income before taxes and before deducting depreciation on the new ship amounted to $250,000 in 1982 and was expected to total $500,000 in 1983. The book value of all assets other than this new vessel totaled $1,250,000 and was expected to remain constant at this level. The income tax rate was 40 percent of taxable income.

The company had sometimes used the tax basis in the past for capitalizing and depreciating costs when this seemed to fit the facts of the case. At other times, it had felt justified in using some basis other than the tax basis. For its financial statements, however, Alexander Cargo Service used only straight-line depreciation or the double-rate, declining-balance method, with the choice depending on the circumstances.

---

[5] Abstracted from an original case, copyright 1967, 1983 by l'Institut pour l'Etude des Méthodes de Direction de l'Entreprise (IMEDE), Lausanne, Switzerland. Published by permission.

a. What depreciation method should have been used for this new ship in the company's financial statements? Explain your reasoning.

b. Using this method, calculate depreciation for 1982. (Only one-half year's depreciation should be charged for the year.)

c. How important was the decision called for in part *a*? Support your answer by citing numbers from this problem.

10

Liabilities and related items

A company's capital structure has great significance to management and outsiders alike. The amount and composition of the liabilities can have a great influence on the profitability of the shareholders' investment and on the risks of investment in the company. This chapter will examine the problems encountered in measuring various kinds of liabilities. Because liability measurement is inseparable from asset measurement in some cases and from expense measurement in others, our examination will cover some of these related topics too. The discussion falls under four major headings:

1. Long-term borrowing.
2. Interperiod income tax allocations.
3. Pension plans.
4. Leases in lessees' financial statements.

LONG-TERM BORROWING

Most large corporations obtain at least part of their funds through long-term borrowing. This kind of debt financing permits shareholders to benefit from the use of relatively low-cost funds to finance high-yield operations. It also allows the company to grow larger than it could if it had to rely on shareholder capital alone. These benefits are obtained at some sacrifice, however. Increasing long-term borrowing relative to the shareholders' equity also increases the risks the shareholders assume. This happens because the residual earnings that accrue to shareholders become more uncertain as the fixed payments required by the long-term debt increase.

In this section we'll examine the nature of long-term borrowing, the market prices and yields on debt securities, accounting measurements of long-term debt and interest expense, and the refunding or restructuring of long-term debt.

The nature of bonds

Corporations often borrow money for long periods from single lenders such as insurance companies. In other cases, they meet their needs by borrowing from many lenders at the same time, each one lending a relatively small percentage of the total. Under these circumstances, a single long-term loan contract is signed by the borrower and a representative of the lenders. The contract is known as an *indenture,* and the lenders' representative is the *trustee.*

Each of the lenders in one of these long-term contractual arrangements receives one or more documents known as bond certificates or *bonds.* These certificates specify the amounts to be paid to the owners of the bonds and the times at which the payments are to be made. The final payment to the bondholder, the amount to be paid on the maturity date (the date on which the contract expires if all its provisions have been met), is called the *maturity value* or *face value* of the bond. Interim interest payments are customarily made semiannually, but they are normally expressed as an annual percentage of the face value. This percentage is called the *coupon rate* or *face rate* of interest. Thus, a $1,000, 12 percent, 20-year bond represents an agreement to pay $1,000 at the end of 20 years

EXHIBIT 10–1. Cash Payments Required for a 20-Year, 12 Percent, $1,000 Bond

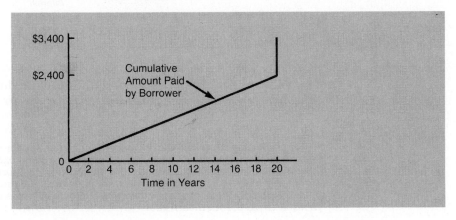

plus $60 (one half of 12 percent of $1,000) at the end of each half-year for 20 years. Exhibit 10–1 illustrates the lifetime pattern of cash payments to the holder of one of these bonds.

Bond values

The value of bonds to investors depends on the *yield to maturity* they could earn on other bonds of comparable risk that are available on the market. Yield to maturity is the rate of interest investors can earn if they buy bonds at a given price, collect the specified interest payments on schedule, and collect the face value from the borrower on the maturity date.

For example, suppose other comparable bonds now yield 14 percent if held to maturity. If bonds are offered with a coupon rate of 12 percent, investors have to figure out how much to pay for these bonds so that they will yield 14 percent, the yield investors can get elsewhere. They do this by calculating the present values of the cash flows they will receive.

Calculating present value. Investors who buy the 12 percent bonds when they are issued become entitled to two kinds of payments for each $1,000 bond they hold: (1) a stream of 40 semiannual payments of $60 each, and (2) a payment of $1,000 at the end of 40 periods, 20 years from the issue date. The present values of these cash flows can be determined by multiplying them by interest factors taken from Tables 3 and 4 in Appendix A.

Because interest is paid twice a year, the usual technique is to use semiannual compounding. A quoted bond yield of 14 percent means that investors can earn 7 percent on their investment every six months.[1] This means using the interest factors in the 7 percent columns of the two tables for 40 six-month periods. The calculations are:

Period	Amount	Interest Factor	Present Value
1 to 40	$60 a period	13.3317	$799.90
40	$1,000	0.0668	66.80
Total			$866.70

The value of this 12 percent bond on the issue date is thus $866.70 to an investor whose comparable alternative is an investment yield-

---

[1] The effective *annual* yield is more than twice the six-months' rate because the bondholders can earn interest of 7 percent in the second half of the year on the 7 percent interest they earned in the first half. If investors can always reinvest the interest they receive at the same rate, the effective annual yield is $(1.07)^2 - 1$ = 14.49 percent. We'll conform to common practice, however, and quote annual yields at twice the six-month rate.

ing 7 percent interest every six months. The $133.30 difference between this amount and the $1,000 maturity value brings the yield on the bond up from 12 percent to 14 percent. This difference is referred to as a *discount*.

Use of bond-yield tables. If investors had to go through the previous calculations every time they considered buying or selling a bond, much time would be wasted unnecessarily. To avoid this, special tables have been prepared for the financial community, based on the kind of calculations just illustrated. A partial set of such tables is included in Appendix A (Tables 5 through 11). The present value of a 20-year, 12 percent bond in a market in which the prevailing yield is 14 percent may be found in Table 8 (the table for a coupon rate of 12 percent) by locating the column for bonds with 20 years to maturity and the row for the 14 percent yield rate. The figure is 86.67, which means that the market price will be $866.70 for each $1,000 of face value—the same amount we obtained using Tables 3 and 4.

Changes in bond prices as maturity approaches. The market value of the bond won't remain $866.70 forever, of course. The day it matures it will be worth $1,000, because that's how much the company will pay the lender at that time. The lowest line in Exhibit 10–2 shows how the market value of a 12 percent bond will change as it approaches the maturity date, other things being equal. For example, if the bond is still outstanding five years after it is issued (15 years before maturity) and the market yield rate is still 14 per-

EXHIBIT 10–2. Market Value of a 12 Percent, $1,000 Bond for 20 Years with Different Market Yield Rates

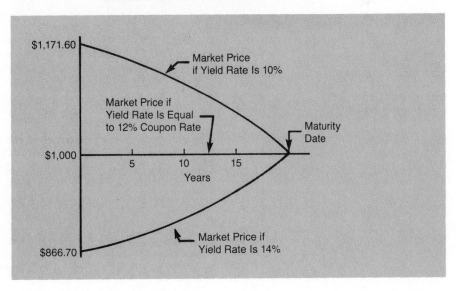

cent at that time, Table 8 indicates the bond will have a value of $875.90. The price will be $894.10 at the end of 10 years and $929.80 after 15 years.

The horizontal line in the middle of the diagram shows the market price of a bond for which the market yield always equals the coupon rate. In such cases the present value of the future stream of payments is always $1,000, and buying a bond for $1,000 will always bring a yield equal to the coupon rate, in this case 12 percent ($120/$1,000 = 12 percent every year).

Finally, the top line in Exhibit 10-2 shows how market prices will move if the bond is issued at a *premium*—that is, at a price higher than its face value. A 20-year, 12 percent bond issued in a 10 percent market should sell for $1,171.60. (The 10 percent row of the 20-year column in Table 8 shows a figure of $117.16 for every $100 in face value.) This premium arises because the company is paying $120 a year, or $20 more than the market expects to receive on $1,000 invested in bonds at 10 percent. The $171.60 is the price the market pays for this extra $20 a year. As the bond approaches maturity, of course, the investor has fewer and fewer of these $20 extra payments to look forward to, and the market price will fall. At the maturity date, the market price will equal the face value.

Effects of changes in market yields.   Market prices change for other reasons, of course. The market's perception of the risk of owning

EXHIBIT 10–3.   Market Value of a 12 Percent, $1,000 Bond with Yield of 14 Percent for Five Years and 10 Percent for the Remaining 15 Years

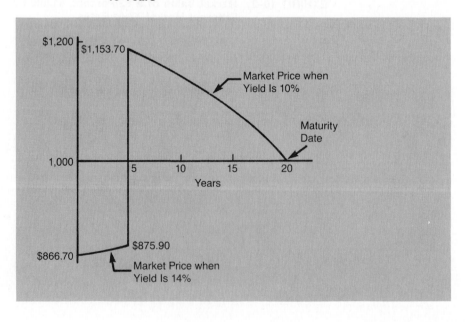

a particular company's bonds may change, or market yields generally may change. For example, suppose market conditions changed five years after our 12 percent bond was issued, so that newly issued bonds of comparable risk were being sold to yield only 10 percent. The $120 annual interest payments would then command a premium. From Table 8 we find that a 12 percent bond with 15 years to maturity in a 10 percent market would command a price of $1,153.70 rather than the $875.90 it brought just before the market changed.

The market price path on this bond is traced by the line in Exhibit 10–3. After rising gradually for five years, the market price jumped dramatically as market yields fell. Assuming market yields remain at 10 percent for the next 15 years, this bond's market price will decline gradually until it reaches face value at maturity. In practice, the path would be much more irregular as market yields move up and down, but it would always be moving toward face value at maturity if the company seemed likely to be able to meet its repayment obligation at that time.

Measuring bond liability and interest expense

The major accounting problem in connection with bonds is to measure the issuing corporation's liability and annual interest expense. We'll examine three situations:

1. The bonds are sold at their face value.
2. The bonds are sold at a discount.
3. The bonds are sold at a premium.

Bonds sold at face value. Bond accounting is simple when bonds are sold at their face value. The initial liability is measured by the amount received from the lenders and remains at that level until the maturity date. A suitable entry to record the sale of $1 million in 14 percent bonds at their face value would be:

Cash	1,000,000	
Bonds Payable		1,000,000

A suitable entry to record the payment at maturity would be:

Bonds Payable	1,000,000	
Cash		1,000,000

In this case, the payment of face value at maturity just cancels out the amount originally received from the lenders, and the only payments to the bondholders for the use of their money are the

$140,000 interest payments made each year. In other words, interest expense is equal to the annual interest payment.

Bonds sold at a discount.   The accounting problem isn't quite as simple when bonds are sold at a discount or at a premium. For example, suppose Reading Company decided late in 19x1 to issue $1 million of 14 percent, 20-year mortgage bonds. (Mortgage bonds are bonds "secured" by mortgages on specified company properties, usually land and buildings, meaning that if the company fails to pay the amounts it has promised to pay when they are due, the bondholders can have the property sold and collect the amounts due them from the proceeds of the sale.)

By the time the bonds were issued on January 1, 19x2, the going market rate of interest had gone up to 16 percent. Therefore, the bonds had to be sold at a discount. The total amount received from the sale was $880,800. The purchasers needed the $119,200 discount from face value to compensate them for accepting annual interest payments of $140,000 (coupon rate times face value) instead of the $160,000 (market rate times face value) they could have obtained by investing their $1 million somewhere else.

The general rule in accounting for liabilities and owners' equities is to record for each source of funds *the amount the investor has invested in the corporation.* Accordingly, the company's accountants first thought of recording the issue of the bonds on Reading Company's books as follows:

```
Cash .........................................  880,800
    Bonds Payable ...........................             880,800
```

Although this entry would have been correct, the controller decided to conform to the more usual practice of recording the face value of the bonds and the discount or premium in two separate accounts, as follows:

```
Cash .........................................  880,800
Discount on Bonds ...........................  119,200
    Bonds Payable ...........................           1,000,000
```

Some consider this treatment more informative because it discloses the final lump-sum payment the borrower is obliged to make (the face value). This provides investors with additional information regarding the magnitude and timing of major cash outflows. The same information could be disclosed in footnotes to the financial statements, of course, but the general practice is to put the face value in the balance sheet itself.

The form of the journal entry doesn't affect the amount of the liability, which should have appeared on the January 1, 19x2, balance sheet as follows:

Bonds payable (face value)	$1,000,000
Less: Unamortized discount on bonds	119,200
Liability to bondholders	$ 880,800

If Reading Company's bonds were to remain outstanding until the maturity date, the bondholders would receive the $1 million face value plus $2.8 million in coupon interest payments ($70,000 every six months for 20 years). The difference between this lifetime total of $3.8 million and the $880,800 proceeds of the issue ($2,919,200) represents the price paid by the corporations for the use of the bondholders' money, or *interest expense*. The $119,200 discount is just as much a component of interest expense as the semiannual payment—after all, the company's alternative was to sell the bonds at a higher coupon rate and higher semiannual payments.

The accounting problem is to decide how much of the $2,919,200 lifetime interest to charge to expense each period. The preferred method of doing this is known as the *effective-interest* method. This method amortizes bond discount (or premium) each period by the amount necessary to keep the ratio of each period's interest expense to the beginning-of-period liability constant throughout the life of the bond issue. This ratio is the yield to maturity or *effective interest rate.*[2]

The effective yield on Reading Company's mortgage bonds was 16 percent. We can verify this by going to the 20-year column of Table 9 in Appendix A, where we find that a price of $88.08 for each $100 in face value is in the row corresponding to an annual yield of 16 percent. As we mentioned earlier, this means a return on investment of 8 percent every six months. It is reasonable, therefore, for the company to calculate interest expense for each six-month period by multiplying 8 percent by the amount of the liability at the beginning of the period. The first six months' interest expense was 0.08 × $880,800 = $70,464.

This interest expense decreased the owners' equity by $70,464 and increased the liability to the bondholders by the same amount, from $880,800 to $951,264. A portion of the liability ($70,000) was current; the remainder ($881,264) was a long-term liability. In other words, the long-term liability increased by $464 during the first six-month period. This portion of the interest will be paid when the bond becomes due at maturity:

---

[2] The Accounting Principles Board made this method mandatory in 1971. Other methods of amortization such as *straight-line* are allowed only if the results obtained are not materially different from those obtained under the effective-interest method.

$$
\begin{array}{ccc}
\text{Interest} & \text{Interest} & \text{Interest} \\
\text{payable} & + \quad \text{payable at} & = \quad \text{expense} \\
\text{currently} & \text{end of 20 years} & \$70{,}464 \\
\$70{,}000 & \$464 &
\end{array}
$$

The entry to record interest expense for the first six months and the cash payment at the end of that period was:

Interest Expense	70,464	
Cash		70,000
Discount on Bonds		464

The credit to Discount on Bonds recorded the increase in the long-term liability during the first six months.

The bonds were reported on the company's June 30, 19x2, balance sheet as follows:

Bonds payable (face value)	$1,000,000
Less: Unamortized portion of	
original discount on bonds	118,736
Liability to bondholders	$ 881,264

The interest expense during the second six-month period was 8 percent of the liability at the beginning of that period, $881,264. Interest expense was thus $70,501, of which $70,000 was payable currently and $501 was payable at the bonds' maturity date. Interest expense was slightly greater during the second six months because the liability was greater during this period ($881,264 instead of $880,800), and it continued to increase as the liability increased. Eventually, the interest during the final six-month period (in year 20) will be 8 percent of $990,741, or $79,259. The interest rate underlying the expense charge is the same throughout the life of the bonds.

Calculating interest expense and the accrual of the amount not paid currently (by a credit to Discount on Bonds) for the other 38 six-month periods produces the liability amounts diagrammed in Exhibit 10–4. The nearer the company comes to the maturity date, the closer the liability comes to the face value of the bonds.

Bonds sold at a premium.   The effective-interest method is also used when bonds are sold for more than their face value—that is, at a premium. For example, Craft Company sold $1 million in 20-year, 14 percent debentures in 19x6. (Debentures are "unsecured" bonds—that is, they are secured only by the company's ability to generate cash flows, not by special claims against specific pieces of property.) The market yields on other bonds comparable in risk and maturity were 12 percent at that time. Craft's bonds, therefore,

EXHIBIT 10–4. Liability to Holders of $1 Million in 20-Year, 14 Percent Bonds Yielding 16 Percent to Maturity

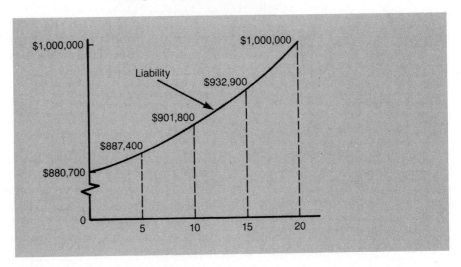

sold at a premium price of $1,150,500 (see the 12 percent row of the 20-year column of Table 9 in Appendix A). The balance sheet should have shown the following liability at that time:

Bonds payable (face value)	$1,000,000
Add: Unamortized premium on bonds	150,500
Liability to bondholders	$1,150,500

Using the effective-interest method, the company calculated interest expense for the first six months as follows:

$$\$1,150,500 \times 12\% \times \tfrac{1}{2} = \$69,030$$

This was $970 less than the $70,000 of cash paid to the bondholders at the end of the first six months. This $970 represented a payment of a portion of the $1,150,500 the company had borrowed six months earlier:

Cash Payment		Interest Expense		Payment of Liability
$70,000	=	$69,030	+	$970

This company had used a separate account to record the initial premium on the issuance of the bonds. The entry to recognize the interest accrual and the payment of cash at the end of the first six months was:

```
Interest Expense ................................. 69,030
Premium on Bonds .............................    970
   Cash ........................................        70,000
```

The debit to Premium on Bonds decreased the liability by that amount, and a balance sheet prepared immediately after this payment showed the following liability:

```
Bonds payable (face value) ........................ $1,000,000
   Add:  Unamortized portion of original
           premium on bonds sold ....................    149,530
Liability to bondholders ........................... $1,149,530
```

Notice what all this amounts to. In purchasing the bonds, the lenders paid $1,150,500 for the privilege of receiving $140,000 a year instead of the $120,000 they could have gotten from investing $1 million elsewhere at 12 percent. That $150,500 will be repaid to them gradually during the 20 years the bonds will be outstanding. As a result, the liability at maturity will be only $1 million, the face value of the bonds.

CALCULATION OF INTEREST AND PRINCIPAL

1. Identify the principal at the beginning of the period.
2. Find the effective yield to maturity when the bonds were first issued.
3. Multiply this yield rate by the beginning-of-period principal—this is the interest expense for the period.
4a. If the interest expense is greater than the payment, add the excess to the beginning-of-period principal to determine the principal at the end of the period.
4b. If the payment is greater than the interest expense, subtract the excess from the beginning-of-period principal to determine the principal at the end of the period.

Retirement and refunding of long-term debt

When a corporation buys its bonds back from the bondholders, the bonds are said to be *retired*. Bonds are sometimes retired at maturity, but other arrangements are also common. For one thing, bond issues are often very large, and it may be more convenient to retire them gradually rather than all at once. Furthermore, a company may not need all the borrowed funds continuously until the maturity date, or it may have an opportunity to obtain substitute financing on more favorable terms prior to that date. In principle, long-term debt will be retired whenever the company can maximize the net present value of future cash flows by doing so. Most bond issues, therefore, provide the issuing corporation with opportunities to retire some or all bonds at early dates.

Debt retirement is sometimes a one-way street, that is, the company pays cash and thereby reduces both its total assets and its total liabilities. In other cases the company merely replaces one bond issue with another. This is known as debt *refunding.* We'll look briefly at each of these situations.

Debt retirement by conversion. Some bonds are *convertible* into shares of common stock. This means the owners of the bonds have the right to exchange their bonds for a specified number of shares of common stock. Convertible bonds give the bondholders an opportunity to share in the benefits if the company is able to use their funds profitably. For this reason, convertible bonds are easier to sell than nonconvertible bonds carrying the same coupon rate. In some cases, the conversion price (the number of common shares obtainable for each bond) is so favorable that everyone expects all the bonds to be converted within a very few years. Such issues are really indirect means of selling common stock.

Debt retirement by serial redemption. A second possibility is to provide for the gradual retirement of the bonds outstanding by making the issue subject to serial redemption—that is, by staggering the due dates of the component securities. Thus, an issue of $100 million of serial bonds may provide for $10 million to mature each year for 10 years, the first maturity coming 11 years after the date of original issue. Serial bonds are usually offered at a range of prices, set to provide higher yields for the longer maturities. Accountants treat each series as a separate issue, using the accounting method described earlier.

Debt retirement by sinking fund. A third device for orderly debt retirement is the sinking fund. Each year the corporation sets aside a certain amount of cash for the sinking fund, and this is then used to purchase company bonds. The trustees of the sinking fund will either buy bonds on the market or require the holders of certain bonds chosen at random to sell them to the sinking fund at specified prices. Bonds the trustees can force bondholders to sell to the company are said to be callable for sinking-fund purposes.

Companies may also take advantage of changes in market conditions and ample cash balances to purchase their own bonds on the open market and retire (cancel) them. For example, on January 2, 19x4, Dawson Company issued $1 million of 20-year, 8 percent bonds with cash proceeds reflecting an 8.5 percent yield to maturity. By January 19x9 (five years later), market yields had gone up to 10 percent, and the market price of Dawson's bonds on January 2, 19x9, was $846,300—as indicated by the 84.63 in the 15-year column, 10 percent row of Table 6 in Appendix A.

Suppose the company buys $100,000 of its bonds at this price, $84,630 in all. The book value of these bonds, reflecting the 8.5 percent yield to maturity five years earlier, can be found by looking at the 8.5 row in the 15-year column of Table 6. The figure is $95.81, which means the book value of the liability is $95,810, and the unamortized discount on bonds is $4,190 ($100,000 − $95,810). The $11,180 difference between the liability ($95,810) and the amount paid ($84,630) would be reported in the income statement for 19x9 as an extraordinary item. A suitable entry to record the purchase and retirement would be:

Bonds Payable	100,000	
Discount on Bonds		4,190
Cash		84,630
Gain on Bond Retirement		11,180

Market prices, it should be emphasized, have no effect on the company's accounts unless the company engages in some market transaction. The company continues to amortize bond discount (or bond premium) on the basis of the *original* yield rate, on the ground that this represents the cost of the financing.

Debt retirement by self-amortization. Another method of reducing indebtedness in an orderly fashion is to take out a self-amortizing loan. In a self-amortizing loan, the borrower pays the lender(s) a specified amount each period for a specified number of periods. Each payment is identical to each of the others. A portion of the payment is for interest, the remainder is a repayment of a portion of the principal. The debt is completely liquidated by the final payment in the series.

For example, Roscoe Products Company borrowed $61,446 on a 10-year note bearing interest at 10 percent a year.[3] Under the terms of this note, Roscoe was to pay the lender $10,000 a year for 10 years, the first payment to be made one year after the date of the borrowing. Interest expense was calculated by the effective-interest method.

Interest expense for the first year was $61,446 × 10 percent = $6,144.60. The difference between this amount and the $10,000 payment was a partial repayment of principal. The company made the following entry:

---

[3] If we know the amount of the loan ($61,446), the term of the loan (10 years), and the interest rate (10 percent), we can calculate the required annual payment by dividing the amount of the loan by the interest factor from Table 4 of Appendix A. In this case, the factor from the 10-year row of the 10 percent column is 6.1446, and the annual payment is $61,446/6.1446 = $10,000.

Notes Payable..................................... 3,855.40
Interest Expense 6,144.60
  Cash 10,000.00

Many self-amortizing loans call for monthly or quarterly payments rather than annual amounts, but the basic principle is the
same: The principal of the loan is repaid gradually during the life
of the loan, not by a single lump-sum payment at the end of that
time.

Bond refunding. For most large corporations, debt is a more or
less permanent component of the capital structure. Far from wishing to reduce its indebtedness, the corporation seeks to maintain
or increase it. When one bond issue matures, it is succeeded by
another. Replacing one bond issue with another is known as refunding.

Refunding is relatively easy when the bonds are callable. Some
bonds are callable for sinking-fund purposes only, but others can
be called for other purposes as well. Callability allows the corporation to refund prior to maturity if conditions seem right. The borrowing corporation can take advantage of declines in money rates
by calling the old higher-yield bonds, replacing them with bonds
at the new lower rates.

To protect the bondholder, the bond contract usually specifies
that an amount greater than the face value of the bond will be
paid in the event of premature retirement. This *call price* normally
varies with the age of the debt, approaching the face value at maturity or at some earlier date.

To illustrate, let's modify the example we used to illustrate bond
retirements. Dawson Company issued $1 million of 20-year, 8 per-
cent bonds on January 2, 19x4, when the market yield was 8.5 percent. Now suppose that five years later the bond market was *more*
favorable to borrowers and an insurance company offered Dawson
a $1,070,000 loan at 7 percent interest for 15 years. The proceeds
would be used to pay off the entire $1 million, 8 percent bond issue
at its call price of $107 for each $100 of face value.

This refunding would have two effects:

1. A reduction in the interest payments each year, from $80,000
   (0.08 × $1,000,000) to $74,900 (0.07 × $1,070,000), a saving of
   $5,100 a year for 15 years.
2. A $70,000 increase in the face value to be paid off at the end
   of 15 years.

Management found this offer attractive because the present value
of the $5,100 series of annual cash savings was greater than the

present value of the $70,000 increase in the face value.[4] Paradoxically, however, the company's income statement in the year the refunding took place showed a $111,900 extraordinary *loss*. Remember that at the end of five years the book value of Dawson's bonds was $958,100. (The bonds were issued initially at a price that reflected an 8.5 percent yield to maturity; the 8.5 row of the 15-year column in Table 6 of Appendix A contains a book value multiplier of 95.81.) The loss reported in 19x9 therefore was calculated by subtracting $958,100 (the book value) from $1,070,000 (the call price), leaving a loss of $111,900.

The reason for this apparent inconsistency—reporting a loss on a transaction that benefited the company—is that the loss actually took place earlier, when the market rate of interest dropped from 8.5 to 7 percent. This loss went unrecorded as long as the company continued to pay the higher rate of interest implicit in the earlier borrowing. Retiring the old debt was an exchange transaction which forced the company to recognize the loss that had already taken place.

INTERPERIOD INCOME TAX ALLOCATIONS

Taxable income, as we have indicated, may differ substantially from the amounts shown in financial statements that are prepared for outside investors. Some of these differences are *permanent*—that is, they lead to tax reductions the company will never have to pay back under any circumstances, or to added taxes the company will never be able to recover. Others arise because of *timing differences;* that is, revenues or expenses appear on the tax return and on the income statement but in different periods. In this section we'll see how these differences affect the company's financial statements.

Product-warranty expense

Some timing differences arise because expenses are included in financial reporting *before* they are allowable as tax deductions. Product-warranty expenses fall in this category in the United States. Expenses and liabilities for product-warranty service are accrued when the related revenues are recognized; warranty expense for

---

[4] These cash flows should be adjusted to reflect the effects of this transaction on the company's income taxes, a technique we'll describe in Chapter 19. If we ignore income taxes and discount the pretax cash flows at 10 percent, compounded annually—a rate we assume Dawson Company can earn on the cash savings as they materialize—the present value of the annual saving is $5,100 × 7.6061 = $38,791. The present value of the $70,000 payment is $70,000 × 0.2394 = $16,758.

income tax purposes is based on expenditures actually made under terms of the warranty, and these come after the revenues are recognized.

The accepted treatment in such cases is to calculate income tax *expense* on the basis of the financial reporting figures. For example, Revere Company started selling a line of products in 19x1 with a one-year repair warranty. Sales of these products in 19x1 totaled $1 million, and income before warranty expense and income taxes was $195,000. The income tax rate in 19x1 was 40 percent.

The estimated warranty costs arising from the year's sales amounted to $50,000. This amount was reflected in the following entry:

Warranty Expense	50,000	
Liability for Product Warranty		50,000

Only $20,000 of warranty-related expenditures were actually made in 19x1, however, leaving a $30,000 liability at the end of the year:

Liability under Product Warranty

Expenditures	20,000	Accruals	50,000
		Bal. 30,000	

For financial reporting, the appropriate warranty expense is $50,000. Only $20,000 was deductible from revenues in calculating taxable income, however. Taxable income, in other words, was $195,000 − $20,000 = $175,000. At the 40 percent tax rate, the current tax liability was $175,000 × 0.4 = $70,000. If this amount had been reported as the income tax expense for the year, the income statement would have shown the following:

Income before warranty expense and income tax	$195,000
Warranty expense	50,000
Income before taxes	145,000
Income tax expense	70,000
Net income	$ 75,000

The apparent income tax rate in this amount is $70,000/$145,000 = 48 percent, a figure we know is too high. If the $50,000 warranty expense had been allowed as a current tax deduction, taxable income would have been only $195,000 − $50,000 = $145,000, and the tax for the year would have been $58,000 rather than $70,000.

Accountants recognize the $12,000 difference between these two tax amounts as a long-term prepayment, using a Deferred Income Taxes account as a prepaid taxes asset account. The entry to record income taxes for the year was:

Income Tax Expense	58,000	
Deferred Income Taxes	12,000	
Income Taxes Payable		70,000

In other words, the company deferred reporting $12,000 of its current income tax payments as income tax expense until some later period.

The situation was reversed in 19x2. The amount accrued for warranty expense in that year was $65,000, but the amounts expended totaled $75,000. This meant that taxable income was $10,000 less than pretax reported income. At a 40 percent tax rate, $4,000 was transferred from the Deferred Income Taxes account. The tax return for 19x2 showed a tax of $80,000, and the entry was:

Income Tax Expense	84,000	
Deferred Income Taxes		4,000
Income Taxes Payable		80,000

Income tax expense for the year was $4,000 more than the tax return showed because warranty expense was $10,000 less than the amount allowed for tax purposes. Part of 19x2's tax obligation ($4,000) had been "prepaid" in 19x1.

These two entries illustrate the process known as *interperiod income tax allocation,* the assignment of income tax expense to the periods in which the related revenues are reported rather than to the periods in which current income tax liabilities are accrued. When this is done, the income tax expense is said to be *normalized.*

The case for the allocation of income taxes to the periods in which the related pretax income is reported is that it is these revenues and expenses which create the tax liability. Congress may decide that these taxes are to be paid earlier or later, but how much is to be paid depends on the profitability of the company's operations. Normalizing the tax is intended to provide a net income amount that is representative of this underlying profitability. If warranty expense is shown at $50,000 but taxes are calculated on the basis of $20,000, the net income figure will be a poor approximation to the company's continuing earning power.

Depreciation

Interperiod income tax allocations arising from warranty expenses and similar items are relatively insignificant for most companies in the United States. In the typical case, however, substantial amounts of cost appear as income tax deductions *before* they appear as expenses in the income statement. Most of these arise from differences between the amounts of depreciation reported on the companies' financial statements and the amounts shown on their income tax returns. The reason is that the depreciation schedules prescribed for federal income tax purposes provide depreciation charges that are recognized over fewer years than depreciation schedules that are used for financial reporting to shareholders and others outside management.

For example, Brubeck Corporation started business on January 1, 19x1. It bought equipment costing $300,000 and placed it in a rented building. This equipment was assigned a five-year life for federal income tax purposes. Annual tax depreciation was based on the percentage schedules prescribed by the accelerated cost recovery system (ACRS). The percentages and amounts for assets in the five-year investment class purchased in 19x1 at a cost of $300,000 were as follows:[5]

Year	Percentage	Amount
19x1	15	$ 45,000
19x2	22	66,000
19x3	21	63,000
19x4	21	63,000
19x5	21	63,000
Total	100	$300,000

Brubeck calculated depreciation for financial reporting on a straight-line basis with a 10-year estimated life and zero estimated end-of-life salvage value—that is, $30,000 a year. Income before depreciation and income taxes was $100,000 in 19x1, and the tax rate was 40 percent. The tax calculation for 19x1 was as follows:

Income before depreciation and taxes	$100,000
Tax depreciation	45,000
Taxable income	$ 55,000
Tax at 40 percent	$ 22,000

Using interperiod income tax allocation, however, the income statement showed the following:

Income before depreciation and taxes	$100,000
Depreciation expense (.10 × $300,000)	30,000
Income before taxes	70,000
Income tax at 40 percent	28,000
Net income	$ 42,000

---

[5] These percentages apply to assets acquired by U.S. taxpayers in and after 1981; they are presented as a means of illustrating the tax allocation process as it applies to depreciation differences. Other sets of percentages are applicable in other taxing jurisdictions, and the percentages in the United States are subject to change.

In other words, income tax allocation led the company to report $6,000 ($28,000 − $22,000) *more* income tax expense in 19x1 than it was currently obligated to pay.

The explanation of this treatment is that the due date for payment of $6,000 of the current income tax expense was postponed, not canceled. By postponing the collection of taxes, the government increased the amount of the company's cash flow it could retain and use during the first half of the assets' lives. The government hoped this would encourage businesses to buy more equipment and stimulate the economy. Payment of these taxes was only deferred, however; it wasn't avoided. As the assets aged, annual tax depreciation would drop below the straight-line figure and the company would have to start paying these deferred amounts.

The basis for this process of tax deferral and eventual payment is illustrated in Exhibit 10–5. This compares the tax depreciation schedule on Brubeck Corporation's $300,000 equipment purchase with straight-line depreciation. Tax depreciation exceeds straight-line depreciation for the first five years, reducing the company's taxable income in those years. In each of the next five years, tax depreciation is zero, meaning that taxable income is $30,000 more than it would be with straight-line depreciation.

The upper part of Exhibit 10–6 shows how the tax deferral affected Brubeck's reported income in 19x1. Its current tax obligation

EXHIBIT 10–5. Depreciation Expense versus Tax Depreciation for Assets Costing $300,000 with 10-Year Life and 5-Year Tax Life

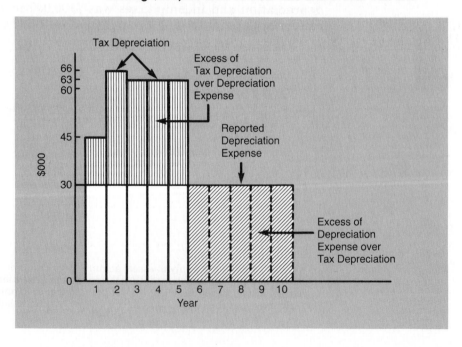

EXHIBIT 10–6. Effect of Income Tax Deferral on Reported Income and Cash Flow

	(1) Straight-Line Depreciation Used For Tax and Reporting	(2) ACRS Depreciation Used for Tax, Straight-Line Used for Reporting — Reported Tax Is the Amount Currently Due	(3) ACRS Depreciation Used for Tax, Straight-Line Used for Reporting — Reported Tax Includes Deferred Tax
Income:			
Income before depreciation and taxes	$100,000	$100,000	$100,000
Depreciation expense	30,000	30,000	30,000
Income before tax	70,000	70,000	70,000
Income tax expense....................	28,000	22,000	28,000
Net income	$ 42,000	$ 48,000	$ 42,000
Cash flow:			
Without deferral			
($100,000 − $28,000)	$ 72,000		
With deferral			
($100,000 − $22,000)		$ 78,000	$ 78,000

was $22,000, equal to 40 percent of Brubeck's $55,000 taxable income ($100,000 − $45,000 ACRS-depreciation). The amounts in column (1) would have been reported if the government hadn't provided the ACRS schedule for tax purposes and if the company believed that straight-line depreciation was the best measure of the decline in the assets' service potential. The amounts in column (2) would have been reported if the tax hadn't been normalized. Column (3) is the income statement the company actually presented.

The net income amounts in columns (1) and (3) are identical, but the net cash flows are greater under the alternative shown in column (3)—$78,000—than under the alternative in column (1) —$72,000. The company saved $6,000 in current tax payments, even though the net income was the same.

An appropriate entry to record the income tax expense for the year under these assumptions would be as follows:

Income Tax Expense	28,000	
Current Taxes Payable		22,000
Deferred Income Taxes		6,000

If Brubeck's income before depreciation and taxes in 19x6 (year 6) once again is $100,000, the tax currently due that year will be $40,000 (40 percent of $100,000), while the normalized expense will be $28,000 (as in Exhibit 10–6). This means that $12,000 of the deferred income tax will have to be reclassified as a current tax liability, as in the following entry:

Income Tax Expense	28,000	
Deferred Income Tax	12,000	
Current Taxes Payable		40,000

With no countervailing influences, the amount of the deferred income tax will be exactly zero at the end of 10 years.

Under this treatment, the deferred portion of the tax is classified as a liability. Many accountants and financial analysts aren't convinced it is really a liability, however. Their argument is that these taxes may never have to be paid, and, if paid, the amounts may be different from the amounts accrued. The liability will never decrease as long as the cumulative difference in tax timing doesn't decrease. And the deferred amounts won't be paid in their entirety unless the corporation is liquidated. Liquidation is highly unlikely, and if it does take place, the deferred taxes may be erased by tax-deductible losses arising in the liquidation process.

The fact remains, however, that the deferral results from a privilege granted to a going concern by the taxing authorities. The taxing authorities can always rescind or reduce this privilege for assets acquired in the future. If this happens, or if the company ceases to grow and allows its depreciable assets to age, current taxable income will exceed current income before taxes—and taxes will exceed tax expense. The deferral can even lead to tax obligations at the time of liquidation even if the assets are sold at a reported loss. Treating deferred taxes as a liability is an effective way of recognizing these facts.

The investment tax credit

The tax laws of many countries provide for complete forgiveness of a portion of income taxes if the taxpayer satisfies specific requirements. A typical provision of this sort is the so-called investment tax credit, which has been available to taxpayers in the United States at various times since it was introduced in 1962.

For example, Trilby Company's equipment purchases one year amounted to $1 million. The investment tax credit was 10 percent of $1 million, or $100,000, and this amount was deducted in full from the amount of taxes to be paid the first year.

The accounting question is whether the entire tax credit should flow through the current income statement or be spread over the estimated life of the depreciable assets. In the *flow-through* method, income tax expense is reduced initially by the full amount of the investment tax credit. A deferred tax liability is recognized only to the extent that the investment tax credit reduces subsequent tax depreciation.

In our example, the law provided that the amount subject to ACRS depreciation was reduced by half of the investment tax credit—$50,000. This means that at a 40 percent tax rate $20,000 of the tax credit (40 percent of $50,000) would be repaid during the ACRS recovery period (e.g., 5 years). In this version of the flow-through method, therefore, only $80,000 of the investment tax credit would flow through to the income statement immediately—the other $20,000 would be treated as a deferred tax credit, to be offset against income tax expense during the ACRS tax recovery period.

The alternative to the flow-through method is the *deferral* method, under which the amount of the investment credit would be spread over the useful life of the property. Assuming a 10-year life and straight-line amortization in the financial statements, only $10,000 of the tax credit would flow through Trilby Company's income statement for the year; the remaining $90,000 would appear in the balance sheet and be amortized over the next nine years.

The case for the flow-through method is that since the investment credit is simply a tax reduction that leaves income before taxes unchanged, income after taxes in the current period should be reduced by the full amount of the tax credit. Advocates of the deferral method, on the other hand, argue that the tax credit is conditional on the purchase and use of equipment, and that it therefore represents a reduction in the cost of the equipment. Recognition of the benefit offered by the credit should be deferred because it is the counterpart of the asset's cost being depreciated over its expected useful life.

While both methods are acceptable for use in the United States and deferral is a better application of accrual accounting, most companies use flow-through. The main difficulty with the deferral method is in classifying the deferred tax credit in the balance sheet. Since the deferral method is predicated on the assumption that the credit represents a reduction in the asset's cost, it should be classified as a contra amount to the asset itself. Similarly, in calculating depreciation each year, a portion of the investment credit should be offset against the depreciation charges that are based on the purchase price of the equipment.

Most companies which use deferral treat the credit either as a liability or as a *deferred credit,* listed in the limbo between the liabilities and owners' equity. This is a way of dodging the issue. It cannot be owners' equity, because this would imply that it reflects a benefit already earned, an assumption that is totally inconsistent with the logic of the deferral method. It can be regarded as a liability, but only if it is assumed to compensate the company for incurring higher operating costs in the future than it would have incurred if it had not purchased the equipment in the first place. The difficulty of verifying this assumption lends further support to our case for listing the deferred investment credit as a reduction of the asset's cost.

LIABILITIES UNDER PENSION PLANS

Some of the more complex questions in the recognition and measurement of liabilities have arisen in connection with employee pension plans. Legislation in the 1970s solved some of the accounting issues, but others linger on. In this section we'll study three topics:

1. Common attributes of pension plans.
2. Accounting for current-service benefits.
3. Accounting for past-service benefits.

Attributes of pension plans

The number of variations in pension plans is virtually limitless, but the most important variations come in a few key elements. First, the plan may be fully vesting, partially vesting, or nonvesting. Under a fully vesting plan, the employees' rights to retirement benefits accrue periodically and cannot be revoked or withdrawn by the employer. If the employees' rights are not vested, they lose all their retirement benefits if they leave the company prior to retirement. Between these two extremes are a host of intermediate arrangements.

Second, the plan may be funded or nonfunded. In a fully funded plan, enough cash has been set aside to meet the expected future costs of all retirement benefits earned to date, assuming that these segregated funds are invested at the rate of interest assumed or specified in the plan. In a nonfunded plan, the employees rely on the employer's future solvency; no cash is set aside until actual payments have to be made.

Some plans are defined-contribution plans, meaning that the company fulfills its obligations by making specified payments to the pension fund; the employees' pensions then depend on the amounts contributed on their behalf and how effectively these funds are invested by the fund administrators.

Other plans are defined-benefit plans, in which the employees' pensions are determined by a formula, usually based on the employees' length of service and average salary during some part of this period. In such cases the company's obligation is to set aside enough funds at some time to pay the amounts required.

Plans in either of these categories may be contributory, meaning that employees pay part of the cost of the plan; others have the employer bear all the costs.

Most pension plans in the United States today must meet the requirements of the Employee Retirement Income Security Act of 1974, more popularly known as ERISA. From an accounting point of view, this very complex legislation is important because it requires rapid vesting of pension rights, immediate full funding of the pension benefits under plans covered by the act and arising from services performed after the act went into effect, and gradual funding of benefits arising from service before that time.

Current-service benefits

In defined-benefit plans, pension expenses in any year arising out of the services provided by employees in that year are referred to as the costs of current-service benefits. They are measured by the present value of the portion of future pension payments attributable to services performed in the current year, discounted at the average rate of interest the assets in the fund are expected to achieve.

The accounting problems of defined-benefit plans are formidable because the company's payments under these plans aren't fixed in advance. Management has to estimate variables such as the employees' average length of service to retirement, average length of life after retirement, average salary during the period on which benefits are based, and the rate of return achieved by any amounts that have been deposited in funds earmarked for the plans. These estimates have to be made by specialists and reviewed frequently. Because of their complexity, we'll go no further with them here.

Defined-contribution plans are a good deal simpler, but they do offer some problems unless the plan merely requires the employer to make specific payments each year to an insurance company or pension-fund trustee. To illustrate a slightly more complicated plan, let's assume Genesee Corporation adopted a pension plan for the first time on January 1, 19x1. Under this plan, the company entered into a contract with each of its employees. This contract required the company, when the employee retired at age 65, to deposit with an insurance company an amount equal to 5 percent of the employee's wages from the date of employment to the date of retirement, compounded annually at 4 percent interest. This money was to be used by the insurance company to provide the employee with a pension.

The contracts for employees hired on or after January 1, 19x1, are accounted for easily. At the time it hires new employees, Genesee has no pension liability to them. At the end of their first year of employment, the company's liability amounts to 5 percent of the employees' wages for the year. (Because interest is compounded annually under this agreement, the year-end liability includes no accrued interest at the end of the first year.) At the end of 1, 2, 3, . . . , n years, the company has a liability arising from the employment contract equal to 5 percent of the employees' wages for the 1, 2, 3, . . . n years plus interest on these amounts compounded at 4 percent.

Although this plan is not funded, each year Genesee should increase its pension liability by an amount equal to 5 percent of the wage payroll for the year, plus 4 percent interest on amounts accrued previously. For example, if the wage payroll for 19x9 is $300,000, and amounts previously accrued for current-service benefits under the pension plan are $500,000, Genesee's 19x9 pension expense arising from these contracts would be the following:

Wage payroll for the year × 5%: $300,000 × 5%	$15,000
Amounts previously accrued × 4%: $500,000 × 4%	20,000
Total pension expense for the year	$35,000

The entry is:

Pension Expense	35,000	
Liability for Pensions		35,000

When payment is made to the insurance company at the time of the employee's retirement, the insurance company takes over the obligation and the entry is:

Liability for Pensions	xxx	
Cash		xxx

Past-service benefits

Current pension accruals of the kind we have just described will be adequate to cover the portion of the retirement benefits arising from employees' services from January 1, 19x1, onward. Genesee's plan also provided benefits for services performed before that date. These are known as past-service benefits.

The company's contracts with employees who were already on the payroll on January 1, 19x1, provided that the amount to be paid to the insurance company at retirement would equal 5 percent of wages, compounded annually at 4 percent from the date of employment, not from the date of the contracts. Thus, on January 1, 19x1,

Genesee had a substantial liability for past-service benefits that had never been reflected in the company's financial statements. This liability was measured by the amounts the company would have accrued in previous years if the plan had been in force then. For an employee who had worked for three years at $12,000 a year, the past service liability was:

First year	$0.05 \times \$12,000 \times (1.04)^2 =$	$ 648.96
Second year	$0.05 \times \$12,000 \times 1.04 \ \ =$	624.00
Third year	$0.05 \times \$12,000 \ \ \ \ \ \ \ \ \ =$	600.00
Total		$1,872.96

In other words, the liability is the future value on January 1, 19x1, of 5 percent of all active employees' earnings in previous years.

The main accounting issue with respect to pension plans is whether the liability for past-service benefits should be recognized immediately or gradually over time. On the one hand, the liability comes into existence at the time the pension plan is adopted. On the other hand, the company assumed this obligation in the expectation that future production costs would be reduced through lower employee turnover, greater company loyalty, and so forth. Most large companies are accruing their past-service liabilities gradually, over periods of 30 years or so. The unaccrued amount is reported in a footnote.

LEASES IN LESSEES' FINANCIAL STATEMENTS

In the past, accountants regarded leases as unfulfilled agreements to buy the use of property. The signing of a lease wasn't regarded as a transaction; the only recognized transaction was the use of the property by the *lessee,* the payment of rent, or the prepayment of rent. Leases are now very common means of acquiring the use of land, buildings, and equipment, however, and these leases often run for many years. As a result, accountants have had to develop a new approach to lease accounting. In this final section, we'll examine some common characteristics of long-term leases and describe situations in which lessees are required to recognize leases in their balance sheets.

Lease characteristics

Many leases serve the same purposes as purchases of property financed by long-term borrowing and have many similar characteristics. For example, to serve its southeastern market, Trevett Company has decided to build a new manufacturing plant in a small town about 50 miles from Atlanta, Georgia. The cost of the land and buildings is $1 million, and it is estimated that the facility will be used for 30 to 40 years. The company doesn't have the liquid assets needed to finance the investment. Its financial position is strong, but a firm of investment bankers has advised Trevett against trying to float a bond issue until additional ownership capital has been obtained. Trevett's present owners are unwilling to increase their commitment in the company and are equally unwilling to endanger their operating control by broadening the ownership base to include new outside owners.

With the conventional avenues to new financing closed off, Trevett has decided to enter into a sale-leaseback agreement with the Globe-Wide Insurance Company. This agreement provides that Trevett will have the plant built to its own specifications, after which the insurance company wil buy the land and building at Trevett's cost ($1 million) and lease it back to Trevett on a 30-year lease. Trevett will pay Globe-Wide $94,778 at the beginning of each year for 30 years and will also pay property taxes, insurance, maintenance, and all other operating costs. All Globe-Wide will do each year is collect the rent. At the end of the initial 30-year lease term, Trevett can either vacate the property or buy it by meeting the best offer received by Globe-Wide at that time.

A sale-leaseback of this type differs from a purchase financed by borrowing in that the lease entitles Trevett to the use of the property for a specified period of time, but it doesn't convey any title to the rights to any residual values at the end of the lease period. If conventional debt financing had been available at an effective interest rate of 8 percent, and if the estimated market value of the property at the end of 30 years is $300,000, the two alternatives might be described as follows:

1. Purchase (financed by borrowing): Pay $80,000 a year (8 percent of $1 million) for 30 years, the interest portion of the loan, and $1 million at the end of the 30 years, the principal of the loan.
2. Sale-leaseback: Pay $94,778 a year for 30 years, starting immediately at the beginning of the first year (the leasing charge per year), and $300,000 at the end of the 30 years, the sale price of the property at that time, if the continued use of the property is desired.

In other words, the choice of lease financing requires Trevett to pay $14,778 more each year than if it had borrowed the money in a more conventional manner. If it leases, however, it will have to pay out $700,000 less ($1 million minus $300,000) 30 years from now.

The effective cost of each of these methods of financing can be calculated from an analysis of the anticipated cash flows. In this case, the cost of conventional borrowing is 8 percent before taxes and 4 percent after taxes at a 50 percent tax rate. The cost of lease financing is 10 percent before taxes and more than 5.25 percent after taxes.[6]

The popularity of leasing stems from its adaptability to a wide variety of specific circumstances and its availability when conventional borrowing is either not feasible or impossible. In addition, leasing is often a considerably cheaper source of funds than additional ownership investment, when used within limits. Leasing therefore affords the stockholder the same kind of leverage that was described earlier in the case of long-term bonds.

Lease capitalization

The concern here is not with the desirability of lease financing, difficult though it is to keep away from that topic. The main interest is the representation of the lease in the company's financial statements. If the plant were financed by conventional borrowing, Trevett's balance sheet would report an increase in fixed assets *and* in long-term debt. Investors considering the purchase of the company's stock would note the greater risk caused by the increased leverage. Furthermore, they would also include the $1 million cost of the plant in its asset base in calculating return on investment.

The lease imposes no less a debt burden than long-term borrowing. If anything, the burden is heavier because the fixed annual payments include the amortization of the principal as well as the interest on the loan. Given this, a strong argument can be made for showing the lessee's rights to use the property and the corresponding liability for future rental payments in the asset and liability sections of the company's balance sheets.

Balance sheet recognition of this sort is known as *lease capitalization*. Leases can be capitalized in much the same manner as any other asset and liability: at the present value of the future obligatory payments under the lease, discounted at an appropriate rate. If the lease payments were capitalized at an interest rate of 10 percent, compounded annually, their present value would be $982,810,[7] and an appropriate entry would be:

Leased Property...............................	982,810	
Lease Liability		982,810

Once leases have been capitalized, both the asset and the liability must be amortized. For example, suppose Trevett decided to amor-

---

[6] At these rates, the present value of the future cash flows under leasing is $1 million. The method of deriving these rates will be discussed in Chapter 19.

[7] $982,810 is $94,778 × 10.3696, the 10.3696 being the sum of the factor for the first payment, 1.0000, and the 9.3696 interest factor (for 10 percent and n = 29).

tize the asset's cost by the straight-line method. The annual depreciation would be $982,810/30 = $32,760. Interest expense, calculated by the effective-interest method, would be $88,803, calculated as follows:

Initial liability	$982,810
First rental payment (paid immediately)	94,778
Principal, first year	$888,032
Interest (10 percent of $888,032)	$ 88,803

Total expense, therefore, would be $32,760 + $88,803 = $121,563, considerably greater than the annual rental. In the later years of the lease, annual expense would be less than if the lease were regarded as a simple rental agreement.

Lessees must capitalize leases if they meet *any one* of the following four criteria:

1. The lease transfers ownership of the property to the lessee by the end of the lease term.
2. The lease contains a bargain (less than fair value) purchase option for the lessee.
3. The lease term is equal to 75 percent or more of the estimated economic life of the leased property.
4. The present value at the beginning of the lease term of the minimum lease payments equals 90 percent or more of the net fair value of the leased property at that time.

SUMMARY

In this chapter, consideration has turned from the forms capital takes once it has been injected into the enterprise to an examination of some problems in accounting for the funds invested by the company's creditors. In the first part of the chapter we outlined a consistent procedure whereby any long-term liability can be capitalized, and illustrated the application of this method to the liability associated with long-term bonds.

We followed this with a discussion of interperiod tax allocation, a practice that is made necessary by differences between the tax and accounting bases for reporting revenues, expenses, gains, and losses. Although these allocations occasionally lead to the recognition of assets, in most cases taxes are deferred and a liability is shown in the balance sheet.

The chapter also examined three topics that represent major issues in contemporary financial reporting: the investment tax credit, pension plans, and long-term leases. Although the accounting profession has identified acceptable and preferred methods of resolving these issues, differences of opinion exist among accountants and readers of financial statements. In all such cases, the reporting company must identify which method it has used.

KEY TERMS

Bond discount	Flow-through method
Bond premium	Income tax allocation
Callable bonds	Investment tax credit
Convertible bonds	Lease capitalization
Coupon rate	Normalization of tax expense
Current-service benefits	Past-service benefits
Debt retirement	Principal
Deferral method	Refunding
Deferred taxes	Self-amortizing loan
Effective-interest method	Sinking fund
Face value	Yield to maturity

INDEPENDENT STUDY PROBLEMS (Solutions in Appendix B)

1. **Accounting for long-term bonds.** The Mountain Electric Company sells a million-dollar issue of 12 percent bonds on a 14 percent basis.

a. What does this mean?
b. Is the price $1,150,500 or $866,700? Why?
c. What is the term of this issue?
d. Calculate interest expense for the first six months. What entry should be made to record the accrual of interest and the payment of the first semiannual coupon?
e. What entry should be made at the second coupon payment?
f. How should this bond issue be shown on the balance sheet one year after it is issued and all interest for the year has been paid?

2. **Income tax allocation.** The Winston Corporation's income before depreciation and taxes in 19x3 was $6 million. Its depreciation for tax purposes was $1.25 million, and the depreciation for financial statement purposes was $850,000.

a. Derive the corporation's income after taxes, assuming a 50 percent tax rate.
b. Present journal entries to account for the year's depreciation and accrual of the income tax liability for the year.

3. **Lease accounting.** Company X has leased a truck from Truck Lessors, Inc., for $2,000 a year, payable at the beginning of each year for five years. Company X is responsible for all taxes, insurance, and maintenance on this truck, and the lease is to be accounted for as a means of borrowing money at 12 percent.

a. Show how this lease would be reflected on a balance sheet prepared immediately after it was signed and the first payment was made.

b. Compute the amount of expense that would be reported on the income statement for the first year of the lease, assuming that depreciation was straight line with zero salvage value.

c. Compute the book value of the asset and of the liability at the beginning of the second year, immediately after the second lease payment.

EXERCISES AND PROBLEMS

4. Calculating bond value. What is the maximum price you would pay for a $1,000, 10 percent bond maturing eight years hence if you required a return of at least 6 percent every six months, compounded semiannually? (Don't use the bond-yield tables except to check your answer.)

5. Self-amortizing loan. The Bell Company borrows $100,000 with the understanding that it will pay the interest and principal on the loan in five equal annual payments, the first payment to be a year from the date the money is borrowed.

a. If the interest rate is 14 percent, what will be the amount of each annual payment?

b. Present a schedule showing the interest and principal components of each of the five payments, assuming a 14 percent interest rate.

c. Prepare journal entries to record the loan and the payment at the end of the first year.

6. Calculating principal and interest. Howell Company borrows $2 million. It will repay the loan, with interest, by making 10 annual payments of $311,638 each at year-end.

a. What is the interest rate on the loan? (Assume annual compounding.)

b. What is the interest expense for the first year? Prepare a journal entry to record the accrual of the first year's interest and the payment to the lender.

c. What is Howell's liability at the end of the first year, after making the first payment?

d. What is interest expense for the second year?

7. Self-amortizing loan; calculating principal amount. Ted Jones purchased a house on January 1, 1944. The cost of the house was $20,000. He paid $2,000 on that date and agreed to pay $1,000 on January 1 of each year, starting in 1945, until the loan was repaid. What was the remaining indebtedness before the payment on January 1, 1984, if the interest rate was 5 percent.

(Prepared by Carl L. Nelson)

8. Self-amortizing loan; calculating number of payments. A company borrowed $20,000 from a bank at an interest rate of 12 percent, compounded annually. It promised to pay the bank $4,000 at the end of each year until the loan was paid off. The final payment would be the amount of the last repayment of principal plus the final year's interest on this amount. This final payment, therefore, would be less than $4,000.

a. How many years will it take to pay off the loan?

b. What will be the amount of the final payment?

(Prepared by Carl L. Nelson)

9. Bond accounting. A corporation issues $10 million in 16 percent, two-year bonds on January 1, 19x5. These bonds are sold to yield 9 percent per half-year. The $800,000 payments are made on each July 1 and January 1; the face value will be paid on January 1, 19x7.

a. How much cash will the company receive?

b. How will the sale affect the borrower's assets, liabilities, and owners' equity?

c. How will the bonds appear on the balance sheet at the time they are sold?

d. How will the liability appear on the December 31, 19x5, balance sheet?

(Prepared by Carl L. Nelson)

10. Bonds payable; missing amounts. Each of the four columns in the following table refers to an independent case. All the data represent amounts in effect on January 1, the day the bonds were issued. The last item in the table, however, relates to the interest expense for the entire first year. Since all the interest rates reflect semiannual payments and semiannual compounding, use the bond-value tables in Appendix A when filling in the missing amounts.

	I	*II*	*III*	*IV*
Bonds payable, face value	$10,000	$200,000	G	J
Market price	A	D	$58,032	K
Yield to maturity	12%	E	H	9%
Coupon interest rate	8%	12%	16%	12%
Life of bond (years)	20	15	I	L
Bond discount (premium)	B	$(7,080)	$1,968	$(24,433)
Interest expense for year 1	C	F	$9,865	$ 11,199

11. Capitalized leases; missing amounts. Determine the missing amounts in each of the following five independent cases.

	I	*II*	*III*	*IV*	*V*
Present value of lease payments	$80,000	$7,828	F	H	K
Depreciation expense, 19x1	A	C	$1,688	$9,326	$5,000
Lease life (years)	10	5	10	I	12
Annual payment	$11,836	$2,000	$4,000	$15,000	L
Interest expense, 19x1	B	D	$2,558	J	M
Depreciable life (years)	10	5	G	7	13
Interest rate	10%	E	12%	15%	8%

The leases begin on January 1, 19x1, and the first lease payment is remitted at that time. The company depreciates its assets on a straight-line basis and assumes zero salvage value.

12. Pension accounting: defined benefit plan. A small company has only one employee, Leroy Williams. Williams started to work for the company

30 years ago, when he was 33 years old. The company established a pension plan at the beginning of this year, when Williams was 63 years old. According to this plan, Williams will receive a pension each year equal to $100 times the number of years he has worked for the company by the time he retires. This pension will be given him every year until his death, the first payment being made one year after the date of his retirement.

The company will amortize and fund the past-service costs during the next two years, and Williams will retire at the end of that time, when he is 65 years old. Williams, being in poor health, is expected to live only three years after his retirement. He will receive the payment due him on the day of his death, however.

Each year the company will also fund an amount equal to the current-service cost. The interest rate to be used in these calculations is 8 percent.

a. Calculate the past-service costs at the present time, when Williams is 63 years old.
b. Calculate the annual amortization amount for the past-service costs.
c. Calculate this year's pension expense.

13. Investment tax credit. In 19x1, Andrew Corporation purchased facilities with a 10-year estimated life, entitling it to a $35,000 investment credit. This investment credit did not reduce the amount subject to ACRS depreciation. Its income before taxes and before reflecting the investment credit was $370,000. The income tax rate was 40 percent.

a. Calculate net income for 19x1 if the investment credit was accounted for on a flow-through basis.
b. Make the same computations, using the deferral method of accounting for the investment credit.
c. Is the difference between your answers to parts a and b large enough to be regarded as significant?

14. Income tax allocation. Pelican Corporation has purchased a machine for $10,296, delivered and installed. The service life of the machine is estimated to be eight years, at the end of which time it is estimated that the machine will have no salvage value. The machine is put into service on the first day of the fiscal year. It is the firm's only depreciable asset.

Pelican uses the straight-line method of depreciation in its financial statements and the accelerated cost recovery system (ACRS) for income tax purposes. It has no other differences between the amounts shown on the income tax return for the year and the amounts shown on the income statement. The ACRS rates, year by year for five years, are as follows: 15 percent, 22 percent, 21 percent, 21 percent, and 21 percent.

Reported income before taxes on income is $6,000 for the first year in which the machine is used. The amount of income taxes currently due as a result of the firm's operations for that year is $2,297.04. The income tax rate is 40 percent.

a. Calculate the amount of income before deductions for depreciation and income taxes were taken.

b. Calculate the net income (after income taxes) that the company will report for the year.
c. What is the amount of deferred income taxes for the year?
d. Assuming that this is the firm's only asset and that the tax rate does not change, calculate the balance in deferred income taxes at the end of each year of the asset's life.

(Adapted from a problem prepared by Charles W. Bastable)

15. Liability transactions. Ralston Company's December 31, 19x4, balance sheet included the following amounts:

Cash	$ 10,000	Accounts payable	$ 24,000
Inventory	15,000	Capital stock	1,000
Land	125,000	Retained earnings	125,000
Total	$150,000	Total	$150,000

The company's independent auditors discovered that the following four transactions which occurred during the first week of January 19x4 had never been recorded:

1. The company bought a truck for $21,000 cash. Although it would be used for five years, ACRS depreciation was 25 percent, 38 percent, and 37 percent during the first three years.
2. Ralston bought a machine for $60,000 cash. Although this machine probably would be used for eight years, ACRS depreciation through 19x8 was as follows, year by year: 15 percent, 22 percent, 21 percent, 21 percent, and 21 percent.
3. As a result of these two purchases, Ralston applied an investment tax credit of $8,100 against its 19x4 federal income tax obligations—$2,100 for the truck and $6,000 for the machine. Half of these amounts were deducted from original cost to determine the amounts subject to ACRS depreciation for tax purposes.
4. Ralston issued a 12 percent, 10-year, $200,000 bond on January 2, 19x4, priced to yield a 13.5 percent return to investors. Interest was to be paid semiannually on June 30 and December 31 of each year.

For both financial reporting and tax reporting, Ralston's income before depreciation, interest, and income tax was $125,000. Ralston expects zero salvage value for its plant assets. For financial reporting, Ralston uses straight-line depreciation and it applies the flow-through method of recognizing investment tax credits. Ralston's tax rate is 40 percent, and the tax payment for 19x4 was to be made in January 19x5.

a. Prepare Ralston's 19x4 income statement.
b. Prepare journal entries to record the additional transactions, the year-end adjustments, and income tax expense for 19x4.
c. Prepare Ralston's balance sheet as of December 31, 19x4.

16. Investment credit; depreciation differences. The Lambert Corporation purchased equipment on January 1, 19x0, at a cost of $10 million. A portion of this expenditure was for elements that made the company eligible for an investment credit of $400,000. For tax purposes, the company was allowed to depreciate the full cost of the equipment less half the investment credit over five years at the following annual rates: 15 percent, 22 percent, 21 percent, 21 percent, and 21 percent.

Management estimated that the equipment would be useful for 20 years, with negligible end-of-life salvage value, and that straight-line depreciation would be appropriate for public financial reporting. The equipment was the Lambert Corporation's only depreciable asset, and the company's income before depreciation and income taxes was $3 million each year. The income tax rate was 40 percent, and the investment credit was to be accounted for by the deferral method.

a. Derive the corporation's net income in 19x3 and 19x9, as reported to the stockholders.
b. Calculate the amounts of deferred income taxes and deferred tax credit at the close of 19x0, 19x2, 19x6, and 19x9.

17.   Lease accounting.   On January 1, 19x0, the Green Company entered into a noncancelable lease agreement under which the Blatt Company would have the use of one of Green's machines for 10 years. This machine was carried on Green's accounting records at $2 million. Payments under the lease agreement, which extended to December 31, 19x9, amounted to $355,080 a year for 10 years, with the first payment coming due in January 19x0, when the lease agreement came into effect. Although the form of the agreement was a lease, for accounting purposes this transaction was treated as a sale by Green and as a purchase by Blatt.

The lease agreement stipulated that the cost of the machine to Blatt was $2.4 million and that the interest rate implicit in the agreement was 10 percent. This was considered fair and adequate compensation to Green for the use of its funds. Blatt expected the machine to have a 10-year life, no salvage value, and a straight-line benefit pattern.

a. Ignoring income taxes, what were Blatt's expenses from this lease in the years ended December 31, 19x0 and 19x1?
b. How much income before income taxes did Green derive from this lease for the years ended December 31, 19x0 and 19x1?

(AICPA adapted)

18.   Lease accounting.   A company needs an additional machine and determines that it can acquire the use of a particular machine in two ways:

1. It can buy the machine for $92,442, paying $10,000 in cash on the date of purchase and promising to pay the remainder and 8 percent interest in 14 equal payments of $10,000 a year, starting one year after the date of purchase. Depreciation would be by the straight-line method over the machine's anticipated useful life of 15 years, with no estimated salvage value.
2. It can lease the machine for 10 years, paying rent of $10,000 at the beginning of each year. The machine is expected to have a market value of $43,121 at the end of the 10 years. The lease contains no purchase or renewal options, and if the company wanted to continue using the machine after the end of 10 years, it would have to negotiate a new lease.

a. Would the balance sheet at the date of acquisition be any different if the asset were purchased rather than leased? If so, how?

b. Calculate income before taxes for the first year under each of these two financing methods, assuming that income before taxes, interest, and depreciation or rent on this machine is $50,000.

19. Bond accounting; refunding. On July 1, 19x2, ABC Corporation sold a $1 million issue of 6 percent, 10-year bonds to an insurance company at a price to yield 8 percent. Interest was payable semiannually, on June 30 and December 31 of each year.

The company paid interest regularly for five years. In 19x7, the need for additional debt capital prompted ABC's management to try to borrow an additional $1 million. The insurance company refused to lend more money to ABC, but ABC's management found a pension trust that was willing to take a $2 million, 10-year issue of 10 percent bonds to yield 9 percent if ABC would pay off its debt to the insurance company. Interest again would be payable semiannually on June 30 and December 31 of each year.

ABC Corporation accepted the pension trust's offer and issued the new 10 percent bonds on June 30, 19x7. Concurrently, it used part of the proceeds from the new 10 percent bond issue to retire the old 6 percent bonds.

a. Calculate the issue price of the 6 percent bond issue on July 1, 19x2.

b. Prepare an entry in general journal form to record the issuance of the bonds on July 1, 19x2. Indicate how the bonds would be reported on the balance sheet as of that date.

c. Prepare an entry in general journal form to record the accrual of interest expense and the interest payment on December 31, 19x2. Indicate how the bonds would be reported on the balance sheet as of that date.

d. Calculate the amount ABC Corporation should have shown as its liability for the 6 percent bonds on a balance sheet as of June 30, 19x7, just after the interest payment but before the bonds were redeemed from the insurance company.

e. Calculate the issue price of the 10 percent bond issue on June 30, 19x7.

f. Prepare an entry in general journal form to record the issuance of the 10 percent bonds on June 30, 19x7. Indicate how the bonds would be reported on the balance sheet as of that date.

g. Calculate the gain or loss, if any, from the retirement of the 6 percent bonds on June 30, 19x7, and prepare a journal entry in general journal form to record the retirement, consistent with each of the following independent assumptions:

   1. The retirement of the 6 percent bonds was effected by the use of the "call" provision, which entitled ABC to require the insurance company to surrender the bonds at their "call price" of $102 for each $100 of face value.

   2. The retirement of the 6 percent bonds was effected by their purchase in the open market at a price to yield 9 percent.

h. Prepare a journal entry in general journal form to record the accrual of interest expense and the interest payment on December 31, 19x7.

Indicate how the bonds would be reported on the balance sheet as of that date.

(Restructured by Hugo Nurnberg)

20. Pension liabilities: discussion question. Global Tire Company is a manufacturer of automobile and truck tires, chemicals, rubber goods, and plastic products. Its sales revenues in 1982 exceeded $2.5 billion, and its net income was almost $35 million. Accruals for employees' pay and benefits amounted to $877 million in 1982. Retained earnings at the end of 1982 amounted to $472 million, and the shareowners' equity totaled $644 million.

One footnote to the financial statements for 1982 read as follows:

> The Company and certain subsidiaries have trusteed retirement plans covering the great majority of their employees. In general, the plans provide for normal retirement at age 65. The domestic plans permit early unreduced retirement at age 55 with 30 years of service. Accounting for the plans is on an accrual basis. Most plans are funded by payments to independent trustees of amounts, computed by independent actuaries, sufficient to provide for current service costs and the amortization of prior service costs over periods not exceeding 30 years.
>
> The total cost for all plans (before reduction for income tax) was $82,209,000 in 1982 and $79,362,000 in 1981.
>
> At January 2, 1982, the date of the most recent actuarial valuation, the actuarially computed value of vested benefits of domestic plans, determined in the manner specified by the Pension Benefit Guaranty Corporation (PBGC), exceeded the pension funds by $515 million; amounts related to foreign subsidiaries are not significant. The decrease of $45 million from that reported in 1981 results from more favorable actuarial assumptions under the PBGC method.

Five years earlier, the company reported that the actuarially computed value of vested pension benefits for employees in the United States exceeded the pension funds and balance sheet accruals by $395 million.

In replying to a question from a securities analyst in 1982, the company's financial vice president made the following statement:

> We began funding [the unfunded vested amount] in 1966 and in 1978 went to a 30-year program, which now has 25 more years to go. We are very much aware that this represents a substantial obligation for Global, but it must be put into perspective. This is not a current liability. It is a projection of the future pension payments we will pay to retired employees, extending from the present through approximately the next 50 years.

a. Since the company began funding its unfunded vested benefits in 1978, what explanation can you offer for the substantial increase in the unfunded amount between 1977 and 1982?

b. The company's treatment of its "prior-service obligation" was in accord with generally accepted accounting principles. Should those principles be modified to require companies such as Global to recognize the past-service obligation more quickly? State the arguments you considered on both sides of this question.

c. Suppose the Financial Accounting Standards Board had issued a new standard in 1983 requiring Global to recognize a major portion of the $515 million unfunded past-service obligation in 1983. If you had been empowered to decide how this change was to be implemented, would you have established the pension liability by a deduction from revenues on the 1983 income statement or by some other means? State the reasons for your choice.

11

The shareowners' equity

The owners' equity has two main components: *contributed capital* and *retained earnings*. Previous chapters focused on changes in owners' equity resulting from current income and the declaration of cash dividends which affect the retained-earnings component. The purpose of this chapter is to examine other transactions that affect either the contributed-capital component alone or both contributed capital and retained earnings simultaneously. This discussion falls under four major headings:

1. Classes of capital stock.
2. Issuance of additional shares.
3. Treasury stock.
4. Contingency reserves.

CLASSES OF CAPITAL STOCK

Each state in the United States has a general incorporation law. Anyone meeting the requirements of this law is entitled to draw up a set of *articles of incorporation* and receive a corporate charter from the state. The owners of the corporation then receive shares of capital stock in exchange for the resources they contribute to the corporation. Two classes of capital stock can be distinguished: common stock and preferred stock.

Common stock

When a corporation has only one class of capital stock, it is usually referred to as *common stock.* In such cases, each share of common stock represents a proportionate share of all the ownership rights in the corporation. Owners of the common stock (and sometimes others with specified voting rights) elect a board of directors to appoint and oversee the company's officers.

The articles of incorporation specify the number of shares of common stock the corporation is authorized to issue and the *par value* of each share. In some cases, the articles will specify that the shares are *no-par* shares, in which case either the articles or the directors will designate a portion of the issue price as the *stated value* of the stock. For most corporations, the number of shares issued is smaller than the number of shares authorized in the articles of incorporation.

Par value had its origin in the concept of legal capital. The amount designated as the legal capital is intended to establish a minimum limit on the owners' equity. In concept, this provides a cushion or margin of protection for the creditors. The economic significance of par or stated value today is minimal, however. The issue price of shares of common stock in the United States is frequently a large multiple of the par or stated value, and the total par value of a company's shares is likely to be only a small fraction of the total of its liabilities. The creditors' protection comes from the amount and continuity of the company's cash flows rather than from the designation of part of the owners' equity as par value or legal capital.

The excess of the issuance price over the par or stated value is reported in the balance sheet under some heading such as Additional Paid-in Capital or Capital in Excess of Par Value. The entry to record the issue of 100,000 shares of $1 par common stock in exchange for $1 million in cash would be as follows:

```
Cash .........................................  1,000,000
    Common Stock ............................              100,000
    Additional Paid-in Capital ................              900,000
```

At any time after the stock is issued and after earnings have been recorded, the owners' equity structure will be as reflected in Exhibit 11–1. In this diagram the left half of the circle represents contributed capital and the right half represents retained earnings. The circle is divided down the middle to emphasize this two-way split; contributed capital isn't necessarily half the total.

EXHIBIT 11–1. Shareowners' Equity: One Class of Stock

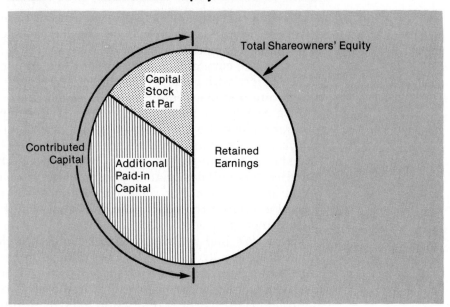

Preferred stock

Some corporations have one or more classes of capital stock in addition to the common stock. These other classes of stock are usually called *preferred* or *preference stock.* Exhibit 11–2 shows the shareowners' equity of a corporation with two classes of preferred stock. Three of the wedges of this diagram represent the par or stated values of the three classes of stock; the remainder of the contributed capital is shown as a single wedge, including the amounts originating in the issuance of all classes of stock. The amounts attributable to the preferred shares aren't reported separately on the balance sheet.

The rights of each class of shares are specified in the articles of incorporation and by-laws, but each share of a given class has the same rights as any other share of that class. Thus, an owner of 1,000 shares of $5 preferred stock receives twice as much dividend money as a holder of 500 shares of this stock.

Shares of preferred stock usually entitle their owners to dividends of a fixed amount that must be paid before any dividends can be paid on the common stock. The owners of preferred ordinarily also have precedence over the common stockholders in any liquidation of assets, up to a specified maximum amount per share. They usually do not have voting rights, however.

EXHIBIT 11–2. Shareowners' Equity: Several Classes of Stock

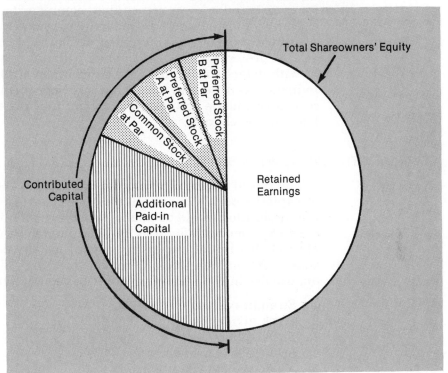

The dividend priority is usually *cumulative,* meaning that no distribution can be made to the common shareholders until all current and back dividends have been paid on the preferred. In most cases, shares of preferred stock are also *callable* at a specified price. This means that the company has the right to repurchase the stock if certain conditions are met, even if the owners of the stock don't wish to sell it. All these characteristics of preferred stock limit the risks of its owners, but at the same time they limit the owners' return on the amounts they have invested in the stock.

A preferred stock differs from a bond in that the stockholders have no legal right to insist on payment of their dividends on specified dates; dividend distributions are decided by the directors. Furthermore, the stock has no maturity date. A corporation may omit or pass the dividend on the preferred indefinitely, although some preferred stocks provide for the transfer of corporate control to the preferred shareholders when the dividends have reached a specified amount in arrears. Thus, preferred stock lies somewhere between bonds and common stock on the risk-return spectrum: It typically offers higher risk and a higher return than bonds, but lower risk and a lower return than common stock.

Many preferred stocks issued in recent years have been *convertible* into a predetermined number of shares of common stock. The sale of preferred stock and bonds with the conversion privilege or with detachable options to buy common stock is sometimes an indirect way of selling common stock. Noteworthy features of such securities and the accounting problems they raise will be discussed later in this chapter.

ISSUING ADDITIONAL COMMON SHARES

The initial source of corporate financing is the sale or issuance of capital stock. Without an adequate base of ownership capital, the corporation would be unable to obtain debt financing and would even experience difficulties in obtaining short-term trade credit. Most of this initial ownership capital usually comes from the issuance of common stock. Common stock may also be issued later on, usually in connection with one of the following:

1. Straight-cash sales.
2. Stock dividends.
3. Stock splits.
4. Securities conversions.
5. Exercise of stock options.
6. Acquisitions of other companies.

We'll discuss the first five of these now, leaving the issuance of shares of stock in exchange for the stock or assets of other companies to Chapter 12.

Cash sales of additional shares

Small numbers of shares of capital stock are often sold to employees as part of company employee-savings plans. The most significant kind of straight-cash sales, however, are sales of additional shares either to the company's current shareowners or to new outside investors. The company is likely to do this because it needs more funds to finance its growth than the company's ongoing operations are able to generate.

Registration requirements. Large corporations wishing to raise capital in this way in the United States must register each new issue with the Securities and Exchange Commission and make a detailed prospectus available to any potential purchaser of the shares. The task of the SEC is to insure that the information provided in the registration statement is complete and credible. SEC approval of a registration statement does not constitute or even imply an endorsement of the shares as a sound investment opportunity.

Preemptive rights. The common shareowners in many companies have the right to purchase any additional shares of common stock the company may offer for sale. Rights of this kind are known as *preemptive rights*. For example, if a company with 1 million shares of common stock outstanding wants to raise capital by selling 100,000 additional shares of stock, each current shareowner will have the right to buy one share of the new issue for every 10 shares he or she now owns.

Some shareowners may not wish to exercise this privilege, of course. They may be short of cash or unwilling to increase the percentage of their total assets they have invested in this particular company's common stock. In such cases, they may try to sell the rights to others. If the price at which the new shares are offered is less than the price at which the old shares are being traded, the rights will be valuable.

For example, the market value of the right to buy a tenth of a new share when the market price is $50 a share and the offer price is $40 should be close to $1. This amount is derived in Exhibit 11–3. These rights are valid only until a specified date, however, and any right that hasn't been exercised by that date becomes worthless.

All new issues aren't offered through rights. The owners of many companies don't have this privilege, and, in other cases, the shareowners may vote to waive their preemptive rights, leaving the com-

EXHIBIT 11–3. Calculating the Value of a Preemptive Right to Purchase One Tenth of a Share of Common Stock

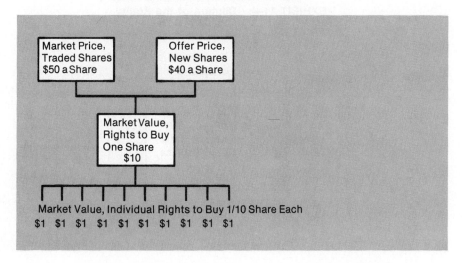

pany free to offer the shares to the general public. These are known as *public offerings,* as opposed to *rights offerings.*

Dilution of the market value of the equity.   When shares of stock are offered to the general public, the existing shareowners are very interested in the price at which these shares are offered. For example, suppose Drake Corporation has 100,000 shares of common stock outstanding with a market value of $30 a share. If the company sells an additional 100,000 shares at $20 a share, a reasonable expectation is that all the shares will trade at $25 a share. If this happens, the market value of the old shareholders' holdings will fall from $3 million to $2.5 million, while the new shareowners will pay $2 million for stock worth $2.5 million ($25 × 100,000 shares).

This transfer of part of the old shareowners' equity to the new shareowners is known as *dilution of the equity* and is illustrated in Exhibit 11–4. This shows the old shareowners giving $5 of the value of their stock to new shareowners to induce them to invest their money in the corporation. The dilution is measured by the difference between the market price before the offer was made and the market price after the new shares were issued, adjusted for other influences on the stock's price.

Offering the new shares at a price lower than the current market price is intended to make the new issue attractive to potential buyers. The reason the existing shareowners may be willing to make this offer has to be that *they expect little or no dilution to take place.* In some cases, for example, the old shareowners and the new shareowners are the same people; that is, the new shares are issued through a rights offering. The old shareowners can then protect themselves either by purchasing the new shares they are

EXHIBIT 11–4.   Dilution of the Equity

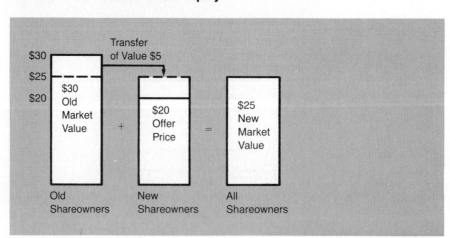

entitled to or by selling their rights at prices reflecting their values.

Existing shareholders may be willing to sell new shares to new shareholders at low prices if they are convinced that management can invest the new capital so effectively that the price of the stock will rise within a reasonable time to the level it would have reached without the new capital or even higher.

For example, if the old shareholders had expected the stock to increase in price to $36 within two years and if it actually goes up to that level as a result of management's ability to invest the new $2 million profitably, the long-term dilution of the equity is zero. In fact, the dilution may even be negative if prices rise faster than they would have without the new infusion of capital into the company. This approach to dilution is illustrated in Exhibit 11–5.

It is difficult to anticipate accurately how new investments will work out, let alone document these expectations. To avoid challenges by dissident stockholders, the board of directors generally tries to set the offer price in a public offering very close to the market price prevailing at the time of the offer.

Dilution of earnings. The funds obtained from the sale of additional shares are unlikely to generate enough income in the short run to keep net income per share unchanged. If the shares are issued to enable the company to retire debt, for example, interest expense will fall and total net income will rise. The percentage increase in the number of shares outstanding will probably be larger than the percentage increase in net income, however, and earnings per share will fall. (Net income is often referred to as *earnings* and net income per share as *earnings per share.*)

EXHIBIT 11–5.   Elimination of Dilution by Effective Investment

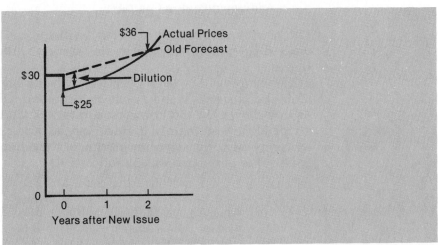

This reduction in earnings per share is referred to as *dilution of the earnings* due to the stock issue. This doesn't mean that the stock issue was unwise; if future earnings per share are higher than they would have been without the new issue, the financing was worthwhile.

Stock dividends

Corporations sometimes increase the number of shares of common stock outstanding without increasing the total amount of resources available to the firm. One way of accomplishing this is to issue what is known as a *stock dividend.*

For example, Space Age Corporation was very successful during its early years of operation, and retained earnings had reached $715,000 by the end of 19x6. The need for funds to finance the company's growth was equally strong, however, and the company therefore had no money to pay dividends. In this situation, the directors declared a 10 percent *stock dividend.* A stock dividend consists of the distribution of additional shares of stock to the existing stockholders in proportion to their holdings. With 55,000 shares outstanding, the Space Age 10 percent dividend consisted of 5,500 shares, one for every 10 outstanding.

This transaction was treated as if the corporation had declared a cash dividend equal to the market value of the 5,500 shares and the stockholders had simultaneously purchased the 5,500 shares at their market price. Because the market price of the stock at the time of the stock dividend was $60, the journal entry was:

Retained Earnings	330,000	
Common Stock		55,000
Additional Paid-in Capital		275,000

The "dividend" reduced retained earnings, and the "stock sale" increased the paid-in capital by the market value of the number of shares.

The shareowners' equity section of the balance sheet before and after the stock dividend is shown schematically in Exhibit 11–6. As this shows, the total owners' equity was unaffected by the stock dividend; it was merely divided into a larger number of shares, each representing a smaller portion of the company than formerly. Book value per share was as follows:

	Before Stock Dividend	After Stock Dividend
Common stock—stated value	$10.00	$10.00
Additional paid-in capital	17.00	20.00
Retained earnings	13.00	6.36
Total	$40.00	$36.36

EXHIBIT 11–6. Effect of a Stock Dividend

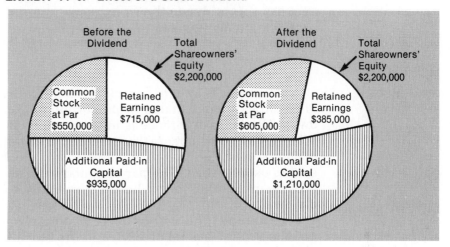

These results were obtained by dividing the amounts in Exhibit 11–6 by 55,000 and 60,500, the numbers of shares outstanding before and after the stock dividend.

It should be evident that the stock dividend in substance is a *paper transaction.* After the dividend, each stockholder had 11 shares which conveyed the same rights as the 10 shares he or she had owned previously. After the dividend, 11 shares had the same $400 book value (11 × $36.36) the owner's 10 shares had had previously.

Although the stock dividend does not give the stockholder any new asset, the market in the stock may be slightly more active than formerly because of the increase in the number of shares outstanding. Many companies also follow the practice of paying the same cash dividend per share after the stock dividend that they had been paying previously, which means increased dividend income for the shareowners.

Furthermore, the market often interprets the declaration of a stock dividend as evidence of management's prediction of continued company growth. Once dividends have been increased, large corporations show a great resistance to reducing them, except under the most extreme conditions. To a large extent, directors avoid dividend cuts by increasing dividends only when they are confident of their ability to maintain them in the future. Maintaining a constant dividend per share, therefore, is likely to increase the total market value of the company's stock because the dividends are assumed to convey management's positive assessment of the firm's long-run earning and dividend-paying potential. In other words, although 11 shares should sell for what 10 shares would have brought previously

$(10 \times \$60 = \$600)$, in fact, they may sell for more (for example, $11 \times \$56 = \$616$). This effect won't persist, however, if the expected cash flows don't materialize.

Stock splits

A stock split is akin to a stock dividend in that each stockholder is given additional shares in proportion to the number he or she owns. The main difference is in the number of shares distributed. When an increase of more than about 20 or 25 percent in the number of shares outstanding is to be achieved, the mechanism of the stock split is usually used. The par or stated value is usually reduced to accompany a stock split, whereas it remains unchanged in a stock dividend.

For example, the market price of Space Age Corporation had risen to $90 by the end of 19x9, and the board of directors decided to declare a two-for-one stock split and to reduce the stated value of the stock from $10 to $5. Since stated value per share was reduced in proportion to the change in the number of shares outstanding, the total stated value remained unchanged. Furthermore, no transfer was made from retained earnings because the generally accepted accounting principle is to treat stock splits as restatements of the existing paid-in capital. Space Age may have made a simple entry such as the following:

Common Stock ($10 par)	605,000	
Common Stock ($5 par)		605,000

The debit removes the old stated value from the owners' equity accounts; the credit puts it back in. (If the change in stated value had been less than proportional to the increase in the number of shares, a transfer from additional paid-in capital would have been made.) The owners' equity section of the balance sheet before and after the stock split are shown in Exhibit 11–7.

EXHIBIT 11–7

SPACE AGE CORPORATION
Shareowners' Equity
December 31, 19x9

	Before Stock Split		After Stock Split	
	Total	Per Share	Total	Per Share
Common stock—stated value	$ 605,000	$10	$ 605,000	$ 5
Additional paid-in capital	1,210,000	20	1,210,000	10
Retained earnings	1,089,000	18	1,089,000	9
Total shareholders' equity	$2,904,000	$48	$2,904,000	$24

Stock splits, like stock dividends, may be signals to the financial markets about the company's future cash flows. For instance, it may be that the market uses the announcement of a split to reevaluate the stream of expected cash flows from the shares. If the consensus is that future dividends will increase, the market price per share is likely to decline less than proportionally to the increase in the number of shares. The price may also be affected by the increase in the number of shares available for trading, thereby making them slightly more marketable. Except for the effects of these two factors, a proportionate change in market price can be expected.

Securities conversions

Corporations often attach conversion privileges to shares of their preferred stock or to their bonds. They do this either to make the securities more attractive to potential investors or to use these *senior securities* (that is, senior to the common stock) as an indirect way of selling common stock to the public. To see how this works, we'll examine a simple issue of convertible preferred stock in some depth and then deal very briefly with convertible debt.

Convertible preferred stock. The convertibility of shares of preferred stock enables their owners to increase the market value of their investment in a company if the market value of its common stock goes up. They can do this by exchanging their preferred shares for shares of common stock whenever the dividend and market price on the common shares have risen above the dividend and market price of the equivalent number of preferred shares.

For example, in 19x1, Taylor, Inc., issued 1,000 shares of convertible preferred stock at an issue price of $100 a share. The annual dividend on the preferred was $5, and each share was convertible into five shares of common stock at the discretion of the holder. The cash dividend on the common stock was 75 cents a share, and the market price of the common shares was $18 a share.

Given these figures, the preferred stockholders had no incentive to exercise their conversion option. By converting a share of preferred into five shares of common, they would have lost $1.25 in dividends and $10 in market value:

	Dividends	Market Value
1 preferred share	$5.00	$100
5 common shares	3.75	90
Difference	$1.25	$ 10

This doesn't mean the conversion option was valueless, however. If earnings and dividends on the common stock continued to rise in the years ahead, the market price of the common would probably rise, too. If that happened, conversion could become very desirable. For example, the cash dividend on the common rose to $1.60 a share in 19x6. The market price of a common share at that time was $40. Conversion of the preferred shares would then give the preferred shareholder $8 in dividends instead of $5, and a market value of $200 (five shares at $40 each). All 1,000 shares of preferred stock were converted into 5,000 shares of $1 par common stock, and these conversions were recorded in the following entry:

Preferred Stock	100,000	
Common Stock		5,000
Additional Paid-in Capital		95,000

The debit to Preferred Stock showed that this form of owners' equity had been extinguished. The credit to Common Stock was the par value of the 5,000 new common shares, and the $95,000 credit to Additional Paid-in Capital showed that the new common shareowners had contributed this amount in excess of the par value of their shares.

In other words, the conversion privilege clearly has value if the price of the common is expected to rise. In practice, most holders of the preferred stock are likely to convert even before the benefits of conversion are as great as this; moreover, the market price of the preferred shares would probably increase in response to the higher value of the common stock.

Issuing convertible securities also involves a cost to the common shareholders. To retire the 1,000 shares of preferred in 19x6, Taylor, Inc., had to issue 5,000 shares of common, worth $40 a share, or $200,000. If the preferred had been callable at $100, however, Taylor could have retired the entire issue with the payment of $100,000 in cash. This $100,000 could have been obtained by issuing only 2,500 shares of common stock at $40 a share. The conversion privilege, in other words, does carry with it a potential dilution of the common equity.

Earnings per share

Calculations of earnings per share of common stock that ignore potential conversions could mislead investors. Suppose Taylor had 20,000 shares of common stock outstanding in 19x5 and net income of $65,000. The total preferred dividend was $1,000 \times \$5 = \$5,000$, and the earnings available to the common shareowners therefore was $\$65,000 - \$5,000 = \$60,000$. If the potential dilution were ignored, earnings per common share would be calculated as follows:

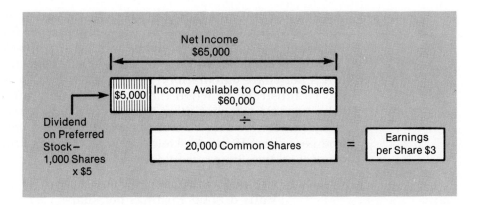

The conversion of all the preferred, however, would raise the number of common shares outstanding to 25,000 and would make the entire $65,000 net income available to the common shareholders. Earnings per share calculated on this basis would be:

$$\frac{\text{Adjusted income available}}{\text{Adjusted number of shares}} = \frac{\$65,000}{25,000} = \$2.60 \text{ a share}$$

Accountants in the United States are required to consider the potential dilutive effects of outstanding convertible preferred stocks when they calculate earnings per share. Two earnings per share amounts are calculated and published: *fully diluted earnings per share,* reflecting *all* existing potential dilutions, and *primary earnings per share,* reflecting potential dilutions only if they are so large as to lead to a reasonable presumption that they have already occurred.

For convertible preferred stock, the dividing line in the United States between a potential dilution that is to be reflected in primary earnings per share and one that is reflected only in the fully diluted earnings per share is based on the relationship between the average Aa corporate bond yield rate (an average market rate on nonconvertible long-term bonds) and the book yield on the preferred stock (ratio of the annual dividend on the preferred to the amounts contributed by the preferred stockholders) *at the time the preferred was issued.*[1] If the book yield was less than two thirds of the Aa yield rate at that time, the preferred is presumed to be equivalent to common stock—and primary earnings per share is calculated as if the conversion has already taken place. If the book yield was greater than two thirds of the Aa yield rate on the issue date, the

---

[1] For securities issued before March 1, 1982, the equivalency test is based on the prime interest rate (applicable to banks' loans to their lowest-risk customers) rather than on the long-term Aa yield rate.

potential dilution is ignored in the calculation of primary earnings per share, but it is reflected in the calculation of fully diluted earnings per share. (If conversion would be *antidilutive*—that is, if it would increase earnings per share— it isn't reflected in either earnings per share calculation.)

To illustrate, if, when the $5 convertible preferred was issued, the Aa yield rate was more than 7.5 percent, primary earnings per share in 19x5 would be $2.60 and no additional calculations would be necessary. If the Aa yield rate was 6 percent on the issue date, however, two figures would be published:

Primary earnings per share $3.00
Fully diluted earnings per share $2.60

Convertible debt.   Bonds are also issued with convertible features, as we saw in Chapter 10. The two-thirds-of-Aa-yield rate is also applied to these to determine whether primary earnings per share should be adjusted for potential dilution. The one difference, however, is that because interest is tax deductible, less than the full amount of the bond interest is added back to net income.

For example, suppose Bradley Corporation had only common stock and $100,000 in 10 percent convertible bonds outstanding, and its taxable income was subject to a 40 percent tax rate. Net income was $48,000, 20,000 common shares were outstanding, and unadjusted earnings per share was $2.40. These amounts are given in the left column of Exhibit 11–8.

To adjust for dilution, the accountant must calculate the net income Bradley would have reported if the debt had been converted into common stock. Without debt, the company would not have had to pay interest at 10 percent on the debt, or $10,000. This was tax deductible, meaning that the aftertax interest cost was $(1.0 - 0.4 = 0.6) \times \$10,000$, or $6,000. Without debt, therefore, the company

EXHIBIT 11–8.   Earnings Per Share with Convertible Bonds Outstanding

	Bonds Outstanding	Bonds Converted
Income before interest and income tax	$90,000	$90,000
Interest (0.10 × $100,000)	10,000	—
Income before taxes	80,000	90,000
Income tax (40 percent)	32,000	36,000
Net income	$48,000	$54,000
Shares outstanding	20,000	25,000
Earnings per share	$ 2.40	$ 2.16

would have reported net income of $54,000 ($48,000 + $6,000), as the right column of Exhibit 11–8 shows.

The $100,000 debt was convertible into 5,000 shares of common stock. Conversion therefore would have increased the number of shares outstanding to 25,000. The revised earnings per share is $54,000/25,000 = $2.16. Whether this would be reported as primary or fully diluted earnings per share depends on how the two-thirds-of-Aa-yield-rate test comes out.

Stock options

Options to buy corporate stock are issued for various reasons. For example, they are sometimes attached to the company's bonds as a means of reducing interest costs and making the bonds more easily marketable.

The most highly publicized stock options are executive stock options, awarded to key corporate executives as part of their compensation. In most option plans, executives are given options to buy at a later date specified numbers of shares at a fixed price, usually the market price at the time the options are granted. If the market price goes up, the executives can exercise some or all of their options and benefit from the gain.

The reason for executive stock options is that they provide key personnel with a strong inducement to perform effectively so that the price of the company's stock will rise. In other words, the executives can't benefit from the options unless the stockholders also benefit.

Because the company receives no direct payment when stock options are *granted* to employees, no changes in the owners' equity can be recognized. The potential dilution must be recognized in the financial statements, however. This is accomplished by disclosing such information as the number of options outstanding and the option price, and by calculating earnings per share on the assumption that all outstanding options have been exercised in full. We'll leave the details of these calculations to more advanced texts.

TREASURY STOCK

Corporations from time to time repurchase shares of their own stock. These repurchased shares are called *treasury stock.*

Objectives of treasury-stock purchases

Share repurchase may have a number of objectives. Some reacquired shares may be used for distribution to executives in bonus or stock option plans. Others may be used for distribution to share-holders as stock dividends, to employees in stock-purchase plans, or to the company's pension funds for long-term investment. Share repurchasing eliminates the necessity to issue new shares for these purposes and thus helps the company avoid the costs and additional reporting requirements associated with new issues.

Share repurchase may also be viewed as a more profitable use of the company's funds than the available alternatives. If the company has more cash than it can invest profitably internally, stock repurchase may prevent a dilution in earnings per share, particularly when market prices seem unjustifiably low.

The negative aspects of these transactions should not be overlooked, however. For one thing, the purchase and sale of treasury stock in any volume can generate short-term movements in the market price of the stock, which might be interpreted as the use of the corporation's funds by "insiders" to influence the price of the stock to their advantage. Similar objections can be raised to the use of the corporation's funds to purchase stock to prevent voting control from being concentrated in unfriendly hands.

A third drawback is that the purchase of treasury stock reduces the company's assets and equities. Treasury stock, in other words, represents a reduction of the stockholders' total investment in the enterprise and may impair the company's ability to discharge its obligations to its creditors. This would hurt not only the creditors but the shareholders and employees as well.

Reporting treasury stock at cost

The customary method of accounting for treasury stock is to include it in the balance sheet as a separate amount, measured at the price paid to acquire it. This is the *cost* method, used by most companies to record temporary reacquisitions of common shares. Under this method, the cost of treasury shares is shown on the balance sheet as a negative element of owners' equity.

For example, suppose Space Age Corporation repurchased for $46,000 a total of 1,000 shares of its common stock after the stock split on December 31, 19x9. This transaction was recorded by the following entry:

Treasury Stock	46,000	
Cash		46,000

The revised December 31, 19x9, balance sheet showed the following:

Common stock—stated value	$ 605,000
Additional paid-in capital	1,210,000
Earnings retained in the business	1,089,000
Total	2,904,000
Less: Treasury stock (at cost)	(46,000)
Total shareholders' equity	$2,858,000

Treasury stock is not an asset. Shares of stock represent portions of the owners' equity in the company. When the shares are repurchased, the assets are reduced and so is the owners' equity. To treat treasury stock as an asset would imply that the company has ownership rights in itself, and this is an impossibility. Treasury shares cannot be voted, nor do they participate in cash dividends or carry any other perquisites of ownership. The purchase of treasury shares represents a partial and perhaps temporary liquidation of the enterprise and represents a reduction in both total assets and total owners' equities. Thus, the amount paid for the stock should be deducted from the shareholders' equity. It should not be included among the assets.

Resale of treasury stock at prices different from their acquisition cost is not reported as a gain or loss in the company's income statement. The company cannot make or lose money by buying and selling a portion of itself, although the equity of the surviving shareholders can be increased or decreased by such actions. The accepted accounting treatment is to add positive differences to the additional paid-in capital and, with some exceptions, to subtract negative differences from retained earnings.

CONTINGENCY RESERVES

Businesses operate in an environment of uncertainty. A previously successful company may suffer serious reverses from events it wasn't able to foresee. To provide for these, management may wish to make deductions from revenues in good years to reflect the possibility that unforeseen events in the future may impair the values of the company's resources.

For example, suppose most of a company's facilities are in an area that is subject to the possibility of earthquakes. Management has decided that outside insurance against earthquake damage is too expensive. Instead, it has decided to show in its financial statements that its investment in plant, equipment, and inventories is subject to the risk of loss due to earthquakes. It has done this by setting up a "reserve for contingencies," a subdivision of the owners' equity calling attention to the *possibility* that a present condition or commitment will lead to a future event that will reduce the company's assets or increase its liabilities. The company's shareowners' equity, including this subdivision, is shown schematically in Exhibit 11–9. Both unshaded segments of this diagram are parts of the retained earnings.

We face two difficulties in attempting to reflect the contingency of an earthquake in the financial statements. First, the probability that an earthquake will occur and that this earthquake will be strong enough to cause damage (that is, will impair the value of assets or give rise to new liabilities) can't be assessed reliably because adequate statistics are unavailable. Earthquakes just don't happen in ways that are predictable enough to support the necessary accounting figures. Second, the amount of the possible loss can't be estimated accurately enough. An earthquake, if it happens, may destroy all of the company, part of it, or none of it.

For these reasons the accounting profession in the United States has taken the position that contingency reserves can't be set up by deductions from revenues in the income statement. Revenue deductions (expense charges) are permitted only if it is deemed probable that a loss has *already* occurred and that it can be estimated accurately enough. In such cases, certain assets are written down or a liability (provision for loss) is established.

Appropriations for losses that don't meet these conditions can be created only by transfers from retained earnings, and they must be shown in the shareowners' equity section of the balance sheet

EXHIBIT 11–9. Shareowners' Equity, Including Contingency Reserve

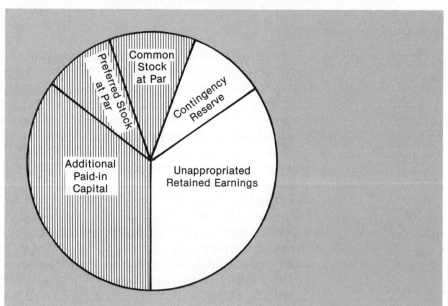

and be clearly identified as appropriations *of retained earnings.* When the losses actually materialize, they are to be charged against revenues, not against appropriations. Furthermore, no part of the appropriations can be transferred to the income statement at any time.

Other types of reserves

The term *reserve* is very imprecise. For one thing, it may imply that it measures the amount of liquid resources that the company keeps on hand for use in times of need. This is not likely to be true.

A second problem is that this term may be used to describe three distinct amounts: appropriations of retained earnings, discussed above; contra assets or *valuation reserves,* such as the reserves (allowances) for depreciation and uncollectibles; and *liability reserves,* such as the reserve (provision) for income taxes. All three are based on estimates and all have credit balances—otherwise, they have nothing in common.

SUMMARY

All corporations have common stock. Some also have one or more classes of preferred stock, with a prior but limited right to dividends. The amounts invested directly in the corporation (contributed capital) are divided into two parts, the par (or stated) values of the shares and the amounts paid in excess of par.

The initial issuance of common stock provides the base for the company's capital structure. Additional shares are issued from time to time, and the proceeds from these issues are also divided between par value and additional paid-in capital. Shareholders are often given preemptive rights to purchase these additional shares so they can avoid having their equity diluted unduly. They may waive these rights, however, to allow the company to issue shares in connection with executive stock options and convertible senior securities and for other purposes. Shares held for conversions and options are included with the number of shares outstanding in certain calculations of earnings per share.

The line between contributed capital and retained earnings is clouded by stock dividends, which require the transfer of amounts from retained earnings to the contributed capital section. Stock dividends and stock splits are generally regarded as signals that the company intends to increase the total cash dividend payment, and the market price of the shares is likely to move higher. It will stay at this higher level, however, only if the cash dividend actually does increase as anticipated.

Corporations in the United States occasionally use funds to repurchase some of their own outstanding shares. These shares are known as treasury stock. They are shown at cost on the balance sheet, deducted from the total of contributed capital and retained earnings to determine the net shareowners' equity.

KEY TERMS

Additional paid-in capital	Preemptive rights
Common stock	Preferred stock
Contingency reserves	Stated value
Convertible securities	Stock dividend
Dilution of earnings	Stock option
Dilution of the equity	Stock split
Earnings per share	Treasury stock
Par value	

INDEPENDENT STUDY PROBLEMS (Solutions in Appendix B)

1. Issuance of common stock for cash; dilution. Angel Rings, Inc., had the following shareowners' equity on January 1, 19x1:

Common stock, $1 par (authorized, 1 million shares)	$ 800,000
Additional paid-in capital	300,000
Retained earnings	500,000
Total	$1,600,000

On January 2, 19x1, the shareowners were given rights to purchase 160,000 new shares of common stock at a price of $4 a share. The market price of the company's stock immediately prior to the announcement of the rights offering was $5 a share. All rights were exercised, and the new shares were issued on February 18, 19x1.

Net income for the year ended December 31, 19x1, was $441,600. A cash dividend of 20 cents a share was declared on December 15, 19x1, and paid on January 15, 19x2.

a. Prepare the shareowners' equity section of the company's balance sheet on December 31, 19x1.
b. Did the issuance of the new shares lead to a dilution of the equity? State the reasons for your answer, including any calculations you find necessary.

2. Stock dividend. Company A's board of directors declared and distributed a stock dividend of one share of common stock for each 20 shares outstanding. Prior to the stock dividend, 20,000 shares were outstanding with a par value of $10 a share. The company recorded the stock dividend at the shares' market value of $30 a share.

State the effect of this transaction on the amounts shown on the company's balance sheet.

3. Treasury stock. On January 1, 19x1, Company B had 100,000 shares of $5 par common stock outstanding. On January 4, 19x1, the company purchased 100 shares of this stock on the market at a price of $30 a share and placed these shares in the treasury. On March 2, 19x1, the company declared a cash dividend on the outstanding shares of common stock at the rate of 30 cents a share; this dividend was distributed on April 5, 19x1. On May 15, 19x1, the company sold its treasury stock at a price of $40 a share.

State the effects of each of these transactions on the company's assets, liabilities, and shareowners' equity. Be careful to specify which portions of the shareowners' equity were affected.

4. Dilution: calculating earnings per share. The Denver Corporation in 19x1 had a net income of $312,000. It had 100,000 shares of common stock outstanding and 10,000 shares of $5 convertible preferred stock. Each share of preferred was convertible into two shares of common.

a. Calculate primary earnings per common share, ignoring the convertibility of the preferred stock.
b. Calculate the fully diluted earnings per common share.

EXERCISES AND PROBLEMS

5. Issuance of stock for cash; book value. On January 8, 19x1, the Alpine Company started operations by issuing 100,000 shares of common stock, $10 par, at a price of $15 a share. No additional shares of stock were issued between that date and December 31, 19x4. Retained earnings of the company as of December 31, 19x4, totaled $2 million.

a. How did the issuance of the stock affect the various components of the shareowners' equity?
b. What was the book value per share of common stock on December 31, 19x4?

6. Purchase of treasury stock. On January 2, 19x5, the Alpine Company (see problem 5) repurchased 1,000 shares of its stock at the market price of $28 a share. This stock was held as treasury stock.

a. How should this treasury stock have been listed on the company's June 30, 19x5, balance sheet?
b. Did the purchase of this treasury stock increase, decrease, or leave unchanged the book value per share of stock issued and outstanding?
c. Should a gain or loss be shown in the 19x5 income statement as a result of the repurchase of the stock? Why?

7. Sale of treasury stock. On July 1, 19x5, the Alpine Company (see problem 6) resold its treasury stock at a price of $34 a share.

a. How did the sale of the treasury stock affect the various components of the shareowners' equity?

b. Should a gain or loss be shown on the 19x5 income statement as a result of the resale of stock? Why?

8. Book value per share; treasury stock. A balance sheet showed the following shareowners' equity section on December 31:

Stockholders' equity:
$5 par value common stock (5,559,500 shares issued)	$27,797,500
Additional paid-in capital	10,960,500
Retained earnings	55,389,500
Treasury stock (9,500 shares)	(153,500)
Total stockholders' equity	$93,994,000

The market price of the stock on December 31 was $25 per share.

a. What was the book value per share of common stock issued and outstanding at the end of the year?

b. Give three alternative explanations for how the "Additional paid-in capital" might have been accumulated. (One phrase or sentence for each will be adequate.)

9. Stock dividend. Assume the corporation in problem 8 declared a 10 percent stock dividend to the owners of the shares outstanding on December 31.

a. How would this transaction affect the various components of the shareowners' equity?

b. What would be the new book value per share?

c. What would be the new book value (on the corporation's books) of the shares owned by an investor who had owned 10 shares of stock prior to the stock dividend?

10. Stock split. Assume that instead of a stock dividend, the corporation in problem 8 declared a two-for-one stock split (two new shares exchanged for each old one) and changed the par value to $3 a share.

a. How would this transaction affect the various components of the shareowners' equity?

b. What would be the new book value per share?

c. What would be the new book value (on the corporation's books) of the shares owned by an investor who had owned 10 shares of stock prior to the stock split?

11. Elements of owners' equity. David Dillon, president of Dillon Company, bought a new desk-top computer. He used a program which he thought would calculate the company's net income, but it only generated the following data for 19x3:

Cost of treasury shares bought July 2, 19x3	$ 19,000
Total liabilities, December 31, 19x3	138,000
Common stock issued, March 14, 19x3	40,000
Declaration of cash dividend, December 10, 19x3	18,000
Owners' equity, January 1, 19x3	280,000
Total assets, December 31, 19x3	$495,000

Although Dillon was disappointed that the amount of net income was not identified, he was astonished to observe that all six amounts were in fact accurate.

Prepare a schedule to calculate Dillon Company's 19x3 net income.

12. Book value per share: missing amounts. Determine the one missing amount in each of the following three independent cases.

	I	II	III
Cash dividend per share	$ 2.25	$ 4.00	C
Common stock, Jan. 1	$ 5,000	B	$ 2,000
Book value per share, Dec. 31	A	$ 5.60	$ 25
Additional paid-in capital, Jan. 1	$16,000	$ 9,000	$118,000
Shares outstanding, Jan. 1	2,500	10,000	8,000
Retained earnings, Jan. 1	$ 9,000	$22,000	$ 56,000
Earnings per share	$ 3.50	$ 6.00	$ 16

13. Calculating earnings per share. The Massena Corporation in 19x1 had a net income of $4,416,000. It had 1 million shares of common stock outstanding and 100,000 shares of $6 convertible preferred. Each share of preferred was convertible into 1.7 shares of common stock.

The company also had $5 million in 9 percent bonds payable, convertible into common shares at a ratio of 18 shares of common for every $1,000 in bonds. The effective tax rate in 19x1 was 40 percent.

a. Calculate primary earnings per common share, ignoring the convertibility of the bonds and the preferred stock.

b. Calculate the fully diluted earnings per common share.

14. Earnings per share: missing amounts. Determine the missing amounts in each of the three independent cases that appear in the table. Each preferred share is convertible into four common shares, and each $1,000 bond is convertible into 15 common shares. Conversion is assumed only for purposes of calculating fully diluted earnings per share, and the company's income tax rate is 40 percent.

	I	II	III
Common shares	20,000	6,000	5,000
$9 preferred shares	5,000	3,000	E
12 percent bonds	$200,000	$90,000	F
Net income	$225,000	C	$57,600
Earnings per share:			
Primary	A	D	$7.20
Fully diluted	B	$2.71	$4.32

15. Issuance of common shares for cash; dilution. The shareowners' equity in Beehive Industries was as follows on January 1, 19x1:

Common stock, no par, stated value, $5 a share
(authorized, 2,000,000 shares; outstanding,
1,800,000 shares) .... $ 9,000,000
Additional paid-in capital 6,300,000
Retained earnings 4,500,000
    Total $19,800,000

The company's shareholders voted in April 19x1 to increase the authorized number of shares of common stock from 2 million to 5 million. In September 19x1, the company gave its common shareholders rights to purchase 450,000 new shares of common stock at a price of $15 a share. All rights were exercised, and the new shares were issued on October 1, 19x1. The market price of Beehive Industries' common stock just prior to the offering was $20 a share.

The company's net income for the year ended December 31, 19x1, was $956,250. Cash dividends of 10 cents a share were declared and paid in May and in November 19x1.

a. Present the shareowners' equity section of the company's balance sheet as of December 31, 19x1.
b. Did the issuance of these shares result in a dilution of the equity? Present figures to support your conclusion.
c. If the earnings per share figure is to be used as an approximation of future earnings per share, should the denominator of the ratio in 19x1 be 1,800,000 shares, 1,912,500 shares, 2,250,000 shares, or some other number? Give the reasons for your choice and any assumptions you had to make.

16. Effects of owners' equity transactions. The composition of the owners' equity section of Grant Corporation's balance sheet was as follows:

Common stock ($10 par) .... $ 50,000
Additional paid-in capital 110,000
Retained earnings 90,000
    Owners' equity $250,000

The following seven events then occurred in sequence:

a. Issued 2,000 new common shares for $65,000.
b. Effected a four-for-one stock split; new par value, $2.50.
c. Declared and paid a $2 cash dividend per share.
d. Declared and distributed a 15 percent stock dividend.
e. Net income was $175,750.
f. Bought 2,200 treasury shares for $35,200.
g. Bought 1,500 additional treasury shares for $16,500.

Set up a matrix consisting of seven rows (a through g), one for each of the seven events listed above, and four columns (1 through 4), one for each of the following four items:

1. Shares outstanding.
2. Retained earnings.
3. Owners' equity.
4. Book value per share.

Show how each of the seven events affected each of the four items, by placing the appropriate letter in each of the 28 (7 × 4) cells, as follows: I = increase, D = decrease, N = no effect.

17. Executive stock options. The stockholders of Topper Corporation voted approval of an executive stock option plan at the annual stockholders' meeting on May 14, 19x0. The vote authorized the board of directors to grant purchase options to key executives up to a maximum of 30,000 shares of the company's previously unissued stock.

The first options were granted on September 10, 19x0. Various executives were given rights to purchase a total of 12,000 shares at $22 a share, the market price of the stock at the close of trading on that date. These options would lapse within five years if they were not exercised.

On June 1, 19x2, officers were given three-year options to buy an additional 15,000 shares at $28 a share, the market price on that date.

Options on 8,000 shares at $22 a share were exercised in November 19x3. The company's stock was then selling at $36 a share.

In 19x4, the stockholders approved the addition of another 20,000 shares to the stock option plan. In September of that year, three-year options were granted on 6,000 shares at $43 a share, the market price at that time.

Options on 4,000 shares at $22 a share and 3,000 shares at $28 a share were exercised in 19x4. The stock was selling at $40 a share at the time.

a. Prepare a footnote to be appended to the 19x0 financial statements, giving adequate disclosure of the stock option plan. The company's fiscal year ends on December 31 each year.

b. Prepare a footnote on the stock option plan for the 19x4 financial statements. Explain your reasons for disclosing each item you have included. Why is it important to disclose this information?

c. Did the exercise of the options in 19x3 and 19x4 constitute dilution of the equity? Explain.

d. What was the effect of all the above transactions on the stockholders' equity in Topper Corporation?

12

Investments, combinations, and consolidations

Investments are company-owned bonds, notes, and stock of other corporations and bonds and notes of government bodies. Sometimes the investment in another company's stock may reflect the occurrence of a business combination; in such cases, consolidated financial statements are usually prepared to report the combined results of the two companies. When companies are quite large and operate in more than one industry, they are also required to provide information about their major industry segments.

In this chapter we'll study the different kinds of investments in securities, the accounting measurements that apply, and some financial reporting practices that come into play. We'll cover the topics in the following order:

1. Investments in bonds and notes.
2. Noncontrolling investments in stocks.
3. Business combinations.
4. Consolidated financial statements.

INVESTMENTS IN BONDS AND NOTES

Corporations often invest in the bonds issued by other corporations or by various government units. They may also hold short-term government notes, bank certificates of deposit, or commercial paper (promissory notes of corporations with the highest credit ratings). Financial corporations (banks, in particular) also hold the promissory notes of other corporations and of individuals.

Short-term marketable securities

Most bonds, government notes, and commercial paper are marketable in the sense that brokers, dealers, and other intermediaries stand ready to buy them at some price or to locate others who are willing to buy. The term *marketable securities* usually is used by nonfinancial corporations, however, to describe the bonds, notes, and commercial paper they have bought with cash temporarily in excess of current operating needs.

Securities of this type usually either will be or can be sold on short notice at prices not significantly lower than current prices. They are reported as current assets and are ordinarily measured at cost. Interest on these notes and bonds should be accrued unless the amounts are too small to be material.

Long-term investments in bonds

Bonds or notes purchased as long-term investments are measured at their amortized cost. *Amortized cost* means the purchase cost less the amortized portion of the investment premium, or the purchase cost plus the amortized portion of the investment discount. For example, suppose Granite Corporation bought $10,000 of XYZ Corporation's 8 percent bonds on July 1, 19x1, five years before their maturity date. The price paid was $9,604, and interest was to be received semiannually, on January 1 and July 1 each year. In other words, Granite bought the bonds at a $396 discount ($10,000 − $9,604). An appropriate entry to record this purchase was:

Investments	9,604	
Cash		9,604

This recorded the decrease in the company's cash asset and the increase in its investments asset.

Granite amortized the $396 discount in such a way as to keep the effective rate of interest constant in every six-month period until the maturity date. It did this by determining the percentage yield to maturity implicit in the $9,604 price, then applying the effective-interest method we described in Chapter 10.

We could determine the yield to maturity the hard way, by trying different possible rates until we found one at which the present value of the future cash receipts from the bonds was exactly $9,604. Fortunately, there's an easier way. All we have to do is turn to Table 6 in Appendix A. Going down the column showing market prices for five years to maturity, we find that when 8 percent bonds with a face value of $100 have a market price of $96.04, the effective market yield to maturity is 9.0 percent (the ninth row in the table).

In other words, bonds with the risk and maturity characteristics of the XYZ bonds were priced on July 1, 19x1, at levels that would earn investors half of 9 percent, or 4.5 percent, every six months. Granite's interest income in the first six months therefore was 4½ percent of $9,604, or $432. Granite was to receive only $400 in cash, however. The $32 difference between these two amounts was the additional investment Granite made in the first six months by agreeing in advance to accept only $400 in cash this period instead of the $432 it would normally expect to receive. An appropriate entry to accrue the interest income on December 31, 19x1, was:

Interest Receivable	400	
Investment	32	
Interest Revenue		432

This showed owners' equity going up by $432, the interest receivable asset going up by $400, and the investment asset going up by $32. Receipt of $400 from XYZ Corporation the next day (January 1, 19x2) converted the interest receivable into cash; the investment was reported in the December 31, 19x1, balance sheet at $9,636 ($9,604 + $32). This pattern continued in later periods as both interest and the investment asset increased until the bonds matured.

CALCULATING INTEREST AND PRINCIPAL ON INVESTMENTS IN BONDS WITH SEMIANNUAL INTEREST PAYMENTS

1. Calculate the percentage yield to maturity at the time of purchase.
2. Multiply the principal amount at the beginning of the period by half this yield percentage—this is interest income for six months.
3. Calculate the difference between interest income and the semiannual interest payment—this difference represents an addition to, or partial payment of, the amount of the investment (principal).
4. Add or subtract this difference to or from the principal at the beginning of the period—this is the principal at the end of the period.

Gains and losses on sales of notes and bonds

If a company buys bonds or notes and holds them to maturity, the entire difference between the purchase price and the maturity value is interest income. If the securities are sold prior to maturity, however, part of the difference between the purchase price and the selling price may be a gain or a loss.

For example, suppose Granite changed its mind about making the XYZ bonds a long-term investment and sold them on January

1, 19x2, at a price of $9,700. The investment in the bonds at that time was $9,636, as we just saw, so the company recognized a $64 gain on the sale ($9,700 − $9,636).

Effect of changes in interest rates

Measuring investments in bonds at their amortized cost may lead to serious misstatements of the investments. Suppose a sharply restrictive national monetary policy drove interest rates up sharply in the six months after Granite bought its XYZ bonds. The effective market interest rate on January 1, 19x2, for bonds of comparable risk and 4½ years to maturity was 8 percent each six-month period. Discounting the future cash flows for nine six-month periods at 8 percent a period gives the following present values:

Periods after January 1, 19x2	Cash Flow	Present Value Multiplier at 8%	Present Value
1 to 9	+$400 a period	6.2469	+$2,499
9	+$10,000	0.5002	+ 5,002
Total			+$7,501

This table tells us that investors on January 1, 19x2, were willing to pay no more than $7,501 for these bonds, the amount they would have to pay to get the same cash-flow stream from another source in the current market. Granite reported its investment in the bonds at their amortized cost of $9,636, however, staying with the original amortization schedule.

Accountants measure bond investments at their amortized cost on the grounds that the company intends to hold the bonds to maturity, at which time market value and unamortized cost will come together at the maturity value.[1] The economic fact, however, is that the owners of fixed-payment securities lose part of their wealth when interest rates rise. Under conventional accounting practice, since this loss is an *unrealized* loss, it is not reported in the income statement. If the intercompany investments in long-term bonds were measured at market value, the loss would be reported as a negative component of current income.

NONCONTROLLING INVESTMENTS IN SHARES OF STOCK

Investments in stocks that constitute 50 percent or less of the voting rights of their corporations are mostly of two types:

1. Long-term investments that don't give their owners significant influence on the investees' actions.

---

[1] Mutual investment funds are an exception to this rule; they measure and report the market value of their portfolios on a daily basis.

2. Long-term investments that do give their owners significant influence on the investees' actions.

Stocks held as short-term investments are encountered so rarely that we'll ignore them here—except to observe that when there are markets in which such shares are traded, a lower-of-cost-or-market approach is used.

Long-term noninfluential investments in stocks

Any ownership of less than 50 percent of the voting shares of a corporation is a *minority interest* in that corporation. If the number of shares is small enough relative to the total, the company won't be able to influence the operating and financial policies of the investee significantly. The only question is: How small is small enough? The rule of thumb in the United States is that ownership of less than 20 percent of the voting stock leads to a presumption that the investor lacks the ability to have significant influence on the investee. This presumption will carry the day unless there is evidence that the investor is able to exert influence on the investee.

The reason for making this distinction is that accountants use different methods to account for investments, depending on whether the investor is able to exert at least a significant amount of influence. For stock investments classified as not significant (generally, those with less than 20 percent of the voting rights), the investment is measured at the lower of the original cost or its current market price. Income is measured by the investor's share in *cash dividends* declared by the investee, plus or minus any gains or losses on sales of investments and minus any write-downs to market value.

The reason for this treatment is that since the investor doesn't own enough shares to influence the investee's board of directors, it has no way of increasing the dividend or of making sure the rest of the cash flows from the investee's operations are invested profitably to generate a larger stream of cash flows in the future.

Long-term influential investments in stocks

The policy of recognizing only dividends as income has been criticized on the grounds that the shareholders benefit eventually from the accumulation of retained earnings, because the investment will produce future cash flows at a satisfactory rate. The accounting method reflecting this reasoning is known as the *equity method.* It is used for *influential* investments—that is, those which give the investor a significant influence over the operating and financial policies of the investee. This is generally presumed to be the case if the investor owns 20 percent or more of the voting rights in the company.

To illustrate this method, let's suppose National Company bought 30,000 shares of Local Company's stock on July 1, 19x1, at a price of $30 a share. The entry was:

Investments 900,000
    Cash 900,000

The $900,000 National paid was equal to 30 percent of Local's $3 million reported owners' equity.

Earnings per share were $3.25, and cash dividends totaled $1.50 a share during the remainder of 19x1. With 100,000 shares outstanding, Local's total net income in this period was $325,000, and its total dividend was $150,000. These amounts are shown in the box at the bottom of Exhibit 12–1. The volume of the entire box represents the net income; the volume of the shaded section stands for

EXHIBIT 12–1. National's Share of Local's Earnings and Dividends

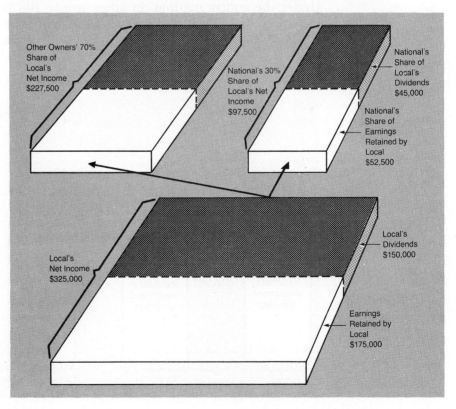

the dividends. National's share in Local's earnings was 30,000 ×
$3.25 = $97,500, or 30 percent of the total. This is represented by
the volume of the box in the upper right-hand portion of the exhibit.
National's share of the dividends paid by Local was 30,000 ×
$1.50 = $45,000, represented by the shaded segment of this smaller
box.

As a result of its 30 percent ownership share, National's income
statement contains 30 percent, or $97,500, of Local's net income.
National's year-end balance sheet reflects asset increases totaling
the same amount. Cash increased by the $45,000 that was realized
as a result of the dividends declared and paid by National during
the year; the remaining, yet-to-be-realized $52,500 equity in Local's
net income appears as an increase in National's investment asset.
National might record these facts by an entry or entries with the
following effects:

Cash 45,000
Investments 52,500
    Revenue from Investments   97,500

Under the equity method, in other words, the investment asset is
measured by the original cost plus the investor's yet-to-be-realized
share in the investee's post-investment earnings.

EXHIBIT 12–2. Income and Investment under the Cost and Equity Methods

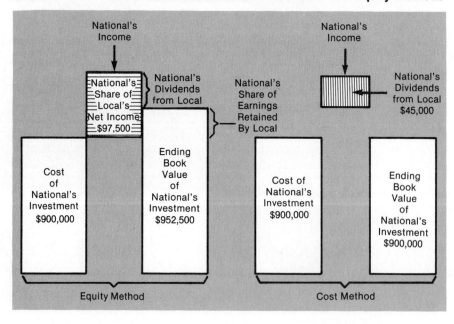

The differences between the cost and equity methods are diagrammed in Exhibit 12–2. The three blocks at the left illustrate the cost method. National would include in its income statement only its $45,000 share in Local's dividends. It would carry the investment at its $900,000 cost unless its market value declined to less than that amount.

The three blocks at the right illustrate the equity method. National's income statement now includes National's full $97,500 share in Local's net income. Some of this amount (the cash dividend) serves to increase National's cash flow; the rest (National's share of the earnings retained by Local) is added to its investment, represented by the right-hand block in the exhibit. This block would appear as the block at the left in a similar diagram drawn for 19x2.

Excess investment cost

If the investment cost exceeds the acquired share of the investee's owners' equity, the excess may be attributable to an unrecorded intangible asset of the investee. This amount is amortized systematically as the investor records its share of the investee's net income or loss; the maximum amortization period in the United States is 40 years.

In our example, if Local's owners' equity had been $2,600,000 instead of $3,000,000 when National bought its shares, National's

EXHIBIT 12–3. Classification of Investments in Stock

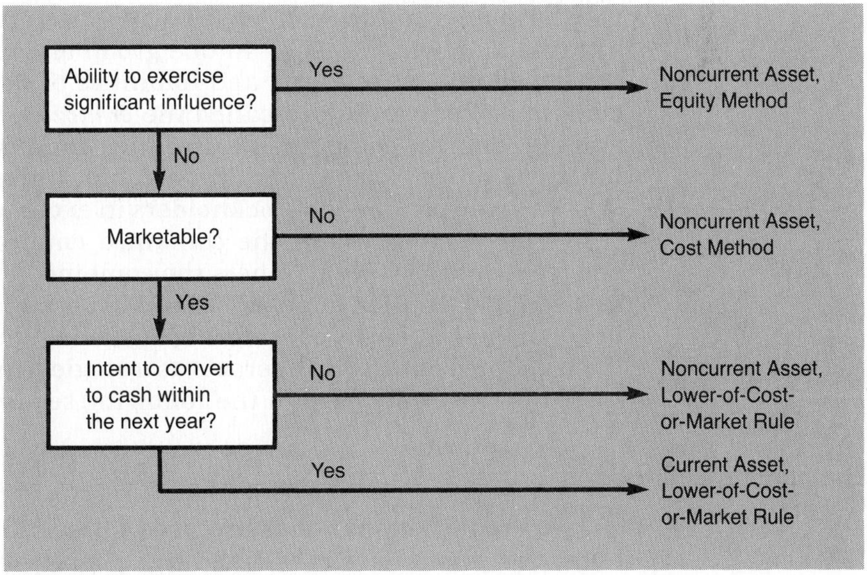

equity in Local's earnings in the second half of 19x1 would have been recorded as $96,000, not $97,500:

Equity in reported income: $325,000 × 30 percent		$97,500
Investment cost	$900,000	
Owners' equity share: $2,600,000 × 30 percent	780,000	
Unrecorded intangible asset	120,000	
Amortization: ½ × 1/40 × $120,000		1,500
Equity in Local's income, as reported by National		$96,000

In summary, we have encountered three methods used to account for investments in another company's stock—cost, lower of cost or market, and equity. Use of a particular method depends on a variety of factors, which are depicted in Exhibit 12–3. The boxes in the left of the diagram identify the factors to be considered, and the financial reporting outcomes appear in the right of the exhibit.

BUSINESS COMBINATIONS

A company's ownership of more than 50 percent of the voting stock of another company gives it a *controlling interest* in that company. Since a controlling interest is often obtained through a business combination, we have to see what business combinations are and how accountants account for them before we can discuss how companies report investments they classify as controlling interests.

Nature of a business combination

A business combination occurs when two companies enter into a transaction which results in one group of common stockholders having equity in the assets and liabilities of both companies. The combining companies are called the *combinor* and the *combinee,* and the resulting company is called the *combined enterprise.* Combinations are effected when the combinor gives cash, securities, or both to the combinee's stockholders in exchange for their shares.

In some combinations, the combined enterprise is operated as one legal entity, while in others the combined enterprise functions as two legal entities—that is, as two separate corporations. We'll begin in this section by considering business combinations in which the combined enterprise operates as a single legal entity. We'll consider the two-entity case in the following section.

The purchase method

Two accounting methods are used to record business combinations: the *purchase method* and the *pooling-of-interests method.*

The two methods are *not* alternatives to each other in the sense that a company might select *either* LIFO *or* FIFO as a basis for determining the cost of its ending inventory. The circumstances surrounding a particular combination dictate which method must be used.

The purchase method reflects the belief that the combinor has *purchased the assets and assumed the liabilities* of the combinee. Paying cash directly to the combinee's stockholders is the usual way to effect a purchase type of combination. The amount of cash that is tendered usually differs from the combinee company's recorded owners' equity. To record a purchase, the combinor must determine how much of the purchase price has been paid for each of the combinee's assets. The question is how much the company would have had to pay to buy each asset in an arm's-length market transaction at the time of the combination. The answer requires the exercise of considerable professional judgment.

To demonstrate, let's suppose Worthy Company pays $220,000 to acquire all the common shares of Able, Inc. Able's combination-date balance sheet shows the following amounts:

Cash	$ 40,000	Liabilities	$ 60,000	
Inventory	90,000	Common stock	50,000	
Machinery	80,000	Retained earnings	100,000	
Total	$210,000	Total	$210,000	

The combinor determines that the fair market value of the inventory is $110,000 and the fair market value of the machinery is $115,000. This information begins to explain why Worthy is willing to pay $220,000, which is $70,000 more than the book value of Able's owners' equity: $20,000 ($110,000 − $90,000) is attributable to undervalued inventory, and $35,000 ($115,000 − $80,000) can be associated with undervalued machinery.

These two amounts explain $55,000 ($20,000 + $35,000) of the $70,000 excess of the purchase price over Able's book value. The remaining $15,000 may be attributable to the present value of the liabilities being lower than their recorded amounts, or it may reflect unrecorded intangible assets. Unrecorded intangible assets may be identified as *goodwill,* or more accurately as *excess of cost over net assets acquired.*[2]

---

[2] Although goodwill is recorded when the purchase price is *greater* than the estimated current value of the combinee's recorded net assets, "negative goodwill" is *not* recorded when the purchase price is *less* than the estimated current value. Instead, the estimates of the current value of plant assets are reduced or the estimated liabilities are increased.

The nature of the purchase method can be demonstrated by considering the accounting entry the combinor (Worthy) might make:

Cash	40,000	
Inventory	110,000	
Machinery	115,000	
Goodwill	15,000	
Liabilities		60,000
Cash		220,000

The total cost of the assets acquired in a purchase combination is dictated by the purchase price paid to effect the combination. When cash is given to the combinee's stockholders, the amount of the purchase price is self-evident. When securities are exchanged, *their* current value is likely to define the amount of the purchase price, unless the market value of the combinee's shares is more readily determinable. In our example, the actual cost of the assets acquired is $280,000 (the $220,000 cash payment plus $60,000 in liabilities taken over).

It should be noted that when the purchase method is used, the current-value amounts recorded become the combined enterprise's costs. For inventories, these costs will flow fairly quickly into the FIFO cost of goods sold but are likely to remain more or less permanently in the LIFO inventory balance. Depreciation is also measured on the new cost basis and the newly recorded goodwill is subject to amortization.

In conclusion, the purchase method reflects the belief that the combinor *purchases* the combinee's assets and liabilities. As is the case in all other types of purchases, a new basis of accountability arises, with the result that some assets and liabilities will be recorded at amounts which differ from the amounts that had previously appeared in the combinee's financial statements.

The pooling-of-interests method

The theory underlying the pooling-of-interests method is based on the following proposition: Instead of the combinee's stockholders *selling* their shares for cash, they *exchange* their stock for shares in the combined enterprise. The transaction is significantly different from a purchase. In a purchase for cash, only the combinor's stockholders are the stockholders of the combined enterprise; in a pooling, both companies' stockholders continue as stockholders of the combined enterprise. As a result, the combined enterprise in a pooling of interests is simply a continuation of the two previous businesses.

This conclusion has three important implications. First, since the combinor hasn't purchased anything, all the combinee's assets and liabilities continue to be measured at the combinee's (book value) amounts. Second, goodwill is *not* recognized despite its undoubtedly having been a factor in determining the number of combinor shares that are given to the combinee's stockholders in exchange for their shares.

The third important effect is that the precombination earnings of both the combinor and the combinee are viewed as being the earnings of the combined enterprise. This means that the retained earnings of both the combinor and the combinee carry over to the combined enterprise. It also means that all the combination-year earnings of both companies are included in the earnings and earnings per share of the combined enterprise, even the portion that was earned before the combination.

To demonstrate the nature of the pooling-of-interests method, let's use the same information we used to illustrate the purchase method in the preceding section, except that Worthy Company (the combinor) gives Able's stockholders shares of its voting common stock instead of cash. Able's balance sheet on the merger date shows the following amounts:

Cash	$ 40,000	Liabilities	$ 60,000
Inventory	90,000	Common stock	50,000
Machinery	80,000	Retained earnings	100,000
Total	$210,000	Total	$210,000

The shares Worthy issues in exchange for Able's shares have a par value of $15,000. If Worthy Company dissolves Able, Inc., immediately after the exchange of shares and treats Able's assets and liabilities as its own from then on, Worthy will add $210,000 to its assets, $60,000 to its liabilities, $50,000 to its paid-in capital ($15,000 in par value and $35,000 in additional paid-in capital), and $100,000 to its retained earnings. A summary entry in general journal form would show the following:

Cash	40,000	
Inventory	90,000	
Machinery	80,000	
Liabilities		60,000
Common Stock		15,000
Additional Paid-in Capital		35,000
Retained Earnings		100,000

Notice that the assets, liabilities, and retained earnings are recorded at the same amounts that had appeared in Able's (the combinee's) financial statements. The only difference is that Worthy divides Able's $50,000 paid-in capital into two parts.[3]

The pooling-of-interests method should be used only when the underlying circumstances indicate that the stockholders of the combinor and the combinee have truly pooled their interests—by becoming stockholders in the combined enterprise.[4] To foster uniform attainment of this objective, the accounting profession in the United States uses a series of 12 conditions which a combination must meet to qualify for treatment as a pooling of interests. For our purposes, the one most pervasive condition is that voting common stock must be exchanged for substantially all the combinee's voting common stock; "substantially all" means at least 90 percent. The 90 percent provision permits cash or other consideration to be exchanged for the remaining shares, or those shares may continue as a minority interest.

In summary, under the pooling-of-interests method the combination is viewed as a nontransaction. As opposed to the combinor purchasing the combinee's assets and liabilities through the acquisition of its outstanding stock, the pooling-of-interests method reflects the two companies' stockholders pooling their interests to become stockholders of one company. Since the combinor is not engaged in a purchase, the current values of the combinee's assets aren't recorded and goodwill isn't recognized.

CONSOLIDATED FINANCIAL STATEMENTS

In many business combinations, the combinee will continue to operate as a legal entity even though all its common stock is owned by the combinor. In these cases, the combinor is called the *parent* company and the combinee is called the *subsidiary* company. In this section, we'll describe how the parent company records a purchase-method combination with its subsidiary, how the parent accounts for its investment as the subsidiary reports earnings and declares dividends, and how most parent companies disclose the combined-enterprise relationship in their public financial reporting.

---

[3] In practice, many more individual accounts would be affected. At a minimum, the original cost of the machinery and its accumulated depreciation would be recorded separately, and separate liability accounts would be used to record accounts payable, wages payable, etc. The entry here has been kept simple to show the basic effects of the event.

[4] Many stock-for-stock combinations in the United States may also qualify as *tax-free* exchanges, thereby making the combinations more attractive to stockholders of prospective combinees. The criteria used by the taxing authorities differ from those used by the accounting profession in deciding whether a given combination can be classified as a pooling of interests.

Recording a purchase-method combination: Two entities

To record the investment in its subsidiary, the parent company sets up an *Investment in Subsidiary* account with an initial balance equal to the purchase price of the shares it acquires. For example, suppose Worthy Company pays cash of $220,000 to acquire all the common shares of Able, Inc. Able's combination-date balance sheet shows the following amounts:

Cash	$ 40,000	Liabilities	$ 60,000	
Inventory	90,000	Common stock	50,000	
Machinery	80,000	Retained earnings	100,000	
Total	$210,000	Total	$210,000	

The fair market value of the inventory is $110,000 and the fair market value of the machinery is $115,000. Goodwill of $15,000 is recognized because this is the amount by which the $220,000 purchase price exceeds the $205,000 fair market value of the assets less the liabilities assumed. Worthy records its investment as follows:

Investment in Subsidiary	220,000	
Cash		220,000

This accounting entry is similar to that of any other cash investment in corporate stock. No entry is recorded by Able, however. It continues to operate as a legal entity, and a corporation makes no entries when its shares are traded among stockholders.

Post-investment accounting: Two entities

A parent and its subsidiary maintain separate accounting records, similar to those they would have if the intercorporate investment didn't exist. The parent applies the equity method just as a company does when it has an influential but noncontrolling interest in another company. For external financial reporting to stockholders, however, parent companies usually prepare consolidated financial statements. Since consolidation is based on the premise that the parent and its subsidiaries constitute a single economic entity, consolidated financial statements contain the same information that would have been presented had the parent and its subsidiary been operating as one legal entity.

A first approximation to consolidated financial statements can be made by adding the comparable accounts of a parent and its subsidiaries to get combined totals. The consolidated cash balance, for example, is the sum of the cash held by the parent and the cash held by the subsidiaries. The combined totals can't always be used without adjustment, however, because some amounts are likely to reflect intercompany relationships. We'll illustrate three major kinds of adjustments, known as *eliminations,* designed to deal with some of these relationships:

1. Intercompany receivables and payables.
2. Intercompany sales.
3. The intercompany investment that created the parent-subsidiary relationship.

Intercompany receivables and payables.   If a subsidiary owes money to the parent, the parent's financial statements will show a receivable and the subsidiary's statements will show a liability. Including these amounts in consolidated receivables and liabilities would overstate both amounts; the consolidated statements would no longer show the financial position of the combined enterprise as a single economic entity facing the outside world.

For example, suppose Worthy and Able have the following accounts receivable and accounts payable at the end of a certain year:

	Worthy	Able	Combined
Accounts receivable......	$100,000	$70,000	$170,000
Accounts payable	80,000	60,000	140,000

Able owes Worthy $25,000 at the end of the year for merchandise Worthy shipped to Able during the year. This means that only $35,000 ($60,000 − $25,000) of Able's accounts payable and $75,000 ($100,000 − $25,000) of Worthy's accounts receivable represent relationships with suppliers or customers outside the combined enterprise. From the point of view of the combined enterprise, the combined totals in the table therefore reflect double counting. We can avoid this by preparing an eliminating entry, as follows:

Accounts Payable	25,000	
Accounts Receivable		25,000

This entry isn't recorded in either company's journal or ledger because it doesn't correct an error in either company's accounts. Instead, it is entered in a special consolidation worksheet, which is prepared solely to facilitate the consolidation process. If a columnar worksheet is used, the receivables and payables lines might appear as follows:

	Worthy	Able	Eliminations	Consolidated
Accounts receivable	$100,000	$70,000	$(25,000)	$145,000
Accounts payable	80,000	60,000	(25,000)	115,000

The amounts in the right-hand column then can be placed in the consolidated balance sheet because they represent amounts owed by and owed to parties outside the combined enterprise.

Intercompany sales. Transactions between a parent company and its subsidiaries affect the income statement as well as the balance sheet. For example, the two companies' records show the following amounts:

	Worthy	Able	Combined
Sales revenues	$700,000	$400,000	$1,100,000
Cost of goods sold	450,000	250,000	700,000
Gross profit	$250,000	$150,000	$ 400,000

The amounts in Worthy's column reflect Worthy's sales of merchandise to outsiders *and* its sales to Able. Worthy's sales to Able had a total price of $52,000 and Worthy's cost of goods sold on these items was $40,000. Able sold all these goods during the same year to outside customers at a $65,000 price, which yielded Able a profit margin of 20 percent of sales ($13,000).

If we look only at the results of the two companies' dealings in these goods, we see the following:

	Worthy	Able	Combined
Sales revenues	$52,000	$65,000	$117,000
Cost of goods sold	40,000	52,000	92,000
Gross profit	$12,000	$13,000	$ 25,000

The $25,000 combined gross profit is correct; merchandise costing the combined enterprise $40,000 was sold to outsiders for $65,000. Combined sales revenues and cost of goods sold, however, are overstated by $52,000. The revenues of the combined enterprise should include only the $65,000 Able got by selling the goods to the public; the consolidated cost of goods sold should include only the $40,000 cost to Worthy. Thus, $52,000 has to be removed both from the sales total and from the total cost of goods sold before the combined enterprise can prepare its income statement. This can be accomplished by another eliminating entry in the worksheet:

Sales Revenues	52,000	
Cost of Goods Sold		52,000

These two lines on the worksheet now show the following:

	Worthy	Able	Eliminations	Consolidated
Sales revenues	$700,000	$400,000	$(52,000)	$1,048,000
Cost of goods sold	450,000	250,000	(52,000)	648,000

The *consolidated* gross profit is identical to the *combined* gross profit in this case because Able's ending inventory included none of the prices it paid Worthy for the merchandise.

The elimination is somewhat different when a portion of intercompany sales is *not* resold to outside customers by year-end. Suppose Able resold only 75 percent of the merchandise at a price of

$47,000. For these goods alone, the two companies' records would show the following at the end of the year:

	Worthy	Able	Combined
Sales revenues	$52,000	$47,000	$99,000
Cost of goods sold................	40,000	39,000	79,000
Gross profit	$12,000	$ 8,000	$20,000
Inventory (25 percent of purchases) ..	—	$13,000	$13,000

It should be clear that the *consolidated* income statement should show sales revenues of only $47,000 from these transactions and a cost of goods sold of $30,000 (75 percent of Worthy's $40,000 cost). The consolidated balance sheet should report the goods remaining on hand at the end of the year at their cost to *Worthy,* $10,000 (25 percent of $40,000). The corrections can be made by the following eliminating entry in the worksheet:

Sales Revenues	52,000	
Cost of Goods Sold		49,000
Inventory		3,000

This entry reduces the combined gross profit arising from these transactions by $3,000, because part of the merchandise wasn't sold to outsiders before the end of the year. The consolidated enterprise, in other words, still hadn't earned 25 percent of the $12,000 profit Worthy recognized on its sales to Able. These calculations are summarized in Exhibit 12–4.

Intercompany investment in stock. The third and final elimination we'll examine is to remove the parent company's investment in the subsidiary's stock. Again, our main task is to eliminate double counting. For example, just after Worthy bought Able's shares, the

EXHIBIT 12–4. Elimination of Effects of Intercompany Sales

	Combined Balances	Consolidated Balances	Amounts Eliminated
Sales revenues:			
$52,000 + $47,000	$99,000		
Sold by Able		$47,000	
Intercompany sale			$52,000
Cost of goods sold:			
$40,000 + (0.75 × $52,000)	79,000		
0.75 × $40,000		30,000	
(0.75 × $52,000) + (0.25 × $40,000)			49,000
Inventory:			
0.25 × $52,000	13,000		
0.25 × $40,000		10,000	
0.25 × ($52,000 − $40,000)			3,000

EXHIBIT 12–5. Worthy Company and Able Company: Balance Sheet Amounts on the Acquisition Date

	Worthy	Able	Combined
Assets			
Cash	$ 60,000	$ 40,000	$100,000
Inventory	70,000	90,000	160,000
Machinery	100,000	80,000	180,000
Investment in subsidiary (Able)	220,000	—	220,000
Total assets	$450,000	$210,000	$660,000
Liabilities and Owners' Equity			
Liabilities	$200,000	$ 60,000	$260,000
Owners' equity:			
Common stock	80,000	50,000	130,000
Retained earnings	170,000	100,000	270,000
Total liabilities and owners' equity	$450,000	$210,000	$660,000

two companies' balance sheets showed the amounts listed in Exhibit 12–5. (For simplicity, we've omitted the classification of Worthy's paid-in capital into its par-value and excess-over-par-value components.)

Unfortunately, the combined amounts in the right-hand column reflect double counting. Worthy's $220,000 investment asset represents its 100 percent share of Able's net assets (assets minus liabilities). We overstate the assets of the combined enterprise if we include both this amount and Able's assets of $210,000 and liabilities of $60,000 in the consolidated totals. For the combined enterprise, the $220,000 investment is simply the company's investment in itself, and that's no asset at all. We know, therefore, that we have to remove $220,000 from the combined asset total.

It would also be wrong to include in the owners' equity section of the consolidated balance sheet the subsidiary's owners' equity when the parent is the one and only stockholder. In this situation, the owners of the parent company's shares of stock are the only owners of the combined enterprise. They are the only ones who have claims to the owners' equity in the combined enterprise. Able's $150,000 owners' equity ($50,000 in common stock and $100,000 in retained earnings) therefore has to be removed from the combined owners' equity amounts before a consolidated balance sheet can be prepared.

Therefore, to prepare a consolidated balance sheet, Worthy has to eliminate the $220,000, $100,000, and $50,000 balances. As a first effort to do this, it might prepare the following entry in the worksheet:

Common Stock	50,000	
Retained Earnings	100,000	
Excess	70,000	
Investment in Subsidiary		220,000

The $70,000 "excess" is the excess of the investment cost ($220,000) over the book value of the owners' equity acquired ($150,000). We discovered earlier that Worthy paid most of this additional amount because the market value of Able's inventory exceeded its book value by $20,000 ($110,000 − $90,000) and the market value of Able's machinery exceeded its book value by $35,000 ($115,000 − $80,000). The remaining $15,000 of the excess was attributed to unrecorded goodwill. In light of this information, the elimination entry in the worksheet can be restated as follows:

Common Stock	50,000	
Retained Earnings	100,000	
Inventory	20,000	
Machinery	35,000	
Goodwill	15,000	
Investment in Subsidiary		220,000

As a result of this elimination entry, Able's inventories, machinery, and goodwill enter the consolidated balance sheet at the same amounts that would have appeared if the combined enterprise had elected to operate as one legal entity.

Minority interest

When the parent owns less than 100 percent of its subsidiary's stock, accountants still prefer to prepare fully consolidated financial statements in most cases. The lack of 100 percent ownership does make it necessary, however, to measure and disclose the equity of the other shareholders of the subsidiary in income and in consolidated net assets—this is referred to as the *minority interest* in those amounts.

The consolidated balance sheet includes all the parent's and all the subsidiary's assets. If the parent has a less-than-wholly-owned subsidiary, however, the minority stockholders of the subsidiary have an equity in a portion of the consolidated assets. The amount of that equity is based on the book value of the subsidiary company's net assets included in the consolidated assets, multiplied by the percentage of subsidiary stock the minority stockholders own.

Let's assume that Worthy pays $180,000 to acquire 80 percent of Able's stock. Neither Worthy nor Able has any amounts receivable from or payable to the other. Able's net tangible assets, including inventories and machinery measured at the amounts equivalent

EXHIBIT 12–6. Worthy Company: Calculation of Purchased Goodwill

	100 Percent	80 Percent
Equity in Able, Inc.'s reported owners' equity:		
Common stock	$ 50,000	$ 40,000
Retained earnings	100,000	80,000
Total	150,000	120,000
Worthy Company's investment cost	220,000	180,000
Excess of cost over reported owners' equity	70,000	60,000
Portion of excess attributable to undervaluation of:		
Inventory	20,000	16,000
Machinery..	35,000	28,000
Total	55,000	44,000
Portion of excess attributable to goodwill	$ 15,000	$ 16,000

assets could be bought for in the market, still total $205,000.[5] Able's owners' equity, as reported in its balance sheet, is $150,000, and Worthy's 80 percent share of this total is $120,000, or $60,000 less than the $180,000 Worthy paid.

The distribution of this $60,000 is shown in the right column in Exhibit 12–6. The left column contains the amounts we derived in the 100-percent example in the previous section. Remember from our earlier discussion that Able's inventories and machinery are reported on its own statements at amounts $20,000 and $35,000 less than Worthy would have to pay to buy equivalent assets in the open market. Its 80 percent share of these amounts is $16,000 and $28,000, as shown in the lower portion of Exhibit 12–6. The other $16,000 of the $60,000 premium over book value is the price Worthy has paid for its share of Able's goodwill.

In other words, in preparing consolidated financial statements, Worthy has to do two things: (1) cancel its $180,000 purchase cost against its 80 percent share of Able's common stock and retained earnings, and (2) recognize the amounts it has paid for unrecorded inventory and machinery values and for goodwill. The elimination entry in the worksheet is:

Common Stock (50,000 × 0.8)	40,000	
Retained Earnings (100,000 × 0.8)	80,000	
Inventory (20,000 × 0.8)	16,000	
Machinery (35,000 × 0.8)	28,000	
Goodwill	16,000	
Investment in Subsidiary		180,000

---

[5]	Cash	$ 40,000
	Inventory	110,000
	Machinery	115,000
	Liabilities	(60,000)
	Total	$205,000

After this entry is made, 20 percent ($30,000) of Able's reported owners' equity ($10,000 listed as common stock and $20,000 as retained earnings) remains "uneliminated." This is the 20 percent equity of Able's minority stockholders. Notice that the amount of the minority interest isn't affected by the fact that the parent paid more for Able's assets than their cost to Able. The minority interest is based on the cost of the assets to Able, not their current market value.

The resulting inventory and machinery figures are peculiar. They include Worthy's own assets at historical cost and Able's assets at a hybrid amount: 80 percent of Able's assets is at Worthy's cost (based on current market value) and the other 20 percent is at Able's cost. This hybrid measurement is inevitable as long as accountants adhere to historical-cost accounting. The addition of $16,000 to the inventory and $28,000 to the machinery and the recognition of $16,000 in goodwill arise because Worthy paid these amounts as part of the purchase price of Able's shares. The remaining portions of the current values of these assets don't appear because the combined enterprise hasn't paid for them.

The acquisition-date balance sheet

The consolidated balance sheet amounts from this example are shown in the right-hand column of Exhibit 12–7. The six items

EXHIBIT 12–7.   Worthy Company and Subsidiaries: Consolidated Balance Sheet Amounts on the Acquisition Date

Assets	Worthy	Able	Eliminations*		Consolidated
Cash	$100,000	$ 40,000			$140,000
Inventory	70,000	90,000	(1)	16,000	176,000
Machinery	100,000	80,000	(1)	28,000	208,000
Investment in subsidiary	180,000	—	(1)	(180,000)	—
Goodwill	—	—	(1)	16,000	16,000
Total assets.....................	$450,000	$210,000			$540,000
Liabilities and Stockholders' Equity					
Liabilities	$200,000	$ 60,000			$260,000
Minority interest	—	—	(2)	30,000	30,000
Stockholders' equity:					
Common stock	80,000	50,000	(1)	(40,000)	80,000
			(2)	(10,000)	
Retained earnings	170,000	100,000	(1)	(80,000)	170,000
			(2)	(20,000)	
Total liabilities and stockholders' equity	$450,000	$210,000			$540,000

* Parentheses signify a decrease.

designated by (1) in the third column are the elimination entry amounts we derived earlier. The three items designated by (2) relate to the minority interest.

Notice that the minority interest is listed between the liabilities and the equity of Worthy's stockholders in the combined enterprise. The subsidiary's minority stockholders aren't creditors, so the minority interest can't be classified as a liability. They aren't shareholders in Worthy's other activities, so they can't be thought of as Worthy's shareholders. Instead, their equity in the combined enterprise is a peculiar kind of owners' equity; they have contributed to and can participate in the performance of only a portion of the combined enterprise, not the entire entity.

Preparation of consolidated financial statements is a demanding technical process and we'll make no effort to explain it in depth. Our purpose has been to foster an appreciation of the significance of the relationships between parent and subsidiary companies. Several final comments are in order before we move on, however. First, the minority interest in the income of a subsidiary must be subtracted to determine the consolidated net income.

Second, the cost of goods sold and depreciation amounts in consolidated income statements must be based on the amounts capitalized for consolidated reporting, not the costs shown in the separate companies' records. The consolidated income statements must also include amortizations of any goodwill capitalized in the consolidation process.

Third, consolidated retained earnings are shown in purchase-method accounting as the retained earnings of the parent company plus the parent's share of earnings retained by the subsidiary from the date of the combination onward.

Consolidation policy

Nonfinancial corporations in the United States sometimes do not consolidate some of their wholly owned subsidiaries. These nonconsolidated subsidiaries fall largely into two categories: (1) customer finance companies and commercial insurance companies, and (2) foreign subsidiaries.

Finance and insurance subsidiaries are usually excluded on the grounds that their operations are so different from those of the parent that to include them would produce distorted statements. For example, the General Motors Acceptance Corporation (GMAC) finances consumer purchases of General Motors automobiles and other products. GMAC assets are almost exclusively the notes of the purchasers of General Motors products, and GMAC finances these assets predominantly by borrowing. Consolidated statements for General Motors and GMAC therefore would show a much higher ratio of debt to equity than is typical for a manufacturing company.

Although a consolidated balance sheet would show a more complete picture of the overall financial position of General Motors, the accounting profession doesn't require consolidation in this case. Instead, General Motors presents separate financial statements for GMAC in its annual report, along with the consolidated statements for the parent company and the rest of its subsidiaries.

Most companies with foreign operations now consolidate the results of operations and the resources of their foreign subsidiaries with those of the parent for external financial reporting. Some foreign subsidiaries are excluded from the consolidation, however, on the grounds that their operations are highly regulated, expropriation is a near possibility, or the repatriation of dividends is prohibited or severely restricted.

The exclusion of foreign subsidiaries from the consolidation should be justified by the circumstances of each individual case. Even when one or more subsidiaries are excluded, however, a U.S. company uses the equity method to account for its investments in any subsidiaries which aren't included in the consolidation. This means that net income isn't affected by the subsidiary's decision to declare dividends or to use earnings to build up the subsidiary's net assets. Possible variations in the ratio of the subsidiary's dividends to its earnings make dividends a very poor measure of the subsidiary's contribution to the parent company's well-being.

SUMMARY

Nonfinancial corporations often hold government and commercial securities to earn a return on temporarily idle funds. Securities held for this purpose ordinarily earn relatively low yields but are highly liquid. They are called *marketable securities.* Most of these temporary investments are in notes, bonds, or other credit instruments with relatively early maturities, and these are stated at their cost.

A company's primary motive for owning other corporations' stock as a longer-term investment is to produce income; short-term marketability is seldom a consideration. When these investments are too small to give their owners any significant influence over the companies they represent, they are stated at the lower of cost or market. When the investments are large enough to give their owners some influence but not control, they are reported on an equity basis; that is, the investor reports as investment revenue the proportionate share of the investee's earnings, not just the dividends received. The investment is measured at cost plus the investor's equity in the increase in the investee's retained earnings since the acquisition was made.

When an investment constitutes a majority of the voting power in the other corporation, the holder is referred to as a parent company. The parent company's financial statements incorporate the parent's investments in its subsidiaries and its equity in their earnings. Most parent companies in the United States present consolidated financial statements, reflecting the consolidated results and year-end position of parent and subsidiary combined. This means the assets, liabilities, revenues, and expenses of the subsidiary are combined with those of the parent.

APPENDIX: POST-COMBINATION ACCOUNTING

Preparing consolidated statements for periods subsequent to the combination date is a difficult task, particularly when the combination is treated as a purchase. To illustrate the process and identify some of the calculations that must be made, we'll follow the Worthy-Able business combination through its first year of operation as a combined enterprise. We'll assume that Worthy paid $180,000 in cash to Able's stockholders on Janury 1, 19x1, in exchange for 80 percent of their shares, as illustrated earlier in Exhibit 12–7.

Worthy decided not to attempt to buy the shares of Able's minority stockholders, and the two companies continued to operate as separate legal entities. Worthy therefore recorded the $180,000 purchase price as an asset, Investment in Subsidiary. The book value of Able's owners' equity was $150,000 on January 1, 19x1 ($210,000 assets − $60,000 liabilities), and Worthy's share in this amount therefore was $120,000 (0.8 × $150,000). Most of the $60,000 excess of the purchase price ($180,000) over book value ($120,000) was deemed to represent Worthy's 80 percent equity in the $20,000 excess of market value over the cost of Able's inventories ($16,000) and in the $35,000 excess of market value over depreciated cost of the machinery ($28,000); the remaining $16,000 ($60,000 − $16,000 − $28,000) was goodwill. We used the consolidation worksheet in Exhibit 12–7 to reflect these amounts in a consolidated balance sheet as of January 1, 19x1.

To prepare consolidated statements for 19x1, Worthy's accountants had to decide how much of the $60,000 Worthy paid in excess of its equity in Able's recorded net assets was to be treated as a determinant of consolidated net income in that year and how much was to appear on the year-end consolidated balance sheet. They also had to determine how much of the two companies' reported income, assets, and liabilities was to appear in the consolidated

EXHIBIT 12–8.   Consolidated Statement Worksheet—First Year after Acquisition Date

	Worthy	Able	Eliminations Debit		Eliminations Credit		Consolidated
Cash	100,000	80,000					180,000
Receivables	90,000	60,000			(2)	6,000	144,000
Inventory	47,000	25,000	(3)	4,800	(1)	3,000	73,800
Machinery (net)	115,000	70,000	(3)	26,000			211,000
Investment in subsidiary	180,000				(3)	180,000	
Goodwill			(3)	15,600			15,600
Liabilities	266,000	30,000	(2)	6,000			290,000
Minority interest					(4)	41,000	41,000
Common stock	80,000	50,000	(3) 40,000 (4) 10,000				80,000
Retained earnings, January 1	170,000	100,000	(3) 80,000 (4) 20,000				170,000
Income statement:							
Sales revenues	372,000	185,000	(1)	30,000			527,000
Cost of goods sold	200,000	90,000	(3)	11,200	(1)	27,000	274,200
Other expenses	156,000	40,000	(3)	2,400			198,400
Minority interest			(4)	11,000			11,000
Net income	16,000	55,000					43,400
Retained earnings, December 31	186,000	155,000					213,400

financial statements. To illustrate this process, let's assume that the two companies' preliminary financial statements contained the amounts shown in the first two columns of Exhibit 12–8. The entries in the Eliminations columns are based on the following additional information:

1. Able's net income in 19x1 amounted to $55,000; Able declared no dividends to its shareholders during the year.
2. Worthy sold merchandise to Able for $30,000 during the year. This was 20 percent above Worthy's cost. At year-end, 60 percent of the $30,000 was still included in Able's inventory.
3. As of December 31, 19x1, there was a $6,000 intercompany debt.
4. Worthy determined that depreciation expense based on the January 1, 19x1, market value of Able's machinery was $2,500 greater than historical-cost depreciation of this asset.
5. Worthy decided to amortize the goodwill created by the business combination over 40 years on a straight-line basis.
6. Able's inventory was measured partly on a FIFO basis and partly on LIFO. Its December 31 inventory included items that still carried the costs they had borne on January 1. The costs of

these items constituted 30 percent of the total cost of Able's January 1 inventory.
7. Worthy had made no entries in its books to record its equity in Able's earnings.

Worthy's first task was to remove intercompany sales and intercompany profits from the financial statements. Worthy's sales revenues included $30,000 of sales to Able rather than to outside customers (item 2 in the list above). Its cost of goods sold on these sales amounted to $25,000 ($30,000/1.2). Able recognized $12,000 (0.4 × $30,000) as part of its cost of goods sold, but the cost to the combined enterprise was only $10,000 (12,000/1.2). In other words, the cost of goods sold had to be reduced by $27,000 [$25,000 + ($12,000 − $10,000)]. Able's inventory included $18,000 (0.6 × $30,000), whereas the cost to the combined enterprises was only $15,000 ($18,000/1.2). The difference, $3,000, was an intercompany profit the combined enterprise hadn't yet earned by the end of 19x1. The eliminating entry therefore was:

(1)

Sales Revenues	30,000	
Cost of Goods Sold		27,000
Inventory		3,000

(In practice, these amounts would be entered only in the consolidation worksheet, not in either company's ledger.)

Worksheet entry (2) eliminated the intercompany debt that was outstanding on December 31, 19x1:

(2)

Liabilities	6,000	
Receivables		6,000

The accountants' next chore was to eliminate the $180,000 cost of Worthy's investment in Able. Worthy's $180,000 purchase cost had to be removed in the consolidation process because it represented Able's net assets at the time of the purchase, and these were already included in the consolidated amounts. Also, 80 percent of the $150,000 book value of Able's owners' equity ($120,000) had to be removed because it didn't represent equity of owners of the combined enterprise. In the absence of any amortization of the three components of the $60,000 difference between these two amounts, the eliminating entry on December 31, 19x1, would have been the same as the entry used in Exhibit 12–7 to eliminate the intercompany investment:

Common Stock (0.8 × $50,000)	40,000	
Retained Earnings (0.8 × $100,000)	80,000	
Inventory (0.8 × $20,000)	16,000	
Machinery (0.8 × $35,000)	28,000	
Goodwill	16,000	
Investment in Subsidiary		180,000

In fact, however, portions of the three asset amounts identified in the original consolidation were applicable to 19x1 revenues: 70 percent of the inventory write-up (0.7 × $16,000 = $11,200); 80 percent of the additional depreciation on the machinery (0.8 × $2,500 = $2,000), and 1/40 of the $16,000 goodwill ($400). The remaining portions of these three assets were applicable to the year-end assets, as follows:

	January 1 Asset		19x1 Expense		December 31 Asset
Inventory	$16,000	=	$11,200	+	$ 4,800
Machinery	28,000	=	2,000	+	26,000
Goodwill	16,000	=	400	+	15,600
Total	$60,000	=	$13,600	+	$46,400

The elimination of the $180,000 initial investment therefore was made in worksheet entry (3):[6]

---

[6] Worthy had to make an entry *in its own books* as of the end of 19x1 as well as this worksheet entry. Because it used the equity method to account for its ownership of Able's stock, it had to increase the investment asset by its equity in the increment to Able's retained earnings, less its share of the amortization of any portion of the purchase cost of the investment. This amounted to $27,400, calculated as follows:

80 percent of Able's $55,000 net income	$44,000	
Additional depreciation (0.8 × $2,500)	− 2,000	
Additional cost of goods sold (0.7 × $16,000)	− 11,200	
Amortization of goodwill ($16,000/40)	− 400	
Yet-to-be-earned intercompany profit [0.6 × 0.2 ($30,000/1.2)]	− 3,000	
Equity in Able's income	$27,400	

The entry to bring Worthy's investment asset up to date as of the end of 19x1 was:

Investment in Subsidiary	27,400	
Equity in Able's Income		27,400

The ending investment balance on Worthy's own balance sheet therefore was $207,400 ($180,000 + $27,400). The $27,400 increment was included in Worthy Company's corporate net income.

(3)

Common Stock (0.8 × $50,000)	40,000	
Retained Earnings (0.8 × $100,000)	80,000	
Inventory (0.3 × $16,000)	4,800	
Machinery [0.8 × ($35,000 − $2,500)]	26,000	
Goodwill (39/40 × $16,000)	15,600	
Cost of Goods Sold (0.7 × $16,000)	11,200	
Other Expenses [(0.8 × $2,500) + ($16,000/40)]	2,400	
Investment in Subsidiary....................		180,000

The final entry in the consolidation worksheet recognized the equity interests of Able's minority stockholders:

(4)

Common Stock (0.2 × $50,000)	10,000	
Retained Earnings (0.2 × $100,000)	20,000	
Income Statement (0.2 × $55,000)	11,000	
Minority Interest (0.2 × $205,000)		41,000

The debits to Common Stock and Retained Earnings remove the final 20 percent of the owners' equity shown in Able's books *at the time of the combination.* The other two amounts in entry (4) identify the minority shareholders' interests in consolidated net income in 19x1 and in the consolidated net assets as of December 31, 19x1.

KEY TERMS

Amortized cost	Goodwill
Business combinations	Intercompany transactions
Combined enterprise	Marketable securities
Combinee	Minority interest
Combinor	Parent company
Consolidated financial statements	Pooling-of-interests method
Eliminations	Purchase method
Equity method	Subsidiary company

INDEPENDENT STUDY PROBLEMS (Solutions in Appendix B)

1. Equity method. The Cantara Company on January 1, 19x1, bought 2,500 shares of the common stock of the Denby Corporation. These shares constituted 25 percent of Denby's outstanding common shares. Cantara paid $30 a share for this stock.

Denby reported a net income of $30,000 in 19x1 and declared dividends of $1.60 a share on its common stock.

a. How much investment income should Cantara report in 19x1 from its investment in Denby?

b. At what amount should Cantara report its investment in Denby on its December 31, 19x1, balance sheet?

2. Goodwill; minority interest. On December 31, 19x1, the Pilot Company paid $92,000 in cash for an 80 percent interest in the Essex Company. The Essex balance sheet on that date showed the following balances in the shareholders' equity:

Common stock	$ 40,000
Additional paid-in capital	20,000
Retained earnings	50,000
Total	$110,000

The appraised value of Essex's tangible assets was equal to their book value on the date of acquisition.

a. What was the amount of the goodwill on the date of the purchase?

b. What was the amount of the minority interest on this date?

3. Long-term investment in bonds. On January 1, 1978, Durant Corporation bought 100 of Russell Company's 12 percent debenture bonds. Although the bonds' maturity value on December 31, 1992, would be $100,000, Durant's investment cost was $87,590. Interest was compounded semiannually, and interest payments were received each June 30 and December 31.

An unanticipated need for cash caused Durant to sell the bonds on January 1, 1983, when the yield rate was 15 percent.

a. Calculate the anticipated yield to maturity on these bonds at the time of purchase.

b. Prepare an entry in general journal form to record Durant's purchase of the bonds in 1978.

c. Calculate Durant's income from these bonds in 1978.

d. How much did Durant receive for the bonds on January 1, 1983? How much gain or loss did it realize on the sale?

e. Prepare an entry in general journal form to record Durant's sale of the bonds in 1983.

4. Intercompany transactions. Alcon Corporation owns 100 percent of the shares of Nonon Company. In 19x1 the two companies had the following income:

	Alcon	Nonon
Sales revenues	$5,000,000	$1,000,000
Dividend income (from Nonon)	50,000	—
Cost of goods sold	(3,000,000)	(700,000)
Other expenses	(1,500,000)	(200,000)
Net Income	$ 550,000	$ 100,000

You have the following additional information:

1. The price Alcon paid for Nonon's shares were equal to the book value of Nonon's net assets at the time the shares were bought.

2. Nonon sold merchandise to Alcon for $250,000 during 19x1. This merchandise had cost Nonon $180,000.
3. Alcon's inventory on December 31, 19x1, included $100,000 of merchandise bought from Nonon. Nonon's cost of this merchandise was $70,000.
4. On December 31, 19x1, Alcon owed Nonon $35,000 for merchandise purchases. This amount was included in Alcon's accounts payable and in Nonon's accounts receivable.
5. Income tax effects of intercompany transactions can be ignored.
6. Alcon didn't use the equity method since it knew consolidated statements would be prepared at year-end.

a. Prepare appropriate elimination entries to reflect this information.
b. Prepare a consolidated income statement for Alcon Corporation and its subsidiary for the year 19x1.

5. Calculating consolidated income, retained earnings, and minority interest. Company X purchased an 80 percent interest in Company Y on January 1, 19x2. The price was $80,000, paid in cash, and the purchase was recorded in the Investments account of Company X. The appraised value of Y's tangible assets was equal to their book value at the time the stock was bought.

The directors of Company Y declared cash dividends in the amount of $10,000 during 19x2.

Company X published no financial statements on a parent-company-only basis; it recorded its investments at cost in its own accounts. Upon receiving Company Y's dividends, it debited Cash and credited Dividend Income. Company X's unconsolidated reported earnings for 19x2 amounted to $55,000, including dividend income. No other transactions between Company X and Company Y took place during the year.

Company X declared cash dividends of $30,000 during 19x2.

The stockholders' equity section of the beginning and ending balance sheets of the two corporations showed the following:

	Company X		Company Y	
	1/1/x2	*12/31/x2*	*1/1/x2*	*12/31/x2*
Common stock.................	$100,000	$100,000	$ 30,000	$ 30,000
Additional paid-in capital	20,000	20,000	10,000	10,000
Retained earnings	375,000	400,000	60,000	65,000
Total	$495,000	$520,000	$100,000	$105,000

Goodwill, if any, was to be amortized in 20 equal annual installments.

a. Calculate Company X's unconsolidated net income, based on the equity method.
b. What would Company X have reported as its investment in Company Y on an unconsolidated balance sheet as of December 31, 19x2, if it had used the equity method?
c. Calculate consolidated net income for 19x2.
d. At what amount would the minority interest be reported in the December 31, 19x2, consolidated balance sheet?

EXERCISES AND PROBLEMS

6. Pooling versus purchase: discussion question. Company P has just acquired all the assets of Company Q by an exchange of stock. Company Q has achieved a notable rate of growth in recent years, both in sales and in earnings, and its stock has been selling at market prices considerably in excess of its book value. The financial statements of Company P are footnoted to indicate that this acquisition was treated as a pooling of interests.

In what ways would next year's reported net income and the end-of-year balance sheet have differed if the acquisition had been treated as a purchase rather than as a pooling of interests?

7. Parent-subsidiary, intercompany inventory profit. World, Inc., is a wholly owned subsidiary of Universal Corporation. During 19x2, Universal sold merchandise to World for $109,200; the goods had cost Universal $84,000 to manufacture. By year-end, 75 percent of the merchandise had been resold for $150,000.

The two companies' individual financial statements contained the following data:

	Universal	World
Sales	$850,000	$418,000
Cost of goods sold	490,000	304,000
Gross margin	$360,000	$114,000
Ending inventory	$ 79,000	$ 36,500

Prepare a schedule which identifies the comparable amounts that should appear in the companies' consolidated financial statements for 19x2.

8. Equity method. On January 2, 19x2, Carson Corporation bought 300 shares of the outstanding common stock of Baldwin, Inc., for $275,000 in cash. Baldwin's owners' equity consisted of 1,000, $5 par-value shares, additional paid-in capital of $285,000, and retained earnings of $410,000. Carson paid an amount in excess of book value because Baldwin had an unrecorded goodwill asset which Carson believed would last for 10 more years.

Baldwin declared and paid a $12,000 cash dividend in July 19x2 and reported net income of $50,000 for the year.

a. How much equity in Baldwin Inc.'s income should be recognized in Carson Corporation's 19x2 income statement?

b. At what amount should the investment in Baldwin, Inc., be reported in Carson Corporation's December 31, 19x2, balance sheet?

9. Long-term investment in bonds. On July 1, 1978, Redwood, Inc., bought 400 debenture bonds which had been issued six months earlier by Saxony Company. The bonds' maturity value on December 31, 1997, would be $400,000. Their coupon interest rate was 10 percent, and interest was paid each June 30 and December 31.

The bonds had been issued on January 1, 1978, to yield 9 percent, but by the time Redwood bought them, it was able to achieve a yield to maturity of 10.5 percent.

Redwood held the bonds until January 1, 1983, when it sold them to Maxwell, Inc. It recorded a $30,800 gain on the sale to Maxwell.

a. What was the cost of the July 1, 1978, investment?
b. What was the interest earned in 1978?
c. What would Redwood's interest income have been in 1978 if it had bought the bonds on January 1, 1978 at Saxony's issue price?
d. What annual yield would Maxwell earn if it held the bonds to maturity?

10. Business combination, minority interest. On January 1, 19x1, Royal Company bought 900 of Yankee, Inc.'s 1,000 outstanding shares of common stock for $162,000. At that time, Yankee's balance sheet showed its outstanding shares at a par value of $10 a share. Yankee's additional paid-in capital amounted to $90,000 and its retained earnings were $80,000. Royal's retained earnings on January 1, 19x1 were $99,000.

The following events occurred during 19x1:

	Royal	Yankee
Operating income	$40,000	$30,000
Dividends declared and paid	3,000	7,000

Cash loan by Royal to Yankee in July, 19x1, $12,000;
  this amount was still outstanding on December 31, 19x1

a. What was Royal Company's unconsolidated 19x1 net income?
b. What was Royal Company's *Investment in Yankee* account balance as of December 31, 19x1?
c. What was consolidated net income for 19x1?
d. What was the minority interest as of December 31, 19x1?

11. Purchase or pooling? Two companies had the following balance sheets on December 31, 19x1:

	Company X	Company Y
Assets		
Current assets	$ 5,500	$1,000
Plant and equipment, net	7,000	1,700
Total assets	$12,500	$2,700
Liabilities and Owners' Equity		
Current liabilities	$ 2,500	$ 500
Common stock ($5 par)	2,000	250
Additional paid-in capital	3,000	750
Retained earnings	5,000	1,200
Total liabilities and owners' equity	$12,500	$2,700

These balance sheets included $200 that Company Y owed Company X for goods Company Y purchased during 19x1 and sold to its customers.

These two companies merged on January 1, 19x2, Company X issuing 100 shares of its common stock in exchange for all the common shares of Company Y. The fair value of a share of Company X's stock at that time was $30.

In 19x2, Company X reported unconsolidated net income of $1,000, including $100 in cash dividends from Company Y. Company X paid $400 in cash dividends to its shareholders. Company Y reported unconsolidated net income of $180. No intercompany sales were made during the year, and the $200 beginning-of-year debt was paid by Company Y during the year.

The appraised value of Company Y's tangible assets was equal to their book value on the date of the merger. As a matter of policy, X's directors insist that any purchased goodwill be amortized in 20 equal annual installments.

a. Should the merger have been accounted for as a purchase or as a pooling of interests? Explain why.
b. Prepare a consolidated balance sheet immediately after the merger.
c. Calculate consolidated net income for the year 19x2.
d. Prepare the owners' equity section of the consolidated balance sheet as of December 31, 19x2.
e. How would your answers to parts b and c have differed if you had answered part a differently?

12. Measurement basis: minority investment.   The market price of the common stock of Epstein Drugs had ranged from $23 to $35 a share during 19x1 and 19x2. Its price in January 19x3 was $32. At that point, Harlow Enterprises offered to buy any or all of the common shares of Epstein Drugs at $40 a share. Epstein's management advised its shareholders to reject this offer, saying the company was worth more than $40 a share, but 350,000 shares were sold to Harlow at that price. Epstein had 1 million shares outstanding at that time.

At the time Harlow made these purchases, Epstein's shareowners' equity was as follows:

Common stock, $5 par	$ 5,000,000
Additional paid-in capital	8,000,000
Retained earnings	4,000,000
Total	$17,000,000

During 19x3, Epstein had a net income of $5 a share and distributed cash dividends of $3 a share.

a. Calculate Harlow's investment income in 19x3 from its ownership of Epstein shares. Harlow amortizes goodwill in 40 equal annual installments.
b. At what amount should Harlow report its investment in Epstein on its December 31, 19x3, balance sheet?
c. An investment analyst commented that consolidated financial statements for Harlow would have been more meaningful than the statements it actually issued. How would consolidated statements differ from nonconsolidated statements? State your reasons for agreeing or disagreeing with the analyst.

13. Consolidated sales and cost of goods sold.   On March 1, 19x1, Company P sold merchandise to its wholly owned subsidiary for $120. Company P had bought this merchandise on February 1, 19x1, for $80. The subsidiary paid Company P on April 5, 19x1, and sold the merchandise on account to an outside customer for $150 on December 15, 19x1.

a. How were these transactions reflected in the unconsolidated income statements for Company P and its subsidiary for the year ended December 31, 19x1?

b. How should these transactions be reflected in the companies' consolidated income statement for the year? Prepare a worksheet elimination entry to produce this result.

c. How would your answers to parts a and b have differed if the merchandise had remained in the subsidiary's inventory on December 31, 19x1?

14. Acquisition-date consolidated balance sheet. On January 3, Prince Company bought 1,600 of the 2,000 outstanding $2.50 par, common shares of Wright, Ltd. Immediately after recording the investment, Prince's balance sheet was as follows:

	Unconsolidated	Consolidated
Assets		
Cash	$180,000	$280,000
Inventory	350,000	640,000
Investment in Wright	160,000	
Goodwill		14,000
Total	$690,000	$934,000
Liabilities and Owners' Equity		
Payables	$440,000	$650,000
Minority interest		34,000
Common stock	20,000	20,000
Retained earnings	230,000	230,000
Total	$690,000	$934,000

Prepare Wright, Ltd.'s balance sheet as of January 3.

15. Consolidated net income, minority interest, retained earnings. Homer Company bought 8,000 shares of the common stock of Cicero Corporation on December 31, 19x3. The purchase price was $12 a share, paid in cash. These shares constituted 80 percent of Cicero Corporation's outstanding common stock. Cicero's balance sheet on that date showed the following shareholders' equity:

Common stock	$ 60,000
Additional paid-in capital	25,000
Retained earnings	35,000
Total	$120,000

The appraised value of Cicero's assets was equal to their book value on the date of the acquisition.

In 19x4, Cicero Corporation had net income of $30,000 and paid $20,000 in dividends to its stockholders. Homer Company's net income for the year amounted to $50,000, including dividends from Cicero but before the year-end adjustment was made in Homer's accounts to bring them in line with the equity method. Neither company included any intercompany profit in the inventory it reported at the end of the year.

a. What was the consolidated net income for 19x4, after providing for minority interests?
b. At what amount would minority interest be shown on the December 31, 19x4, consolidated balance sheet?
c. How much of Cicero's retained earnings would be shown in consolidated retained earnings as of December 31, 19x4?

16. Business combination: alternative methods.   Company A and Company B were completely independent. Neither had invested in the other; neither had ever bought goods or services from the other. These two companies merged at the beginning of this year. Immediately before the merger, their balance sheets showed the following:

	Company A	Company B
Assets		
Cash	$290	$ 30
Other current assets	90	60
Property and equipment (net)	120	60
Total	$500	$150
Liabilities and Owners' Equity		
Liabilities	$100	$ 50
Common stock	50	15
Additional paid-in capital	150	45
Retained earnings	200	40
Total	$500	$150

The amounts shown for common stock were the total par values of the shares.

a. Assume Company A purchased all the outstanding common stock of Company B for $160 cash and operated B as a subsidiary. The appraised value of the property and equipment was equal to its book value. What would A's consolidated balance sheet show immediately after the acquisition?
b. Assume Company A acquired all the outstanding stock of Company B, issuing in exchange its own stock with a market value of $160 (par $40). The merger of the two companies was treated as a pooling of interests. After the merger, B ceased to exist as a legal entity. What would appear on A's post-combination balance sheet?
c. For the year preceding the merger, net income was $50 for Company A and $11 for Company B (after depreciation of $6). Assuming the same operating revenues and expenses for the year after the merger except as they may be affected by the accounting method, what net income would be reported under each of the two circumstances described above? (Where appropriate, assume that company policy calls for goodwill to be written off on a straight-line basis over a five-year period.)
d. Compare the results under the two sets of circumstances. Which is more attractive to a management that is interested in putting its best foot forward?

17. Business combination, minority interest. On January 1, 19x4, Paxton Company bought 90 percent of Nicely Corporation's common stock by paying $325,000 cash to Nicely stockholders. The two companies' January 1, 19x4, pre-combination balance sheets showed the following:

	Paxton	Nicely
Assets		
Cash	$ 500,000	$ 80,000
Receivables	440,000	150,000
Land	60,000	170,000
Total	$1,000,000	$400,000
Liabilities and Owners' Equity		
Payables.......................	$ 300,000	$100,000
Common stock	400,000	100,000
Retained earnings	300,000	200,000
Total	$1,000,000	$400,000

It was determined that the market value of Nicely's land was $350,000. The two companies then began operating as parent and subsidiary.

On December 31, 19x4, Nicely informed all its stockholders that it had a net income of $20,000 during 19x4 ($82,000 sales − $62,000 expenses), and that on December 24 its board of directors had declared an $8,000 cash dividend payable on January 30, 19x5, to stockholders of record as of December 31, 19x4.

During 19x4, Paxton's sales revenues were $175,000, its cost of goods sold and other expenses totaled $150,000, it declared a $13,000 cash dividend, and there were no sales between Paxton and Nicely.

a. Prepare Paxton's post-combination unconsolidated balance sheet as of January 1, 19x4.
b. Prepare the companies' consolidated balance sheet as of January 1, 19x4.
c. What was Paxton's unconsolidated income for 19x4?
d. What was the consolidated net income for 19x4?

18. Business combination, journal entries. Larsen Corporation has identified the following five scenarios through which it might acquire a controlling or significant interest in Garcia, Ltd.

1. Larsen pays $202,000 cash to buy 100 percent of Garcia's outstanding shares, and the combined enterprise is operated as one legal entity.
2. Larsen pays $202,000 cash to buy 100 percent of Garcia's outstanding shares, and the combined enterprise is operated as a parent and subsidiary.
3. Larsen pays $135,000 cash to buy 70 percent of Garcia's outstanding shares, and thereby creates a parent-subsidiary relationship.
4. Larsen pays $81,000 cash to buy 40 percent of Garcia's outstanding shares.
5. Larsen exchanges 4,800 of its $1 par-value common shares for all Garcia's outstanding shares. The market values per share were: Larsen

$5 and Garcia $2.40. The combined enterprise is operated as one legal entity.

The transaction would occur on January 1, 19x4, when Garcia's balance sheet is expected to appear as follows:

Assets

Cash.........................	$ 40,000
Inventory	80,000
Machinery	180,000
Total	$300,000

Liabilities and Owners' Equity

Payables	$140,000
Common stock ($2 par)	20,000
Additional paid-in capital	90,000
Retained earnings	50,000
Total	$300,000

The market value of the inventory is expected to be $90,000, and the market value of the machinery is expected to be $200,000.

Prepare a journal entry Larsen would find appropriate under each of the five scenarios.

19. Post-combination earnings. Larsen Corporation (see problem 18) acquired stock of Garcia, Ltd., on January 1, 19x4. Three of the five scenarios described in problem 18—scenarios 2, 3, and 4—resulted in Garcia continuing to operate as a legal entity. The estimates in problem 18 proved to be correct.

The following information relates to the two companies' operations in 19x4:

	Larsen	Garcia
Sales revenues	$350,000	$190,000
Expenses:		
Cost of goods sold	140,000	70,000
Depreciation	20,000	18,000
Other expenses	100,000	42,000
Total expenses	260,000	130,000
Net income	$ 90,000	$ 60,000

Dividends declared and paid were $15,000 by Larsen and $10,000 by Garcia. Garcia didn't buy or sell machinery during 19x4, and 20 percent of its January 1 inventory remained unsold at year-end. Larsen amortized goodwill over 10 years on a straight-line basis.

a. For scenarios 2, 3, and 4 identified in problem 18, what was Larsen Corporation's net income in 19x4?
b. For scenarios 2 and 3, prepare the 19x4 consolidated income statement.
c. For scenarios 1 and 5, prepare Larsen's 19x4 income statement.

20. Business combination. On November 30, 19x3, the Fair Deal Corporation exchanged 10,000 shares of its $5 par common stock for a 100 percent ownership in Strate & Shute, Inc. At that time, Fair Deal stock was selling at a market price of $40 per share; Strate & Shute was a family-owned corporation and there was no market in its shares. The acquisition was treated as a pooling of interests.

Balance sheets drawn up for the two corporations as of November 30, 19x3, just before the acquisition transaction was consummated, showed the following (in summary form):

	Fair Deal	Strate & Shute
Assets		
Assets	$1,000,000	$250,000
Owners' Equity		
Common stock	$ 200,000	$100,000
Additional paid-in capital	300,000	70,000
Retained earnings	500,000	80,000
Total owners' equity	$1,000,000	$250,000

Earnings for the two companies for 19x3 were:

	Fair Deal	Strate & Shute
January 1–November 30	$120,000	$40,000
December 1–December 31	20,000	5,000
Total	$140,000	$45,000

There were no intercompany sales during the year. No dividends were declared by either company during the year. A set of consolidated financial statements was prepared at the end of 19x3.

a. At what amounts would goodwill and retained earnings appear on the consolidated balance sheet at December 31, 19x3?
b. Calculate consolidated net income for the year. (Goodwill, if any, is to be amortized in equal amounts for 20 years.)
c. How would your answers to parts a and b have differed if the Strate & Shute stock had been acquired in exchange for $394,000 in cash?

21. Business combination. Below are the balance sheets of Single and Multiple Corporations as of December 31, 19x3:

	Multiple	Single
Assets		
Assets	$3,400,000	$156,000
Liabilities and Owners' Equity		
Liabilities	$ 650,000	$ 50,000
Capital stock, 32,000 shares		32,000
Capital stock, 800,000 shares	800,000	
Capital contributed in excess of par value	600,000	17,000
Retained earnings	1,350,000	57,000
Total	$3,400,000	$156,000

The appraised value of Single's tangible assets was equal to their book value at that time.

At the start of 19x4, Multiple paid $190,000 in cash for the 32,000 shares of Single. The two companies then began operating as parent and subsidiary.

The two companies' unconsolidated income statements for 19x4, drawn up before the end-of-year adjustments were made to reflect the equity method, were as follows:

	Multiple	Single
Sales	$10,000,000	$800,000
Expenses	8,700,000	700,000
Operating income	1,300,000	100,000
Dividend received	40,000	
Income before taxes	$ 1,340,000	$100,000

No intercompany sales took place during 19x4, and consolidated income before taxes was taxed at a rate of 50 percent.

a.   Would the merger have been accounted for as a purchase or as a pooling of interests? Why?
b.   Prepare the combination-date consolidated balance sheet.
c.   Present a consolidated income statement for 19x4. Goodwill, if any, was to be amortized equally over seven years.
d.   How, if at all, would your answers to the questions above have differed if the shares of Single had been obtained in exchange for 20,000 shares of Multiple's stock, valued at $9.50 a share?

22.   Advantages of consolidated statements.   Indico, Inc., has its headquarters in a country in which corporations are not required to follow U.S. generally accepted accounting principles in preparing their financial statements. Indico has one subsidiary, Dilex, Inc. Indico established Dilex in 19x1 by buying 100,000 shares of its $1 par common stock for $500,000. No other shares were issued, either then or later.

The income statements of the two companies for the year 19x7 were as follows:

	Indico	Dilex
Sales revenue	$150,000	$600,000
Dividend income (from Dilex)	40,000	—
Total revenue	190,000	600,000
Cost of goods sold	85,000	420,000
Selling and administrative expenses	45,000	53,000
Interest expense........................	—	22,000
Income tax expense	10,000	30,000
Net income	$ 50,000	$ 75,000

Dilex's sales revenues included $50,000 in sales to Indico; the cost of goods sold attributable to these sales was $35,000.

The two companies' balance sheets as of December 31, 19x7, contained the following information:

	Indico	Dilex
Assets		
Current assets:		
Cash	$ 10,000	$ 25,000
Accounts receivable	20,000	170,000
Inventories	30,000	205,000
Total current assets	60,000	400,000
Investment in subsidiary	500,000	—
Plant and equipment (net)	140,000	670,000
Total assets	$700,000	$1,070,000
Liabilities		
Current liabilities:		
Accounts payable	$ 5,000	$ 35,000
Taxes payable	5,000	10,000
Total current liabilities	10,000	45,000
Bonds payable	—	275,000
Total liabilities	$ 10,000	$ 320,000
Shareowners' Equity		
Common stock	$200,000	$ 100,000
Additional paid-in capital	100,000	400,000
Retained earnings	390,000	250,000
Total shareowners' equity	$690,000	$ 750,000

On December 31, Indico owed Dilex $2,000 for purchases of merchandise, and this amount was included in the accounts payable. Indico's inventory included merchandise purchased from Dilex at a price of $3,000. Dilex's cost of this merchandise was $1,800.

a. Prepare a set of 19x7 consolidated financial statements for Indico and its subsidiary.

b. Indico has never published either consolidated financial statements or the separate financial statements of Dilex. A group of Indico's shareholders have asked management to publish consolidated statements for 19x7. The company's treasurer has opposed this but has suggested meeting the shareowners' needs by shifting to the equity method in the parent company's statements. Evaluate this suggestion, indicating the benefits, if any, consolidated statements would give the shareholders and whether the equity method would be an adequate substitute for consolidation. Use numbers from the problem to support your arguments.

Part three

FINANCIAL REPORTING

13

The statement of changes in financial position

A business's operating performance is usually measured by its earnings, based on accrual accounting and the application of suitable revenue-recognition criteria. The results of this measurement process are communicated through the income statement, which sets forth the enterprise's revenues, expenses, gains, and losses. Unfortunately, the income statement doesn't show the effects of all the events which affected the company's liquidity—its ability to meet its cash obligations on time—nor does it reflect all the flows of resources into or out of the company during the period.

To overcome these deficiencies, a second performance-related statement is prepared—the *statement of changes in financial position,* or *funds statement.* Whenever a balance sheet and an income statement are prepared subject to review by independent public accountants, a statement of changes in financial position is also prepared, encompassing the same time interval covered by the income statement. This statement measures the flows of funds into and out of the company during a specified period of time. It shows how the events of the period affected the company's liquidity, where management obtained funds during the period, and how management used these funds. The abbreviated funds statement in Exhibit 13–1 is constructed to emphasize these three sets of variables. We'll see in a moment how current operations provide funds and what an increase in liquidity means.

The purpose of this chapter is to explain what the funds statement is, how it is prepared, how it relates to the income statement, and how it is used. In the first two sections we'll study statements

EXHIBIT 13–1

XYZ COMPANY
Statement of Changes in Financial Position
For the Year Ended December 31, 19x1

Sources of funds:		
Current operations		$500,000
Borrowing........................		200,000
Sale of plant assets		100,000
Total sources of funds		800,000
Uses of funds:		
Purchase of plant assets	$450,000	
Cash dividends	300,000	
Total uses of funds		750,000
Increase in liquidity		$ 50,000

that use the widely used working-capital format. We'll then examine statements reflecting cash flows and conclude with an analysis
of the usefulness of these statements.

SOURCES AND USES OF WORKING CAPITAL

The term *funds* denotes cash or any other form of liquid resources. To most people, *funds* is used interchangeably with *cash;*
in corporate finance, *funds* is occasionally used to denote all of
an enterprise's financial resources. *Funds* therefore is a term which
should be used only when there is a common understanding of
the context in which it is being used.

Defining funds as working capital

A strong case can be made for constructing funds statements
to show the flows of *cash* into and out of the company. Although
cash-based statements are now coming into favor, most companies
define funds as working capital, and their funds statements show
the sources and uses of working capital. The thinking is that fluctuations in the relationships of the various components of working
capital are likely to be temporary—flows of working capital are
therefore more meaningful in analyses of longer-term trends. For
this reason, we'll discuss the working-capital format first and postpone discussion of the cash format until later in this chapter.

The funds equation

To learn how funds statements are constructed, we first need
to understand how working capital relates to the other components

of the balance sheet. Working capital, as we pointed out in Chapter 2, is the difference between total current assets and total current liabilities. Let's recall that the basic accounting equation is:

$$\text{Assets} = \text{Liabilities} + \text{Owners' Equity} \qquad (1)$$

We can proceed further by observing that

$$\text{Current Assets} + \text{Noncurrent Assets} = \text{Current Liabilities} + \text{Noncurrent Liabilities} + \text{Owners' Equity} \qquad (2)$$

Upon subtracting noncurrent assets and current liabilities from both sides of the equation, we derive:

$$\text{Current Assets} - \text{Current Liabilities} = \text{Noncurrent Liabilities} + \text{Owners' Equity} - \text{Noncurrent Assets} \qquad (3)$$

And since working capital is measured by subtracting current liabilities from current assets, equation (3) can be restated as:

$$\text{Working Capital} = \text{Noncurrent Liabilities} + \text{Owners' Equity} - \text{Noncurrent Assets} \qquad (4)$$

In Equation (4), all the current items are on the left side of the equation and all the noncurrent items are on the right.

Finally, if we subtract the amount for each of these quantities from the comparable amount on a later date, the equation becomes

$$\text{Change in Working Capital} = \text{Change in Noncurrent Liabilities} + \text{Change in Owners' Equity} - \text{Change in Noncurrent Assets} \qquad (5)$$

Classes of transactions

The statement of changes in financial position reflects all transactions that produce at least one change on the left side of equation (5) *and* at least one change on the right side—that is, transactions which affect at least one current element and one noncurrent element on the balance sheet. Since the right side contains changes in three classes of noncurrent elements and these changes can be either upward or downward, there are six different classes of trans-

EXHIBIT 13–2. Transactions Affecting Working Capital

Change in a Noncurrent Account	Sample Transaction	Effect on Working Capital
1. Increase noncurrent liabilities	Issue bonds	Increase
2. Increase owners' equity	Issue stock	Increase
3. Decrease noncurrent assets	Sell land	Increase
4. Decrease noncurrent liabilities	Retire bonds	Decrease
5. Decrease owners' equity	Declare cash dividend	Decrease
6. Increase noncurrent assets	Buy machinery	Decrease

actions which constitute sources or uses of funds. These are listed in Exhibit 13–2. The three transactions which cause increases in working capital are identified as *sources* of working capital; the three transactions which result in decreases in working capital are called *uses* of working capital. The statement of changes in financial position therefore identifies the three types of sources and the three types of uses. If uses exceed sources, working capital decreases by that amount.

Transactions which affect only current items don't appear in the funds statement. Examples are purchasing inventory or collecting receivables. These transactions affect only the left side of equation (4), causing shifts between current items but having no net effect on total working capital. A transaction that affects only current items therefore neither provides nor uses working capital.

Other transactions affect only noncurrent items—that is, only items appearing on the right side of equation (4). Only the right side of the equation is affected, and there is no effect on either the right-side total or the left-side total. Transactions in this class appear in the statement of changes in financial position if they consist of flows of noncurrent resources into and out of the business. An example is the purchase of land with a long-term mortgage loan. Even though working capital isn't affected by this transaction, it taps one of the company's sources of funds (mortgage lenders) to enable it to acquire a useful resource (land). The transaction therefore is treated in the funds statement as both a source and a use of working capital.

Working capital from operations

In Exhibit 13–2 we used the issuance of stock as our example of an inflow of funds from an increase in owners' equity. Profitable operations also increase owners' equity through the increase in retained earnings. Whether the occurrence of net income is also a source of working capital depends on the types of assets and liabilities that are affected. This can be explained by recalling the nature of earnings.

Net income, as we pointed out in Chapter 2, is the excess of revenues over expenses. Revenues measure increases in assets such as cash or accounts receivable. Expenses measure decreases in assets or the creation of liabilities. Hence, net income is a measure of the growth of the company's *net assets* (assets net of liabilities).

Although net income is the basis for measuring the change in net assets resulting from current operations, it isn't necessarily also the appropriate basis for measuring the net change in *current* assets and *current* liabilities which results from operations. In fact, net income would serve this additional function only if all the period's revenues represented only increases in current assets *and* if all the period's expenses represented only decreases in current assets and increases in current liabilities.

We know, however, that some revenue and expense amounts do *not* represent changes in current assets or current liabilities. As a result, net income is not a measure of the amount of working capital provided by operations. Companies therefore must go beyond net income to measure the extent to which their operations are either a source or a use of working capital. What we really want is a funds-flow schedule that is analogous to the income statement—that is, a schedule showing the amount of funds each income statement item has provided or consumed.

For example, suppose an income statement has only the following items:

Sales revenues		$100,000
Cost of goods sold	$60,000	
Depreciation	5,000	
Income taxes	8,000	
Other expenses	15,000	88,000
Net income		$ 12,000

Sales revenues measure inflows of cash or accounts receivable. Since both of these are components of working capital, sales revenues belong on a schedule showing the amount of funds provided by operations. The cost of goods sold reflects the costs of items taken from inventory. Since inventory is a component of working capital, the cost of goods sold is also a determinant of funds provided by operations. Depreciation, on the other hand, measures a reduction in plant assets, not a reduction in working capital. It therefore doesn't belong in the funds-flow schedule.

Most of the income tax expense usually measures current payments of cash or increases in current liabilities, and these portions belong in the funds-flow schedule. If some of the income tax expense reflects an increase in deferred income taxes, however, this portion doesn't represent an outflow of working capital. To illustrate, if we find that the deferred portion of current income tax expense is $1,000, then only $7,000 of the $8,000 total belongs on the schedule of funds provided by operations.

Assuming that other expenses arise entirely from the payment of cash, the use of current inventories, or increases in wages payable or other current liabilities, the schedule of funds provided by operations is as follows:

	Net Income	Funds Provided by Operations
Sales revenues/inflows of funds	$100,000	$100,000
Expenses/outflows of funds:		
Cost of goods sold	60,000	60,000
Depreciation	5,000	—
Income taxes	8,000	7,000
Other expenses	15,000	15,000
Total expenses/outflows	88,000	82,000
Net income/net funds provided	$ 12,000	$ 18,000

Most funds statements derive the amount of funds provided by operations indirectly, starting with net income and adding or subtracting amounts that appear on the income statement but don't belong on a schedule of funds provided by operations. In our simple illustration, the presentation would be:

Net income	$12,000
Add: Depreciation	5,000
Increase in deferred income tax	1,000
Funds provided by operations	$18,000

We'll examine the accountant's method in more detail in the next section.

PREPARING THE STATEMENT

The first step in funds-statement preparation is to establish the net change in the amount of funds on hand between the beginning and the end of the period. When the company adopts the working-capital format, the change to be identified is the change in the company's working capital.

Exhibit 13–3 contains Peabody, Inc.'s balance sheets as of January 1 and December 31, 19x1. On the basis of these data, we can prepare a schedule of working-capital changes. In summary form, it appears as follows:

	January 1	December 31	Increase in Working Capital
Current assets	$190,000	$194,000	$ 4,000
Current liabilities	90,000	82,000	8,000
Working capital	$100,000	$112,000	$12,000

Both the $4,000 increase in current assets *and* the $8,000 decrease in current liabilities represent increases in working capital.

Our basic approach will be to analyze each noncurrent item in the comparative balance sheets. The objective is to determine whether the indicated change affected working capital—and if so, in what amount. We've already seen from equation (5) that increases and decreases in all the noncurrent balance sheet amounts will yield the same net change as the change in working capital. We've listed all these increases and decreases in Exhibit 13–4. If we can explain all these changes, we'll have explained the change in working capital.

Exhibits 13–5 and 13–6 provide additional data we'll need as we try to explain the balance sheet changes. The only other information we'll need comes from the president's letter to the shareholders, noting that the company spent $50,000 to buy new machinery in 19x1.

EXHIBIT 13–3

PEABODY, INC.
Comparative Balance Sheets
January 1 and December 31, 19x1

	January 1	December 31
Assets		
Current assets:		
Cash	$ 30,000	$ 14,000
Accounts receivable	70,000	85,000
Inventories	90,000	95,000
Total current assets	190,000	194,000
Plant assets:		
Machinery	290,000	310,000
Accumulated depreciation	90,000	75,000
Total plant assets	200,000	235,000
Total assets	$390,000	$429,000
Liabilities and Owners' Equity		
Current liabilities:		
Accounts payable	$ 79,000	$ 69,000
Salaries payable	1,000	1,000
Taxes payable	10,000	12,000
Total current liabilities	90,000	82,000
Noncurrent liabilities:		
Bonds payable	90,000	80,000
Deferred income taxes	15,000	20,000
Total noncurrent liabilities	105,000	100,000
Owners' equity:		
Common stock	20,000	30,000
Additional paid-in capital	80,000	120,000
Retained earnings	95,000	97,000
Total owners' equity	195,000	247,000
Total liabilities and owners' equity	$390,000	$429,000

EXHIBIT 13–4

PEABODY, INC.
Schedule of Changes in Noncurrent Assets,
Noncurrent Liabilities, and Owners' Equity
For the Year Ended December 31, 19x1

	January 1	December 31	Increase (Decrease)
Noncurrent liabilities:			
Bonds payable	$ 90,000	$ 80,000	$(10,000)
Deferred income taxes	15,000	20,000	5,000
Owners' equity:			
Common stock	20,000	30,000	10,000
Additional paid-in capital	80,000	120,000	40,000
Retained earnings	95,000	97,000	2,000
Total noncurrent liabilities and owners' equity	300,000	347,000	47,000
Plant assets:			
Machinery	290,000	310,000	20,000
Accumulated depreciation	90,000	75,000	15,000
Total plant assets	200,000	235,000	35,000
Working capital	$100,000	$112,000	$ 12,000

EXHIBIT 13–5

PEABODY, INC.
Income Statement
For the Year Ended December 31, 19x1

Sales revenue		$400,000
Expenses:		
Cost of goods sold	$240,000	
Depreciation	11,000	
Salaries	55,500	
Interest	7,000	
Loss on sale of machinery	1,000	
Miscellaneous expenses	20,500	
Income taxes	26,000	361,000
Net income		$ 39,000

EXHIBIT 13–6

PEABODY, INC.
Schedule of Changes in Owners' Equity
For the Year Ended December 31, 19x1

	Common Stock (par)	Additional Paid-in Capital	Retained Earnings
Balance, January 1	$20,000	$ 80,000	$95,000
Net income	—	—	39,000
Stock dividends	3,500	16,500	(20,000)
Cash dividends	—	—	(17,000)
Shares issued	6,500	23,500	—
Balance, December 31	$30,000	$120,000	$97,000

Retained earnings

We can start with any balance sheet element, but we prefer to begin by accounting for the change in retained earnings: for Peabody, a $2,000 increase in 19x1. First, the income statement identified net income of $39,000. This means the resources flowing into the company during 19x1 as a result of the year's operations brought $39,000 more net assets into the company than operations took out. What now needs to be determined is whether operations were also a $39,000 source of funds in 19x1.

We've already said that net income reflects changes in all assets and liabilities—that is, both current and noncurrent assets and liabilities. *Funds provided* invariably is different from net income; accountants therefore use net income only as a first approximation to funds provided by operations since it has the advantage of providing a visible link between the funds statement and the income statement.

We indicated earlier that depreciation expense and the deferred portion of income tax expense are the kinds of items that cause funds provided by operations to differ from net income. When we analyze the related balance sheet amounts, we will be able to identify the noncurrent components of net income to determine the amount of funds provided by operations. For the moment, however, we'll direct our attention to the other items underlying the $2,000 increase in retained earnings during 19x1—to see what effect, if any, they had on Peabody's working capital.

The right-hand column of Exhibit 13–6 shows two changes other than the change due to net income:

Stock dividend	$20,000
Cash dividend	17,000

Together, these two events removed $37,000 from retained earnings, leaving a net increase of only $2,000.

The stock dividend had no effect on the company's working capital. It was accomplished by a simple transfer from one noncurrent element in the balance sheet to two other noncurrent elements. In entry form, this transfer was as follows:

Retained Earnings	20,000	
Common Stock		3,500
Additional Paid-in Capital		16,500

The cash dividends, on the other hand, clearly constituted a use of funds and therefore appear in this section of the statement of changes in financial position. Declaration of the dividends created a current liability, and any event which increases current liabilities decreases working capital, by definition. It doesn't matter whether the cash was actually distributed in 19x1. Indeed, the subsequent cash payment doesn't affect working capital because it decreases both a current liability and a current asset by equal amounts.

Common stock and additional paid-in capital

The balance sheet changes in the other two elements of owners' equity were as follows:

	January 1	December 31	Increase
Common stock	$20,000	$ 30,000	$10,000
Additional paid-in capital	80,000	120,000	40,000

This shows that additional shares with a total par value of $10,000 were issued during the year, adding a total of $50,000 to paid-in capital. Our analysis of retained earnings has already revealed that part of this change was due to a stock dividend. If we express this information in T-account form, we see the following:

Common Stock			Additional Paid-in Capital		
	Jan. 1	20,000		Jan. 1	80,000
	Stock			Stock	
	dividend	3,500		dividend	16,500
	?	?		?	?
	Dec. 31	30,000		Dec. 31	120,000

The unexplained changes in these two components of the owners' equity ($6,500 in common stock and $23,500 in additional paid-in capital) can only have come from the issuance of additional shares of stock. As a result, $30,000 ($6,500 + $23,500) is listed as a source of working capital in the statement of changes in financial position.

Plant assets

Now that we've accounted for all the changes in owners' equity, it's time to shift to another balance sheet item. Exhibit 13–4 provided the following information on the original cost of Peabody's plant assets:

	January 1	December 31	Increase
Machinery (original cost)	$290,000	$310,000	$20,000

We were also told that $50,000 had been expended during 19x1 to acquire new machinery. Although it is immediately apparent that this $50,000 was a use of working capital, the original cost of the machinery on hand increased by only $20,000. This suggests that there was a sale of used machinery during the period, machinery with an original cost of $30,000 ($50,000 − $20,000).

Although we would be correct in recognizing that the sale of machinery was a source of working capital, it is likely that the amount of the proceeds was a sum other than the machine's $30,000 original cost. Reference to Peabody's 19x1 income statement (see Exhibit 13–5) indicates that the sale resulted in a $1,000 loss. This tells us that the proceeds were $1,000 less than the machine's book value. The book value of a depreciable asset is its cost ($30,000 in this case) less its accumulated depreciation, an amount we haven't determined yet.

To determine the amount of the accumulated depreciation, we have to turn to the reported change in this balance sheet element:

	January 1	December 31	(Decrease)
Accumulated depreciation	$90,000	$75,000	$(15,000)

Reference to Peabody's income statement (see Exhibit 13–5) indicates that the depreciation expense was $11,000. Our knowledge of accounting for depreciation tells us that its recognition as an expense in the income statement also results in an increase in the accumulated depreciation that appears in the balance sheet.

At this point, it will be helpful to summarize in T-account form what we know and what we don't know about Peabody's accumulated depreciation:

Accumulated Depreciation

?	Jan. 1	90,000
	Expense	11,000
	Dec. 31	75,000

As this shows, although depreciation for the year *increased* the amount of accumulated depreciation, the year-end balance was actually *smaller* than the balance at the beginning of the year. The explanation is that the sale of machinery reduced the amount of accumulated depreciation. To produce a net reduction of $15,000 in the face of an $11,000 depreciation addition, the accumulated depreciation on the machinery sold must have been $26,000.

This calculation enables us to derive the amount of the proceeds from the sale of machinery. The book value of the machinery sold was $4,000 (the original cost of $30,000 less accumulated depreciation of $26,000). A loss of $1,000 was reported in the income statement (see Exhibit 13–6). The proceeds therefore must have been only $3,000 ($4,000 − $1,000). The entry to record the sale could have been as follows:

Cash	3,000	
Accumulated Depreciation	26,000	
Loss on Sale of Machinery	1,000	
Machinery		30,000

Two lines in this entry enter into the preparation of the funds statement. The most obvious is the $3,000 increase in funds from the proceeds of the sale—this appears as a source of funds. Not so obvious is the role of the $1,000 loss on the sale. We pointed out earlier that a company's operations are an important source of working capital. We use net income as our first approximation to the amount of funds provided by operations, but adjustments have to be made to convert net income into an amount representing the effects of operations on working capital. One adjustment is designed to prevent the miscounting that arises from the inclusion in net income of a loss on the sale of a noncurrent asset.

Let's see how this works. We've already seen that the sale of the machinery reduced plant assets (a noncurrent element in the balance sheet) by $4,000. In our analysis of the transaction, however, we identified only $3,000 as a source of funds, because the proceeds from the sale amounted to only $3,000. The other $1,000 (the loss) was deducted from revenues in the calculation of net income. Thus, the $1,000 was reflected in our initial estimate of the impact of operations on working capital. Although this amount was deducted correctly in the calculation of net income, deducting it for the purpose of measuring the operating funds flow was a mistake which we are now in a position to correct. The $1,000 didn't constitute a current use of working capital—no cash was disbursed and no current liability was created. Net income, in other words, *understated* by $1,000 the amount of funds provided by operations. To correct this, we must *add* the $1,000 loss to the net income amount when we prepare the funds statement.

To summarize, our analysis of the changes in plant assets thus far has identified three amounts that will appear in the statement of changes in financial position:

1. The $50,000 purchase of new machinery is a use of working capital.
2. The $3,000 proceeds from the sale of used machinery is a source of working capital.
3. The $1,000 loss is added to net income to avoid understating the amount of funds provided by operations.

Depreciation

We pointed out that depreciation during the year reduced plant assets by $11,000, but we didn't show how this enters into the preparation of the funds statement. *Depreciation doesn't affect working capital;* instead, it represents the estimated reduction in a *noncurrent* asset. For example, if equipment is purchased for $100,000 and $20,000 depreciation is recorded the following year, this $20,000 affects assets only by reducing the equipment's book value from $100,000 to $80,000; working capital remains unchanged.

Although depreciation has no effect on working capital, it does enter into the procedure used in preparing funds statements. Like the loss on the sale of machinery, depreciation was deducted from revenues in the calculation of net income. Since depreciation doesn't measure a use of working capital, deducting it from revenues makes net income understate the amount of funds provided by operations. To correct this, we must add the depreciation— $11,000 in our example—to the net income if our purpose is to calculate the amount of funds provided by operations.

An additional comment is in order here. Companies often list depreciation as the *first* addback to reported earnings, and for manufacturing enterprises annual depreciation is usually a relatively significant amount. Readers sometimes observe merely that depreciation appears in the statement of changes in financial position as a positive factor in arriving at the amount of working capital provided by operations. They are then tempted to conclude that depreciation is a *separate* source of working capital, similar to earnings and the issuance of securities.

This conclusion is far from the truth. Accounting for depreciation is a means of allocating the cost of plant assets to individual fiscal periods in a systematic manner. Depreciation charges neither recover nor create funds. Revenue-producing activities are the sources of funds from operations. If funds-producing revenues exceed funds-reducing expenses during a fiscal period, funds are available to cover expenditures other than these expenses. If these revenues don't exceed these expenses, no funds are made available, no matter how much or how little depreciation is charged. The role of the depreciation addback is to reverse a deduction which was appropriately made for income measurement purposes but has no relevance to the funds-flow calculation.

Depreciation can have indirect effects on funds, however. First, depreciation charges affect reported income and hence may affect managerial decisions such as those on pricing and dividends. Second, depreciation deductions on the company's income tax returns affect taxable income and thus the amount of income taxes that accrue in the year of deduction. The result is that an aftertax funds benefit is attributable to the tax deductibility of depreciation. (This effect stems from the depreciation deductions on the tax returns, which may differ from depreciation expense on the income statement.) Third, to the extent that depreciation is included as a reimbursable cost in cost-plus contracts, a contractor can increase the current level of revenues.

Bonds payable

We've spent a good deal of time analyzing the relationships between changes in plant assets and changes in working capital. Most other relationships are simpler than these and can be disposed of more quickly. To begin with, Peabody's balance sheets provide the following information on bonds payable:

	January 1	December 31	(Decrease)
Bonds payable	$90,000	$80,000	$(10,000)

Although we try to look for gross changes rather than net changes, in this case we have no additional information to indicate that there had been any transactions other than the early retirement of a portion of Peabody's bonds.[1] Even at this point, however, we cannot assume that the use of working capital was necessarily $10,000. We turn to the income statement to determine if there had been a gain or a loss on the early retirement. Since Peabody reported no gain or loss in the income statement for 19x1, we can reasonably conclude that $10,000 was the amount of working capital used to retire bonds that year.

If a gain or a loss does occur, the amount of the retirement payment is calculated by subtracting the gain from or adding the loss to the change in bonds payable. This amount is then disclosed as a use of working capital. In addition, a loss is added back to net income, just as we added Peabody's loss on the sale of machinery, and for the same reasons. A gain would be *subtracted* from net income—to avoid including it *both* in funds provided by operations *and* as an element of the uses of funds.

For example, suppose Peabody had reported a $1,000 gain on the retirement of the bonds payable. Its income would have been $1,000 greater—but the amount of funds provided by operations wouldn't have been increased. On the other hand, it would have used only $9,000 ($10,000 − $1,000) to retire the bonds. So, instead of a single $10,000 item in the funds statement, the company would have reported a $9,000 use of funds and a $1,000 reduction in the reported amount of funds provided by operations. *The algebraic sum of the sources, uses, and adjustments related to any balance sheet component will always equal the net change in the balance sheet amount.*

---

[1] Noncurrent bonds payable may also be reduced as portions of the bonds approach maturity and are reclassified as current liabilities. Since Peabody had no bonds payable among its year-end current liabilities, however, we must assume that the bonds were actually retired. And since the company had no bonds payable among its beginning-of-year current liabilities (indicating no imminent maturities at that time), the retirements must have been early retirements.

Deferred income taxes

The second noncurrent liability appearing in Peabody's comparative balance sheets is deferred taxes:

	January 1	December 31	Increase
Deferred income taxes	$15,000	$20,000	$5,000

We recall from our discussion in Chapter 10 that deferred income taxes refers to amounts that are included in a company's income tax expense but that are not payable within the next year. The circumstances that cause such a deferral are the so-called *timing differences* between accounting income and taxable income.

The implication for the statement of changes in financial position is that even though tax expense was correctly stated for income measurement, the deferred portion has no effect on working capital. As a result, we add to reported income the increase in the *deferred* amount. This allows working capital provided by operations to reflect the effect of only that portion of the tax expense which in fact reduced a current asset or increased a current liability.

Completing the statement

Peabody's statement of changes in financial position for the year 19x1 is shown in Exhibit 13–7. This statement shows all the sources of funds, starting with funds provided by operations, all the uses of funds, and the change in the working capital balance, appearing as a residual. It reveals that the main internal source of funds, current operations, was inadequate to cover both the cash dividend and the company's purchases of machinery. The company was growing faster, in other words, than its internal sources could support.

The statement also shows that the company retired debt, meeting its needs for additional funds by issuing common stock. In other words, despite its growth, the company was moving its capital structure toward a less risky mixture of more owners' equity and less debt.

Some funds statements include an increase in working capital as a use of funds or a decrease as a source or funds, making the total of the sources equal to the total of the uses. This has the advantage of showing that the company's working capital requirements often place the same kinds of demands on the company's financial resources as dividends, capital expenditure programs, and debt retirements. The format illustrated in Exhibit 13–7 is widely used, however, and seems easier to understand.

EXHIBIT 13–7

PEABODY, INC.
Statement of Changes in Financial Position
For the Year Ended December 31, 19x1

Sources of working capital:
Operations:

Net income			$39,000
Add: Depreciation	$11,000		
Deferred income taxes	5,000		
Loss on sale of machinery	1,000	17,000	
Working capital provided by operations			$56,000
Sale of common stock			30,000
Sale of machinery			3,000
Total sources of working capital			89,000

Uses of working capital:

Purchases of machinery	50,000	
Cash dividends	17,000	
Debt retirement	10,000	
Total uses of working capital		77,000
Increase in working capital		$12,000

The all-resources concept

Earlier in this chapter, we pointed out that some transactions which consist of flows of noncurrent resources into and out of the business are shown in the funds statement even though they neither increase nor decrease the amount of working capital. The objective of the statement is to report the effects of all changes in financial position, not just those that affect working capital. The statement therefore includes significant transactions involving flows of non-current resources even if working capital is not affected. Statements prepared on this basis are said to reflect the all-resources concept. To recognize changes in all resources, these transactions are disclosed as both sources *and* uses of working capital; three examples follow:

Example A. Issue a three-year promissory note to acquire land at a cost of $12,000.

Source of working capital:
Issue long-term note .... $ 12,000

Use of working capital:
Purchase land .... $ 12,000

Example B. Acquire a $250,000 building for $50,000 cash and a $200,000 mortgage note.

Source of working capital:
Issue mortgage note $200,000

Use of working capital
Purchase building $250,000

Example C.   Issue 400 shares of stock in exchange for 50 of the company's outstanding convertible debenture bonds with $50,000 book value and $50,000 face value.

> Source of working capital:
> Issue common stock $50,000
>
> Use of working capital:
> Retire debentures $50,000

In each example, each side of the transaction has a significant effect on the company's financial position. By applying the all-resources concept, we can produce funds statements that more fully reflect these significant effects.

Funds from operations—revisited

Our discussion of operations as a source of funds identified some of the adjustments to net income most frequently encountered in practice. In the context of the Peabody illustration, we discussed depreciation, deferred income taxes, and the loss on a sale of non-current assets. There are also three other adjustments with which we will want to be familiar.

When the company has intangible assets it is amortizing, each period's income statement absorbs a portion of the assets' original cost. Although income is properly reduced as a result, the company's funds are unaffected—the effect on funds took place when the asset was acquired. Like depreciation expense, the amount amortized each period must be added back to net income to arrive at working capital provided by operations.

A second additional adjustment is called for if the company has bonds outstanding that were issued at a discount or at a premium. Interest expense each period equals the current accrual of cash interest payable (based on the coupon rate) plus (or minus) an amortization of the original bond discount (premium). Only the amounts of the current cash payments affect working capital; net income must be adjusted by the amount of the amortization to determine the amount of funds provided by operations.

For example, suppose net income is $100,000 after the deduction of $30,000 in interest expense. The coupon payments applicable to this period total $32,000, indicating that operations provide $2,000 ($32,000 − $30,000) *less* working capital than the income amount implies. Assuming this is the only adjustment, the calculation of funds provided by operations is as follows:

> Net income $100,000
> Less: Amortization of bond premium   2,000
> Funds provided by operations . . . . $ 98,000

Assuming a beginning-of-year liability of $315,000 and no other bond transactions during the year, the amortization of the premium would appear on the comparative balance sheets as follows:

	January 1	December 31	Decrease
Bonds payable (including premium)	$315,000	$313,000	$2,000

Amortization of the premium in this case accounts for the entire change in this balance sheet element.

If the bonds were sold initially at a discount, on the other hand, a portion of this discount will be included in interest expense each year. Interest expense will be greater than cash interest, and the amount of the net liability will increase as the discount is amortized. The amount of the amortization therefore must be *added* to net income to determine the amount of funds provided by operations.

The third adjustment to net income arises when a company's earnings include its equity interest in an affiliated company's income. This happens when the company uses the equity method to account for its investment in either an unconsolidated subsidiary or an investee in which it has a significant interest. An adjustment is needed because recognition of the affiliate's income affected the investor's *noncurrent* investment asset—with no effect on working capital. Although income is properly recorded, the equity interest in the affiliate's income is subtracted to arrive at working capital provided by operations.[2]

In summary, to determine working capital provided by operations, the accountant uses net income as the starting point and then makes adjustments to reflect the components of income which had no effect on working capital. Exhibit 13–8 lists the adjustments made most often. Additive adjustments are made for items that have unfavorable effects on income but don't affect working capital. Subtractive adjustments are made for items that have favorable effects on income but no effects on working capital.

THE CASH-FLOW FORMAT

We have identified working capital as the most common medium by which to prepare the statement of changes in financial position. An increasingly popular alternative, however, is to adopt a *cash* format.[3] Cash reflects a more short-run orientation than working capital because it focuses on immediate cash-paying ability.

---

[2] If cash dividends were received or accrued, the adjustment would reflect only the *undistributed* portion of the equity interest in the affiliate's income.

[3] Another alternative is to define funds as *cash and marketable securities,* marketable securities being near-cash in the sense that they can be liquidated quickly with little or no loss.

EXHIBIT 13–8. Adjustments to Derive Working Capital from Operations

		Adjust by	
Income Element		Adding	Subtracting
1. Depreciation of plant assets		x	
2. Amortization of intangible assets...........		x	
3. Deferred income taxes		x*	
4. Sale of noncurrent asset			
Gain			x
Loss		x	
5. Undistributed affiliate earnings			x
6. Early extinguishment of debt			
Gain			x
Loss		x	
7. Interest expense			
Long-term premium amortized			x
Long-term discount amortized		x	

* Subtract if the amount of the deferral is negative.

Distinctive features of the cash-format statement

The basic difference in the statement of changes in financial position is that a cash-format statement identifies sources of cash and uses of cash. To calculate the amounts of sources and uses, the accountant analyzes each balance sheet element—other than cash itself—to determine whether changes in that element affected cash, and by what amount. Several differences from the working-capital approach emerge. For example:

1. Whereas issuing a 30-day or six-month note to borrow money is not a source of working capital, it is a source of cash.
2. Whereas the purchase or sale of marketable securities does not affect working capital, it does appear in a funds statement prepared on a cash-format basis.
3. Whereas *declaration* of a cash dividend is a use of working capital, it is *payment* of the dividend that is a use of cash.

In addition, transactions involving accounts receivable, inventory, accounts payable, and taxes payable are sources or uses of cash. Since such transactions almost always relate directly to operations, they are examined in the process of calculating *cash provided by operations*.

Cash provided by operations

When discussing *working capital provided by operations,* we identified seven items that affect net income but do not also affect working capital. As a result, adjustments are made to transform net income into a working-capital dimension. In the cash format, we encounter a similar task—namely, to convert net income into *cash* provided by operations. To achieve this objective, we recognize that nearly every component of income requires adjustment.

Consider, for example, that although Peabody, Inc.'s 19x1 sales revenue was $400,000, the cash received from customers was not necessarily $400,000. Peabody's comparative balance sheets (Exhibit 13–3) indicated a $15,000 ($85,000 − $70,000) increase in accounts receivable. Since a $15,000 increase in receivables signifies that sales exceeded collections by $15,000, the accountant concludes that cash collections were only $385,000 ($400,000 − $15,000).

We can apply this approach to each item in the income statement, adjusting it for changes in related balance sheet elements other than cash. For example, the cost of goods sold will be a good measure of the current cash outlay for merchandise only if inventories and accounts payable remain constant. This is easy to test. Going back to Exhibit 13–5, we find that Peabody's cost of goods sold in 19x1 was $240,000. This amount is shown in the upper left-hand block in Exhibit 13–9. The difference between the cost of goods sold and the total amount paid to suppliers of merchandise is the algebraic sum of the changes in inventories and accounts payable. From Exhibit 13–3 we find that the inventory increased by $5,000 during the year; purchases therefore must have amounted to $245,000 ($240,000 + $5,000), as shown in the oval at the upper right in Exhibit 13–9. The balance sheets also show that accounts payable decreased by $10,000 during the year, indicating that payments to suppliers exceeded purchases by this amount. Payments therefore totaled $255,000, as shown in the lower left-hand block. (Actually, some accounts payable may have arisen from the purchase of plant assets, but we have no way of separating out this component.)

By carrying out similar calculations on each item in the income statement, we can derive the amount of cash provided by operations. These two sets of numbers are shown in Exhibit 13–10. Depreciation and the loss on the sale of machinery don't appear in the calculation of cash flow because they don't measure current disbursements of cash. Salary payments, on the other hand, are equal to salary expense because the amount of salaries payable in the year-end balance sheet was identical to the amount payable on January 1. Current income tax payments are $7,000 less than current income tax

EXHIBIT 13–9. Determining Cash Outflow

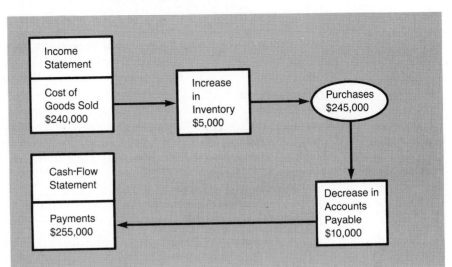

expense because current taxes payable increased by $2,000 and deferred taxes increased by $5,000.

We can also calculate the amount of cash provided by operations by adding and subtracting noncash changes in the balance sheet, just as we calculated the amount of working capital provided by operations by adjusting net income for nonworking-capital changes. These calculations are shown in the upper portion of Exhibit 13–11, with the analogous working-capital calculations shown in the first column. The $28,000 net cash flow from operations was

EXHIBIT 13–10. Income versus Cash Provided by Operations

	Income Provided by Operations	Cash Provided by Operations
Sales revenues/collections	$400,000	$385,000
Expenses/payments:		
Cost of goods sold/payments to suppliers	240,000	255,000
Depreciation	11,000	—
Salaries	55,500	55,500
Interest	7,000	7,000
Loss on sale of machinery	1,000	—
Miscellaneous expenses	20,500	20,500
Income tax	26,000	19,000
Total expenses/payments	361,000	357,000
Net income/net cash flow	$ 39,000	$ 28,000

EXHIBIT 13–11

PEABODY, INC.
Changes in Financial Position (Working Capital and Cash Flow)
For the Year Ended December 31, 19x1

	Working Capital	Cash
Sources of funds:		
Operations:		
Net income	$39,000	$ 39,000
Add: Depreciation	11,000	11,000
Deferred taxes	5,000	5,000
Loss on sale of machinery	1,000	1,000
Increase in taxes payable		2,000
Less: Increase in receivables.....................		(15,000)
Increase in inventories		(5,000)
Decrease in accounts payable		(10,000)
Funds provided by operations	56,000	28,000
Sale of common stock	30,000	30,000
Sale of machinery	3,000	3,000
Total sources of funds......................	89,000	61,000
Uses of funds:		
Purchase of machinery	50,000	50,000
Cash dividends	17,000	17,000
Debt retirement...................................	10,000	10,000
Total uses of funds	77,000	77,000
Increase (decrease) in working capital (cash)	$12,000	$(16,000)

only half of the $56,000 of working capital provided by the same source. All the other sources and uses of cash were identical in amount to the other sources and uses of working capital.

The end result was that the cash balance decreased by $16,000, whereas working capital *increased* by $12,000. The $28,000 difference between these two figures is identical to the difference between the net cash flow from operations and the amount of working capital provided by operations.[4]

USING FUNDS-FLOW ANALYSIS

The purpose of the statement of changes in financial position is to offer insights not otherwise available from either an income statement or a balance sheet. It is useful mainly because it throws light on management's investing and financing practices. The uses

---

[4] In practice, other differences may arise. For example, a dividend declared but not yet paid is a use of working capital but not a use of cash; borrowing on a short-term note is a source of cash but not a source of working capital. Credit purchases of plant assets also cause the use of working capital to differ from the amount of cash used for this purpose.

a company makes of its funds have a considerable influence on its future profitability and on the risks investors in the company are exposed to. Knowledge of how management gets the funds to finance these activities is important for the same reason.

Sources of funds

The sources of business funds can be grouped into four main categories:

1. Current operations.
2. Borrowing.
3. Issuance of additional shares of the company's capital stock.
4. Sale of assets not originally acquired for resale.

Funds from current operations have four important advantages: (1) they come from a continuing source, the result of a myriad of individual actions and decisions, not the result of intermittent activity; (2) their source is the one most completely under management's control; (3) they provide a base which is essential if management wishes to raise additional funds by borrowing or by issuing additional shares of stock; and (4) they expose the company to no additional risks of the kind generally associated with borrowing.

Funds from the issuance of additional shares of capital stock also expose the company to no additional risks and provide part of the equity base for borrowing. Companies issue new shares primarily in connection with mergers or acquisitions of other companies, or from the conversion of convertible bonds or preferred stock. Public sales of new shares are relatively rare, partly because the costs of floating new issues can't be justified unless large sums are required.

Borrowing also has advantages. Investors in bonds may accept lower yields than investors in the company's common stock require. Furthermore, the company can deduct interest as an expense on its income tax returns, further reducing the cost of debt. Borrowing also gives the company access to the funds controlled by certain types of investors who don't participate in equity markets.

Borrowing increases the riskiness of investments in the company, however. Interest or principal may fall due for payment just when the company finds itself temporarily short of cash. The company may have to curtail its other activities to make these payments or, in extreme cases, may fail to make the payments, causing it to fall into bankruptcy or receivership.

Given these factors, investors need to appraise the relative amounts of funds the company obtains from borrowing and from other sources. Is the company using enough debt to profit from the advantages of borrowing? Is it using too much debt, increasing the riskiness of investments in the company to too high a level? The amount that constitutes "enough" or "too much" depends on the industry, the company's existing financial structure, the state of financial markets, the company's own dynamics, and the investor's preferences.

Analysts ordinarily expect funds from operations to cover a major portion of most companies' needs for funds in most periods. In some periods, however, internally generated funds may be relatively small or even negative. For a development-stage company, for example, or an established enterprise heavily engaged in research and product development, current operations are likely to generate small amounts of funds relative to management's needs.

Uses of funds

The manner in which a company uses funds can also be revealing. The relative amounts of funds that are used to decrease the company's debt, pay cash dividends, and expand its productive capacity can disclose a great deal about its managerial priorities. Parties with specialized interests—creditors seeking to be paid and stockholders interested in cash dividends, for example—want to assess the company's past patterns of funds use.

Another key comparison the funds statement permits is the relationship between the company's purchases of plant assets and the amount of funds provided by operations. The more of its expenditures it can finance internally, the less exposed it is to weaknesses and disruptions in the financial markets.

The funds-flow perspective

Some readers of financial statements could become so enamored of funds-flow analysis that they might conclude it is a valid *substitute* for profitability analysis. The fallacy lies in their failure to appreciate that these two types of analysis are complementary. One is concerned with profitability, the other with changes in financial structure and liquidity. One matches each period's revenues and expenses to document growth or decline in the long run; the other summarizes each period's events in terms of their short-run effects. Both statements are essential to a proper understanding of the results of the current period's activities; neither serves all purposes by itself.

SUMMARY

The objective of the income statement is to summarize the economic productivity of the company's resources during the period.

Cash-flow statements summarize the receipts and disbursements of cash and are intended to measure the business's ability to meet its short-term needs for cash. Statements of changes in financial position, in contrast, are designed to show how the company obtained and used financial resources during the period. The relationships between the structure of the resources provided and the amounts devoted to such uses as dividends, property additions, and debt retirement are important information for the evaluation of the company's financial management and for future planning by management.

This chapter has tried to explain what funds flows are and has presented a simple method that can be used to develop funds statements from income statement and balance sheet information. The method itself is less important, however, than the relationships between the funds statement and the other financial statements with which it is coupled.

APPENDIX: WORKSHEET ANALYSIS

The analysis in this chapter was conducted informally, more or less on the back of an envelope. In practice, an organized approach is generally necessary to keep the analysis under control to prevent errors and to discover information that might otherwise go unnoticed. The procedure we'll describe consists of four steps:

1. Enter the balance sheet amounts or changes in a worksheet consisting of a set of T-accounts, one for each balance sheet element.
2. Set up three additional analytical T-accounts: Funds Provided by Operations, Other Sources of Funds, and Uses of Funds.
3. Using the income statement and any other available information, construct a set of entries the company could have made to produce the balance sheet changes which actually occurred, and enter these in the worksheet.
4. Transcribe the amounts in the three analytical T-accounts and put them in a statement format.

Exhibit 13–12 is the worksheet showing Peabody's balance sheet changes for 19x1, with funds defined as *working capital*. A single T-account contains the net change in working capital; changes in individual components of working capital are irrelevant when the working-capital format is used. The worksheet entries for the transactions described in this chapter are as follows:

1. Net income:

Funds Provided by Operations	39,000	
Retained Earnings		39,000

This entry shows that net income increased the balance in retained earnings and provided $39,000 in working capital. The debit to the Funds Provided by Operations analytical account actually represents a debit to Working Capital; we use the separate account to enable us to assemble the amounts which, taken together, will give us the amount of funds provided by operations.

2. *Cash dividends:*

Retained Earnings	17,000	
Uses of Funds		17,000

This shows that the declaration of dividends reduced the balance in retained earnings and required the use of working capital. The credit to Uses of Funds actually represents a credit to Working Capi-

EXHIBIT 13–12

PEABODY, INC.
T-Account Worksheet for Funds Statement Preparation
For the Year Ended December 31, 19x1

Machinery		Deferred Income Taxes	
Net change 20,000			Net change 5,000

Accumulated Depreciation		Common Stock	
Net change 15,000			Net change 10,000

Bonds Payable		Additional Paid-in Capital	
Net change 10,000			Net change 40,000

Working Capital		Retained Earnings	
Net change 12,000			Net change 2,000

Funds Provided by Operations		Uses of Funds	

Other Sources of Funds	

tal; again, we use a separate analytical account to help us assemble data for use in preparing the funds statement.

3. *Stock dividend:*

Retained Earnings	20,000	
Common Stock		3,500
Additional Paid-in Capital		16,500

This shows the effects of the stock dividend. None of the three analytical accounts is affected because the stock dividend neither provided nor used working capital, nor did it constitute a flow of resources into or out of the company.

4. *Issue of common stock:*

Other Sources of Funds	30,000	
Common Stock		6,500
Additional Paid-in Capital		23,500

This shows the amount of working capital provided by the sale of new shares of the company's common stock. Together with entry 3, it accounts for the entire change in common stock and additional paid-in capital. These elements play no further role in the analysis.

5. *Sale of machinery:*

Other Sources of Funds	3,000	
Funds Provided by Operations	1,000	
Accumulated Depreciation	26,000	
Machinery		30,000

The debit to Other Sources of Funds identifies the proceeds from the sale of machinery, while the $1,000 debit to Funds Provided by Operations places the loss on the sale in a position to be added to net income. The debit to Accumulated Depreciation and the credit to Machinery remove the record of the machinery from the balance sheet.

6. *Purchases of machinery:*

Machinery	50,000	
Uses of Funds		50,000

This shows the effect on working capital and on the machinery asset of the company's purchases of machinery during the year.

7.   *Depreciation:*

Funds Provided by Operations.....................	11,000	
Accumulated Depreciation		11,000

The debit to Funds Provided by Operations recognizes the need to add the year's depreciation expense back to net income for funds statement purposes. The credit to Accumulated Depreciation brings the balance in that account to the amount shown on the year-end balance sheet.

8.   *Retirement of bonds:*

Bonds Payable	10,000	
Uses of Funds		10,000

This identifies the use of working capital to retire outstanding bonds payable during the year.

9.   *Deferral of income taxes:*

Funds Provided by Operations.....................	5,000	
Deferred Income Taxes		5,000

The debit to Funds Provided by Operations is our final addition to net income to identify the amount of funds provided by operations. The credit to Deferred Income Taxes brings the balance in this T-account up to the amount shown on the year-end balance sheet.

Exhibit 13–13 shows the T-account worksheet with all the analytical entries posted to the T-accounts. The entries in the T-accounts representing noncurrent balance sheet elements account for all the changes in those elements. No entry has been made in the Working Capital T-account, because the entries we would have made there were made in the three analytical T-accounts. The algebraic sum of the balances in those three accounts is equal to the net change in the working capital balance:

Debit balances:	
Funds provided by operations	$56,000
Other sources of funds	33,000
Total	89,000
Credit balance: Uses of funds	77,000
Net change in working capital (debit)	$12,000

Since all other balance sheet changes have been accounted for, our work is complete. The only step remaining is to assemble the amounts shown in the three analytical accounts in a form suitable for funds statement presentation.

EXHIBIT 13-13

PEABODY, INC.
Completed Funds Statement Worksheet
For the Year Ended December 31, 19x1

Machinery			
Net change	20,000		
(6)	50,000	(5)	30,000

Accumulated Depreciation			
Net change	15,000		
(5)	26,000	(7)	11,000

Bonds Payable			
Net change	10,000		
(8)	10,000		

Deferred Income Taxes		
	Net change	5,000
	(9)	5,000

Common Stock		
	Net change	10,000
	(3)	3,500
	(4)	6,500

Additional Paid-in Capital		
	Net change	40,000
	(3)	16,500
	(4)	23,500

Retained Earnings			
		Net change	2,000
(2)	17,000	(1)	39,000
(3)	20,000		

Working Capital	
Net change	12,000

Funds Provided by Operations

(1)	Income	39,000
(5)	Loss on sale of machinery	1,000
(7)	Depreciation	11,000
(9)	Deferred income taxes	5,000
	Bal. 56,000	

Other Sources of Funds

(4)	Sale of stock	30,000
(5)	Sale of machinery	3,000
	Bal. 33,000	

Uses of Funds

(2)	Dividends	17,000
(6)	Machinery purchases	50,000
(8)	Debt retirement	10,000
	Bal. 77,000	

KEY TERMS

All-resources concept
Funds-flow analysis
Funds from current operations
Net cash flow

Sources of funds
Statement of changes in financial
   position
Uses of funds

INDEPENDENT STUDY PROBLEMS (Solutions in Appendix B)

1. **Analysis of plant and equipment changes.** Below are certain balances from Placque Corporation's financial statements:

Balance Sheet	19x2	19x3
Plant and equipment	$8,500	$8,900
Accumulated depreciation	3,300	3,600

Income Statement	
Depreciation expense	$ 900
Loss on retirements	400

A note to the financial statements reports that property with an original cost of $1,300 and accumulated depreciation of $600 was sold during 19x3 for $300.

a. List the transactions that affected the plant and equipment and accumulated depreciation during the year.

b. Indicate how, if at all, each of these would be shown on a statement of changes in financial position.

2. **Preparing a funds statement.** The following figures (in $000) have been taken from Anderson Company's balance sheets for the beginning and end of the year 19x1:

	Beginning	Ending
Current assets	$56,746	$ 77,091
Long-term marketable securities, at cost	—	1,005
Property, plant and equipment, at cost	31,414	49,096
Accumulated depreciation	(13,237)	(18,421)
Total assets	$74,923	$108,771
Current liabilities	$42,536	$ 48,898
Bonds payable	—	7,000
Deferred income taxes........................	4,362	4,899
Total liabilities	46,898	60,797
Preferred stock, at par ($100 per share)	1,347	1,123
Common stock, at par ($1 per share)............	4,317	4,492
Additional paid-in capital	7,179	19,014
Retained earnings.............................	15,182	23,345
Total liabilities and owners' equity	$74,923	$108,771

Additional information on transactions during 19x1:

1. Net income for the year, $8,243,000.
2. Preferred dividends declared and paid, $80,000.
3. Preferred stock repurchased and retired, 2,240 shares; the purchase price exceeded the par value by $37,000, and this excess was charged correctly to additional paid-in capital.
4. Common stock issued, 175,000 shares.
5. Depreciation (on income statement), $5,501,000.
6. Cost of property, plant, and equipment acquired, $18,082,000.

Prepare a statement of changes in financial position for the year, using the working-capital format.

3. Working capital provided by operations. Andy, Inc.'s 19x6 income statement was as follows:

Revenue from sales	$325,400	
Less: Estimated customer defaults	4,100	
Net sales		$321,300
Equity in Wilson Corporation's earnings		12,000
Total revenues		333,300
Expenses:		
Cost of goods sold	178,600	
Salaries	68,800	
Depreciation	14,900	
Insurance	1,000	
Research and development	2,500	
Patent amortization	1,800	
Interest	21,300	
Income tax:		
Current	13,200	
Deferred	3,100	16,300
Total expenses		305,200
Net income		$ 28,100

You have the following additional information:

1. 70 percent of gross revenues from sales were on account.
2. All the $184,000 merchandise purchases were on account.
3. Salaries payable totaled $3,200 at year-end.
4. Amortization of premium on bonds payable was $2,700.
5. No dividends were received from other corporations.
6. Andy declared cash dividends of $8,000.

Prepare a schedule which calculates the amount of working capital provided by operations.

4. Cash provided by operations. Andy, Inc. (see problem 3), showed the following changes in its working-capital elements in 19x6:

	Increase (Decrease) in Working Capital
Cash	$ 1,000
Marketable securities	3,200
Accounts receivable	(14,300)
Allowance for uncollectibles	(3,800)
Inventory	5,400
Prepaid insurance	1,400
Accounts payable (for merchandise)	(11,300)
Salaries payable	4,100
Dividends payable	6,000
Decrease in working capital	$(8,300)

Using this information, together with that in problem 3, prepare a schedule which calculates the amount of cash provided by operations.

EXERCISES AND PROBLEMS

5. **Changes in plant and equipment.**   The Granada Corporation's income statement for 19x1 showed depreciation of $150,000 and a $42,000 loss on the sale of equipment. The amount of accumulated depreciation increased by $37,000 between the beginning and the end of the year, and the original cost of the company's plant and equipment went from $1 million at the beginning of the year to $2 million on December 31, 19x1. The original cost of the equipment retired during the year amounted to $175,000.

Which changes in plant and equipment would appear on the funds statement for the year? Where would they appear and in what amounts?

6. **Changes in plant and equipment.**   A note to the financial statements of Solo Corporation revealed the following:

	Plant and Equipment	Accumulated Depreciation
Beginning balance	$650,000	$200,000
Additions	210,000	45,000
Retirements.............	(140,000)	(110,000)
Ending balance...........	$720,000	$135,000

One item on the company's income statement for the year was a gain on the sale of equipment, $15,000.

Which of these items would appear on the statement of changes in financial position for the year, and how would they be shown?

7. **Interpretation: funds flow versus income flow.**   Arkville Transit Company operates a network of bus lines in a small city. The company can abandon a bus route only with the approval of the city government, which also regulates the fares it charges bus riders. Last year, Arkville Transit reported a small operating loss, and earnings are unlikely to improve in the near future. The following income statement for last year is likely to be typical of those to be prepared for the next few years:

Fares and other revenues		$1,000,000
Expenses:		
Salaries and wages	$650,000	
Fuel and lubricants	170,000	
Depreciation	100,000	
Tires and batteries	20,000	
Repair parts...................	30,000	
Other expenses	40,000	
Total expenses		1,010,000
Net income (Loss)		$ (10,000)

The company's balance sheet showed the following amounts at the beginning and end of last year:

	Beginning of Year	End of Year
Assets		
Current assets:		
Cash.....................................	$ 100,000	$ 90,000
Receivables	50,000	40,000
Inventories	150,000	160,000
Total current assets	300,000	290,000
Plant and equipment (net)	940,000	920,000
Total assets	$1,240,000	$1,210,000
Liabilities and Stockholders' Equity		
Current liabilities:		
Accounts payable	$ 66,000	$ 147,000
Salaries payable	4,000	3,000
Total current liabilities	70,000	150,000
Bonds payable	100,000	—
Common stock............................	260,000	260,000
Retained earnings	810,000	800,000
Total liabilities and stockholders' equity	$1,240,000	$1,210,000

John Bergson bought an 80 percent interest in this company late last year for $200,000. When shown the income statement above, he replied, "Good! That's just what I'd hoped for."

Bergson is a professional investor, not given to letting sentiment or emotion affect his investment decisions. Furthermore, he has little time to devote to active participation in the management of the companies he invests in.

a. How did he probably justify his decision to invest in Arkville Transit Company?

b. What plans does he probably have for his investment in Arkville transit? How do these plans differ from the actions of the previous owners? Do you think he is likely to achieve his objectives? Support your answers with numbers from the problem.

8. Preparing a funds statement. General Ferry Corporation reported the following balance sheets in a recent year:

	Jan. 1, 19x3		Dec. 31, 19x3	
Assets				
Current assets:				
Cash.....................................		$ 15		$ 10
Accounts receivable		10		15
Inventory		40		60
Total current assets		65		85
Plant and equipment.....................	$100		$113	
Less: Accumulated depreciation	40	60	45	68
Total assets		$125		$153
Liabilities and Owners' Equity				
Current liabilities				
Accounts payable		$ 10		$ 12
Bank loan payable......................		20		40
Total current liabilities		30		52
Deferred income taxes		5		7
Shareholders' equity:				
Common stock ($1 par)	$ 25		$ 29	
Additional paid-in capital	15		20	
Retained earnings	50	90	45	94
Total liabilities and owner's equity		$125		$153

Additional information:

1. Net income for the year (including $1 gain on sale of plant and equipment), $5.
2. Cash dividends declared and paid during the year, $10.
3. Depreciation on plant and equipment during the year, $8.
4. Plant and equipment acquired during the year:
   For cash, $10.
   For four new shares of common stock, $9.

Prepare a statement of changes in financial position using the working-capital format.

9. Sources and uses of funds. Summit Company had the following transactions during 19x5.

1. Bought equipment for $150,000. Paid 10 percent cash and signed a three-year note for the balance.
2. Used temporarily idle cash to buy government securities for $14,000.
3. Issued 10,000, $2 par value preferred shares for $10.50 a share.
4. Reclassified a $50,000 note payable as a current liability, in recognition of its November 30, 19x6, maturity date.
5. On December 31, 19x5, issued a $1 million, 20-year, 12 percent mortgage bond for $880,000.
6. Declared a $12,000 cash dividend payable on January 20, 19x6.
7. Bought 1,200 treasury shares for $22 a share.
8. Sold real estate for $40,000, yielding a $15,000 gain.
9. Bondholders converted 220 of the company's $1,000 debenture bonds. These bonds had a net-of-unamortized-discount balance of $196,000.

In exchange, Summit issued 8,800 common shares which had a market value of $24 a share.

10. Sold the government securities (item 2) for $15,000.

11. Sold the treasury shares (item 7) for $25,000.

Determine whether each of these items was a source or a use of working capital, and identify the amount of each item's working capital effect.

10. Preparing funds statement; contrast with cash-flow statement. Hartwell Stores operates a chain of retail hardware stores. Its income statement for 19x5 showed the following:

Gross sales		$120
Less: Estimated customer defaults	$ 2	
Cost of goods sold	80	
Wages and salaries	15	
Depreciation	5	
Income tax expense	4	
Miscellaneous operating expense	8	114
Net income		$ 6

The following amounts were taken from the company's balance sheets at the beginning and end of 19x5:

	January 1	December 31
Assets		
Cash	$10	$ 8
Accounts receivable (net)	20	23
Inventory (at cost)	15	19
Plant and equipment (net)	30	35
Total assets	$75	$85
Liabilities and Owners' Equity		
Accounts payable	$11	$17
Bonds payable (long-term)	22	21
Deferred income taxes	3	4
Common stock	25	31
Retained earnings	14	12
Total liabilities and owners' equity	$75	$85

You have the following additional information:

1. The company declared and paid $5 in cash dividends to its shareholders in 19x5.
2. A stock dividend of $3 was declared and distributed.
3. Equipment with an original cost of $7 and accumulated depreciation of $6 was sold. There was neither a gain nor a loss on this transaction.
4. All accounts payable arose from the purchase of merchandise.

a. Prepare a statement of changes in financial position for 19x5, using the working-capital format.

b. Prepare a second funds statement, using the cash format.

11. Preparing a funds statement; cash flow from operations. You have the following information about the financial affairs of XYZ Company:

Balance sheets:

	Beginning of Year		End of Year
Assets			
Current assets:			
Cash		$ 2	$ 1
Accounts receivable		3	4
Inventories		5	6
Total current assets		10	11
Land, plant, and equipment, cost	$20		$29
Less: Accumulated depreciation	8	12	9	20
Total assets		$22	$31
Liabilities and Owners' Equity			
Current liabilities:			
Accounts payable		$ 4	$ 3
Taxes payable		1	2
Notes payable		—	2
Total current liabilities		5	7
Bonds payable		—	5
Deferred taxes		3	4
Total liabilities		8	16
Owners' equity:			
Common stock	$ 4		$ 5
Additional paid-in capital	2		4
Retained earnings	8		6
Total owners' equity		14	15
Total liabilities and owners' equity		$22	$31

Income statement:

Sales revenues		$51
Operating expenses:		
Cost of goods sold	$25	
Depreciation	4	
Other	15	44
Operating income		7
Gain on sale of equipment		2
Income before taxes		9
Income tax expense		4
Net income		$ 5

Additional information:

1. Land purchased during the year in exchange for bonds, $5.
2. Cash dividends declared and paid, $4.
3. Stock dividends, capitalized at $3.
4. Original cost of plant and equipment retired and sold during the year, $7.

a. Prepare a statement of changes in financial position using the working-capital format.
b. Was the amount of cash provided by operations more or less than the amount of working capital provided by operations? Explain briefly.

12. Preparing and interpreting a funds statement. Traydown Corporation's financial position went from bad to worse during 19x8, although net income showed a satisfactory increase over that of prior years. Despite the company's negotiation of a $100,000 bank loan early in 19x8, the cash balance decreased to a dangerous point by the end of the year. The balance sheets showed the following:

TRAYDOWN CORPORATION
Comparative Balance Sheets
($000)

	December 31, 19x7	December 31, 19x8
Assets		
Current assets:		
Cash	$ 50	$ 30
Receivables	200	220
Inventories	150	200
Total current assets	400	450
Buildings and fixtures	300	280
Less: Accumulated depreciation	(90)	(70)
Total buildings and fixtures............	210	210
Total assets	$610	$660
Liabilities and Stockholders' Equity		
Current liabilities:		
Accounts and wages payable	$200	$180
Bank loan payable	50	150
Total current liabilities	250	330
Mortgage payable	70	55
Deferred income taxes	20	23
Long-term note payable	10	12
Total liabilities	350	420
Stockholders' equity:		
Common stock (par)	140	130
Retained earnings	120	110
Total stockholders' equity	260	240
Total liabilities and stockholders' equity	$610	$660

Notes (all figures in $000):

1. Net income for 19x8 was $29.
2. Total sales were approximately the same in 19x8 as in 19x7.
3. A building with an original cost of $52 and accumulated depreciation of $30 was sold for $56, cash.
4. Depreciation for the year was $10.
5. Cash dividends paid were $23.
6. One stockholder sold her common stock back to the company for $26, cash. The par value of this stock was $10, and the remaining $16 of the repurchase price was charged to retained earnings.

a. Prepare a schedule of working-capital changes.
b. Prepare a statement of changes in financial position using the working-capital format.

c. Prepare a brief report, addressed to the loan officers of the company's bank, commenting on any items in your statement you think would help them reach a decision on renewing or increasing the bank's loan to the company. They have a statement of forecasted cash flows for 19x9 but feel that the 19x8 funds statement can provide additional information the forecast does not give.

13. Preparing a funds statement; impact of inflation. A company's annual report showed the following balance sheets for the beginning and end of its most recent fiscal year:

	Beginning	End	Change
Assets			
Current assets:			
Cash	$ 10	$ 20	+$10
Accounts receivable	30	51	+ 21
Inventory	50	45	− 5
Total current assets	90	116	+ 26
Investments in other corporations	80	50	− 30
Fixed assets $220	$228	+$ 8	
Less: Accumulated depreciation 120	124	+ 4	
Total fixed assets	100	104	+ 4
Total assets	$270	$270	—
Liabilities and Shareowners' Equity			
Current liabilities:			
Accounts payable	$ 40	$ 35	−$ 5
Dividends payable	—	2	+ 2
Total current liabilities	40	37	− 3
Bonds payable	40	—	− 40
Deferred income taxes	20	23	+ 3
Total liabilities	100	60	− 40
Shareowners' equity:			
Common stock (par) .... $ 25	$ 30	+$ 5	
Additional paid-in capital 65	90	+ 25	
Retained earnings 80	90	+ 10	
Total shareowners' equity	170	210	+ 40
Total liabilities and shareowners' equity ...	$270	$270	—

You have the following additional information:

1. Net income for the year, $30.
2. Cash dividends declared during the year, $8.
3. Stock dividends declared during the year (par value $2), $12.
4. Depreciation on fixed assets for the year, $18.
5. Purchases of fixed assets during the year.
   For cash, $21.
   In exchange for stock (par value $3), $18.
6. Cash proceeds from sale of fixed assets during the year, $2.
7. Cash proceeds from sale of investments during the year, $42; no investments were purchased during the year, and all investments are shown on the balance sheet at cost.
8. All accounts payable were to vendors of merchandise bought for resale.

a. Prepare a statement of changes in financial position using the working-capital format.

b. Prepare a statement of changes in financial position using the cash format.

c. The year in question was a year of severe inflation. Judging from the funds statement and from information in the problem, do you think the actions taken by management were appropriate in an inflationary situation?

14. Preparing a funds statement. The net changes in the balance sheet of X Company for the year 19x1 are shown here:

	Debit	Credit
Investments		$25,000
Land	$ 3,200	
Buildings	35,000	
Machinery	6,000	
Office equipment		1,500
Accumulated depreciation:		
Buildings		2,000
Machinery		900
Office equipment	600	
Discount on bonds	2,000	
Bonds payable		40,000
Capital stock—preferred	10,000	
Capital stock—common		12,400
Premium on common stock		5,600
Retained earnings		6,800
Working capital	37,400	
Total	$94,200	$94,200

Additional information:

1. Cash dividends of $18,000 were declared December 15, 19x1, payable January 15, 19x2. A 2 percent stock dividend on the common stock was issued March 31, 19x1, when the market value was $12.50 per share.
2. The investments were sold for $27,500.
3. A building which cost $45,000 and had a depreciated basis of $40,500 was sold for $50,000.
4. The following entry was made to record an exchange of an old machine for a new one:

Machinery	13,000	
Accumulated Depreciation—Machinery	5,000	
Machinery		7,000
Cash		11,000

5. A fully depreciated office machine which cost $1,500 was written off.
6. Preferred stock of $10,000 par value was redeemed for $10,200.
7. The company sold 1,000 shares of its common stock (par value $10) on June 15, 19x1, for $15 a share. There were 13,240 shares outstanding on December 31, 19x1.

Prepare a statement of changes in financial position for the year 19x1 using the working-capital format.

(AICPA adapted)

15. Preparing and interpreting a funds statement. Apex Company's financial statements for 19x2 showed the following (all figures are in $000):

Balance Sheets

	December 31, 19x1	December 31, 19x2
Assets		
Current assets:		
Cash	$ 2,250	$ 2,133
Accounts receivable, net	1,064	1,382
Inventories	936	1,179
Total current assets	4,694	4,250
Long-term assets:		
Land	198	273
Buildings, machinery, and equipment	6,750	6,700
Less: Accumulated depreciation	(2,000)	(2,270)
Investments in subsidiaries	3,002	3,018
Goodwill	100	90
Total assets	$12,300	$12,505
Liabilities and Shareowners' Equity		
Current liabilities:		
Accounts payable	$ 2,350	$ 1,080
Taxes payable	650	550
Dividends payable	—	—
Total current liabilities	3,000	1,980
Long-term liabilities:		
Bonds payable	—	1,000
Bond premium	—	72
Liability for pensions	150	150
Deferred income taxes	90	110
Total liabilities	3,240	3,312
Shareowners' equity:		
Common stock, at par	1,500	1,510
Additional paid-in capital	1,910	2,000
Appropriation for contingencies	300	400
Retained earnings	5,350	5,283
Total liabilities and shareowners' equity	$12,300	$12,505

Income Statement
For the Year Ended December 31, 19x2

Sales		$ 9,880
Income from unconsolidated subsidiaries		206
Gain on sale of land		15
Total		10,101
Expenses:		
Cost of goods sold	$7,414	
Selling and administrative expenses	1,843	
Amortization of goodwill	10	
Bond interest expense	97	
Income taxes	354	
Total expenses		9,718
Net income		$ 383

Additional information:

1. All the company's subsidiaries were in the United States. Income on investments in unconsolidated subsidiaries was recognized on an equity basis.
2. Expenses for the year included depreciation in the amount of $496,000.
3. The only dividend declared during the year on Apex common stock was the cash dividend declared during December and payable on January 20, 19x3.
4. Buildings, equipment, and machinery purchased in 19x2 cost $246,000.
5. Apex Company issued stock during the year in exchange for land. No other common stock transactions occurred during the year.
6. Bonds were issued on January 2, 19x2, with a 10 percent coupon rate.

a. Prepare a statement of changes in financial position for the year using the working-capital format.
b. What does this funds statement tell you about management's financial policies and practices?

16. Using funds statements to explain changes in financial status. Mastik Company was incorporated in 1977 by two young electronics engineers, Frank Orsini and Rosemary Newman, to manufacture and market a new electronic relay they had developed. The initial share capital consisted of 10,000 shares, divided equally between the two founders. Each founder paid the company $10,000 in cash for those shares. An additional block of 2,000 shares was issued in 1979 to a friend of the founders in exchange for $5 a share, paid in cash.

The company's first product was highly successful, and in 1979 operations were transferred to a larger building which the company leased for five years. Purchase of additional equipment at that time was financed by a five-year loan from an equipment finance company. This same company also granted loans for equipment purchased in subsequent years.

Mastik's sales continued to grow at a rapid rate as new products and services were introduced. Net income grew even faster, as shown in the following table:

	1980	1981	1982
Sales	$194,000	$318,000	$390,000
Expenses:			
Wages and salaries	87,000	178,000	191,000
Materials and supplies	58,000	75,000	94,000
Rent	12,000	12,000	12,000
Depreciation	5,000	7,000	8,000
Other operating expenses (including interest)	20,000	22,000	31,000
Income taxes	4,000	8,000	18,000
Total expenses	186,000	302,000	354,000
Net income	$ 8,000	$ 16,000	$ 36,000

In March 1983, Mastik's commercial bank notified management that the company's bank balance had fallen to less than the minimum required by the bank. The bank was unwilling to extend additional credit unless the company was able to broaden its ownership base and attract more stockholder capital. The company's balance sheets for the previous four years were as follows:

	1979	1980	1981	1982
Assets				
Current assets:				
Cash	$18,000	$ 21,000	$ 15,000	$ 8,000
Accounts receivable	20,000	29,000	48,000	74,000
Inventories	11,000	15,000	30,000	55,000
Prepayments	2,000	3,000	4,000	5,000
Total current assets	51,000	68,000	97,000	142,000
Plant assets:				
Machinery and equipment	50,000	60,000	65,000	82,000
Less: Accumulated depreciation	(6,000)	(11,000)	(18,000)	(26,000)
Net plant assets	44,000	49,000	47,000	56,000
Total assets	$95,000	$117,000	$144,000	$198,000
Liabilities and Stockholders' Equity				
Current liabilities:				
Accounts payable	$ 3,000	$ 6,000	$ 10,000	$ 14,000
Wages and taxes payable	4,000	5,000	9,000	20,000
Notes payable to bank	2,000	7,000	12,000	20,000
Total current liabilities	9,000	18,000	31,000	54,000
Equipment loan payable	30,000	35,000	30,000	25,000
Notes payable to stockholders	4,000	4,000	7,000	12,000
Total liabilities	43,000	57,000	68,000	91,000
Stockholders' equity:				
Common stock	30,000	30,000	30,000	30,000
Retained earnings	22,000	30,000	46,000	77,000
Total stockholders' equity	52,000	60,000	76,000	107,000
Total liabilities and stockholders' equity ..	$95,000	$117,000	$144,000	$198,000

Orsini and Newman were stunned by this news. They didn't understand how they had gotten into such a difficult position, since they had never reported a loss, even in their first year of operations, their customers were all good credit risks, and finished goods were always shipped soon after completion.

Prepare a report for Orsini and Newman, explaining what had happened.

14

Financial reporting and changing prices

All measurement systems take two factors into consideration: the attribute to be measured and the measuring unit. In conventional financial statements, two attributes are measured: Most monetary assets (mainly cash and receivables) are measured at their values to the company, and nonmonetary assets are generally measured at their *historical cost*. Since different resources are acquired at different times, both the balance sheet and the income statement will contain costs measured at the prices that prevailed in many different periods. Accountants can eliminate these inconsistencies by measuring resources at their *current costs*, the costs that would have to be incurred to replace them on the measurement date. (When current cost is the attribute to be measured, monetary assets are measured at their current values to the company; to minimize confusion in terminology, we'll also refer to these amounts as current costs.)

Both historical cost and current cost can be measured in either nominal-dollar or constant-dollar measuring units, leading to the four possible combinations shown in Exhibit 14–1:

Historical cost/nominal dollars (the traditional approach).

Historical cost/constant dollars.

Current cost/nominal dollars.

Current cost/constant dollars.

A nominal-dollar measuring unit makes no adjustment for changes in the general price level—which we generally refer to as price

EXHIBIT 14–1. Dimensions of Accounting Measurement

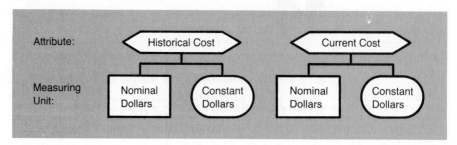

inflation or (rarely) deflation. A constant-dollar measuring unit, on the other hand, recognizes that changes in the general price level cause the value (purchasing power) of one period's dollars to be different from the value of the dollars which measure other periods' transactions. Rather than counting the number of dollars, this approach counts units of constant purchasing power.

Our objectives in this chapter are to explain how price changes of various kinds affect traditional financial statements and to describe techniques accountants can use in lieu of the conventional accounting measures (the historical-cost/nominal dollar combination in the upper left-hand box in Exhibit 14–1).

EFFECTS OF PRICE CHANGES ON THE MEANING OF FINANCIAL STATEMENTS

The meaning of conventional historical-cost/nominal-dollar financial statements is affected by price changes in different ways, depending on whether the general price level remains steady.

Impact of changes in replacement prices

Changes in the prices a company has to pay for the resources it uses don't affect the meaning of the accounting numbers unless the business already has some of these resources among its assets. Ownership of these resources means that historical costs reach the income statement after the periods in which those costs were current.

For example, if the purchase price of merchandise goes up by $10, the cost of goods sold may still be measured at the old price if costs flow to the income statement on a FIFO basis. The effect of this time lag is illustrated in Exhibit 14–2. When purchase prices and selling prices go up in 19x2, the lag in getting the new purchase prices into the income statement produces a gross margin which

EXHIBIT 14–2. Lag in Expense Reporting after Purchase-Price Change

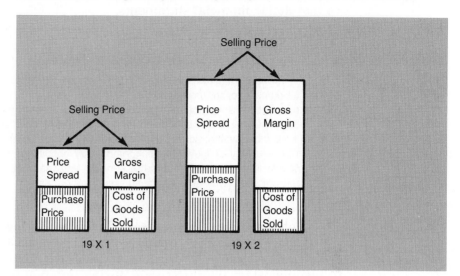

exceeds the difference between the current selling price and the current cost of the merchandise.

This lag effect is even more pronounced in connection with changes in the prices of buildings and equipment. Buildings and equipment last for many years, and the 1983 income statement may include some depreciation charges based on the much lower building construction prices of 1963 and equipment prices of 1973. Historical-cost lags can continue to affect net income amounts long after the cost changes have taken place.

Impact of changes in the general price level

Changes in the general price level have two effects on conventional financial statements. First, they reduce the comparability of the statements of different years. For example, a company's net income may have doubled between 1970 and 1980, but the purchasing power of a dollar in 1980 was less than half the purchasing power of a dollar of 1970 income. In constant dollars, net income didn't advance at all.

The second effect of changes in the general price level is to generate gains or losses in the purchasing power of the company's monetary assets and liabilities, and these gains and losses don't appear in conventional income statements. For example, if a company holds $100,000 in cash throughout a period in which the general price level rises by 10 percent, its cash will lose 10 percent of its purchasing power. This loss does not appear in historical-cost/nominal-dollar financial statements.

TERMINOLOGY REMINDER

Monetary assets consist of cash and the rights to receive specified amounts of cash, usually at specified times, such as accounts receivable, notes receivable, and nonconvertible bonds. *Monetary liabilities* consist of obligations to pay specified amounts of cash, usually at specified times. Accounts payable, notes payable, and bonds payable are monetary liabilities; warranty obligations are nonmonetary obligations because they are liquidated by the performance of services and the passage of time rather than by the payment of specified quantities of cash.

Holders of monetary assets suffer losses during a period of inflation because the fixed amounts of money their assets represent will buy progressively fewer goods and services. Conversely, those who owe monetary liabilities gain during inflation because their debts will be repaid with money having less purchasing power than the money they borrowed. Lenders know this is likely to happen, however, and they charge higher rates of interest to compensate themselves for absorbing the purchasing-power loss which is the complement of the borrowers' purchasing-power gains. (Their loans are monetary assets, which lose purchasing power in inflation.) The problem is that the higher interest rates appear in the conventional income statements of the borrowers; the purchasing power gains do not.

CURRENT-COST/NOMINAL-DOLLAR MEASUREMENTS

Some defects of conventional financial statements can be addressed by statements based on the measurement of current costs in nominal dollars. In particular, these statements are designed to remove the effects of lags between the acquisition of resources and their use in the generation of revenues. In this section, we'll show how measurements of the current costs of inventories and goods sold can be made and how they can be used. We'll also include a brief discussion of the application of current cost to measurements of plant assets and depreciation.

Current-cost inventory accounting

In a current-cost measurement system, inventories, plant assets, cost of goods sold, and depreciation are measured at their current costs instead of their historical costs. The current cost of a company's inventories on any date is the amount the company would have to spend to replace them at the prices prevailing on that date. The current cost of goods sold is their replacement cost on the date of the sale.

To illustrate, we'll assume that Atlas Company, which buys and sells plastic sheeting, began 19x4 with 100,000 yards of sheeting in inventory. Its purchases and sales in 19x4 and the year-end inventory were as follows:

Purchases	340,000 yards
Sales	400,000 yards
Ending inventory	40,000 yards

The purchase price of replacement merchandise was 25 cents a yard all year until December 31, when Atlas's supplier announced a major increase in the price to 40 cents a yard.

If Atlas had used a current-cost measurement system in 19x4, it would have reported a cost of goods sold of $100,000, calculated as follows:

Yards Sold	×	Current Cost per Yard at Time of Sale	=	Current Cost of Goods Sold
400,000		$0.25		$100,000

The current cost of the inventory was $25,000 (100,000 yards × $0.25) on December 31, 19x3, and $16,000 (40,000 yards × $0.40) on December 31, 19x4.

Holding gains and losses

A company that holds inventories when prices change will have holding gains and losses as well as income from manufacturing or merchandising operations. A *holding gain* results from the holding of a nonmonetary asset at the time the price of that asset increases; a *holding loss* results from the holding of a nonmonetary asset at the time the price of that asset decreases.

We measure inventory holding gains and losses by the changes in the *purchase prices* of the items in inventory. The idea is that a purchase before the date of a price change is a substitute for a purchase after that date. By buying early, the company gets the benefit or incurs the penalty of buying at the old price.

As we saw earlier, the price of plastic sheeting held steady throughout 19x4 but increased by $0.15 a yard on December 31,

EXHIBIT 14–3

ATLAS COMPANY
Current-Cost Income Statement
For the Year Ended December 31, 19x4

Sales revenues (at $0.35)	$140,000
Current cost of goods sold (at $0.25)	100,000
Current-cost margin	40,000
Inventory holding gain	6,000
Net income	$ 46,000

19x4, under the impact of a sudden shortage of supplies. The holding gain for the year is calculated as follows:

Yards in Inventory at Time of Price Change	×	Amount of Price Change	=	Holding Gain
40,000		+$0.15		$6,000

Holding gains and losses are included in income statements prepared on a current-cost/nominal-dollar basis, as in Exhibit 14–3. (To simplify the exhibit, we have assumed that selling and administrative expenses and income taxes were zero.) The first three lines in this statement show the calculation of the *current-cost margin*— the spread between the current selling price and the current purchase price *on the date of each sale.* Sales revenues amounted to 400,000 yards at 35 cents a yard, a total of $140,000. The $100,000 current cost of goods sold is the same quantity at 25 cents a yard, the price which prevailed when all the sales took place. Subtracting $100,000 from the revenues produces the current-cost margin on the third line of the exhibit.

The current-cost margin per unit remained steady at 10 cents a yard throughout 19x4. If the company had been able to buy and sell sheeting simultaneously, thereby eliminating the need to carry inventory, the current-cost margin would have been its sole source of income. Because it had inventory, however, and because replacement prices rose at the end of 19x4, Atlas had a holding gain. Adding the holding gain to the current-cost margin produces the current-cost net income on the bottom line of Exhibit 14–3.

Comparison with FIFO-cost/nominal-dollar accounting

While current costs aren't used in the basic financial statements in the United States, they are analytically useful because they enable us to estimate how much of historical-cost income results from holding gains and losses. Current-cost income includes *all* the holding gains and losses arising during the period; historical-cost income *may* include holding gains and losses but these are likely to appear in the income statements of periods *after* the periods in which they arise. Furthermore, a current-cost income statement *discloses* the amount of holding gain or loss; historical-cost income statements *conceal* this amount. We'll demonstrate these differences by comparing current-cost/nominal-dollar income with FIFO-cost/nominal-dollar income.

FIFO-cost income is likely to include undisclosed amounts of inventory holding gains in periods of rising prices. Atlas began the year 19x4 with an inventory of 100,000 yards of plastic sheeting. The unit cost of the last 100,000 yards of sheeting bought in 19x3 was 20 cents a yard; this therefore became the FIFO unit cost of the January 1, 19x4, inventory (100,000 × $0.20 = $20,000). It was only at the end of 19x3 that the price increased to 25 cents a yard, the price Atlas paid when it bought 340,000 yards of sheeting in 19x4 for $85,000 (340,000 × $0.25).

The income statement in Exhibit 14–4 shows the result of using the FIFO-cost method in 19x4. The $10,000 FIFO cost of the inventory at the end of the year is based on the most recent unit cost of 25 cents a yard (40,000 yards × $0.25 = $10,000).

The two differences between FIFO net income and net income on a current-cost/nominal-dollar basis (ignoring income taxes and selling and administrative expenses) are summarized in Exhibit 14–5. First, the 19x4 FIFO-cost gross margin included $5,000 of inventory holding gains which actually arose in 19x3. This happened because the FIFO cost of the first 100,000 yards sold in 19x4 was the FIFO cost of the opening inventory, 100,000 yards × $0.20 = $20,000, whereas current cost was 25 cents a yard, or $25,000. In other words, $5,000 of the FIFO-cost margin for 19x4 represented the holding gain that had taken place in 19x3, when the replacement cost of the inventory rose by 5 cents a yard (from $0.20 to $0.25) —100,000 × $0.05 = $5,000.

EXHIBIT 14–4

ATLAS COMPANY
FIFO-Based Income Statement
For the Year Ended December 31, 19x4

Sales revenues (400,000 × $0.35)		$140,000
Cost of goods sold:		
Beginning inventory (100,000 × $0.20)	$ 20,000	
Purchases (340,000 × $0.25)	85,000	
FIFO cost of goods available	105,000	
Ending inventory (40,000 × $0.25)	10,000	
FIFO cost of goods sold (100,000 × $0.20) +		
(300,000 × $0.25)		95,000
Net income		$ 45,000

EXHIBIT 14–5

ATLAS COMPANY
FIFO-Cost versus Current-Cost Income
For the Year Ended December 31, 19x4

	FIFO Cost	Current Cost	Difference
Sales revenues	$140,000	$140,000	—
Cost of goods sold	95,000	100,000	$ 5,000
Operating margin	45,000	40,000	5,000
Holding gain	—	6,000	(6,000)
Net income	$ 45,000	$ 46,000	$(1,000)

Accountants say that this $5,000 was *realized* through the sale of plastic sheeting in 19x4. (What they mean by the term *realized* is that this amount was included in income in that year; it doesn't necessarily mean that all customer purchases were for cash.) In contrast, the 40,000 yards of sheeting in the ending inventory contained an *unrealized* holding gain of 15 cents a yard because their FIFO cost was 25 cents, or 15 cents less than their 40 cent current replacement cost at that time. The realized inventory holding gains and losses—that is, the amounts included in reported income for the year—are referred to as *inventory profits and losses.* Atlas Company's $5,000 realized holding gain in 19x4 appears in Exhibit 14–5 as the difference between the FIFO cost of goods sold and the current cost of goods sold. The FIFO-cost income statement would have been more informative if the year's income had been subdivided as follows:

Merchandising income	$40,000
Inventory profit	5,000
Net income	$45,000

The other difference between FIFO-cost income and current-cost income is that current-cost income includes *all* the holding gains and losses which actually took place during the year ($6,000 in this case) and reports them separately. We can reconcile the differ-

EXHIBIT 14–6.   Atlas Company: Calculation of Realized Holding Gain, 19x4

Unrealized holding gains, beginning of period [100,000 × ($0.25 − $0.20)]	$ 5,000
Add: Holding gains (losses) arising during the period	6,000
Total	11,000
Less: Unrealized holding gains, end of period [40,000 × ($0.40 − $0.25)	6,000
Holding gains (losses) realized during the period [inventory profits (losses)]	$ 5,000

ence between the $5,000 FIFO-based inventory profit and the $6,000 current-cost/nominal-dollar holding gain by means of the calculation in Exhibit 14–6.

Comparison of current-cost income with LIFO-cost income

Differences between current-cost income and LIFO-cost income can be analyzed with the help of the same techniques we applied to FIFO-cost income comparisons:

1. The nominal-dollar realized holding gain or loss is the difference between the LIFO cost of goods sold and their current replacement cost at the time of revenue recognition.
2. The nominal-dollar unrealized inventory holding gain on any inventory date is the difference between the LIFO cost of the inventory and its current replacement cost on that date.

During and after a period of prolonged inflation, the LIFO cost of most companies' inventories is likely to be substantially lower than their current replacement cost—that is, LIFO companies are likely to have substantial unrealized inventory holding gains—but the LIFO cost of goods sold in any period is likely to be very close to the current cost of goods sold except for periods in which inventory levels fall.

For example, suppose Atlas Company had adopted LIFO as of January 1, 19x3, when it had 100,000 yards of plastic sheeting in inventory. Until that time, the company had used FIFO to cost its inventories, and the FIFO cost of the December 31, 19x2, inventory therefore became the cost of the LIFO base quantity on January 1, 19x3. The FIFO cost of this quantity was 20 cents a yard, or $20,000. The current replacement cost on that date was also 20 cents a yard, so there was no unrealized inventory holding gain.

The quantity purchased in 19x3 was equal to the quantity sold, and the ending inventory quantity was equal to the beginning quantity. This means that the LIFO cost of the ending inventory was the same as the LIFO cost of the inventory at the beginning of the year (100,000 yards at 20 cents).

The purchase price remained constant at 20 cents a yard throughout 19x3 but rose to 25 cents a yard on December 31. The holding gain in 19x3 therefore was $5,000:

Inventory at Time of Price Increase	×	Price Increase	=	Inventory Holding Gain
100,000 yards		$0.05		$5,000

None of this holding gain entered the LIFO-cost income statement, however. Both the current cost of goods sold and the LIFO cost of goods sold were measured at the current 19x3 purchase price. This meant that the LIFO-cost gross margin was identical to the current-cost gross margin.

The situation was very different in 19x4. Sales exceeded purchases by 60,000 yards. This means that $12,000 (60,000 × $0.20) would have been removed from the inventory and added to the cost of 19x4 purchases to determine the LIFO cost of goods sold in 19x4. Since the current cost of goods sold was 25 cents a yard in 19x4, Atlas would have included a $3,000 inventory holding gain in its LIFO-cost gross margin:

Current cost of goods sold, last 60,000 yards: 60,000 × $0.25	$15,000
LIFO cost of goods sold, last 60,000 yards: 60,000 × $0.20	12,000
Realized holding gain: 60,000 × ($0.25 − $0.20)	$ 3,000

The realized holding gain would have been much larger if the company had gone on LIFO much earlier, when the cost of the inventory was, say, 10 cents a yard.

The results of this simple example can be summarized succinctly, as follows:

Year	Holding Gain Arising During Year	Realized Holding Gain During Year	Unrealized Holding Gain, End of Year
19x3	$5,000	$ 0	$5,000
19x4	6,000	3,000	8,000*

* $5,000 + ($6,000 − $3,000) = $8,000.

(Remember that the replacement price rose by 15 cents on December 31, 19x4, producing a holding gain that year of $6,000 on the 40,000-yard year-end inventory.)

The lesson to be learned from this simple illustration is that the amount of inventory holding gain to be included in reported income (the realized holding gain) bears no necessary relationship to the amount of holding gain actually arising during the period. The company could even be including a realized holding *gain* in its LIFO-cost gross margin if it had an inventory reduction in a year in which replacement prices were falling, thus creating holding *losses*.

The main cause of a realized holding gain under LIFO is a reduction in the quantity of inventory. Any such reduction is known as a *LIFO liquidation* because it brings the unit costs of earlier periods' LIFO layers into the determination of the cost of goods sold.[1] Since

---

[1] If the overall inventory level remains steady but the inventories of some items decrease significantly, the LIFO cost of goods sold may differ significantly from the current cost of goods sold. Any such decreases are LIFO liquidations even if the overall inventory level remains constant or increases.

these earlier unit costs are likely to be lower than current unit cost, a LIFO liquidation is likely to produce a higher net income than the company would have reported if it had been able and willing to acquire enough goods during the year to keep the inventory at its beginning-of-year level.

Under LIFO, therefore, some of the holding gains that weren't recognized when the prices (current costs) were rising affect the reported income of periods in which inventory levels are reduced. LIFO cost neither reports unrealized holding gains when they occur nor identifies them as holding gains when they are included in income (realized). As we saw in our brief example, Atlas's 60,000-yard inventory reduction in 19x4 would have brought $3,000 of the 19x3 inventory holding gain into the 19x4 LIFO gross margin. This realized holding gain or "inventory liquidation profit" wouldn't have been reported separately in the LIFO-cost income statement.

Current costs and plant assets

Current-cost measurements can also be made of plant assets and depreciation. These measurements in a period of rising prices result in the following:

1. The current cost of plant assets is greater than the historical cost.
2. Higher depreciation expense causes current-cost operating income to be lower than historical-cost operating income.
3. Current-cost income will include holding gains on plant assets.

To see how current-cost measurements are applied to plant assets, we'll assume Gray Company bought a machine in January 19x1 for $20,000. Gray expected the machine to last 20 years, and it was depreciated at a straight-line rate of $1,000 a year.

The manufacturer of this machine went out of business in 19x3, but other companies continued to make roughly comparable machines. Because specific replacement prices aren't available, we have to approximate them by constructing a series of *index numbers*. Unlike the consumer price index, which most people are familiar with and which measures the average price change of a broad range of goods and services, these indexes are prepared specifically to gauge the price changes of narrow classes of assets.

To simplify our calculations, we'll assume that replacement prices change each year on December 31 and then remain steady for 12 months. Our price indexes for this type of equipment were as follows:

> January 1, 19x1 120
> January 1, 19x9 180
> December 31, 19x9 204

EXHIBIT 14–7. Gray Company: Calculation of Current Cost of Machine, 19x9

	Historical Cost	Price Relative	Current Cost
January 1, 19x9:			
Machine	$20,000	150%	$30,000
Accumulated depreciation (8/20)	8,000	150	12,000
Undepreciated cost	$12,000	150	$18,000
Depreciation, 19x9	$ 1,000	150	$ 1,500
December 31, 19x9:			
Machine	$20,000	170	$34,000
Accumulated depreciation (9/20)	9,000	170	15,300
Undepreciated cost	$11,000	170	$18,700

The first two numbers tell us that machinery prices were 120 percent of the base-period level at the beginning of 19x1 and 180 percent of the base-period level at the beginning of 19x9 and throughout that year (due to our simplifying assumption that prices don't change during the year). By dividing these two numbers, we find that the prices prevailing at the beginning of 19x9 were 180/120 = 150 percent of the prices prevailing at the beginning of 19x1, when the machine was acquired. The comparable ratio on December 31, 19x9, was 170 percent (204/120).

These ratios are used in Exhibit 14–7 to determine the current cost of Gray Company's machine in 19x9. At beginning-of-year prices, the machine had an undepreciated current cost of $18,000 at the beginning of 19x9 (the third line in the right-hand column). Current-cost depreciation for the year was $1,500, reducing undepreciated current cost to $16,500 just before the year-end price increase. The price increase then pushed the current cost of the machine up to $18,700 (the bottom line of the exhibit). The nominal-dollar equipment holding gain therefore was $2,200 ($18,700 − $16,500). The realized holding gain for the year was only $500, however (the difference between the $1,000 historical-cost depreciation and the $1,500 current-cost depreciation).

Exhibit 14–8 compares Gray Company's historical-cost and current-cost/nominal-dollar income statements. We start by assuming a $9,000 income before depreciation (any other number would do as well) and no income taxes. The first column shows the conventional historical-cost amounts; the second column shows the current-cost income statement, reflecting both the operating income and the holding gain for the year. Net income is different by $1,700 ($9,700 − $8,000). The historical-cost income statement classifies the $500 realized holding gain as an *undisclosed* component of oper-

EXHIBIT 14–8. Gray Company: Income Calculated on Historical-Cost and Current-Cost/Nominal-Dollar Bases, 19x9

	Historical-Cost Basis	Current-Cost Basis
Income before depreciation	$9,000	$9,000
Depreciation	1,000	1,500
Operating income	8,000	7,500
Holding gain	—	2,200
Net income	$8,000	$9,700

ating income; current-cost income excludes this amount (because it actually arose in previous years) but reports the entire 19x9 holding gain on a separate line.

Advantages of current-cost disclosures

Advocates of current-cost measurements point to the ability of these measurements to provide better data for certain purposes. We'll discuss three of these arguments briefly:

1. Better measures of sustainable income.
2. Better comparisons of the returns on investment achieved by companies with different asset structures.
3. Better measures of managerial performance.

Sustainable income. Conventional net income is likely to overstate or understate the income level the company can sustain on a continuing basis. The reason is that current expense charges for depreciation and for some portions of materials or merchandise costs are likely to be different from the amounts the company will have to spend for these resources each year, on the average, to maintain the physical operating volume at its current level. Current-cost measures this quantity better than historical cost.

Return on investment. The historical rate of return on investment tends to be overstated when resource prices are rising, both because income includes amounts that must be reinvested simply to replace the resources the company is using up, and because investments in plant assets and perhaps in inventory as well are understated. This overstatement of the rate of return is greater for companies with extensive investments in inventories and equipment than for those with more rapid asset-turnover rates. It is also greater for older companies, whose equipment is older and whose inventories, if on LIFO, will be much more understated than those of younger companies. Current cost reduces this noncomparability.

Managerial performance. Because some changes in purchase prices enter the income statement only after a time lag, the net income amount includes a component which results almost exclusively from the increase in purchase prices rather than from management's skill in managing the company's resources. Furthermore, this component of net income is reported neither separately nor consistently. Investors, therefore, find it difficult to appraise management's ability to anticipate and respond to changes in resource prices. Current-cost measurements try to address that problem.

Current-cost measurement and interpretation problems

Objections to current costing fall into two classes: (1) measurement difficulties and (2) interpretation difficulties.

Measurement difficulties. The most important measurement difficulties are in getting reliable price quotations or price indexes which measure the same bundle of assets the company wishes to apply them to. These problems are compounded if technological changes have taken place since the assets were acquired. Technological change forces a shift to the second definition of replacement cost—the amount necessary to maintain productive capacity. Measuring this quantity calls for the exercise of judgment. For example, if the new equipment available is 10 percent more expensive, produces 15 percent more units per hour, and costs 2 percent more to operate each hour, it's not clear whether replacement costs have gone up or down.

These and other difficulties come together in an obstacle of still another sort. Development of comprehensive current-cost data would add to the costs of companies' data-gathering systems. These costs would be lower once the measurement systems were operating smoothly, but they wouldn't be negligible even then.

Interpretation difficulties. Objections to current-cost accounting are also raised on the grounds that the current-cost data, even if accurate, are difficult to interpret. First, changes in the relative prices of different assets may lead to changes in the mix of assets used. This means that when replacements are made, they won't be made in the same proportions as existing assets. This would make current replacement cost totals less meaningful as predictors of future cash flows.

Second, current cost may not be a good measure of the amounts the company will actually pay to replace its present inventory and physical capacity sometime in the future, when conditions are very different from those prevailing today. Again, replacement cost may not be a useful predictor of future cash flow.

Third, market conditions may prevent the company from passing along increases in purchase prices; holding gains therefore may be more illusory than real. Conversely, the current-cost margin may understate the company's ability to generate cash flows in the future if the company operates in markets in which increases in selling prices occur later than purchase-price increases. In other words, the holding gains are real, but the current-cost margin is misleading.

All this probably can be summed up in the observation that accounting data are never as precise as they seem. Judgment is essential. The readers of financial statements must decide whether current-cost information, despite its limitations, aids their ability to understand and interpret companies' financial positions and prospects.

CONSTANT-DOLLAR MEASUREMENTS

Both historical-cost and current-cost financial statements can be expressed in constant dollars. To use constant dollars, accountants must restate each dollar number, by the use of index numbers, in dollars that have the purchasing power of those on a selected date. The date accountants generally use is the end of the *current* year.

For example, suppose a company bought land for $10,000 in 19x3 when the consumer price index (CPI) was 120. The year 19x8 has just ended, and the CPI has risen to 180. To restate the nominal-dollar historical cost of the land in constant dollars of December 31, 19x8, purchasing power, we need merely multiply it by the ratio of the CPI index numbers on the two dates:

$$\text{Historical cost in constant dollars} = \text{Historical cost} \times \text{Relative index}$$
$$= \$10,000 \times \frac{180}{120} = \$15,000$$

Elimination of nominal holding gains and losses

Proponents of a constant-dollar measuring unit believe that inflation-induced holding gains aren't real and therefore should be excluded from reported gains relating to inventory and plant assets. One way of accomplishing that is to restate each historical-cost or current-cost number with an index number reflecting changes in the general price level. Holding gains then would appear only if the replacement prices of the company's nonmonetary assets rose more rapidly than the general price level; holding losses would appear if replacement prices fell, held steady, or rose less rapidly than the general price level.

To illustrate, let's assume that the current cost of the land is estimated to be $19,000. In other words, although the general price level has increased by 50 percent $(180/120 - 1.0)$, the value of the land has increased even more, by 90 percent $[(\$19{,}000 - \$10{,}000)/\$10{,}000]$. Historical/cost/nominal-dollar accounting reports the $10,000 cost of the asset and no income or gain during the five-year period. Historical-cost/constant-dollar accounting reports the land at $15,000 $(\$10{,}000 \times 180/120)$. No income or gain is recognized, however, because all we have done is change the measuring unit. Changing the measuring unit doesn't make an owner better or worse off than before, just as measuring weight in kilograms instead of in pounds doesn't signify an instantaneous loss of weight (70 kilograms is the same as 154 pounds, not 84 units less).

Current-cost accounting takes us in a different direction. Current-cost/nominal-dollar accounting reports the land at its $19,000 current cost and recognizes the $9,000 increase as a *holding gain*. Current-cost/constant-dollar accounting, in contrast, responds both to specific price changes and to general price changes. While the land is written up to its $19,000 current cost, the entire $9,000 increase

EXHIBIT 14–9. Nominal and Real Holding Gains

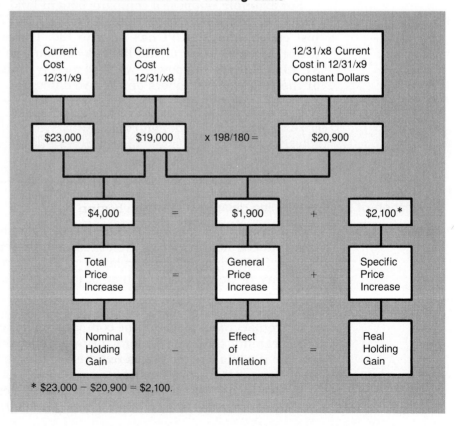

* $23,000 − $20,900 = $2,100.

isn't recognized as the holding gain. Instead, the holding gain is $4,000—the difference between the $19,000 current cost and the $15,000 constant-dollar equivalent of the $10,000 historical cost. While the current-cost/nominal-dollar holding gain measures the nominal increase in the asset's cost and therefore recognizes the *nominal holding gain,* current-cost/constant-dollar accounting isolates the $5,000 general price level component of the $9,000 nominal gain and recognizes only the *real holding gain* of $4,000. In other words, the company's purchasing power has actually increased because it has held land instead of assets whose nominal-value changes have paralleled the increase in the general price level index.

Exhibit 14–9 diagrams this holding-gain difference by using data for the following year (19x9) when the year-end CPI is 198 and the current cost of the land is $23,000. While both current-cost methods measure the land at $23,000, the *nominal* holding gain is $4,000 ($23,000 − $19,000) and the *real* holding gain is $2,100 [$23,000 − ($19,000 × 198/180)]. The $1,900 difference ($4,000 − $2,100) is the effect of inflation.

Calculating purchasing-power gains and losses

Constant-dollar measurements also perform another function: determination of gains or losses resulting from the company's *net monetary position* (total monetary assets minus total monetary liabilities). Accountants calculate the purchasing-power gain or loss for a period by restating in end-of-period constant dollars: (1) the beginning-of-period monetary balances, and (2) the monetary transactions which occurred during the period, and then comparing the adjusted total with the actual net monetary position at the end of the period.

To illustrate, we'll assume that Walsh Company had the following monetary balances at the beginning and end of 19x3:

	January 1	December 31
Monetary assets	$120,000	$170,000
Monetary liabilities	80,000	105,000
Net monetary position	$ 40,000	$ 65,000

Walsh first adjusted its January 1, 19x3, net monetary position to end-of-year constant dollars. The consumer price index (CPI) was as follows in 19x3:

Date or Period	CPI
January 19x3	100
Average 19x3	107
December 19x3	114

We can adjust the net monetary assets on January 1, 19x3, to end-of-year constant dollars by multiplying by 114/100: $40,000 × 114/100 = $45,600. In other words, the company would have needed $45,600 at the end of 19x3 to buy the same package of goods and services as $40,000 would have commanded in January of that year. If Walsh hadn't engaged in any monetary transactions during the year, it would have had the same net monetary assets ($40,000) on hand at year-end as it had on January 1—but this amount would have been $5,600 ($45,600 − $40,000) less than would have been needed to buy the goods and services $40,000 could have bought in January.

Walsh's next task was to restate the year's monetary transactions in dollars of year-end purchasing power. It had the following transactions affecting monetary items in 19x3:

a.	Credit sales	$145,000
b.	Collection of receivables	60,000
c.	Inventory purchases on credit	65,000
d.	Payments of monetary liabilities	70,000
e.	Payments of current operating expenses	30,000
f.	Stock issue	25,000
g.	Machinery purchase on credit	50,000

These seven transactions had the following effects on the company's net monetary position:

a.	Credit sales increased the monetary asset, accounts receivable	+$145,000
b.	The collection of receivables increased one monetary asset (cash) and reduced another (accounts receivable); it therefore had no effect on Walsh's net monetary position	—
c.	Inventory purchases reduced Walsh's net monetary position because they either created a monetary liability (accounts payable) or were an immediate reduction in cash	− 65,000
d.	The payments of monetary liabilities decreased total monetary assets and total monetary liabilities by the same amount; they therefore had no effect on Walsh's net monetary position	—
e.	Payments of operating expenses decreased Walsh's cash balance and net monetary position	− 30,000
f.	The stock issue increased cash; therefore, it increased the company's net monetary position	+ 25,000
g.	The purchase of machinery on credit created a monetary liability, thereby reducing the net monetary position	− 50,000
	Net effect of monetary transactions	+$ 25,000

The $25,000 net effect of these transactions accounted for the full increase in the company's net monetary position from $40,000 at the beginning of 19x3 to $65,000 at the end of the year.

Sales, collections, purchases, and payments occurred relatively evenly throughout the year; Walsh therefore could adjust them to constant dollars by using the ratio of the year-end price index to

EXHIBIT 14–10. Walsh Company: Calculating Purchasing-Power Loss, 19x3

	Nominal Dollars	Relative Index	Constant Dollars
Net monetary position, January 1, 19x3	$40,000	114/100	$45,600
Net monetary transactions, 19x3	+25,000	114/107	+26,636
Total			72,236
Net monetary position, December 31, 19x3	$65,000	114/114	65,000
Purchasing-power loss, 19x3			$ 7,236

the average price index for the year: 114/107. The machinery purchase and stock issue were unique events, but Walsh decided to simplify the analysis by assuming that both events took place when the CPI was at the average for the year. Again, the appropriate adjustment ratio is 114/107.

The net adjustment of the company's monetary transactions in 19x3 is shown in the second line of Exhibit 14–10. (We could have adjusted the transactions one by one, but this wasn't necessary because of Walsh's simplifying assumption that all transactions took place when the general price level index was at its average for the year.) The net effect of the monetary transactions was to bring in $26,636 in year-end purchasing power. This amount is greater than the actual dollars received because the receipts came at a time when their purchasing power was greater than it would have been at year-end.

The calculation of the purchasing-power loss in 19x3—expressed in end-of-year constant dollars—is summarized at the bottom of Exhibit 14–10. Restating both the beginning-of-year $40,000 net monetary assets and the components of the $25,000 increase yields $72,236 as the constant-dollar purchasing power the company should have had at the end of 19x3. Since the actual purchasing power on hand at year-end was only $65,000, a $7,236 loss in purchasing power ($72,236 − $65,000) occurred during the year.

FINANCIAL REPORTING REQUIREMENTS

The Financial Accounting Standards Board requires large U.S. companies to supplement their basic financial statements with disclosures relating to changing prices. The requirements apply to publicly held corporations which have either inventory and gross plant assets in excess of $125 million or total assets greater than $1 billion. Approximately 1,500 companies therefore publish chang-

EXHIBIT 14–11

E. I. du PONT de NEMOURS AND COMPANY
Comparative Historical-Dollar, Constant-Dollar, and
Current-Cost Income Statements, 1980
($ millions)

	As Reported in the Primary Statements (historical dollars)	Adjusted for General Inflation (average 1980 constant dollars)	Adjusted for Changes in Specific Prices (average 1980 current costs)
Sales and other income	$13,801	$13,801	$13,801
Cost of goods sold and other operating charges	10,293	10,420	10,437
Selling, general, and adminis- trative expenses	1,466	1,466	1,466
Depreciation and obsolescence	804	1,156	1,109
Interest on borrowings	110	110	110
Total.......................	12,673	13,152	13,122
Earnings before income taxes and minority interests	1,128	649	679
Provision for income taxes	402	402	402
Earnings before minority interests	726	247	277
Minority interests in earnings of consolidated subsidiaries	10	10	10
Income from continuing operations	$ 716	$ 237	$ 267
Effective income tax rate	36%	62%	59%
Purchasing power gain attributable to holding net monetary liabilities		$ 85	$ 85

ing-prices information each year in their annual reports to stockholders.[2]

Exhibit 14–11 shows, in abbreviated form, the information provided by the Du Pont Company in its 1980 annual report. The first column shows data from the historical-cost/nominal-dollar income statement, the second column shows historical-cost/constant-dollar data, and the third column shows current-cost data, all for the 1980 fiscal year. Both current-cost and constant-dollar adjustments in this exhibit are based on the *average* consumer price index for 1980, rather than the end-of-year index numbers we've been using in our illustrations.

The narrative accompanying this schedule called particular attention to the income tax rate comparison, which appears toward the bottom of Exhibit 14–11, showing that income taxes took 62 percent or 59 percent of the adjusted income amounts, as opposed

---

[2] These data have been processed for public use by Professor Miklos Vasarhelyi and the staff of the Accounting Research Center of the Graduate School of Business of Columbia University, under the auspices of the Financial Accounting Standards Board. The data can be obtained in processed form from the board.

EXHIBIT 14–12

E. I. du PONT de NEMOURS AND COMPANY
Comparison of Selected Financial Data in Historical Dollars,
Constant Dollars, and Current Costs*

	1980	1979	1978	1977	1976
Sales:					
Historical dollars	$13,652	$12,572	$10,584	$ 9,435	$ 8,361
Constant dollars	13,652	14,272	13,368	12,830	12,103
Income from continuing operations:					
Historical dollars	716	939	787	545	459
Constant dollars	237	620	585	522	421
Current costs	267	554			
Earnings per share from continuing operations:					
Historical dollars	4.83	6.42	5.39	3.69	3.10
Constant dollars	1.55	4.21	3.97	3.50	2.81
Current costs	1.76	3.75			
Gain attributable to holding net monetary liabilities	85	102	109	109	77
Excess of constant-dollar over current-cost increase in value of inventories and net plants and properties	240	—			
Stockholders' equity at year-end:					
Historical dollars	5,690	5,312	4,760	4,317	4,030
Constant dollars	10,251	10,273	9,832	9,491	9,203
Current costs	10,365	10,585			
Dividends paid per common share:					
Historical dollars	2.75	2.75	2.42	1.92	1.75
Constant dollars	2.75	3.12	3.05	2.61	2.53
Market price per common share at year-end:					
Historical dollars	42.00	40.38	42.00	40.13	45.04
Constant dollars	40.11	43.34	51.09	53.21	63.78
Average CPI-U (1967 = 100)	246.8	217.4	195.4	181.5	170.5

* Dollars in millions, except per share; all constant dollar and current cost data in average 1980 dollars.

to the 36 percent nominal rate on historical-cost/nominal-dollar income. Notice also that the final line in this table shows a purchasing power *gain* in 1980, because Du Pont had *net monetary liabilities;* that is, its monetary liabilities exceeded its monetary assets.

Exhibit 14–12 shows part of the five-year comparative summary Du Pont provided in its 1980 supplementary disclosure statement. Some current-cost data were available only for two years because Du Pont, like most other affected companies, didn't publish current-cost calculations before 1979.

Several comparisons from these tables are worth noting. Although nominal-dollar sales increased from $8,361 to $13,652 million, inflation accounted for most of this increase. Du Pont was a so-called growth company, but the growth was far less dramatic than the nominal-dollar amounts implied. Furthermore, the nominal-dollar increases in income and earnings per share showed up as decreases when restated in constant dollars—because a dollar of income could buy much less in 1980 than in 1976 and because plant assets and some inventories used in 1980 had been acquired by the expenditure of dollars having much more purchasing power than dollars had in 1980.

The decrease in current-cost/constant-dollar income from 1979 to 1980 (53 percent), the only year for which we can make this comparison, was much more pronounced than the historical-cost/ nominal-dollar decrease (25 percent), reflecting mainly the impact of the higher current-cost depreciation charges. In other words, sustainable income suffered much more in 1980 than the conventional income statements implied.

Finally, the $240 million item for 1980—located in the middle of Exhibit 14–12—shows that the *general* price level rose faster in 1980 than the *specific* replacement prices of the company's inventories and plant assets. This would have been identified as a "real holding loss" if the terminology in this chapter had been used in this schedule.

The restatement of sales, dividends, and market prices could have been made by anyone. Both the CPI and the historical amounts of these items were publicly available. The most important elements in these supplemental disclosures therefore are the restatement of the income amounts and the calculation of the purchasing-power gains and losses, the current costs of the inventories and plant assets, and the holding gains and losses.

SUMMARY

The historical costs of the resources used in any period reflect a mixture of current and past resource prices. Historical-cost accounting therefore reflects movements in resource prices only with a lag, and this lag may be either long or short, depending on the company's asset structure. The result is to lead the income statement to overstate or understate the resources the company can distribute or pay in taxes without reducing its operating capacity. It also reduces the value of the income statement as a measure of managerial and company performance.

Measuring resources used and on hand at their current replacement costs has been proposed as a way of remedying these defects of historical-cost accounting. Under current-cost accounting, a company would recognize holding gains and losses when replacement prices change rather than later when resources are used. The operating profit margin would measure the difference between revenues and current costs at the time of revenue recognition. The income statement, therefore, would include both realized and unrealized holding gains and losses.

Current-cost statements reflect only changes in specific prices, not the effects of changes in the general price level. A portion of holding gains and losses measured for nonmonetary assets under current-cost accounting may not be real if the general price level changed concurrently with changes in the prices of the company's specific assets. Furthermore, current-cost accounting ignores changes in the purchasing power of the company's net monetary position.

Restating financial statements in units of purchasing power has been proposed as a means of adjusting for changes in the purchasing power of the monetary unit. Broad general price level indexes such as the consumer price index in the United States are used for this purpose, applied either to conventional accounting data or to current-cost amounts.

Neither current costs nor general price level adjustments are acceptable in the United States as the primary basis for financial reporting. Large corporations, however, are required to disclose the effects of changing prices on their income and resources.

KEY TERMS

Constant dollars	Nominal dollars
Consumer price index	Nominal holding gain/loss
Current cost	Purchasing-power gain/loss
Current-cost margin	Real holding gain/loss
General price level	Realized holding gain/loss
Index numbers	Relative index
Inflation	Replacement cost
Net monetary position	Unrealized holding gain/loss

INDEPENDENT STUDY PROBLEMS (Solutions in Appendix B)

1. Calculating inventory holding gains and losses. Company A had 50,000 units of merchandise in inventory on January 1, 19x1. The replacement cost of these units at that time was $2 a unit.

The company bought 40,000 units between January 1 and May 15, 19x1, at a cost of $2 each. It sold 55,000 units during this period at a price of $3 each.

On May 16, 19x1, Company A's supplier increased the wholesale price of this merchandise from $2 to $2.20. The company bought 60,000 units at this price between May 16 and the end of the year and sold 35,000 units at an average price of $3.10. Replacement cost remained at $2.20 a unit through the end of 19x1. The company's inventory on December 31, 19x1, amounted to 60,000 units.

a. Calculate the nominal-dollar current cost of goods sold in 19x1 and the current cost of the inventory on December 31, 19x1.
b. Calculate the holding gain or loss for the year.
c. Calculate the current cost margin for the year.

2. Company without inventories. Company B is in the same business as Company A (see problem 1) but carries no inventories. Between January 1 and May 15, 19x1, it bought 55,000 units of merchandise at a cost of $2 each; it sold 55,000 units during this period at a price of $3 each. Between May 16 and December 31, 19x1, it bought 35,000 units at $2.20 a unit and sold 35,000 units at a price of $3.10 each.

a. Calculate the nominal-dollar current cost of goods sold, the inventory holding gain or loss which arose during the year, and the current-cost margin for the year.
b. What conclusion can you draw from a comparison of Company B's performance with that of Company A?

3. Realized inventory holding gains and losses. Company A (see problem 1) uses the FIFO method to cost inventories and the merchandise it sells. On January 1, 19x1, the FIFO cost of its inventory was $1.95 a unit.

a. Calculate the FIFO cost of goods sold during 19x1 and the FIFO cost of the December 31, 19x1, inventory.
b. Calculate the unrealized inventory holding gain or loss on January 1 and on December 31, 19x1.
c. Calculate the amount of inventory holding gain or loss that was included in pretax income for 19x1. How would this amount be reported to the shareholders?

4. Equipment holding gains and losses. Company C had the following equipment in its factory on January 1, 19x9:

Year of Purchase	Original Cost	Accumulated Depreciation January 1	Depreciation for 19x9
19x0	$150,000	$90,000	$10,000
19x2	45,000	21,000	3,000
19x5	60,000	16,000	4,000

The replacement cost index for equipment of this kind traced the following path:

Year	Index
19x0	100
19x2	110
19x5	150
19x9:	
Beginning of year	180
Average for year	190
End of year	200

No equipment was purchased or retired during 19x9.

a. Calculate the unrealized equipment holding gain or loss as of January 1, 19x9.
b. Calculate depreciation for 19x9 on a current-cost basis.
c. Calculate the realized equipment holding gain or loss for 19x9. Where and in what manner would this be reported to investors?
d. Calculate the unrealized equipment holding gain or loss as of December 31, 19x9.
e. Calculate the total equipment holding gain or loss arising during the year 19x9 (including both the realized and unrealized portions).

5. Purchasing-power gain or loss. Gregory Company presented the following nominal-dollar/historical-cost balance sheets in its annual financial report for 19x9:

	January 1	December 31
Assets		
Current assets:		
Cash	$ 10	$ 15
Accounts receivable	20	40
Inventory	30	35
Total current assets	60	90
Plant and equipment	200	220
Less: Accumulated depreciation	(80)	(83)
Total assets	$180	$227
Liabilities and Shareowners' Equity		
Current liabilities:		
Accounts payable	$ 5	$ 7
Notes payable	10	30
Total current liabilities	15	37
Bonds payable	10	10
Total liabilities	25	47
Common stock	100	100
Retained earnings	55	80
Total liabilities and shareowners' equity	$180	$227

The following transactions affecting monetary assets and liabilities took place in 19x9:

1. Sales on account, $320.
2. Purchases of merchandise on account, $170.
3. Purchases of equipment on account, $40.
4. Payments to merchandise and equipment suppliers on account, $208.
5. Collections from customers on account, $300.
6. Payment of employees' salaries and other expenses, $100.
7. Sale of equipment for cash, $3.
8. Borrowings from bank, $20.
9. Declaration and payment of cash dividends, $10.

The general price level index traced the following path during the year:

January 1, 19x9 180
Average, 19x9 190
December 31, 19x9 200

All purchases, collections, and payments can be assumed to have taken place evenly throughout the year.

a. Calculate the company's net monetary position on January 1 and on December 31.
b. Calculate the effect of each of the nine events listed on Gregory Company's net monetary position.
c. Calculate Gregory's net purchasing-power gain or loss for the year, expressed in dollars with December 31, 19x9, purchasing power. Carry your calculations to two decimal places.

EXERCISES AND PROBLEMS

6. Calculating inventory holding gains and losses. Company X started the year 19x8 with an inventory of 50,000 units of merchandise. The replacement cost of this merchandise was $2 a unit on January 1; it rose to $2.50 on March 22, to $2.80 on July 1, and to $3.00 on September 16. It remained at $3.00 to the end of the year.

The following purchases and sales were made during 19x8:

Period	Purchases	Sales
1/1–3/21	60,000 × $2.00	45,000 × $2.70
3/22–6/30	70,000 × 2.50	65,000 × 3.20
7/1–9/15	50,000 × 2.80	65,000 × 3.40
9/16–12/31	40,000 × 3.00	60,000 × 3.50
Total	220,000	235,000

The company had 35,000 units in inventory at the end of 19x8.

a. Calculate the current cost of goods sold in 19x1 and the current cost of the inventory on December 31, 19x8.
b. Calculate the holding gain or loss for the year.
c. Calculate the current-cost margin for the year.

7. Realized inventory holding gains and losses. Company X (see problem 6) used LIFO to account for its inventories and the cost of goods sold. The LIFO cost of its January 1, 19x8, inventores was:

Base quantity	30,000 units × $1.00	$30,000
19x2 layer	16,000 units × 1.40	22,400
19x5 layer	4,000 units × 1.60	6,400
Total	50,000 units	$58,800

a. Calculate the LIFO cost of goods sold during 19x8 and the LIFO cost of the December 31, 19x8, inventory.
b. Calculate the unrealized inventory holding gain or loss (1) on January 1, 19x8, and (2) on December 31, 19x8.
c. Calculate the amount of inventory holding gain or loss that was included in pretax income for 19x8. How would this amount be reported to the shareholders?

8. Replacement-cost depreciation: discussion question. Miller Enterprises, Inc., is incorporated in a country in which corporations aren't required to base their financial statements on generally accepted accounting principles. In view of the steadily rising costs of equipment and building construction in that country, Miller's controller has suggested basing depreciation each year on replacement cost. Depreciation each year would be reflected in a journal entry of the following form:

Depreciation	X	
Accumulated Depreciation		Y
Reserve for Replacement		Z

in which X is the depreciation charge based on replacement cost and Y is the depreciation charge based on acquisition cost.

a. What effect would the proposed method have on net income during a period of rising equipment costs? Would this effect continue after equipment costs stopped rising? Explain.

b. If the controller's proposal were accepted, how would you interpret the "reserve for replacement"? Would it appear on the income statement for the year or would it go directly to the year-end balance sheet? In which section of the statement should it appear? State your reasons.

c. If a machine is replaced at the end of its anticipated useful life by an identical machine with a higher replacement cost, will the reserve for replacement equal the difference between the original cost of the first machine and the cost of its replacement? Explain.

9. Current costing. Company Y had 10,000 pounds of product in inventory on January 1, 19x2. The replacement cost of that inventory on that date was $10 a pound. The following events took place during 19x2:

January 30:	Supplier announced a price increase to $11 a pound.
February 20:	Company sold 3,000 pounds at a price of $15 a pound.
May 15:	Supplier announced a price increase to $12 a pound.
June 6:	Company sold 4,000 pounds at a price of $15 a pound.
September 15:	Company bought 5,000 pounds at a price of $12 a pound.
December 10:	Supplier announced a price decrease to $11.50 a pound.

a. Calculate the cost of goods sold and the cost of the ending inventory on a current-cost/nominal-dollar basis.

b. Calculate the inventory holding gain or loss arising during the year.

10. Realized inventory holding gains and losses. Company Y (see problem 9) used FIFO to account for its inventories and the cost of goods sold in 19x2. The FIFO inventory cost on January 1, 19x2, was $9.80 a pound. The market value of the year-end inventory was greater than its cost.

a. Calculate the FIFO cost of goods sold for 19x2.

b. Calculate the amount of the unrealized holding gain, if any, (1) at the beginning of 19x2 and (2) at the end of 19x2.

c. How much of the FIFO gross margin consisted of realized holding gains and losses?

11. Realized inventory holding gains and losses (LIFO). Suppose Company Y (see problem 9) used LIFO to cost its inventory and the cost of goods sold in 19x2. The LIFO cost of the January 1, 19x2, inventory was as follows:

Base quantity	6,000 pounds	$6.00	$36,000
19x0 layer	3,000 pounds	8.50	25,500
19x1 layer	1,000 pounds	9.50	9,500
Total	10,000 pounds		$71,000

a. Calculate the LIFO cost of goods sold for 19x2.
b. Calculate the amount of the unrealized holding gain, if any, (1) at the beginning of 19x2 and (2) at the end of 19x2.
c. How much of the LIFO gross margin consisted of realized holding gains and losses?

12. Supplying missing figures. You have the following information from three companies for a recent year:

	Company A	Company B	Company C
Current cost, beginning inventory	$100	$ E	$ 50
Current cost, ending inventory	110	150	65
Current cost of goods sold	315	650	J
Historical cost, beginning inventory	A	120	45
Historical cost, ending inventory	65	110	K
Historical cost of goods sold	320	F	285
Holding gain (loss) arising during the year	B	20	L
Holding gain (loss) realized during the year	C	G	(5)
Unrealized holding gain, beginning of year	40	80	M
Unrealized holding gain, end of year	D	H	Zero

a. Make the calculations necessary to supply the missing data.
b. Identify each company as a probable user of FIFO or a probable user of LIFO. Explain how you reached your conclusion in each case.

13. Purchasing-power gains and losses. Company M presented the following information on assets and liabilities in its 19x1 annual report:

	January 1	December 31
Cash	$ 20	$ 19
Accounts receivable	40	50
Inventory (LIFO)	50	55
Plant and equipment (net)	100	110
Accounts payable	10	8
Notes payable	20	24

Transactions during the year had the effect of increasing the company's net monetary position by $7 in nominal dollars.

The general price level index at the end of the year was 150. It was 125 at the beginning of the year and 140, on the average, during the year.

a. Calculate Company M's net monetary position on January 1 and on December 31, 19x1.
b. Calculate the purchasing-power gain or loss in 19x1 on the company's holdings of net monetary assets.

14. Inventory profits, holding gains. Royce Corporation was founded late in 19x1. It bought inventory before year-end and therefore was able to engage in merchandise transactions throughout 19x2. Listed below are the events that related to Royce's inventory transactions.

December 29, 19x1	Buy 15,000 @ $2.00
January 6, 19x2	Replacement cost = $2.15
January 7–August 11	Sell 6,000 @ $7.00
August 12	Replacement cost = $2.20
August 13–December 29	Sell 4,000 @ $8.50
September 20	Buy 12,000 @ $2.20
December 30, 19x2	Replacement cost = $2.30

During 19x2, Royce's other expenses totaled $20,000, and income taxes should be ignored.

a. Using FIFO cost, calculate the 19x2 net income and the inventory amount that will appear in the December 31, 19x2, balance sheet.
b. Prepare the same accounting measurements using the current-cost/nominal-dollar approach.
c. Calculate the amount of inventory profit or loss included in the FIFO-cost/nominal-dollar net income you calculated in answer to part a.
d. Reconcile the amount of inventory profit contained in your answer to part c with the holding gain appearing in your answer to part b.

15. Realized/unrealized holding gains. Royce Corporation (see problem 14) experienced the following events in 19x3 (the year after the events described in problem 14):

January 2–April 9	Sell 9,000 @ $9.00
April 10	Replacement cost = $2.38
July 9	Buy 24,000 @ $2.38
April 11–December 29	Sell 11,000 @ $10.00
December 30	Replacement cost = $2.45

During 19x3, Royce's other expenses totaled $55,000; income taxes should be ignored.

a. Using FIFO cost, calculate the 19x3 net income and the inventory amount that will appear in the December 31, 19x3, balance sheet.
b. Prepare the same accounting measurements using the current-cost/nominal-dollar approach.
c. Calculate the amounts of the realized and unrealized portions of the holding gain or loss in 19x3, and reconcile these amounts with the unrealized inventory holding gains as of January 1 and December 31, 19x3.

16. Holding gains/losses, nominal and real. Webster, Inc., a manufacturing company, bought a parcel of land for $400,000 cash in 19x1. Although its original intention had been to build a plant on the property, Webster's president began to doubt in 19x4 that construction would be undertaken, mainly because inflation had caused construction costs to rise dramatically. The company had determined, however, that the market value of the land had also risen dramatically during the first three years of ownership, as follows:

	Increase	
	Absolute	Percent
19x1 cost, $400,000		
19x2 market, $468,000	$ 68,000	17.0%
19x3 market, $550,000	82,000	17.5
19x4 market, $616,000	66,000	12.0
	$216,000	54.0

Although impressed by the 54 percent *increase* in value, the president was reminded that the just-published consumer price index for 19x4 indicated an identical 54 percent *decrease* in the purchasing power of the dollar between 19x1 and 19x4. Since the president's immediate reaction was that there was something sinister about this coincidence, the accountants assembled the following CPI numbers from published sources: 19x1 = 100, 19x2 = 110, 19x3 = 132, 19x4 = 154.

Prepare a schedule which identifies the real holding gains or losses experienced by Webster, Inc., during each of the three years it owned the land.

17. Purchasing-power gain and loss. The following information is available for Companies A and B (in $000):

	Company A		Company B	
	Jan. 1	Dec. 31	Jan. 1	Dec. 31
Cash	$150	$170	$ 60	$ 70
Accounts receivable	180	200	40	40
Inventory	110	90	320	275
Total	$440	$460	$420	$385
Accounts payable	$ 30	$ 40	$ 20	$ 30
Bonds payable	200	200	160	130
Owners' equity	210	220	240	225
Total	$440	$460	$420	$385

The general price level index was 100 as of January 1 and 116 as of December 31. The December 31 index was 108 percent of the average of the index during the year. Monetary-flow transactions occurred uniformly during the year.

a.   What was the nominal-dollar increase or decrease in each company's net monetary position during the year?

b.   What was the purchasing-power gain or loss experienced by each company?

c. Explain how and why the year's inflation affected the two companies differently.

18. Using LIFO to keep holding gains off the income statement. The Ethereal Spirits Company is a wholesale distributor of wines and liquors. It measures all its inventories on a LIFO basis. Increments to the LIFO inventories in any year are measured at the prices paid for the first units purchased during the year.

One of Ethereal's products is Sonoma Mountain Red, produced and bottled by the Carson Brothers Winery in California. Ethereal's inventory of this product on January 1, 19x9, was as follows:

	No. of Gallons	LIFO Cost Per Unit	Total
Base quantity	1,000	$1.50	$1,500
19x2 layer	200	2.00	400
19x7 layer	100	2.20	220
Total	1,300		$2,120

The price charged by Carson Brothers was $2.50 a gallon on January 1, 19x9, and remained at that level until October 15, 19x9, when it was increased to $2.75. Ethereal's purchases and sales during 19x9 were as follows:

	Gallons Purchased	Gallons Sold
Prior to October 15.............................	8,000	6,000
From October 15 to December 31	3,000	4,000
Total	11,000	10,000

a. Calculate the current cost of goods sold in 19x9 and the current cost of the December 31, 19x9, inventory.
b. Calculate the LIFO cost of goods sold for 19x9 and the LIFO cost of the December 31, 19x9, inventory.
c. Calculate the total inventory holding gain or loss arising during 19x9, including both the realized and the unrealized components.
d. Using data from this problem, comment on the proposition that LIFO keeps inventory holding gains and losses out of the income statement as long as the number of units purchased in any year equals or exceeds the number of units sold.

19. Purchasing-power gain or loss. As of January 1, 19x6, the monetary assets of Monarch, Ltd., were $11,000; its monetary liabilities were $6,000.

Sales of merchandise amounting to $60,000 occurred uniformly during the year, and land which had cost $20,000 in 19x3 was sold in March for $36,000. Inventory costing $12,000 was bought at a steady rate during the year, and $26,000 of operating expenses, occurring uniformly throughout 19x6, had immediate effects on Monarch's net monetary position.

Monarch bought a computer in February for $19,000 and purchased machinery in March for $40,000. During February the company sold treasury shares of common stock for $30,000, in July it paid off $4,000 of its long-term notes with $4,000 cash, and in November it expended $38,000 to retire shares of preferred stock.

The following consumer price index numbers relate to 19x6:

	Consumer Price Index
January 1	110
February	111
March	112
July	121
November	126
December 31	132
19x6 average	120

Using the end-of-year purchasing power as the constant dollar, calculate the gain or loss in purchasing power resulting from changes in Monarch's net monetary position during 19x6.

20. Interpreting published information. In its 1979 annual report, Upward, Inc., had a section entitled, *Supplementary Information—Effect of Changing Prices.* The presentation consisted of two schedules and one footnote. Excerpted information from Schedule A was as follows (in $ millions, except per-share amounts):

	As Reported in the Traditional Statements	Adjusted for General Inflation (historical cost/constant dollars)	Adjusted for Changes in Specific Prices (current costs)
Cost of goods sold	$15,991	$16,093	$16,074
Depreciation, depletion, and amortization	624	880	980
Earnings before income taxes and minority interest	2,391	2,033	1,952
Minority interest in earnings of consolidated affiliates	29	16	13
Net earnings applicable to common stock	1,409	1,064	986
Earnings per common share	$ 6.20	$ 4.68	$ 4.34

Schedule B is presented in its entirety. The amounts shown in both schedules for "Net earnings applicable to common stock" and "Earnings per common share" don't reflect the loss or gain in the general purchasing power of net monetary items. The footnote read as follows:

At December 31, 1979, the current cost of inventory was $5,251 million and of property, plant, and equipment was $7,004 million. Estimated current costs applicable to the sum of such amounts held during all or part of 1979 increased by approximately $1,111 million, which was $329 million less than the $1,440 million increase which could be expected because of general inflation.

Schedule B
Current-Cost Information in Dollars of 1979 Purchasing Power
(in average 1979 dollars)*

	1979	1978	1977	1976	1975
Sales of products and services to customers	$22,461	$21,867	$20,984	$20,015	$19,022
Cost of goods sold	16,074	15,548	14,793	14,145	13,914
Selling, general, and administrative expense	3,716	3,566	3,606	3,360	3,018
Depreciation, depletion, and amortization	980	1,000	986	979	1,006
Interest and other financial charges	258	249	238	222	251
Other income	(519)	(466)	(467)	(350)	(235)
Earnings before income taxes and minority interest	1,952	1,970	1,828	1,659	1,068
Provision for income taxes	953	995	926	853	620
Minority interest in earnings of consolidated affiliates	13	13	20	26	26
Net earnings applicable to common stock	$ 986	$ 962	$ 882	$ 780	$ 422
Earnings per common share	$ 4.34	$ 4.22	$ 3.88	$ 3.45	$ 1.88
Average consumer price index (1967 = 100)	217.4	195.4	181.5	170.5	161.2
(Loss)/gain in general purchasing power of net monetary items	$ (209)	$ (128)	$ (61)	$ (20)	$ 19
Dividends declared per common share	2.75	2.78	2.52	2.17	2.16
Market price per common share at year end	47⅞	50½	58¼	69⅜	60¼

* In $ millions, except per-share amounts.

a. Make the following specific calculations:
1. Sales for each of the five years, expressed in nominal dollars.
2. Sales for each of the five years, expressed in dollars of 1967 purchasing power.
3. The percentage increase in sales, year by year, during the five-year period—in nominal terms and in real terms.
4. The 1976 cost of goods sold, as it would appear in Schedule B (the five-year summary) in the company's 1980 annual report, encompassing the years 1976–80 and expressed in dollars of 1980 purchasing power. The consumer price index for 1980 was 246.8.

b. Why was the cost of goods sold less when adjusted for changes in specific prices than when adjusted for general inflation?

c. When comparing "adjusted for changes in specific prices" data with amounts "as reported in the traditional statements," why did the cost of goods sold change so insignificantly relative to the change in depreciation, depletion, and amortization?

d. What conclusions can be reached by comparing these supplementary data with the company's traditional balance sheet's disclosure of inventories ($3,161 million) and property, plant, and equipment ($4,613 million)?

e. What observations can be made with respect to the company's net monetary position?

f. Upward, Inc., is generally regarded as a "growth company," meaning that the trend in sales, earnings, and dividends is upward. Is this a valid categorization of this company? Support your conclusions with data from this problem.

21. Interpreting adjusted data. Upon its formation on January 1, the Nuovo Company bought inventories at a cost of $2,000 and equipment at a cost of $4,000. The balance sheet at that point was as follows:

Assets		Liabilities and Owners' Equity	
Cash	$1,000	Liabilities	$1,500
Inventory	2,000	Capital stock	5,500
Equipment	4,000	Retained earnings	0
Total	$7,000	Total	$7,000

On that date, of course, the figures for inventory and equipment represented not only original cost but current cost as well. (The Nuovo Company operated in a country which had no income taxes. Its monetary unit was the dollar.)

The income statement for the first year of operations was computed both on a conventional historical-cost basis and on a replacement-cost basis, using *average* replacement costs for the year. This produced the following amounts:

	Historical-Cost Basis	Replacement-Cost Basis
Sales	$6,000	$6,000
Cost of goods sold	4,100	4,400
Depreciation	600	612
Other expenses	900	900
Net income	$ 400	$ 88

The year-end balance sheet was also stated on an historical-cost basis and on a replacement-cost basis, using *year-end* replacement prices to determine Inventory and Equipment balances. The amounts were:

		Historical-Cost Basis		Replacement-Cost Basis
Assets				
Cash		$2,100		$2,100
Inventory		2,300		2,400
Equipment	$4,000		$4,160	
Less: Accumulated depreciation	600		624	
Equipment, net		3,400		3,536
Total assets		$7,800		$8,036
Liabilities and Owners' Equity				
Liabilities		$1,900		$1,900
Common stock		5,500		5,500
Retained earnings		400		88
Accumulated holding gains		—		548
Total liabilities and owners' equity		$7,800		$8,036

The amount shown for "Accumulated holding gains" was the total of the following:

Realized holding gains:
Cost of goods sold: $4,400 — $4,100 .... $300
Depreciation: $612 — $600 12
Unrealized holding gains:
Inventory: $2,400 — $2,300 100
Equipment: $3,536 — $3,400 136
Total accumulated holding gain $548

Further investigation revealed that the general price level on December 31 had reached 110 percent of the January 1 level. The average for the year was 105 percent of the January 1 level. Purchases and sales were made at steady rates throughout the year.

After examining these amounts, the company's purchasing agent commented that although operating income on a replacement-cost basis was not satisfactory, the holding gains experienced during the period were very gratifying. The marketing vice president, on the other hand, rejected the replacement-cost amounts, saying the marketing people had done a good job selling the company's products at a good margin over their cost. No bookkeeper was going to take that achievement away from them.

In the treasurer's view, the holding gain wasn't a real gain because the purchasing power of the dollar had fallen during the year. Working quickly on the back of an envelope, the treasurer produced the following calculation:

1. Assets, January 1 .... $7,000
2. Liabilities, January 1 1,500
3. Net assets, January 1 (1 — 2) $5,500
4. Purchasing power index, December 31 .... 110%
5. Adjusted net assets, January 1, at end-of-year prices (3 × 4) $6,050
6. Adjusted net assets, December 31 (from balance sheet) 5,900
7. Loss in purchasing power during the year (5 — 6) .... $ 150

a. What position would you take in this argument? Prepare a short statement defending your position, indicating your reasons for accepting or rejecting the arguments advanced by the purchasing agent, the marketing vice president, and the treasurer. Your statement should not include numerical calculations but should describe the concept the net income measure should reflect.

b. If accounting reports had been stated in year-end constant dollars, would this company have reported a profit or a loss on its ordinary operations (exclusive of holding gains and losses)? Explain.

c. What changes in management policies would you recommend for the future if events during the next several years seem likely to follow the pattern set this year?

d. Prepare a nonnumerical analysis of the difference between the treasurer's estimate of a $150 loss in purchasing power and the $88 net income calculated on a replacement cost basis. In other words, identify the sources of this difference but don't attempt to quantify their effects.

15

Financial-statement analysis

Corporate financial statements summarize part of the company's history. Their main purpose, however, is to help managers and investors make decisions that will affect the company's future. The study of financial statements for this purpose is known as *financial-statement analysis.* The purpose of this chapter is to explain what financial-statement analysis is and what it is expected to accomplish. We'll also introduce some of the devices financial analysts use. The chapter has four parts:

1. The basic tools of financial analysis.
2. Measures of profitability.
3. Measures of debt-paying ability and risk.
4. Measures of efficiency.

THE BASIC TOOLS OF FINANCIAL-STATEMENT ANALYSIS

To appreciate the nature of financial-statement analysis, we need to recognize that a number in isolation is meaningless. To be told, for example, that Grant Company earned $60 million this year conveys no substantive information. We don't know whether this was good or bad, desirable or undesirable, worthy of replication or not. What we need is a frame of reference in the form of a benchmark so that the $60 million net income can be evaluated in an appropriate context.

Performance benchmarks

Readers of financial statements generally use three main kinds of performance benchmarks. The most common is performance in one or more prior periods. Thus, if we're told that Grant's net income was $75 million last year, we can conclude that this year's $60 million net income represented a 20 percent reduction.

A second commonly used benchmark is the income earned by comparable companies or average industry income. Learning that a competitor, Nickel, Inc., earned only $40 million enables us to calculate that Grant's earnings were 50 percent larger than Nickel's.

Additional insight can be obtained by using both benchmarks simultaneously. Assuming Nickel earned $30 million last year, we can display all four income amounts—two companies, two years—as follows:

	Net Income ($ millions)		Percentage Increase (Decrease)
	19x1	19x2	
Grant Company............	$75	$60	(20%)
Nickel, Inc................	30	40	33
Percentage advantage......	150%	50%	

Although Grant's income was 50 percent larger than Nickel's in 19x2, it had been 150 percent larger than Nickel's in 19x1. The concurrent use of two benchmarks enables us to see that even though Grant's income continued to exceed Nickel's earnings, Grant's relative position was declining.

The third benchmark with which to analyze financial results is the anticipated outcome. The notion of "anticipated outcome" is not as well defined as the other two benchmarks. Within the company itself, budgeted amounts would serve this function, and this will be discussed further in Chapter 20. For external parties, however, it is much more difficult to identify an anticipated outcome. Although some companies provide their bankers with projected financial statements, and some corporation presidents announce publicly the income their company expects to earn during the coming year, analysts and investors usually have to determine for themselves the amount of income they expect companies to earn.

However definitive or official the expectation, users of financial statements do evaluate results against the amounts that had been anticipated or hoped for. To give this benchmark an added dimension, it should be used in conjunction with the other two guides. In our example, the 20 percent decline in Grant's income is seen in an altogether different light if earnings had been expected to decrease by 35 percent than if they had been expected to increase by 10 percent.

The role of ratios

The basic building block in financial-statement analysis is the *ratio,* a percentage or decimal relationship of one number with another. Ratios are an important means by which benchmarks are used to analyze financial statements; the three different ways to use ratios are as follows:

1. *Structural analysis* entails examining the relationship between two financial-statement items or groups of items in the same period, such as relating the amount of cash on hand to total current liabilities.
2. *Time-series analysis* involves comparing individual financial-statement ratios of the same company in different time periods.
3. *Cross-sectional analysis* refers to comparing the company's financial-statement items with those of other companies in the same industry or with some market-wide measure or measures.

The advantage of ratios is that they bring the numbers being expressed as ratios down to a common scale. A company may be twice as large as it was 10 years ago, for example, so comparing total expenses in the two periods won't be as useful as comparing the expense/revenue *ratios* in the two periods.

Stating relationships on a common scale doesn't necessarily make them perfectly comparable, however. A high ratio may be appropriate for a company in one industry but not for a company in another industry or for a company at a different stage in its development or for a much larger or smaller company.

Both time-series analysis and cross-sectional analysis may be distorted by inflation or unusual business conditions. Time-series comparisons tend to be distorted by inflation to a larger extent than cross-sectional comparisons because all observations in a cross-sectional analysis are made in the same time period, with the same general price level. The analyst's problem is to decide how serious these distortions are and how to adjust for them.

For these reasons, we can't prescribe an ideal value for any ratio. The ideal varies with the circumstances the individual company finds itself in. Our objective will be to provide some insight into whether high ratios are likely to signal strengths or weaknesses in different circumstances.

To do this, we'll use the financial statements of a hypothetical company, Alpha Company. Exhibit 15–1 presents Alpha's balance sheets as of the end of 19x1 and 19x2. Exhibit 15–2 shows the compa-

EXHIBIT 15–1

ALPHA COMPANY
Balance Sheets
December 31, 19x1 and 19x2

	19x1	19x2
Assets		
Current assets:		
Cash	$ 4,300	$ 2,600
Receivables	17,100	19,800
Inventories	28,700	35,900
Total current assets	50,100	58,300
Plant assets	44,800	50,500
Less: Accumulated depreciation	18,100	19,400
Net plant assets	26,700	31,100
Total assets	$76,800	$89,400
Liabilities and Shareholders' Equity		
Current liabilities:		
Accounts payable	$ 4,800	$ 6,600
Notes payable	6,200	15,500
Federal income taxes	2,200	2,100
Total current liabilities	13,200	24,200
Long-term debt	17,400	11,700
Total liabilities	30,600	35,900
Shareholders' equity:		
8 percent preferred stock, par value $10 (700 shares)	7,000	7,000
Common stock, par value $5 (2,000 shares in 19x2, 1,800 shares in 19x1)	9,000	10,000
Additional paid-in capital	9,900	12,600
Retained earnings	20,300	23,900
Total shareholders' equity	46,200	53,500
Total liabilities and shareholders' equity	$76,800	$89,400

ny's income statement for 19x2, and Exhibit 15–3 is the statement of changes in retained earnings for 19x2. We'll introduce the company's funds statement later in the chapter.

MEASURES OF PROFITABILITY

Investors become and remain stockholders in a company because they believe that dividends and capital gains (increases in the market price of the stock) will compare favorably with the amounts they can earn on alternative investments of comparable risk. The most important determinant of future dividends and capital gains is the corporation's future earnings, and the first source of data for use in forecasting future earnings is the corporation's past-earnings record.

EXHIBIT 15–2

ALPHA COMPANY
Income Statement
For the Year Ended December 31, 19x2

Sales revenue		$105,460
Expenses:		
Cost of goods sold (except depreciation)	$57,700	
Depreciation	2,500	
Research and development	4,630	
Selling and administration	27,470	92,300
Income before interest and taxes		13,160
Interest expense		2,500
Income before taxes		10,660
Income taxes		4,200
Net income		$ 6,460

Three ratios used widely as measures of the company's past-earnings record are:

1. Earnings per share of common stock.
2. Return on common equity.
3. Return on assets.

We'll discuss each of these in turn and then describe a way of breaking the return-on-assets ratio down into two component ratios, the asset-turnover ratio and the profit-margin ratio. We'll also discuss the concept of the quality of earnings and the dividend-payout ratio.

Earnings per common share

The most widely used measure of financial performance is net aftertax earnings per common share, usually referred to as *earnings per share.* As we saw in Chapter 11, dividends the holders of preferred stock are entitled to must be subtracted from net income

EXHIBIT 15–3

ALPHA COMPANY
Statement of Changes in Retained Earnings
For the Year Ended December 31, 19x2

Retained earnings, January 1, 19x2		$20,300
Add: Net income, 19x2		6,460
Total		26,760
Less: Dividends on preferred stock	$ 560	
Dividends on common stock	2,300	
Total dividends		2,860
Retained earnings, December 31, 19x2		$23,900

to get earnings applicable to the common stock. The 19x2 calculation for the Alpha Company is:

$$\frac{\text{Net income} - \text{Preferred dividends}}{\text{No. of common shares}} = \frac{\$6,460 - \$560}{2,000}$$
$$= \$2.95 \text{ per share}$$

Earnings-per-share amounts are used to compare one year's earnings with those of prior years. They are also combined with other data, such as market price per share, to reveal relationships the analyst wishes to examine. The relationship between a company's earnings per share and a market index of earnings (total earnings of a large sample of corporations) can be particularly useful in predicting the company's future earnings.

Both the numerator and the denominator of this ratio need to be studied carefully. The dilution adjustments we discussed in Chapter 11 are now made routinely and we needn't dwell on them here. What we need to concentrate on is the earnings numerator. For one thing, analysts distinguish between earnings from ordinary, continuing operations and earnings from operations about to be discontinued and from the effects of extraordinary events. In fact, even ordinary operating earnings have to be examined carefully because many items that are unusual or nonrecurring but do not meet the accounting profession's test to be *extraordinary* are included in ordinary income. The total amount of income or loss from these sources is likely to fluctuate more widely than income from other sources. The analyst should be alert to identify the underlying movements in earnings from these fluctuations.

Quality of earnings

Analysts also study the company's financial statements to appraise what they refer to as the *quality of earnings*. Quality has many dimensions. Some refer to the company's accounting policies. Companies using FIFO for inventories, straight-line depreciation, the flow-through method of accounting for the investment credit, and pooling-of-interests accounting for business combinations are likely to report greater earnings than comparable companies using LIFO, accelerated depreciation, investment-credit deferral, and the purchase method of accounting for business combinations.

Quality also depends on the nature of the company's products and markets. It is important to know whether the bulk of current earnings comes from growing business segments or from declining segments, from domestic markets or foreign markets, from a few large customers or many small ones, and so on. The publication of segment-income data, including a geographic breakdown, provides analysts with the raw material to analyze these aspects of quality.

A third aspect of earnings quality is the extent to which current earnings are affected by current expenditures on research and development or promotional marketing activities. Sales revenues from these activities won't be recognized until some time in the future, but their costs show up among the current year's expenses. Similarly, if equipment-replacement prices have been rising rapidly, current depreciation charges are likely to be much lower than they will be in the future when the present equipment is replaced. In fact, a good deal of our discussion in earlier chapters was designed to provide the foundation for an analysis of the quality of earnings.

Return on common equity

The absolute amount of income is an inadequate measure of profitability because it does not indicate how much had to be invested to achieve it. One way to put earnings and investment amounts together is to compute the rate of return on common equity—that is, the ratio of net income available to common shareholders to the *book value* of the common shareholders' equity in the company. For Alpha, the book value of the common equity was the total of capital stock at par value, additional paid-in capital, and retained earnings, adding up to $46,500 at the end of 19x2.[1] The rate of return on common equity, therefore, was as follows:

$$\frac{\text{Net income} - \text{Preferred dividends}}{\text{Common equity}} = \frac{\$6,460 - \$560}{\$46,500} = 12.7 \text{ percent}$$

In reaching a judgment as to whether this represents good or bad performance, a number of questions must be answered. For example, how does this amount compare with the return of other companies in the industry and in industry in general? Is this company's rate of return holding steady, going up, or declining? How wide are the year-to-year fluctuations in rate of return?

The rate of return on common equity can also be calculated in

---

[1] Earnings may be related to the investment at the beginning of the year, the investment at the end of the year, or an average of the two. We have used year-end investment because it is generally the most convenient.

another way, with the market value of the common shares as the denominator of the ratio. After all, book value represents investment decisions investors made in the past. The current question is: How large a return is the company making on the amounts investors are *now* willing to invest in this company?

This ratio is calculated routinely but in an inverted form; that is, one of the most widely quoted ratios in the financial press is the *price/earnings ratio,* usually referred to simply as the *P/E ratio.* For example, if Alpha's common stock was being traded on the market at a price of $29.50 a share at the end of 19x2, the P/E ratio was $29.50/$2.95 = 10. This is simply the reciprocal of the earnings/market value ratio: $2.95/$29.50 = 10 percent.

Return on assets and the leverage effect

A corporation's return on its common equity is a consequence of two factors: (1) its return on assets, and (2) the extent to which *financial leverage* is used by the company. Return on assets is measured by the ratio of earnings *before interest* to total assets. The percentage of total assets that is supplied by creditors and preferred shareholders represents the leverage used by the company.[2]

Pretax analysis. The leverage effect can be seen most easily in an analysis of pretax amounts. For example, Alpha Company had $89,400 in assets and $13,160 in income before interest and taxes in 19x2 (from Exhibits 15–1 and 15–2). Its pretax rate of return on assets was:

$$\frac{\text{Income before interest and taxes}}{\text{Total assets}} = \frac{\$13,160}{\$89,400} = 14.7 \text{ percent}$$

The reason for using earnings *before* interest and dividends as the numerator in this ratio is that the denominator represents all assets, not just those supplied by the shareholders. To be comparable, the earnings amount should measure earnings before distributions to either creditors (interest) or shareholders (dividends).

By using leverage, the company was able to earn a much higher return on its common equity than it earned on its total assets. If

---

[2] Leverage can also be measured by the ratio of *long-term* debt and preferred stock to the book value of the common stock, or as the ratio of *interest-bearing* debt and preferred stock to common equity. Our measure, which uses total liabilities in the numerator and total assets in the denominator, is appropriate when the comparison is to be made between return on total assets and return on the common shareholders' equity in those assets, as it is here.

EXHIBIT 15–4. **Pretax Effect of Financial Leverage**

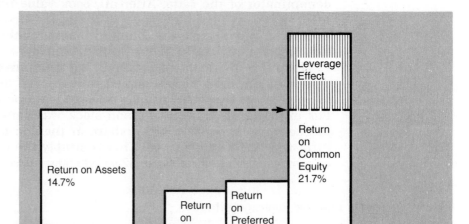

the income tax rate had been zero, the earnings available to the common stockholder would have been $13,160 less the $2,500 interest expense and the $560 dividends on the preferred stock, or $10,100:

Income before interest and income taxes $13,160	−	Interest expense $2,500	−	Preferred dividends $560	=	Pretax leveraged income $10,100

The book value of the common stockholders' equity was $46,500 (from Exhibit 15–1). The pretax rate of return on common equity therefore was:

$$\frac{\text{Pretax income on common equity}}{\text{Common stockholders' equity}} = \frac{\$10,100}{\$46,500} = 21.7 \text{ percent}$$

The leverage effect in this case is illustrated in Exhibit 15–4. This was successful leverage because the 7 percent average interest cost of debt ($2,500 interest/$35,900 total liabilities) and the 8 percent cost of preferred stock were less than the overall earnings rate on total assets (14.7 percent). The common shareholders, in other words, gained the full 14.7 percent on their own investment plus more than half the return on the assets financed by creditors and preferred stockholders. To get this additional return, the common stockholders had to assume the greater *risk* (uncertainty of the rate of return on their investment) arising from the increased fixed burden of debt service. ("Debt service" is the total of the payments for interest and principal in any period.)

Three technical aspects of this analysis are worth noting. First, some liabilities, such as accounts payable and accrued taxes payable, lead to no recognized interest expense. The presence of these liabilities in the mix reduces the average interest cost of the company's debts to less than the interest rate on those liabilities which do give rise to recognized interest expense.

Second, year-end liability balances may be a very poor approximation to the *average* amount of liabilities outstanding during the year, which may have been much larger or much smaller than the year-end amounts. These variations within the year make leverage analysis much less precise than it appears to be.

Finally, both interest and preferred-dividend rates are the historical rates in effect when the debt was incurred or the preferred stock was issued. They don't necessarily represent the current costs of those kinds of capital. Alpha's pretax costs of *new* borrowing in 19x2 may have been much higher than the historical rates reflected in this analysis. For current leveraging decisions, management has to compare current borrowing rates with the anticipated returns on additional investments in assets.

Aftertax analysis. The aftertax analysis is likely to be even more dramatic than the pretax analysis because tax deductibility reduces the nominal aftertax cost of debt. The analysis is in three steps:

1. Calculate the aftertax rate of return on common equity for the actual capital structure.
2. Recalculate the aftertax rate of return on equity on the assumption that common stock was the company's sole source of capital.
3. Compare these two rates; the difference between them is the leverage effect.

The first of these steps is simple. We subtract the dividends on any preferred stock outstanding from net income and divide the difference by the common shareholders' equity. Since dividends are not tax deductible, the aftertax rate of return on equity is the same 12.7 percent we calculated in the preceding section.

To make the second calculation, we have to find out what tax rate is applicable to the portion of "earnings before interest and taxes" that interest deductibility has shielded from income taxation.

EXHIBIT 15–5. Aftertax Effect of Financial Leverage

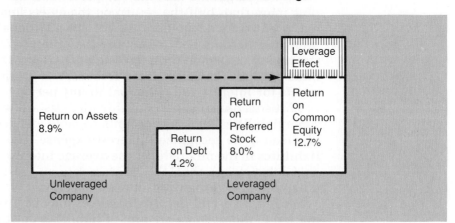

The correct tax rate for this adjustment is the marginal tax rate—that is, the rate on the next i dollars of taxable income.

In the absence of debt financing, Alpha's taxable income in 19x2 would have been $2,500 greater, and the income taxes would have been increased by 40 percent of $2,500, or $1,000, if we assume a 40 percent marginal tax rate.[3] Income taxes, therefore, would have been $4,200 + $1,000 = $5,200, and aftertax income would have been $13,160 − $5,200 = $7,960. The aftertax return on assets therefore was:

$$\frac{\text{Adjusted aftertax income}}{\text{Total assets}} = \frac{\$7,960}{\$89,400} = 8.9 \text{ percent}$$

This is the return Alpha would have earned on the common equity if no debt or preferred financing had been used.

The aftertax leverage effect is illustrated in Exhibit 15–5. As this shows, the use of debt and preferred stock raised Alpha's return on its common equity from 8.9 percent to 12.7 percent. The aftertax cost of debt was only 4.2 percent (60 percent of 7 percent) because the interest was deductible from taxable income.

The same calculations can be performed with market values substituted for book values in the denominator.

---

[3] Alpha's income tax expense was calculated at the rate of 30 percent of the first $640 of income before taxes and 40 percent of all amounts in excess of $640. Since the $2,500 interest deduction reduced income before taxes from $13,160 to $10,660, its impact on taxes must be measured by the tax rate applicable to a reduction in that portion of the income range, 40 percent. (These rates and the dollar limit for the lower rate are purely illustrative; in practice, both the rates and the limit will differ, depending on the location of the company's operations and the revenue needs of the taxing authorities.)

Successful versus unsuccessful leverage. Leverage works both ways, of course. If the overall return on assets is lower than the rates of return on debt and preferred stock, the rate of return on the common equity will be lower than the return on assets and may even be negative. The rate of return on the common equity will be equal to the rate of return on assets when the rate of return on assets (ROA) equals the average rate of return required by lenders and preferred stockholders. We can express this in an equation:

$$\text{ROA} = \frac{r_p P + r_d D}{P + D}$$

where P is the amount of preferred equity, D is the amount of debt, r_p is the dividend rate on the preferred, and r_d is the aftertax interest expense rate on the debt.

In this case, with preferred of $7,000, debt of $35,900, an 8 percent preferred stock, and a 4.2 percent average aftertax cost of debt, the average aftertax rate of return on assets has to be only 4.82 percent for the return on common equity to be equal to return on assets:

$$\text{ROA} = \frac{0.08 \times \$7{,}000 + 0.042 \times \$35{,}900}{\$7{,}000 + \$35{,}900} = 4.82 \text{ percent}$$

If return on assets is higher than that, leverage will be successful; if return on assets is lower, leverage will be unsuccessful.

The relationship between return on assets and return on equity is diagrammed in Exhibit 15–6. The line of the relationship is shown as a straight line. This won't always be true, partly because different tax rates are likely to apply to different portions of the taxable income and partly because the tax status of losses depends on the company's tax history. The basic relationship holds, however; the success or failure of leverage depends on the relationship between the return on assets and the aftertax book rate of return on senior securities.

The possibility of unsuccessful leverage adds to the risks of investment in this company, and the market will adjust the prices it is willing to pay for the company's stocks and bonds to reflect this risk. In simple terms, the common stock will have a lower price/earnings ratio than a comparable company with no leverage.

Percentage-of-sales ratios

The rate of return on assets is the product of two factors: (1) the rate of asset turnover, and (2) the profit margin. This relationship can be stated in the form of an equation:

$$\begin{aligned} \text{Return on assets} &= \text{Asset turnover} \times \text{Profit margin} \\ &= \frac{\text{Sales}}{\text{Assets}} \times \frac{\text{Income}}{\text{Sales}} \end{aligned}$$

We'll discuss profit-margin ratios here, leaving asset-turnover ratios for the final section of this chapter.

The profit-margin ratio and other percentage-of-sales ratios are widely used in profitability analysis, mainly to identify trends or intercompany differences. In calculating the overall profit-margin ratio, we need to use the same income amount that we use in the return-on-investment comparisons. If return on investment is calculated as a return on assets, as in our present example, then the income amount should be before interest but after taxes, the tax amount being adjusted to eliminate the leverage effect, as described in the preceding subsection.

EXHIBIT 15–6. Effect of Variations in Return on Assets on Leveraging Success

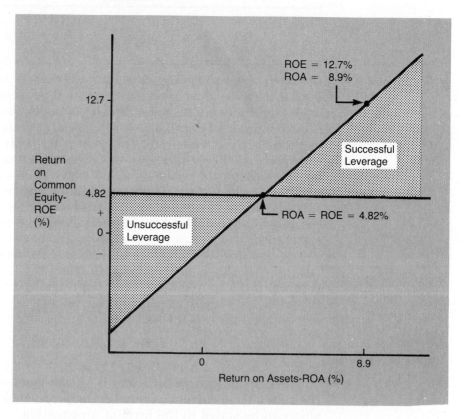

Alpha's adjusted income after taxes, as we saw a moment ago, was $13,160 − $5,200 = $7,960. Its profit margin for 19x2 was:

$$\frac{\text{Adjusted net income}}{\text{Sales revenue}} = \frac{\$7,960}{\$105,460} = 7.5 \text{ percent}$$

If return on investment is measured by the rate of return on equity, the numerator should be the amount of income available to the common stockholders (net income minus preferred dividends).

The overall profit-margin ratio is usually supplemented by various subordinated ratios, such as the *operating ratio* (the ratio of operating expenses to operating revenues), the *gross-margin ratio* (the ratio of the total gross margin to gross revenues), and the *research-and-development ratio* (the ratio of research and development expenses to gross revenues). These ratios are useful both in intercompany comparisons and in analyzing trends in the company's own performance. A rising operating ratio, for example, may be a signal of operating difficulties; an operating ratio higher than competitors' ratios may be a signal of competitive weakness. Alternatively, a high and rising operating ratio may signal a shift by the company to an aggressive marketing strategy, in which low profit margins are accompanied by large increases in sales volume, now or in the future.

This dual interpretation reinforces a point we made earlier. The ratio is only an analytical tool. A high ratio may be a good sign or a bad sign, and the analyst can decide which it is only by placing it in the context of other ratios and other available information.

The payout ratio and the rate of growth

Potential purchasers of a company's stock are buying not only dividends at the current rate but also prospects of future growth (or decline). This growth is provided, in large part, by the reinvestment of funds provided by operations. An index of the company's commitment to growth is the *payout ratio:*

$$\text{Payout ratio} = \frac{\text{Dividends per share}}{\text{Earnings per share}} = \frac{\$1.15^*}{\$2.95} = 39 \text{ percent}$$

* $2,300 (Exhibit 15–3)/2,000 (Exhibit 15–1).

The payout ratio is often used with two related ratios: (1) the price/earnings ratio which was discussed earlier, and (2) the yield ratio. With the current period's cash dividend as the *sole* measure of an investor's return, the yield ratio is the rate of return relative to the current market price per share. The following illustration assumes the market price of a common share of Alpha Company was $29.50.

Yield ratio	Price/earnings ratio	Payout ratio
$\dfrac{\text{Dividends per share}}{\text{Market price per share}} \times$	$\dfrac{\text{Market price per share}}{\text{Earnings per share}} =$	$\dfrac{\text{Dividends per share}}{\text{Earnings per share}}$
$\dfrac{\$1.15}{\$29.50}$	$\dfrac{\$29.50}{\$2.95}$	$\dfrac{\$1.15}{\$2.95}$
3.9%	10	39%

Investors are interested in both dividend yield and capital appreciation. The price/earnings ratio indicates the market's current disposition toward a company's stock, and it may also offer some clues about future capital appreciation.

Alpha paid dividends equal to 39 percent of its earnings (its payout ratio); the 61 percent that was retained is called its *retention ratio*. The retention ratio, together with the return on common equity we discussed earlier, enables financial analysts to address the question of how effectively the company can use the funds it retains and reinvests in the business. The resulting measure is called the *sustainable-growth ratio:*

Sustainable-growth ratio = Return on equity × Retention ratio
= 12.7% × 0.61 = 7.75 percent

This is also the $3,600 increase in retained earnings divided by the $46,500 common stockholders' equity. This shows us that in 19x2 the book value of Alpha's stockholders' equity was growing at a rate of 7.75 percent a year; if all other relationships were steady, earnings presumably were growing at the same rate.[4] The higher the return on equity and the higher the retention rate, the higher the rate of growth in earnings the company can sustain.

Market-value ratio

The rate of return on equity is likely to be reflected in the *market-value ratio:*

---

[4] This statement isn't strictly accurate because we are using the end-of-year balance sheet amounts in the return-on-equity ratio. If we had used the average owners' equity for the year, the sustainable-growth ratio would have been slightly higher.

$$\text{Market-value ratio} = \frac{\text{Market price per share}}{\text{Book value per share}}$$

Problems of asset measurement aside, companies with higher rates of return on equity will have higher stock prices relative to the current book value of the stock than comparable companies (with similar risk characteristics) having lower return-on-equity ratios, as long as the market believes the company can continue to generate these returns on the funds reinvested in the business. Earnings retention means the stockholders are exchanging current cash dividends in the expectation of receiving greater cash dividends or increased market prices in the future. If the company can't use the cash profitably, the return on equity will fall, the growth rate will drop, and the market-value ratio will decline.

The size of the market-value ratio depends on investors' appraisals of the ability of book values to measure the present value of the company's future cash flows. The book value of Alpha's common stock in 19x2 was $46,500/2,000 = $23.25 a share. The market price was $29.50, and the market-value ratio was $29.50/$23.25 = 1.27. This could reflect a relatively low asset-measurement profile—LIFO inventory measurement, for example. Alternatively, it could mean that the company's assets would likely yield a higher rate of return than investors considered normal.

MEASURES OF DEBT-PAYING ABILITY AND RISK

Both lenders and investors in stocks are interested not only in profitability but also in the risks associated with investments in individual companies. Lenders think of risk as the uncertainty about whether they will receive the amounts due them and on time; equity investors see it as the degree of uncertainty surrounding their estimates of the rate of return on their investments. Financial-statement analysis includes three techniques for evaluating risk:

1. Analysis of the capital structure.
2. Analysis of the sources and uses of funds.
3. Coverage analysis.

Analysis of the asset-liability structure

One kind of analysis of the sources and uses of funds is a study of the *structure* of the company's assets and of its liabilities and owners' equity.

Debt structure. The order in which the sources of funds are listed in the balance sheet corresponds to two important characteristics: the interest cost of obtaining the funds and the risk they bring with them. Current accounts payable and wages payable are attractive sources of funds because they have no explicit interest cost. Current notes payable do have explicit interest costs, but the rates of interest on these notes are likely to be lower than on longer-term debt, at least in times of interest-rate stability. Despite these attractive features, current liabilities aren't unmixed blessings. Their main drawback is that they must be paid in a relatively short time. The *risk* cost is therefore high because payment may fall due just when the company finds itself temporarily short of cash.

Long-term debt, in contrast, typically carries a higher interest rate in periods of financial-market stability. Its advantage is that it poses less immediate threat to the company's solvency—that is, its ability to pay its debts when they come due. For instance, a company ordinarily can pick a convenient time to refinance long-term debt before it falls due, thereby minimizing the likelihood that it will fall due when the company lacks ready cash.

Finally, funds obtained from shareholders through the sale of stock or retention of earnings carry no risk of insolvency. The company has no contractual obligation to make payments on specified dates, even to the preferred shareholders. In return for removing this risk from the corporation, the stockholders expect a higher yield on their investment than that earned by the company's creditors. This desired yield can and should be considered a cost of stockholder capital.

The relative importance of debt in the capital structure is measured by several different ratios, of which we'll consider only three. The first of these, the *long-term-debt ratio,* is obtained by dividing the book value of the long-term debt by the book value of the owners' equity. For Alpha at the end of 19x2 this ratio was:

$$\frac{\text{Long-term debt}}{\text{Pfd. stock} + \text{Common equity}} = \frac{\$11,700}{\$7,000 + \$46,500} = 21.9 \text{ percent}$$

The long-term-debt ratio is used as a measure of risk. Because only near-term debt retirement and interest requirements constitute immediate threats to the company's solvency, however, this ratio applies more to long-term than to short-term risks.

A more inclusive ratio is the *debt/equity ratio,* the ratio of total liabilities to total owners' equity:

$$\frac{\text{Total liabilities}}{\text{Total owners' equity}} = \frac{\$35,900}{\$53,500} = 67.1 \text{ percent}$$

A variant of this ratio is the ratio of total liabilities to total assets; both give essentially the same information.

The debt/equity ratio is a more inclusive measure of risk than the long-term-debt ratio, but it still doesn't give much information on near-term risks. In 19x2, for example, Alpha Company increased its short-term debt and decreased its long-term debt. As a result, the debt/equity ratio remained almost constant, but the ratio of current liabilities to total liabilities increased from 43.1 percent at the end of 19x1 ($13,200/$30,600) to 67.4 percent a year later ($24,200/$35,900). Other things being equal, this represented an increase in risk.

The main difficulty in interpreting these ratios is that they can be affected significantly by the company's asset-measurement policies. The choices of inventory method, depreciation method, and similar matters affect the capital-structure ratios just as they affect the profitability ratios.

One way to get around this difficulty is to use market values instead of book values to measure the liabilities and owners' equity which enter into the calculation of the capital-structure ratios. The advantage of market values is that they provide a more up-to-date measure of the debt burden. Market values of debt represent the present value of future debt service payments under current market conditions. For example, if the market rate of interest is 12 percent, a company with $1 million of 8 percent debt incurred when the market yield was 8 percent has a smaller debt burden than a company with a $1 million issue of 12 percent bonds of the same maturity but issued when the market yield was 12 percent. Each will appear on the balance sheet as a $1 million liability, but the market value of the 8 percent issue will be much smaller, reflecting its smaller burden to the company.

Asset structure. The way the company's funds have been used is also significant. Current assets are more liquid than plant and equipment, for example; that is, they can be made available more quickly to meet unexpected cash needs. Investments in current assets may also be highly profitable if they enable the company to increase total revenues or reduce total operating costs. Beyond some point, however, additional investments in current assets add less than enough to income to provide an adequate rate of return on the additional investment; idle cash balances, for example, earn nothing.

With these relationships in mind, analysts can use asset-structure ratios to see how management is using the company's funds. For instance, two of Alpha's asset-structure ratios for 19x2 reflected a clear decline in the company's liquidity:

	19x1	19x2
Cash/assets	5.6%	2.9%
Cash and receivables/assets	27.9	25.1

This was a favorable change if it resulted from a reduction in the amount of idle assets, an unfavorable change if it resulted from the company's inability to generate enough cash to meet its needs.

Working-capital ratios. Whether a company is liquid enough depends on its ability to meet short-term demands for cash. Analysts frequently use two balance sheet ratios to throw light on this question: the current ratio and the quick ratio.

The current ratio is the ratio of total current assets to total current liabilities. Looking back at Exhibit 15–1, we see that Alpha Company's current ratio at the end of 19x2 was:

$$\frac{\text{Current assets}}{\text{Current liabilities}} = \frac{\$58,300}{\$24,200} = 2.41$$

Since the comparable ratio at the beginning of the year was $50,100/$13,200 = 3.80, the company's activities during the year obviously caused a substantial weakening in its current position.

A high current ratio isn't an unmixed blessing. It shows that the company is financing a large proportion of its current assets from long-term sources—long-term debt and owners' equity. This provides a cushion or margin of safety against possible short-term downswings in the company's business. This reduces financial risk but it is also costly. As we pointed out earlier, short-term credit is likely to be cheaper than long-term credit, and a high current ratio means the company is either unable or unwilling to use this cheaper credit as extensively as a company with a low ratio.

One shortcoming of the current ratio is that it can be controlled by management. We'll illustrate this by using Alpha Company's working-capital data as of December 31, 19x1 and 19x2—as they appeared in Exhibit 15–1:

	December 31	
	19x1	19x2
Current assets	$50,100	$58,300
Current liabilities	13,200	24,200
Working capital	$36,900	$34,100
Current ratio	3.80	2.41

While the working capital fell by $2,800 ($36,900 − $34,100), or 7.6 percent, the current ratio decreased by almost five times that much, 36.6 percent [(3.80 − 2.41)/3.80].

Management may prefer that analysts not be confronted with

this downward movement. Since $12,500 of Alpha's current liabilities were scheduled to be paid early the following month anyway, management could have ordered these payments to be made during the third week of December. As a result, both current assets and current liabilities would have been reduced by $12,500, bringing the current ratio up to 3.91 ($45,800/$11,700). Although the absolute decrease in working capital would have remained $2,800, the increase in the current ratio from 3.80 to 3.91 would have implied that Alpha was relatively more liquid on December 31 than it had been one year earlier.

A second defect of the current ratio is that its level depends on the method used to measure inventories. Other things being equal, a company using FIFO or average costing will have a higher current ratio after purchase prices have been rising than a company measuring inventories on a LIFO basis. Fortunately, inventory-replacement-cost data are now available for many companies, and these data give the analyst the raw materials to make adjustments to eliminate this source of noncomparability.

A third shortcoming of the current ratio is that it conveys no information on the *composition* of the current assets. Clearly, a dollar of cash or even of accounts receivable is more readily available to meet obligations than a dollar of most kinds of inventory. A measure designed to overcome this defect is the *quick ratio* (or *acid-test ratio*). This is the ratio of cash, short-term marketable securities, and short-term receivables to current liabilities. This ratio for Alpha was as follows at the end of 19x2:

$$\frac{\text{Quick assets}}{\text{Current liabilities}} = \frac{\$2,600 + \$19,800}{\$24,200} = 0.93$$

This represented a sharp decline from the previous year's value of ($4,300 + $17,100)/$13,200 = 1.62, reflecting the large increase in inventory and current notes payable. This shift might be regarded as a cause for some concern.

Funds-flow analysis

The main defect of all the balance sheet ratios is that they represent static relationships. Very few companies have enough cash or liquid assets at the beginning of the year to cover all the payments they will have to make during the year. Nor should they, because this would tie up the company's funds unnecessarily. Instead, they rely on the cash coming in during the year to cover most of their cash obligations.

For this reason, the best guarantee that a company will be able to pay its bills when they come due is an ample excess of cash receipts from operations over cash disbursements required by operations. Whether Alpha's current ratio of 2.41 or its quick ratio of 0.93 represented an adequate margin of safety depended on the variability of the cash-flow stream, the ability to renew or replace its existing short-term obligations with other short-term obligations, and the ability to reduce the amount of its current assets without impairing its operating performance.

Management uses a *cash budget* to determine whether the anticipated cash receipts from operations are likely to be adequate to meet the company's needs for cash during the coming period, and we'll discuss cash budgets in Chapter 20. Outside investors have no access to the cash budget, however, and must try to approximate it by other means. The handiest tool for this purpose is the statement of changes in financial position (funds statement).

Alpha's funds statement for 19x2, prepared by the methods described in Chapter 13, is presented in Exhibit 15–7. Since this company had no deferred taxes and no reported nonoperating gains and losses, funds from operations were the total of net income and depreciation. If this continued at the same level in 19x3, it wouldn't be big enough to cover dividends and plant and equipment expenditures at the 19x2 level. The analyst would have to estimate (1) how large the company's capital expenditures would be in 19x3 and (2) whether other sources of funds would be available in 19x3 to meet those needs.

The funds statement, of course, isn't a cash-flow statement, but it may serve the same purpose. Some changes in short-term receiva-

EXHIBIT 15–7

ALPHA COMPANY
Statement of Changes in Financial Position
For the Year Ended December 31, 19x2

Sources of funds:		
From operations:		
Net income		$ 6,460
Depreciation		2,500
Total from operations		8,960
From sale of common stock		3,700
From sale of plant assets		500
Total sources of funds		13,160
Uses of funds:		
To retire long-term debt	$5,700	
To pay dividends	2,860	
To purchase plant assets	7,400	
Total uses of funds		15,960
Decrease in working capital		$ 2,800

bles and payables are temporary, and, in the absence of growth, increases in one period will be offset by decreases in the next period. If the company's growth rate is rapid, however, the analyst will have to make explicit forecasts of the effect of this growth on the company's cash flows.

Coverage ratios

Although funds-flow statements and cash-flow statements are probably the most valuable single basis for judging debt-paying ability, *coverage ratios* are also widely used for this purpose. Like the funds statement, a coverage ratio deals with *dynamics,* measuring a relationship between two sets of *flows.* The basic coverage ratio is the *times-charges-earned ratio,* the ratio of income before interest and taxes to interest and preferred dividend requirements. On this basis, the Alpha ratio for 19x2 was:

$$\frac{\text{Income before interest and taxes}}{\text{Interest} + \text{Preferred dividends}} = \frac{\$13,160}{\$3,060} = 4.3$$

In other words, the company's earnings could shrink to 23 percent (1.0/4.3) of their 19x2 size and still be adequate to cover the interest and preferred dividend requirements.[5]

The times-charges-earned ratio is obviously incomplete. Interest and preferred-dividend payments aren't the only payments the company is committed to make on a continuing basis. A company's fixed obligations also include such items as property taxes, rentals, scheduled retirements of maturing debt, and even management salaries and other operating costs that wouldn't shrink quickly in the face of a reduction in the company's operating volume. A better ratio therefore is a ratio of the cash flow available to cover fixed-cash payments of all kinds. This is the *fixed-charges ratio:*

$$\text{Fixed-charges ratio} = \frac{\text{Cash flow before fixed charges}}{\text{Total fixed charges}}$$

To calculate the (numerator) amount of cash flow available, we must identify the fixed costs we subtracted in calculating the cash flow from operations and add them back. The (denominator) total fixed charges consist of both the fixed operating cash payments

---

[5] Preferred dividends are not deductible from revenues in computing taxable income. Therefore, the amount entered in the coverage ratio formula ought to be the *pretax* amounts necessary to provide for preferred dividends. This added refinement can be left for more advanced texts on the grounds that it will be important only if the coverage ratio is very low.

and other fixed cash payments (such as interest and preferred dividends):

$$\frac{\text{Cash flow from operations} + \text{Fixed operating cash payments}}{\text{Fixed operating cash payments} + \text{Other fixed cash payments}}$$

Outsiders don't have full access to the amounts entering into the calculation of this ratio, but they have enough information to approximate it. We'll return to this idea in Chapter 20 in which we discuss a technique known as *break-even analysis*.

No matter which coverage ratio is used, however, it has to be examined in conjunction with some measure of *volatility*—that is, the amplitude of fluctuations in annual earnings or operating cash flows before taxes and interest. Presumably, the higher the earnings volatility, the higher the coverage ratio should be.

MEASURES OF EFFICIENCY

As we pointed out earlier, a company's profitability depends on the profit margin on sales *and* on the amount of assets required to support a given sales volume. The main danger in focusing profitability analysis on revenue-based income or expense ratios is that they don't measure economic efficiency in any absolute sense. Businesses such as grocery chains and meat-packing companies operate with exceptionally narrow margins on sales and rely on a large sales volume to cover operating expenses and yield a satisfactory return on investment. Others, such as high-fashion clothing shops and yacht manufacturers, take the opposite tack and operate with low volume and high markups.

The solution to this problem is to supplement the profit-margin ratios with *asset-turnover ratios.* We'll take a brief look at three of these:

1. Total-asset turnover.
2. Receivables turnover, or collection period.
3. Inventory turnover.

Total-asset turnover

The principal turnover ratio is the ratio of total sales to total assets. Using year-end total assets as the base, this ratio for Alpha in 19x2 was:

$$\frac{\text{Sales revenue}}{\text{Total assets}} = \frac{\$105,460}{\$89,400} = 1.18$$

In other words, $1 of assets was required to support every $1.18 of sales.

Once again, the main use of this kind of ratio is to identify ways in which the company is departing from its own previous operating pattern or from that of its competitors. Turnover and percentage-of-sales ratios must be examined together, in parallel—the significance of a change in one can be appraised only if movements in the other are known.

The main shortcoming of these ratios is that they are sensitive to variations in asset-measurement and revenue-recognition practices. We've said enough about these in general to make repetition here unnecessary, but if all the accounting policy differences between two companies run in the same direction—that is, one company's policies all lead to higher asset figures than the other's—the asset-turnover ratios may be very difficult to compare.

The significance of total-asset turnover lies in the following relationship. A company invests in assets to produce sales revenue, and sales revenue in turn generates income. All told, a company invests in assets to be able to earn income. This relationship can be depicted as follows:

Asset turnover		Profit margin		Return on assets
$\dfrac{\text{Sales revenue}}{\text{Total assets}}$	$\times$	$\dfrac{\text{Adjusted income}}{\text{Sales revenue}}$	$=$	$\dfrac{\text{Adjusted income}}{\text{Total assets}}$
$\dfrac{\$105,460}{\$\ 89,400}$		$\dfrac{\$\ 7,960}{\$105,460}$		$\dfrac{\$\ 7,960}{\$89,400}$
1.18		7.55%		8.9%

Although the three ratios were calculated individually, it is readily apparent that having computed any two of these ratios, the third can be determined very easily. The significant implication, however, is that to maximize return on assets, a company must try to maximize its asset turnover while holding its profit margin constant or maximize its profit margin while holding its asset turnover constant.

Receivables turnover and the collection period

The efficiency of individual kinds of assets may be easier to appraise than overall efficiency. Again, we use turnover ratios to measure efficiency. For example, the *receivables-turnover ratio* is usually calculated as the ratio of annual sales revenues to accounts receivable on some date. Based on 19x2 year-end receivables balances, this ratio for Alpha was:

$$\frac{\text{Sales revenues}}{\text{Receivables}} = \frac{\$105,460}{\$19,800} = 5.3$$

This ratio implies that the company's receivables "turned over" or went through the cycle of collection and regeneration 5.3 times during the year.

A related and perhaps more easily understood statistic is the *collection period*—the number of days' sales in accounts receivable. On the basis of a 360-day year, ($105,460 ÷ 360 =) $292.94 is the average daily sales. Dividing the accounts-receivable balance by this amount produces $19,800 ÷ $292.94 = 68, the number of days' sales in accounts receivable. This can also be calculated by dividing the number of days by the receivables-turnover ratio: 360/5.3 = 68 days.

These ratios are regarded as indicators of (1) the liquidity of the receivables, (2) the quality of the receivables, and (3) management's credit-granting policies. A low turnover ratio—that is, a long collection period—means that in the normal course of business, receivables are turned into cash somewhat slowly. A collection period that is long relative to the normal credit period in the industry indicates either that the company is using a liberal credit policy to stimulate sales or that the receivables are of low quality, with many customers failing to pay their bills on time. If Alpha's terms of sale call for payment within 30 days, for example, its 68-day collection period would be regarded as quite long.

Neither ratio is very precise. The year-end receivables may be lower than their average for the year; sales revenues may include revenues from cash sales. An aging of the receivables would give a much better indication of the quality of those receivables; a weighted average of the collection times during the year would be more indicative of the collection period. This means that once again the emphasis must be less on the absolute size of the ratio than on trends and intercompany comparisons.

A high turnover of receivables may not always be the most efficient policy for a company. It may be the consequence of a tight credit policy and a vigorous collection program that unduly restricts the volume of sales. A loosening of credit standards will often increase receivables by a larger percentage than the increase in sales, but the increase in profit may be considerably higher than the company's desired rate of return on the added investment.

Inventory turnover

Another ratio similar in purpose to the receivables-turnover ratio is the *inventory-turnover ratio.* Inventory and revenue accounting data are not precisely comparable: The former are on a cost basis, while the latter represent selling prices. Strictly speaking, therefore, the number of days' inventory on hand can be calculated only if the cost of goods sold is known, in which case the ratio is cost of goods sold per day divided by inventory. The same purpose can be served by a sales/inventory ratio, however, and inventory turnover is often calculated on this basis.

Fortunately, we have Alpha's cost of goods sold for 19x2. Based on the year-end inventory, the 19x2 inventory-turnover ratio for Alpha was:

$$\frac{\text{Cost of goods sold}}{\text{Inventories}} = \frac{\$57{,}700}{\$35{,}900} = 1.61$$

The number of days' inventory on hand therefore was 360/1.61= 224 days.

A low ratio is indicative of slow-moving inventory, and a ratio that is falling or lower than competitors' or both is a sign of potential danger. On the other hand, a company may deliberately carry large inventories to reduce the loss of sales caused by inadequate stocks and to avail itself of economies of large purchase or production lots. Nevertheless, a falling ratio is presumptive evidence of a decline in liquidity, high carrying costs, and potential future losses from obsolescence.

Inventory-turnover ratios are subject to the same defects as receivables-turnover ratios. They say little about the quality of the year-end inventory mix, nor do they reflect seasonal variations in sales and inventories. Probably even more important, however, are the effects of the company's inventory-measurement methods. During and after a period of generally rising prices, for example, LIFO inventories will have higher turnover ratios than FIFO inventories. When replacement-cost data are available, they can be substituted for the historical-cost amounts to make the ratios more comparable over time and among companies.

SUMMARY

Outside financial analysts use the data in corporate financial statements to help them predict corporations' future earnings (profitability analysis) and debt-paying ability (solvency analysis). Various ratios are calculated for these purposes. Other ratios indicating the efficiency of asset utilization are related both to profitability analysis and to solvency analysis. A representative set of ratios in each of these three categories is listed in Exhibit 15–8.

The validity of these kinds of analysis is conditioned not only

EXHIBIT 15–8. Selected Financial Ratios

Profitability

Profit-margin ratio
$$\frac{\text{Net income}}{\text{Total revenue}}$$

Earnings per common share
$$\frac{\text{Net income} - \text{Preferred dividends}}{\text{No. of common shares outstanding}}$$

Return on common equity
$$\frac{\text{Net income} - \text{Preferred dividends}}{\text{Common equity}}$$

Return on assets
$$\frac{\text{Adjusted net income}}{\text{Total assets}} \quad \text{or} \quad \left(\frac{\text{Sales}}{\text{Assets}} \times \frac{\text{Income}}{\text{Sales}}\right)$$

Payout ratio
$$\frac{\text{Common dividends}}{\text{Income applicable to common shareholders}}$$

Price/earnings ratio
$$\frac{\text{Market price per common share}}{\text{Earnings per common share}}$$

Debt-Paying Ability and Risk

Current ratio
$$\frac{\text{Current assets}}{\text{Current liabilities}}$$

Quick ratio
$$\frac{\text{Cash} + \text{Marketable securities} + \text{Receivables}}{\text{Current liabilities}}$$

Debt/equity ratio
$$\frac{\text{Total liabilities}}{\text{Total owners' equity}}$$

Long-term-debt ratio
$$\frac{\text{Long-term debt}}{\text{Total owners' equity}}$$

Times-charges-earned
$$\frac{\text{Net income before interest} + \text{Taxes}}{\text{Interest} + \text{Preferred dividends}}$$

Fixed-charges ratio
$$\frac{\text{Cash flow before fixed charges}}{\text{Total fixed charges}}$$

Efficiency

Accounts-receivable turnover
$$\frac{\text{Sales revenues}}{\text{Receivables}}$$

Inventory turnover
$$\frac{\text{Cost of goods sold}}{\text{Inventories}}$$

Total-asset turnover
$$\frac{\text{Sales revenues}}{\text{Total assets}}$$

by the comparability of past and future but also by the quality of the underlying data. The measurement methods used in preparing company financial statements have great effects on the ratios discussed in this chapter, and these effects must be considered when the ratios are interpreted.

While financial statements provide data and information in absolute-number terms, ratios enable analysts to obtain insights in relative terms as well. Although ratios have therefore become the most popular means of analyzing financial statements, their role is in fact limited to *identifying* critical aspects of a company's financial results and nothing more. Ratios deal with the issues of what and how; they do not address the overriding question of why. Ratios direct the analyst to the areas that may require investigation; they do not themselves offer answers. Ratios point out symptoms, sometimes even a series of symptoms; they say nothing about underlying causes.

KEY TERMS

Collection period	Payout ratio
Coverage ratios	Price/earnings ratio
Current ratio	Profit-margin ratio
Debt/equity ratio	Quality of earnings
Earnings per share	Quick ratio
Fixed-charges ratio	Receivables turnover
Inventory turnover	Return on assets
Leverage	Return on common equity
Long-term-debt ratio	Retention ratio
Market-value ratio	Sustainable-growth ratio
Operating ratio	Times-charges-earned ratio

INDEPENDENT STUDY PROBLEMS (Solutions in Appendix B)

1. Calculating return on equity. Barnes Company had net income after taxes of $106 million for 19x4, $111.3 million for 19x5, and $109.1 million for 19x6. Preferred dividends were $10 million in each year. The shareholders' equity section of the company's balance sheets during this period showed the following:

	12/31/x3	12/31/x4	12/31/x5	12/31/x6
Preferred stock	$ 170,000,000	$ 170,000,000	$ 170,000,000	$ 170,000,000
Common stock, $1 par	50,000,000	50,000,000	52,000,000	52,000,000
Additional paid-in capital	200,000,000	200,000,000	238,000,000	238,000,000
Retained earnings	580,000,000	626,000,000	677,300,000	724,400,000
Total	$1,000,000,000	$1,046,000,000	$1,137,300,000	$1,184,400,000

a. Compute the earnings per common share in 19x4, 19x5, and 19x6, basing your calculations on the number of shares outstanding at the end of the year.
b. Compute the book value per common share at each balance sheet date.
c. Compute the return on common equity for 19x4, 19x5, and 19x6. In each case, base your calculations on average common equity for the year.

2.   Effect of transactions on ratios.   A company has just sold one of its buildings at a price equal to its book value and has used the proceeds from the sale to retire long-term bonds payable. The price paid to retire the bonds was equal to the amount at which they were shown on the balance sheet. Upon selling the building, the company entered into a lease with the new owner.

a. If the new lease is treated as an operating lease, not requiring lease capitalization, how will this series of transactions affect:
 1.   The debt/equity ratio?
 2.   The current ratio?
 3.   The asset-turnover ratio?
b. If the new lease is treated as a repurchase of the property (requiring lease capitalization), how will this series of transactions affect these three ratios?

3.   Effect of leverage.   The following data have been taken from the financial statements of a manufacturing company:

Total assets	$100,000
Interest expense	$ 2,000
Tax rate	45%
Return on common equity	7.2%
Debt/equity ratio	0.25

The company had no preferred stock outstanding.

a. Calculate the overall rate of profitability (return on assets).
b. Did the company use leverage successfully?

EXERCISES AND PROBLEMS

4.   Effects of transactions on selected ratios.   Casey Company has a current ratio of 3.0, a quick ratio of 1.5, a receivables turnover of 6.1, and an inventory turnover of 4.5. How will each of the transactions listed here affect these ratios?

a. Purchase of merchandise for cash.
b. Purchase of merchandise on credit.
c. Sale of a marketable security at cost (that is, at zero gain or loss).
d. Sale of merchandise at a profit for cash.

5.   Using ratios: missing amounts.   In each of the three independent cases in the table, determine the missing amounts.

	I	II	III
Owners' equity (all "common")	$104,000	F	K
Total-asset turnover	A	6.5	L
Return on common equity	0.25	0.3	M
Return on assets	B	G	0.35
Profit-margin ratio	0.05	H	N
Debt/equity ratio	0.6	I	0.37
Sales	C	J	$600,000
Total assets	D	$120,000	P
Net income	E	$ 24,000	$ 90,000

6. Using ratios to calculate unknowns. For each of the following three independent cases, use the data provided to determine the unknown quantity:

a. What is the cash balance:

Profit margin ratio	8%	Number of current assets	3
Accounts receivables turnover	10	Current ratio	2.5
Gross margin/sales ratio	22%	Net income	$40,000
Inventory turnover	13	Current liabilities	$50,000

b. What is the profit-margin ratio?

Book value per share	$1.50	Owners' equity	$75,000
Earnings per share	$0.40	Total liabilities	$50,000
Total-asset turnover	8		

c. What is the total of the liabilities?

Total-asset turnover	12	Dividend yield ratio	5%
Price/earnings ratio	8	Debt/equity ratio	0.4
Profit-margin ratio	2%	Cash dividends	$24,000

7. Using ratios to determine balance sheet amounts. The December 31, 19x5, balance sheet of Ratio, Inc., is presented with some omissions. The items listed are the only items in the balance sheet. Amounts indicated by question marks can be calculated from the additional information given.

Assets

Cash	$ 25,000
Accounts receivable (net)	?
Inventory	?
Plant and equipment (net)	294,000
Total assets	$432,000

Liabilities and Stockholders' Equity

Accounts payable (trade)	$?
Income taxes payable (current)	25,000
Long-term debt	?
Common stock	300,000
Retained earnings	?
Total liabilities and stockholders' equity	$?

Additional information:

Current ratio (at year-end) .... 1.5 to 1
Total liabilities divided by total stockholders' equity (at year-end) 0.8
Inventory turnover:
  Based on sales and ending inventory .... 15 times
  Based on cost of goods sold and ending inventory .... 10.5 times
Gross margin for 19x5 .... $315,000

a. Calculate Ratio's trade accounts payable on December 31, 19x5.
b. Calculate retained earnings on December 31, 19x5.
c. Determine the cost of Ratio's inventory on December 31, 19x5.

(AICPA adapted)

8. Leverage exercise.   Company X and Company Y are identical in all
respects except for their capital structure. Company X obtained $1 million
in assets from the issuance of 100,000 shares of common stock. It has no
debt. Company Y obtained $500,000 in assets by issuing 20-year, 8 percent
bonds at their face value; it obtained another $500,000 by issuing 50,000
shares of common stock. Each company had $1 million in sales revenue
and earnings before interest and income taxes (EBIT) of $150,000. The
income tax rate was 50 percent.

a. Calculate earnings per share for each company. Did Company Y use
    leverage successfully?
b. How would your answer change if each company had sales of $350,000
    and EBIT of $60,000?

9. Effects of transactions on ratios.   A company's current ratio was in
excess of 1.0, the times-charges-earned ratio was 3.0, and the ratio of earnings before interest and income taxes to net sales was 0.15. Net income
was positive. Each of the following transactions occurred independently
of the others:

1. Issued common stock in exchange for cash.
2. Sold building for cash at a price in excess of book value.
3. Declared and paid cash dividend on common stock.
4. Paid cash to retire long-term debt.
5. Paid accounts payable 30 days after receipt of merchandise.
6. Issued a long-term note payable in exchange for land.
7. Sold goods costing $10,000 on current account for $15,000.
8. Issued common stock in exchange for outstanding convertible preferred
    stock.
9. Issued common stock in exchange for outstanding convertible bonds.

For each of these transactions, *taken by itself* (all other things unchanged), state whether each of the following ratios will increase, decrease,
or remain the same:

a. Current ratio.
b. Times-charges-earned ratio.
c. Debt/assets ratio.
d. Net income/sales ratio.

10. Leverage exercise. Doud Company has a return on common equity of 12 percent, based on net income of $12,000 (after income taxes). Its debt/owners'-equity ratio is 50 percent and the income tax rate is 40 percent. Interest expense is $4,600 a year.

a. Calculate total assets.
b. Calculate earnings before interest and income taxes (EBIT).
c. Calculate the before-tax rate of return on total assets.
d. Calculate the aftertax rate of return on total assets.
e. Is this company using leverage successfully? Explain.

11. Trend analysis: interpretation of ratios. Analysis of a company's financial statements reveals the following information for three consecutive years:

	19x1	19x2	19x3
Return on common equity	8.1%	9.7%	10.5%
Current ratio	2.5:1	2.7:1	2.6:1
Earnings per share	$1.62	$2.04	$2.31
Times charges earned	10.0	4.2	3.9
Debt/equity ratio	1:5	2:3	9:11

The tax rate was 50 percent in each of these years, and 50,000 shares of common stock were outstanding throughout the entire three-year peiod.

a. Did the company's basic profitability increase during this period? Support your position with figures developed from the information supplied.
b. Did the shareowners' risk increase? Cite figures to support your position.

12. Effects of transactions on ratios. An analyst is interested in the effects of various events on the following four measures of a company's performance:

1. Working capital, $40,000.
2. Current ratio, 3:1.
3. Total debt/equity ratio, 0.6.
4. Return on common equity, 25 percent.

Determine the effect of each of the 10 events listed below on each of the four measures of performance:

a. Declared a $10,000 cash dividend.
b. Declared and distributed a 12 percent common stock dividend to common stockholders: $8 market value, $1 par value per share.
c. Adjustment to record $6,500 estimated customer defaults.
d. Adjustment to record $9,000 expected future warranty claims.
e. Paid the $10,000 cash dividend.
f. Wrote off $4,100 receivables as uncollectible.
g. Paid $5,600 to satisfy warranty claims.
h. Use flow-through method to record investment tax credit.
i. Changed from FIFO to LIFO prior to a period of increasing prices.

j. Changed revenue recognition from point of delivery to completion of production.

Use a matrix consisting of 10 rows (*a* through *j*) and four columns (1 through 4). In each of the 40 cells, place the appropriate letter as follows: *I* = increase, *D* = decrease, *N* = no effect.

13.   Intercompany comparisons of profitability.   Companies A, B, and C are three of the largest merchandising companies in the United States. We have the following data on these companies for a recent year (in $000):

	Company A	Company B	Company C
Rank (by sales) among merchandising firms	26	11	2
Sales revenues	$627,349	$1,293,765	$5,458,824
Assets	120,363	274,603	884,001
Shareholders' equity	43,554	163,317	627,366
Net income	11,477	8,327	55,897
Interest expense	3,994	5,342	13,088

a. Calculate income as a percentage of sales, asset turnover, return on assets, return on equity, and debt/asset ratio for each company. Assume a 50 percent income tax rate.

b. For return on common equity, Company A ranked first, Company B ranked 46th, and Company C ranked 39th among the merchandising companies on the list. Basing your analysis on the financial-statement data alone, prepare an explanation of the difference between the relative sales ranking and the relative return on common equity ranking.

14.   Effect of financing method.   A company needs approximately $1 million in new capital to finance its expansion program. Management is undecided whether to obtain the needed funds from the sale of bonds or from the sale of additional shares of common stock. You have the following information:

1.   Number of shares of stock now outstanding: 300,000.
2.   Current annual earnings after taxes: $1.2 million ($4 a share).
3.   Anticipated increase in earnings (before interest and income taxes) from investment of additional capital: $400,000.
4.   The proposed bond issue would consist of 20-year, 14 percent bonds with a face value of $1 million, to be sold to an insurance company at their face value.
5.   The proposed stock issue would consist of 40,000 shares of common stock, to be sold at a price of $25 a share.
6.   The effective income tax rate is 40 percent.
7.   The company now has no long-term debt.

a. Calculate the anticipated earnings per share under each method of financing.

b. How great an effect is this decision likely to have on the riskiness of investments in the company's common stock?

15. Quality of earnings: effect of inventory method. Alpha Company and Omega Company are both engaged in the smelting and refining of copper. The year 19x8 was a poor year for the copper industry in general, with rates of return on assets clustering mainly between 1 and 2 percent. The following data were taken from the balance sheets of these two companies as of the beginning and end of that year:

	December 31, 19x7	December 31, 19x8
Alpha Company inventories (LIFO)	$ 32,825,000	$ 26,450,000
Omega Company inventories		
(FIFO, lower of cost or market)	77,140,000	63,750,000
Alpha Company total assets	128,448,000	119,856,000
Omega Company total assets	312,660,000	285,918,000

Neither company had any interest-bearing debt at any time during 19x8.

Alpha adopted LIFO 15 years before 19x8, when copper prices were about half the level they had reached at the beginning of 19x8. Its inventories had grown about 10 percent in that period.

The market prices of copper and copper ores were the same on December 31, 19x8, as they had been on January 1, 19x8.

The income statements for the two companies for the year ended December 31, 19x8, were as follows:

	Alpha	Omega
Sales	$95,000,000	$215,000,000
Cost of goods sold	74,300,000	180,000,000
Depreciation	3,700,000	9,000,000
Other expenses	9,000,000	20,000,000
Total expenses	87,000,000	209,000,000
Income before taxes	8,000,000	6,000,000
Income taxes	4,000,000	3,000,000
Net income	$ 4,000,000	$ 3,000,000

a. Using the average of the beginning-of-year and end-of-year figures as the base, calculate each company's return on assets in 19x8.

b. Which of these companies appears to have been more profitable in 19x8? Support your answer with figures insofar as you can and indicate how the differences in the companies' inventory methods influenced your conclusion.

c. How would your answer to part b have differed if the prices of copper and copper ores had been 10 percent lower throughout 19x8 than at the end of 19x8?

16. Evaluating receivables and credit policy. Delta Company and Gamma Company sell similar lines of products. The manager of Delta Company has collected the following statistics:

	Delta	Gamma
Sales, 19x3	$7,000,000	$5,000,000
Estimated customer defaults, 19x3	35,000	50,000
Income before interest and taxes, 19x3	600,000	500,000
Total assets, December 31, 19x3	4,800,000	4,000,000
Accounts receivable, December 31, 19x3	800,000	750,000

The manager wants answers to the following questions. You are expected to answer the questions if possible. If the information provided is not adequate for a satisfactory answer, state the additional information you need and explain how you would use it to answer the question.

a. Which company has the more liberal credit policy?
b. Which company has the more liquid receivables?
c. By how much will Delta's accounts receivable increase during 19x4?
d. Which company is managing its accounts receivable more profitably?

17.   Manipulation of financial ratios.   On December 15, 19x1, the controller of Redwood, Inc., gave the president a copy of an estimated year-end balance sheet for the company, containing the following figures:

Assets

Cash	$ 300,000
Accounts receivable	120,000
Inventories	180,000
Plant and equipment (net)	900,000
Total assets	$1,500,000

Liabilities and Shareowners' Equity

Accounts payable	$ 300,000
Long-term debt	100,000
Common stock	800,000
Retained earnings	300,000
Total liabilities and shareowners' equity	$1,500,000

The president was concerned that the quick ratio was so low and asked the controller to suggest some way of improving this ratio in the two weeks remaining before the end of the year.

a. Calculate the quick ratio.
b. What suggestion probably would be the easiest to implement? Would carrying out this suggestion impose any costs on the company?
c. What action might analysts take that would either neutralize this kind of year-end "window dressing" or make it unnecessary?

18.   Inadequacy of position ratios.   At the beginning of 19x2, Davis Company's current ratio was 3.25, the quick ratio was 1.25, and the ratio of long-term debt to the common shareholders' equity was 0.3. The return on equity in 19x1 was 15 percent. All these ratios were well within the range regarded by financial analysts as satisfactory for this industry.

Davis Company had begun a plant-expansion program in 19x1. To finance the completion of that program in 19x2 and 19x3, the company negotiated an additional long-term loan of $7 million early in 19x2. Market conditions deteriorated during 19x2, however. Sales volume fell from $25 million in 19x1 to $20 million in 19x2, while net income fell from $3 million to $400,000. Davis's cash position deteriorated even more severely, and in December 19x2 it was unable to make its scheduled payments to its creditors.

Davis's income statement for 19x2 and condensed balance sheets for the beginning and end of the year were as follows:

DAVIS COMPANY
Statement of Income
For the Year Ended December 31, 19x2
($ millions)

Sales revenue	$20.00
Expenses:	
Cost of goods sold*	13.7
Selling and administrative expense	4.1
Interest expense	1.5
Income tax expense	0.3
Net income	$ 0.4

* Schedule of cost of goods sold:		
Materials inventory, January 1	$ 2.7	
Purchases of materials	10.8	
Cost of materials available	13.5	
Materials inventory, December 31	4.9	
Cost of materials used	8.6	
Factory labor	5.9	
Factory depreciation	0.5	
Other factory costs	2.3	
Total costs of production	17.3	
Less: Cost of added finished goods inventory	3.6	
Cost of Goods Sold	$13.7	

DAVIS COMPANY
Condensed Balance Sheets
December 31, 19x1 and 19x2
($ millions)

	19x1	*19x2*		*19x1*	*19x2*
Cash	$ 1.0	$ 0.2	Accounts payable	$ 1.0	$ 4.7
Accounts receivable	4.0	6.3	Notes payable	3.0	3.0
Inventory	8.0	13.8	Taxes payable	—	0.3
Net plant and equipment	17.0	20.5	Interest payable	—	0.4
			Long-term debt	6.0	13.0
			Common stock	5.5	5.5
			Add'l paid-in capital	2.5	2.5
			Retained earnings	12.0	11.4
			Total liabilities and		
Total assets	$30.0	$40.8	shareholders' equity	$30.0	$40.8

a. Calculate the current ratio, quick ratio, and long-term debt/equity ratio at the end of 19x2.
b. Prepare an analysis to explain what led to Davis's inability to pay its creditors on schedule in 19x2.
c. Comment on the usefulness of position ratios such as the quick ratio as indicators of short-term bill-paying ability.

19. Comparison of two companies. Here are the income statements and balance sheets of Franklin Company and Morgan Company, taken from their annual reports for the year ended December 31, 19x1:

Income Statement
For the Year 19x1

	Franklin Company	Morgan Company
Sales	$8,000,000	$7,000,000
Cost of goods sold	6,000,000	4,700,000
Selling, general, and administrative expenses ...	1,200,000	1,900,000
Interest on debt	—	70,000
Income before taxes	800,000	330,000
Income taxes	390,000	160,000
Net income	$ 410,000	$ 170,000
Dividends declared	$ 100,000	$ 70,000

Condensed Balance Sheets
As of December 31, 19x1

	Franklin Company	Morgan Company
Assets		
Cash.......................................	$ 300,000	$ 300,000
Accounts receivable	800,000	650,000
Inventory	1,300,000	850,000
Net plant and equipment	2,100,000	1,500,000
Total assets	$4,500,000	$3,300,000
Liabilities and Owners' Equity		
Accounts payable	$ 710,000	$ 400,000
Taxes payable	390,000	160,000
Long-term debt.............................	—	1,400,000
Common stock	2,200,000	800,000
Retained earnings	1,200,000	540,000
Total liabilities and owners' equity	$4,500,000	$3,300,000

On the basis of the available information, which do you consider to be (1) more liquid? (2) more solvent? (3) more profitable? Explain your conclusions.

20. Effect of accounting methods.   Dalton Company two years ago established two subsidiary corporations to develop two new markets. The two companies started with identical sets of assets and no liabilities. Dalton distributed the stock of these two companies to its shareholders, and, thereafter, they operated independently of each other and of Dalton.

One of these companies, Littler, Inc., elected to use the LIFO inventory method, the deferral method of accounting for the investment credit, and accelerated depreciation. The other company, Bigler Enterprises, used FIFO, the flow-through method, and straight-line depreciation. The income tax rate was 50 percent, and ACRS-depreciation was 15 percent in the first year and 22 percent in the second year.

The balance sheets of the two companies at the end of last year, their second year of operation, contained the following information:

	Littler	Bigler
Assets		
Current assets:		
Cash	$ 4,100	$ 3,200
Accounts receivable	7,000	7,000
Inventory	10,000	12,000
Total current assets	21,100	22,200
Plant and equipment	20,000	20,000
Less: Accumulated depreciation	(7,200)	(4,000)
Total assets	$33,900	$38,200
Liabilities and Shareowners' Equity		
Current liabilities:		
Accounts payable	$ 2,500	$ 2,500
Taxes payable	1,000	1,100
Total current liabilities	3,500	3,600
Long-term debt	10,000	10,000
Deferred income taxes	100	1,700
Deferred investment tax credits	1,600	—
Total liabilities	15,200	15,300
Common stock	5,000	5,000
Additional paid-in capital	10,000	10,000
Retained earnings	3,700	7,900
Total liabilities and shareowners' equity	$33,900	$38,200

The two companies' income statements for last year showed the following:

	Littler	Bigler
Sales revenues	$75,000	$75,000
Cost of goods sold	51,000	50,000
Gross margin	24,000	25,000
Selling and administrative expenses*	10,000	8,800
Interest expense	1,000	1,000
Income tax expense	6,300	7,600
Net income	$ 6,700	$ 7,600

* Includes depreciation.

The two companies have had identical sales volumes and have paid identical amounts as dividends each year. Inventory replacement costs have been rising at a rate of about 10 percent a year. Neither company made any capital expenditures last year.

Prepare an analysis comparing the profitability of these two companies, taking into consideration the differences in their accounting policies insofar as you are able.

(Suggested by Charles W. Bastable)

21. Intercompany comparisons: profitability analysis. Anderson, Ltd., and Zoysia, Inc., are incorporated and operate in a country in which generally accepted accounting principles are followed but the income tax rate is only 25 percent. The two companies offer the same general line of products to the same potential customers.

The following data were taken from the 19x1 financial statements of these two companies:

	Anderson	Zoysia
Cash	$ 8,000	$ 24,000
Accounts receivable	17,000	19,200
Inventories	27,200	29,568
Prepaid expenses	2,000	4,000
Property and equipment	100,000	220,000
Accumulated depreciation	(62,400)	(57,152)
Total	$ 91,800	$239,616
Current liabilities	$ 20,000	$ 40,000
Long-term debt—6 percent	40,000	—
Long-term debt—9 percent	—	20,000
Stockholders' equity	31,800	179,616
Total	$ 91,800	$239,616
Sales	$204,000	$460,800
Cost of goods sold	(163,200)	(354,816)
Other expenses	(22,440)	(46,080)
Interest	(2,400)	(1,800)
Income taxes	(3,990)	(14,526)
Net income	$ 11,970	$ 43,578

Anderson's long-term debt was obtained about 10 years earlier. Its low interest rate constituted a subsidy from a state economic development agency. Zoysia's long-term debt also arose about 10 years before 19x1, but it was a straight financial-market transaction, with no government subsidy.

All sales in both companies are on account and there are only minor seasonal variations in sales.

a. Compare the current debt-paying ability of the two firms. To what extent can the inventories be looked upon as a means of paying debts due in 30 days? In 60 days?

b. Compare the profitability of the two firms. What factors account for the difference?

c. Compare the long-term debt-paying ability of the two firms.

MANAGERIAL ACCOUNTING

16

Managerial accounting: Introduction to incremental analysis

Until now, we've been discussing management's perspective with respect to its financial reporting obligations to people outside the management group—that is, *financial accounting*. In this chapter and the seven that follow, we'll examine the processes and means by which a company's accounting staff can help management plan and control the company's activities—that is, *managerial accounting*.

The accounting staff and accounting system play a very important role in control processes. In fact, a company's chief accounting officer usually bears the title of *controller*. We'll begin our discussion of managerial accounting, however, with an examination of the accounting requirements of managerial planning, postponing any discussion of control processes until Chapter 21. Our objective in this chapter is to explain some basic concepts underlying the kinds of information accountants can provide to help management make two kinds of planning decisions: (1) how the company will use its existing capacity; and (2) what prices to publish on regularly offered products.

PLANNING PROCESSES

One of management's most important functions is to decide how to use the resources available to it—which products or services to produce, how and where to produce and market them, and on what terms. These decisions are the essence of managerial *planning*.

Managers make planning decisions in many different ways. In general, however, the decision process is likely to include the elements listed in Exhibit 16–1. The wavy ribbon segments in this diagram represent external inputs to the decision, the ovals identify processes, and the rectangular blocks identify the results of these processes.

Before management can make decisions, it has to understand the organization's goals. The reason is that decisions must be goal-oriented, based on the anticipated effects of management's actions on progress toward the organization's goals. If the goal is to increase profit, then the effects of the decision on profit have to be identified. In a not-for-profit organization, on the other hand, service goals are likely to replace the profit goals we find in profit-seeking businesses, and these should be incorporated in the decision process.

Given a goal or set of goals, decision making begins when someone recognizes the need for a decision. This usually means noticing that an opportunity to obtain or use resources has arisen or that a problem in the company's use of resources needs resolution. This step is represented by the oval in the upper left corner in Exhibit 16–1.

Next, management needs to identify the major alternative actions it might take to resolve the issue. In the simplest situations, only two alternatives need be considered: act or don't act, accept a proposal or reject it. In other situations, management may be able to identify three, four, or even more plausible solutions.

EXHIBIT 16–1.   Elements of a Decision

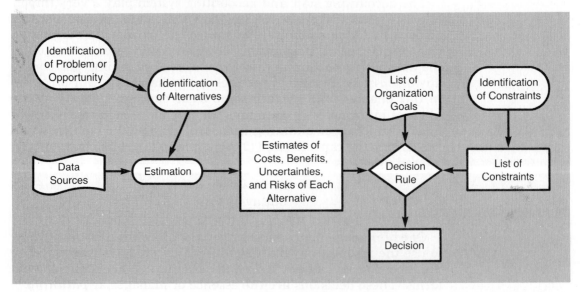

Once the alternatives have been identified, management should estimate the costs and benefits each alternative appears likely to generate, accompanied by a list of the uncertainties in the estimates and the risks each alternative would expose the organization to. Benefits in each case should be measured in units that represent progress toward the organization's goals.

The next step is to identify the constraints, or limits, on management's freedom of action in regard to the decision at hand. For example, materials or labor may be in short supply and environmental pollution must be kept below specified levels. Some constraints apply to all decisions (e.g., a flat prohibition against trade in certain areas); others are particular to the specific decision situation (e.g., only 1,400 service-hours are available this month).

The final step is to choose and apply a method of comparing the alternatives with one another. This is known as a *decision rule* and is represented by the diamond-shaped block in Exhibit 16–1, where all the other elements in the decision come together. A decision rule for a business organization might be: Select the alternative which appears to be most likely to maximize the present value of the company's future cash flows without violating any of the constraints. In the next three sections, we'll describe the concepts underlying an uncomplicated decision rule which can be applied to short-term, capacity-utilization decisions when the outcome of each alternative can be predicted with certainty.

BASIC CONCEPTS FOR RESOURCE-ALLOCATION DECISIONS

Decisions, in the final analysis, hinge on management's perceptions of the costs, benefits, and risks associated with each alternative it has been able to identify. Our objective in this section is to explain how the principal costs and benefits of business activity should be measured for decision-making purposes.

Cash flows

While financial accounting measures costs and benefits on an accrual basis, managerial decision making defines both costs and benefits in terms of cash flows. *Benefits* consist of cash receipts (or reductions in cash outlays); *costs* consist of cash outlays (or reductions in cash receipts).

The reason for this emphasis on cash flows is that in most circumstances cash is the only resource management can use to get productive goods and services and to reward the owners. If the company has no cash and can't get any, it won't be able to meet its payroll or pay its suppliers, no matter how many receivables or how much equpment it has. On the other hand, if cash is coming in, it can be used to buy materials and pay employees. Noncash resource outflows, such as depreciation on existing equipment, reduce net income but they don't reduce management's immediate ability to meet its obligations.

The incremental principle

Each possible course of action available to management will produce future cash flows. Management's choice of one course of action brings with it the cash flows associated with that action, but it keeps the company from experiencing the cash flows associated with other possible actions. In other words, the *effect* of a decision consists of the *differences* between the cash flows associated with the chosen course of action and the cash flows associated with a rejected alternative.

This idea is illustrated in Exhibit 16–2. It is the basis for the *incremental principle,* which states that decisions should be based on perceived differences among the alternatives management is considering. Any difference between the cash flow associated with one course of action and the cash flow associated with an alternative is referred to as a *differential cash flow,* or an *incremental cash flow.* If the incremental cash flow is negative—that is, if the proposal calls for a larger cash outflow or a smaller cash inflow in a particular time period than an alternative—we say it is an *incremental cash outlay* or an *incremental cost.* If the incremental cash flow is positive, we say it is an *incremental cash receipt.*

The algebraic sum of the incremental cash flows associated with a proposed course of action relative to an alternative in any time period is the *incremental net cash flow* in that period. If the incre-

EXHIBIT 16–2.   Cash Flows Attributable to a Proposed Action

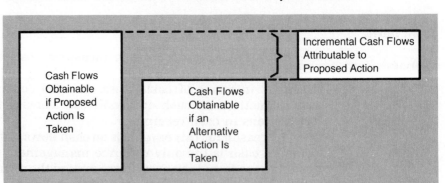

mental receipts exceed the incremental costs in a period, we say that this alternative has an *incremental net cash receipt* or incremental net cash inflow in that period. If the total of the incremental outlays exceeds the total of the incremental receipts, we have an *incremental net cash outlay* or an incremental net cash outflow. Because this terminology sounds awkward, we usually use the terms *incremental profit* and *incremental loss* instead.

TERMINOLOGY

Incremental profit or *incremental loss* in any period is the difference between the algebraic sum of the cash flows associated with a proposed course of action and the algebraic sum of the cash flows associated with an alternative course of action.

Time horizon of the decision

Some decisions affect the cash flows of only one period. We refer to these as *tactical decisions,* and the incremental cash flow can be stated as a single amount—the algebraic difference between the alternatives' net cash flows in the affected period. Single-period estimates of incremental net cash flows can also be used if the sign of the incremental net cash inflow appears likely to be the same in *each* future period.

Other decisions affect the company's future cash flows in such a way that choosing one alternative instead of another is likely to result in an incremental net cash receipt in one or more periods *and* an incremental net cash outlay in one or more other periods. We refer to these as *investment decisions.* For these decisions, both the *timing* and the *amounts* of the cash flows are important. Rather than try to deal with both dimensions of costs and benefits at once, we'll limit our discussion in this chapter to tactical decisions. We'll return to investment decisions in Chapter 19.

Opportunity cost

We defined incremental cost as the negative difference between the cash flow from one alternative and the cash flow from another. The incremental costs associated with a proposal therefore must include any cash *inflows* that will be *lost* if that proposal is accepted. Any such portions of the incremental cost are called the *opportunity cost* of the resources the proposal would divert from another use. It is the value of a forgone opportunity.

For example, Van Horn Company manufactures and sells lawn-mowers. It has a stockpile of 10,000 reels, designed originally for use in manually operated mowers. The marketing manager has proposed that these reels be used in a low-priced power mower for a special promotion by a regional chain of hardware stores. No cash outlay need be made to obtain these reels—the company already owns them—but the reels nevertheless have an incremental cost (an opportunity cost) because Lawntex Company, one of two remaining manufacturers of manually operated mowers, has offered to buy them for $10 each. The incremental cost (and opportunity cost) of the reels therefore is $100,000 ($10 × 10,000):

(1) Cash Flow if Proposal Is Accepted	(2) Cash Flow if Proposal Is Rejected	(3) Incremental Cash Flow (1) − (2)
0	+$100,000	−$100,000

Opportunity cost is a component of incremental cost because *an action which eliminates a cash inflow is equivalent to an action which produces a cash outflow.*

Sunk cost

In our discussion of opportunity cost, we made no mention of the amounts Van Horn paid to obtain the reels. The reason is that management's present decision on the use of the reels cannot affect the cash outlay that was made to obtain them in the first place.

The original cost of the reels is an example of a *sunk cost,* defined as any cash outflow which will be unaffected by the decision to be made. Cash outlays which haven't yet been made may also be sunk costs, if the decision won't affect them. For example, Van Horn Company will pay the plant manager's salary each month whether the marketing manager's proposal is accepted or rejected. This portion of the company's net cash flow will be the same no matter which of these two alternatives is selected. The plant manager's salary therefore is a sunk cost with respect to the marketing manager's proposal and need not be included in the analysis.

Time lags

Time lags between payments for resources and collections from customers can affect management's decisions because they deprive the company of the use of cash during the lags. If the lags are long enough, the decision should be treated as an investment decision and the analysis should be based on the methods we'll outline in Chapter 19. If the time lags are relatively short, however, they generally can be ignored in incremental analysis for tactical decisions. In such cases, incremental cash receipts are assumed to be equal to incremental revenues, and incremental cash outlays are assumed to be equal to the incremental costs of the resources consumed. Incremental profit therefore will approximate the effect of the decision on the company's income before taxes.

SHORT-TERM COST-VOLUME RELATIONSHIPS

Many resource-allocation decisions focus on management's efforts to use existing capacity profitably. Increasing or decreasing the amount of capacity takes time and, in the meantime, management must try to do its best with what it has.

The question in a decision of this kind is whether to increase or decrease the rate of output of a particular product or service within existing capacity limits. For this purpose, management needs to estimate how costs will change when the rate of output increases or decreases.

Variable costs

Every business has at least some subunits (e.g., departments) engaged in *responsive activities*. A responsive activity is any activity imposed on an organizational subunit by activities outside that subunit. Manufacturing is a responsive activity, meeting demands arising from marketing activities. Preparing employee payrolls is a responsive activity, meeting demands arising from all the company's activities.

Some costs of responsive activities go up or down in total almost automatically in response to small changes in operating volume. Operating volume, or level of activity, is the rate at which resources are used (pounds of materials per hour) or at which goods or services are produced (meals served per week). Any cost that must be increased in total if the company is to achieve a small increase in the level of activity is a *variable cost.*

The diagrams in Exhibit 16–3 represent the behavior of a cost element—operating supplies, in this case—which is *proportionally* variable with volume. Each dot in the left-hand diagram stands for the cost and volume recorded in one specific month in the past, adjusted for changes in the prices the company paid to obtain these supplies. The line which seems to fit the pattern of the relationship described by the dots indicates the cost of the operating supplies

EXHIBIT 16–3. Proportionally Variable Cost

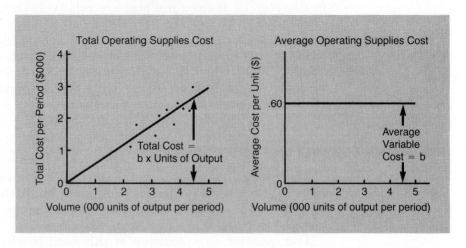

this company might be expected to use at each level of activity, on the average, if future conditions are like those of the past.

The line fitted to the observations plotted in Exhibit 16–3 is described by the equation:

$$C = bV$$

in which C = total cost per month, V = the volume of activity, measured by units of output, and b = the rate of variable cost per unit of output. In this case, average variable cost is constant (and equal to b) per unit of output throughout the entire volume range, as shown in the right-hand diagram in Exhibit 16–3.

Fixed costs: Responsive activities

Costs that don't change in total as a necessary result of small changes in volume are known as *fixed costs*. Some of these are the fixed costs of responsive activities, also known as *capacity costs*. They are the costs of the resources management uses to provide or maintain current operating capacity. The horizontal line in the left-hand panel of Exhibit 16–4, for example, represents the relationship between the total cost of property taxes each month and the volume of activity. The line of relationship is given by the formula:

$$C = a$$

in which a represents the total cost of property taxes each month. Since the total depreciation cost doesn't vary as a result of output

EXHIBIT 16–4. Fixed Cost

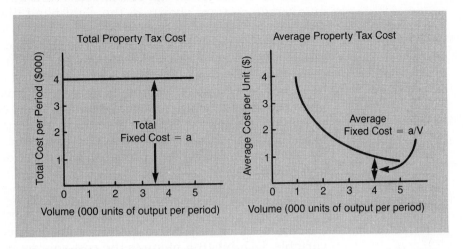

changes, the cost per unit of output decreases as the rate of output per period increases. At any output (V), the average cost is a/V. This is shown in the right-hand panel of Exhibit 16–4.

Some capacity costs are affected by variations in volume—but in large steps rather than gradually. These are called *stepped costs*. For example, the left-hand diagram in Exhibit 16–5 shows the estimated total cost of supervisory time in one of Van Horn's factory departments. In this case, the basic supervisory force can handle all volumes up to 2,500 units of output a month. For sustained operations above this level, additional supervisory time must be provided,

EXHIBIT 16–5. Stepped Fixed Cost

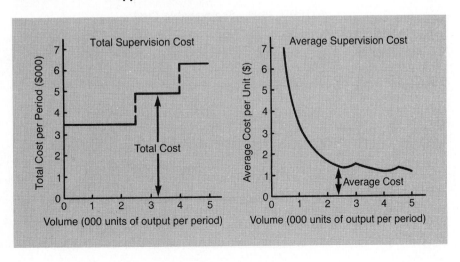

and the total cost jumps up. The effects of this kind of cost behavior on average cost are shown in the right-hand diagram in Exhibit 16–5.

Whether stepped costs are likely to be classified as fixed or variable costs depends on the width of the steps. In our illustration, only three broad steps are identified and supervision costs are likely to be classified as fixed. If volume is likely to fluctuate between 2,500 and 4,000 units a month, for example, supervisory costs are expected to remain constant at $4,900 a month. In contrast, if the total cost of another cost element moves up a step each time volume increases by 500 units, management probably will think of that element as a variable cost.

Semivariable costs

Some costs of responsive activities are partly fixed and partly variable. Exhibit 16–6 pictures the cost-volume relationship of one of these costs. The diagram at the left shows that power consumption increases as volume rises, but not in proportion to the change in volume. The explanation is that some uses of power—lighting, for example—do not respond to variations in volume. This kind of cost can be described by an equation which combines elements from the two equations cited earlier:

$$C = a + bV$$

in which both a and b are positive. Dividing both sides by V, we get:

$$\text{Average cost} = \frac{C}{V} = \frac{a}{V} + b$$

EXHIBIT 16–6.   Semivariable Cost

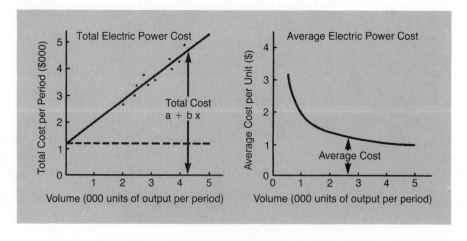

As output (V) increases, a/V decreases and so does average cost per unit (C/V).

The linearity assumption

The total-cost lines in Exhibits 16–3, 16–4, and 16–6 were drawn as straight lines, with no discontinuities or changes in slope. In most cases, these lines should be drawn to cover only part of the total volume range from zero to capacity, the portion known as the *relevant range* or the *customary range*. The lines should be cut off before they extend to low volumes, both because the company probably has had little or no experience with these low volumes and because management would probably change the amount of its fixed costs if volume actually were to fall this low. (Discretionary activities such as window washing are likely to be curtailed, fewer lights would be used, and so on.) Extending the lines to the right of the customary range is equally hazardous because the shape of the lines in that zone is likely to depend on such factors as the methods management uses (overtime, subcontracting, etc.) and the amount of time it has to gear up to operate at those volumes.

Even though the cost lines aren't wholly reliable outside the customary range, in most cases a straight line is a reasonable representation of cost variability within this portion of the range. This being the case, it does no harm to extend the lines beyond the confines of the customary range as long as we don't interpret the extensions literally. Extending the lines in this way does have the positive advantage of allowing us to describe the relationships within the customary range in simple, linear equations, as we have done in this section.

Fixed costs: Programmed activities

Every business organization has a second group of fixed costs, fundamentally different from capacity costs relating to responsive activities. These are the costs of *programmed activities,* undertaken at management's initiative to meet objectives other than demands for service imposed on the business from outside. Programmed activities determine the company's scope and direction. Some of them are *innovative,* designed to enable the company to change the way it operates—by developing new products, acquiring other companies, improving operating methods, and so forth. Others are *promotional,* intended to stimulate demands for the company's goods and services; most selling activities fall in this category.

The costs of programmed activities are generally agreed upon at the beginning of each planning period. They may be changed during the period, but any such changes are not *necessitated* by changes in volume. In other words, they are discretionary fixed costs. Because these costs don't respond to changes in volume, average programmed cost per unit will be low if volume turns out to be high and high if volume is low.

Some organization units engaged in programmed activities perform responsive activities as well. For example, sales branch offices may be responsible both for performing the clerical operations necessary to process customer orders and for delivering products to the customers. If a significant portion of the costs of the responsive activities in a unit of this sort appears likely to be variable, an effort to estimate the rate of variability may be useful.

Estimating cost variability

Estimating the rate at which costs vary with volume isn't easy. For one thing, it isn't always clear how volume should be measured. If a department produces only one kind of product or service, volume can be measured by the number of units produced. In the more typical multiproduct situation, however, the units produced are so dissimilar that physical output totals are meaningless—one automobile plus one bicycle doesn't add up to two of anything. The usual solution is to use some measure of input, such as the number of labor-hours or machine-hours.

Having chosen a measure of volume, we still have to develop a method of estimating the rate at which costs change in response to changes in volume. Most analysts prefer to use the statistical method known as *least-squares regression analysis.* This approach uses a set of equations to position a line of relationship on a diagram like the left-hand diagram in Exhibit 16–6. This line, known as a *regression* line, is drawn in such a way that the dots in the diagram are closer to this line than to any other that might be drawn in its place.[1]

A simpler approach is to rely on the judgment of experienced personnel. This approach, known as the *inspection-of-accounts* method, requires someone to classify each kind of cost as wholly fixed, wholly variable, or a mixture of the two. The analyst then estimates the monthly amount for each fixed-cost element and the average unit cost for each proportionally variable element.

The inspection-of-accounts method is less scientific than regression analysis, but it can be used when historical data are inadequate for some reason. It should also be used to check the results of regres-

---

[1] The calculation of a linear regression line by the least-squares method is outlined in the appendix to this chapter.

sion analysis; a little personal judgment may be necessary to find the truth.

USING COST-VARIABILITY DATA TO ESTIMATE INCREMENTAL COST

Estimates of short-term relationships between costs and volume are useful in a wide range of decision situations. A study of two such situations will help illustrate this point: (1) pricing additional business, and (2) discontinuing a product. Examination of these problems will also show that all the relevant considerations can't always be quantified, so that accounting data alone don't determine what the decision should be.

Pricing additional business

Most companies do most of their business with customers who buy the products and services that are the company's regular stock in trade. Opportunities sometimes arise, however, to fill special orders for products that aren't part of the regular line. For example, the purchasing agent of Wilde Company, which operates a chain of automotive and hardware stores, asked Van Horn's sales manager whether Van Horn would be interested in manufacturing 2,000 power mowers to be sold by Wilde under its own brand name, Wilcut. Van Horn could have this order at a price of $48 a unit. Production capacity was easily adequate to handle this order, and the marketing manager saw no reason why sales of Wilcut mowers would affect sales of Van Horn's regular mowers. Van Horn's controller agreed to estimate the cost of filling this special order.

Starting with existing cost estimates for Van Horn's Zephyr mower, which was very similar to the Wilcut mower, the controller estimated that the Wilcut mowers would have to be sold to Wilde at a price of $55.80 if they were to generate a normal profit margin. The calculation was as follows:

Manufacturing cost:	
Materials	$25.80
Labor	7.00
Other	9.35
Total manufacturing cost	42.15
Selling expense	1.45
Administrative expense	2.90
Total cost	46.50
Desired profit margin (20 percent)	9.30
Target price	$55.80

The manufacturing vice president was eager to have the company accept this order. Without it, some factory employees would have to go on a reduced workweek, which would affect employee morale and imperil the success of the company's efforts to increase labor productivity. The manufacturing vice president therefore prepared an alternative cost estimate, reflected in the following estimate of incremental net cash flow:

	Per Unit	Total	
Incremental sales revenues	$48.00		$96,000
Incremental costs:			
Incremental variable costs:			
Variable materials..................	25.80	$51,600	
Variable labor	7.00	14,000	
Other variable factory costs	5.00	10,000	
Variable administrative costs	0.20	400	
Incremental variable cost	38.00	76,000	
Incremental fixed factory costs		2,000	
Total incremental costs........			78,000
Incremental net cash receipts			$18,000

In this analysis, the manufacturing vice president accepted the original estimates of labor and materials costs as fully incremental costs because they represented employee salaries and materials-purchase costs that would not be incurred if the proposal were rejected.

The variable portions of other factory costs also were fully incremental, and these were estimated at $5 a unit. Fixed factory costs were mostly sunk, however, and the manufacturing vice president excluded these from the analysis. The idea was to include only those fixed factory costs likely to be added to the total by acceptance of the order. The only likely increment here seemed to be a slight increase in supervisory costs, adding up to about $2,000 for the contract as a whole. Fixed costs, in other words, can be incremental but not necessarily in the proportions implied by the average fixed cost per unit.

The selling and administrative expense figures in the original estimates were based on average cost/revenue ratios for the company as a whole. The only selling and administrative costs to be affected by the acceptance of this order were clerical costs in the accounting department, which seemed likely to go up by about 20 cents for each additional unit manufactured and sold. This increment is listed on the fourth line of the table of incremental variable costs.

These estimates are all presented as definite amounts, with no allowances for uncertainty or errors of estimation. We noted in Exhibit 16–1 that decision making calls for estimates of the uncertainties and risks associated with each potential course of action. In this case, the proposal didn't appear likely to expose the company to any special risks, but the estimates of cash flows were far from certain. The main uncertainties centered on the accuracy of the manufacturing vice president's assumption that Wilcut sales wouldn't affect revenues from Van Horn's other models. The president, for example, was afraid that the company's regular customers, mostly small independent dealers, would regard this as unfair to them and might shift to competitors' lines. The controller suggested that the low price might lead competitors to retaliate by price cutting on models that competed directly with Van Horn's own branded models. Another worry was that if the sales force were encouraged to cut the price this time, it would want to do so again and again. This would undermine the company's entire pricing structure.

The sales manager had a different perspective, pointing out that Van Horn had been losing market share in recent years by not participating in the rapidly growing portion of total mower sales handled by mail-order houses and other large retail distributors. This initial order would give the company valuable experience in dealing in this market and might lay the groundwork for a substantial penetration of the market in the future.

How this argument was resolved is unimportant here, but it does illustrate two things. First, a purely quantitative analysis is unlikely to resolve the issues in decision making involving major policy questions. Second, the arguments summarized represent the typical range of managerial reactions to the use of incremental-cost data. How the issues are resolved in any case will depend on management's considered judgment on the validity of the arguments raised in this illustration.[2]

Dropping an unprofitable product

Van Horn's management also faced another problem. Its Estate power mower, with a volume of about 5,000 units a year, was selling at a price that was $4.10 less than the average cost assigned to it. Van Horn's president asked the controller to prepare an estimate of the financial impact of discontinuing sales of the Estate mower.

The controller's first step was to ask the sales manager whether

---

[2] Although managers often rely on their own judgment to resolve issues arising from the uncertainties surrounding their estimates of incremental costs and benefits, formal techniques of varying levels of complexity and sophistication are widely available and highly useful for dealing with many of these issues. See, for example, D. Warner North, "A Tutorial Introduction to Decision Theory," in *Accounting for Managerial Decision Making,* 2d ed., ed. Don T. DeCoster, Kavasseri V. Ramanathan, and Gary L. Sundem (Los Angeles: Melville Publishing Co., 1978), pp. 15–36; or Robert S. Kaplan, *Advanced Management Accounting* (Englewood Cliffs, N.J.: Prentice-Hall, 1982), pp. 181–204.

withdrawal of the Estate mower would affect the company's sales of any of its other mowers. The sales manager reported that if this item were dropped, many buyers would switch to the company's Suburban mower, a somewhat less expensive model with many of the same features as the Estate mower. Sales of the Suburban mower seemed likely to increase by about 3,000 units a year if the Estate mower were dropped. None of the company's other models would be affected.

The controller's next step was to prepare estimates of the variable cost of manufacturing and selling these two mowers. These estimates were as follows:

	Estate	Suburban
Variable factory costs:		
Materials	$32.00	$27.50
Labor	12.00	7.50
Other	6.00	5.00
Total	50.00	40.00
Variable selling cost	3.50	3.00
Variable administrative cost	0.20	0.20
Total variable cost..........	$53.70	$43.20

Variable selling costs in this table represented the commissions the company's sales force received on all sales of the regular lines of mowers.

Finally, the controller tried to estimate how dropping the Estate mowers would affect the fixed factory costs. This effect was not measured by the average fixed cost but had to be estimated from an item-by-item analysis. After careful study, the manufacturing vice president reported that $27,000 of the factory's fixed costs, which were fixed as long as *any* Estate mowers were manufactured, could be eliminated if *none* were produced. Production of an additional 3,000 Suburban mowers a year wouldn't lead to any increases in fixed factory costs.

The analysis of this proposal is summarized in Exhibit 16–7. The estimates in column (2), taken alone, indicate that the company would lose $54,500 in net cash receipts if it discontinued production and sales of the Estate mower. Column (4), however, shows that $50,400 of this loss would be offset by the increased net cash receipts from increased sales of the Suburban mower.

The net effect of the discontinuation proposal is shown in column (5). It indicates that withdrawing the Estate mower would reduce net cash receipts by about $4,100 a year. The company therefore probably should continue to manufacture and sell Estate mowers for now. Their incremental contribution to the company's net cash

EXHIBIT 16–7. Van Horn Company: Incremental Net Cash Flow from Proposal to Discontinue Sales of Estate Mowers

	Cash-Flow Effects of Forgone Sales of Estate Mowers		Cash-Flow Effects of Additional Sales of Suburban Mowers		(5) Incremental Effects on Net Cash Flow
	(1) Per Unit	(2) Total	(3) Per Unit	(4) Total	(2) − (4)
Effect on receipts	−$70.00	−$350,000	+$60.00	+$180,000	−$170,000
Effect on costs:					
Variable costs	− 53.70	− 268,500	+ 43.20	+ 129,600	− 138,900
Fixed factory costs		− 27,000		—	− 27,000
Total effect on costs . . .		− 295,500		+ 129,600	− 165,900
Effect on cash flow		−$ 54,500		+$ 50,400	−$ 4,100

flow is so small, however, that management might prefer to spend its time developing markets for other products—unless it could find ways to improve the cash flows from the Estate mower business.

The use of averages

Average labor and materials costs were used in both these illustrations, but only as a means of estimating the total labor and materials costs associated with each alternative. The average of the other factory costs and the averages of selling and administrative expenses didn't enter the analysis, however, because these costs weren't expected to be proportionally variable with volume. We use averages only when they are valid predictors of totals—that is, when total cost appears likely to vary proportionally with variations in volume.

A simple example should demonstrate this point. Suppose Van Horn's service department now serves 2,000 customers at an average cost of $10 a month. It has an opportunity to pick up an additional 500 customers without affecting the volume of business it does with its present customers or the prices they pay. The additional volume will reduce the department's average cost to $9.75 a month per customer, but the new customers will pay only $9 a month for service. Serving these potential new customers therefore appears to be a losing business.

A careful analysis shows that the new business will be marginally profitable if the present estimates are valid. The correct comparison is as follows:

	Incremental Total	Incremental per Customer
Incremental receipts: 500 × $9	$4,500	$9.00
Incremental cost:		
Cost to service 2,500 customers:		
2,500 × $9.75 .... $24,375		
Cost to service 2,000 customers:		
2,000 × $10 20,000		
Total incremental cost	4,375	8.75
Incremental profit	$ 125	$0.25

The reason the incremental analysis shows an incremental profit instead of a loss is that some of the department's costs won't rise proportionally with volume. The incremental cost for the additional customers will average $4,375/500 = $8.75 a customer, and this is less than the incremental receipts of $9. If the cost increment weren't less than $10, the average wouldn't fall. The revised average will always be between the original average and the increment.

Identifying the increment

The incremental receipts attributed to proposals to expand total volume may not be the receipts actually collected from the new customers. The analytical rule is to compare the total receipts if the expansion proposal is accepted with the total receipts obtainable without expansion.

Suppose the service department's present business is to service four different 500-customer groups who are now paying $15, $12, $10.50, and $8.50 a month, respectively. If we make the simplifying assumption that all the customers are alike except for the prices they pay, then the department will be able to increase its net cash receipts without expanding its total volume. How? By servicing the new group of customers at a price of $9 a month *instead of* servicing the *least* profitable group of its present customers—those paying only $8.50 a month—the department can increase its pretax net cash inflow by $250 a month [500 × ($9.00 − $8.50)]. It can do this without increasing its physical volume or increasing its total costs. This being the case, the expansion decision has to hinge on whether the $8.50 price is high enough to cover the incremental costs of expansion—and in this case we know it falls $0.25 short of the incremental costs, which average $8.75 a customer.

Exhibit 16–8 shows this comparison graphically. Group A customers contribute $6.25 more than incremental cost; group D customers contribute $0.25 less than incremental cost. The 2,000 most profitable customers are the 1,500 in the first three existing groups, plus the 500 in the new group. All these can be served without increasing total volume and without incurring incremental costs

EXHIBIT 16–8.   Identifying Incremental Receipts

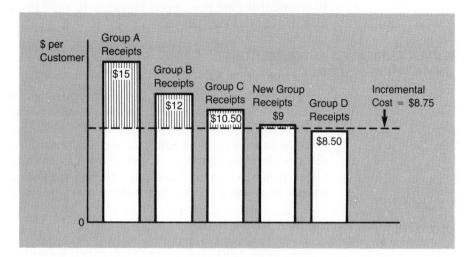

of $8.75 a customer. The only reason for incurring the incremental costs necessary to expand volume is to enable the company to serve customer group D, and this is clearly unprofitable. Van Horn presumably should either charge more for its services to customers in this group or discontinue service to them.

The conclusion from all this is that when resources are interchangeable, the same incremental cost figure applies to *each* portion of total volume, not just to the volume provided by potential new customers. Each group of customers—current and prospective—can be regarded as the incremental group.

Different costs for different purposes

The illustrations in this chapter demonstrate a point we haven't made explicit until now: Each decision calls for its own definition of incremental cost. For decisions that affect only a small percentage of total volume for short periods of time, only short-term variable costs are likely to be incremental. For decisions that affect a large amount of volume, affect volume for a long time, or call for major differences in the amount of marketing, production, development, or administrative effort, incremental cost will include fixed costs as well as variable costs.

For example, if Van Horn is considering discontinuing the service business entirely, the average incremental cost may be closer to $9.75 than to $8.75 because many fixed costs are incremental with respect to that decision. The cost of servicing *one* more customer, however, may very well be less than $8.75 because that customer's work may fit easily into an idle period in the daily schedule. Incremental cost may even be close to zero for a decision to make one additional service call.

USING ESTIMATED AVERAGE COST IN CATALOG-PRICING DECISIONS

Most pricing decisions apply not to a single order but to a succession of customer orders or inquiries over many months. We'll refer to these as *catalog-pricing decisions.* These decisions call for a great deal of managerial judgment and understanding. Cost estimates almost always enter in, but not always in the same way. We'll conclude this chapter by taking a brief look at some of the ways estimates of average costs can help management set product prices.

Catalog-pricing decisions: A simple model

A simple approach to catalog pricing is to estimate the effect of price on volume and the effect of volume on cost, selecting the price that seems likely to produce the greatest spread between total revenue and total cost. For example, suppose a company estimates the following price-volume relationship:

Price	Units Sold	Revenue
$1.25	10,000	$12,500
1.50	8,000	12,000
1.75	6,000	10,500

Estimated total costs, including production, selling, and administrative costs, are as follows:

Units Sold	Total Cost
10,000	$10,000
8,000	9,000
6,000	8,000

Putting these two sets of estimates together yields the following profit estimates:

Price	Units Sold	Revenue	Cost	Profit
$1.25	10,000	$12,500	$10,000	$2,500
1.50	**8,000**	**12,000**	**9,000**	**3,000**
1.75	6,000	10,500	8,000	2,500

The optimal price in this case is $1.50.

Cost-based formula pricing

This short-term profit-maximization model is very difficult to apply, partly because price-volume relationships are difficult to predict, partly because price is only one element in an overall marketing strategy, and partly for other reasons. One alternative is *cost-based formula pricing,* in which an established percentage markup is added to an estimate of the product's average cost to obtain a target price. The average cost in the formula may be an estimate of the average *variable* cost of producing the product, or an estimate of average *total* cost (usually referred to as *full cost*).

Pricing based on average variable cost.   Prices based on average variable cost are common in retailing, where the only variable cost of any significance may be the cost of the merchandise itself. For example, suppose Drake Markets is ready to place a new product on its shelves. The cost of the merchandise is $1 a unit and Drake's customary markup in the department in which this new item will be sold is 70 percent. The indicated retail price therefore would be $1.70.

Drake's merchandise buyers, who are responsible for product pricing, know that comparable products are sold in competitors' stores at prices ranging from $1.45 to $1.55. The $1 variable cost allows them to compete by setting a price in that range, because they know that any price in excess of $1 will contribute to covering the department's fixed costs. At a price of $1.50 and volume of 10,000 units a month, the contribution would be $5,000 [($1.50 − $1.00) × 10,000].

Pricing based on average full cost.   The advantage of using average variable cost in the formula base is that it allows management to see the short-run profit implications of volume variations more clearly. It fails, however, to identify the amount of cost the product must cover in the long run if it is to avoid generating a loss. Formulas based on average full cost are designed to provide this information.

For example, suppose Gander Company has only one product, with fixed costs of $5,000 a month and variable costs of $1 a unit. The profit necessary to produce the desired rate of return on investment is $2,000 a month. The plant was designed to operate efficiently at volumes between 8,000 and 12,000 units a month, with 10,000 units being regarded as normal.

At a 10,000-unit level, total costs will be $5,000 + $1 × 10,000 = $15,000. Average cost will be $15,000/10,000 = $1.50. The desired profit margin is $2,000/10,000 = $0.20 a unit. The full-cost-based price therefore might be $1.70:

Average variable cost	$1.00
Average fixed cost	0.50
Profit markup	0.20
Target price	$1.70

A perceptive manager will be quick to point out that this product will generate a profit of $0.20 a unit only if volume reaches the 10,000-unit level. Income before taxes at this and other volumes would be as follows:

	6,000 units	8,000 units	10,000 units	12,000 units
Revenues (at $1.70)	$10,200	$13,600	$17,000	$20,400
Expenses:				
Variable (at $1)	6,000	8,000	10,000	12,000
Fixed	5,000	5,000	5,000	5,000
Total expenses......................	11,000	13,000	15,000	17,000
Income (loss) before taxes	$ (800)	$ 600	$ 2,000	$ 3,400

As this table shows, full-cost pricing is far from a sure road to profitability. It has some advantages, however. First, full-cost data may help management identify a price that won't be unduly attractive to potential competitors. In other words, cost data may help management forecast what sacrifices competitors are making or would have to make to manufacture a similar product and thereby provide management with a means of estimating a competitive price level.

Second, full-cost pricing may appear to reduce the uncertainty surrounding the pricing decision. One company's sales depend as much on the prices its competitors charge as on its own prices. Competitors' cost structures for a given product are likely to be quite similar, however, and the full-cost formula may help the company forecast its competitors' prices. It may decide to set the price at this level and concentrate on other ingredients of the marketing mix, such as advertising, field selling, and customer service, to get customers to buy the company's wares.

Variable-cost amounts serve this purpose less satisfactorily than full cost. For example, suppose a company with many products is considering adding a new product to its line. The estimated variable cost is $15 a unit; the estimated full cost is $20. The company's average markup on other products with the same market characteristics is 30 percent of average full cost or 120 percent of variable cost. The two cost-based pricing formulas would yield the following:

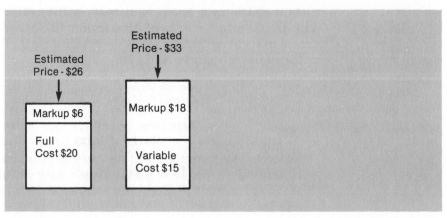

The full-cost price is lower than the variable-cost price in this case because this new product uses less expensive capacity than the average existing product. We can see this by calculating the average ratio of full cost to variable cost. If P = price, F = full cost, and V = variable cost, we have the following two normal relationships:

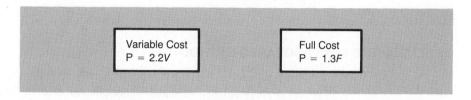

| Variable Cost | Full Cost |
| $P = 2.2V$ | $P = 1.3F$ |

The relationship between variable cost and full cost for the average product can be derived by putting these two formulas together:

$$2.2V = 1.3F$$

Full cost for an average product, in other words, is 2.2/1.3, or about 170 percent of its variable cost. The full cost of the new product, in contrast, is only $20/$15 = 133 percent of variable cost.

Why is this significant? If this company can produce the new product in facilities with a low full-cost/variable-cost ratio, so can its competitors. A price based on the average for all products, therefore, very likely would be higher than the prices competitors will charge for comparable products. Thus, a variable-cost pricing formula may be a poorer prediction of market price than a full-cost pricing formula.

SUMMARY

The basic approach to quantitative analysis for management decisions is to estimate the incremental cash flows, the *differences* between the anticipated results of a proposed course of action and the anticipated results of the action the company would take if the proposal were rejected.

Incremental analysis is a powerful concept, but one which is by no means easily applied in all cases. In simple situations, for example, a product's variable cost may be a good estimate of the cost of increasing product output, but revenue effects may be extremely difficult to forecast. In other cases, many fixed costs will also be affected, particularly if large amounts of business are affected by the decision.

This chapter has indicated how costs can be classified into fixed and variable costs to make them more readily usable in decision making. We have also examined a number of cost concepts, such as sunk cost and opportunity cost, to obtain a better understanding of how incremental analysis can be used in decision making. Finally, we've shown how estimates of average full cost may be used to estimate the price the market might bear on a continuing basis. Our task in the next two chapters is to describe the methods accountants use to estimate average variable cost and average full cost for individual products.

APPENDIX: THE LEAST-SQUARES METHOD

The process of fitting a line to approximate the relationship between a dependent variable (cost) and one or more independent variables (volume, average lot size) is known as *regression analysis*. The formula describing the relationship is known as a *regression equation*. With only one independent variable, the process is known as *simple regression;* with two or more independent variables, the analysis becomes one of *multiple regression*.

In this appendix, we'll describe the calculations required by simple regression to fit a straight line to a set of data points by the method of least squares. The equation for a straight line is

$$y = a + bx$$

where

y = the dependent variable (total cost)
a = a constant (total fixed cost)
x = the independent variable (volume)
b = the variation (variable cost per unit) of the dependent variable for a unit variation in the independent variable

These relationships are represented graphically in Exhibit 16–9. By moving one unit of x to the right, the total cost increases by b; this is the *slope* of the regression line. The constant, a, is the *y-intercept*. The object of regression analysis is to estimate the values of a and b.

The first step is to record a number of paired values of x and y. Each pair of values (one for x and one for y) represents a single observation. Enough observations must be made to allow the analyst to conclude that the resulting regression equation and the values of a and b are reliable enough to be used. Furthermore, these observations should cover all portions of the likely range of the independent variable. And if conditions (input prices, technology, or methods) change during the period in which the observations are made, observations made before the change should be either adjusted (e.g., by a price index) or discarded.

EXHIBIT 16–9. Equation for a Straight Line

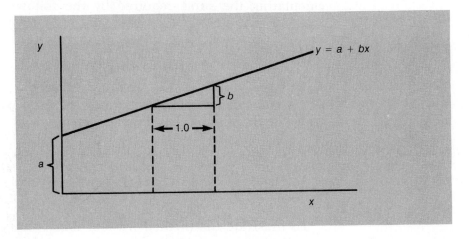

The objective of simple linear regression analysis based on the least-squares method is illustrated in Exhibit 16–10. Each observed value of y is labeled y_o and this value is plotted as a point in the exhibit. [A fully correct label would be (y_o, x_o) but since our interest is in the values of y, we've used the simpler notation.] The symbol y_c stands for the value of y calculated from the regression equation for any given value of x. As the expression in the lower right of the diagram shows, the objective of least-squares regression analysis is to find the line which minimizes the sum of the squares of the differences $(y_o - y_c)$ between y_o and y_c for each y_o.

The regression equation for a straight line that has this property

EXHIBIT 16–10. A Least-Squares Regression Line

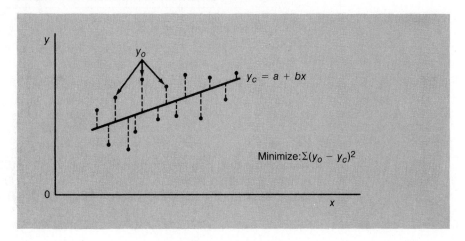

and represents the relationship between y and x can be found by calculating the sums required by the following two equations, known as the *normal equations,* and solving for a and b:

$$\Sigma y = an + b\Sigma x$$
$$\Sigma xy = a\Sigma x + b\Sigma x^2$$

in which n = the number of observations of x and y.

To make these normal equations easier to work with, we can translate them into the following form:

$$a = \frac{\Sigma y}{n} - \frac{b\Sigma x}{n} \tag{1}$$

$$b = \frac{n\Sigma xy - \Sigma x\Sigma y}{n\Sigma x^2 - (\Sigma x)^2} \tag{2}$$

To illustrate the method without unnecessary arithmetic, let's suppose we have six cost/volume observations from which we wish to estimate the relationship between cost and volume. The observations and the computational quantities required by the two normal equations are as follows:

Volume	Cost		
x	y	xy	x^2
3	5	15	9
4	6	24	16
5	6	30	25
6	9	54	36
7	9	63	49
8	10	80	64
$\Sigma =$ 33	45	266	199

With six observations, $n = 6$.

Substituting these amounts in the normal equations, we get the following:

$$a = \frac{45}{6} - \left(\frac{33}{6}\right)b \tag{1}$$

$$b = \frac{6 \times 266 - 33 \times 45}{6 \times 199 - (33)^2} \tag{2}$$

Solving equation (2), we find that b equals $111/105 = 1.057$. Putting this in equation (1) yields a value of $a = 7.500 - 5.814 = 1.686$. The regression line therefore is described by the following equation:

$$y = \$1.686 + \$1.057x$$

We can use this formula to predict the cost that will be incurred at any volume in the normal volume range. At a volume of 3, for example, cost should be $1.686 + 3 \times \$1.057 = \$4.857$. This is $0.143 less than the amount observed at that volume. Repeating this calculation for each of the other observed volumes, we get the following comparison:

Volume	Observed Cost	Calculated Cost	Deviation	Deviation²
x	y_o	y_c	$(y_o - y_c)$	$(y_o - y_c)^2$
3	$ 5	$ 4.857	+ $0.143	$0.0204
4	6	5.914	+ 0.086	0.0074
5	6	6.971	− 0.971	0.9428
6	9	8.028	+ 0.972	0.9448
7	9	9.085	− 0.085	0.0072
8	10	10.142	− 0.142	0.0202
$\Sigma =$				1.9428

If we were to alter either a or b, the sum of the squared deviations would be greater than 1.9428.

Before management uses a regression equation, it needs to know how closely it has fit the observed facts in the past and then whether it is likely to continue to describe the relationship in the future. This requires the calculation of various measures of reliability. One such measure is the *coefficient of determination* (r^2):

$$r^2 = 1 - \frac{\Sigma(y_o - y_c)^2}{\Sigma(y - \bar{y})^2}$$

($\bar{y}$ is the mean of the observed values of y.)

The general term for the degree of association between variables is *correlation*. If all the observations fall on the regression line, $\Sigma (y_o - y_c)^2$ will be 0, and r^2 will be equal to 1. This is known as *perfect correlation*. On the other hand, if the deviations from the predicted values are as great as the deviations from the mean, then $\Sigma(y_o - y_c)^2 / \Sigma(y_o - \bar{y})^2$ will equal 1, and r^2 will equal 0. This is known as no correlation or *zero correlation*. In our simple illustration, r^2 is 0.91, meaning that by introducing variations in volume as a possible way of predicting variations in cost, we accounted for 91 percent of the variation of the squared deviations from the mean.[3]

[3] For a more complete discussion of regression analysis and measures of reliability, see Wayne E. Leininger, *Quantitative Methods in Accounting* (New York: D. Van Nostrand, 1980), pp. 95–123; for a more advanced treatment, see Edmond Valinvaud, *Statistical Methods of Econometrics,* 2d rev. ed. (New York: American Elsevier, 1970), chaps. 3–10.

KEY TERMS

Capacity cost
Cash flow
Constraint
Decision rule
Fixed cost
Incremental cost
Incremental principle
Incremental profit
Least-squares method

Managerial accounting
Opportunity cost
Planning
Programmed activity
Regression analysis
Responsive activity
Sunk cost
Variable cost

INDEPENDENT STUDY PROBLEMS (Solutions in Appendix B)

1. Cost-volume relationships. The Johnson Works has prepared the following estimates of average total factory cost at different volumes:

Weekly Volume (units)	Average Cost per Unit
1	$11.00
2	6.00
3	4.33
4	3.50
5	3.00
6	2.67
7	2.43
8	2.25
9	2.22
10	2.30

a. Calculate average variable cost at each volume. (For this purpose, assume that total fixed cost is the same at all volumes.)
b. Calculate average fixed cost at each volume.
c. Assuming the company is now operating at a weekly volume of nine units, calculate the cost relevant to a decision to increase the rate of operations to 10 units a week.

2. Opportunity cost. Nancy Smith bought 100 shares in Hydrophonics, Ltd., on January 15, 19x1, paying $15 a share. She bought an additional 100 shares on March 18, 19x4, paying $20 a share. The market price of this stock fell rapidly in 19x5, reaching a low of $6 a share. Early in 19x6 the market price had recovered to $8 a share. At that point General Enterprises, Inc., offered to buy all shares tendered to it at a price of $10 a share.

What cost should Smith use in evaluating this offer?

3. Identifying incremental costs. Marmon, Inc., owns two delivery trucks. The costs of owning and operating these trucks are as follows:

	Truck A	Truck B
Yearly fixed costs:		
Garage space	$ 800	$ 800
Depreciation	2,400	2,000
Registration and insurance	1,500	1,500
Maintenance	500	500
Variable costs:		
Drivers' wages and benefits	$15 an hour	$15 an hour
Gasoline and oil	0.20 a mile	0.22 a mile
Maintenance	0.08 a mile	0.10 a mile

Marmon normally operates truck A 1,800 hours a year; truck B is used only 650 hours. On the average, trucks in service cover 15 miles in an hour. The company rents garage space for its trucks in a nearby garage. The garaging contract for either truck can be canceled on one month's notice. Maintenance is provided by a local truck-repair shop.

Marmon has just purchased merchandise in a liquidation sale and must pick this merchandise up next week. Unfortunately, truck A is now fully scheduled for regular deliveries all next week. Truck B isn't scheduled for use next week, but it can't be used to pick up the new merchandise because it is too wide for the loading platform where the merchandise is located. Truck B could be used for truck A's regular deliveries, thereby releasing truck A to pick up the merchandise, but Marmon's management is concerned that that would be too costly.

Management estimates that the merchandise-moving job will take one full week. If truck A were used to move the merchandise, it would travel 400 miles and use 40 hours of a driver's time. Truck B, if used in the regular delivery service while truck A was on this special assignment, would operate 40 hours and cover 600 miles. The additional truck driver would be hired for the week on a contract basis at the regular wage-and-benefits cost of $15 an hour.

As an alternative, an independent trucking company has offered to pick up and deliver the purchased merchandise to Marmon's warehouse for $780.

a. Should Marmon use truck A to pick up this merchandise, or should it use the independent trucker? Show your calculations and indicate how you treated each cost element. (You may assume a year of 50 weeks.)

b. Because truck B is used so little, management is considering scrapping it and using an independent trucker to make the deliveries it is now used for. Assuming truck B now has no significant scrap value, what is the highest annual amount Marmon could afford to pay an independent trucker each year instead of using truck B? Show your calculations. (Ignore income taxes.)

4. Desirability of reducing prices. The manager of the university print shop is trying to decide whether to meet the prices and delivery-time performance of local commercial printing shops on small printing jobs. The commercial shops quote prices that are 10 percent lower than the university shop's schedule and also offer faster delivery at no extra charge. Until now, university departments have been required to use the university shop for this sort of work, but a mounting volume of complaints has led the university controller to authorize the use of off-campus shops. The university shop will continue to do large-volume jobs and confidential work, such as examinations and research reports. The university shop would require the same amount of equipment it now has, even if it were to let small jobs go outside.

At its present operating volume of 2,000 labor-hours a month, the operating costs of the university print shop are:

Paper stock	Varies with nature of work
Labor	$8 a labor-hour
Other processing costs	$6 a labor-hour

All labor is regarded as wholly variable with volume; other processing costs include $8,000 of fixed costs, the remainder being wholly and proportionally variable with volume and volume being measured in terms of labor-hours.

Approximately 600 labor-hours a month are now being spent on the work affected by the decision. Materials cost on this work is approximately $6,000 a month, and the amount now being charged by the university shop to other university departments for this work is $15,000 a month.

The shop manager is convinced the shop will lose the work unless it meets both the competitive price and the competitive delivery time. To permit faster deliveries, an additional 80 hours of labor a month would be required in excess of the 600 labor-hours now devoted to this work. Fixed costs would not be affected by this choice between these two alternatives.

Which alternative should the manager choose? Show your calculations.

EXERCISES AND PROBLEMS

5. Effect of special order. Relay Corporation manufactures batons. Relay can manufacture 300,000 batons a year at a total variable cost of $750,000 and a total fixed cost of $450,000. Relay's prediction is that 240,000 batons will be sold at the regular price of $5 each. In addition, a special order has been placed by a customer for 60,000 batons at a 40 percent discount off the regular price.

By what amount will income before income taxes be increased or decreased as a result of this special order?

(AICPA adapted)

6. Make or buy decision. Buck Company manufactures Part No. 1700 for use in its production cycle. The costs per unit for 5,000 units of Part No. 1700 are as follows:

Variable materials costs	$ 2
Variable labor costs	12
Other variable costs	5
Fixed costs	7
Total cost	$26

Hollow Company has offered to sell Buck 5,000 units of Part No. 1700 for $27 a unit. If Buck accepts this offer, some of the facilities presently used to manufacture Part No. 1700 can be used in the manufacture of Part No. 1211, thereby reducing the company's cost of manufacturing Part No. 1211 by $40,000. In addition, if the company stops making Part No. 1700, it can reduce its total fixed factory cost by $15,000.

What is the incremental profit or loss to be obtained by accepting Hollow's offer?

(AICPA adapted)

7. Cost-volume relationship. From the following estimates of total cost at different hourly volumes, calculate for each volume of activity: (*a*) average total cost, (*b*) average fixed cost, (*c*) average variable cost, and (*d*) the incremental cost of producing the final unit. Assume that total fixed cost is the same at all volumes.

Units	Cost
0	$100
1	200
2	250
3	290
4	330
5	370
6	410
7	450
8	500
9	570
10	670

8. Exercises in incremental analysis.

a. Light Company has 2,000 obsolete light fixtures that are carried in inventory at a manufacturing cost of $30,000. If the fixtures are reworked for $10,000, they can be sold for $18,000. Alternatively, the fixtures can be sold for $3,000 to a jobber in a distant city. In a decision model used to analyze the reworking proposal, what is the opportunity cost?

b. Woody Company, which manufactures sneakers, has enough idle capacity to accept a special order of 20,000 pairs of sneakers at $6 a pair. The normal selling price is $10 a pair. Variable manufacturing costs are $4.50 a pair, and fixed manufacturing costs are $1.50 a pair. Woody will incur no incremental selling expenses as a result of the special order, nor will total fixed manufacturing costs be affected. What will be the effect on income before taxes if the special order can be accepted without affecting other sales?

c. Argus Company, a manufacturer of lamps, budgeted sales of 400,000 lamps at $20 a unit for the year 19x0. Variable manufacturing costs were budgeted at $8 a unit, and fixed manufacturing costs were budgeted at $5 a unit. A special offer to buy 40,000 lamps for $11.50 each was received by Argus in April 19x0. Argus had enough plant capacity to manufacture the additional quantity of lamps; the production would have to be done by the regular work force on an overtime basis, however, at an estimated additional cost of $1.50 per lamp. Argus would incur no incremental selling expenses as a result of the special order. What would be the effect on income before taxes if the special order could be accepted without affecting normal sales?

d. Cardinal Company needs 20,000 units of a certain part to use in its production cycle. The following information is available on costs per unit:

Cost to Cardinal to make the part:
Materials (variable)	$ 4
Labor (variable)	16
Other variable.....................	8
Fixed	10
Total........................	$38

Cost to Cardinal if it buys the part
from Oriole Company $36

If Cardinal buys the part from Oriole instead of making it, Cardinal will not be able to use the released facilities in another manufacturing activity. Sixty percent of the fixed costs will continue if Cardinal buys the part from Oriole. In deciding whether to make or buy the part, what estimate of the incremental cost of making the part would you use?

e. Motor Company manufactures 10,000 units of part CRX-16 for use in its production annually. The following costs are reported:

Materials (variable)	$ 20,000
Labor (variable)	55,000
Other variable	45,000
Fixed	70,000
Total	$190,000

Valve Company has offered to sell Motor 10,000 units of part CRX-16 for $18 a unit. If Motor accepts the offer, some of the facilities presently used to manufacture part CRX-16 can be rented to a third party at an annual rental of $15,000. Additionally, $4 a unit of the other fixed costs will be eliminated. Should Motor accept Valve's offer, and why?

(AICPA adapted)

9. Identifying sunk costs. The Meredith Machine Company entered into a contract to manufacture certain specially designed processing equipment for a foreign buyer. When the equipment was completed and in the testing stage, currency controls which nullified all import contracts were instituted by the government to which the purchaser was subject. The manufacturing costs incurred by the Meredith Company up to that time amounted to $700,000. The scrap value of the equipment was estimated to be approximately $80,000.

No purchaser could be found for the equipment in its existing form, but one company was interested if certain major modifications were made. This company offered $500,000; the estimated cost of modification to fit the revised specifications was $200,000.

What action should the Meredith Company have taken? To what extent was the decision affected by the manufacturing cost the company had already incurred?

10. Analyzing costs. John Robinson lives 28 miles from his place of work. He drives his automobile to and from work five days a week, 50 weeks a year, and estimates his expenses as follows:

Gasoline	$0.08 a mile
Parking	$3 a day
Depreciation	$200 a month
Maintenance and repairs	$500 a year
Insurance	$750 a year

A fellow worker has asked John to give him a ride to and from work each day. Even though this would add seven miles each morning and each afternoon, the travel time would be the same as it had been because John would then drive on a toll road which charges a 75 cent toll in each direction.

If John is determined not to make a profit from doing his co-worker a favor but doesn't want to lose money, what amount should he charge each week? Show your calculations.

11. Drawing a regression line. The following table shows departmental output and total departmental labor cost for each of the past 12 months:

	Output (no. of units)	Labor Cost
January	35	$27,600
February	63	20,700
March	132	28,200
April	150	33,000
May	125	30,400
June	111	25,500
July	116	24,300
August	98	23,200
September	135	24,000
October	120	27,300
November	114	20,700
December	140	30,000

a. Plot these data on a sheet of graph paper and draw a straight line which seems to fit the observations most closely. Fit this line visually; do not use the least-squares method described in the appendix to this chapter.

b. Derive the mathematical equation which describes the line you drew in answer to part a.

c. Use the least-squares method described in the appendix to this chapter to derive another mathematical equation to describe the apparent relationship between total labor cost and output in this case.

d. Compare the equations in your answers to parts b and c. How similar are they? Why aren't they identical?

12. Taking on additional business. A printing company is considering an opportunity to print a new monthly magazine for an organization of professional social workers. The organization isn't wealthy, and it can't pay more than $1 a copy to have its new magazine printed, or $10,000 a month for the anticipated press run of 10,000 copies a month. The printing company would like to help out, but only if it can recover its costs plus a margin of 5 percent of cost to allow for contingencies. If the contingencies don't materialize, the company will make a small profit.

The total cost of labor, paper stock, and ink would vary in direct proportion to the number of copies printed. The printing company's other costs, which average $4 a labor-hour at the company's current operating volume of 8,000 labor-hours a month, would fall to an average of $3.90 a labor-hour as the new magazine would increase the company's volume to 8,500 labor-hours a month. Management has drawn up the following profit estimate for the new magazine:

Revenue per hour		$20.00
Costs per hour:		
Labor	$12.00	
Paper stock and ink	5.00	
Miscellaneous	3.90	20.90
Profit/(loss) per hour		$ (0.90)

The print shop supervisor says the miscellaneous costs are sunk costs and should be ignored. Since the anticipated margin over the costs of labor, paper stock, and ink amounts to $3 an hour, the job should be taken on.

Prepare an analysis and make a recommendation. If your analysis indicates the proposal should be rejected, prepare a response to be made to the social workers' representative.

13.   Identifying incremental costs. A company has four large presses of approximately the same capacity. Each was run at close to its full capacity during 19x8. Each machine is depreciated separately; a declining-charge method is used. Data for each press are:

	No. 1	No. 2	No. 3	No. 4
Date acquired	1/1/x0	1/1/x4	1/1/x6	1/1/x7
Cost	$100,000	$120,000	$145,000	$175,000
Operating costs—19x8:				
Labor	$ 11,000	$ 10,500	$ 10,000	$ 9,500
Maintenance	3,800	2,400	2,000	1,000
Repairs	600	1,200	800	500
Depreciation	3,500	5,400	7,800	10,800
Total	$ 18,900	$ 19,500	$ 20,600	$ 21,800

It is expected that activity in 19x9 will be substantially less than in 19x8. As a result, one machine is to be put on standby. It has been proposed that No. 4 should be that machine on the grounds that it has the highest operating cost. A standby machine would require neither maintenance nor repairs.

Do you agree with this proposal? Explain, citing figures from the problem.

14. Pricing additional business. Harley Company operates a contracting business. Its supervisors and administrative personnel are paid monthly salaries: Salaries of administrative personnel, including employee benefits, amount to $10,450 a month; supervisors work a total of 350 hours a month at salaries amounting to $4,550, again including the costs of employee benefits. The company's other employees are paid only for the hours they work, and this amount varies from week to week.

Costs other than materials and employees' salaries and wages amount to $6,000 a month plus $0.10 for each hour worked by the hourly paid employees. In an average month, the hourly paid employees work 2,000 hours, earn $20,000, and use materials costing $30,000. The company's managerial and physical capacity is large enough to handle a total volume of business amounting to 2,500 hours of work by the hourly paid employees.

Harley has an opportunity to enter a bid on a contracting job at Burns Products, Inc. The work would be done next month and would require materials costing $4,800 and 300 hours of work by hourly paid employees at wages and benefits totaling $11 an hour. The company's supervisors would spend 50 hours supervising work on this contract.

If Harley doesn't win this contract, it will use 1,500 hours of hourly paid employees' time next month, at wages and benefits of $10 an hour. Total materials costs will amount to $22,500 on that work, and revenues will amount to $58,000.

a. Calculate Harley Company's anticipated income before taxes if it fails to win the Burns Products contract.
b. Calculate Harley Company's anticipated average cost per hour of hourly paid employees' time (1) if it wins the Burns Products contract, and (2) if it fails to win the contract.
c. What is the minimum price Harley could bid on the Burns Products contract without losing money as a result of entering into this contract? Show your calculations.
d. Comment on the relevance of your answers to parts a and b to your answer to part c, explaining either how you were able to use those answers or why you didn't use them.

15. Costs for pricing. Harley Company's management (see problem 14) has established that the ratio of total materials cost to hourly labor time varies significantly from contract to contract. Hourly wage rates also vary from contract to contract, but the variations occur within a relatively narrow range.

a. Is it likely that Harley's management would find a cost-based pricing formula useful? If so, explain how it would be constructed and how it would be used. If not, explain why it wouldn't be helpful.
b. If you were deciding for Harley, would you enter a bid on the Burns Products contract (see problem 14) close to the minimum price you calculated in answer to part c or considerably higher? Explain why and identify the factors other than those described in these two problems that you would consider in deciding how much to bid on this contract.

16. Simple pricing model. Middleton Enterprises, Inc., owns a baseball stadium with a seating capacity of 5,000. The fixed costs of operating this stadium are $15,000 a year, and variable costs are 10 cents per spectator per game. These variable costs actually increase in steps, with an increase of 500 spectators requiring a $50 increase in costs, but management sees no harm in converting this $50 increment into an average.

One hundred games are played each year, and the average attendance is 1,000 spectators a game. Fixed costs, therefore, average 15 cents per spectator per game. The stadium is adequate for all games except a special series of five exhibition games with major-league teams. For each of these five games, the estimated demand is as follows:

If the Price Is—	Then Estimated Attendance Is—
$3.00	2,000
2.50	6,000
2.00	9,000
1.75	11,000
1.50	16,000
1.00	20,000

The company can rent a nearby stadium (25,000 capacity) for a fee of $2,000 for each game plus 10 percent of gross receipts. In addition, the company would still have the variable costs of 10 cents per spectator per game.

Assuming that the price charged will be one of the six alternatives above, present a table that will indicate the admission price that will be most profitable for the company and also whether the larger stadium should be rented. Show all calculations.

17. Discontinuing a product. Company X manufactures and sells more than 200 products to industrial customers. Management is now reviewing one of these, product T. Although this product seemed highly promising when it was introduced two years ago, competitive developments have cut into its market, and the marketing manager says no one will be buying it three years from now. You have been given the following estimates:

	This Year	Next Year	Year after Next
Sales	$1,000,000	$ 600,000	$ 200,000
Costs:			
Variable factory	500,000	300,000	100,000
Fixed factory	250,000	150,000	50,000
Development	200,000	200,000	200,000
Direct selling	150,000	120,000	60,000
Total costs	1,100,000	770,000	410,000
Product margin	$ (100,000)	$(170,000)	$(210,000)

Further investigation reveals that:

1. The charges for fixed factory costs in the table are based on averages. When production of this product is discontinued, $70,000 in fixed factory costs will be eliminated each year.

2. The company spent $1 million to acquire the rights to this product. This amount is being amortized over a five-year period at $200,000 a year, and $600,000 remains unamortized today.
3. Direct selling costs are all traceable to this product and consist of items such as sales-force salaries and travel expenses.
4. Investment in working capital to support this product is negligible.

Prepare an analysis to help management decide whether to discontinue manufacturing and selling product T right now or keep it in the line for one, two, or three years.

18. Costs for pricing. The Hardy School is a nonprofit organization providing educational programs for gifted children. The school has two divisions: a lower school, for children six to nine years old, and an upper school, for 10- to 13-year-old children. Both divisions and the school's administrative offices are in a single building. This building is occupied under a lease which still has two years to run. The annual rental is $12,000, which is less than the school would have to pay to lease comparable facilities today.

The school year has just ended, all bills have been paid, and the school has $4,700 in its bank account. The board of trustees is meeting next week to set the tuition rates for next year. Tuition this past year was a flat $3,800 per pupil, and 60 pupils were enrolled in each division. Space is available to take as many as 70 pupils in each division, and no more.

The school's treasurer has just finished drawing up a tentative cost budget for next year. This shows the following:

Upper school	$234,000
Lower school	222,000
Administration (including rent, heat, light, and so forth)	60,000
Total	$516,000

Based on past experience, the treasurer expects to raise $18,000 next year in charitable contributions from alumni and educational foundations. The school has no endowment funds of its own.

The finance committee plans to recommend an increase in the tuition rate to $4,150 because that will balance the budget. The treasurer wants to set the tuition at $4,300 because this represents full cost. The school's principal is reluctant to see any increase in the tuition rate because some of the gifted children in the school might not be able to continue. More important, parents of six-year-old children might be less willing to enroll these children because the total commitment for the next eight years would be even greater than it is now. Those with children in the upper school might be less likely to withdraw these children from the school because their future commitment would be smaller. No one has any firm estimate of the effect of a tuition increase on enrollment, however.

a. Prepare an estimate or estimates of average costs the board might use in reaching a decision on the tuition question.
b. Prepare your own recommendation, including a concise statement of your reasons for favoring the action you are recommending.

19. Make or buy; maximum purchase price; long term versus short term. The Grandview Corporation has been manufacturing a chemical compound known as corolite. Its entire output of this compound, about 100,000 gallons a year, has been used in the production of several of the company's finished products.

Grandview uses 10,000 gallons of corolite a year in the manufacture of blivets in a separate factory. A gallon of corolite is used for each dozen blivets manufactured. You have the following cost estimates:

	Corolite	Blivets
Annual volume	100,000 gal.	10,000 doz.
Materials	$4/gal.	$2/doz.*
Labor	8/gal.	5/doz.
Other variable	6/gal.	3/doz.
Fixed	5/gal.	4/doz.
Total cost	$23/gal.	$14/doz.*

* Plus 1 gallon of corolite per dozen.

The Boxboro Corporation has just developed a substitute for corolite, known as formulane, and has offered to sell 10,000 gallons of this product to Grandview for use in the manufacture of blivets during the coming year. The price would be $20.50 a gallon. Formulane has one advantage over corolite: It can be used directly in the manufacture of blivets without further processing in the blivets plant. Management estimates this would reduce the labor cost of manufacturing blivets by $1 a dozen, or 20 percent of the total labor cost of this product in the blivets factory.

The manager of the blivets factory has asked top management to approve the purchase of 10,000 gallons of formulane from Boxboro, on the basis of the following cost comparison:

Purchase price of formulane	$20.50
Reduction in processing time:	
20 percent of ($5 + $3 + $4)	2.40
Net cost of formulane	$18.10
Cost of corolite	23.00
Net saving	$ 4.90

The manager of the corolite plant has objected, saying the corolite plant's fixed costs would go on anyway; therefore, the net cost of formulane to Grandview would be $18.10 + $5.00 = $23.10.

Total fixed costs in the blivets plant wouldn't change if formulane were to be substituted for corolite. "Other variable" costs in each factory vary in proportion to changes in labor costs.

a. Should Grandview buy formulane from the Boxboro Company? Summarize the figures on which your answer is based and show how you calculated them.
b. Calculate the maximum price Grandview could afford to pay Boxboro for an order of 10,000 gallons of formulane.
c. Suppose Grandview was considering discontinuing the manufacture

of corolite entirely, using formulane obtained from Boxboro in all products now based on corolite. Formulane has the same advantages over corolite in all these products as in the manufacture of blivets. Would the maximum purchase price of formulane probably be greater, less, or equal to the maximum purchase price you calculated in your answer to part *b?* Explain.

20. Closing a factory. Arcadia Corporation has its home office in Ohio and leases factory buildings in Texas, Montana, and Maine, all of which produce the same product. The operations of the Maine factory have been unprofitable for a number of years. The lease on the Maine building will expire at the end of this year, and Arcadia's management has decided to cease operations there rather than renew the lease. This factory's machinery and equipment will be sold. Arcadia expects the proceeds from the sale of these assets will exceed their book value by an amount just adequate to cover all termination costs.

Prior to the decision to close the Maine plant, Arcadia's management had prepared the following projection of operating results for the next year:

	Total	Texas	Montana	Maine
Sales revenue	$4,300,000	$2,200,000	$1,400,000	$700,000
Fixed costs:				
Factory	1,100,000	560,000	280,000	260,000
Selling and administrative	350,000	210,000	110,000	30,000
Variable costs	1,450,000	665,000	425,000	360,000
Home office costs	500,000	225,000	175,000	100,000
Total operating expense	3,400,000	1,660,000	990,000	750,000
Operating income (loss) before taxes	$ 900,000	$ 540,000	$ 410,000	$ (50,000)

Home-office costs are divided among the factories in proportion to their labor costs and will remain $500,000 in total even after the Maine factory is closed.

Arcadia would like to continue serving the customers now being served by the Maine factory, if it can do so economically. Accordingly, management is considering the following alternatives, all based on the assumption that the selling price remains $25 a unit:

Alternative 1.. Close the Maine factory and expand the operations of the Montana factory by using space presently idle there. This move would result in the following changes in operations at the Montana factory:

a. Sales revenue would increase by 50 percent.
b. Factory fixed costs would increase by 20 percent.
c. Selling and administrative fixed costs would increase by 10 percent.
d. Average variable costs would be $8 a unit.

Alternative 2. Close the Maine factory and enter into a long-term contract with an independent manufacturer to serve the area's customers.

This manufacturer would pay Arcadia a royalty of $4 a unit based on an estimate of 30,000 units being sold.

Alternative 3.   Close the Maine factory and discontinue serving its present customers.

Prepare an analysis to help management decide which of these three alternatives is the most desirable for Arcadia.

(AICPA adapted; restructured by Hugo Nurnberg)

21.   Special order.   Anchor Company manufactures several different styles of jewelry cases. Management estimates that during the third quarter of 19x6 the company will be operating at 80 percent of maximum capacity. Because the company desires a higher utilization of plant capacity, the company will consider accepting a special order.

Anchor has received special-order inquiries from two companies. The first order is from JCP, Inc., which would like to market a jewelry case similar to one of Anchor's cases. The JCP jewelry case would be marketed under JCP's own label. JCP, Inc., has offered Anchor $5.75 per jewelry case for 20,000 cases to be shipped by the end of the quarter. The cost data for the Anchor jewelry case, which is similar to the specifications of the JCP special order, are as follows:

Regular selling price per unit	$9.00
Costs per unit:	
Materials	$2.50
Labor: 0.5 hours × $6	3.00
Other: 0.25 machine-hours × $4	1.00
Total	$6.50

According to the specifications provided by JCP, Inc., the special-order case requires materials that are less expensive than those in Anchor's regular case. Consequently, the materials would cost only $2.25 a case. Management has estimated that the remaining costs, labor time, and machine time would be the same as on the Anchor jewelry case.

The second special order was submitted by the Krage Company for 7,500 jewelry cases at $7.50 a case. These cases would be marketed under the Krage label and would have to be shipped by the end of the quarter. The Krage jewelry case is different from any jewelry case in the Anchor line, however. The estimated unit costs of this case are as follows:

Materials	$3.25
Labor: 0.5 hours × $6	3.00
Other: 0.5 machine-hours × $4	2.00
Total	$8.25

In addition, Anchor would have to buy a $2,500 special device to manufacture these cases and would have to spend an additional $1,500 to install and adjust this device for use on this product. The device would be discarded once the special order was completed.

Anchor's cost estimates include provisions for costs other than materials and labor at their estimated average of $4 a machine-hour. Factory fixed costs are expected to amount to $18,000 a month ($216,000 for the year), and the factory's maximum capacity under normal conditions is 90,000 machine-hours a year or 7,500 machine-hours a month.

Anchor will have the entire third quarter to work on the special order, if it decides to accept one of them. Production of its regular products will increase in the fourth quarter, leaving no capacity available for filling a special order. Management doesn't expect any repeat sales to be generated by either special order, and company policy precludes Anchor from subcontracting any portion of an order which isn't expected to generate repeat sales.

Should Anchor Company accept either special order? Justify your answer and show your calculations.

(CMA adapted)

17

Classifying operating costs; process costing

Accountants analyze and record current operating costs for various reasons—to provide data management can use in estimating the future effects of its present decisions, to distinguish between the cost of goods sold and the cost of the ending inventory for financial reporting and tax purposes, to help management judge the effectiveness and efficiency of current operations, and in some cases to establish the amounts customers or others should be charged for the company's goods or services. Our purpose in this chapter is to describe the main aspects of the systems accountants use to classify and record costs for these purposes, with an emphasis on operations used exclusively to produce a single product or service. These systems are the central focus of the branch of accounting known as *cost accounting*.

THREE DIMENSIONS OF COSTS

The typical system for classifying and recording operating costs has three dimensions: organization unit, object of expenditure, and activity. We'll examine each of these briefly.

Organizational classification

From an accounting viewpoint, an organization can be regarded as a group of interrelated *cost centers*. A cost center is any department or other unit of the organization or any portion of such a unit for which management chooses to accumulate operating costs. In general, this first dimension of the costing structure parallels the company's organization chart.

Exhibit 17–1 shows the main elements of the organization structure of Apex Company, a small manufacturer of industrial coatings and pesticides. Each block in this diagram represents a *responsibility center,* defined as an organization segment headed by a single person, answerable to higher authority, and obligated to perform certain tasks at agreed-upon levels of efficiency and effectiveness. Although Apex is a small company, each responsibility center in the bottom row has two or more subordinate units that would appear in the next row if we had decided to display them in our chart.

Beginning with the block for the chief operating officer—the president—each block in the chart contains the title of the manager and the accounting code number of the responsibility center it represents. The first two digits of the code identify the company's principal responsibility centers, those in the middle three rows. The third digit is always zero except for department subdivisions such as those shown in the bottom row of the exhibit. The fourth digit is used to identify any further subdivisions of the base-level responsibility centers. The number 2421, for example, might be used to

EXHIBIT 17–1. Apex Company: Partial Organization Chart and Organizational Account Codes

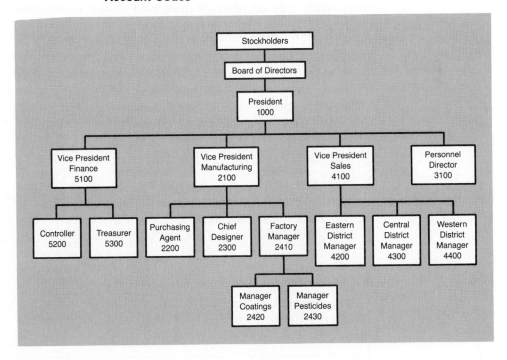

identify the mixing room in the coatings department; number 2422 might identify the coatings department's maintenance shop.

The primary basis for assigning costs to organization units is *traceability;* that is, each cost is assigned to the lowest block in the organization chart to which it is traceable. A cost is said to be traceable to a cost center if it is incurred entirely to support the activities of that cost center or of cost centers subordinate to it. For example, the factory manager's salary is traceable only to the factory as a whole, while the salary of the manager of the coatings department is traceable *both* to the factory *and* to the coatings department.

Object-of-expenditure classification

The second basis for classifying operating costs is by the kinds of resources used in operations (supervision, electric power, etc.). We call this an object-of-expenditure classification (electric power is the object obtained by the expenditure). The purpose of the object-of-expenditure classification is to make the relationships between costs and their determinants easier to identify. This means that the costs in any one cost account should show roughly similar patterns of response to the various determinants of cost.

For example, if the costs of lubricating oil vary with the number of hours the machines are run and if the costs of cleaning supplies vary with the number of hours of labor used, these two costs

EXHIBIT 17–2.   Apex Company: Chart of Factory Cost Accounts

Department		2410 Factory Management	2420 Coatings Department	2430 Pesticides Department
01	Materials	2410.01	2420.01	2430.01
02	Processing labor	2410.02	2420.02	2430.02
11	Supervision	2410.11	2420.11	2430.11
12	Labor—travel time	2410.12	2420.12	2430.12
13	Labor—idle time	2410.13	2420.13	2430.13
14	Labor—clerical	2410.14	2420.14	2430.14
15	Labor—other	2410.15	2420.15	2430.15
21	Overtime premium	2410.21	2420.21	2430.21
22	Vacation and holiday pay	2410.22	2420.22	2430.22
23	Payroll taxes	2410.23	2420.23	2430.23
24	Pensions	2410.24	2420.24	2430.24
31	Travel allowances	2410.31	2420.31	2430.31
51	Tools	2410.51	2420.51	2430.51
52	Supplies	2410.52	2420.52	2430.52
53	Equipment rental	2410.53	2420.53	2430.53
54	Depreciation	2410.54	2420.54	2430.54
61	Insurance	2410.61	2420.61	2430.61
71	Other	2410.71	2420.71	2430.71

shouldn't be in the same object-of-expenditure account. Putting them together would obscure the underlying cost-volume relationships.

Exhibit 17–2 shows the account coding system used in Apex's factory. The object-of-expenditure account titles and code numbers are shown at the left; the full two-dimensional account codes are shown in the three columns at the right. When a cost is incurred, it must be classified both by cost center and by object of expenditure. If John Jones works a full eight hours repairing equipment in the coatings department at an hourly rate of $12, the account 2420.15 (Coatings Labor—Other) will be charged with $96 (8 × $12).

Activity classification

While the object-of-expenditure classification shows *which* resources are used and the organizational classification shows *where,* the activity classification shows *why.* Some business activities are designed to induce customers to buy merchandise or place orders; these are known as order-getting activities. Others are undertaken to provide services to outside customers or to manufacture finished products; these are called end-product activities. Still others are service and support activities, undertaken to support activities in the other two classes.

While cost-accounting systems may identify the costs of individual order-getting, service, and support activities, our concern in this chapter and the next is with end-product activities. Most of these consist of the production of goods or services for outside clients or customers—such as automobiles, restaurant meals, and hospital patient care.

The end-product activities in factories result in the production of identifiable quantities of individual products. The process of measuring the costs of these activities is known as *product costing;* the total cost assigned to a particular product is known as *product cost.* Product cost can be calculated in any of four main ways, as in the following table:

Method	*Basis*	
Process costing	Full-cost basis	Variable-cost basis
Job order costing	Full-cost basis	Variable-cost basis

This chapter will be devoted to a description of process costing, first on a full-cost basis and then on a variable-cost basis; job order costing will be discussed in Chapter 18.

PROCESS COSTING: FULL-COST BASIS

In process costing, the focal point is the goods or services produced in a production center in a specific period of time. If costing

---

TERMINOLOGY

A *production center* is a specific set of facilities in which end-product activities take place—the production of goods or services for inventory or delivery to customers.

---

is on a full-cost basis, each unit produced is assigned a proportionate share of *all* the costs of operating the production center in that period. The calculation is:

$$\text{Average unit cost} = \frac{\text{Total production costs for the period}}{\text{Total units of product manufactured}}$$

Output homogeneity

Costs in process costing are divided by a single divisor (units, pounds, bottles filled, etc.). This means that all units of output must be *homogeneous;* that is, they must be measurable in the same units so that we can add them together. In other words, process costing can be used in any production process which turns out a single kind of product (e.g., cement or flour) or performs a single operation (e.g., filling bottles of uniform size) for long periods at a time.

If a factory produces more than one kind of end product, it still may be able to use process costing if a common measure of output can be found for each of its production centers. For example, ABC Company's factory has three production centers—departments A, B, and C. The factory manufactures two very different products. Each production center, however, has a single kind of output, and process costing can be used. The costs of materials issued by the storeroom, labor, and other resources used by these three production centers are listed in the following table, along with the departments' outputs:

Department	Costs	Output
A	$200,000	100,000 pounds
B	100,000	40,000 gallons
C	310,000	50,000 boxes
Total ...	$610,000	

Department A produces semiprocessed products which it transfer to departments B and C. Its output is 100,000 pounds of semiprocessed products, at an average cost of $2 a pound ($200,000/100,000). These amounts are shown in the block at the left center of Exhibit 17–3. Department A transfers 30,000 pounds of semiprocessed products and $60,000 of its costs (30,000 × $2) to department B; the other 70,000 pounds (and $140,000 of costs) go to department C. The total cost of department B therefore is $160,000 ($100,000 of its own costs and $60,000 transferred from department A), and its finished output has a unit cost of $4 a gallon ($160,000/40,000), as shown in the block in the upper right-hand corner of the exhibit. Department C has total costs of $450,000 ($310,000 plus $140,000 from department A) and a unit cost of $9 a box ($450,000/50,000). All $610,000 of the factory's costs are now assigned to finished products:

Department B: 40,000 gallons × $4	$160,000
Department C: 50,000 boxes × $9	450,000
Total.................................	$610,000

Apex Company has a slightly simpler structure. It has only two production centers—the coatings department and the pesticides de-

Exhibit 17–3. Calculating Departmental Unit Cost

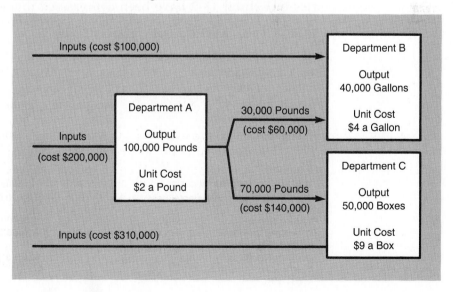

partment. The unit-cost divisor in the coatings department is the number of *gallons* of coatings manufactured; unit cost in the pesticides department is cost per *pound*.

Determining product cost: Direct product costs

The term *direct* in cost accounting means *readily traceable* to a specified costing entity (e.g., a department); the term *indirect* means *not readily traceable* to the costing entity in question. A cost may be fully traceable (direct) to one costing entity (e.g., a department) but not traceable (indirect) to another (e.g., a specific product). In using these terms, accountants specify the costing entity they are applying them to; otherwise, the meaning isn't clear.

Product cost in process costing consists of two broad classes of costs: (1) costs which are *direct costs* of the production centers in which the product is manufactured and therefore are also direct costs of the product, and (2) costs which are direct costs of cost centers which provide necessary service and support to two or more production centers. Costs in this second category are *indirect* costs of the output of individual production centers.

In full-costing systems, all the direct costs of a production center (department) are direct costs of the products passing through that production center, and all are assigned to those products. The direct costs of the two production centers in Apex Company's factory in May 19x1 are shown in the upper portion of Exhibit 17–4, along with the costs that are direct to the factory management support center but indirect to the production centers. To simplify the presentation, the 18 object-of-expenditure direct departmental cost categories in Exhibit 17–2 have been compressed into six.

EXHIBIT 17–4.   Apex Company: Factory Costs

	Service Center (Factory Management)	Production Centers	
		Coatings Department	Pesticides Department
Materials	—	$150,000	$ 50,000
Processing labor	—	30,000	30,000
Other labor	$35,000	5,000	10,000
Supplies	1,000	6,000	10,000
Depreciation	2,000	4,000	15,000
Other direct departmental costs	7,000	25,000	20,000
Total direct departmental cost	$45,000	$220,000	$135,000
Product output		100,000 gallons	300,000 pounds
Processing labor-hours		10,000 hours	5,000 hours
Average direct product cost:			
Coatings: $220,000/100,000		$2.20 a gallon	
Pesticides: $135,000/300,000			$0.45 a pound

Physical production data and labor-hour statistics for the two production centers are shown in the lower part of the exhibit. The bottom line shows that each unit of product in each production center is assigned the average of the direct costs in that production center—$2.20 a gallon in coatings and $0.45 a pound in pesticides.

Determining product costs: Indirect product costs

The direct costs of Apex's factory management cost center aren't traceable to either the coatings department or the pesticides department. Instead, they are incurred to support the operations of *both* production centers. Factory management is an example of a *service center;* its direct costs are indirect costs with respect to the operations of the two production centers. Although these costs aren't readily traceable to individual production centers, they are just as necessary to produce coatings and pesticides as the direct costs of operating the coatings and pesticides departments. If product cost is to include all the costs required by the manufacture of the product—as it is when product cost is prepared on a *full-cost* basis—some means must be found to assign a portion of these indirect costs to each unit of product.[1]

Apex assigns the costs of factory management to individual products by means of an *apportionment rate,* defined as the ratio of total factory management cost to total processing labor-hours in the two production centers combined:

$$\text{Apportionment rate} = \frac{\text{Total factory management cost}}{\text{Total processing labor-hours}} = \frac{\$45,000}{15,000} = \$3 \text{ an hour}$$

Since the coatings department used 10,000 processing labor-hours in May, it was assigned $30,000 (10,000 hours × $3) in factory management costs for product costing purposes; the pesticides department was assigned the remaining $15,000 (5,000 hours × $3).

Apex uses total processing labor-hours to distribute factory management costs because this is a measurable characteristic of each product and because total factory management cost appears to vary in the long run with the number of processing labor-hours. In the long view, therefore, the production of a gallon of coatings requiring

---

[1] The costs of Apex's nonfactory cost centers aren't assigned to individual products and don't enter this illustration. In general, the causal relationships between production and administrative costs above the factory level are extremely remote and difficult to identify. Costs in these categories are seldom assigned to individual products except in situations in which the price the customer pays is tied by formula to cost.

1/10 of a labor-hour can be said to cause the company to spend $1/10 \times \$3 = \$0.30$ of the company's factory management costs.

The full-costing calculations for Apex's two products in May 19x1 are summarized as follows:

	Coatings	Pesticides
Production costs:		
Direct costs	$220,000	$135,000
Indirect costs	30,000	15,000
Total	$250,000	$150,000
Production output	100,000 gallons	300,000 pounds
Unit cost	$2.50 a gallon	$0.50 a pound

Apportionment of factory management costs therefore raised the average cost of a gallon of coatings by $0.30 (from $2.20 to $2.50) and the cost of pesticides by $0.05 a pound (from $0.45 to $0.50).

Apportionment versus allocation of indirect costs

Apex Company is able to use a single apportionment rate to assign factory management costs to individual products because this appears to approximate the long-term relationship between production volume and total factory management cost. This simple solution may be unsatisfactory if some elements of factory management cost are determined by one product characteristic (e.g., processing labor) while other elements are determined by one or more other product characteristics (e.g., weight of raw materials). To obtain more accurate product costs in these situations, the accountant may decide to use two or even more apportionment rates, one for each major group of cost elements.

The costing problem is even more complex if various elements of factory management cost are affected by the production center in which production takes place. For example, an hour of processing labor in the pesticides department may require more factory management support than a labor-hour in the coatings department. This could happen if pesticides hours required more machine maintenance or scheduling services from factory management. In other words, the level of Apex's indirect costs is determined by characteristics of the *production centers* (number of maintenance hours used) rather than by some characteristic that is common to all the end products (number of processing labor-hours). In such cases, an hour in one department can be said to cause more factory management cost than an hour in another department.

This situation calls for *interdepartmental allocation,* a two-stage process. In the first stage, indirect costs are reassigned (allocated) to the various production centers; in the second stage, the costs allocated to a production center are combined with the production center's direct costs to yield the numerator of the product costing rate in that production center. This costing rate is then used to apportion both the direct costs and the indirect costs to the units of product produced during the period, as shown in the following diagram:

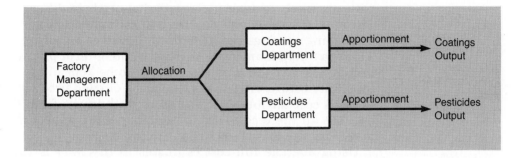

Although we'll examine interdepartmental allocations in depth in the next chapter, we can illustrate the procedure using the Apex example. If Apex had determined that 80 percent of the factory management support cost was allocable to the pesticides department, we'd have the following result:

	Coatings	Pesticides
Production costs:		
Direct costs	$220,000	$135,000
Indirect costs:		
0.2 × $45,000	9,000	
0.8 × $45,000		36,000
Total	$229,000	$171,000
Production output	100,000 gallons	300,000 pounds
Unit cost	$2.29 a gallon	$0.57 a pound

Product costs for external financial reporting

Unit costs calculated by the full-costing method we've just described are useful in calculating the cost of goods sold and the cost of product inventories for external financial reporting. Each period's operating costs are assigned to work in process and to finished goods by one of the methods described in Chapter 8—FIFO, LIFO, or average costing.[2] Transfers of costs from the finished goods inventory to the cost of goods sold are also determined by one of

---

[2] For an explanation of how this is done, see Gordon Shillinglaw, *Managerial Cost Accounting,* 5th ed. (Homewood, Ill.: Richard D. Irwin, 1982), chap. 14.

these three methods, by exactly the same processes companies use to account for the costs of purchased goods.

Average full cost in managerial decision making

Management may find unit costs based on full costing useful in managerial decision making, even though fixed and variable costs are likely to enter incremental analysis in different ways. For example, management may need to estimate the incremental cost of keeping coatings products on the market on a long-term basis. This may help management establish long-term pricing targets or decide whether the products deserve to be kept in the line for the indefinite future. Eventually, the price of each product must cover the full cost attributable to it or be withdrawn from the market, because all these costs are incremental with respect to a decision to market the product on a continuing basis.

Using average full-cost estimates in this way is valid if three major assumptions hold true:

1. The amount of indirect costs apportioned to a product is a reasonable approximation to the amount caused by this product; that is, this amount of cost could be eliminated eventually if the product were discontinued.
2. The unit prices of resource inputs are at the levels anticipated during the period covered by the decision management needs to make.
3. Departmental volume is at the level at which the facilities were designed to operate; that is, fixed costs are spread over the volume they were intended to support.

The first of these assumptions is violated if the apportionments or allocations don't really measure the indirect costs caused by the product. The second assumption is most likely to be violated in periods of rapid price changes—mostly during inflation. The second and third assumptions may be violated if the cost calculation is based on the historical costs of only one period: If volume in that period is abnormally high or low, the average fixed cost will be lower or higher than management has reason to expect. This error can be avoided by performing the calculation on estimated data rather than on actual historical data.

PROCESS COSTING: VARIABLE-COSTING BASIS

Full-cost data, no matter how carefully constructed and no matter how useful for their intended purposes, don't identify the short-run variable costs that are affected by variations in the use of operating capacity. To provide unit costs that are more useful and to introduce more flexibility into cost data generally, some companies calculate product cost on a *variable-costing* basis (sometimes called *direct costing*).

Variable costing segregates the variable component of manufacturing costs in product cost records and subsequently in internal profit performance reports. *Under variable costing, unit cost is defined as the estimated increase in total variable cost which results from the production of an additional unit of the product.* Fixed manufacturing costs are excluded from product cost completely because they are unaffected by the volume of units produced.

For example, Apex Company's coatings department's operating costs show the following behavior pattern:

	Fixed Cost per Month	Variable Cost per Gallon
Materials	—	$1.50
Processing labor	—	0.30
Other labor	$ 4,000	0.01
Supplies	2,000	0.04
Depreciation	4,000	—
Other direct costs	15,000	0.10
Factory management costs*	25,000	0.05
Total	$50,000	$2.00

* The variable elements of factory management costs vary in proportion to the number of processing labor-hours. Processing labor time in coatings is proportionately variable with the volume of production. The provision for variable factory management costs can be included in the departmental costing rate, as in this table, or established as a separate apportionment rate.

Under variable costing, the cost of each gallon of output in the coatings department is $2.00.

Variable costing for easier cost estimation

The cost amounts in this chapter represent the coatings department's anticipated experience in a time when operations are at the volume level for which the facilities were designed, 100,000 gallons a month. We refer to this as *normal volume.* We'll now assume the department has a good deal of idle capacity because it is processing only 80,000 gallons a month. In light of this low volume, management has made some reductions in its fixed-cost structure, mainly a $500 a month reduction in equipment rentals below the normal amount.

Apex's management is considering a proposal to market coatings in a new geographic area, with an estimated sales volume of 10,000 gallons a month in the first year. The question is whether this is in the company's best interests in the short run.

This increment is clearly within existing capacity limits. Relying on its variable costing data, management estimates that the increment in total variable cost will be $20,000 a month (10,000 gallons × $2). Although management sees no reason why the variability on this incremental volume would depart from the normal $2 rate, departmental equipment rental costs would have to go back up to their normal level, an increase of $500 a month over their present level.

Apex's entry into the new market would be through a regional distributor. Apex would charge the distributor $2.70 a gallon, and the distributor would pay all freight, taxes, and regional marketing costs. Apex's selling and administrative expenses would be likely to increase by about $1,000 a month, the salary of one additional clerk in the accounting department. The first year's monthly incremental profit before income taxes therefore is estimated to be as follows:

	Per Unit	Total
Sales revenues	$2.70	$27,000
Less: Variable costs	2.00	20,000
Contribution margin	0.70	7,000
Less: Incremental fixed costs*		1,500
Incremental profit		$ 5,500

* $500 in manufacturing costs; $1,000 in selling and administrative costs.

Variable costing contributes two insights to management. First, by identifying the variable costs of producing a gallon of coatings, variable costing gives management a basis on which to estimate the increment in these components of total cost. Second, by *not* including fixed costs in factory unit cost, variable costing calls attention to fixed costs by reporting them as separate totals for the period. With fixed costs highlighted in this way, management presumably would avoid the temptation to assume that the increment in fixed cost would be zero or that it could be approximated by multiplying the change in volume by the average fixed cost per gallon at normal volume.

Variable costing also gives management a clearer view of the impact on profit of errors in its forecasts of sales volume. For example, suppose management decides to extend its operations into the new market this year, thereby increasing the fixed factory costs of the coatings department by $500 a month and selling and administrative expenses by $1,000. With the information made available by variable costing, management can quite easily prepare the following estimates of profit sensitivity:

	Incremental Gallons per Month		
	5,000	10,000	15,000
Sales revenues ($2.70)	$13,500	$27,000	$40,500
Less: Variable costs ($2.00)	10,000	20,000	30,000
Contribution margin ($0.70)	3,500	7,000	10,500
Less: Incremental fixed costs	1,500	1,500	1,500
Incremental profit	$ 2,000	$ 5,500	$ 9,000

Management is likely to be reassured by this indication that the new market will generate an incremental profit even if the incremental volume turns out to be only half the forecasted amount.

Variable costing: The negative side

A full evaluation of variable costing requires more background than we have been able to provide in this brief description. We must caution, however, that variable costing isn't the answer to all problems in all situations.

First, product costs derived by variable costing imply that variable costs are linearly proportional to variations in operating volume in the short run. If this assumption isn't valid, variable costing may produce misleading estimates of product cost.

Second, product costs yielded by variable costing can be misinterpreted, just as full-costing product costs can be misinterpreted. If management is led to believe that these are the *only* costs to be affected by volume-determining actions, it will overlook any changes in fixed costs that are likely to take place in the short run.

Third, many decisions have a time horizon that extends beyond the immediate period. Apex's management, for example, should determine whether its venture into the new market is strictly a short-term expedient to soak up idle capacity this year or whether it is a foray into a promising market for ongoing penetration in the future. If the venture is to succeed on an ongoing basis, revenues from the new market must be large enough to cover all the costs attributable to it—and these will include many costs that won't change in the short run, as long as operating capacity remains unchanged. At least some of the coatings department's fixed costs could be eliminated in time if the company decided to reduce its capacity rather than use it to supply all its existing customers and those in the new market as well. By the same token, a company introducing a new product needs to know how much cost the product will cause, on the average, at a volume appropriate to the capacity of the facilities it requires. At least some of these costs will be fixed in the short run.

Full-cost data may not answer these long-term questions either, because one or more of the three assumptions we identified earlier may be invalid; that is, allocations of service and support costs may be inappropriate, input prices may be out of date, or the volume denominator may not represent the designed capacity of the production facilities. Even so, full cost is likely to approximate long-term incremental cost better than short-run average variable cost.

This suggests that management may wish to calculate product cost on at least two bases—a variable-costing basis for use in decisions with short time horizons and a more comprehensive basis for financial accounting and long-term decisions. These latter unit costs are likely to be closer to full cost than to variable cost.

IMPACT OF INFLATION

So far we've been assuming that unit costs are likely to be the same from period to period as long as volume remains unchanged. One factor that may interfere with this happy assumption is the impact of systematic changes in the level of input prices—generally associated today with periods of persistent price inflation.

Inflation's impact is uneven, as we pointed out in Chapter 14. Some input prices may remain unchanged or even decrease, even though prices generally are mounting rapidly. Furthermore, product costs determined by processing actual transactions data will reflect various combinations of past and current input prices. The depreciation-cost component, for example, will reflect prices in many previous periods, while operating labor costs reflect current wage rates.

Systems for measuring unit costs can respond to inflation in two ways. First, product costs emerging from the routine processing of current transactions can be calculated to reflect the current-costing approach we outlined in Chapter 14; that is, each resource input can be measured at an estimate of its current replacement cost rather than its historical cost. The main purpose of this change is to keep management abreast of the current impact of resource price changes—to identify the profit spreads we referred to in Chapter 14 as the *sustainable gross margin.* In some countries, product costs calculated in this fashion can also be applied to the inventories and cost of goods sold in company financial statements, but in the United States they now are presented by large companies as supplementary financial information only.

Second, estimates of future unit costs should be based on estimates of future trends in input prices and production efficiency during the period affected by the decision. For a decision applicable to the next six months only, adjustments may not be large. For decisions on extended construction contracts, however, adjustments in at least some input costs are likely to be substantial. Again, the adjustments should be made input by input, not on the basis of the consumer price index. What matters is what will happen to the prices of resources the company actually uses, not the prices of a general resource package.

IMPACT OF THE LEARNING CURVE

Two factors other than resource price changes may induce period-to-period changes in the unit costs of manufactured products. One is change in technology—the installation of new equipment designed to reduce operating costs. The other is the company's ability to learn to produce more efficiently, with no change in technology. This second effect is less obvious than the effects of technological change and therefore requires a brief explanation.

Nature of the learning curve

Cost analysts have found that the effect of experience on operating costs often follows a highly predictable pattern from period to period. This pattern can be represented both algebraically and graphically and is known as an *experience curve* or *learning curve.* It applies primarily to the labor component of operating cost.

The basis for the learning curve is that repetition leads to familiarity, which leads to improved productivity. The first time a new operation is performed, both the personnel and the operating procedures are untried. As the operation is repeated, the work goes more smoothly and labor costs go down. This is likely to continue until the possibilities for improvement under the existing technology have been exhausted.

The effect of experience on cost is summarized in the *learning ratio* or *improvement ratio:*

$$\text{Learning ratio} = \frac{\text{Average labor cost for the first } 2X \text{ units}}{\text{Average labor cost for the first } X \text{ units}}$$

If the average labor cost for the first 500 units is $12.50 and the average labor cost for the first 1,000 units is $10, the learning ratio is 80 percent:

$$\text{Learning ratio} = \frac{\$10}{\$12.50} = 80 \text{ percent}$$

In other words, every time *cumulative* output doubles, *cumulative* average cost declines to 80 percent of its previous level. Since the average cost of the first 1,000 units was $10, the average cost of the first 2,000 units will be expected to be 20 percent less, or $8 a unit.

The effect of learning shows up clearly when the equations are plotted on graph paper. An 80 percent learning curve is shown in Exhibit 17–5. The diagram at the left is plotted on ordinary graph paper. It shows costs declining rapidly at first and then more slowly. If the curve were extended, further reductions would eventually become small enough to be ignored. The right diagram shows the same relationship on logarithmic paper. It is a straight line because the *rate* of decrease is constant.

If producing a second 1,000 units will reduce cumulative average cost from $10 to $8, the cost of the second 1,000 units will have to be only $6,000, or $6 each:

	Total Cost	Units	Average Cost
First 2,000 units	$16,000	2,000	$ 8
First 1,000 units	10,000	1,000	10
Second 1,000 units	$ 6,000	1,000	$ 6

Defining the learning curve in terms of this incremental relationship would be useful, but the mathematical formula is more difficult to work with. As a result, learning-curve improvement ratios are usually stated as percentage reductions in cumulative average labor

EXHIBIT 17–5.   An 80 Percent Learning Curve

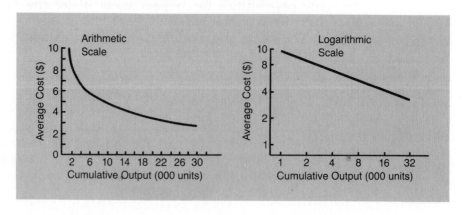

cost. Incremental cost can be calculated by solving an equation for two different cumulative production totals, then subtracting one from the other.

Although most processes improve as the company gains experience with them, learning curves apply mainly in processes that can be thought of as new. Most are based on companies' experiences with new products or new models, but the same pattern can be found in new factories as well. All that is necessary is repetitive production over an extended time—and effective management.

Learning-curve applications

The main impact of learning-curve analysis is likely to be on data collected for use in decision making, particularly in connection with product pricing and marketing strategy decisions. For example, suppose Laurel Company has been asked to bid on an order for 4,000 units of a product which has already had a run of 4,000 units at an average labor cost of $64 with an 80 percent improvement curve. The incremental labor cost of the next 4,000 units can then be computed as follows:

New average cost: 80 percent of $64	$51.20
New total cost: 8,000 × $51.20	$409,600
Old total cost: 4,000 × $64	256,000
Total incremental cost	153,600
Average incremental cost: $153,600/4,000	$38.40

An ability to forecast this cost reduction may make the difference between landing and losing a profitable order.

SUMMARY

Accounting systems typically classify operating costs by organization unit, by object of expenditure, and by activity (products produced or services rendered by the company). The activity classification is the most important—it is used in financial accounting, in managerial decision making, and sometimes in calculating the amounts due from customers or reimbursement agencies. It is also the most difficult, because activity costs ordinarily must include costs that can't be traced unequivocally to specific activities.

This chapter has described two different bases of measuring the costs of goods or services in operations in which the output of individual production centers is essentially homogeneous—that is, in process-costing situations. The full-costing basis provides unit cost data for use in financial accounting and in certain kinds of managerial decisions with a long-term focus. Variable costing—in which product cost is limited to the variable costs of production—provides unit cost data which are useful in short-term utilization-of-capacity decisions.

Historical product cost data of these kinds may need to be adjusted for managerial use because input prices are changing (e.g., in inflationary periods), because the company has installed new facilities incorporating more modern technology, or because management and the work force have learned how to use the existing facilities more efficiently. The learning effect is often predictable on the basis of identifiable learning curves.

KEY TERMS

Allocation	Normal volume
Apportionment	Object of expenditure
Cost accounting	Process costing
Cost center	Product cost
Direct cost	Production center
Full costing	Service center
Indirect cost	Traceability
Learning curve	Variable costing

INDEPENDENT STUDY PROBLEMS (Solutions in Appendix B)

1. Chart of cost accounts. Zebra Company has 84 employees: 56 in manufacturing, 18 in marketing and sales, and 10 in administrative positions. Its manufacturing employees occupy three quarters of the space in a single-story building in a suburban industrial park; the remainder of the space is divided equally between administrative staff and the marketing division, which includes the finished goods storage area.

Part of the factory area is used to assemble low-priced vacuum cleaners from purchased parts; most of the rest is used to cut, stamp, bend, and assemble sheet metal into air-conditioning ducts. The remainder of the factory area is used for parts storage, the factory manager's office, and a small maintenance shop.

Zebra Company's cost account structure is very simple. Last month's operating cost report showed the following:

Salaries	$ 55,000
Wages	82,000
Materials	157,000
Depreciation	22,000
Freight	23,000
Insurance	8,000
Heat	6,000
Telephone	4,000
Electricity	5,000
Travel and entertainment	9,000
Property taxes	18,000
Postage	3,000
Supplies	7,000
Miscellaneous	15,000

a. What changes would you suggest making in the chart of cost accounts? Be as specific as you can and state the reasons for your recommendations.

b. Offer at least one plausible explanation of Zebra's previous lack of interest in making the changes you are recommending.

2. Unit costs: multiple departments. Flax Company manufactures two products, PDX and QYK. The company's factory has only four production centers (departments), each performing a single operation on each product. Both products are processed first in production department A. PDX is then finished in production department B, while QYK goes to production department C and then to production department D for finishing.

The costs and production volumes of Flax Company's production departments in a normal month are as follows:

Department	Variable Costs	Fixed Costs	Output (units)
A	$30,000	$10,000	50,000
B	20,000	5,000	12,500
C	24,000	15,000	37,500
D	15,000	12,000	37,500
Total	$89,000	$42,000	

a. Calculate the unit cost of each of the company's two products on a full-costing basis.

b. Recalculate unit costs on a variable-costing basis.

c. Why are the relative variable costs of these two products so different from their relative full costs?

3. Unit costs: apportionment. Flax Company's accountants (see problem 2) have just discovered that the costs supplied in problem 2 are only the direct costs of the four production departments. The costs of the factory's service centers amount to $27,500 a month. Although service-center costs are fixed costs, major expansions or contractions of production department capacity are likely to call for proportional changes in service-center capacity.

An analysis indicates that most of the work done in the service centers relates to the amount of labor time required by the work of the production departments. A unit of product QYK requires 50 percent more labor time than a unit of product PDX.

a. Apportion the total cost of the service centers to the two products in proportion to total labor time, and calculate the average full cost of each product.

b. At the unit cost you calculated in answer to part *a,* QYK has a very narrow profit margin. The sales manager suggests that apportioning service-center costs in proportion to the number of units of output would distribute these costs more fairly. Perform the calculations necessary to carry out this suggestion.

c. Should the sales manager's proposal be implemented? What does "more fairly" mean in this context? Explain your reasoning.

EXERCISES AND PROBLEMS

4. Discussion question. University Hospital's main operating room is the scene of many operations, ranging from simple diagnostic procedures requiring the assistance of one nurse to complex microsurgery requiring a large team of surgeons, nurses, and other professional staff. The costs of all operating personnel except surgeons and the costs of all equipment and supplies used in the operating room are charged to the operating room cost center in the hospital's accounts.

Each operating room patient is charged the estimated average cost of the operating room per operating room hour, multiplied by the number of hours (or fraction) the patient spends there. In that way, patients requiring more operating room time are charged more than those who are in the operating room only briefly.

Is this a good example of an appropriate process-costing situation? Explain.

5. Unit cost: full costing. Troy Company makes inexpensive plastic pens. Its factory has three production centers, each responsible for one process: molding, filling, and packing. It has two service centers: administration and maintenance. The direct factory costs of these five cost centers last month were as follows:

	Administration	Maintenance	Molding	Filling	Packing
Materials	—	$ 600	$ 5,000	$10,000	$ 4,000
Salaries and wages	$ 7,500	3,200	7,000	6,000	8,000
Depreciation	100	700	2,500	1,000	100
Rent	12,000	—	—	—	—
Power	1,200	—	—	—	—
Other	4,200	500	1,500	2,000	900
Total	$25,000	$5,000	$16,000	$19,000	$13,000

The factory produced 500,000 pens last month.

Determine the unit cost in each of the three production centers and develop a combined apportionment rate for the two service centers last month.

6. Unit cost: variable costing. Materials costs in Troy Company's factory (see problem 5) are proportionally variable with volume in all four cost centers that have materials costs. Salaries and wages are 20 percent fixed and 80 percent variable with volume in the three production centers, and 100 percent fixed in the two service centers. Depreciation and rent are entirely fixed in all cost centers. Power costs are 65 percent fixed and 35 percent variable. "Other" costs are 90 percent fixed and 10 percent variable in factory administration and 50 percent fixed and 50 percent variable in each of the other four cost centers.

a. Calculate unit cost on a variable-costing basis.
b. What reasons might management have for preferring this unit cost calculation to the calculation you made in answer to problem 5? What disadvantages does it have?

7. Allocation and apportionment. Troy Company's managers (see problems 5 and 6) have found that most of the company's competitors buy molded pen casings in bulk from manufacturers of molded plastic products rather than do their own molding. You have the following additional information about Troy Company's factory:

1. The $12,000 monthly rental cost is for the use of the factory building. The five cost centers occupy the following percentages of the space in this building: administration, 20 percent; maintenance, 5 percent; molding, 35 percent; filling, 15 percent; packing, 25 percent.
2. A consulting engineer has estimated that 50 percent of the power consumption is for interior lighting in the building, 5 percent is used by equipment in the factory's administrative offices, 10 percent is used in maintenance, 20 percent is used in molding, and 15 percent is used in the filling operation.
3. 60 percent of the time of maintenance personnel is spent in the molding department; virtually all the remaining 40 percent is spent in the filling department.
4. No other relationship has been established between administrative and maintenance costs and characteristics of the three production centers.

a. Allocate the cost of rent and power among the five cost centers in the proportions indicated.
b. Allocate the cost of maintenance (including its share of rent and power costs) to the molding and filling departments.
c. Calculate the average unit cost for last month, in four parts: molding, filling, packing, and administration. Each of these four parts should include the costs you allocated to these four cost centers in answer to parts a and b.
d. How, if at all, would the unit costs you calculated in answer to part c bear on management's interest in competitors' use of independent molding companies? What factors limit their usefulness in this connection?

8. Apportionment versus allocation. The president of Troy Company (see problem 7) believes that a more accurate product cost can be derived if, after the allocations in parts a and b have been made, the remaining costs of factory administration are allocated to the three production centers in proportion to their relative percentages of the total of all other costs, including the costs allocated to them in answer to parts a and b.

a. Perform this allocation and calculate the unit cost for last month, with three components: molding, filling, and packing.
b. Calculate the differences between the unit costs you developed in answer to part a and those you calculated in answer to problem 7, part c.
c. What does the president mean by "more accurate" unit costs? Why might this added accuracy be important? Are the unit costs produced by the final allocation called for in part a more accurate than those you developed in answer to problem 7, part c? Explain.

9. Classification of costs. Stan Brown is the manager of one of Griffin Company's five processing departments. Stan has an excellent understanding of the technical intricacies of his department's work tasks and he is quite adept as a motivator of people.

As a conscientious manager, however, Stan is disturbed by his inability to fathom the managerial significance of cost data. Stan knows that some costs vary with volume while others don't. He also recognizes that some costs are incurred exclusively by his department while others are shared. For starters, Stan wants to know if these different dimensions of cost can be considered concurrently.

Stan didn't pursue the matter until he was somewhat taken aback to learn that last month his department incurred costs of more than $100,000 for the first time during his seven months on the job. The nature and amounts of the costs were as follows:

Materials used	$ 11,200
Home-office support	16,200
Stan Brown's salary	2,400
Janitorial services	2,300
Quality control inspection	1,800
Processing labor	59,400
Building depreciation	4,100
Machinery depreciation	8,600
Heat, light, and power	1,700
Fire insurance	1,900
Total	$109,600

Each department uses its own machines. Depreciation is calculated on the basis of the machines' useful lives, and the cost of fire insurance is assigned on the basis of the original cost of each department's machines. Janitorial cost is based on the square footage of each department's work area, and the cost of the inspection staff is assigned as a predetermined fee for each unit completed and transferred to another processing department. The heat, light, and power costs are charged to each department on the basis of the number of worker-hours used. Although Stan doesn't know how the home-office charge is determined, he has noticed that it increases by $100 each month, no matter what happens to volume.

Prepare a table classifying the department's costs as (*a*) variable or fixed, and (*b*) direct or indirect.

10.   Average full cost.   Dandy Panda Company manufactures toys. Its factory has four production centers—stuffed animals, dolls, figurines, and packaging—and three service centers—administration, scheduling, and maintenance. It has the following factory costs and output per month:

	Variable Costs	Fixed Costs	Output (units)
Stuffed animals	$21,000	$ 3,000	5,000
Dolls	12,000	3,000	1,000
Figurines	13,000	5,000	2,000
Packaging	8,000	1,000	8,000
Administration	—	10,000	
Scheduling	—	6,000	
Maintenance	4,000	2,000	
Total	$58,000	$30,000	

Packaging operations are essentially the same for each product, so the output of the packaging center consists of the sum of the outputs of the other three production centers.

a. Calculate the average direct cost of each of the company's products.
b. Apportion all service-center costs to products on the basis of their direct production costs and calculate average full cost on that basis.
c. Apportion all service-center costs to products on the basis of the number of units of output and calculate average full cost on that basis.
d. How would you choose between your answer to part b and your answer to part c? In other words, under what circumstances would you recommend that management use the unit costs in part b in preference to the unit costs in part c?

11. Average variable cost.   Dandy Panda Company (see problem 10) has an opportunity to accept a special order for 1,000 figurines, to be manufactured and delivered to the customer at the rate of 500 units a month. You have the following information in addition to the data in problem 10:

1. Variable maintenance department costs vary in response to variations in the number of maintenance hours used.
2. The maintenance costs in problem 10 cover 250 hours of maintenance service. The figurines department uses 120 of those hours and this usage is proportionally variable with figurine output.
3. The packaging department uses 10 maintenance service hours and this usage is completely fixed.
4. Acceptance of the special order for figurines would require a 10 percent increase in the fixed costs of the figurines production center in each of the two months in which production would take place.
5. Acceptance of the figurines order would have no effect on the fixed costs of any cost center except those of the figurines production center.
6. Acceptance of the figurines order would have no effect on the company's other business.

a. Calculate the average unit cost of figurines on a variable-costing basis.
b. If the offer price of the special order is $10 a unit and the sales force would receive a 3 percent commission on the sale, should Dandy Panda accept the order? Show your calculations.

12. Chart of cost accounts; unit cost.   Marina Corporation bottles soft drinks. It had the following operating costs in June:

1. Employees' salaries and wages: factory management, $3,500; bottling crews, $5,000; factory maintenance staff, $1,500; sales force, $5,700; executive office, $4,500.
2. Rent: factory building, $3,200; executive offices, $1,800; sales offices, $2,500; executive office equipment, $200.
3. Materials used: sugar, $2,500; flavorings, $1,000; carbon dioxide, $300.

4. Depreciation: factory equipment, $2,100; executive office equipment, $100; sales force vehicles, $500.
5. Electricity: factory, $800; executive offices, $150; sales offices, $200.
6. Telephone: factory, $100; executive offices, $400; sales offices, $600.
7. Water: factory, $400; executive offices, $50; sales offices, $100.
8. Supplies used: factory, $600; executive offices, $800; sales offices, $400.

Marina Corporation had 1,000 cases of soft drinks in inventory at the start of business on June 1. It bottled 10,000 cases in June and had 1,500 cases in inventory at the close of business on June 30. Inventories of work in process were negligible at the end of each working day.

a. Establish a two-dimensional chart of cost accounts for Marina Corporation—by organization unit and object of expenditure—and use these accounts to classify the company's costs in June.
b. Should Marina Company add an activity dimension to its chart of cost accounts? State your reasons.
c. Calculate the average cost of manufacturing a case of soft drinks in June.
d. Calculate the cost of goods sold on a FIFO basis. The FIFO cost of the June 1 inventory of soft drinks was $2,000.

13. Learning curve. Cheryl Corporation purchased the exclusive right to produce a newly patented industrial tool. The first run, consisting of 600 units, was manufactured in August and it had a direct-labor cost of $18,000. Later in August, there was a second run of 600 units which brought the total direct-labor cost for the month to $32,400.

Cheryl's engineering staff stated that a similar rate of improvement would be experienced in producing another 1,200 units in September, and that it would recur in the manufacture of an additional batch of 2,400 units in October. The engineers had reason to believe, however, that a comparable rate of improvement would not be experienced beyond the first 4,800 units.

a. What was Cheryl Corporation's learning ratio?
b. What was the anticipated total incremental direct-labor cost to produce 1,200 units in September?
c. What was the anticipated average incremental direct-labor cost per unit to produce 2,400 additional units in October?
d. What was the anticipated average direct-labor cost per unit for the first 4,800 units produced?
e. Cheryl's management believes the company can be competitive if it can reduce the cumulative average direct labor cost of the tool to $20 on the first 9,600 units to be produced. The company expects to produce 4,800 units in November. What cumulative learning ratio must the company experience in November to meet the $20 target? What incremental learning ratio will be necessary to produce this result?

14. Multiple products. Larkin Company's factory has four production centers and an administrative service center. It manufactures five different products, but each production center performs an identical set of operations on each product it processes. Production costs in a typical month are as follows:

	Variable Costs	Fixed Costs	Output (units)
Production A	$20,000	$ 4,000	16,000
Production B	10,000	5,000	10,000
Production C	25,000	8,000	16,000
Production D	12,000	8,000	16,000
Administration	—	20,000	
Total	$67,000	$45,000	

Production in a typical month is as follows:

Product	Output (units)	Production Centers Used
X	5,000	A, B, D
XL	8,000	A, C, D
Y	2,000	B, C
YL	3,000	A, B, C
Z	3,000	C, D

a. Calculate the average direct cost in each production center.
b. Calculate the average full cost of each product, using an apportionment rate based on units of output to apportion administrative costs.
c. Calculate the cost of each product on a variable-costing basis.
d. Larkin Company is considering adding a new product, YM, to its line. YM would be identical to Y, except that it would be processed further in production center D. Monthly volume probably would average 1,000 units, and production capacity is now available to manufacture this volume. Prepare a brief report summarizing the estimated cost implications of the proposal to add this new product.

15. Cost classification systems. Ace Maintenance Company provides routine equipment maintenance service and performs equipment repairs for a large number of industrial users in the New York metropolitan area. The company will service or repair almost any factory equipment and has built a reputation for prompt, efficient service.

Ace Maintenance was founded 10 years ago by Paul Mace, a highly gifted salesman and administrator. Mace is still president of the company, doing most of the direct selling himself. His vice president, Don Wynant, is responsible for hiring all service personnel and for the day-to-day operation of the service end of the business.

The company's operating cost accounts for a typical month show the following balances:

	Executive Office	Accounting	Operations
Salaries and wages	$10,000	$3,000	$26,000
Overtime premiums	—	—	1,100
Materials and supplies	500	450	1,000
Repair parts	—	—	14,000
Utilities	1,200	—	—
Payroll taxes	300	120	1,200
Pension plan	700	150	1,300
Travel	100	—	2,100
Advertising	200	—	—
Insurance	800	—	—
Taxes	900	—	—
Rent	2,500	—	—
Miscellaneous	400	30	600
Total	$17,600	$3,750	$47,300

A large industrial service company has offered to buy Mace's interest in the business. Mace would retire and his place would be taken by a president and a salaried sales manager.

a. The company's chart of accounts has three departmental codes (one each for the executive office, accounting, and operations) and the 13 object-of-expenditure classifications listed in the table. In what ways, if any, will the chart of accounts have to be changed to meet the needs of the new owners and the new manager? Give reasons for your suggestions.

b. What problems would you be likely to encounter in trying to carry out your suggestions?

16. Full costing; implications for production decisions. Segal Corporation owns and operates two factories. Factory A manufactures an industrial material, which it sells both to Segal's factory B and to outside customers. Factory costs and volumes are now at the following levels:

	Factory A	Factory B
Costs:		
Variable:		
From factory A	—	$ 80,000
Other	$150,000	100,000
Fixed	50,000	40,000
Total costs	$200,000	$220,000
Volume (units)	100,000	20,000

Factory A charges factory B its average full cost of production for each unit of the industrial material it transfers to factory B. Each unit of factory B's output requires two units of materials from factory A. The costs of these units are included in factory B's variable costs in the table.

Segal's management is considering increasing factory B's output by 20 percent. This additional output would then be processed further in a new factory. The costs of processing these units would be as follows:

> Variable processing costs .... $3 a unit
> Fixed processing costs .... $8,000 a month

Both factory A and factory B have ample capacity to supply the new factory's requirements of factory B's output, with no increases in their fixed costs.

a. Calculate the average unit cost of the new product if Segal Corporation uses the same method of transferring costs from factory B to the new factory as it uses to transfer industrial materials from factory A to factory B.

b. Calculate the average incremental manufacturing cost attributable to the decision to establish the new factory and use it to process a portion of factory B's output.

c. Prepare a brief explanation of any difference between your answers to parts *a* and *b*. If your two answers are identical, explain why.

17. Average full cost; departmental inventories.

Edgeware Company's factory manufactures a single product, which passes through four production departments in succession, starting with department A. To allow for possible irregularities in delivery schedules, each department except department A usually maintains a small inventory of the output of the immediately preceding department. The cumulative cost of work completed by one department is transferred to the next department; the cumulative cost of transfers from department D is credited to department D and charged to the finished goods inventory. Each department's costs are accounted for on a FIFO basis.

You have the following information for the month of May:

| | | | Unprocessed Units in ||
Department	Direct Costs	Units Started and Completed	Beginning Inventory	Ending Inventory
A	$60,000	100,000	0	0
B	22,000	100,000	10,000	10,000
C	27,000	90,000	0	10,000
D	15,000	100,000	10,000	0
Service	24,000			

None of the production departments had done any of its work on the units in its inventory at the beginning or at the end of the month.

a. Calculate the average direct cost in each department in May.

b. Calculate the average full cost of producing a unit of finished product in May. Service costs are apportioned only to units finished by department D during the month.

c. The beginning inventory in department B had a FIFO cost of 50 cents a unit. How much cost was transferred from department B to department C in May? What was the average of those costs?

d. The average cost you calculated in answer to part *c* should be slightly different from the average cost you calculated in answer to part *a*. Why did that difference arise? Assuming that the difference is significantly large in some months, for what purpose or purposes would you use the unit cost in your answer to part *a* in preference to the unit cost in your answer to part *c*? Why?

e. What additional costing problems would have to be solved if the beginning and ending inventories in any department were partly processed by that department?

18.   Allocation and apportionment of costs.   Computeronics Corporation is engaged in two types of service: preparation of business payrolls by computer for various outside customers, and word processing of documents and briefs for law firms. In addition to maintaining a task-oriented production department for each of these services, Computeronics has a marketing group and a staff of technicians responsible for equipment repairs and preventive maintenance.

Although Computeronics has been profitable during its four-year corporate life, it recently began to encounter intense competition. Top management decided it needed to know more about its costs. It soon discovered that no information was available on either the source or the distribution of the company's costs. Costs therefore were carefully tabulated on a departmental basis for the first time. The table identifies the direct costs incurred by each of the company's departments in October.

	Materials, Parts, and Supplies	Salaries, Wages, and Benefits	Other Expenses
Top management	$ 4,100	$ 67,700	$ 12,200
Marketing group—department A	6,300	39,800	13,900
Technical staff—department B	23,800	69,400	26,800
Word processing—department C	29,500	216,000	54,500
Payroll preparation—department D	53,300	162,000	24,700
Total	$117,000	$554,900	$132,100

In addition, Computeronics had $80,000 of costs which weren't incurred for the exclusive benefit of any one department. These costs were primarily for rent, insurance, and utilities.

Top management decided to assign costs as follows:

Rent, insurance, and utilities: equally to departments A, B, C, and D.

Marketing: 30 percent to C and 70 percent to D.

Technical staff: to C and D proportional to their salaries, wages, and benefits costs.

Top management: to A, B, C, and D proportional to their direct costs.

Word-processing customers were charged $1.20 a page, and 750,560 pages were processed and billed in October. Payroll-preparation cost $1.75 per employee-week, of which 230,500 were processed and billed in October.

a. Using management's cost-assignment methods, calculate the unit cost in Computeronics Corporation's payroll-preparation department and in its word-processing department.

b. Did top management's method of assigning costs yield valid results? Justify your conclusion on this point, including a statement of what you think the word *valid* means in this context.

19. Variable costing; full costing. Plymouth Corporation converted its department 23 to the manufacture of a new product. Production of this product was begun in November, and the department incurred the following costs that month:

	Fixed Cost per Month	Variable Cost per Unit
Materials		$ 0.90
Processing labor		12.40
Other labor	$ 8,000	
Supplies		0.20
Depreciation	24,000	
Other costs	28,000	0.30
Total	$60,000	$13.80

During November, 8,000 units were completed; 6,000 units were sold for $23 a unit.

The general manager of department 23 proudly informed top management that $10,200 had been earned. This conclusion was challenged by a cost analyst at Plymouth's headquarters on the basis of the following calculation:

Sales revenue (6,000 × $23)		$138,000
Variable expenses (6,000 × $13.80)	$82,800	
Fixed expenses	60,000	142,800
Net loss................................		$ 4,800

a. Which measure of department 23's November performance is valid? State reasons and implications.

b. Assume that Plymouth uses FIFO costing and that in December 15,000 units were completed and 14,000 units were sold (again, at $23 a unit). Calculate income or loss (1) as the general manager would calculate it, and (2) as the cost analyst would calculate it. Ignore income taxes.

c. What are the relative merits of the two income-calculation methods you used in answer to part b?

18

Job order costing

The second major system of measuring the costs of products or services is *job order costing.* In job order costing, the costing focus is the specific product, service contract, batch of products, or other distinctly identifiable component or segment of the company's total output. The main purpose of this chapter is to explain how companies determine the costs of individual job orders, first on a full-cost basis and then on a variable-cost basis. Although job order costing is used in many kinds of businesses, including advertising agencies, research laboratories, and small service businesses, we'll illustrate its use in manufacturing, where it is most firmly established.

JOB ORDER COSTING: FULL-COST BASIS

Job order costing is used only when work is performed on a batch or job order basis—that is, when the goods or services the company produces can be identified with specific projects, contracts, customers, or production batches while the work is going on. In other words, whereas process costing is used for the continuous production of homogeneous output, job order costing relates to the production of nonsimilar batches of different products. In most cases, individual production centers (departments) work on many jobs concurrently or in rapid succession (e.g., advertising copy, job printing, and furniture manufacture).

EXHIBIT 18–1. Job Cost Sheet

LION CORPORATION Job Cost Sheet						
Job No. 111					Quantity 320	
Description Flister blidgets, large					Date 5/7/x1	
Direct Materials			Direct Labor		Factory Overhead	
Quantity	Item	Cost	Hours	Cost	Department	Cost
340 688	Frames #22A Brackets #31X	$510 344 854	30	$360	C	$450

The job cost sheet

Production in a job order operation ("job shop") begins when someone in authority issues a production order, job order, or project order. This identifies the work to be done and may also specify the resources to be used. An identifying name or number is assigned to the job, and a *job cost sheet* is prepared, calling for the information provided in Exhibit 18–1. This sheet (which may actually be a portion of a computer's memory) is used to accumulate the costs of a job. As Exhibit 18–1 shows, these costs fall into three categories: direct materials, direct labor, and factory overhead. We'll define each of these categories in this section and explain how accountants decide how much cost in each category to enter on the job cost sheet.

Direct materials costs

In job order costing, as in process costing, we start by identifying the costs we can trace readily to the costing entity, in this case the individual job. These are the direct costs of the job. The costs of materials which are traced to a job therefore are the *direct materials costs* of that job.

Direct materials data are likely to be entered on *materials requisitions,* which instruct storeroom personnel to deliver these materials—that is, *issue* them—to the production people who will use them on jobs. The costs of these materials are then transferred from the materials inventory records to the job cost sheet. For example, mate-

rials costing $854 were issued to production supervisors in Lion
Corporation's factory for use on Job No. 111. These were classified
as direct materials costs of that job and entered in the job cost
sheet in Exhibit 18–1. The entry to record the issuance of these
materials was:

Work in Process Inventory 854
    Materials Inventory   854

This entry recorded the change in the status of the inventory but
didn't change the total of the company's assets. Similar entries were
made to record all other direct materials costs in May; the total
was $133,000.

Both accounts in the entry above are *control accounts*. A control
account is used to reduce the amount of detail in a ledger: The
balance in a control account must equal the total of the balances
in the detailed records it controls. The debit of $854 to Work in
Process Inventory was necessary because $854 was entered on a
job cost sheet. Otherwise, the balance in the Work in Process Inventory account wouldn't have equaled the total of the costs on the
job cost sheets. By the same token, the $854 credit to Materials Inven-
tory showed that this amount was removed from one part or another
of the detailed materials inventory record, often known as a *stores
ledger*. (Referring back to the first three columns of Exhibit 18–1,
we find that $510 was removed from the stores ledger card for
Frames #22A and $344 was removed from the card for Brackets
#31X.)

This relationship between the Work in Process Inventory account
and the job cost sheets is illustrated in Exhibit 18–2. This shows
the balance in the Work in Process Inventory account and the cost
totals of all the job orders in process on May 8, 19x1. For simplicity,
we're assuming that the work in process inventory on this date
consisted of only four jobs—Nos. 101, 104, 109, and 111.

As we said earlier, three kinds of costs are entered on the typical
factory job cost sheet: direct materials and two categories of costs
we haven't explained yet—direct labor and factory overhead. It
should be apparent, however, that since direct labor and factory
overhead costs are entered on the job cost sheets, along with direct
materials costs, the control account balance must reflect these
amounts, too.

Materials issued as direct materials sometimes are returned to
the storeroom unused as *returned materials,* either because they
weren't needed or because they were defective in some sense. When
this happens, the costs of these materials should be removed from
the job cost sheet to which they have been charged. In other words,

EXHIBIT 18–2. Relationship between Work in Process Inventory Account and Job Order Cost Sheets, May 8, 19x1

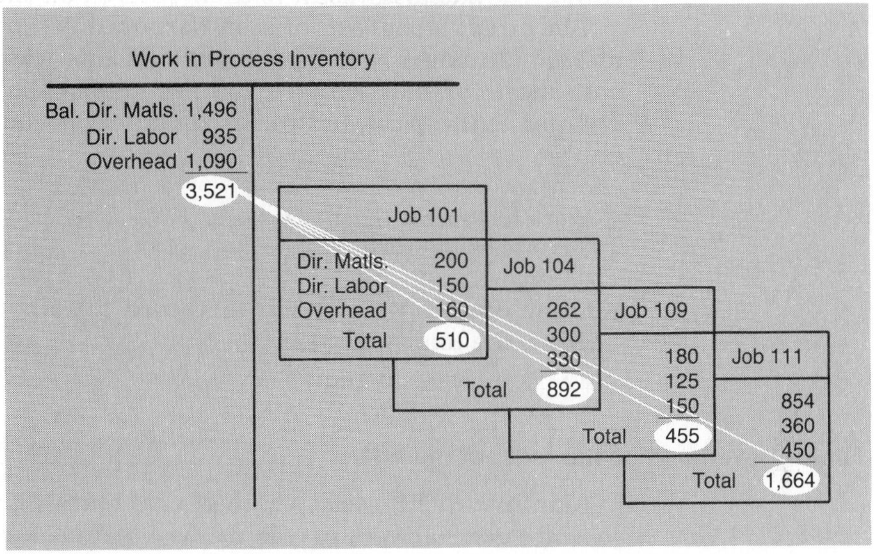

the cost of direct materials is the *net* cost of the materials used on the job, after deducting the costs of any materials which were issued for use on the job but weren't used.

To keep the balance in the control account at the correct level, the accountants must also remove the costs of any of these returned materials from the Work in Process Inventory account:

Materials Inventory xxx
    Work in Process Inventory xxx

If the materials are defective, their costs can be removed from the Materials Inventory account and treated as a loss or as a reduction in the amount payable to the supplier, depending on whether the supplier can be persuaded to accept responsibility for the defects.

Direct-labor costs

The costs of the time employees spend working on individual job orders are known as *direct-labor costs*. Lion Corporation uses *time tickets* to record the time factory employees work on specific jobs. Each employee fills in a time ticket each time he or she works on a job. This ticket identifies the employee, the job, and the times the employee began and finished working on that job. Someone in the accounting department then calculates the direct-labor time and locates the employee's hourly wage rate in the personnel records. The dollar amount is then entered on the job cost sheet.

The direct-labor costs of Lion Corporation's job No. 111 amounted to $360 (30 hours × $12 an hour), and this was entered on the job cost sheet for that job (see Exhibit 18–1). The same amount was charged to the Work in Process Inventory account by the following entry:

```
Work in Process Inventory ...........................   360
      Wages Payable  .....................................         360
```

Similar entries were made to record all other direct-labor costs in May; the total was $122,000.

Factory overhead costs: Indirect materials

Manufacturing costs which aren't readily traceable to specific jobs are generally known as *factory overhead costs.* Some of these are *indirect materials* or *supplies,* materials issued to production centers not for use on specific jobs but to enable the centers to operate effectively. Examples are lubricants for power equipment and cleaning compounds.

Indirect materials costs, like other factory overhead costs, are just as necessary in the production of finished products as direct materials and direct labor. They can't be recorded on the job cost sheets, however, because they can't be traced readily to individual jobs. This also means they can't be recorded in the Work in Process Inventory account when they are incurred, because doing so would destroy the equality of the balance in this control account and the sum of the balances in the job cost sheets. Instead, Lion Corporation records the costs of indirect materials in object-of-expenditure accounts for the departments they are issued to. Lion's factory has three production departments—A, B, and C—and the company made the following summary entry to record the issuance of factory indirect materials in May 19x1:

```
Indirect Materials—Department A ..................   3,200
Indirect Materials—Department B ..................   7,500
Indirect Materials—Department C ..................     900
      Materials Inventory  ...........................           11,600
```

This entry established departmental responsibility for the use of these materials but did not assign these costs to individual job orders. We'll return in a moment to the method Lion Corporation used to assign some of these costs to each job order.

Factory overhead: Indirect labor

Employees in each department in Lion Corporation's factory spend at least some of their time on tasks that aren't readily traceable to specific jobs. All this work falls into the general category of *indirect labor*—cleaning floors, maintaining equipment, and waiting while equipment is repaired are three examples. Since this time isn't readily traceable to individual jobs, the costs of indirect labor time can't be entered on the job cost sheets or in the Work in Process Inventory control account. Instead, Lion Corporation records them in departmental object-of-expenditure accounts. The entry for May 19x1 was:

Indirect Labor—Department A	5,200	
Indirect Labor—Department B	14,100	
Indirect Labor—Department C	6,500	
Wages Payable		25,800

Other factory overhead

Lion Corporation's factory incurred many other overhead costs in May—electric power, depreciation, and property taxes are only three examples. The totals of these other overhead costs of the three production departments in May were as follows:

Department A	$ 38,400
Department B	49,600
Department C	21,700
Total	$109,700

The entries to record these costs as they were incurred took the same general form as entries recording indirect materials and indirect labor but with the credits going to accounts such as Accumulated Depreciation and Accounts Payable.

Production department costs: A preliminary recapitulation

Lion Corporation's factory had materials inventories costing $231,000 on May 1, 19x1. It bought materials on credit for $125,000 during the month of May and issued direct materials costing $133,000 and indirect materials costing $11,600 during the month. Its Materials Inventory account showed the following at the end of the month:

Materials Inventory

Bal. 5/1	231,000	Direct materials	133,000
Purchases	125,000	Indirect materials	11,600
	356,000		144,600

Bal. 5/31 211,400

The costs of materials issued during the month were recorded as follows:

Work in process (direct materials)	$133,000
Department A (indirect materials)	3,200
Department B (indirect materials)	7,500
Department C (indirect materials)	900
Total	$144,600

The factory's three production departments incurred labor costs of $147,800 in May, and these were distributed as follows:

Work in process (direct labor)	$122,000
Department A (indirect labor)	5,200
Department B (indirect labor)	14,100
Department C (indirect labor)	6,500
Total	$147,800

Combining indirect materials and indirect labor costs with the other overhead costs charged to the three production departments in May gives us the following overhead cost totals:

	Department A	Department B	Department C	Total
Indirect materials........	$ 3,200	$ 7,500	$ 900	$ 11,600
Indirect labor	5,200	14,100	6,500	25,800
Other overhead	38,400	49,600	21,700	109,700
Total overhead....	$46,800	$71,200	$29,100	$147,100

Our next chore is to find out how the company decided how much of these costs to assign to each job the factory worked on in May.

Overhead costing rates

When product costs are determined on a full-cost basis, the cost of each product must include an appropriate share of all production costs, including necessary factory overhead costs. By their very nature, overhead costs can't be traced readily to specific job orders; instead, they are assigned to jobs by means of *averages* known as *burden rates, overhead rates,* or *indirect-cost rates.*

Averages are always relationships between two quantities. In this case, we need to relate overhead cost to some other quantity which represents the amount of production in the factory. Sometimes we can measure the amount of production by the number of units manufactured—pounds of cement, gallons of antifreeze, etc. Lion Corporation can't do this, however, because its factory makes many different products. A bookcase isn't the same as a floor lamp or an umbrella stand, and we can't add the number of units of each to get a total which makes any sense.

In situations such as this, accountants usually look for some other quantity they can measure for each job—the number of direct labor-hours used, the amount of direct labor cost, or the amount of raw material used, to mention just three possibilities. For example, an overhead rate with the number of direct labor-hours as the denominator is calculated as follows:

$$\text{Overhead rate} = \frac{\text{Total overhead cost}}{\text{Total volume (direct labor-hours)}}$$

Ideally, we'd like to find a measure of volume that is most closely correlated with long-term changes in the overhead cost. If we can't find one measure that does this better than others, we'll probably choose the one that's easiest to measure.

Predetermined overhead rates

Overhead rates measuring the average overhead cost in each period are often used in costing government contracts; *predetermined* rates are more common elsewhere. A predetermined overhead rate is based on *estimates* of overhead cost and production volume. These estimates are made before the beginning of the period, usually the company's fiscal year, and the resulting rates are generally used without change throughout the period, no matter what the actual experience is. If the rates are to reflect the estimated average overhead cost in a "normal" or typical month, they'll be calculated as follows:

$$\text{Overhead rate} = \frac{\text{Estimated overhead costs in a normal month}}{\text{Estimated total volume in a normal month}}$$

Lion Corporation made several preliminary calculations of overhead rates at the beginning of 19x1. The first of these was a factory-wide rate based on estimates of the overhead costs the factory would incur if it operated steadily at the volume it was designed for (*normal volume*). Normal volume is smaller than maximum volume, because facilities are generally designed with enough capacity to handle most of the probable peak demand; the expected average therefore is bound to be smaller than the expected peak.

Lion's management estimated that the need for overhead costs in most departments was determined primarily by the amount of direct labor time, so this first tentative overhead rate had the number of direct labor-hours as its denominator. A total of 16,000 factory direct labor-hours would be recorded if all departments were at normal volume, and factory overhead at that volume was expected to be $148,000 a month. An overhead rate based on these estimates would have been $9.25 an hour:

$$\text{Overhead rate} = \frac{\$148,000}{16,000} = \$9.25 \text{ an hour}$$

Using this rate, the company would assign $185 in factory overhead cost to a job requiring 20 direct labor-hours (20 × $9.25).

Departmental overhead rates

Lion's management was uncomfortable with the factory-wide overhead rate because the ratio of overhead cost to the number of direct labor-hours differed substantially from department to department, and because the factory's three production departments' respective shares in the amount of work done were likely to vary from job to job. Some jobs might require only assembly work, done in department B with little overhead cost; other jobs would require a good deal of machining, performed in departments A and C which had heavy overhead costs. Using a single overhead rate, therefore, would overstate the costs of some jobs and understate the costs attributable to others.

To accommodate job-to-job differences in the use of various factory departments, Lion's management decided to use departmental rates.[1] Exhibit 18–3 identifies the estimated overhead costs at normal volume in each of the company's three production departments in 19x1. Management decided to use the number of machine-hours as the denominator of the overhead rate in department A because most of its overhead costs were more closely related to the amount of machine time than to the amount of labor time. Overhead costs

---

[1] In practice, a composite rate may be used for several production departments which appear to have roughly similar overhead cost patterns. In some cases, a single department may be subdivided for product-costing purposes into two or more overhead cost centers, each with its own overhead rate. We'll refer to all of these as *departmental rates*.

EXHIBIT 18–3. Lion Corporation: Budgeted Monthly Factory Overhead Costs at Normal Volume for the Year 19x1

	Department			
	A	B	C	Total
Indirect labor	$ 6,000	$15,000	$ 7,000	$ 28,000
Indirect materials	3,000	7,000	1,000	11,000
Power	4,000	2,000	4,000	10,000
Depreciation	7,000	4,000	5,000	16,000
Building services	10,000	16,000	4,000	30,000
Equipment maintenance	9,000	6,000	3,000	18,000
Factory management	8,000	12,000	4,000	24,000
Other	1,000	8,000	2,000	11,000
Total	$48,000	$70,000	$30,000	$148,000
Direct labor-hours		10,000	2,000	
Machine-hours	8,000			
Overhead rate per machine-hour	$6			
Overhead rate per direct labor-hour		$7	$15	

in departments B and C were largely labor-related, and the number of direct labor-hours seemed to be an appropriate denominator for the overhead rate in these departments.

The impact of management's decision to departmentalize the overhead rates can be seen by examining the overhead costs assignable to two of Lion Corporation's products, X and Y. Each unit of these products requires 20 hours of direct labor. Product X is produced entirely in department B; product Y is manufactured in department C. A factory-wide overhead rate would assign an overhead cost of 20 × $9.25 = $185 to each unit of each of these products. If departmental rates are used, however, product X will be assigned a cost of 20 × $7 = $140, while the overhead cost of a unit of product Y will be 20 × $15 = $300. This is a substantial difference.

Assigning overhead costs to job orders

The process of assigning factory overhead costs to individual job orders is commonly called the *application* or *absorption* of overhead. Every time work is performed on a job order, some overhead is assigned to it or "absorbed" by it. For example, job No. 111 in Lion Corporation's factory required 30 hours of direct labor in department C. With a departmental overhead rate of $15 an hour, $450 of department C's overhead was assigned to this job.

The amounts absorbed are recorded on individual job cost sheets for the job orders on which the work was done. The same amounts are assigned to the Work in Process Inventory account. Lion Corporation's entry to record the application of factory overhead costs to job No. 111 in May was as follows:

Work in Process Inventory 450
    Factory Overhead Applied—Department C   450

Factory Overhead Applied—Department C is an offsetting account to the department's various overhead accounts. The credit to this account represents the assignment of $450 of these costs to the work in process inventory.

Cost of jobs finished and sold

We pointed out in Chapter 5 that when production is completed, the costs assigned to the completed products are transferred from a work in process inventory account to a finished goods inventory account. The job cost sheets provide the basis for this transfer.

For example, work on job No. 111 was completed in June and the assignment of costs to this job was completed when $450 of overhead cost was entered on the job cost sheet. The entries we've described so far produced the amounts we showed in Exhibit 18–1 and now summarize in Exhibit 18–4. Completion of this job calls for an entry such as the following:

Finished Goods Inventory 1,664
    Work in Process Inventory   1,664

This entry records this job's change in status from an in-process asset to a finished goods asset.

Once costs enter the Finished Goods Inventory account, they make their way to the cost of goods sold by the same route as any

EXHIBIT 18–4.   Elements of Job Order Cost

Job Order Cost Sheet Job No. 111		
Direct materials	$ 854	*Direct materials:* the costs of materials that can be traced readily to individual job orders.
Direct labor	360	*Direct labor:* the costs of the time employees spend working directly on individual job orders.
Factory overhead	450	*Factory overhead:* all factory costs not readily traceable to individual job orders; assigned to jobs by means of averages known as overhead rates.
Total	$1,664	

other cost of salable merchandise—that is, on a FIFO, LIFO, or average-costing basis. Job No. 111 consisted of 320 units of finished products, so the average unit cost was $5.20 ($1,664/320). When sales call for the transfer to the cost of goods sold of the unit costs of, say, 300 units from job No. 111, the entry will be as follows (300 × $5.20 = $1,560):

Cost of Goods Sold	1,560	
Finished Goods Inventory		1,560

Overhead under- or overabsorbed

The total amount of overhead absorbed in any period is the sum of the amounts assigned to individual job orders during the period. This amount can also be determined by applying the following formula:

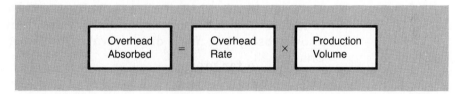

For example, Lion Corporation used 1,800 hours of direct labor in department C in June 19x1. The total amount of overhead absorbed by production in that department in June therefore was $27,000 (1,800 × $15). The company's system, in other words, identified $27,000 as the overhead cost of creating new inventory assets during the month.

When predetermined overhead rates are used, the total cost absorbed in any period is likely to differ from the actual amount of overhead incurred in that period. For example, the actual overhead costs in department C in June 19x1 were as follows:

Indirect labor	$ 6,500
Indirect materials	900
Power	4,100
Depreciation	5,000
Other direct overhead	1,800
Building services	3,200
Equipment maintenance	3,600
Factory management	4,000
Total	$29,100

Only $27,000 of this total was absorbed by production; the remaining $2,100 is known as a factory overhead cost *variance* or *underabsorbed overhead*. (If the amount absorbed exceeds the actual overhead cost, the excess is labeled *overabsorbed*.)

Over- and underabsorption of factory overhead arises in a number of ways, most notably the following:

1. *Actual costs differ* from the amounts that would normally be expected at the production volume actually achieved during the period.
2. *Production volume differs* from the volume used to set the overhead rate.

The first of these effects is probably self-evident. If volume holds steady but the company spends more than it expected to when it set the overhead rate, it won't absorb the extra costs. And if it spends less than it expected, it will overabsorb its overhead.

The volume effect works the same way. Department C's $15 overhead rate, for example, was based on the assumption that normal volume would amount to 2,000 direct labor-hours. At that volume, the full $30,000 in estimated overhead costs will be absorbed. If volume is smaller than that, however, the amount absorbed will be smaller. In the extreme case, if volume falls to zero, no overhead costs will be absorbed at all. Low volume, in other words, is likely to lead to underabsorption; volume greater than normal will lead to overabsorption. We'll discuss ways of quantifying this effect in Chapter 23.

External reporting of under- or overabsorbed overhead

When overhead is either over- or underabsorbed, the company has to decide how to treat the over- or underabsorbed portion in the financial statements it prepares for its shareholders and others outside the organization. Three alternatives might be considered:

1. Divide the under- or overabsorption in any period between the income statement and the balance sheet in direct proportion to the distribution of the overhead absorbed during the period.
2. Report the under- or overabsorption in full as a loss or a gain on the income statement for the period in which it arises.
3. Carry any such amounts to the balance sheet for the end of the period, to be added to or offset against similar amounts arising in preceding or succeeding periods.

The first of these solutions will be adopted if the objective is to have inventory cost and the cost of goods sold approximate the actual average cost of production in the period. The second alternative will be selected if the objective is to measure the inventory at its normal cost, with the effects of all departures from normal appearing in the income statement.

The argument supporting the second alternative is that inefficiencies due to overspending or underproduction are costs of the period rather than costs of the products manufactured during the period. If volume is low, for example, some fixed costs incurred to provide the capacity to produce will go unabsorbed. In other words, these are the costs of the goods that *weren't* produced, not costs of the goods that *were* produced.

The cost of providing the idle portion of capacity fits the definition of a *loss*—a cost unaccompanied by any benefit. Since losses are reported in the income statement when they are identified, unabsorbed overhead costs should be treated as an expense or a loss of the current period. A predetermined overhead rate, in other words, is the *preferred* basis for product costing, not a poor substitute for an historical rate that is adopted for reasons of convenience.

In practice, the under- or overabsorbed overhead is generally included in the income statement for the period in which it arises. Some portion of it may be placed in an interim-period balance sheet if management expects it to be offset later in the year, but this practice isn't extended to annual reporting. The under- or overabsorbed overhead will be split between inventory and the cost of goods sold only if it is large enough to have a material effect on the financial statements *and* it either represents overabsorption or is likely to be recoverable from the sale of the inventory in later periods.

REMINDER: COST DISTRIBUTION

The factory costs to be accounted for in any period are the costs of the beginning inventories, the costs of materials purchased, and the factory operating costs of that period. These costs are accounted for by assigning them to the ending inventories, to the cost of goods sold, or to the over(under)absorbed overhead. This requirement is illustrated in the following diagram, using a simple set of hypothetical costs:

Beginning Inventory: Raw Materials Work in Process Finished Goods }	$40		Cost of Goods Sold	$75
Materials Purchased	$30		Underabsorbed Overhead	$10
Labor and Other Resources Used in the Factory	$50		Ending Inventory: Raw Materials Work in Process Finished Goods }	$35

Costs to Account for $120   Costs Accounted for $120

The over(under)absorbed overhead is either assigned in its entirety to the cost of goods sold or divided between the cost of goods sold and the ending inventory.

Cost classification problems

Some factory costs are classified as overhead even though they are or appear to be traceable to individual job orders. Some of these are classified as overhead because the cost and effort required to trace them to individual jobs are prohibitive—for example, the costs of the glue and upholstery nails used in making furniture. Others are classified as overhead because other costs incurred for the same object of expenditure and for similar purposes aren't traceable to individual jobs. For example, some jobs require work to be performed on customers' premises. The costs of employees' travel to and from the customers' places of business can be classified as direct costs of specific jobs if the travel is always exclusively for a single customer. Most travel time is likely to be shared by several customers, however, and the costs of this travel are classified as overhead. If the averaging procedure includes multicustomer travel costs as overhead, then classifying single-customer travel time and cost as a direct cost would constitute double counting. The result: Single-customer travel time costs in these situations are also classified as overhead.

A slightly different problem arises in connection with *overtime premiums*. Factory employees are paid more than their regular (*straight-time*) wage rates for hours they work in excess of some specified number. The difference between the straight-time wage rate and the special rate is the overtime premium. If the straight-time wage rate is $10 an hour, the employee ordinarily will be paid $15 (time and a half) for overtime work. The overtime premium is $5 an hour.

Overtime premiums almost always should be classified as overhead; that is, the cost of an overtime hour spent on a specific job order should be distributed as follows:

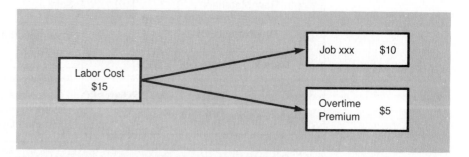

The reason for this is that the job which management schedules for the overtime period is no more responsible for the overtime premium than another job which management puts on the production schedule earlier in the day. This is true even if the job processed in the overtime period has been accepted as a rush order—it could just as well have been processed earlier in the day, with some other job moved to the premium period. Overtime results from the *total* demand on the production facilities, and *all* production shares in the responsibility for the overtime. This isn't to say that management shouldn't charge the rush-order customer a high price for fast service—that's a question of pricing strategy or tactics, not a costing question.

INTERDEPARTMENTAL COST ALLOCATIONS

Some costs of operating a factory aren't specifically traceable to the production departments in which the products are actually manufactured. Depreciation on the factory building and the plant manager's salary are two examples; the cost of production scheduling is another. Lion Corporation's predetermined overhead rates included provisions for these costs. In this section we'll explain briefly how the company did this.

Service and support centers

Costs which aren't readily traceable to factory production centers are traceable to other cost centers in the factory, those providing service or support to the production centers. The plant manager's salary, for example, can be traced to the factory's administrative office; the wages of the equipment maintenance crew are traceable to the equipment maintenance department.

For simplicity, we'll refer to all service and support centers as *service centers*, regardless of the kind of service or support they provide. The relationships between these service centers and the production centers are diagrammed in Exhibit 18–5. To keep this exhibit relatively simple, we've diagrammed it to show only two service centers and two production centers, even though Lion Corporation has three production centers and three service centers.

EXHIBIT 18–5. Product Flows versus Service Flows

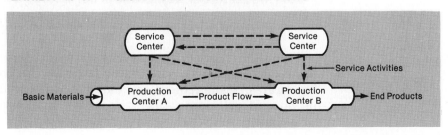

As the diagram shows, service centers ordinarily provide their services to the production centers and sometimes to each other as well. In general, they don't work directly on job orders; jobs don't even pass through them on their way to completion.

Interdepartmental allocations

Lion Corporation uses the service flows represented by the dashed lines in Exhibit 18–5 to assign the costs of its three factory service centers to its production centers, using a process known as *allocation*. The direct costs of the service centers thereby become indirect costs of the production centers. These indirect costs are then included in the numerators of the three departmental overhead rates. The amounts shown in Exhibit 18–3 as building services, equipment maintenance, and factory management costs were all allocated amounts. In total, these allocations accounted for almost half the factory's overhead costs at normal volume; in department A, allocated building service, equipment maintenance, and factory management costs accounted for $27,000, or 56.25 percent of the department's $48,000 total estimated overhead cost at normal volume.

TERMINOLOGY REMINDER

A *direct cost* in accounting is a cost that is *traceable* to a specified costing entity. A complete definition should specify the costing entity the cost is traceable to. *Direct materials* and *direct labor,* however, are generally understood to be costs traceable to specific end products, such as jobs, projects, or contracts, and no further specification is needed.

Unless otherwise specified or evident from the context, *indirect materials* and *indirect labor* aren't traceable to specific end products. Indirect labor and indirect materials costs are traceable to other costing entities, however, such as specific cost centers. Indirect labor, for example, may be indirect with respect to jobs but direct with respect to a particular production center because it is traceable in its entirety to that production center (e.g., salaries of departmental supervisors). In such cases, indirect labor is a component of the *direct departmental overhead* of the production center—that is, all overhead costs that are traceable to that specific production center.

The allocations in this case were made *before the year began,* so that management could include them in the predetermined overhead rates. Management estimated that if the factory operated at its normal volume in 19x1, the costs of the three service centers would be as follows:

	Building Services	Equipment Maintenance	Factory Management
Indirect labor*	$ 6,000	$13,000	$15,000
Indirect materials*	1,000	1,500	1,000
Power...................	2,200	500	300
Depreciation	15,000	1,000	500
Property taxes	8,000	—	—
Other direct overhead....	1,800	1,000	4,200
Total	$34,000	$17,000	$21,000

* In practice, the labor and materials costs in service departments are likely to bear titles other than indirect labor and indirect materials. These titles are used here to keep the exhibits compact.

Lion Corporation's allocations

The accountants' task was to find a way of allocating these costs among the three production departments so that the allocations most closely approximate the amounts of service department cost attributable to the operations of each production department. They decided to proceed sequentially, starting with the building services department's costs, on the grounds that building services used far less of the services of the other two service departments than it provided to them.[2] They allocated building services costs in proportion to the amount of floor space the other departments occupied, as follows:

Department	(1) Floor Space Occupied (sq. ft.)	(2) Cost Allocated (1) × $0.40*
Equipment maintenance	2,500	$ 1,000
Factory management.........	7,500	3,000
Production A	25,000	10,000
Production B	40,000	16,000
Production C	10,000	4,000
Total	85,000	$34,000

* $34,000/85,000 = $0.40.

The allocation rate of $0.40 a square foot was the ratio of estimated building services costs ($34,000) to the amount of floor space occupied by the other five cost centers (85,000 square feet). This allocation reflects an assumption that the cost of providing building services is determined by the amount of floor space the factory requires.

[2] Service departments often provide services to each other. In such cases, allocations can be determined by iteration, or as the solutions to a set of simultaneous equations.

In the second allocation, the company distributed the estimated monthly costs of equipment maintenance to the three production centers, where all the maintenance services were likely to be performed. Estimated usage statistics and cost allocations were as follows:

Production Department	(1) Equipment Maintenance Hours Used	(2) Cost Allocated (1) × $15*
A	600	$ 9,000
B	400	6,000
C	200	3,000
Total	1,200	$18,000

* $18,000/1,200 = $15.

The total estimated maintenance cost at normal volume in 19x1 amounted to $18,000, including $1,000 as maintenance's share of building services costs. The assumptions here are that the usage of maintenance services is the *cause* of maintenance costs and that these are roughly proportional to the amount of usage in the long run.

Lion Corporation's final allocation was an allocation of factory management costs—scheduling, recordkeeping, and overall factory administration. Here the accountants faced a new problem. In allocating building services costs they had a reasonable measure of the amount of building *capacity* each department required, and in allocating equipment maintenance costs they had a good measure of service *usage*. For factory management, however, no measure of capacity or usage could be found which represented satisfactorily the factors that cause factory management costs to be incurred. Factory management costs were necessary to the operation of the three production centers, however, and therefore had to be included in overhead rates to reflect the full-cost concept.

The accountants decided to distribute these costs in proportion to the amounts of direct labor and overhead costs the three departments were to incur during the year. They reasoned that factory management costs were incurred to support the activities of the other departments, and activity in this case could best be measured by *total cost added* (all departmental costs except direct materials costs). Direct materials costs were excluded because few of Lion Corporation's factory management activities were devoted to the management of materials. The total cost in all departments combined was expected to amount to $300,000 in 19x1, as shown in column (5) of Exhibit 18–6. Factory management costs were expected to total $24,000 ($21,000 + $3,000) in allocated building ser-

EXHIBIT 18–6. Lion Corporation: Allocation of Factory Management Costs

	(1)	(2)	(3)	(4)	(5)	(6)
			__ Allocations __		Total Cost Added	Allocated Costs of Factory Management
Production Department	Direct Labor	Direct Overhead	Building Services	Main-tenance	(1) + (2) + (3) + (4)	8%* × (5)
A	$ 60,000	$21,000	$10,000	$ 9,000	$100,000	$ 8,000
B	92,000	36,000	16,000	6,000	150,000	12,000
C	24,000	19,000	4,000	3,000	50,000	4,000
Total	$176,000	$76,000	$30,000	$18,000	$300,000	$24,000

* $24,000/$300,000 = 8 percent.

vices costs. The allocation rate therefore was 8 percent of the total cost added. The allocations based on this rate are shown in column (6) of Exhibit 18–6.

The three sets of allocations Lion Corporation made in developing its factory overhead rates in 19x1 are summarized in the lower portion of Exhibit 18–7. The end result is that all the costs associated with operations at normal volume are assigned to the three production departments. The amounts in the three right-hand columns are those we presented earlier in Exhibit 18–3.

JOB ORDER COSTING: VARIABLE-COST BASIS

We pointed out in Chapter 16 that decisions with short time horizons require estimates of the short-term variability of operating

EXHIBIT 18–7. Lion Corporation: Estimated Factory Overhead Cost Allocation for 19x1

	Building Services	Equipment Maintenance	Factory Management	Production Department		
				A	B	C
Indirect labor	$ 6,000	$13,000	$15,000	$ 6,000	$15,000	$ 7,000
Indirect materials	1,000	1,500	1,000	3,000	7,000	1,000
Power	2,200	500	300	4,000	2,000	4,000
Depreciation	15,000	1,000	500	7,000	4,000	5,000
Property taxes	8,000	—	—	—	—	—
Other direct overhead	1,800	1,000	4,200	1,000	8,000	2,000
Total direct overhead	34,000	17,000	21,000	21,000	36,000	19,000
Building services	(34,000)	1,000	3,000	10,000	16,000	4,000
Equipment maintenance		(18,000)	—	9,000	6,000	3,000
Factory management			(24,000)	8,000	12,000	4,000
Total				$48,000	$70,000	$30,000

EXHIBIT 18–8.   Lion Corporation, Department C: Estimates of Fixed and Variable Overhead Costs

	Fixed Cost per Month	Variable Cost per Direct Labor-Hour
Indirect labor	$ 4,000	$1.50
Indirect materials	200	0.40
Power	—	2.00
Depreciation	5,000	—
Other direct departmental overheads	1,600	0.20
Building services	4,000	—
Equipment maintenance	1,200	0.90
Factory management	4,000	—
Total	$20,000	$5.00

costs in response to variations in operating volume. In Chapter 17 we showed how accountants can measure product costs to meet this need. We referred to systems designed to accomplish this as *variable-costing* systems.

Variable costing differs from full costing in job order costing only in the treatment of factory overhead. Direct labor and direct materials costs are typically assumed to be proportionally variable with volume, and therefore are assigned to product units in the manner described earlier in this chapter. The variable-costing difference is that factory overhead is included in product cost by means of overhead rates that cover only the variable components of the various overhead cost elements.

For example, suppose an analysis of the overhead costs in Lion Corporation's department C has provided the estimates shown in Exhibit 18–8. In this case, the overhead rate would be $5 a direct labor-hour. Job No. 111, requiring 30 direct labor-hours in this department, would be charged $150 (30 hours × $5 an hour) for variable overhead. No charge would be made for any portion of the $20,000 in fixed costs.

Developing the overhead rate

Four of the cost elements in Exhibit 18–8 are semivariable. Indirect labor, for example, has a normal monthly expenditure of $4,000 plus increments of $1.50 a direct labor-hour in response to the use of the department's facilities. By further subdividing the chart of accounts, we could do a better job of separating the fixed component of actual indirect labor from the variable component. Supervision, for example, is ordinarily fixed within fairly wide volume ranges, and a separate object-of-expenditure account could be (and probably would be) established to accumulate these costs.

Product inspection and quality control labor, on the other hand, may contain both a fixed component and a variable component, and the accountant may be unable to label any particular hour of this kind of indirect labor as part of the fixed component or the variable component. Fortunately, this is no barrier to variable costing. Since the overhead rate is predetermined, the only requirement is that a *rate of variability* be estimated for each cost element.

Allocations in variable costing

Allocations of building services and factory management costs are treated as completely fixed in department C. They therefore don't enter into product cost under variable costing. Equipment maintenance costs, on the other hand, contain both a fixed component and a variable component. The problem is to estimate the response of costs in the *equipment maintenance* department to variations in the volume of activity in *production* department C.

For example, suppose an analysis of the costs of the equipment maintenance department indicates that at the department's normal volume of 1,200 *maintenance hours,* fixed costs are expected to be $6,000 a month; variable costs are expected to total $10 a *maintenance hour.* Further investigation shows that department C's *consumption* of equipment maintenance services is expected to amount to 20 hours a month plus 9 *maintenance hours* for every 100 *direct labor-hours* in department C. If we measure each of these hours at equipment maintenance's variable cost of $10 a maintenance hour, we get the following:

Department C's fixed usage: 20 hours × $10 .... $200 a month
Department C's variable usage: (9 hours × $10)/100 .... $0.90 a direct labor-hour

In other words, although the equipment maintenance department's variable cost of providing an hour of service is $10, none of this should be treated as a variable cost of the departments using the services unless their service *usage* is also variable.[3]

---

[3] The average fixed cost of providing equipment maintenance services is $5 an hour ($6,000 divided by 1,200 maintenance hours). The $1,200 estimated fixed costs of equipment maintenance in department C, as shown in Exhibit 18–8, has two components: (1) $300 for its fixed *usage* of 20 hours times the sum of the fixed and variable costs of maintenance services ($5 + $10); and (2) the $900 in the fixed costs of equipment maintenance assignable to department C's expected usage of equipment maintenance services at normal volume ($5 × 9/100 × 2,000). This allocation doesn't enter into the product-costing rates in variable costing.

Absorption and underabsorption of factory overhead

Use of variable costing in department C would lead to the absorption of only $9,000 of variable factory overhead in June 19x1 (1,800 direct labor-hours × $5 an hour). A suitable entry to record this absorption would be:

Work in Process Inventory............................	9,000	
Variable Overhead Cost Applied—Department C ..		9,000

But remember that the department was actually charged overhead costs totaling $29,100 in June.[4] The amount of overhead unassigned to products (unabsorbed) therefore would be $20,100. This amount is due partly to variations in the rate of spending, as it was in our full-costing example, but most of it is the result of our deliberate decision to exclude fixed costs from the overhead rates.

Exclusion of fixed costs from inventory in this manner is unacceptable for external financial reporting in the United States. Under generally accepted accounting principles, some procedure must be adopted to assign an appropriate portion of the year's fixed costs to the goods in inventory at the end of each year (FIFO) or to the inventory addition, if any (LIFO). One way to handle this is to segment the full-cost overhead rate, with one segment covering variable overhead costs and another segment covering fixed overheads. In this way both the short-term variability information and the inventory costing data will be available at the same time.

COSTS AND BENEFITS OF JOB ORDER COSTING

The appropriate product-costing method is determined in the first instance by the nature of the production process. Job order costing can't be used when production consists of continuous flows of identical product units; process costing won't provide information useful to management if production consists of a highly disparate and changing product mix. Job order costing is a costly accounting method, however, and management should use it only if it appears likely to produce benefits which exceed its costs. We'll conclude this chapter with a brief review of the potential benefits from job order costing, and a comment on the costs of operating a job order costing system.

---

[4] Adoption of variable costing might affect the methods used to distribute the fixed costs of service departments. Discussion of any changes of that sort doesn't bear on the issue we're examining here, however, and we'll defer any further mention of those changes to Chapter 22.

Cost estimation

Management needs estimates of product costs in connection with decisions such as whether to produce and sell specific products, whether to accept specific orders, and how to price its products. Job order costing helps management estimate the costs attributable to product-related decisions.

First, the file of costs of completed job orders provides data which management can use in preparing estimates of the amounts of direct materials, direct labor, and departmental time that potential new jobs will require. An estimated job order cost can be built up in exactly the same way as historical job order cost: estimated direct materials, estimated direct labor, and estimated overhead absorption. New jobs are seldom totally unrelated to work the company has done in the past. For the most part, therefore, management can specify the operations required by the new job and determine how much cost these operations required in the past.

Job order costing's second contribution to product-cost estimation is in the development of predetermined overhead rates. Even without consulting historical job-cost files, experienced cost estimators may be able to estimate direct materials, direct labor, and departmental time requirements fairly accurately. Departmental overhead cost averages are much more difficult to estimate, however, because they aren't determined by the characteristics of the job itself. Predetermined overhead rates allow management to estimate the overhead costs associated with the jobs.

Finally, recording the amount of direct materials, direct labor, and departmental time actually required by a job order allows management to check the accuracy of the estimates it prepared before undertaking the job. Management can use these comparisons to adjust its estimates in the future.

Cost control

Management needs information to determine whether costs are being controlled effectively. If production consists mainly of repeated batches of regular products, job cost data can be used to develop and monitor the accuracy of performance standards for product costs. Management may calculate job order costs either routinely for this purpose or intermittently, when it has reason to believe the performance standards are out of date. We'll return in Chapter 22 to study the ways management can use cost-performance standards of this sort.

Cost-performance standards are much more difficult to establish when each job order is unique than when most job orders consist of the manufacture of repeated batches of regular products. In these situations, cost-control efforts are likely to center on the individual job order. Job cost data then permit management to compare the actual costs incurred on each job with the costs estimated for that job.

Costs of job order costing

The benefits of job order costing aren't obtained without incurring costs. In fact, job order costing is the most expensive method of determining product cost. It requires a number of clerical operations which can be avoided in simpler systems. The most obvious of these operations is entering data on job cost sheets. Without job order costing, job cost sheets aren't needed, and the processes of sorting and tabulating materials requisitions and labor time tickets by job can be eliminated. In fact, without job order costing, the company may not even have to prepare labor time tickets at all. And management can simplify the materials requisitions to identify only the departments receiving the materials, not the job orders for which they are used.

Using job order cost sheets as a basis for cost estimation is also costly in that it requires a filing system and a means of data retrieval. For example, suppose management estimates that a proposed new job will require the use of operation 42X and wants to know how much time that operation will take. If the job cost file is to be used for this purpose, the time spent on operation 42X has to be both clearly identified in the job cost sheets and coded in such a way that management can extract this information in a timely fashion.

In short, the costing method is determined to a large extent by the nature of the production process. Even so, management may not use the more expensive job order costing method even if production is on a job order basis, if it judges that the incremental costs of the costing system exceed the probable incremental benefits. In such cases, broad cost averages might be used, subject to judgmental adjustments to reflect management's past experience.[5]

SUMMARY

The second major method of measuring the costs of products or services is job order costing, which is used when the focus of

---

[5] For example, Apex Company, which provided our illustration of process costing in Chapter 17, actually produces several kinds of coatings in the coatings department and several kinds of pesticides in the pesticides department, with products passing through these departments in large batches. Apex Company chooses to ignore product-to-product differences in each department in its costing routine, however, because these differences are largely in materials costs and adjustments for differences in materials costs can be made easily outside the process costing system, without the expense of job order costing.

production is the individual batch, project, contract, or assignment. Three categories of costs are assigned to specific job orders: direct materials, direct labor, and factory overhead. Direct materials and direct labor are traced uniquely to individual jobs; factory overhead is assigned to jobs by means of averages known as overhead rates.

Except in special cost-reimbursement situations, overhead rates are usually predetermined; once the amount of materials, labor, or machine time used on a job is known, the overhead cost of the job can be calculated, even if actual overhead costs are still unknown at that time. Overhead rates are also likely to be departmentalized: that is, each department or production center is given its own rate, used for assigning overhead costs to the work it does. This requires the allocation of the costs of service departments to the various production departments.

Job order costing can be based on either full cost or variable cost. Under full costing, the objective is to estimate the cost attributable to the product in the long run. Under variable costing, the accountant tries to approximate the effect on total cost of short-run variations in the volume of production.

The most difficult part of this process is the development of meaningful allocation rates. Allocations of service and support center costs based on usage or capacity required provide useful estimates of the service-center components of product cost; allocations based on broad measures of activity in the departments supported by the support activities are likely to be less useful and may even be misleading. Accountants are careful to develop allocations which are tied clearly to the specific purposes for which the allocations are required, whether for inventory costing, short-run decision making, or long-term decisions.

Management can use job order costing to improve the quality of its cost estimates and to obtain useful information on the company's success in meeting product cost-performance standards. Job order costing systems are expensive, however, and management needs to decide whether the added benefits are great enough to justify the added costs.

KEY TERMS

Allocations	Job cost sheet
Control account	Job order costing
Direct costs	Normal volume
Direct labor	Overhead absorbed
Direct materials	Overhead rate
Factory overhead	Under-/overabsorbed overhead
Indirect costs	

INDEPENDENT STUDY PROBLEMS (Solutions in Appendix B)

1.   Job cost and overhead variance.   Chailly, Inc., uses a job order costing system in its factory with a predetermined overhead rate based on direct labor-hours. You are given the following information:

1.   Job No. 423 was started on March 3 and finished on March 28.
2.   Other data:

	Job No. 423	All Jobs (in March)	Estimated Annual Amount at Normal Volume
Direct labor-hours	60	10,000	100,000
Direct labor cost................	$400	$ 60,000	$ 350,000
Direct materials cost	$800	$150,000	$1,300,000

3.   Factory overhead budgeted for the entire year was $900,000; actual overhead for the month of March was $106,000.

a.   Compute the cost of Job. No. 423.
b.   Calculate the amount of overhead over- or underabsorbed in March.

2.   Job order costing: predetermined overhead rate.   Webber Corporation has a job order costing system and a plantwide predetermined overhead rate of $4 a direct labor hour. You have the following data:

1.   Inventory balances on December 1:

Materials	$10,000
Work in process	15,000
Finished goods	20,000

2.   Data recorded during December:

Materials purchased	$16,000
Direct materials issued	18,000
Direct labor, 5,000 hours	48,000
Manufacturing overhead (actual)	17,000
Cost of goods finished	80,000

3.   Finished goods inventory on December 31: $23,000.

a.   Calculate the cost of the materials inventory and the cost of the work in process inventory on December 31.
b.   What was the cost of goods sold during December?
c.   What was the over- or underabsorbed overhead in December?

3.   Departmental overhead rates.   The Robertson Company has been using a single overhead rate for its entire factory. An alternative has been proposed: departmental overhead rates. You are given the following information:

1.   Three products (A, B, C) are produced in three departments (1, 2, 3).
2.   Labor-hours required for a unit of each product are:

	Department			
	1	2	3	Total
Product A	2	1	1	4
Product B	0	2	2	4
Product C	2	3	3	8

3. Products produced in a normal year: A—40,000 units; B—40,000 units; and C—10,000 units.
4. Overhead incurred in a normal year: department 1—$400,000; department 2—$300,000; and department 3—$100,000.

Should the company use a plantwide overhead rate or department overhead rates? Why? (In either case, the overhead rate or rates would be based on direct labor-hours.)

4. Interdepartmental allocations. A factory has two production departments (Able and Baker) and four service departments (building, office, storeroom, and maintenance). The company uses predetermined departmental overhead rates for product costing on a full-costing basis.

To develop these overhead costing rates, the company allocates normal service department costs to the two production departments sequentially, using the following statistics for operations at normal volume:

	Direct Labor Hours	Total Labor- Hours	Percent- age of Floor Space	Main- tenance Hours	Percent- age of Requi- sitions	Direct Overhead Costs
Building	—	500	—	—	—	$ 5,000
Office	—	600	15	10	—	6,370
Storeroom	—	300	10	—	—	2,260
Maintenance	—	500	5	—	5	6,000
Able	5,000	5,600	40	150	35	2,770
Baker	2,000	2,500	30	250	60	3,100
Total						$25,500

a. Prepare a table to develop departmental full-cost overhead rates for Able and Baker, based on direct labor-hours. You should distribute the service department costs in the following sequence and on the following bases:

Building .... Percentage of floor space
Office .... Total labor-hours
Storeroom .... Percentage of requisitions
Maintenance .... Maintenance hours

b. Calculate the amount of overhead assigned to the following two jobs, using the allocated rates you developed in answer to part a:

	Job 123	Job 321
Direct labor-hours—Able	5	2
Direct labor-hours—Baker	2	5

5. Variable costing. A company manufactures many products. Each product passes through two production departments, which have the following cost structures:

	Department A	Department B
Normal monthly volume	5,000 direct labor-hours	10,000 pounds of materials
Monthly fixed costs at normal volume	$10,000	$40,000
Monthly variable costs at normal volume	15,000	20,000

Two job orders that went through the factory last month had the following results:

	Job 1 (product X)		Job 2 (product Y)	
	Quantity	Cost	Quantity	Cost
Direct inputs:				
Direct materials	480 lbs.	$2,400	1,500 lbs.	$4,800
Direct labor:				
Department A	180 hrs.	1,620	100 hrs.	900
Department B	60 hrs.	420	40 hrs.	280
Output	600 units		1,000 units	

a. Calculate the unit cost of each of these jobs on a full-costing basis.
b. Recalculate unit costs on a variable-costing basis.
c. Why are the relative variable costs of these two products so different from their relative full costs?

EXERCISES AND PROBLEMS

6. Job order costs. A factory uses a job order costing system. You have the following information about the factory's operations last week:

1. Direct labor and direct materials used:

Job Order	Direct Materials	Direct Labor-Hours
878	$ 250	46
882	412	32
891	346	18
905	1,215	81
906	811	20
910	1,440	62
912	196	10
Total	$4,670	269

2. The direct labor wage rate was $8 an hour.
3. Actual factory overhead costs for the week totaled $1,545. They were applied to jobs at a rate of $5 a direct labor-hour.
4. Jobs completed: Nos. 878, 882, 905.
5. The factory had no work in process at the beginning of the week.

a. Prepare a summary table that will show all the costs assigned to each job.

b. Calculate the cost of the work in process at the end of the week.

c. Calculate the amount of overhead over- or underabsorbed last week.

7. Manufacturing transactions. Goodhue Chemical Company buys chemicals in bulk and packages them for sale to local customers. The company's activities last month included the following:

1. Ordered from a supplier 30 55-gallon drums of chemicals. The price of the chemicals was $60 a drum, plus a $5 returnable deposit on the drum. In addition, Goodhue was responsible for paying freight and delivery charges on these chemicals.
2. Received 27 of the drums ordered in item 1.
3. Paid freight charges of $108 for delivery of the 27 drums.
4. Returned two drums of chemicals to the supplier for full credit as defective merchandise; the supplier agreed to pay the return freight charges on these two drums and also to reimburse Goodhue for freight costs on the original shipment of these drums.
5. Paid the bill due to the supplier after deducting the amount paid for incoming freight charges on the two defective drums.
6. Paid 12 months' property taxes on factory building, $8,700.
7. Bought 5,500 empty quart tins on credit at a total cost of $475, delivered and labeled.
8. Paid each of five temporary employees $5 an hour; each of these employees worked 16 hours filling the tins with chemicals and putting them on the shelves.
9. Paid factory janitor's regularly monthly salary, $1,100, for 170 hours' work sweeping floors, moving materials, etc.
10. Received utility bills for telephone and electric service in the factory last month, $850.
11. Returned 25 empty drums to the supplier for credit against the next purchase.
12. Applied factory overhead costs to the tin-filling job at the rate of $2 a direct labor-hour.
13. Sold 4,400 tins of chemicals on account at a price of 80 cents each.

a. Calculate the cost of the tin-filling job in total and per tin, with separate amounts for direct materials, direct labor, and factory overhead.

b. For each cost described above that you didn't assign to the tin-filling job, explain why you excluded it.

c. Calculate the cost of goods sold and the gross margin on sales of tinned chemicals from this batch last month.

8. Factory overhead. Answer each of these three unrelated questions.

a. Empire Corporation budgeted overhead at $374,000 for November for department G based on a budgeted volume of 110,000 direct labor-hours. The overhead costs were assigned to job orders by means of a predetermined overhead rate per direct labor hour based on budgeted overhead cost at budgeted volume. Actual overhead was $374,000 and actual direct labor-hours were 114,000. What was the over- or underabsorbed overhead for November?

b. Ingleside Shoe Company applied factory overhead by means of a predetermined overhead rate based on direct labor cost, reflecting normal overhead cost at normal volume. Data for 19x2 were as follows:

Normal direct-labor cost.........	$180,000
Underabsorbed overhead	2,000
Actual direct-labor cost	190,000
Normal overhead cost	270,000

It was discovered subsequently that both when establishing the overhead rate and when calculating actual overhead, $45,000 of indirect labor had been treated as sales salaries expense. What was the correct over- or underabsorbed overhead for 19x2?

c. Erie, Inc., wanted to determine the fixed portion of its factory electricity costs. Although one of the vice presidents had stated that electricity costs varied with direct labor-hours, no one had been able to estimate the fixed and variable elements of factory electricity cost. The data in the following table are representative of the company's experience:

Month	Direct Labor-Hours	Electricity Cost
July	23,000	$4,360
August	26,000	4,710

What was the fixed portion of Erie, Inc.'s factory electricity cost?

9. Calculating variable product cost. A company has three production departments, each with its own full-cost overhead rate:

Department A	$2 per pound of materials
Department B	$3 per machine-hour
Department C	$4 per direct labor-hour

You are told that at normal volume variable costs account for 40 percent of the overhead cost in department A, 30 percent of the overhead cost in department B, and 60 percent of the overhead cost in department C.

A job lot of 1,000 units of product X was manufactured in April. This job used 2,000 pounds of materials (in department A), 400 machine-hours in department B, and 200 direct labor-hours in department C.

a. Calculate the overhead cost of this job lot on a full-costing basis.
b. Calculate the overhead cost of this job lot on a variable-costing basis.
c. What do you do with the costs that are included in part a but excluded in part b?

10. Fill in the blanks. Dowbar Company manufactures candlesticks on a job order basis, using a plantwide overhead rate based on normal volume. You have the following data for three recent years:

	19x1	19x2	19x3
Overhead rate per direct labor-hour	A	D	$ 3.20
Actual direct labor-hours	B	9,000	8,000
Normal direct labor-hours	8,000	8,500	G
Overhead absorbed	$30,000	$27,900	H
Actual overhead	29,000	E	27,000
Overhead over(under)absorbed	C	(600)	I
Overhead cost at normal direct labor-hours	24,000	F	28,800

Make the necessary calculations and supply the missing amounts in this table.

11. Effect of predetermined overhead rate. Bates Company has been using a relatively small percentage of its capacity for the past year and this is likely to persist. You have the following data:

1. Estimated factory overhead cost at normal volume (10,000 direct labor-hours a month), $40,000.
2. Estimated factory overhead cost at estimated actual volume (8,000 direct labor-hours a month), $36,000.
3. Actual factory overhead cost at actual volume for April (7,500 direct labor-hours), $37,000.

a. Calculate a predetermined overhead rate on the basis of normal volume.
b. Calculate the amount of overhead under- or overabsorbed during April.
c. Would the amount of overhead under- or overabsorbed have been increased or reduced if the overhead rate had been based on estimated actual volume? Would you have preferred this alternative? Explain.

12. Classifying labor costs. A factory department has four direct production workers. They work an eight-hour day plus occasional overtime. The pay for overtime hours is 150 percent of the regular-time rate.

Three jobs (Nos. 125, 127, and 129) were in process when the employees reported for work on the morning of July 6. Operations were begun during the day on four new jobs (Nos. 126, 128, 130, and 131). Work was completed on Jobs 125, 126, 127, and 130. The following time tickets were filed for the day's work:

Employee	Hourly Wage Rate	Job No.	Hours
Abt, J.	$4.00	127	1
		126	5
		Lubrication	1
		128	1
Davis, P.	6.00	125	1
		127	2
		130	2
		Training	3
		Clean-up	1
Rogers, L.	5.00	128	4
		Sweeping	1
		130	3
		128	2
Thomas, G.	7.00	129	1
		Maintenance	2
		129	1
		131	4
		130	2

These time tickets are listed in the sequence in which the work was performed.

Prior labor costs on jobs in process at the beginning of the day were as follows: Job 125, $28; Job 127, $73; Job 129, $48. Completed jobs were transferred to the finished goods storeroom.

a. Calculate the total direct-labor cost for the day. How much should be entered on each of the job order cost sheets? How much would you classify as overhead cost?
b. Indicate any alternative(s) you considered and rejected in answering part a and give reasons for your choice(s).
c. Calculate the direct-labor cost of the goods finished.
d. Calculate the direct-labor cost of the work in process at the end of the day.

13. Calculating over(under)absorbed overhead. Grace Manufacturing Company uses a job order costing system with a predetermined factory-wide overhead rate based on normal volume. The factory's normal operating volume is 100,000 pounds of direct material a month, and its estimated overhead cost at that volume is $93,000 a month.

a. Calculate the amount of under- or overabsorbed overhead in months in which the following data were recorded (production volume was equal to sales volume in each case):
   1. Volume, 90,000 pounds; overhead cost, $90,000.
   2. Volume, 110,000 pounds; overhead cost, $99,000.
   3. Volume, 80,000 pounds; overhead cost, $86,000.
   4. Volume, 100,000 pounds; overhead cost, $95,000.
b. Grace Manufacturing estimates that half its estimated overhead cost at normal volume will vary in direct proportion to variations in volume above and below the normal level. If a predetermined overhead rate based on variable costing were used, how much overhead cost would be absorbed in each of the four situations described in part a? How much overhead cost would be deducted from revenues in each situation?

14. Distributing manufacturing costs. The Eagleby Company uses a job order costing system with a predetermined factory-wide overhead rate based on normal volume. The overhead rate in 19x1 was $2.50 a direct labor-hour. Over(under)absorbed overhead is included in full each month as a component of the cost of goods sold.

On May 1 and May 31, 19x1, the company had the following inventories:

	May 1	May 31
Raw materials	$20,000	$17,000
Work in process	13,000	15,000
Finished goods	32,000	32,500

You have the following information about the factory's transactions during May 19x1:

1. Raw materials purchased: $8,000.
2. Direct labor used: 5,000 hours, $45,000.

3. Factory overhead cost: $14,000.
4. Indirect materials used: None.

a. Calculate the cost of direct materials used during May.
b. Prepare a schedule showing (1) the costs to be accounted for during May and (2) the amounts of these costs to be assigned to each inventory category and to the cost of goods sold.
c. How much of the cost of goods sold represented over(under)absorbed overhead?

15. Single versus multiple overhead rates.   The Franklin Company's factory has a drill press department with six style A, three style B, and two style C machines. These machines have the following characteristics:

	Machine Style A	Machine Style B	Machine Style C
Cost—each machine	$4,000	$6,000	$9,000
Space occupied—each machine (sq. ft.)	20	50	60
Horsepower-hours per month—each machine	850	1,600	3,000
Hourly wage rate, machine operators	$11.00	$13.20	$15.60
Operating hours per month at normal volume—each machine	184	160	150

A machine operator operates only one machine at a time; the number of direct labor-hours is, therefore, equal to the number of machine-hours.

The normal overhead costs of the drill press department for one month are as follows:

Depreciation, taxes, and insurance—buildings	$1,820
Depreciation, taxes, and insurance—machinery	1,200
Heat and light	520
Power	1,590
Miscellaneous	660
Total	$5,790

a. Calculate a full-cost overhead rate applicable to all the machines in this department, expressed as a percentage of direct-labor cost.
b. Allocate the departmental overhead costs among the three machine styles and calculate a separate full-cost overhead rate for each machine style, expressed as a rate per machine-hour. (Miscellaneous costs are to be divided equally among the 11 machines in the department.)
c. Job No. 2051 was run on one of the style C machines and required 15 hours of machine-time. Compare the amount of overhead costs that would be assigned to this job under the two different costing systems implicit in parts a and b. How would you choose between the two?

16. Costing individual jobs.   Broxbo Manufacturing Company uses a job order costing system. On July 1, the cost of the work in process was $2,700, made up as follows:

Job No.	Direct Materials	Direct Labor	Overhead
101	$ 620	$640	$340
102	730	250	120
Total	$1,350	$890	$460

Finished goods on this same date amounted to $4,000, representing the cost of Job No. 100.

During July, direct materials cost, direct labor cost, and direct labor-hours were:

Job No.	Direct Material Cost	Direct Labor Cost	Direct Labor-Hours
101	$ 100	$ 860	200
102	200	1,900	300
103	1,500	780	150
104	2,000	820	200
105	3,000	245	50
Total	$6,800	$4,605	900

In a normal month, the factory is expected to operate at a volume of 1,000 direct labor-hours, and factory overhead is expected to amount to $3,000. Actual factory overhead cost for July was $2,950.

Job Nos. 101, 102, and 103 were completed during July and were placed in the finished goods storeroom.

Job Nos. 100, 101, and 102 were delivered to customers during July at a billed price of $15,000.

a. Calculate the total cost assigned to each job order.

b. What was the total gross margin on Job Nos. 100, 101, and 102?

c. What was the amount of the over- or underabsorbed overhead for the month?

d. For what purposes might management wish to use the information summarized in your answers above? Is this information well suited to these purposes?

17. Calculating interdepartmental allocations. Minkin Enterprises, Inc., operates a factory with two production departments, a service department, and a factory office. All factory overhead costs except the costs of building ownership and operation are assigned initially to the departments they are traceable to. The costs of building ownership and operation are accumulated in a separate set of accounts.

In developing predetermined departmental overhead rates, Minkin Enterprises first distributes the estimated building ownership and operation costs among the four factory departments in proportion to the amount of floor space each occupies. The estimated costs of the factory office, including its share of building ownership and operation costs, are then reassigned to the other three factory departments in proportion to the number of employees in each department. Finally, the estimated costs of the factory service department are divided between the two production departments in proportion to the amount of service each is expected to provide.

Estimated overhead costs and statistics for next year are as follows:

	Production No. 1	Production No. 2	Factory Service	Factory Office	Building Ownership and Operation
Traceable overhead costs per month	$10,925	$6,550	$5,975	$3,150	$7,000
Floor space (sq. ft.)	9,000	7,000	3,000	1,000	—
Number of employees	35	60	5	3	2
Service-hours used per month	400	200	—	—	—
Machine-hours per month	5,000	—	—	—	—
Direct labor-hours per month	—	9,000	—	—	—

a. Using the company's method, allocate the estimated costs.
b. Calculate predetermined overhead rates for the two production departments: No. 1, based on machine-hours; No. 2, based on direct labor-hours.

18. Calculating inventory costs; proposed allocation of overhead variance. On November 30, a fire destroyed the plant and factory offices of the Swadburg Company. The following data survived the fire:

1. From the balance sheet at November 1, you find the beginning inventories: materials, $5,000; work in process, $15,000; finished goods, $27,500.
2. The factory overhead rate in use during November was 80 cents per dollar of direct material cost.
3. Total sales for the month amounted to $60,000. The gross profit margin constituted 25 percent of selling price.
4. Purchases of materials during November amounted to $30,000.
5. The payroll records show wages accrued during November as $25,000, of which $3,000 was for indirect labor.
6. The charges to factory overhead accounts totaled $18,000. Of this, $2,000 was for indirect materials and $3,000 was for indirect labor.
7. The cost of goods finished during November was $52,000.
8. Underabsorbed overhead amounted to $400. This amount was not deducted in the computation of the gross profit margin (item 3 above).

a. Calculate the amount of cost that had been assigned to the inventories of raw materials, work in process, and finished goods that were on hand at the time of the fire on November 30.
b. The Swadburg Company's management has claimed that a portion of the underabsorbed overhead should be assigned to the inventory, thereby increasing the amount due from the insurance company. The insurance company has denied this claim, and you have been called upon to arbitrate the dispute. What answer would you give? What arguments would you advance to support it?

19.   Analyzing effects of transactions; clerical errors.   The Sandrex Company uses a job order cost accounting system. Direct-labor costs are charged daily to Work in Process and credited to Wages Payable on the basis of time tickets. Direct materials costs are charged to Work in Process and credited to Materials Inventory. Factory overhead costs are charged initially to a Factory Overhead account. Overhead costs are charged to the Work in Process account by means of a predetermined overhead rate of $2 a direct labor-hour. The costs of goods finished are transferred from Work in Process to a Finished Goods account at the time each job is completed. A perpetual inventory system is used for both materials and finished goods.

Following are some of the events that took place in 19x1:

1.   Goods manufactured in 19x0 at a cost of $8,000 were sold on credit for $14,000. The job cost sheets for these goods showed a total of $2,000 for materials, $3,000 for direct labor, and $3,000 for overhead.

2.   Factory overhead was charged to a job on which 480 direct labor-hours were recorded during 19x1. The job was still unfinished at the end of the year.

3.   It was discovered prior to the end of 19x1 that an error in analyzing a batch of time cards resulted in treating 500 hours of direct labor at $5 an hour as indirect labor (that is, the charge was made to Factory Overhead). The job on which this labor was used was finished but not sold in 19x1.

4.   Materials costing $5,000 and supplies costing $500 were issued from the factory storeroom. Of the materials, $1,000 was for use in constructing new display cases in the company's salesrooms. The display cases were completed and placed in use during 19x1. The remaining materials were issued to the factory for specific job orders which were still in process at the end of 19x1. Of the supplies, $100 was for the immediate use of the sales office, and the remainder was for general factory use.

5.   Prior to the end of 19x1, it was discovered that $1,000 of direct materials had been charged to the wrong job. At the time this error was discovered, both jobs had been completed but not yet sold.

6.   Prior to the end of the year, it was discovered that an error had been made in adding up the direct labor-hours on a certain job order which had been completed and the products sold during 19x1. The dollar amount of direct labor was added correctly, but the hours were overstated by 100.

7.   At the end of 19x1, factory wages earned but still unpaid amounted to $3,000 for direct labor (at $10 an hour) and $1,000 for indirect labor. Time tickets for these amounts of labor had not yet been processed. Employer's payroll taxes on these wages were 9 percent. This company treats all payroll taxes as overhead. The direct labor was expended on jobs that were still in process at the end of 19x1.

Indicate how discovery of these facts would affect the cost assigned to the work in process inventory at the end of the year, the cost of the finished goods inventory, or the cost of goods sold. Each event should be regarded as independent of the others.

20. Discussion question: interdepartmental cost allocation. A company's own power-generating department provides electric power to four factory departments. Two of these are production centers (A and B) and two are service centers (X and Y). Power consumption isn't measured; instead, it is assumed to vary in proportion to the number of horsepower-hours used by the equipment in the four user departments. The cost of operating the power-generating department is expected to be $4,000 a month plus 40 cents per horsepower-hour. The amount of fixed cost is determined mainly by the amount of power-generating capacity the power department has and will increase or decrease roughly in proportion to the capacity provided.

The estimated volume of activity in each of the four power-using departments, as measured by the number of horsepower-hours, is as follows:

	Production Centers		Service Centers		
	A	B	X	Y	Total
Horsepower-hours needed at capacity production	10,000	20,000	12,000	8,000	50,000
Horsepower-hours used in an average month	8,000	13,000	7,000	6,000	34,000

You have been asked to help management develop predetermined departmental overhead rates for each of the two production centers. The rates are to be full-cost rates, each representing the average cost attributable in the long run to the activities of the production center in question.

What dollar amount of estimated power-department cost should be assigned to each production center and each service center for this purpose? Give reasons for your answer, including your reasons for allocating or not allocating power-department costs to the two service centers.

21. Overhead rates under variable costing. The management of Leininger Company has decided to use variable costing for cost-estimating purposes. Full-cost figures will be entered on the job order cost sheets and in the financial accounts. The estimated overhead costs of factory department 77 at a normal value of 4,000 direct labor-hours a month are as follows:

Supervision	$ 4,000
Indirect labor	6,000
Fringe benefits	8,400
Supplies	1,200
Power	1,000
Depreciation	800
Miscellaneous	600
Total	$22,000

You have the following additional information.

1. Supervision costs remain at $4,000 a month for any volume between 3,000 and 5,000 direct labor-hours. If volume drops below 3,000 hours,

supervision can be cut to $2,800; if volume exceeds 5,000 hours, supervision costs will go up to $5,000 a month.
2. One third of indirect labor costs at normal volume are fixed; two thirds are proportional to the number of direct labor-hours.
3. Fringe benefits amount to 20 percent of labor cost, including direct labor, supervision, and indirect labor. Direct labor wage rates average $8 an hour.
4. Supplies and power costs should be proportional to the number of direct labor-hours.
5. Depreciation and miscellaneous overhead costs are entirely fixed.
6. The volume of activity ordinarily fluctuates between 3,200 and 4,600 direct labor-hours.

Calculate overhead rates for this department, both for variable costing and for full costing.

22. Interpreting job cost data. Dan Roman is a contractor specializing in small house-remodeling jobs. Most of his employees are specialists who work for other contractors as well, so the size of his payroll rises and falls with fluctuations in the amount of work to be done. Higher wage rates are paid to the more highly skilled workers, but the average rate in the construction industry in Roman's area is about $11 an hour and Roman uses this rate in preparing estimates of job order costs.

Roman recently installed a job order costing system and now has the following labor cost data:

Job Number	Estimated Labor-Hours	Estimated Labor Cost	Actual Labor-Hours	Actual Labor Cost
47	600	$6,600	650	$ 8,125
48	400	4,400	380	4,520
50	900	9,900	1,000	13,100
51	200	2,200	210	2,400
52	500	5,500	460	5,290
54	700	7,700	750	9,150
55	800	8,800	820	9,840

During the period covered by these figures, Roman submitted bids on 18 jobs. Other contractors underbid him on 11 of these; he was the low bidder on the seven jobs shown. Roman's profit margin was considerably lower than that of most of his competitors during this period.

a. What advice can you give Roman on the basis of these figures? Do they help explain his low profit margin? Is there anything he can do about it?
b. What further data would you probably find in Roman's job cost sheets that would throw more light on these questions?
c. Would charging overhead costs to individual job orders provide Roman with useful information?

23. Product cost under variable costing. Gaddis Corporation owns and operates two factories. One manufactures component parts, either for sale to outside customers or for use in the company's other factory.

Each factory uses a job order costing system with a factory-wide predetermined overhead rate based on estimated overhead costs at normal volume, determined as follows:

	Factory A	Factory B
Overhead cost at normal volume:		
Variable	$10,000	$ 8,000
Fixed	50,000	12,000
Total	$60,000	$20,000
Normal monthly volume	20,000 machine-hours	10,000 direct labor-hours
Overhead rate	$3 per machine-hour	$2 per direct labor-hour

Management is considering the possibility of using factory B to manufacture a new product, product X. Monthly volume would amount to 5,000 units, which would require 1,000 direct labor-hours in factory B at a direct labor wage rate of $8 an hour, add $25,000 to factory B's direct materials costs, and increase factory B's fixed overhead by $500 a month. Factory B's variable overhead costs would vary in proportion to the number of direct labor-hours used.

All the direct materials for product X would be component parts manufactured in factory A. Their costs would be:

Direct materials	$11,000
Direct labor	8,000
Factory overhead	6,000
Total	$25,000

Fixed overhead costs in factory A would be unaffected by the manufacture of the parts necessary to make product X.

Gaddis Corporation's marketing vice president asked the controller for cost estimates to be used in an analysis of the sensitivity of the company's income to errors in the forecasts of sales volume for product X. The controller provided these estimates from the data supplied here. When asked why the company didn't use variable costing to determine product costs on a regular basis, the controller replied that prices had to cover fixed costs too. Besides, full-cost data could be adjusted to a variable-costing basis any time management needed estimates of variable cost.

a. Calculate the unit cost of product X on a variable-costing basis.
b. Comment on the controller's argument, including an analysis of the differences between your answer to part *a* and the cost of product B on a full-costing basis.

24. Departmental overhead rates; allocations. The Sender Company has four product departments (machine No. 1, machine No. 2, assembly, and painting) and three service departments (storage, maintenance, and office) but uses a plantwide overhead rate based on direct labor-hours. At normal volume, 100,600 direct labor-hours would be used and factory overhead costs would be as follows:

Indirect labor and supervision:
Machine No. 1	$33,000
Machine No. 2	22,000
Assembly	11,000
Painting	7,000
Storage	44,000
Maintenance	32,700

Indirect materials and supplies:
Machine No. 1	2,200
Machine No. 2	1,100
Assembly	3,300
Painting	3,400
Maintenance	2,800

Other:
Rent of factory	96,000
Depreciation of machinery and equipment	44,000
Insurance and taxes on machinery and equipment	2,400
Compensation insurance at $2 per $100 of labor payroll	19,494
Power	66,000
Factory office salaries	52,800
General superintendence	55,000
Miscellaneous office costs	21,620
Heat and light	72,000
Miscellaneous storage charges (insurance and so forth)	3,686

You have the following additional information about the various departments:

Department	Area (sq. ft.)	Cost of Machinery and Equipment	Raw Materials Used	Horsepower Rating	Direct Labor-Hours	Direct Labor Payroll	Number of Employees
Machine No. 1	65,000	$220,000	$520,000	2,000	48,000	$440,000	100
Machine No. 2	55,000	110,000	180,000	1,000	17,600	220,000	60
Assembly	44,000	55,000		100	24,000	110,000	30
Painting	32,000	22,000	90,000	200	11,000	55,000	15
Storage	22,000	11,000					14
Office	11,000	5,500					11
Maintenance	11,000	16,500					10
Total	240,000	$440,000	$790,000	3,300	100,600	$825,000	240

a. Calculate a plantwide overhead rate on a full-cost basis.

b. Calculate departmental overhead rates based on full costing. For this purpose you will need to distribute some of the general overhead costs among the seven departments and then allocate the costs of the service departments among the four production departments. You should allocate office and general superintendence costs on the basis of direct labor-hours, maintenance on the basis of machinery and equipment cost, and storage costs on the basis of materials (direct and indirect) used.

c. How would the use of these departmental overhead rates instead of the plantwide rate affect the cost assigned to a job order requiring 100 direct labor-hours in machine No. 1, 200 direct labor-hours in machine No. 2, 20 hours in assembly, and 10 hours in painting?

d. Someone has questioned the allocation you made in answer to part *b,* saying that the allocation bases appear to be arbitrary. Formulate a reply, including a statement of what each overhead rate ought to mean and comparing the rates you have developed against that standard. You may either agree or disagree with the critic of your allocations, but if you agree you should indicate how you would change the procedure. *No calculations are required by this question.*

19

The capital-expenditure decision

The decisions described in Chapter 16 could be based on estimates of their effects on the organization's cash flows in a single time period no longer than a year. This approach is inadequate when management is faced with an *investment problem.* An investment problem is a situation requiring management to decide whether to expend cash in one or more time periods to obtain cash inflows in another time period or periods.

One of the most important types of investment problems is the *capital-expenditure decision,* in which an initial cash outlay (the capital expenditure) is made in the expectation that it will produce cash receipts in a later year or years. Typical examples are proposals to build, acquire, replace, or expand long-lived productive assets. The purpose of this chapter is to see how management can analyze and solve problems of this sort.

THE NET PRESENT VALUE APPROACH

The most widely recommended method of evaluating proposals to make capital expenditures is to calculate for each proposal the net present value of the anticipated cash flows, using an interest rate representing the company's minimum acceptable rate of return on investment. This is referred to as *discounted-cash-flow (DCF)* analysis. Since we examined the present value concept in detail in Chapter 6, we'll spend this chapter studying how this concept is applied in discounted-cash-flow analysis.

TERMINOLOGY REMINDER

The *present value* of a future sum is the amount which, if invested now at compound interest at the specified rate, will grow to an amount equal to the future sum at the specified future date.

The procedure

In the basic form of discounted-cash-flow analysis, all estimates are treated as equivalent to amounts that can be predicted with certainty. The analysis in this form consists of four steps:

1. Identify the proposal and at least one alternative to accepting it.
2. Estimate the cash flows, year by year, that would result if the proposal were accepted; make a similar set of estimates for each alternative being considered. Enter these estimates in a table known as a *timetable,* in which each row identifies a period or point in time and each column lists a series of cash flows associated with a particular alternative.
3. Determine—by the process known as *discounting*—the *net present value* of the estimated cash flows associated with each alternative. The net present value of an alternative is the algebraic sum of the present values of the estimated cash inflows (*receipts*) and estimated cash outflows (*outlays*) associated with that alternative.
4. Choose the alternative with the highest net present value.

Step 1: Identify the alternatives. Barclay Company is considering a proposal to invest $34,000 (proposal A). To evaluate this proposal, management has to identify at least one alternative to accepting it. If it has no alternative, it has no decision to make. In this case management has decided to introduce only one alternative: *reject proposal A.*

Step 2: Estimate the cash flows. One way to proceed would be to estimate the cash flows for the entire company under each alternative. This might be necessary for truly major capital-expenditure proposals that would affect the basic nature and structure of the company's operations. A simpler approach, adequate for most capital-expenditure decisions, is to select one alternative as a benchmark and measure the cash flows of each other alternative as differences from that benchmark. In this case management has selected "reject proposal A" as the benchmark alternative. The estimated cash flows relative to this benchmark are shown in the following table:

Years from Now	Cash Flow
0	−$34,000
1	+ 10,000
2	+ 10,000
3	+ 10,000
4	+ 10,000
5	+ 10,000
Total	+$16,000

In this table, cash receipts are identified by + signs; the cash outlay is identified by a − sign. Since the anticipated annual cash inflows (receipts) in this case are identical, we can also show them in the timetable as a five-year annuity of $10,000 a year.

Step 3:   Estimate the net present value of each alternative.   The prices investors pay for Barclay Company's stocks and bonds establish the rate of return they demand as their reward for investing in the company. This demanded rate is known as the *cost of capital* and is discussed more fully in the appendix to this chapter.

Barclay estimates that its cost of capital is 10 percent; its management therefore insists that the capital expenditures it makes offer the promise of a rate of return of 10 percent or more. To test an expenditure's ability to earn this much, Barclay's management determines the estimated present value of the expected cash flows at an interest rate of 10 percent, compounded annually. The present value multiplier for a five-year annuity at 10 percent (from Table 4 of Appendix A) is 3.7908, and the present values of the anticipated cash flows associated with this proposal are as follows:

Years from Now	Cash Flow	Present Value at 10 Percent Multiplier	Amount
0	−$34,000	1.0000	−$34,000
1 to 5	+ 10,000 a year	3.7908	+ 37,908
Net present value......			+$ 3,908

Step 4:   Choose the best alternative.   Barclay Company has recognized only one alternative to accepting proposal A: reject proposal A and continue present operations unchanged. The cash flows in the tables above represent the *differences* between the results with proposal A and the results with this benchmark alternative. The estimated net present value in the table above therefore is an *incre-*

EXHIBIT 19–1.　Present Value of Competing Alternatives

	(1)	(2)	(3)	(4)	(5)
			Proposal B		Proposal C
Years from Now	Present Value Multiplier at 10 Percent*	Cash Flow	Present Value (1) × (2)	Cash Flow	Present Value (4) × (1)
0	1.0000	−$56,000	−$56,000	−$45,000	−$45,000
1	0.9091	+ 16,000	+ 14,546	+ 15,000	+ 13,636
2	0.8264	+ 16,000	+ 13,222	+ 15,000	+ 12,396
3	0.7513	+ 16,000	+ 12,021	+ 15,000	+ 11,270
4	0.6830	+ 16,000	+ 10,928	+ 10,000	+ 6,830
5	0.6209	+ 16,000	+ 9,934	+ 5,000	+ 3,105
Net present value			+$ 4,651		+$ 2,237

* From Table 3, Appendix A.

mental net present value, the *difference* between the net present value of proposal A and the net present value of the benchmark alternative. The difference in net present value is positive in this case, meaning that the cash flows proposal A is expected to generate will be more than enough to recover the $34,000 initial outlay and to provide a 10 percent rate of return on the company's investment. The excess cash flows have a present value of $3,908. Since the company finds 10 percent an acceptable rate of return, it should be happy to accept proposal A.

Multiple alternatives

　　The procedure we've just described can be applied without modification to proposals with several alternatives. This is particularly important because for major capital-expenditure proposals, management should insist that a real effort be made to identify one or more substitute proposals that might fill the same needs in different ways. Once this has been done, management should select the proposal with the highest positive net present value; if none of the proposals has a positive net present value, all should be rejected.

　　For example, we saw earlier that proposal A has an estimated net present value of $3,908. Instead of accepting this proposal, however, management could accept either proposal B or proposal C. The cash flows and multipliers for proposals B and C are shown in Exhibit 19–1. Proposal B offers a higher net present value than proposal A; the net present value of proposal C is lower than that of either of the other two. Proposal B therefore should be chosen.

Reasons for the net-present-value approach

We use net present value as the measure of the desirability of a capital-expenditure proposal mainly for two reasons:

1. It provides a means of testing whether the estimated cash inflows are adequate to cover the cost of capital *and* recover the outlays required by the proposal.
2. It takes into account differences in the *timing* of the cash flows associated with individual proposals.

Capital recovery. Net present value is the present value of the cash flows that aren't needed to recover the initial outlay or cover the cost of capital. To illustrate, let's go back to proposal A, for which the initial outlays are expected to be $34,000. The first year's interest at 10 percent, therefore, amounts to $3,400. Since $10,000 in cash is received, the remaining $6,600 can be treated as a partial recovery of the original investment. This leaves an unrecovered balance of $27,400 at the end of the first year. Interest on that amount in the second year is $2,740, leaving $7,260 of the second year's cash receipts to be treated as a recovery of another portion of the initial outlay.

Continuing these calculations for three more years produces the following table:

Year	(1) Unrecovered Investment, Beginning of Year	(2) Interest at 10 Percent	(3) Amortization of Investment [$10,000 − (2)]	(4) Unrecovered Investment, End of Year (1) − (3)
1	$34,000	$3,400	$6,600	$27,400
2	27,400	2,740	7,260	20,140
3	20,140	2,014	7,986	12,154
4	12,154	1,215	8,785	3,369
5	3,369	337	9,663	(6,294)

By the end of the fifth year, the entire investment has been recovered, despite annual interest payments at a 10 percent rate, and the company still has $6,294 left over (Exhibit 19–2). In other words, Barclay could have paid more than 10 percent interest from the cash inflows stemming from this investment. As we said earlier, the $6,294 net present value is the future value of $3,908 five years later, compounded annually at 10 percent.

Timing differences. A second important feature of net present value is that it takes into account the timing of the anticipated

EXHIBIT 19–2. The Investment-Recovery Pattern

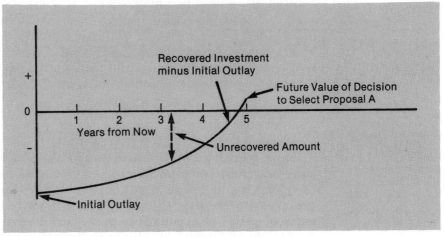

cash flows. For example, suppose Barclay Company can invest in any or all of the following proposals:

Years from Now	Net Cash Receipts (+) or Cash Outlays (−)		
	Proposal X	Proposal Y	Proposal Z
0	−$13,000	−$13,000	−$13,000
1	+ 1,000	+ 5,000	+ 9,000
2	+ 5,000	+ 5,000	+ 5,000
3	+ 9,000	+ 5,000	+ 1,000
Total cash flow	+$ 2,000	+$ 2,000	+$ 2,000

These three proposals have identical lifetime total cash flows, but they are far from equally desirable. Proposal Z is the best because cash is received earlier under this proposal than under either of the others. Proposal X is the worst of the three.

These differences appear clearly in present-value calculations. Assuming a 10 percent interest rate, the net present values of these proposals are:

Years from Now	Present Value Multipliers	Proposal X	Proposal Y	Proposal Z
0	1.0000	−$13,000	−$13,000	−$13,000
1	0.9091	+ 909	+ 4,545	+ 8,182
2	0.8264	+ 4,132	+ 4,132	+ 4,132
3	0.7513	+ 6,762	+ 3,757	+ 751
Net present value		−$ 1,197	−$ 566	+$ 65

The present value multipliers in this table came from the 10 percent column of Table 3 in Appendix A.

In this case, proposals X and Y promise a return on investment of less than 10 percent; only proposal Z promises a return in excess of 10 percent. Therefore, only proposal Z should be accepted. The net present value measure, in other words, permits management to compare proposals which differ in the timing of their cash flows.

Internal rate of return

Some managers are accustomed to evaluating company activities—and their personal investment activities as well—by the rate of return the activities produce. For this reason some companies prefer to use the *internal rate of return* to measure the incremental value of a capital-expenditure proposal. The internal rate of return is the rate of interest at which the incremental net present value of a proposal is zero. Calculating the internal rate of return is a three-step, trial-and-error process:

Step 1: Discount all cash flows at a trial rate.   We have already performed this step. The net present value of the cash flows at 10 percent is $3,908. This indicates that the rate of return is greater than 10 percent, but it doesn't show how much greater.

Step 2: Discount all cash flows at a second trial rate.   Since we now know that the internal rate of return is higher than 10 percent, a reasonable second trial rate is 15 percent. The multipliers and present values at this rate are:

Years from Now	Cash Flow	Present Value at 15 Percent	
		Multiplier	Amount
0	−$34,000	1.0000	−$34,000
1–5	+ 10,000 a year	3.3522	+ 33,522
Net present value			−$ 478

The present value of the cash receipts at a 15 percent discount rate is only $33,522, producing a negative net present value. This means that the cash inflows aren't big enough to produce a rate of return as high as 15 percent.

Step 3: Interpolate.   The internal rate of return from proposal A is greater than 10 percent because the cash inflows are expected to be more than adequate to cover a 10 percent cost of capital; the estimated net present value is positive at 10 percent. We also know that the internal rate of return is less than 15 percent because the cash inflows are expected to be less than adequate to cover a 15

EXHIBIT 19–3. Interpolating to Approximate the Internal Rate of Return

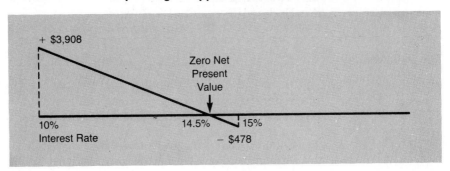

percent cost of capital; the estimated net present value is negative at 15 percent.

The correct rate therefore is somewhere between 10 and 15 percent. To locate it precisely, we could discount the cash flows at various interest rates between 10 and 15 percent until we found the rate at which proposal A's estimated net present value was zero. In general, however, an approximation obtained by interpolating between two points on a graph, as in Exhibit 19–3, will be close enough. We can make this same calculation algebraically, as follows:

$$\text{Approximate rate} = 10\% + \frac{\$3,908}{\$3,908 + \$478} \times (15\% - 10\%) = 14.5\%$$

($3,908 + $478 = $4,386 is the total distance between + $3,908 and − $478.)

ESTIMATING CASH FLOWS

Any subdivision of the cash flows associated with a capital-expenditure proposal is partly arbitrary. All that matters is the amount and timing of the cash flows; whether some are called capital outlays while others are called maintenance expenses is relevant only insofar as the classification coincides with the classification scheme used by the taxing authorities to determine the tax effects of the outlays. Even so, we find it convenient to distinguish four components of the cash-flow stream:

1. The initial outlay.
2. Secondary investment outlays.

3. Operating cash flows.
4. End-of-life residual values.

The initial outlay

The initial outlay consists of all the cash outflows that must take place before significant operating cash receipts or cash cost savings begin to flow in. It contains some or all of the following:

1. Cash outlays for plant and equipment.
2. Opportunity costs of existing facilities to be incorporated in the proposal.
3. Outlays for working capital.
4. Disposal values of facilities to be displaced by the proposal.
5. Immediate income tax effects.

Plant and equipment. For most proposals, the major outlays are for the acquisition and installation of physical facilities. For example, a proposal to modernize Barclay Company's factory is expected to require the following outlays before the investment begins to bring in cash receipts:

Equipment	$80,000
Installation	10,000
Training and test runs	7,000
Total	$97,000

If these outlays are spread over a period longer than a few months, accuracy will be served if they are split up and entered into the cash-flow timetable at the amounts corresponding to each time period. In this case, however, Barclay's management estimates that they'll all take place within a very short time, which we'll refer to as the *zero date* for present value calculations.

Existing facilities used. One of Barclay's present machines, now idle, will be put back in service only if the modernization proposal is approved. No cash needs to be paid for this machine; the company already owns it. Even so, it belongs in the timetable of cash flows. By accepting the proposal, management will make this machine unavailable for any other use. This proposal, therefore, should be charged for the machine's value in its best other use—that is, its opportunity cost.

In this case, Barclay's management has decided that the machine will be sold if it isn't needed for the modernization proposal. The estimated sale price is $12,000. This is part of the investment outlay because, in accepting the proposal, the company is depriving itself of $12,000 in cash:

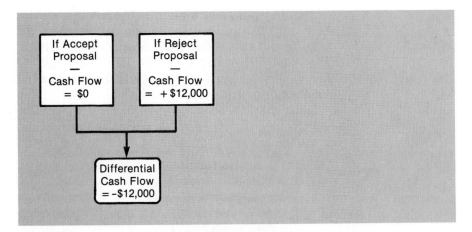

A *cash receipt forgone is always equivalent to a cash outlay.* The book value of the equipment doesn't measure either current or future cash flows, of course, and therefore should be ignored.

Working capital. Capital-expenditure proposals often require outlays for resources other than land, buildings, and equipment. Cash outlays for product development, working capital, or market research are just as much a part of the investment required by a capital-expenditure proposal as are outlays for plant assets.

The only additional outlays required by our illustrative modernization proposal are for working capital. To use the new equipment effectively, management will have to increase inventories by $5,000. Suppliers will finance only $3,000 of this amount. In addition, management will have to immobilize $1,000 of its cash balances to support the additional activity the proposal will generate. Putting these estimates together, we get an estimated working-capital requirement of $3,000, all to be provided at the time the equipment is put in place:

Cash	$1,000
Inventory	5,000
Accounts payable	(3,000)
Working capital	$3,000

The proposal also calls for a further increase in working capital, as additional receivables are created by the first year's operations. Although it is often convenient to include this increase as part of the initial outlay, we'll handle it as part of the *operating* cash flow because it actually arises when sales revenues exceed collections from customers in the period of sales expansion.

Displaced facilities. The cash flows we've mentioned so far haven't included one determinant of the initial outlay. If the proposal is accepted, Barclay's management can dispose of a machine serving a standby purpose. This machine has a tax basis (book value) of only $1,000, but once again opportunity cost, not book value, is the right measure of the cash flow. Opportunity cost is measured by the machine's scrap value, $6,000. The displaced machine, in other words, can finance $6,000 of the gross pretax outlays the proposal will require.

This may become clearer if we recognize that we're really comparing two alternatives in our cash-flow estimates:

A	B
Accept the Proposal and Dispose of Existing Standby Equipment +$6,000	Reject the Proposal and Keep the Standby Equipment +$0

The only way to get the $6,000 cash inflow is to accept this proposal. It therefore becomes a cash inflow attributable to the proposal and must be included in the timetable.

Tax effects of the initial outlay

Income taxes are cash flows. Like other cash flows, their amount and timing can affect the present value of capital-expenditure proposals.

Each country has its own taxing rules, and individual states, provinces, and local government bodies may also tax the organization's income. These rules are often extremely complex; they also change frequently. For these reasons we can only illustrate how some kinds of tax provisions can affect the cash flows, if they happen to be applicable.

Tax rates also vary and different tax rates may apply to different portions of the taxable income stream. To simplify the presentation, we'll assume that a tax rate of 40 percent is applied to all amounts that enter into the calculation of taxable income. We'll also assume that the company has taxable income from other sources to offset any losses the proposal generates for tax purposes. Losses therefore are also subject to the 40 percent tax rate.

Our initial outlay has four separate kinds of tax effects: a tax credit, a tax deduction, a tax-deductible loss, and a taxable gain. (A tax credit is a direct reduction in the amount of tax due; a tax deduction is a reduction in the amount of taxable income.)

Tax credit. Many governments offer tax credits to induce businesses to invest in facilities or to increase their inventories, thereby providing jobs and stimulating the economy. In our illustration, the $80,000 outlay for new equipment is eligible for a 10 percent tax credit. This will reduce the tax by $8,000, and this amount should be deducted in calculating the initial outlay.

Tax deduction. Both the purchase price and the installation cost of the new equipment will be capitalized and depreciated for tax purposes over a period of years. The $7,000 in training and test-run costs, however, will be fully deductible from taxable revenues right away. At a 40 percent tax rate, this will reduce current taxes by $2,800. The aftertax outlay for these items therefore is $7,000 − $2,800 = $4,200.

Tax-deductible loss. We have already seen that accepting the proposal will deprive the company of the $12,000 cash flow from selling an idle machine. It will also deprive the company of the right to enter the loss from the sale of the machine on the current income tax return. The loss for tax purposes is the difference between the proceeds from the sale and the book value for tax purposes (the "tax basis"), which in this case happens to be $20,000:

Sale value	$12,000
Tax basis	20,000
Tax-deductible loss	$ 8,000

Since the sale of this machine would reduce taxable income, it would also reduce taxes. Using the machine will deprive the company of this reduction. It thus becomes another incremental cash outflow arising from the proposed expenditure. At a tax rate of 40 percent, the tax effect is $3,200. The aftertax cash inflow is:

Sale value forgone		$12,000
Tax basis	$20,000	
Sales value	12,000	
Tax-deductible loss	8,000	
Tax rate	× 40%	
Tax increase due to loss deferred		3,200
Aftertax cash outflow		$15,200

Taxable gain. The final element in the initial outlay calculation, the sale of the displaced machine, also has a tax effect. The market value of this machine is $6,000 and the tax basis is $1,000, so the taxable gain is $5,000. The cash flows are:

Market value	+$6,000
Tax on the gain: 40% × $5,000	− 2,000
Aftertax cash flow	+$4,000

The aftertax investment outlay. All these figures are summarized in Exhibit 19–4. In this case the net difference between the pretax and aftertax amounts is relatively small, less than 6 percent; in

EXHIBIT 19–4. Calculation of Incremental Aftertax Initial Outlay

Item	Incremental Outlay before Tax	Tax Effect	Incremental Outlay after Tax
Equipment, installed	$ 90,000	$(8,000)	$ 82,000
Working capital	3,000	0	3,000
Training and test runs	7,000	(2,800)	4,200
Surplus equipment used	12,000	3,200	15,200
Equipment displaced	(6,000)	2,000	(4,000)
Total	$(106,000)	$(5,600)	$(100,400)

Alternative format:

Item	If Accept Proposal	If Reject Proposal	Incremental Cash Flow
Equipment, installed	−$82,000	0	−$ 82,000
Working capital	− 3,000	0	− 3,000
Training and test runs	− 4,200	0	− 4,200
Surplus equipment used	0	+$15,200	− 15,200
Equipment displaced	+ 4,000	0	+ 4,000
Net outlay	−$85,200	+$15,200	−$100,400

other cases it can be much greater. In the exhibit's alternative format, minus signs identify cash outlays and plus signs identify cash receipts. The alternative form of display has the advantage of showing the alternatives clearly, but it obscures the tax adjustment.

Secondary investment outlays

Management can often predict special outlays that will have to be made in later time periods to keep the investment alive. These, too, may be for equipment or for additional working capital. Each has to be examined for its tax implications.

Secondary investment outlays of this sort are no different in concept from the initial outlay and need no further discussion here. The only secondary investment outlay Barclay's management anticipates for the plant modernization proposal is $20,000 to replace equipment at the end of the fifth year. This, too, will be eligible for a 10 percent investment credit ($2,000), thereby reducing the aftertax cash outlay to $18,000.

Operating cash flows

The incremental operating cash flow in our illustrative modernization proposal is expected to come partly from increased sales volume and partly from reduced operating costs. Once again we could present the cash flows under our two alternatives in two columns, with an incremental column at the right:

Years from Zero Date	If Accept Proposal	If Reject Proposal	Incremental Cash Flow
n	X	Y	X − Y

In this case, however, management has much less confidence in its ability to forecast the absolute results under each alternative than in its ability to forecast the differences *between* them. Although costs and therefore expenses are expected to increase from year to year, the gap between the two alternatives is expected to remain roughly constant at $9,000 a year in increased revenues and $16,000 in reduced operating expenses (other than depreciation and income taxes), a total of $25,000.

Translating income into cash flow. The $25,000 increment we just described is an increase in operating income before depreciation and income taxes. What we want, of course, is the increment in cash flow. In this illustration we have only one adjustment to make to convert operating income into the pretax cash flow—to reflect a $2,000, one-time increase in accounts receivable during the first year of operations. In other words, the first year's net incremental cash flow before taxes will be $2,000 less than incremental operating income, because the incremental collections from customers will be $2,000 less than the first year's increase in sales revenues. The first year's pretax operating cash flows therefore are expected to be as follows:

Increase in collections: $9,000 − $2,000 .... $ 7,000
Decrease in disbursements 16,000
Incremental pretax cash inflow, first year $23,000

Adjusting for income taxes. The next step in the analysis is to calculate the effect of the estimated increments in operating income on the company's income taxes. In this calculation, we start with the pretax cash flows. In doing so, however, we recognize that the spread between taxable income (based on the revenues and expenses shown on the company's income tax returns) is likely to differ significantly from the amount of the pretax cash flow. One reason for the difference between these two amounts is the effect of accrual accounting on taxable income, such as in the treatment of product warranty costs. Another difference exists because of government attempts to influence taxpayer behavior by disallowing certain kinds of cash outflows as deductible expenses in calculating taxable income (e.g., court fines and penalties in some taxing jurisdictions) or by accelerating or decelerating the recognition of certain kinds of revenues or expenses.

The only significant differences between pretax cash flows and incremental taxable income in our illustration are the first-year increase in receivables we just described and incremental tax depreciation. Depreciation charges aren't cash flows, but they do enter into the calculation of taxable income and therefore do affect the aftertax cash flow.

Tax depreciation on the new facilities required by the proposal is governed by the "accelerated cost recovery system" (ACRS) adopted in the United States in 1981. The tax life on the new equipment and on the secondary investment five years after the zero date is five years, even though the original facilities are expected to last 10 years. The applicable ACRS schedule for this equipment (in percentages of original cost less half the investment credit) is as follows:

Year	Percentage
1	15
2	22
3	21
4	21
5	21

The existing equipment being incorporated in the project, with a present tax basis of $20,000, is depreciated for tax purposes at a straight-line amount of $5,000 a year. The standby equipment replaced by the proposal has a tax basis of $1,000, which is now depreciated by the straight-line method at $500 a year.

Depreciation calculated on these bases is summarized in Exhibit

EXHIBIT 19–5. Calculation of Incremental Tax Depreciation

Year	(1) New Equipment	(2) Present Equipment	(3) Total	(4) Tax Depreciation if Proposal Is Rejected	(5) Incremental Tax Depreciation (3) − (4)
1	$12,900*	$5,000	$17,900	$500	$17,400
2	18,920*	5,000	23,920	500	23,420
3	18,060*	5,000	23,060	—	23,060
4	18,060*	5,000	23,060	—	23,060
5	18,060*	—	18,060	—	18,060
6	2,850†	—	2,850	—	2,850
7	4,180†	—	4,180	—	4,180
8	3,990†	—	3,990	—	3,990
9	3,990†	—	3,990	—	3,990
10	3,990†	—	3,990	—	3,990

* Depreciation of $90,000 cost of new equipment, less half the investment credit ($4,000).
† Depreciation of $20,000 original cost of equipment purchased by secondary outlay, less half the investment credit ($1,000).

EXHIBIT 19–6. Calculation of Aftertax Operating Cash Flows

Year	(1) Incremental Income before Depreciation and Income Tax	(2) Incremental Tax Depreciation	(3) Incremental Taxable Income (1) − (2)	(4) Incremental Income Tax 40% × (3)	(5) Incremental Cash Flow before Income Tax	(6) Incremental Cash Flow (5) − (4)
1	$ 25,000	$ 17,400	$ 7,600	$ 3,040	+$ 23,000	+$ 19,960
2	25,000	23,420	1,580	632	+ 25,000	+ 24,368
3	25,000	23,060	1,940	776	+ 25,000	+ 24,224
4	25,000	23,060	1,940	776	+ 25,000	+ 24,224
5	25,000	18,060	6,940	2,776	+ 25,000	+ 22,224
6	25,000	2,850	22,150	8,860	+ 25,000	+ 16,140
7	25,000	4,180	20,820	8,328	+ 25,000	+ 16,672
8	25,000	3,990	21,010	8,404	+ 25,000	+ 16,596
9	25,000	3,990	21,010	8,404	+ 25,000	+ 16,596
10	25,000	3,990	21,010	8,404	+ 25,000	+ 16,596
Total	$250,000	$124,000	$126,000	$50,400	+$248,000	+$197,600

19–5. Our reason for deducting tax depreciation on the displaced equipment may be easier to understand if it is recognized as a simple time shift. If the proposal is accepted, the equipment will be replaced and $1,000 will be deducted immediately in the calculation of taxable income. We incorporated this $1,000 deduction in our calculation of the tax effect of the initial outlay. If the proposal is rejected, on the other hand, the equipment will be retained and Barclay Company will deduct the $1,000 on its tax returns during the next two years.

Aftertax operating cash flows. Given the before-tax cash flows and the tax depreciation amounts, we can calculate taxable income, income tax effects, and aftertax cash flows. Exhibit 19–6 summarizes the operating cash-flow calculations. The amounts in column (1) show the estimated effect of the proposal on the company's tax returns, except for tax depreciation. The next three columns are used to calculate the income tax effect. Column (5) shows the estimated pretax cash flows, in this case identical to the amounts in column (1) except for the $2,000 increment in accounts receivable in the first year. The incremental cash flow is then found by subtracting the incremental tax in column (4) from the pretax cash flow.

Notice how the rapid depreciation schedules provided by the taxing authority have turned a level annual pretax cash flow into an irregular stream that is much larger in the first five years than in the final five years of this proposal's estimated useful life. This makes the proposal more valuable than if only the straight-line method were available, because the present value of near-term cash flows is greater than the present value of distant cash flows.

End-of-life residual value

The final cash flow associated with a capital-expenditure proposal is the cash value of the facilities and working capital remaining when the project's life comes to an end. This value is usually referred to as the residual value or, less elegantly, salvage value. Salvage values are quite important for short-lived investments, less so for projects with long lives. To find out whether salvage values are important, we should always prepare rough estimates except for extremely long-lived projects.

Pretax residual values. Management expects the plant modernization expenditures to be productive for about 10 years, for the reasons we'll describe in the section headed "Economic Life." At the end of that time, the company can renovate the facilities once more or liquidate them. If it liquidates, it can reasonably expect to recover most of its investment in working capital, together with the salvage value of the remaining equipment. Removal costs and severance pay for employees who will leave the company's employ if the operation is terminated should be deducted from these amounts.

Barclay's management anticipates only the pretax incremental residual values shown in Exhibit 19–7. This shows that the company expects to be able to recover $10,000 from the sale of equipment *and* $5,000 from the liquidation of the incremental working capital

EXHIBIT 19–7. Calculation of Incremental Pretax Residual Value

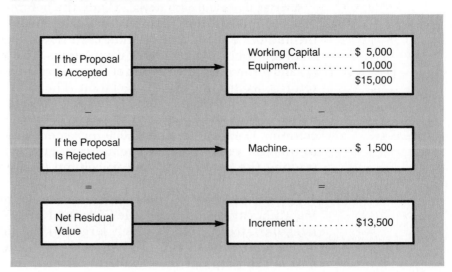

required by today's proposal, a total of $15,000. The incremental residual value is $1,500 less than $15,000, however. If the proposal is rejected, the company will keep its standby machine instead of selling it now. The estimated sale value of that machine 10 years from now is $1,500, and this must be deducted in calculating the pretax incremental residual value.

Notice how we are handling the old standby machine in this analysis. The anticipated cash flows associated with this machine are as follows:

Years from Now	If Proposal Is Accepted	If Proposal Is Rejected	Incremental Cash Flow
0	+$6,000	—	+$6,000
10	—	+$1,500	− 1,500

Our approach is to enter the $6,000 as a negative determinant of the initial outlay (see Exhibit 19–4) and the $1,500 forgone residual value 10 years from now as a negative determinant of net residual value. The effect is to subtract a total of $4,500 ($6,000 − $1,500) from the lifetime cash inflows arising from this proposed investment.

Tax effect on residual value. The calculation of the end-of-life residual value is summarized in Exhibit 19–8. As the first line shows, no tax adjustment applies to the recovery value of the working capital. The reason is that the $5,000 estimated liquidation value of the incremental working capital ($1,000 in cash, $2,000 in receivables, $5,000 in inventories, less $3,000 in trade payables) is just equal to its tax basis, and no taxable gain or loss will arise.

The equipment, however, will have a zero tax basis at the end of 10 years. Both the initial equipment and the equipment acquired by the secondary outlay will be fully depreciated, and the standby equipment that will be retained if the proposal is rejected will also be fully depreciated if it is held for 10 more years. The entire cash flow from the sale of the equipment therefore is exposed to income taxes. The incremental residual value associated with this capital-

EXHIBIT 19–8. Calculation of End-of-Life Residual Value

	Incremental Pretax Cash Flow	Incremental Income Tax	Incremental Aftertax Cash Flow
Working capital	$ 5,000	—	$ 5,000
Equipment	10,000	$4,000	6,000
Total	15,000	4,000	11,000
Less: Standby equipment	1,500	600	900
Net residual value	$13,500	$3,400	$10,100

expenditure proposal therefore is $10,100, the amount shown in the lower right-hand corner of Exhibit 19–8.

CALCULATING NET PRESENT VALUE

Once the cash flows have been estimated, calculating net present value is relatively simple. The first step is to enter the cash flows in a timetable, as in the first three columns of Exhibit 19–9. The first column shows the initial outlay, the renovation outlay five years later, and the end-of-life residual value. These are added to the operating cash flows to get the total cash-flow amounts in column (3).

The second step is to calculate the minimum acceptable rate of return. For Barclay Company, this is 10 percent after taxes.

The third step is to take present value multipliers from present value tables and apply these to the cash flows. The result of this step is shown in the right-hand column of the exhibit.

These calculations show that the net present value of the modernization proposal is $17,989, the total of the amounts in the right-hand column. This means that, if the estimates are correct, the future operating cash receipts will be enough to pay back the amounts invested ($100,400 and $18,000) and pay interest on these amounts at an annual rate of 10 percent after taxes, with enough

EXHIBIT 19–9. Calculation of Net Present Value

Years from Now	(1) Investment Cash Flow after Taxes	(2) Operating Cash Flow after Taxes‡	(3) Total Cash Flow after Taxes (1) + (2)	(4) Present Value at 10% Multiplier*	(5) Amount (3) × (4)
0	−$100,400†		−$100,400	1.0000	−$100,400
1		+$19,960	+ 19,960	0.9091	+ 18,146
2		+ 24,368	+ 24,368	0.8264	+ 20,138
3		+ 24,224	+ 24,224	0.7513	+ 18,199
4		+ 24,224	+ 24,224	0.6830	+ 16,545
5	− 18,000	+ 22,224	+ 4,224	0.6209	+ 2,623
6		+ 16,140	+ 16,140	0.5645	+ 9,111
7		+ 16,672	+ 16,672	0.5132	+ 8,556
8		+ 16,596	+ 16,596	0.4665	+ 7,742
9		+ 16,596	+ 16,596	0.4241	+ 7,038
10	+ 10,100§	+ 16,596	+ 26,696	0.3855	+ 10,291
Net present value					+$ 17,989

* From Appendix A, Table 3.
† From Exhibit 19–4.
‡ From Exhibit 19–6.
§ From Exhibit 19–8.

left over to increase the company's value now by $17,989. Other things being equal, the proposal should be accepted.

ECONOMIC LIFE

Cash flows in the preceding example were estimated for a 10-year period. This period was selected because management estimated that the investment had an economic life of 10 years. The economic life of an investment is the length of time before the combination of assets, people, and purposes it embodies will have to be reconstituted or disbanded.

In practice, the economic life of an investment is often defined to coincide with the economic life of one or more of the major tangible assets acquired at the time the investment is made. These assets may be replaced at the end of this period, either because the costs of owning and operating them are high relative to the costs of owning and operating replacement assets then available, or because the replacement assets can produce a greater quantity or variety of output. Alternatively, economic life may come to an end because the revenues from the products or services provided can no longer cover the costs of providing them, including a return on the investment. In such cases, the assets may be sold or diverted to other uses.

SOME RECURRING QUESTIONS

The illustrations in this chapter have given implicit answers to a number of potentially troublesome analytical questions. We need to examine several of these before we move on to other material:

1. Why did we ignore the unamortized costs of existing facilities or programs, except in connection with tax calculations?
2. Why did we make no provision for annual depreciation charges on newly acquired facilities?
3. How do internal cost allocations and absorptions enter into the estimates of incremental cash flows?
4. Why don't we include in the cash-flow stream estimates of the cash flows from long-term borrowing, interest payments, and debt-retirement transactions?
5. How should the impact of inflation be allowed for?

Unamortized costs

Management often finds it difficult to ignore amounts spent in the past to provide equipment or to develop new products. Suppose, for example, an automobile company has spent $2 billion to design, test, tool, and market a new automobile model. Sales have been disappointing, and management is considering discontinuing the model. Only $1.5 billion of the development and marketing costs have been amortized, however, leaving $500 million in tooling costs to be written off now if the company decides to drop the model from the line.

The $500 million in unamortized costs is irrelevant to the decision to discontinue the model—it is not a cash flow. Even so, it may influence the decision:

1. Money is always spent to create value. Belief that a value has been created is slow to die, and managers are often reluctant to terminate an old project. ("It's a shame to write off all that money. If we just put in another $500 million, the model is sure to take hold.")

2. Managers often think of costs as amounts to be recovered. If not recovered as originally intended, they have to be charged against something else. ("We can't accept that proposal. It won't cover amortization of the costs of tooling we already have.") Result: Proposals that don't bring in enough cash to cover depreciation of past outlays as well as future cash outlays may be turned down.

These are two examples of the *sunk-cost fallacy*, the notion that costs not yet amortized are somehow relevant to decision making. One of these makes it harder to get rid of old projects; the other makes it harder to adopt new ones. The relevant concept in both cases is opportunity cost: What is the present salvage value of the investment, and by how much will that salvage value decline if the investment is not liquidated now? The amounts invested in the past are sunk costs; neither they nor amortizations of them are relevant to today's decisions.

Depreciation on new facilities

Annual depreciation charges on the equipment required by Barclay's plant modernization proposal were not reflected in the $25,000 annual cash flow. Depreciation charges don't measure current cash outlays. This doesn't mean that present value calculations overlook depreciation, however. Accountants recognize depreciation for financial reporting by spreading it systematically over the assets' estimated lives. They reflect it in present value analysis by entering two amounts in the cash-flow timetable—the initial outlay and the end-of-life salvage value—at the times these cash flows take place.

For example, on an investment proposal calling for an outlay of $100,400 now and an estimated residual value of $10,100 in 10 years, the lifetime depreciation amounts to $90,300. This enters the timetable in the following way:

Time	Cash Flow
0	−$100,400
10	+ 10,100
Total	−$ 90,300

Entering depreciation again in the form of annual deductions from cash receipts would be double counting.

Allocations and cost absorption

A third source of difficulty is the practice of reassigning overhead costs by means of overhead rates and interdepartmental cost allocations. A company, for instance, may apply factory overhead to products by means of a predetermined overhead rate of $2 a direct labor-dollar. It is very unlikely, however, that the company will save $2 in overhead for every dollar of direct labor it saves. In fact, most labor-saving investments actually increase total company overhead rather than the other way around.

Interdepartmental cost allocations can be misleading in a similar way. In our example, plant modernization will decrease the amount of floor space required by the operations affected by the proposal. This will reduce the amount of building occupancy costs allocated to these operations. The opportunity cost of the space saved is zero, however, because the company has no way of using it or renting it out. The cash-flow estimates must ignore this apparent difference in costs.

The treatment of interest

Timetables for capital-expenditure proposals show neither borrowings as cash inflows nor interest and debt retirements as cash outflows. The reason is that the capital-expenditure decision controls the investment of *all* the long-term funds available to the company, not just the funds invested by the shareowners. Since the discounting process implicitly provides for the rewards both the long-term lenders and the shareowners require, they don't have to be deducted a second time.

For example, take Barclay Company's proposal A, the one discussed at the beginning of this chapter. The initial cash outlay required by that proposal is $34,000, the estimated future cash receipts amount to $10,000 a year for five years, and the present value of the future cash receipts is $37,908. The left block in Exhibit 19–10 shows that the sum of the net cash flows in the five-year period is +$16,000; the right block shows that the net present value is only +$3,908. The $12,092 difference between these two amounts

EXHIBIT 19–10. Calculation of Implicit Interest

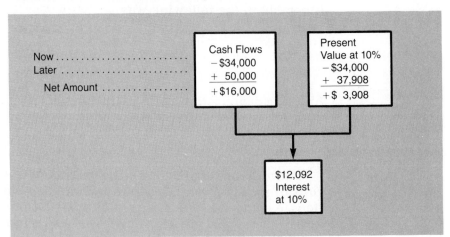

represents interest at 10 percent on the investment for the full life of the proposed expenditure.

The explanation is that the amounts in the left block represent the present values of the cash flows at a *zero* rate of interest. The amounts in the right column are smaller because interest at 10 percent has been subtracted. This being the case, charging interest explicitly against the cash flows generated by a proposal would be double counting.

Adjusting for inflation

Inflation affects both the cost of capital and the cash flows emanating from capital expenditures. The aftertax cost of debt capital in the United States, for example, rose from less than 3 percent in the mid-1950s to 9 percent and more in the early 1980s, as investors sought to compensate themselves for the declining purchasing power of the money they would be receiving in return for the use of their funds. Inflation also affected the cash flows during this period. Equipment that was originally expected to produce labor savings at labor costs of $5 an hour turned out to yield savings of $10 an hour as wage rates and employee benefits rose.

Management should build its expectations of future prices and wage rates into its cash-flow forecasts. As the cost of capital goes up, with its built-in adjustment for inflation, the apparent desirability of capital-expenditure proposals will fall unless the cash-flow estimates are adjusted accordingly. Some proposals will benefit, as their cash-flow rates advance more rapidly than the rate of inflation; others will suffer, as the markets in which they operate fail to provide benefits matching the rate of inflationary change. This means that multiplying currently anticipated cash flows by some general-purpose index of the overall inflation rate won't work. Management has to be willing to distinguish between proposals that will benefit from inflation or resist its inroads and others that will suffer.

DISINVESTMENT DECISIONS

All the investment problems we have looked at so far have been proposals to tie up company funds in plant, equipment, and working capital. A similar kind of problem arises when someone proposes to sell a factory, withdraw from a market area, or discontinue selling a product—converting the amounts invested in those activities into ready cash. These are *disinvestment problems.*

For example, Barclay sells one of its products to other companies which process it on equipment that is no longer being manufactured. Sales of Barclay's product have been declining for some time, as customers have been replacing their old equipment with machines which don't use this product. Management now forecasts that sales will continue for the next five years, but at steadily declining amounts. If Barclay discontinues marketing the product now, it can sell the trade name and liquidate working capital, making about $500,000 in cash available for other uses almost immediately. This amount is shown in column (1) of Exhibit 19–11. If Barclay continues to market the product for the next five years, however, management expects the product to generate the cash-flow stream shown in column (2). (All these cash flows are aftertax cash flows.)

This problem is in substance no different from any of the other problems we have been looking at. To see why this is true, let's turn the problem around. Instead of thinking of this as a proposal

EXHIBIT 19–11. Net Present Value of Disinvestment Decision

Years from Now	(1) Cash Flows from Dropping the Product	(2) Cash Flows from Keeping the Product	(3) Differential Cash Flows (2) − (1)	(4) Present Value at 10% Multiplier	(5) Present Value at 10% Amount
0	+$500,000		−$500,000	1.0000	−$500,000
1	0	+$250,000	+ 250,000	0.9091	+ 227,275
2	0	+ 200,000	+ 200,000	0.8264	+ 165,280
3	0	+ 150,000	+ 150,000	0.7513	+ 112,695
4	0	+ 100,000	+ 100,000	0.6830	+ 68,300
5	0	+ 50,000	+ 50,000	0.6209	+ 31,045
Net present value.					+$104,595

to sell the rights to manufacture and market the product, we can think of it as a proposal to keep it in the line. To do that, the company must forgo an immediate cash inflow of $500,000. Doing that is just like investing $500,000 to keep the product flowing. If we look at it that way, we can subtract column (1) from column (2) instead of the other way around, and get the incremental or differential cash flows shown in column (3).

If the minimum acceptable rate of return is 10 percent, and if we assume that cash flows are concentrated at the end of each year, the present value of keeping this product in the line is $104,595, as shown at the bottom of column (5). Barclay Company should continue to exploit the product rather than accept the outsider's offer to buy the rights to manufacture and market it. Management can review the situation next year if another offer can be generated at that time—and so on each year until the calculation produces a *negative* net present value, which is then the signal to disinvest.

OTHER MEASURES OF INVESTMENT VALUE

Two simpler measures than net present value and the internal rate of return are sometimes used in the evaluation of capital-expenditure proposals: (1) payback period and (2) average return on investment.

Payback period

The payback period is the time that will elapse before net cash receipts will cumulate to an amount equal to the initial outlay. The shorter the payback period, the better the project, or so it is assumed.

If cash flows are uneven, the payback period should be calculated by adding cash flows until the total equals the initial outlay. Otherwise it can be calculated by applying the following formula:

$$\text{Payback period (years)} = \frac{\text{Investment outlay}}{\text{Average annual cash receipts}}$$

For example, if the installed cost of a piece of equipment is $50,000 and it will produce cash operating savings of $10,000 a year, it has a payback period of five years:

$$\frac{\text{Investment}}{\text{Annual cash receipts}} = \frac{\$50,000}{\$10,000} = 5 \text{ years}$$

The main defect of payback period is that it ignores the estimated useful life of the proposed facilities. If the facilities will have to be replaced five years from now, the project will have achieved no net earnings for the company. The company will have invested $50,000 at a zero rate of return. Or, if a large portion of the investment outlay is for working capital with a high end-of-life recovery value, the project may be more desirable than another with a lower payback period but no end-of-life salvage value.

Average return on investment

A second method is to compute for each proposal the expected average return on investment. This may be defined in many ways, perhaps most commonly by the following formula:

$$\frac{\text{Average}}{\text{return}} = \frac{\text{Average cash receipts} - \text{Average annual depreciation}}{\text{Average lifetime investment}}$$

The average lifetime investment figure depends on the method used to calculate depreciation. The use of straight-line depreciation for accounting purposes presumes that investment declines in a linear fashion as facilities age. The average investment under this assumption is halfway between the amount of the initial outlay and the residual investment at the end of the project's life, measured by the recoverable value of the facilities and working capital at that time.

For example, the project for which payback period was computed earlier required an initial outlay of $50,000 and had no end-of-life salvage value. Average investment is thus $25,000. Assuming that the life of this project is expected to be 10 years, average annual depreciation is $5,000, and the average before-tax return on investment is 20 percent:

$$\frac{\text{Average net earnings}}{\text{Average investment}} = \frac{\$10,000 - \$5,000}{\$25,000} = 20 \text{ percent}$$

This method does consider the expected life of the facilities, and it does consider the amount of end-of-life salvage. It fails, however, to allow for differences in the timing of outlays and receipts. By this method, a project in which no receipts appear until the 10th year will appear to be just as profitable as a project in which most of the cash is received in the first few years of the project's life, as long as the average is the same.

SUMMARY

Many of management's resource-allocation problems can be classified as investment problems. Decision models for investment problems must provide a mechanism for comparing incremental cash outflows in one or more time periods with the incremental cash inflows in another time period or periods.

The model that does this most satisfactorily is the net present value model, in which all anticipated incremental cash flows are discounted to their present equivalents at an interest rate based on the cost of capital. Other things being equal, the alternative with the greatest positive net present value should be selected; proposals with negative net present values should be rejected. A related technique is the calculation of each project's internal rate of return, which can then be compared directly with the cost of capital.

In calculating net present value or the internal rate of return, the analyst has to estimate the economic life of the investment, the amount and timing of the investment outlays, the amount and timing of the operating cash flows, and the end-of-life salvage value attributable to the proposal. All these estimates should reflect differential or incremental cash flows, not accounting allocations made for other purposes. Sunk costs should be ignored. The differentials should be measured from a benchmark that will be acceptable to the company, and opportunity costs should be taken into account as well.

APPENDIX: THE COST OF CAPITAL

Businesses must be careful to make investments that will produce an adequate rate of return. The money they have to invest comes from their stockholders and from lenders, and these investors expect to be rewarded for letting the company use their money.

Cost of debt capital

The cost of debt capital is the rate of interest that equates the present value of the future stream of interest payments (after allowing for income tax effects) and maturity date repayment of face value to the current net proceeds from sale of the debt instruments.

For example, assume that bonds with a coupon rate of 9 percent and a 20-year maturity can be sold at their face value. After providing for the tax deductibility of interest at a tax rate of 50 percent, the aftertax cost of this debt offering is 4.5 percent.

The cost of debt capital at any time is a combination of (1) the interest rate the company would have to pay if the lenders incurred no risk by lending to the company, and (2) a premium to compensate the lenders for the perceived risks of lending to this particular company. The risk-free interest rate—the first component of the cost of debt capital—also consists of two parts: the "real" cost of money and a premium reflecting the rate of inflation the market expects the economy to experience.

Cost of equity capital

The cost of equity capital can be defined as the rate of discount stockholders apply to the expected future receipts from stock ownership to determine the price they are willing to pay. To determine this rate, we need data on the market price of the stock and the stockholders' future expectations. The latter information being unavailable, the analyst typically falls back on a study of past relationships between market prices, dividends, and capital appreciation.

As a simple illustration of the concept, if a stock is selling for $50 per share and the company's earnings are stable at $5 a share, this is some evidence that the marginal stockholders in the company are willing to pay $10 for each dollar of earnings. To attract additional funds into the company, therefore, management must be able to communicate an expectation that these funds will also earn a return of at least 10 percent on investments, and perhaps more.

The cost of equity capital includes risk-free and risk-premium components, similar in concept to these two components of the cost of debt capital. The size of the risk-free component depends on market forces in general, rather than on the characteristics of individual companies, and it includes a provision for the rate of inflation equity investors are anticipating.

The size of the risk premium depends on the perceived risks of investing in that company relative to the risks of investing in the market generally. The so-called capital-asset pricing model links the size of the risk premium to the contribution the stock makes to the variability of a diversified portfolio. Companies whose stock prices are very sensitive to movements in the stock market will have high risk premiums, and vice versa.[1]

Weighted average cost of capital

Most companies use both debt capital and equity capital. Public utility companies have a high proportion of debt, mining companies relatively little. A company's average cost of capital will depend not only on the costs of the two kinds of capital but also on the proportions in which they are to be used.

What this means is that the minimum acceptable rate of return

---

[1] James H. Lorie and Mary T. Hamilton, *The Stock Market: Theories and Evidence* (Homewood, Ill.: Richard D. Irwin, 1973).

should be based on a weighted average of the costs of both debt and equity capital. The weights should represent the relative place each has in the company's financing plans:

	Aftertax Capital Cost	Weight	Weighted Cost
Debt	4.5%	40%	1.8%
Equity	12.0	60	7.2
Total			9.0%

If the company's investments do not yield a rate of return at least as great as the cost of capital, they will dilute the company's earnings and likely impair its ability to secure additional funds on a balanced basis in the future.

KEY TERMS

Average return on investment
Capital expenditure
Cost of capital
Discounted cash flow
Economic life
End-of-life salvage value

Internal rate of return
Investment problem
Net present value
Payback period
Zero date

INDEPENDENT STUDY PROBLEMS (Solutions in Appendix B)

TAX DEPRECIATION NOTE

Depreciation rates and amounts for tax purposes vary from country to country and from time to time. Solutions to the problems in this chapter should assume that tax depreciation on new assets is based on the percentages applicable in the United States to property placed in service during 1981 or later. These percentages are embodied in the accelerated cost recovery system (ACRS) prescribed by the U.S. government, as follows:

Year	3-Year Property	5-Year Property	10-Year Property	Buildings
1	25%	15%	8%	175%
2	38	22	14	of the
3	37	21	12	straight-line
4		21	10	rate, applied
5		21	10	to the
6			10	declining
7			9	balance
8			9	
9			9	
10			9	

1. Calculating present value and internal rate of return. Calculate net present value at 10 percent, compounded annually, and the internal rate of return for each of the following capital-expenditure proposals. You should assume that the initial outlay is made immediately and each subsequent cash flow takes place at the end of the year in which it arises. All cash flows have been adjusted to reflect the impact of income taxes.

a. Initial outlay $10,000
   Annual cash receipts . . . . $ 1,750
   Estimated life . . . . 10 years
   End-of-life residual value . . . . None

b. Initial outlay $10,000
   Annual cash receipts:
      First five years . . . . $ 2,000
      Second five years . . . . $ 1,500
   Estimated life . . . . 10 years
   End-of-life residual value . . . . None

c. Initial outlay $10,000
   Annual cash receipts:
      First five years . . . . $ 1,500
      Second five years . . . . $ 2,000
   Estimated life . . . . 10 years
   End-of-life residual value . . . . None

d. Initial outlay $10,000
   Annual cash receipts . . . . $ 1,350
   Estimated life . . . . 10 years
   End-of-life residual value . . . . $ 4,000

e. Initial outlay $10,000
   Annual cash receipts . . . . $ 1,750
   Estimated life . . . . 15 years
   End-of-life residual value . . . . None

2. Calculating payback period and average return on investment. For each capital-expenditure proposal described in problem 1, calculate the payback period and the average return on investment, using average lifetime investment as the denominator.

3. Estimating cash flows: make or buy decision. Arnold Machine Company has been having a neighboring company perform certain operations on a part used in its product at a cost of 50 cents per piece. The annual production of this part is expected to average 6,000 pieces.

Arnold Machine Company can perform this operation itself by bringing two machines into operation: a spare lathe which has a net tax basis of $2,000 and a new machine which can be purchased at a price of $7,000. The new machine is expected to last seven years. The old machine has a remaining physical life of at least 10 years and could be sold now for approximately $1,500. The final salvage value of both machines is considered negligible. In performing the operation itself, Arnold will incur out-of-pocket costs for direct labor, power, supplies, and so forth, of 20 cents per piece.

The old machine is being depreciated for tax purposes at a straight-line amount of $500 a year. The new machine would be classified as a "five-year property" for tax purposes (see "Tax Depreciation Note" above). The income tax rate is 40 percent.

a. Arrange the pretax cash flows in a timetable.
b. Calculate the aftertax cash flows and arrange them in a timetable.

4. Estimating aftertax cash flows.   Under a proposal just submitted by the production manager of Romano Company, proposed new facilities will cost $100,000, half of which will be capitalized for tax purposes. The rest will be expensed immediately. A government investment incentive device known as an investment credit allows the company an immediate tax rebate of 10 percent of the capitalized portion of the outlay. Tax depreciation will be based on the amount capitalized, less half the amount capitalized.

The proposal will also require a $10,000 increase in working capital.

Cash operating savings are expected to amount to $20,000 a year for 10 years. The new facilities would be classified as "five-year property" for income tax purposes (see "Tax Depreciation Note" above). The income tax rate is 40 percent.

a. Calculate the aftertax initial cash outlay for this proposal.
b. Calculate the aftertax cash savings for each of the first two years of the life of the facilities.

5. Calculating present value and internal rate of return.   The expected life of a proposed facility is 10 years, the installed cost will be $65,000, and the expected end-of-life salvage value is zero. The new facilities will replace facilities now in use which have a tax basis (book value) of $32,000 and a market value of $10,000.

The new facilities, if acquired, will be classified as "five-year property" for income tax purposes (see "Tax Depreciation Note" above). No investment credit is available, but $15,000 of the new facility's installed cost can be expensed immediately for tax purposes. The facilities to be replaced are now being depreciated for tax purposes by the straight-line method down to an end-of-life salvage value of zero.

A staff analyst has prepared the following estimates of the annual pretax savings from this proposal:

	At Present	After New Installation	Savings
Labor	$32,500	$23,000	$ 9,500
Materials wastage	6,200	1,000	5,200
Depreciation (10% of cost)	4,000	6,500	(2,500)
Supplies, repairs, and power	11,600	6,400	5,200
General factory management			
(5% of labor)	1,625	1,150	475
Insurance and miscellaneous	1,900	2,000	(100)
Total	$57,825	$40,050	$17,775

All these costs except general factory management are direct costs of the facilities. General factory management consists of the costs of building depreciation, the plant manager's salary, and similar items. In a year of normal volume, these average 5 percent of facilities labor costs.

The income tax rate is 40 percent, and all savings are assumed to take place at the end of each year. The tax rate applies to all taxable income, including gains and losses on the sale of equipment.

a. Prepare a timetable of the estimated incremental cash flows associated with this proposal.

b. Calculate the estimated incremental aftertax present value of this proposal at 12 percent, compounded annually. If 12 percent is the aftertax minimum rate of return, should this proposal be accepted?

EXERCISES AND PROBLEMS

6. Present value exercises. Prepare a timetable of cash flows for each of the following independent proposals, calculate the net present value, and indicate whether the outlay should be made. You may decide to accept some, all, or none of these proposals. The minimum acceptable rate of return is 10 percent. All cash flows have been adjusted to reflect the impact of income taxes.

a. Immediate outlay, $100; cash to be received at one-year intervals for 10 years, the first to be received exactly one year after the immediate outlay, $15 a year.

b. Immediate outlay, $67; cash receipts, $20 a year for five years, starting one year after the immediate outlay.

c. Immediate outlay, $100; cash receipts $15 a year for five years, starting one year after the immediate outlay, plus one additional receipt of $75 10 years after the immediate outlay.

d. Immediate outlay, $67; cash receipts: $35 one year later, $30 two years later, $20 three years later, $10 four years later, and $5 five years later.

e. Immediate outlay, $67; cash receipts: $5 one year later, $10 two years later, $20 three years later, $30 four years later, and $35 five years later.

7. Mutually exclusive proposals. The company can accept only one of the proposals described in problem 6. Which one would you recommend? Why would you recommend it?

8. Internal rate of return. Calculate the internal rate of return for each of the exercises in problem 6. Do these calculations point to the same recommendations you made in answer in problems 6 and 7? Does this seem reasonable?

9. Payback period and average return on investment. Calculate the payback period and the average return on average investment for each of the situations described in problem 6. Assume straight-line depreciation for purposes of calculating average investment. How satisfactory is each of these measures as a device for ranking investment proposals? In your analysis of this question, you should use net present value and the internal rate of return as comparison standards.

10. Present value exercises. Heslin, Inc., invested in a machine with a useful life of five years and no salvage value. The annual cash inflow from operations, net of income taxes, was $1,000. Heslin used a minimum acceptable rate of return of 12 percent.

a. Assuming this investment just satisfied the company's minimum rate of return on investment, what was the amount of the original investment?

b. Assuming the amount of the original investment was $3,500, what was the net present value, rounded to the nearest dollar?

(AICPA adapted)

11. Net present value: three exercises. Answer each of the following three independent questions.

a. Thomson Company is planning to invest $80,000 on January 1, 19x1, in a three-year project. The aftertax cash inflow will be $30,000 in 19x1 and $36,000 in 19x2. Assuming the internal rate of return is 10 percent and each cash inflow occurs at year-end, what will the aftertax cash inflow be in 19x3?

b. On January 1, 19x4, Jackson Corporation purchased for $520,000 a new machine with a useful life of seven years and no salvage value. The machine is expected to produce an aftertax cash flow of $120,000 at each year-end. If Jackson's minimum internal rate of return on this kind of expenditure is 14 percent, what was the net present value of the machine on January 1, 19x4?

c. Victoria, Inc., invested in a four-year project that would yield a 12 percent annual rate of return. The aftertax cash inflow that was expected at the end of each of the four years was $4,000, $4,400, $4,800, and $5,500. If the positive net present value was $3,492, what was the amount of the original investment?

(AICPA adapted)

12. Value of tax benefits. Freedom Corporation acquired a truck at a cost of $50,000. The estimated life was four years, but the truck was classified as "three-year property" for income tax purposes (see "Tax Depreciation Note" above). The estimated salvage value was zero, the relevant interest rate was 8 percent after taxes, and the income tax rate was 40 percent.

What was the present value of the tax benefits resulting from using the three-year tax recovery factors (instead of four-year, straight-line depreciation) for tax purposes?

(AICPA adapted)

13. Discussion question: effect of past purchase price. David and Zelda are co-owners of 1,000 shares of the common stock of Arlington Farms, Inc., an industrial conglomerate. They bought these shares five years ago at a price of $46 a share. The market price of a share of Arlington Farms common stock is now $12.50.

Zelda thinks the stock should be sold now because the company's future seems dim. David agrees with Zelda's forecast but thinks the stock should be kept because selling it now would prevent them from recovering their investment. David and Zelda live in a country in which losses on the sale of securities lead to income tax reductions only if the taxpayer has similar taxable capital gains on sales of other securities. For this reason, their tax advisor thinks they should keep their Arlington Farms stock until they have enough offsetting capital gains.

What position do you take in this argument? What flaws do you find in the position(s) you rejected?

14. Amortization schedule. A machine costs $29,910 payable immediately in cash. Use of this machine is expected to reduce cash outflows by $10,000 a year for five years. The controller has calculated that the internal rate of return from the purchase of this machine would be 20 percent. Cash flows take place at one-year intervals and interest is compounded annually.

Without using the interest tables, prepare a schedule showing the amount of each annual cash flow that can be regarded as a recovery of part of the $29,910 investment in the machine and the amount to be regarded as a return on investment (to the nearest dollar).

15. Indifference point. Ander Company can invest $4,980 in a piece of equipment with a three-year life. The minimum desired rate of return is 10 percent after taxes and the annual expected cash savings amount to $2,500 (net of taxes) and will be received at year-end. What is the amount by which the annual cash flows could change before the company would be indifferent to acquiring the equipment?

(CMA adapted)

16. Disinvestment proposal: estimating cash flows. J. T. Long, owner of the Long Office Building, was recently approached by a buyer for that property. The offer consisted of $200,000 down plus $50,000 at the end of each of the next five years—a total of $450,000.

Long had bought the land and built the building 15 years earlier. The land had cost $40,000; the building had cost $600,000. Annual depreciation for tax purposes had been charged at a straight-line rate of $20,000 a year.

The appraised value of the land at the time of the offer was $100,000. The remaining useful life of the building at that time seemed to be about 10 years. At the end of that time, the land and building probably could be sold to a developer for $150,000. The amount of working capital required to support the operation of this building was negligible and seemed likely to remain so.

Long expected future income to be about $30,000 a year for the remaining life, calculated as here:

Yearly revenues from office rental		$79,000
Yearly expenses:		
Taxes	$ 4,000	
Repairs	12,000	
Depreciation	20,000	
Heat and miscellaneous	13,000	49,000
Total income		$30,000

The cash flows from ownership of the property each year would become available to Long at the end of the year.

a. Prepare a timetable of the pretax cash flows associated with this proposal.
b. Disinvestment decisions of this sort should take into consideration the tax consequences of the different alternatives. Which of the cash flows you identified in part *a* would have to be adjusted, and what information would you need to make these adjustments?

17.   Sensitivity of rate of return.   The initial investment outlay is $40,000, of which $30,000 will be capitalized for tax purposes. The remaining $10,000 of the initial outlay will be expensed immediately for tax purposes. Before-tax operating cash receipts will be $12,000 a year for five years; these amounts will be received at the end of each year. Estimated end-of-life salvage value is zero.

The $30,000 capitalized portion of the initial outlay is to acquire a vehicle which is classified as a "three-year property" for income tax purposes (see "Tax Depreciation Note" above). The income tax rate is 40 percent of taxable income. Taxes are paid or tax credits are received immediately, as soon as the taxable or tax-deductible transaction takes place.

a. What is the estimated present value of this proposal at an annual after-tax interest rate of 8 percent?
b. What is the aftertax internal rate of return?
c. What would be the internal rate of return if end-of-life salvage were $5,000 but annual "capital recovery" (depreciation) for tax purposes continued to be based on zero salvage?
d. What would be the rate of return on investment if economic life were six years, with zero salvage value, and all other estimates were as listed above?
e. What would be the rate of return if economic life were five years, salvage value were zero, and the required equipment were classified as a "five-year property" for income tax purposes?
f. Prepare a short commentary on the relationships indicated by your answers to the preceding parts of this question.

18.   Cost-reducing investment.   An investment in equipment would reduce factory labor costs by $15,000 a year for 10 years. Factory overhead costs are assigned to products by means of a predetermined overhead rate of 75 percent of direct-labor cost. Forty percent of factory overhead costs at normal volume are proportionally variable with volume. Maintenance and energy requirements of the new machine would increase fixed factory overhead costs by $2,000 a year.

The equipment would cost $72,000 and would be classified as "five-year property" for income tax purposes (see "Tax Depreciation Note" above). The company expects the equipment to have no residual value at the end of 10 years.

The company has a minimum acceptable aftertax return on investment of 10 percent. The income tax rate is 40 percent. All operating and tax cash flows are assumed to occur at year-end, except for the initial outlay for the equipment.

a. Prepare a timetable of estimated cash flows for this proposal.

b. Calculate estimated net present value. Should the investment be made?

19. Investment in new facilities: relevant benchmark. Artling Corporation manufactures four products in four identical processing operations. The only differences among the four products are in the raw materials used. The facilities are completely interchangeable, although newer machines have higher depreciation and generally lower operating costs than older machines. Processing costs (that is, all costs other than materials costs) are determined by the machines used, not by the product being manufactured.

The company is now considering a proposal to acquire a fifth set of processing facilities to manufacture a new, higher grade of product, using a more expensive raw material that has just come on the market. All machines, new as well as old, would still be completely interchangeable, but the new machine would probably be used to make the new product.

The following table shows the selling prices of the five products and all the costs per pound that would be incurred in the factory to operate the machines:

Product/Machine	Selling Price	Materials Cost	Depreciation	Other Factory Costs	Gross Margin
A/1	$0.70	$0.15	$0.08	$0.31	$0.16
B/2	0.76	0.20	0.08	0.30	0.18
C/3	0.83	0.25	0.09	0.28	0.21
D/4	0.91	0.30	0.09	0.29	0.23
E*/5*	1.00	0.35	0.10	0.29	0.26

Depreciation cost per pound is an average straight-line rate based on estimated annual production of 100,000 pounds of each product and an estimated life of 10 years. Estimated salvage value of the production equipment is zero; in fact, once the facilities are installed, their only market value is their scrap value, which is negligible.

In support of the proposal to add the fifth product (product E) and corresponding facilities (machine 5), Artling Company's sales manager has pointed out that this would increase the company's gross margin by $26,000 ($0.26 a pound on an added sales volume of 100,000 pounds annually). Incremental variable selling and administrative costs amounting to 5 percent of sales would reduce this by $5,000, but this would still leave $21,000 to provide a handsome rate of return on investment.

Calculate the incremental annual cash flow that you would use in deciding whether the proposed investment is adequately profitable. State your reasoning. Ignore income taxes.

20. Make or buy decision. Griffa Machine Company has been purchasing from a neighboring company a part used in one of its products. The purchase price of this part is 95 cents each, and the expected average annual production is 6,000 parts.

The methods department of the Griffa Machine Company has submitted a proposal to manufacture this part in the company's own plant. To do this, the company would have to purchase a new machine at a price of $10,800. It would also use a lathe now owned by the company but not in current use. This lathe has an estimated market value now of $1,000, but its book value is $2,000. Depreciation for tax purposes on the old lathe is at a straight-line rate of $400 a year. The new machine would be classified as a five-year asset for income tax purposes (see "Tax Depreciation Note" above). Griffa's management believes that both machines would be usable for 10 years if the proposal were accepted, and the final salvage value of both machines is assumed to be negligible.

The incremental costs of operating the two machines, other than depreciation costs, would be as follows:

	Unit Cost
Direct labor, 0.05 hour at $8 an hour	$0.40
Direct materials	0.10
Power, supplies, and so forth	0.05

All other factory costs would be unaffected by the decision to manufacture this part. The company uses an overhead rate of $3 per direct labor-hour to absorb factory overhead costs.

Assuming an income tax rate of 40 percent and a minimum acceptable rate of return on investment of 12 percent after taxes, should this proposal be accepted?

21. Maximum purchase price. Company Z has contracted to supply a government agency with 50,000 units of a product each year for the next five years. A certain component of this product can be either manufactured by Company Z or purchased from the X Corporation, which has indicated a willingness to enter into a subcontract for 50,000 units of the component each year for five years if the price offered is satisfactory. These alternative methods of procurement are regarded as equally dependable.

If Company Z decides to manufacture the component, it expects the following to occur:

1. A special-purpose machine costing $110,000 will have to be purchased. No other equipment will be required.
2. The machine will be classified as "five-year property" for income tax purposes (see "Tax Depreciation Note" above), and management doesn't expect the machine to be useful beyond the five-year contract period.
3. No investment credit is available.
4. Estimated salvage value at the end of five years is $10,000.
5. The manufacturing operation will require 1,000 feet of productive floor space. This space is available in a building owned by Company Z and will not be needed for any other purpose in the foreseeable future. The costs of maintaining this building (including repairs, utilities, taxes, and depreciation) amount to $2 per square foot of productive floor space per year.

6. Variable manufacturing costs—materials, direct labor, and so forth—are estimated to be 50 cents a unit.
7. Fixed factory costs other than those mentioned in items 1 through 4—such as supervision—are estimated at $20,000 a year.
8. Income taxes are computed at the rate of 40 percent of taxable income or taxable savings.
9. The policy of Company Z is to subcontract if and only if the costs saved by manufacturing instead of subcontracting provide less than a 10 percent annual return on investment. For this purpose, return on investment is defined as the relationship between cost saving, after provision for income taxes, and the capital investment that will have to be made to permit Company Z to manufacture the component in its own plant.

What is the maximum price per unit which Company Z should be willing to offer to the X Corporation? Make explicit any assumptions you believe to be necessary in solving the problem.

22. Adjusting for inflation. Nelson Company plans to introduce a new product, requiring immediate outlays of $200,000 for equipment and $100,000 for working capital. The product will sell at a price of $18 a unit the first two years. The price will increase to $20 in the third year and then increase another $1 each year for the next five years to reach a final plateau at $25 a unit in the eighth year. Operating cash outlays for manufacturing costs will be as follows:

	First Year	Annual Rate of Increase
Direct materials	$5 a unit	10%
Direct labor	2 a unit	5
Variable overhead	1 a unit	8
Fixed overhead	$50,000	4

The additional equipment required by this new product will be classified as "five-year property" for income tax purposes (see "Tax Depreciation Note" above). No investment tax credits are available for this equipment purchase, and the company expects it to have a zero net residual value at the end of the product's life cycle, which management expects will be at the end of 10 years. Management intends to depreciate the $200,000 equipment cost for financial reporting at a straight-line amount of $20,000 a year for 10 years. Working capital investments can be recovered without gain or loss at the end of the product's life.

Sales and production volume are expected to reach 10,000 units the first year, 20,000 the second year, and 25,000 in the third year, continuing at that level through the eighth year, then decline to 20,000 in the ninth year and 15,000 units in the 10th year as substitute products take over.

To achieve these volumes, marketing expenditures will be $90,000 the first year and $60,000 the second year, rising each year thereafter by 5 percent of the previous year's expenditure until the 10th year. Marketing outlays in the 10th year will be cut to half the level they would otherwise reach in that year, as the product is gradually phased out.

The income tax rate is expected to be 40 percent for the entire period and the required rate of return is 15 percent after taxes. It should be assumed that each year's operating cash flows are received at year-end and that income taxes on the year's taxable income are also paid at year-end. Annual compounding is appropriate. Nelson Company expects to have ample taxable income from other sources to enable it to capture the tax benefits of any operating loss the new product will incur in any year.

a. Prepare a timetable for cash flows for this proposal.
b. Should Nelson Company's management accept it and introduce the new product? Show calculations to support your recommendation.

23. Expansion proposal. The management of Taunton Cotton Company is considering the acquisition of new spinning machinery, partially to replace certain less efficient equipment and partially to increase total productive capacity. Market surveys indicate that the anticipated increase in productive capacity can be disposed of only by additional sales effort coupled with a price reduction. Pertinent data are as indicated:

Cost of new equipment, including freight and installation	$55,000
Cost of removal of equipment replaced, rearrangement and revamping, and so forth, to be charged to expense for tax purposes	25,000
Net book value (tax basis) of equipment replaced (original cost: $40,000)	8,000
Amount to be realized from sale of equipment replaced	5,000
Expected salvage value, new equipment (end of 10 years)	0

	Present		Proposed	
Annual Processing Costs	Dollars	Per Lb.	Dollars	Per Lb.
Labor.....................................	$120,000	$0.0600	$135,000	$0.0540
Supplies, repairs, and power	80,000	0.0400	93,000	0.0372
Taxes, insurance, and miscellaneous	20,000	0.0100	22,000	0.0088
Depreciation (10% of cost, straight-line)	4,000	0.0020	5,500	0.0022
Total	$224,000	$0.1120	$255,500	$0.1022

Annual production:	
Present	2,000,000 lbs.
Proposed	2,500,000 lbs.
Estimated manufacturing margin per lb. (estimated selling price minus estimated material cost):	
Present	$ 0.150
Proposed (allowing for reduction of ½¢ in selling price)	0.145
Estimated additional selling and administrative expenses:	
Commissions	$ 5,000
Branch office sales expense (including advertising)	11,000
Billing and miscellaneous administrative	1,500
Total	$17,500

Depreciation for tax purposes on present equipment has been by the straight-line method at 10 percent of cost. The new equipment would be classified as "five-year property" for income tax purposes (see "Tax Depreciation Note" above). The income tax rate is 40 percent.

a. Prepare a timetable of the estimated pretax cash flows, and make the necessary adjustments for the effects of income taxation.

b. Would you recommend the expenditure if a 12 percent return after taxes is required?

24. Multiple alternatives: cash flows from income data. David Adams burst into the office of his supervisor, the works manager, to announce that a new machine which had just come out should be bought to replace the one used in the manufacture of product W. To support his argument, he presented the following comparative income statements for product W:

	Using the Present Machine	Using the New Machine
Sales revenues	$200,000	$200,000
Expenses:		
Factory direct materials	50,000	50,000
Factory direct labor	40,000	30,000
Machinery depreciation	5,000	10,000
Other factory overhead (200 percent of direct labor)	80,000	60,000
Selling and administrative expenses (15 percent of sales)	30,000	30,000
Total expenses	205,000	180,000
Income (loss) before taxes	(5,000)	20,000
Less: Income taxes	2,000	8,000
Net income (loss)	$ (3,000)	$ 12,000

"The cost of the present machine is a sunk cost," Adams said. "The new machine will cost us $110,000, and since it will increase our net income by $15,000 a year, it will bring us a good deal more than the 10 percent annual aftertax return on investment we want."

Upon investigation, you discover the following additional information:

1. Machine data:

	Present Machine	New Machine
Expected life	Not applicable	10 years
Original cost	$55,000	$110,000
Tax depreciation to date	27,000	0
Present trade-in value	10,000	Not applicable
Expected trade-in value after 7 years	5,000	35,000
Expected trade-in value after 10 years	0	10,000
Capacity in units per year	60,000	80,000
Expected output (units per year)	50,000	50,000

2. If the present machine isn't disposed of now, it can be used for the next 10 years in the manufacture of product W. The price of product W and the cash flows required to operate either machine are expected to rise slightly from year to year, but these increases are expected to offset each other. Estimates can be based on the data in 1 above.

3. All the company's requirements of product W are manufactured in a single plant, along with a number of other products. Product W is now being assigned 25 percent of the total factory overhead cost other than

equipment depreciation. Factory overhead other than equipment depreciation can be predicted from the following formula:

$$\$240{,}000 + 0.5 \times \text{Direct labor cost}$$

Installation of the new machine would add $500 a year in electric power costs over and above the amounts indicated by this formula.

4. Tax depreciation on the old machine has been calculated with the sum-of-the-years'-digits method, based on a 10-year life and zero salvage. The new machine would be classified as "five-year property" for income tax purposes (see "Tax Depreciation Note" above).

5. Gains and losses on the sale of equipment would be taxed at the regular tax rate, and no "investment credit" is available. Depreciation for internal financial reporting is calculated on a straight-line basis.

6. If production of product W were discontinued, the present machine could be disposed of. None of the present fixed factory overhead costs other than equipment depreciation would be affected by the discontinuation of product W, nor would there be any saving in selling and administrative expenses. Working capital of $10,000 would be released for use elsewhere, however.

a. Identify the major alternatives the company should consider.

b. Present and support a recommendation as to the desirability of continuing the manufacture of product W and purchasing the new machine, indicating the anticipated consequences of each alternative you identified in answer to part a.

20

Budgetary planning

We defined *planning* in Chapter 16 as the process by which management decides how to use the resources available to it. Five different kinds of planning fit this definition, each appropriate to a particular decision-making environment within the company:

1. *Strategic planning*—establishing the basic directions top management wants the organization to take.
2. *Long-range periodic planning*—translating the strategic plan into preliminary action proposals and making rough estimates of the resources required to carry them out.
3. *Short-range periodic planning (budgeting)*—developing a coordinated program to govern the use of all the organization's resources in a single short period, usually the first year of the long-range plan.
4. *Project and situation planning*—making final decisions to use specific portions of the organization's resources in specific ways.
5. *Scheduling*—determining in detail what needs to be done to carry out the planned program, establishing timetables for the performance of these tasks, and seeing to it that people, materials, facilities, and funds are available in the necessary quantities at the necessary times and places to carry out the plan.

The diagram in Exhibit 20–1 traces the relationships among these processes. The progression moves from the top of the chart toward the bottom, from the general to the specific, from the tentative to the firm commitment. What the diagram doesn't show is that project

EXHIBIT 20–1.   Managerial Planning Processes

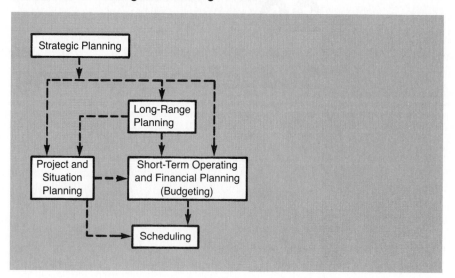

and situation planning often take place within the context of the annual budgeting process, as well as at other times.

We discussed instances of project or situation planning in the preceding four chapters. The purpose of this chapter is to show why and how management engages in short-term operating and financial planning, or budgeting. The chapter has three parts:

1. A discussion of the form and purposes of budgeting and the annual budgetary plan.
2. A step-by-step illustration of the budgetary planning process.
3. A survey of accounting's role in budgetary planning.

BUDGETARY PLANNING: FORM AND PURPOSE

The short-term operating and financial plan, or *budget,* lists the resources the organization has decided to use during a period. It also shows where the organization plans to get these resources, where and how it plans to use them, and what it expects to accomplish during this period. It assembles the project and situation decisions that have already been made, incorporates a preliminary forecast of those still to be made and implemented during the period, and presents the results as an integrated, coordinated plan for the period.

The best way to understand budgeting is to follow the steps an organization takes in developing a budget. Before we get into an example, however, we need to look briefly at four questions:

1. What are the various parts of the budget?
2. How does the budget relate to the structure of the organization?
3. What are the goals budgeting is expected to attain?
4. What criteria should be applied in budgeting?

Components of the budget

We usually classify the parts of the budget into two groups, operating budgets and financial budgets. *Operating budgets* list the amounts of goods and services the organization plans to consume during the operating period and the benefits it expects these activities to produce. In most organizations, the resources consumed are generally represented by cost figures as well as by physical quantities; in a profit-oriented company, benefits are represented by revenues. *Financial budgets,* on the other hand, show how much money the organization plans to spend during the period and where it plans to get the funds to finance these expenditures.

Each block in Exhibit 20–2 represents one or more parts of the overall budget of a manufacturing company. For convenience, we'll refer to each part as a budget, although we find it useful to remember that these are all part of a single budgetary plan.

EXHIBIT 20–2. Budget Components

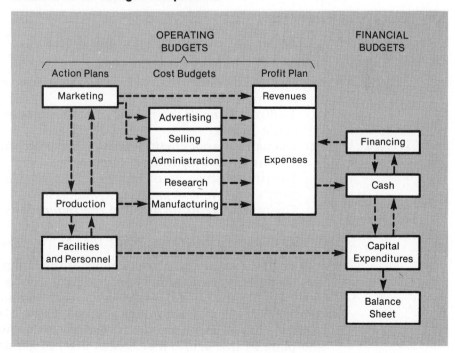

The organizational dimension

The budget also has an organizational dimension. All but the smallest organizations are subdivided, with different people responsible for the operation of the various subdivisions. In small organizations, one layer of subdivisions is enough—one *department* for purchasing, another for production, another for selling, and so forth. In larger organizations, the departments will be subdivisions of larger units, each one a subdivision of the whole. A sales *division,* for example, may include a dozen or more branch offices. And if the branches are numerous, they are likely to be grouped into regions, each with a regional manager reporting to the division manager.

The organizational dimension of the budget doesn't appear in Exhibit 20–2. Each division, each department has its own portion of the overall plan. Departmental budgets are narrow in scope, dealing with only one or two elements. Divisional budgets are more comprehensive—divisions with both sales and production operations even have their own profit plans and may have divisional balance sheets and partial financing plans. Overall financing remains a head-office responsibility, however, and most organizations control cash mainly in the head office.

The purposes of budgeting

The annual budgetary planning process has at least six major objectives:

1.   To force managers to *analyze* the company's activities critically and creatively.
2.   To direct some of the management's attention from the present to the *future.*
3.   To enable management to *anticipate* problems or opportunities in time to deal with them effectively.
4.   To reinforce managers' *motivation* to work to achieve the company's goals and objectives.
5.   To give managers an ongoing *reminder* of the actions they have agreed to.
6.   To provide a *reference point* for control reporting.

The first four of these are benefits of the budgeting *process.* The final two items are advantages of the budget documents themselves. For example, the budget is intended to serve managers as a constant reminder of the plan they have adopted. As such, it provides a blueprint they can consult from time to time as they work to implement the plan. In this sense, it serves as a set of general instructions to the department and division managers, reflecting the actions they have agreed to take and the results they have agreed to strive for.

Decision criteria in budgeting

Budgeting, like other forms of planning, is a process focusing on a set of decisions. For this purpose, each manager typically submits proposals to higher management. Higher management then decides whether to approve these proposals as they stand, modify them in some way, or return them to the originators for revision and resubmission.

Higher management needs to examine individual proposals from four points of view: (1) Do the anticipated *benefits* of proposed expenditures justify the costs? (2) Are the estimates *realistic*? (3) Is the proposal *consistent* with the company's strategic plans and with the proposals of other parts of the organization? and (4) Is it *feasible* in light of the company's financial, marketing, and production capacities?

The budgeting process is more iterative than this description is likely to imply; that is, tentative budgets are proposed, discussed, and revised again and again as they move upward toward final approval. The process is a progressive dialogue; an executive seldom receives a budget proposal from a subordinate without having discussed vital aspects of it ahead of time. Through vertical and horizontal communication within the management group, these plans are adjusted and readjusted until they become integrated and realizable objectives consistent with overall company policies.

Yet another function of some portions of the budget is to define *spending limits.* For example, budgeted advertising expenditures may be the maximum amount the advertising manager can spend. Budgeting is in its essence a planning process, however, not a limiting process. The budgeting procedure should allow for changes in the amount or pattern of the budgeted expenditures as conditions change or as management gains more knowledge of its resources and opportunities.

PREPARING THE ANNUAL BUDGET

The development of a formal budgetary plan requires careful examination of the interrelationships among its various components. Although the complexity of this process cannot be conveyed effectively in a few pages, a very simple example may at least identify the issues. Since a manufacturing illustration would be too complex for our purposes at this point, let's see how the management of a small publishing house, Darwin Books, Inc., developed its annual budget for 19x2.

The organization

Activities at Darwin Books fall broadly into three major categories: manuscript procurement, production, and sales. *Production,* in this case, consists mainly of editing manuscripts, preparing them for typesetting, proofreading, and designing book covers and dust jackets. All printing and binding of books is done on contract by outside printers.

The company has two main product lines—textbooks for college and university use and textbooks for secondary schools. This split provides the basis for the company's organization chart, portions of which are shown in Exhibit 20–3. The vice president who serves as division manager of a textbook division is responsible for both manuscript procurement and sales. He has a force of field representatives, organized into four regional groups, each headed by a regional manager with the title of field editor. The financial vice president is in charge of all financial activities, including coordination of the annual budget.

The marketing plan

Darwin's fiscal year begins July 1. Early in March 19x2, John Truro, the company's president, asked each textbook division man-

EXHIBIT 20–3. Darwin Books, Inc.: Partial Organization Chart

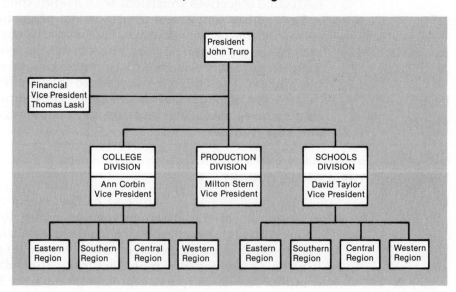

ager to submit a tentative marketing plan, showing the size and composition of the field organization, the promotional pattern to be followed, and anticipated revenues and expenses.

Ann Corbin, manager of the college division, started by preparing an up-to-date list of the book titles that were then available or were scheduled for production for use during the next fiscal year. She gave copies of this list to her field editors and asked each of them to spell out in detail a promotional program for the coming year, estimate its cost, and predict the resulting sales volume. Dave Taylor, the schools division manager, followed a similar procedure.

Both division managers reviewed the projected sales and the underlying marketing plans with their field editors. Corbin, for example, compared the proposed expense/sales ratio for each region with the 19x1 ratio and with the ratios in other regions. She compared the proposed increase in selling expense in each region with the projected increase in sales volume. She encouraged her western region field editor to hire an additional field representative to work actively in locating new manuscripts for textbooks in the natural sciences, and her comments and suggestions led to changes in each of the regional plans.

At one point, she turned down a proposal of the southern region field editor to expand the field staff to increase the number of contacts with junior colleges in the area. Darwin Books had few titles that were appropriate for use in the junior college market. Corbin felt that any promotional effort in this market should be concentrated on a few departments in some of the larger junior colleges. This would not require an increase in the size of the field sales force.

After working with the field editors, the two division managers presented the following tentative sales and expense budgets to Tom Laski, the financial vice president:

	College Division	Schools Division
Sales revenues	$4,200,000	$2,700,000
Less: Returns	180,000	20,000
Net sales	$4,020,000	$2,680,000
Marketing and administration:		
Division office salaries	$ 100,000	$ 85,000
Field salaries	400,000	300,000
Travel and entertainment	130,000	80,000
Advertising	50,000	50,000
Miscellaneous	40,000	50,000
Total marketing and administrative expenses	$ 720,000	$ 565,000

Laski questioned Dave Taylor, the schools division manager, on the slow growth in sales in his division and the high ratio of marketing expenses to sales. Taylor blamed both of these on the lack of any large-volume titles in the list. Darwin Books was a relative newcomer in the schools market, with a line of innovative texts, but none of these had broken through with sales to the large school districts which accounted for the bulk of textbook purchases.

After further analysis of his proposal, Taylor agreed that the proposed budget for miscellaneous marketing and administrative expenses could be reduced by $20,000 and the travel and entertainment budget could be reduced by $10,000 without reducing forecasted sales revenues. These changes reduced the tentative divisional budget for marketing and administrative expenses to $535,000. Laski endorsed these changes but pointed out that Truro would want to discuss the schools division's future with Taylor at the final budget review session in June.

The production plan

At this point, Laski asked the textbook division managers to meet in his office with Milt Stern, the production manager. The textbook division managers gave Stern their proposed schedules for new books and new editions and their estimates of sales for each title on the active list. They reviewed inventory figures and identified titles that should be allowed to go out of print as soon as present stocks were exhausted.

Stern complained that the manuscript-preparation schedules

EXHIBIT 20–4

DARWIN BOOKS, INC.
Tentative Profit Plan
For the Year Ending June 30, 19x3

	College Division	Schools Division	Total
Net sales	$4,020,000	$2,680,000	$6,700,000
Divisional expenses:			
Printing and binding	2,400,000	1,700,000	4,100,000
Copy editing	120,000	80,000	200,000
Authors' royalties	480,000	250,000	730,000
Marketing and administration	720,000	535,000	1,255,000
Total divisional expenses	3,720,000	2,565,000	6,285,000
Divisional profit	$ 300,000	$ 115,000	415,000
General administrative expenses			300,000
Income before income taxes			115,000
Income taxes			50,000
Net income			$ 65,000

were too heavily concentrated in the autumn months. Although many of his copy editors were part-time employees, some tasks had to be done by full-time personnel, and they simply couldn't handle the projected peak load. Darwin Books had solved this problem occasionally in the past by delaying publication dates for several books, but this time it seemed more sensible to authorize an increase in the size of Stern's full-time staff.

The profit plan and the cash budget

After his meeting with the division vice presidents, Laski assembled the available data into a tentative profit plan for the coming year. This plan is summarized in Exhibit 20–4. He also received proposals for such items as dividends and purchases of furniture and equipment, and then prepared the following tentative cash budget for the coming year:

Cash receipts:		
Customers		$6,500,000
Other sources		100,000
Total cash receipts		6,600,000
Cash disbursements:		
Salaries	$1,350,000	
Printing	4,500,000	
Other suppliers	210,000	
Authors' royalties	700,000	
Taxes	50,000	
Dividends	40,000	
Furniture and equipment purchases	100,000	
Total cash disbursements		6,950,000
Cash deficit		$ 350,000

Some disbursements on this list can be classified as *discretionary outlays,* meaning that most and maybe all of the marketing and production goals embodied in the current operating plan could be achieved even if the expenditures leading to these disbursements weren't made. Dividends, research and development outlays, and most disbursements for the purchase of furniture and equipment are discretionary in this sense; some manufacturing overhead costs, advertising and selling expenses, and general administrative expenses may also be discretionary, at least in the short run.

As the table shows, Darwin's expected cash receipts were $350,000 less than anticipated disbursements. This left management with several options to investigate, mainly the following:

1. Reduce existing cash balances.
2. Defer payments to suppliers.
3. Press customers for faster payment.

4. Curtail discretionary spending plans.
5. Borrow.
6. Revise marketing plans.
7. Reduce dividends.

Although the choices here are top management's responsibility, the financial executives are usually expected to analyze the alternatives and make recommendations. In practice, they are likely to work closely with the division managers and other senior operating managers, so that the final budget will reflect the consensus of top management before it is presented to the board of directors for approval.

The main problem at this point is to find adequate criteria to guide management's choices among these alternatives. In this case, management felt that any reduction in the dividend would have had an unacceptable effect on the market price of the company's stock. This alternative, therefore, was regarded as a last resort.

Courses of action. Reductions in the proposed amount of capital expenditures often can produce a marked improvement in the company's short-term cash position, and may not have harmful long-term effects. Many proposals fail to pass muster when subjected to the kinds of tests described in Chapter 19. Others may meet the company's cost-of-capital tests but still have to be rejected or postponed because management values the benefits of other discretionary outlays more highly.

Laski's review of the capital-expenditure proposals at Darwin Books led him to recommend deleting proposals requiring outlays of $45,000 in fiscal 19x3. Proposals accounting for the remaining $55,000 in requested capital outlays appeared likely to meet Darwin's capital-expenditure tests or other criteria management was likely to apply, so Laski left them in the tentative budget for the moment.

Reducing the tentative budget for disbursements for furniture and equipment by $45,000 reduced the estimated cash deficit from $350,000 to $305,000, still a substantial gap. One way to reduce a deficit of this size is to reduce the company's bank balances or to liquidate any holdings of short-term marketable securities. In this case, Laski's analysis indicated that reduction of the cash balance would jeopardize the company's ability to meet its payrolls and other obligations on time, and Darwin Books had no marketable securities to liquidate. Its credit rating was very good, however, and Laski was able to get a commitment for a $200,000 line of credit from a local bank, at 10 percent interest. By projecting the time at which the borrowed funds would be needed, Laski estimated that the borrowing against the line of credit would increase interest payments by $15,000 and decrease tax payments in 19x3 by $6,000.

The additional borrowing, therefore, would reduce the cash gap by $191,000 ($200,000 − $15,000 + $6,000).

With a remaining cash deficit of $114,000 ($350,000 − $45,000 − $191,000), Laski knew that more drastic measures would be necessary. Previous consultations with the division managers had convinced him that significant further reductions in discretionary divisional outlays wouldn't be feasible. As a start, he asked both the company's credit manager and purchasing agent whether they could help solve 19x3's anticipated cash-flow problem by pressing customers for prompt payment of their bills or by deferring some supplier payments to fiscal 19x4.

Laski approached these possibilities with a great deal of caution. Unless a company's collection efforts have been lax, faster collections from customers ordinarily can be achieved only at the cost of lost sales because of a more restrictive credit policy. If the profit contribution from sales exceeds the benefits from faster collections, a tighter credit policy would be self-defeating. In this case, since Darwin's customers were generally prompt in their payments, neither Laski nor the credit manager saw much chance of help from this source in 19x3.

Slower payments to suppliers also had to be approached very carefully. A reputation as a slow payer can weaken a company's credit rating and increase its purchasing costs. In this case, however, the purchasing agent agreed that payments to the company's printers could be reduced by $100,000 in 19x3 without adverse effects. Darwin had always paid its printers before the end of the normal credit period, and slowing the rate of payment would only be taking advantage of a privilege already available to the company. In most cases, the printers would hardly notice this change in Darwin's practice.

Final resolution. The slowdown in payments to the printers, together with the paring of the capital budget and the additional borrowing, left an estimated cash deficit of only $14,000 for 19x3. To close this gap, Laski decided to recommend reducing the budget for capital expenditures by an additional $14,000. Few of the capital-expenditure proposals remaining after the initial $45,000 reduction were ready for final approval, and a $14,000 reduction in the capital budget would require a more thorough scrutiny of the proposals as they came up for final approval during the year. The poorest of these proposals—including some which would help department heads meet their personal objectives without increasing the company's net present value—would likely be rejected when they came up for approval later on.

The changes Laski suggested to prevent the cash deficit inherent in the initial budget proposal can be summarized as follows:

Reductions in proposed capital outlays:		
Submarginal proposals	$ 45,000	
Low-priority proposals	14,000	
Total reductions in proposed capital outlays		$ 59,000
Deferral of payments to suppliers		100,000
Additional borrowing	200,000	
Less: Aftertax cost of additional borrowing ($15,000 − $6,000)	9,000	
Net effect of additional borrowing		191,000
Total reduction in cash deficit		$350,000

Both the tentative profit plan and the tentative cash budget were modified to reflect these changes. The board of directors reviewed and approved the revised plans but indicated their dissatisfaction with the profit level being achieved. Truro was asked to work with his division managers on ways to improve profit performance, with particular attention to the schools division. A full-fledged review of the schools division was scheduled for an autumn board meeting.

Budgeting as a decision-making process

Budget approval is top management's signal that the methods selected and the ends to be achieved are acceptable. When top management receives a proposed profit plan, it can (1) accept it, (2) send it back for revision, or (3) take steps to terminate the operation. In practice, some question is almost always raised about the adequacy of the plan, thus ruling out immediate acceptance. Termination, on the other hand, is unlikely to be ordered unless such a decision had been considered before and deferred to give the division manager an opportunity to come up with a viable alternative.

The result is a response pattern such as that schematized in Exhibit 20–5. Management's rejection of an initial proposal, represented by the *No* arrow under the top diamond, ordinarily starts the process again, as lower management seeks ways to improve the anticipated results. This is shown by the arrows looping back into the block at the upper left-hand corner of the exhibit.

Notice that three of the blocks at the right of the diagram represent decisions to accept and implement the budget. These decisions reflect top management's conclusion that existing management can't be expected to surpass the performance levels embodied in the proposals being accepted. This is important because one purpose of the budget, as we mentioned earlier, is to serve as a standard against which the performance of division and department managers can be evaluated. Top management's approval of a budget, therefore, carries with it a commitment to recognize the budgeted performance levels as satisfactory if actual conditions are as antici-

EXHIBIT 20–5. System Responses to Proposed Profit Plan

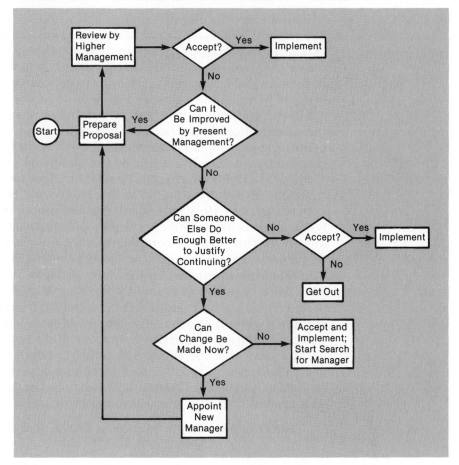

pated. If top management is unwilling to make this commitment, the proposal should be routed back into the loop for another revision and review.

Meeting the budget constraints in this illustration was a good deal easier than it usually is in practice. Internal politics, personal idiosyncracies, and genuine disagreements as to the feasibility and effectiveness of various parts of the plan often make budgeting a painful and time-consuming process. We don't wish to ignore these factors, but we see no reason to dwell on them at length. Our objective has been to make it quite clear that budgeting is a creative, decision-oriented process. It may also be the most important single phase in the management control process, in that much of what the organization will do is decided at this time.

THE CAPITAL BUDGET

At the time of annual budget preparation, division managers or department heads are asked to submit tentative lists of the capital expenditure proposals they plan to make during the coming year—major projects individually and in detail, minor projects grouped in meaningful categories. Preliminary estimates of the anticipated benefits of major projects and groups of minor projects are ordinarily submitted along with the preliminary requests for budget inclusion. These lists are combined with schedules of planned expenditures on projects which already will have been approved and inaugurated before the beginning of the fiscal year.

For Darwin Books, the 19x3 capital budget took the form of the schedule in Exhibit 20–6. (For simplicity, we have assumed that expenditures in 19x3 will equal disbursements in that year.) Darwin's projects are relatively simple, with little carryover from year to year. In this case the company planned to spend $13,000 in 19x3 on projects approved and started in previous years, plus another $28,000 on new projects. Future outlays necessary to complete projects were expected to amount to another $1,500.

Budget inclusion seldom serves as the final authorization to undertake a capital-expenditure project. Most budgeting systems require submission of a written appropriation request for each proposal at the time the sponsor is ready to begin committing funds to it. The main purpose is to give the sponsor more time to plan as well as to consider events that have occurred since the budget was prepared. It also gives the company more flexibility in that

EXHIBIT 20–6. Darwin Books, Inc.: Capital Budget for the Year Ending June 30, 19x3

	Expenditures		
	Previous Years	19x3	Future Years
Prior-year approvals:			
Office addition	$45,000	$ 5,000	
Telephone system	2,000	8,000	
Subtotal	$47,000	13,000	
Current-year approvals:			
Forklift trucks		12,000	
Furniture and equipment:			
College division		3,000	
Schools division		4,000	$ 500
Production divison		2,000	
Administrative offices		7,000	1,000
Subtotal		28,000	$1,500
Total current expenditures		$41,000	

all of its resources aren't fully committed at the start of the year. If an emergency or an extraordinarily profitable opportunity arises during the year, projects can be initiated at once without upsetting the overall budget figure. It will be necessary to delay or cancel other projects only if additional investment funds can't be obtained from other sources on short notice.

Each appropriation request must show the reasons the sponsor believes it should be undertaken. For many projects, this includes a detailed estimate of future cash flows, from either reduced costs or expansion of capacity. For others, the justification is more qualitative, with the sponsor's assertion that the benefits will be substantial even though they are now unmeasurable. One part of good capital budget administration is to encourage efforts to estimate both costs and benefits.

In large companies, final approval authority for small projects is usually delegated to managers at lower levels. Department heads may approve individual projects smaller than, say, $10,000; division managers may have authority to approve projects up to some higher amount, such as $100,000; and the president may be able to approve projects up to amounts as large as $500,000 or even more, with the limit depending on the size of the company and its history. Final decisions on the largest projects, however, are almost always made or ratified by the board of directors.

Delegated approval authority is almost always limited and subject to review. Lower-level managers are still expected to apply company profitability standards to proposals within their authority limits, and they are usually subject to limits on the total amounts they can approve. These limits are embodied in lump-sum budget provisions for groups of small proposals in each responsibility center.

COST-VOLUME-PROFIT ANALYSIS

The outcomes of few decisions can be predicted with certainty. One major uncertainty is the operating volume management will be able to achieve. One technique management uses to help judge the sensitivity of results to errors in forecasting operating volume is known as *cost-volume-profit analysis*. In this section we'll describe this technique, illustrate how it can be used in a budgeting context, and point out some of its limitations.

Basic calculations

The objective of cost-volume-profit analysis is to identify three quantities: (1) the rate at which profit varies in response to variations in sales, (2) the break-even sales volume, and (3) the spread between anticipated volume and break-even volume.

For example, Darwin Books' tentative profit plan for fiscal 19x3 showed estimated pretax income of only $115,000 (see Exhibit 20–4), and even this was reduced by $15,000 by the contemplated additional borrowing. Laski knew that Truro and the executive committee would want to know how sensitive this estimate was to errors in forecasts of divisional sales. Failure to reach the budgeted sales levels would decrease both net income and the cash flow from operations, thus jeopardizing the company's ability to pay cash dividends and finance its other discretionary outlays.

Laski and the two division managers reviewed the divisional budgets and agreed on the following estimates:

	College Division	Schools Division
Volume (number of books)	300,000	500,000
Average revenue per book	$13.40	$5.36
Variable cost per book	$ 9.60	$3.90
Total divisional fixed cost	$840,000	$615,000

Despite obvious book-to-book variations in variable unit cost and price, Laski felt these averages were likely to be stable enough for use in cost-volume-profit analysis.

The estimates for each division can be stated algebraically. For the college division, total revenue, R, at volume V is:

$$R = \$13.4\,V \tag{1}$$

Total divisional cost, C, at volume V is:

$$C = \$840,000 + \$9.6\,V \tag{2}$$

The division will break even at the volume at which $R = C$. This volume can be identified by equating the right-hand sides of equations (1) and (2) and solving for V:

$$\$13.4\,V = \$840,000 + \$9.6\,V$$
$$V = 221,053 \text{ books}$$

This is known as the divisional *break-even volume* or *break-even point*.

We can get the same result using *contribution-margin* estimates.

TERMINOLOGY

Contribution margin is the difference between the revenue from a product or service and the short-term variable costs of producing and selling that product or service.

At a price of $13.40, an average college division book has a contribution margin of $13.40 − $9.60 = $3.80. The break-even point can be located by finding out how many books must be sold to produce a *total* contribution margin equal to the budgeted fixed costs. This is obtained by dividing total fixed cost by the contribution margin per unit:

$$\text{Break-even volume} = \frac{\$840,000}{\$3.80} = 221,053 \text{ books}$$

In monetary terms, the division's break-even point is reached when it has revenues of $2,962,110 (221,053 × $13.40).

A companion to the break-even volume is the *margin of safety,* the difference between the break-even volume and the actual or anticipated volume of activity. The college division's budgeted volume for the year was 300,000 books. The estimated margin of safety therefore was:

$$\text{Margin of safety} = 300,000 - 221,053 = 78,947 \text{ books}$$

In other words, the division will cover its total costs even if volume turns out to be 78,947 books fewer than management is anticipating.

Break-even and profit-volume charts

This same analysis is presented graphically in Exhibit 20–7 in a diagram we call a *break-even chart* or profit-volume chart. These charts can be constructed in various ways, but in this case total revenue and total variable cost are represented by straight lines rising from the origin. The vertical spread between these two lines at any volume measures the total contribution margin at that volume. Total fixed cost is entered in the chart by drawing the total-cost line parallel to the total-variable-cost line, but $840,000 higher in this case.

A glance at the chart in Exhibit 20–7 reveals three key estimates:

1. If fixed costs are at planned levels and no sales are made, the division will lose $840,000 because the fixed costs won't be covered.
2. As volume increases, the contribution margin from sales will cover more and more of the fixed costs until at a 221,053-book sales volume the division will just break even.
3. At the anticipated sales volume of 300,000 books in 19x3, the division will earn a profit (represented by the vertical distance

EXHIBIT 20–7. Darwin Books, Inc.: College Division Profit-Volume Chart

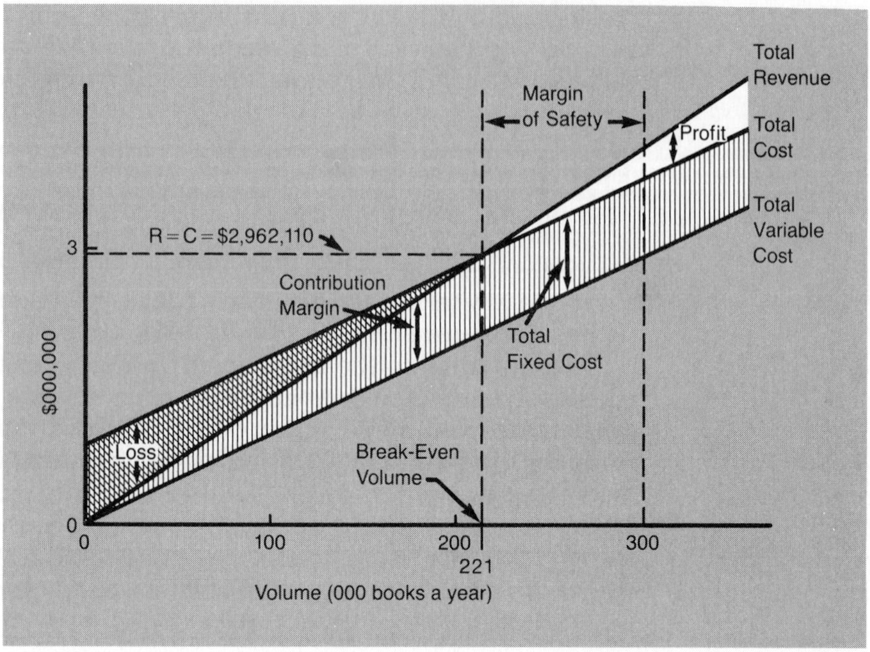

between the total-revenue and total-cost lines at that volume) and the margin of safety will be 78,947 books.

Multiproduct analysis

Calculating the break-even volume and the overall contribution-margin ratio is more difficult if volume consists of more than one product. One reason is that the products' contribution margins are likely to differ. Another is that a common physical measuring unit may be hard to find. A few words on the methods accountants use to deal with these problems are in order.

Differing contribution margins. The break-even volume and average contribution margin in a multiproduct company can be heavily influenced by the *product mix,* the percentages of total sales accounted for by the company's various products or services. Darwin Books' budgeted fixed expenses in 19x3 amounted to $1,770,000 ($840,000 in the college division, $615,000 in the schools division, $300,000 in general administrative expenses, and $15,000 in interest expense). The budgeted contribution margin in the college division was $3.80 a book; in the schools division it was only $1.46 ($5.36

— $3.90). The budgeted average contribution margin at the budgeted product mix was as follows:

	College Division	Schools Division	Total
Per book:			
Sales revenue	$13.40	$5.36	
Variable costs	9.60	3.90	
Contribution margin	3.80	1.46	
Sales volume (number of books)	300,000	500,000	800,000
Total contribution margin	$1,140,000	$730,000	$1,870,000
Average contribution margin per book			$2.3375

At the budgeted product mix, the break-even volume for the company as a whole was 757,219 books ($1,770,000/$2.3375), leaving a margin of safety of only 42,781 books at the budgeted sales volume of 800,000 books.

Suppose, however, actual sales amounted to 250,000 books in the college division and 550,000 books in the schools division. The total volume is still 800,000 books, but the average contribution margin has fallen to $2.19125 a book [(250,000 × $3.80 + 550,000 × $1.46)/ 800,000]. The break-even volume is now 807,758 books ($1,770,-000/$2.19125), 7,758 more than the company sold. Operating below the break-even volume, the company suffered a loss.

This means that management may wish to analyze the sensitivity of its income (and its cash flows, as well) in two directions—sensitivity to volume and sensitivity to mix. The result will be a two-way matrix of income estimates rather than a simple schedule. The amounts in the cells of the following partial matrix are estimates of the pretax income or loss at each of nine volume/mix combinations:

	Budgeted Income/(Loss) before Taxes when College Division Unit Sales Account for		
	30% of Total	37.5% of Total	45% of Total
Volume (no. of books):			
700,000	$(256,600)	$(133,750)	$ (10,900)
800,000	(40,400)	100,000	240,400
900,000	175,800	333,750	491,700
Average contribution margin per book	$2.162	$2.3375	$2.513
Break-even point (number of books)	818,686	757,219	704,337

Management's willingness to make discretionary outlays will be very different if it anticipates that the college division is more likely to provide less than 37.5 percent of total physical sales than if it expects the product mix to be richer.

Differing units of measurement. Darwin Books measures sales volume in each of its divisions in physical units, the number of books sold. This measure obscures many differences in the size and importance of the books sold—a heavy dictionary receives the same weight as a 64-page workbook. In other situations, measuring total volume in physical units may be impossible—a business which engages in both sales and service, for example.

The only feasible measure of volume in most such cases is revenue dollars. Expressing Darwin's budgeted contribution margins as percentages of budgeted net sales dollars give us Exhibit 20–8. Budgeted income before taxes can be represented by the following formula:

$$\begin{array}{l} \text{Income/(loss)} = \text{Average contri-} \\ \text{before tax} \quad \text{bution margin} \end{array} \times \text{Sales revenue} - \text{Fixed cost}$$
$$= 0.2791R - \$1,770,000$$

The break-even volume then can be calculated in the usual way:

$$\text{Break-even volume} = \frac{\text{Total fixed cost}}{\text{Average contribution margin}} = \frac{\$1,770,000}{0.2791}$$
$$= 6,342,000 \text{ revenue dollars}$$

A break-even or profit-volume chart can be drawn with dollars of revenue on the horizontal axis.

Either of the two formulas in the preceding paragraph can be used to calculate the budgeted income for 19x3. First we can use the income formula:

Contribution margin (from Exhibit 20–8)	$1,870,000
Fixed costs	1,770,000
Income before tax	$ 100,000

EXHIBIT 20–8. Darwin Books, Inc.: Contribution-Margin Percentages

	College Division	Schools Division	Total
Sales revenues (see Exhibit 20–4)	$4,020,000	$2,680,000	$6,700,000
Variable costs:			
300,000 × $9.60	2,880,000		4,830,000
500,000 × $3.90		1,950,000 }	
Contribution margin	$1,140,000	$ 730,000	$1,870,000
Contribution margin:			
Percentage of sales	28.36%	27.24%	27.91%

Alternatively, we can calculate the margin of safety and apply the contribution-margin percentage:

Budgeted sales revenue	$6,700,000
Break-even sales revenue	6,342,000
Margin of safety (revenue dollars)	358,000
Contribution-margin percentage (from Exhibit 20–8)	27.91%
Income before tax ($358,000 × 0.2791)	$ 100,000

Aftertax analysis

Cost-volume-profit analysis can also be applied on an aftertax basis. For example, if Darwin Books' pretax income or loss is subject to income taxes at a flat rate of 40 percent, the budgeted income or loss can be calculated from the following formula:

$$\text{Net income/(loss} = (1 - 0.4)(0.2791R - \$1,770,000)$$
$$= 0.16746R - \$1,062,000$$

The break-even volume is still $6,342,000 ($1,062,000/0.16746) because we have simply reduced both the fixed costs and the contribution margin by the same percentage. Imposition of a 40 percent tax, however, does affect the *amount* of aftertax income that is earned when volume exceeds the break-even point.

Charting dividend and target profit requirements

Cost-volume-profit analysis can be adapted to include preselected requirements for dividends, net income, or return on investment. For example, suppose Darwin Books has net assets of $1 million and a 10 percent aftertax cost of capital. Its target income therefore is $100,000 (10 percent × $1 million). This can be treated as an additional aftertax fixed expense, and the revised break-even formula is as follows:

$$\text{Target volume} = 0.16746R - \$1,062,000 - \$100,000$$
$$= \$6,939,000$$

Budgeted sales in 19x3 were only $6,700,000, or $239,000 less than the target volume.

This analysis is diagrammed in Exhibit 20–9. The diagram has been deliberately drawn offscale to emphasize the spreads between the lines. The spread between the Total Requirements and Total Cost before Taxes lines to the left of the break-even volume is based on the assumption that the company has tax carryforwards that will permit it to recover taxes paid in previous years.

This chart points out the gap between budgeted volume and target volume. The company can meet its income target in any of

EXHIBIT 20–9. Darwin Books, Inc.: Profit Chart Incorporating Fixed Income Target

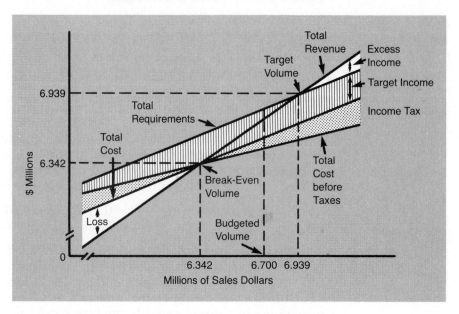

three ways: (1) by increasing volume, (2) by increasing the average contribution margin, or (3) by reducing the level of fixed costs. Before adopting a proposed budget, management must determine whether any of these actions is likely to be both effective and consistent with the company's long-term goals.

Assumptions and limitations

Cost-volume-profit analysis is useful in budgetary planning, but care must be exercised to insure that it isn't misused or misinterpreted. First, the revenues and costs in a typical analysis are unlikely to be exactly equal to operating cash receipts and disbursements. Management may wish to construct cash-based charts if short-term cash flows are the focus of attention. Darwin Books' management, for example, should have used a cash-based chart because of the cash-flow difficulties it was experiencing.

Actually, the usual break-even chart may not be a perfect predictor of short-term net income. The typical cost-volume-profit analysis assumes that all units sold have identical effects on variable expenses and on revenues. Unit costs may vary systematically during the year, and the amounts actually reported as the cost of goods sold will depend on the inventory costing method used. Similarly,

EXHIBIT 20–10. Customary Volume Range

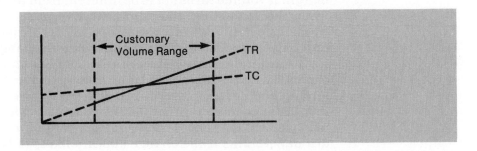

if production volume differs from sales volume in a manufacturing company, the amount of fixed overhead costs absorbed by production may differ from the amount of fixed overhead costs absorbed by sales.

A second major assumption in cost-volume-profit analysis is that the cost and revenue functions can be represented by linear equations or straight lines on the break-even chart. This assumption isn't made because management believes the relationships are linear from zero volume to capacity; instead, it reflects an assumption that the charts are to be used to describe cost and revenue behavior within a limited portion of this total range, as in Exhibit 20–10. This limited portion of the range is known as the *relevant range* or the *customary range*. Within this range, the responses of costs and revenues to changes in physical volume are likely to be linear or very close to linear. The portions of the lines extending outside the customary range aren't used. Extending the lines beyond the customary range, as in Exhibit 20–10, is useful because it allows us to describe the relationships between these limits in simple linear equations.

If volume moves toward the edge or outside the customary volume range and appears likely to stay there, management may change its evaluation of those activities which are at least partly discretionary. As a result, the actual break-even volume is likely to be lower than the break-even volume on the chart. Similarly, the profit spread at high volumes is likely to be narrower than the chart implies, as cost control seems less urgent and fringe activities seem more attractive in that more benevolent climate.

Third, despite the introduction of an independent variable (volume) which can take any of a large number of values, cost-volume-profit analysis is essentially static. It illustrates the profit *normally* associated with *steady* operation at various operating volumes within the customary volume range, given a specified marketing and administrative plan. It shows what will happen to the profit margin if volume turns out to be different from the level anticipated when the marketing and administrative plan was proposed and if management adjusts the scope of its responsive activities promptly and efficiently every time volume changes.

As this implies, cost-volume-profit analysis ignores a number of dynamic forces. One is that when volume moves rapidly from one level to another, the costs of responsive activities may respond either faster or more slowly than the chart indicates. Another is that management may choose deliberately not to adjust its cost structure to a new volume if the change appears likely to be temporary. For example, it will accept the costs of idle time or off-budgeted overtime premiums rather than contract or expand the work force for temporary valleys and peaks in demand.

Finally, the profit chart reflects a given set of marketing and administrative plans. If management doesn't like what it sees, it can draw up a new set of plans. These then can be reflected in a new chart showing the new level of fixed costs, the new relationship between variable costs and revenues, and the new estimated break-even point. This is how break-even analysis is supposed to be used; one chart isn't expected to include all the options open to management.

THE ROLE OF ACCOUNTING

Budgetary planning is a management process and a responsibility of the company's line managers. Accounting and other staff personnel don't make the plans. They do have several important roles to play, however, and a few words about each of these should be useful to round out our discussion of budgetary planning:

1. They provide data for use in preparing estimates.
2. They analyze and interpret these data.
3. They design and operate the budgeting procedures.
4. They consolidate and review the budgetary proposals originating in various parts of the organization.

1. **Data collection.** The estimates managers use in making budgeting decisions reflect their forecasts of the future consequences of those decisions. To make those estimates, however, managers usually draw very heavily on records of what happened in the past. The future may be very different from the past, but it is likely to be closer to the past than to estimates drawn at random. In other words, managers are more comfortable adjusting past figures than starting fresh, with no underlying data at all.

One function of the accounting system, therefore, is to provide a record of the costs and benefits of the company's various activities in considerable detail. Ideally, these data should enable management to identify the responses of costs, expenses, revenues, and cash flows to various kinds of managerial actions. For example, the management of our illustrative company, Darwin Books, would like to know how sales and expenses in the college division responded in the past to increases in advertising and field-selling effort. It probably would also like to know what would happen to net income if revenues were to fall, say, 10 percent short of their forecasted levels.

2. Data analysis. Accounting's contribution doesn't stop with data collection. The accounting numbers need to be interpreted, adjusted to allow for changes in company-specific, industry-specific, and economy-wide conditions, and recombined in various ways. Since accountants know more about their own numbers than anyone else, it is understandable that they do a good deal of this analytical work.

3. Budget administration. The headquarters financial staffs, often including others as well as accountants, play two other roles in the budgeting process. The first of these is that they are responsible for designing and securing support for the procedural aspects of periodic planning, mainly the questions of what is to be budgeted, when, and by whom. This is ordinarily done by the budget staff, working closely with operating executives. The final version is likely to be summarized in a budget manual, spelling out deadlines for various budget components, assigning responsibilities for budget preparation, prescribing forms, and describing the overall budget pattern.

4. Consolidation and review. The final role of accountants and others on the central financial staff is in the review and coordination phase of budgeting. Although the operating managers have the main responsibility for developing operating and financial plans, the central financial staff is responsible for putting the pieces together.

Even if budget proposals have been reviewed carefully and critically all the way up the line within a given segment of the organization, the corporate financial staff members often have the authority to subject these proposals to their own tests of feasibility and profitability. They are always free to seek clarification or to question whether other alternatives have been investigated, and, in some cases, they even have the power to ask individual managers to revise their proposals.

We must emphasize, however, that in taking any action of this sort, the controller, budget director, or other financial executive is acting as the agent of the chief executive. Planning is a managerial function first, a technical operation second.

SUMMARY

Periodic planning, or budgeting, is not simply a matter of forecasting what the future may offer. It is a creative process in which managers at all levels are expected to evaluate and compare different possible courses of action, selecting those which seem most likely to meet company goals. Budgeting, in other words, is a decision-making process.

In this chapter we have tried to describe the complexity and dynamism of the budgeting process without getting bogged down in complicated numerical examples. In our illustration, budget preparation was initiated by top management, but the major effort took place at the divisional level as the division managers developed their marketing plans and translated them into production requirements and profit estimates. These plans were reviewed, revised, and consolidated before being presented to top management for final approval. They came together eventually in a profit plan, cash budget, and capital budget that were both feasible and acceptable to top management.

Budgeting always takes place in an environment of uncertainty. Cost-volume-profit analysis is designed to help management evaluate the uncertainties surrounding the forecasts of operating volume. Location of the break-even point and calculation of the margin of safety and profit response ratios of different marketing and administrative plans may increase management's ability to choose plans which appear likely to be most consistent with the company's overall goals.

Accounting and other financial personnel have vital roles to play in the budgetary process. They provide, interpret, and analyze data; design and administer the budgeting procedures; review the proposals submitted by managers in various parts of the organization; and consolidate the final proposals into a feasible, workable plan.

KEY TERMS

Authorization limit	Long-range planning
Break-even point	Margin of safety
Budget	Marketing plan
Budgeting	Production plan
Capital budget	Profit plan
Cash budget	Profit-volume chart
Contribution margin	Project and situation planning
Cost-volume-profit analysis	Scheduling
Customary volume range	Strategic planning

INDEPENDENT STUDY PROBLEMS (Solutions in Appendix B)

1. **Profit-volume diagrams.** Cranby Company manufactures and sells a single product. You have the following data:

Fixed costs	$32,000 a month
Variable costs	$3 a unit
Selling price	$5 a unit
Anticipated sales	20,000 units

a. Construct a profit-volume chart.
b. Calculate the break-even point, the margin of safety, and the anticipated income before taxes at the anticipated sales volume.
c. The company is considering increasing the selling price to $5.50. At this price it expects to sell 18,000 units.
   1. Recalculate the break-even point, the margin of safety, and the anticipated income before taxes.
   2. Redraw the profit-volume chart, showing both the old and the new profit spreads.
   3. How many units would have to be sold at the new price to produce a 10 percent increase in total income before taxes?
d. The sales manager has offered a counterproposal. The price would be reduced to $4.60, and an additional $4,000 a month would be spent on advertising.
   1. Recalculate the break-even point.
   2. How many units would have to be sold at the new price to produce a 10 percent increase in total income before taxes?

2. **Use of contribution-margin ratios.** Carillo Company sells two products, A and B, with contribution-margin ratios of 40 and 30 percent and selling prices of $5 and $2.50 a unit. Fixed costs amount to $72,000 a month. Monthly sales average 30,0000 units of product A and 40,000 units of product B.

a. If the company spends an additional $9,700 on sales promotion, sales of product A can be increased to 40,000 units a month. Sales of product B will fall to 32,000 units a month if this is done, however, as some customers shift from one product to the other. Should this proposal be accepted?
b. As an alternative to the proposal in part a, management is considering redesigning product A and reducing the price of product B to give both products more market appeal. The variable cost of product A would be increased by 10 cents a unit; the price of product B would be reduced by 10 cents a unit. Unit sales of each product would increase by 5,000 units a month. What action would you recommend?

3. **Developing a profit plan and cash budget; feasibility test.** Darnell Company is organized in three divisions, each with a division manager, a small office staff, and its own sales force. The various divisions sell different kinds of products and deal with different groups of customers.

The company's budget director has received the following proposals and estimates for next year from the division managers:

	Division A	Division B	Division C
Divisional marketing costs amounting to	$ 150	$ 500	$ 300
Will produce revenues of	1,000	3,000	2,100
And cost of goods sold of	650	1,650	1,260
Administrative expenses to support these			
activities will total	150	300	200
Accounts receivable will increase by	10	200	50
Inventories will exceed this year's			
ending balances by	50	100	50
Accounts payable will increase by	15	50	80

The expenses of the company's central management are tentatively budgeted at $400 for the year, to be paid in cash. Cash purchases of equipment amounting to $130 and cash dividends of $350 are also proposed. Of the equipment purchases, $60 is to replace existing equipment and $70 is for expansion. The expansion proposals, which management has approved in principle, will have no effect on next year's income statement.

Depreciation is included in the administrative expense figures above as follows: central management, $10; division A, $5; division B, $15; division C, $20.

a. Prepare a tentative profit plan and cash budget for next year, on the assumption that all these proposals are approved.

b. The company will start next year with a cash balance of $290 and an unused line of bank credit of $100. The minimum cash balance is 5 percent of sales. Is the tentative plan feasible?

EXERCISES AND PROBLEMS

4. Profit-volume exercises.   Each of the following exercises is independent of the others.

Exercise A.   Oliver Company plans to market a new product. Based on its market studies, Oliver estimates it can sell 5,500 units in 19x1. The selling price will be $2 a unit. Variable costs are estimated to be 40 percent of the selling price. Fixed costs are estimated to be $6,000.

a. Calculate the break-even point (in units).
b. Calculate the margin of safety.

Exercise B.   Breiden Company sells rodaks for $6 a unit. Variable costs are $2 a unit. Fixed costs are $37,500.

a. How many rodaks must be sold if the company is to realize income before income taxes of 15 percent of sales revenue?
b. How many rodaks must be sold if the company is to realize income before taxes of $10,000?

Exercise C.   At a break-even point of 400 units sold, the variable costs were $400 and the fixed costs were $200. How much will the 401st unit sold contribute to income before income taxes?

(AICPA adapted)

5. Profit-volume exercises. Each of the following exercises is independent of the others.

Exercise A. Label Corporation's product A has sales of $300,000, variable costs of $240,000, and fixed costs of $40,000.

a. Assuming the cost relationship is linear, calculate the break-even volume.
b. How much income before taxes would product A generate if its sales volume increased by 20 percent?

Exercise B. Dallas Corporation wishes to market a new product for $1.50 a unit. Fixed costs to manufacture and market this product are $100,000 if volume is less than 500,000 units and $140,000 if volume is 500,000 units or more. The contribution margin is 20 percent. How many units must be sold to realize income before taxes from this product of $100,000?

Exercise C. Freedom, Inc., has projected the following annual costs based on 40,000 units of production and sales:

	Total Annual Costs	Variable Portion's Percent of Total Annual Costs
Direct material	$400,000	100%
Direct labor	360,000	75
Manufacturing overhead	300,000	40
Selling and administrative	200,000	25

a. Compute Freedom's unit selling price that will yield income before taxes of 10 percent of sales revenues if sales are 40,000 units.
b. Assume management selects a selling price of $30 a unit. Compute Freedom's dollar sales that will yield a projected 10 percent margin on sales, assuming the above variable fixed-cost relationships are valid.

(AICPA adapted)

6. Covering minimum return on investment requirements. Degas Company sells products with an average pretax contribution margin of 35 percent of sales. Fixed costs amount to $500,000 a year, and the income tax rate is 40 percent.

To support its production and marketing activities, the company must maintain net assets of $700,000 plus an amount equal to 10 percent of sales. The company's management wishes to maintain a rate of return on net assets of at least 12 percent after taxes.

a. Calculate the minimum dollar sales volume at which the company can generate its desired rate of return on investment.
b. What is the company's net income at this volume? What is the margin of safety?

7. Break-even exercises. Answer each of the following independent questions.

a. Thomas Company sells products P, Q, and R. Thomas sells three units of P for each unit of R, and two units of Q for each unit of P. The contribution margins are $1.00 per unit of P, $1.50 per unit of Q, and $3.00 per unit of R. If fixed costs are $600,000, how many units of P would Thomas sell at the break-even point?

b. Felder Company is a medium-sized manufacturer of lamps. During 19x9, a new line called Twilight was made available to Felder's customers. The break-even point for sales of Twilight was $400,000 with a contribution margin of 40 percent. If income before taxes was $200,000, what were the revenues from sales?

c. Rawlings, Ltd., had break-even sales of $1 million and variable costs of $3.50 a unit. Rawlings wants to sell an additional 50,000 units at the same selling price to generate income before taxes equal to 10 percent of the new revenue generated by the additional sales. If Rawlings expects the contribution margin to remain at 30 percent of sales revenues, what is the maximum amount of additional fixed costs that could be incurred?

(AICPA adapted)

8. Break-even exercise: multiproduct company. Danvers Corporation has two products, for which you have the following data:

	Product A	Product B
Sales volume (units)	200,000	300,000
Selling price per unit	$2	$3
Contribution-margin/Sales	30%	40%
Direct fixed costs	$120,000	$200,000
Indirect fixed costs	30,000	60,000

a. Calculate a break-even dollar sales volume for each product. State any assumptions you had to make.

b. Calculate a break-even dollar sales volume for the company as a whole. State any assumptions you had to make.

c. Compare the break-even point you calculated in part b with the sum of the break-even points you calculated in part a. Explain why these two figures are or aren't identical.

9. Effect of changes on break-even point. During 19x1, Arapahoe Company sold 300,000 units of product and had a net income (after taxes) of $60,000. The contribution margin was $1 a unit before taxes, and the selling price was $2.50. Fixed costs were $200,000, and the income tax rate was 40 percent.

For 19x2, variable costs went up 10 cents a unit, fixed costs went up $22,000, and income taxes increased to a rate of 50 percent.

a. What was the break-even sales volume for 19x1, in dollars?

b. What will be the break-even sales dollars for 19x2 if the selling price is not changed?

c. How many units will have to be sold to make a net income of $60,000 in 19x2 if the selling price is not changed?

d. By how much will the selling price have to be increased if the break-even point, in units, is to be the same in 19x2 as in 19x1?

e. At what selling price would the company continue to make $60,000 net income after taxes on sales of 300,000 units?

10. Product-line budgeting. Hammersmith, Ltd., has three regional factories, each of which manufactures all the company's products. The sales force is also organized geographically in 10 regional divisions, and each sales representative has a geographic territory in which he or she is the company's sole representative.

In the past, the annual budgeting process started with the development of tentative sales and marketing plans by the regional sales managers. These were then used to estimate the requirements for production and for administrative support. After review and revision, the final budget was structured along organizational lines.

Hammersmith's management became convinced in the early 1980s that this approach was preventing the development of coherent, aggressive marketing plans for individual products. Four product managers were appointed, each one responsible for setting objectives and developing marketing programs for one of the company's four main product groups. The regional manufacturing and sales organizations remained; the product managers were planners and coordinators without direct-line authority over factory or sales personnel.

In line with this change, top management decided that all future budgets would be drawn up on a product-line basis. Each product manager would draw up a proposed marketing and production plan for his or her line, working closely with the head-office sales and production staffs.

What problems do you foresee in the new system? How would you try to anticipate them and minimize their importance?

11. Tentative cash budget. The management of Cranmore Manufacturing Company at the beginning of 19x2 anticipated (1) a decrease in sales as compared with 19x1 because of production time lost in converting to new products, and (2) a considerably smaller profit margin due to higher material and labor costs. The controller was asked to prepare a cash budget based on estimated 19x2 sales of $2.4 million (a decrease of $300,000) and, in particular, to forecast the cash position at the close of 19x2.

The treasurer's forecast of certain balance sheet and other items was as follows:

Accounts receivable (net)	$ 35,000 decrease
Accounts payable	20,000 decrease
Inventories	17,000 increase
Additions to plant (gross)	125,000
Additions to retained earnings appropriated for contingencies	25,000
Income for 19x2 (after depreciation but before income taxes)	95,000
Depreciation expense, 19x2	48,000
Income taxes for 19x2 (payable in 19x3)	45,000
Dividend payments (at 19x1 rates)	30,000

The cash balance on January 1, 19x2, was $54,000, and the tax liability on that date, arising from 19x1 taxable income, amounted to $93,000. The company had no bank loans outstanding.

a. Assuming that any balance sheet items not listed above would be unchanged, prepare a schedule of forecasted cash receipts and cash disbursements for 19x2, and determine the expected cash balance as of December 31, 19x2.

b. What action would you expect management to take when it sees the cash flow estimates for the year?

12. Budgeting decisions: identifying criteria and data required. A consulting firm has a professional staff of 10, giving it a capacity to provide 1,500 hours of consulting service in an average month. Commitments to and from the company's present clients will require the firm to provide them with approximately 1,000 hours of service in each of the next six months, yielding revenues of approximately $40,000 a month and project-related expenses of $10,000 a month. Salaries of the professional staff amount to $25,000 a month; rent, and other office expenses average $8,000 a month.

The firm would like to submit bids for four additional consulting projects to be completed during the next six months. The staff has been working closely on these with the prospective clients and are quite convinced that the firm will be given the assignments if it can promise completion within the six-month period. The estimates for these four projects are as follows:

	Project A	Project B	Project C	Project D
Hours per month	125	250	375	450
Consulting fees to be charged to the client each month	$5,000	$6,000	$16,500	$22,500
Unreimbursed project expenses per month (other than salaries of professional staff, rent, and other office expenses)	$ 100	$ 500	$ 7,500	$ 9,000

a. What should the firm do? Show your calculations.
b. What criterion or criteria did you use in reaching your conclusions?
c. What other kinds of information about these projects would you, as the budget officer, find useful and perhaps essential in the development of a budget for the next six months?

13. Contribution-margin analysis. Davis Company produces two products and anticipates, with no changes in prices or programs from the previous year, the following relationships for costs, prices, and volume:

	Product A		Product B
Revenues	$3.00 a unit		$5.00 a unit
Variable costs	$1.50 a unit		$2.00 a unit
Direct fixed costs	$45,000		$60,000
Indirect fixed costs		$57,000	
Volume	60,000 units		40,000 units

Although no relationship between indirect fixed cost and any other variable has been established, the Davis Company allocates indirect fixed costs between the two products in proportion to their dollar sales volumes.

Management is considering each of the following independent proposals:

1. An outlay of $20,000 for advertising which would result in anticipated volume of 50,000 units of A and 50,000 units of B. The individual who

proposes this move states that "B is the high-margin product—this is what we want."

2. A change in production methods which would increase the annual outlay for common fixed costs by $10,000 but would reduce the variable costs of product A by 10 cents a unit and the variable costs of product B by 15 cents a unit. This change would also expand the capacity of production of A from 70,000 units to 80,000 units, but the sales would not be expected to increase.

3. A reduction of the price of B to $4.75 which would increase the volume of B to 45,000 units. This would require a $5,000 increase in B's fixed costs. Sales volume of A would be unaffected.

4. An increase in wage rates for direct labor. This increase would raise the variable costs of A by 10 cents a unit and of B by 15 cents a unit. If the increase were granted, management would increase the selling price of each product by 15 cents. Sales of A would decrease by 5,000 units; sales of B would decrease by 2,000 units.

a. Calculate the effect of each of these proposals on the company's income before taxes.

b. Indicate in each case whether the change would be likely to increase the margin of safety, decrease it, or leave it unchanged.

14. Budgeting cash receipts and cash disbursements. Alumabilt, Inc., is making an effort to manage its cash more effectively and profitably. It therefore is developing a forecast of two critical components of March 19x3 cash receipts and cash disbursements.

Sales in March are expected to be $3,200,000: 90 percent cash sales and 10 percent credit sales. Accounts receivable as of March 1 are $300,000: one quarter represents January credit sales, the remainder represents February sales. Pre-19x3 receivables either have been collected or were written off as uncollectible.

Alumabilt believes that its past experience with collecting accounts receivable is likely to continue as follows:

In the month of sale	20%
In the first month after the month of sale	50%
In the second month after the month of sale	25%
Written off as uncollectible at the end of the second month after the month of sale	5%

Alumabilt has also prepared the following information relating to inventory payments during March 19x3:

Cost of Inventory on hand, March 1	$180,000
Estimated cost of goods sold for March	900,000
Estimated cost of inventory on hand, March 31	160,000
Estimated payments in March for pre-March purchases......	210,000
Percentage of March purchases expected to be paid in March	80%

a. What are the expected cash receipts for March 19x3?

b. What are the expected cash disbursements for inventory for March 19x3?

(AICPA adapted)

15. Budgeting decisions: ranking competing proposals. You have just been appointed budget director of a manufacturing company, responsible for reviewing and coordinating the budget proposals submitted by the company's operating executives. On your first day on the job you are given the following summaries of budget proposals for each of the company's three products:

	Product A	Product B	Product C
Sales revenues	$240,000	$120,000	$40,000
Expenses:			
Manufacturing cost of the goods sold	120,000	72,000	28,000
Sales salaries	32,000	12,000	4,000
Travel and entertainment	48,000	16,000	4,800
Advertising	20,000	4,000	2,400
Total expenses	220,000	104,000	39,200
Product profit margin	$ 20,000	$ 16,000	$ 800

All three products are sold by the same sales force. The advertising costs in each of the budget proposals are specific to the particular product line, however; that is, each advertising figure in the table is the amount the company proposes spending to advertise that particular product.

The three products are manufactured in the same factory, but each product has its own production line in the factory. The finishing operation on each product must be performed on highly sophisticated equipment, however, and this equipment is so expensive that separate installations for each product line would be uneconomical. For this reason the factory has only one finishing department, which performs the finishing operations on all the company's products.

The manufacturing cost of goods sold figures in the budget proposals summarized above were made up as follows:

	Product A	Product B	Product C
Direct materials	$ 16,000	$10,000	$ 4,500
Direct labor:			
Finishing department	8,000	12,800	2,000
Other departments	28,000	10,000	6,000
Overhead:			
Finishing department	12,000	19,200	3,000
Other departments	56,000	20,000	12,500
Total cost of goods sold	$120,000	$72,000	$28,000

The finishing department has a total practical capacity of 2,500 hours a month. The budget proposals summarized above call for the following amount of time in the finishing department:

Product A .... 1,000 hours
Product B .... 1,600 hours
Product C ....   250 hours

Finishing work can also be performed by independent local firms at a cost of $25 an hour.

a. Outline the steps you would take in reviewing the proposed budgets for the three product lines. Illustrate each step, using figures supplied here, and indicate how you would decide how much finishing work should be performed by outside contractors.

b. What additional classifications of these costs would help you in making the budgeting decisions your review procedures would require? Explain how these classifications would help.

16. Budgeting decisions: profitability and feasibility. The president of Ethelred, Inc., has a commitment from the company's bank for a loan of $100,000 if the company needs it during the coming year. No other outside source of cash will be available during the year.

Ethelred provides bookkeeping services to local business firms and other organizations and has been growing rapidly in recent years. Its experience has been that accounts receivable increase as its sales volume increases. A $10 increase in annual sales volume will require a $1 increase in accounts receivable.

If the company continues its present operations, maintaining its sales force at current levels, total sales volume will increase next year by $100,000 and reported income will be:

Sales	$1,100,000
Expenses (including $10,000 depreciation)	980,000
Net income	$ 120,000

The company's present facilities will be adequate to handle this sales volume, requiring capital expenditures of only $12,000 for routine replacement of furniture and equipment.

The company's president would like to add another sales representative to contact a new group of potential customers. Additional data-processing equipment would have to be rented to handle any business the new sales representative brought in. These changes would increase Ethelred's annual operating expenses by the following amounts:

Sales representative's salary and expenses	$22,000
Equipment rental	30,000
Other expenses	60,000 + 10% of added sales

The president believes that the additional sales volume from this market would amount to $50,000 in the first year, but it might amount to nothing at all. If the operation proved successful, revenues in later years would be substantially higher.

Ethelred's shareholders have received cash dividends of $50,000 in each of the last three years, and the board of directors has tentatively decided to increase the dividend next year to $60,000 if the cash flow is adequate. It also wishes to contribute $20,000 to the local art museum as a community service.

a. Are these proposals feasible? Prepare a tentative profit plan and a tentative cash budget to support your answer. You may assume that all expenses other than depreciation and all equipment expenditures must be accompanied by immediate cash payments.

b. What action should the president take? If you conclude that you lack enough information on which to base a recommendation, identify the issues which still need to be resolved before a recommendation can be made.

17. Revising a proposed budget. Noting substantial increases in the proposed levels of marketing and administrative costs over those of the current year, Darnell Company's budget director asked the company's three division managers for additional information to be used in reviewing the divisional budget proposals summarized in problem 3. It wasn't clear how much of the increases were due to changes in prices and how much resulted from changes in the amount or structure of marketing effort.

To supplement the forecasted results for the proposed marketing plans, the budget director asked each division manager for estimates of the following:

1. This year's results.
2. The results to be expected next year if this year's marketing program were to be continued unchanged.
3. The results to be expected next year if marketing and administrative expenses were to be kept at this year's levels (an "austerity budget").

With the help of personnel from the central market research and controller's departments, the division managers supplied the following additional data:

	Division A	Division B	Division C
Expected results this year from this year's program:			
Sales	$800	$2,000	$2,000
Cost of goods sold	496	1,200	1,200
Marketing expenses	120	380	280
Administrative expenses	110	200	190
Accounts receivable, year-end	40	350	330
Inventories, year-end	195	320	360
Accounts payable, year-end	60	120	550
Expected results next year if this year's program were to be repeated:			
Sales	840	2,400	2,000
Cost of goods sold	546	1,392	1,260
Marketing expenses	125	400	300
Administrative expenses	120	220	200
Accounts receivable, year-end	42	400	330
Inventories, year-end	215	368	360
Accounts payable, year-end	64	141	550
Expected results under austerity budget:			
Sales	820	2,100	1,900
Cost of goods sold	533	1,218	1,197
Marketing expenses	120	380	280
Administrative expenses	110	200	190
Accounts receivable, year-end	41	360	314
Inventories, year-end	205	324	332
Accounts payable, year-end	62	124	517

Central administrative expenses for the current year are expected to total $380, cash purchases of equipment will amount to $120, and cash dividends of $300 will be paid. Depreciation expenses included in the administrative expenses are: central management, $10; division A, $5; division B, $15; division C, $20.

a. Calculate expected net income for the current year.

b. Prepare a profit plan on the assumption that current marketing programs will be continued next year. (Central administrative expenses would be at their proposed level, $400.)

c. Prepare an austerity budget profit plan on the assumption that marketing and administrative expenses next year are held to this year's level. (Under an austerity budget, central administrative expenses would amount to $395.)

d. Assuming that these estimates are sound, and basing your recommendations solely on the figures given in these two problems, what action should Darnell's management take on the budget proposals?

18. Contribution-margin analysis: interdependent products. Mazini Company manufactures a number of products, three of which can be described as follows:

	Rinsol	Sudsit	Sansgrit
Price per case	$7.60	$12.00	$15.00
Cost per case:			
Direct materials	3.00	3.50	6.00
Direct labor...................	1.00	1.00	1.50
Factory overhead	2.00	2.00	3.00
Administration	0.38	0.60	0.75
Total cost	6.38	7.10	11.25
Marketing profit per case	$1.22	$ 4.90	$ 3.75
Total marketing costs	$400,000	$4,000,000	$800,000
Number of cases sold	400,000	1,000,000	200,000

You have the following additional information:

1. Factory overhead is assigned to products by means of an overhead rate of 200 percent of direct-labor cost.

2. The variable portion of factory overhead cost amounts to 60 percent of direct-labor cost.

3. Fixed-factory overhead costs will remain constant for all feasible production volumes of these three products. If production of any one of them were to be discontinued entirely, however, the company could reduce its fixed factory overhead by $200,000.

4. Administrative costs are assigned to products at amounts equal to 5 percent of sales. Investigation shows that the variable portion of this amounts to 30 cents a case.

5. The marketing costs are all fixed. Discontinuation of any product would reduce the amounts shown by 75 percent.

a. Using the company's methods of cost assignment, calculate income before taxes for each of these three products.

b. Judging solely from the information provided, would you recommend that any of these three products be discontinued? Show your calculations.

c. You are told further that sale of a case of Rinsol causes the company to lose the sale of three tenths of a case of Sudsit. Sale of a case of Sansgrit, however, increases sales of Sudsit by one tenth of a case. No other interproduct relationships can be identified. What recommendation would you make now? Show your calculations.

19. Using contribution-margin data; interdependent products. Albegata Company produces four products, Alpha, Beta, Gamma, and Delta. Its income statement for the past year showed the following (in $000):

	Alpha	Beta	Gamma	Delta	Total
Units sold.........................	400	300	200	2,000	—
Sales revenues	$4,000	$3,000	$2,000	$1,000	$10,000
Cost of goods sold:					
Direct material...................	1,500	1,000	500	500	3,500
Direct labor	1,000	1,000	300	200	2,500
Factory overhead absorbed	400	400	120	80	1,000
Total	2,900	2,400	920	780	7,000
Gross margin.....................	1,100	600	1,080	220	3,000
Selling expenses:					
Sales commissions	120	90	60	30	300
Direct fixed costs	200	60	60	60	380
Indirect fixed costs	480	360	240	120	1,200
Administrative expenses:					
Order processing	30	50	20	20	120
General administration..........	320	240	160	80	800
Total operating expense	1,150	800	540	310	2,800
Net income (loss) before tax	$ (50)	$ (200)	$ 540	$ (90)	$ 200

It is believed that no external force in the foreseeable future will alter the picture. At the board of directors' meeting, it is decided that something must be done in view of the low overall profit rate (2 percent on sales) and the net loss on all except one product line.

At your request, the following additional information is furnished by the company:

1. Sales commissions are paid to the company's sales force at the rate of 3 percent of sales.

2. Order-processing costs are assigned to products on the basis of the amount of time spent by office employees in recording orders, preparing invoices, and recording the amounts collected from customers. Order-processing costs increase in steps, but the steps are narrow enough to justify classifying these costs as variable.

3. Analysis of factory overhead and fixed operating expenses:

	Alpha	Beta	Gamma	Delta
Factory overhead:				
Variable (with direct-labor cost)	$150	$200	$100	$ 60
Fixed, but escapable if the line is shut down	150	100	10	10
Fixed and inescapable if the line is shut down	100	100	10	10
Direct selling expense:				
Fixed, escapable only by shutdown.................	180	60	50	60
Fixed, inescapable by shutdown	20	—	10	—
Indirect fixed selling expense:				
Escapable by shutdown...........................	200	210	200	110
Inescapable by shutdown	280	150	40	10
General administrative expense:				
Fixed, escapable only by shutdown.................	20	40	10	50
Fixed, inescapable by shutdown	300	200	150	30

4. Products Beta and Alpha share the same equipment, and this is now fully utilized. A unit of Alpha requires the same number of machine-hours as a unit of Beta. For competitive reasons, the selling price of neither product can be increased. The marketing manager has no doubt the company could get enough additional orders of either of these products to utilize the equipment fully if production of the other were to be discontinued, with no change in any marketing costs except sales commissions.

5. Product Delta is looked on as a loss leader, since it is feared that sales of Gamma would fall by as much as 20 percent if Delta were dropped from the company's line. Alpha and Beta, on the other hand, are sold to other types of buyers, and their sales would not be affected.

a. Give recommendations when only the additional information in items 1, 2, and 3 is known. (All recommendations should be supported by computations showing estimated improvement in profits.)

b. Give recommendations when only the additional information in items 1, 2, 3, and 4 is known.

c. Give recommendations when all the above information is known.

20. Budgeting: benefits and implementation problems. "This budget is a big nuisance," said Hiram Baumgartner, president of Colleyford, Inc., the U.S. subsidiary of a large European manufacturer of electrical and electronic products. "I have to spend most of my time on it for the better part of a month, and I don't know how many hours my controller puts in on it. As far as I'm concerned, it's just another report I have to make."

Colleyford operated one small electronics factory in upstate New York but otherwise imported all its needs from parent-company factories in Europe and Japan. It operated primarily in the northeastern United States and on the West Coast and had fairly large product-distribution warehouses in New York and San Francisco.

For budgeting purposes, Colleyford used the parent company's product-classification scheme. It marketed products in six of the parent's product categories:

1. Lighting products.
2. Electronic tubes and transistors.

3. Components for computers and industrial communications equipment.
4. Radios, television receivers, and phonographs.
5. Industrial equipment and parts.
6. Service and repair.

Some products were marketed through wholesalers, while others were sold directly to industrial consumers by the company's own sales force. Colleyford had a sales force of approximately 40 men and women. Although some of them tended to concentrate on one or two product groups, they all handled all the company's lines.

Baumgartner was allowed to manufacture any product his plant was equipped to produce. The types and amounts of this production were included in the budget that he submitted to headquarters each November. The parent-company headquarters then informed him which factories would supply his remaining requirements. The prices charged for these intergroup transfers were established by the head office in advance of budget preparation.

Two or three staff executives from the parent company's headquarters ordinarily spent a week or so at the Colleyford offices while the budget was being prepared and were also in frequent communication by telephone. They offered their advice and suggestions and raised questions about parts of the budget proposal as it was in process. Baumgartner usually presented his budget to the parent company in person at the end of November; and the final budget received from headquarters in December was ordinarily almost identical to the one Baumgartner submitted.

a. What benefits might Baumgartner reap from the company's system of budgetary planning? Comment on possible reasons for his attitude toward the budget and offer suggestions as to what might be done to give him a more favorable view of the budgetary process.
b. Discuss the problems of data classification in Colleyford, Inc. What kinds of data should the profit plan include, and how should these data be subdivided and classified?

21

The control process: Reporting profits to management

The budgetary plan emerging from the managerial planning process described in Chapter 20 provides a basis for overall *control* reporting. Managerial control consists of management's efforts to prevent unwanted departures from planned results, to keep track of events and their results, to interpret information on departures from the plan, and to take action in response to this information. The purpose of this chapter is to show how management uses accounting measurements of income, assets, and liabilities to control major segments of the business.

THE ORGANIZATIONAL SETTING

Profit-performance reports can be issued for any segment of the company's business. A business segment is any portion of the business for which both revenues and expenses can be identified. The organization units responsible for business segments may be called divisions, groups, subsidiary companies, or departments. We'll use the term *division* to identify them all.

Companies in which the managers reporting to the chief executive officer are responsible for generating profits in specific business segments are generally referred to as *decentralized* companies. Their major operating divisions are known as *profit centers*. In this section we'll see how these and other kinds of organization units fit into the decentralized company.

Profit centers

The profit center is intended to function much like an independent business. It has four main characteristics:

1. It has a defined profit objective.
2. Its management has authority to make decisions affecting the major determinants of profit.
3. Its management is expected to use profit-oriented decision rules.
4. Its management is accountable to higher management for the amount of profit generated.

The result is that the typical profit center is a division selling a limited number of product lines or serving a specific geographic area. It encompasses both the means of providing goods or services and the means of marketing them.

Top management always limits division managers' authority, even in companies which are highly decentralized. Top management is likely to make all the major decisions on financing and capital expenditures, for example, and require that divisions conform to overall company policies and that each division's activities be coordinated with those of other divisions. Although other restrictions are also common, a true profit center should have at least three kinds of authority, within the limits established by company policy:

1. Freedom to choose its customers.
2. Freedom to choose the sources of supply for most of the materials and other goods and services it buys.
3. Authority to decide how many people to use in pursuing its profit goals and how to use them.

Why companies decentralize

Companies decentralize because they want their division managers to act, within limits, as though they were administering independent companies. They expect this kind of behavior to yield benefits such as the following:

1. Decisions will be made more quickly, with less red tape.
2. Decisions will be of higher quality, because the decentralized manager can devote more time to individual decisions and bring more specialized knowledge to bear on these decisions than top management could.
3. Division managers will recognize that specific parts of the company's income are the result of their own efforts, and this recognition will reinforce their motivation to strive for greater profits.

4. Top management will have more time to concentrate on strategic planning and other higher-level activities.
5. More people will gain experience in making profit-based decisions, and this will increase the number of experienced candidates for senior managerial positions.

Decentralization can also produce harmful effects. First, subordinate managers may make mistakes that managers with more experience might be able to avoid. Second, some actions which increase one division's profits may hurt other divisions and the entire company as well; this is called *suboptimization*. Third, decentralized companies are likely to have more staff personnel, both because more managers need staff assistance and because top management needs staff to help provide central guidance and oversight of decentralized operations. Finally, the quest for short-term profits may cause division managers to underemphasize nonfinancial objectives or to shortchange the future.

A company shouldn't decentralize unless it is confident it can keep the harmful effects at levels commensurate with the value of the benefits to be reaped.

Service centers

Many organization units in decentralized companies are classified as service centers. A *service center* is a unit providing services or support to other units in the organization. The relationships between service centers and profit centers are illustrated in Exhibit 21–1. These service centers have three common characteristics:

1. The volume of production, service, or support they provide is determined elsewhere in the company.

EXHIBIT 21–1. Relationships between Service Centers and Profit Centers

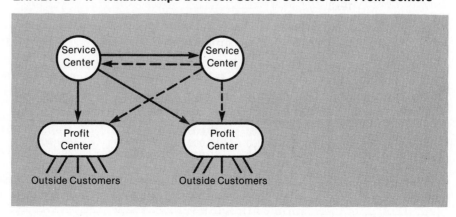

2. Their managers are evaluated on the basis of cost, quality, effectiveness, and other internal performance criteria, not on a profit basis.

3. The activities they perform are evaluated either jointly with other activities or on the basis of benefit criteria other than profit (e.g., amount of cost saved or public goodwill created).

Service centers in corporate headquarters help top management analyze the strategic plans and implementation proposals submitted by the division managers. They also advise and assist the division managers on technical matters, supplementing the efforts of the divisions' own staff analysts. In addition, corporate service centers may administer the controls top management has established to set limits within which the division managers are free to exercise their authority. And they help top management review and evaluate the performance of individual divisions and their managers. In a sense, dealing with central staff is the price division managers pay for the authority they've been given.

DIVISIONAL PROFIT-PERFORMANCE STANDARDS

Top management is likely to use periodic reports to provide two kinds of *scorecard* control information on the profit performance of the company's divisions:

1. To identify *activities* which seem to be either particularly good or particularly poor uses of the company's resources (*economic evaluation*).

2. To evaluate the effectiveness and efficiency of individual *managers* in the organization (*managerial evaluation*).

EXHIBIT 21–2.   Darwin Books, Inc.: College Division Profit Report for the Month Ended June 30, 19x3

	Current Month			Entire Year		
	Actual	Budget	Over/(Under) Budget	Actual	Budget	Over/(Under) Budget
Net sales	$320,000	$300,000	$20,000	$4,250,000	$4,020,000	$230,000
Expenses:						
Printing and binding	192,000	180,000	12,000	2,580,000	2,400,000	180,000
Copy editing	11,000	10,000	1,000	118,000	120,000	(2,000)
Advertising and selling	48,000	50,000	(2,000)	567,000	580,000	(13,000)
Authors' royalties	42,000	39,000	3,000	485,000	480,000	5,000
Administration	10,000	9,000	1,000	143,000	140,000	3,000
Total expenses	303,000	288,000	15,000	3,893,000	3,720,000	173,000
Division income	$ 17,000	$ 12,000	$ 5,000	$ 357,000	$ 300,000	$ 57,000

(Scorecard controls are summary reports on the overall performance of various activities or organization segments and of the
managers responsible for them.)

For example, Darwin Books, Inc., a publisher of textbooks, has
two profit centers. Exhibit 21–2 shows the divisional income statement for one of these profit centers—the college division—for the
final month of the 19x3 fiscal year. Top management is likely to
want to know whether divisional incomes of $17,000 this month
and $357,000 for the year as a whole are adequate returns on the
company's investment of managerial time and financial capital in
the college division, and whether these amounts are as large as
the division's management should have been able to achieve this
year.

Profit standards in economic evaluation

Economic evaluation is the process by which higher management decides whether a division's activities produce benefits commensurate with their costs. For a revenue-generating division (e.g.,
a profit center), the question is whether the division's activities
are generating enough income to justify the funds invested in it.
In other words, is the division generating an adequate rate of return
on investment?

To answer this question, we should compare the return the division is getting with a standard based on the cost of capital, applied
uniformly to all divisions in a given risk category. Differences in
the market environment don't justify the use of different standards
for different divisions; top management's only concern is whether
invested capital produces more than it costs. Adequate economic
performance in a hostile environment justifies continuation; poor
economic performance in a favorable environment calls for discontinuation unless the situation can be turned around.

Profit standards in managerial evaluation

Standards used in evaluating division managers' profit performance need to be tested against two major criteria:

1. Current *attainability* by competent division managers.
2. Consistency with the degree of profit *controllability*.

Attainability. Attainability is a highly qualitative characteristic.
In this context, it refers to levels of performance which the division
managers themselves believe they can reach. The attainability criterion is important because standards which are unattainable will
be perceived as unfair by the division managers. This means that

they won't *internalize* these standards; that is, they won't accept them as goals worthy of their efforts.

The attainable level of performance must be determined division by division. Profit differences can be created by variations in the age or condition of production facilities; by differences in local wage structures, transportation costs, or raw materials prices; by differences in the types of products handled or customers served; or by differences in the degree of competition faced in the marketplace. This means that the standard must be adapted to each division's situation each period—otherwise, it may not be attainable.

Controllability.   Profit standards for use in managerial evaluation must also satisfy the *controllability* criterion, which specifies that the manager being evaluated must have authority to influence the variables which may create differences between actual performance and the performance standard. The controllability criterion is important because divisional profit reports are intended to reinforce the division manager's *motivation* to pursue goals which are consistent with the company's overall profit goals. Differences between reported profits and the managerial performance standard (*profit variances*) won't have that effect if they result from forces the manager can't control.

The profit plan.   The performance standard which comes closest to satisfying both the attainability and the controllability criteria is the current *profit plan,* adjusted for the effects of unforeseen changes in the economic environment. As we pointed out in Chapter 20, most profit plans are established jointly by profit-responsible executives, their subordinates, and their immediate superiors. Once established, the profit plan becomes a commitment—by the profit center manager to strive to carry it out and by higher management to accept the achievement of planned results as satisfactory managerial performance. If superiors are unwilling to make this commitment, they should reject the plan and either demand a new one or find a new manager for the profit center.

Two safeguards are essential if this standard is to be used in managerial evaluation. First, top management has to carry out a rigorous, critical review of all budget proposals, usually with strong central-staff participation (i.e., by a corporate service center). Second, management has to include *improvement targets* in the budgeting process. Low profit levels may be acceptable for a while, but they can't be tolerated in the long run. Recognizing this, top management should judge division managers' performance at least as much by the quality of their budget proposals as by their current profit performance.

Failure to produce the results anticipated in the annual plan doesn't necessarily imply managerial failure. Many noncontrollable factors may have influenced the results. For this reason, most internal profit reports include analyses or commentaries on the differences between actual and budgeted performance. The commentaries, in calling attention to unusual events which affected income favorably or unfavorably, may indicate whether these effects are expected to continue and what actions management is taking to cope with, or to capitalize on, the situation.

Qualitative commentaries on profit variances are often supported and supplemented by quantitative breakdowns of the aggregate profit variance in each segment of the business. The variance can be subdivided to identify the effects of any influences management thinks are likely to be significant.[1]

MEASURING DIVISIONAL PROFIT

For *economic evaluation,* divisional profit should reflect all the revenues, expenses, gains, and losses attributable to each division and its activities, together with an estimate of the resources committed to the support of those activities. For *managerial evaluation,* divisional profit should be measured in such a way that the differences between reported profit and the profit plan result from actions and events over which division management has some influence.

Given these two criteria—for economic evaluation and for managerial evaluation—let's examine four possible measures of divisional profit performance:

1. Profit contribution.
2. Net income.
3. Return on investment.
4. Residual income.

Profit contribution

The profit contribution of any business segment is calculated by subtracting the fixed costs traceable to the segment from the segment's contribution margin. (We defined contribution margin in Chapter 20 as the spread between the total revenues of the segment and the variable costs occasioned by those revenues.) Exhibit 21–3 shows how the monthly profit report of Darwin Books' college division can be restructured in a profit-contribution format. (To avoid clutter, we've omitted the year-to-date totals presented in Exhibit 21–2.) Darwin classifies printing and binding expenses and

---

[1] For one analytical scheme, see Gordon Shillinglaw, *Managerial Cost Accounting,* 5th ed. (Homewood, Ill.: Richard D. Irwin, Inc., 1982), chap. 27.

EXHIBIT 21–3. Darwin Books, Inc.: College Division Profit Contribution Report for the Month Ended June 30, 19x3

	Actual	Budget	Over/(Under) Budget
Net sales	$320,000	$300,000	$20,000
Variable expenses:			
Printing and binding	192,000	180,000	12,000
Authors' royalties	42,000	39,000	3,000
Total variable expenses	234,000	219,000	15,000
Contribution margin	86,000	81,000	5,000
Traceable fixed expenses:			
Copy editing	11,000	10,000	1,000
Advertising and selling	48,000	50,000	(2,000)
Administration	10,000	9,000	1,000
Total traceable fixed expenses	69,000	69,000	—
Profit contribution	17,000	12,000	5,000
Indirect fixed expenses:			
Head-office charges	14,000	10,000	4,000
Income before taxes	3,000	2,000	1,000
Income tax	1,200	800	400
Net income	$ 1,800	$ 1,200	$ 600

authors' royalties as wholly variable with sales volume; the other three categories of divisional expenses are classified as fixed.

Because Darwin Books allocates none of the expenses of its corporate head office routinely to the divisions, the college division's *profit contribution* in Exhibit 21–3 is equal to the *divisional income* total in Exhibit 21–2. When head-office expenses are allocated to divisions, a division's income will be less than its profit contribution. We'll discuss the role of the allocations at the bottom of Exhibit 21–3 in the next section.

One advantage of the profit-contribution format is that it emphasizes the sensitivity of profit to variations in the use of the capacity established by the structure of fixed costs. A 10 percent increase in the college division's sales volume, for example, presumably would increase the contribution margin by 10 percent (from $86,000 to $94,600) but would leave the fixed costs unchanged.

Profit contribution fails to satisfy either the economic evaluation criterion or the managerial evaluation criterion, however. It is unsatisfactory for economic evaluation, both because it overlooks centrally administered costs attributable to the division and because it doesn't reflect divisional investment at all. It does come closer to meeting the needs of managerial evaluation, because it is likely to encompass most of the income statement elements the division manager can influence (and only those elements). Its drawback is that it ignores the investments under the division manager's control.

A division may be able to increase its profit contribution by increasing its investments in inventories and receivables. Unless the profit-performance measure reflects these investments, it will provide a misleading impression of managerial performance. The manager will get credit for the benefits of the investment without being evaluated for the costs of the investment.

Net income

Under the profit-contribution approach, company fixed costs which can't be traced to individual divisions or other revenue segments—that is, indirect fixed costs—aren't distributed among the segments. *Company net income is the sum of the profit contributions of the various revenue segments (divisions) less the total of the indirect fixed costs.* To move from profit contribution to net income for individual segments, as we did at the bottom of Exhibit 21–3, we have to find some way of allocating indirect fixed costs.

An ideal solution would be to allocate to each segment the fixed costs the company could eliminate if it were to withdraw from that segment. To try to approximate this, we might subdivide the indirect fixed costs into groups, each of which has its own set of determinants, and then allocate the costs in each group to the segments in proportion to the segments' shares of these determinants. The cost of office space in a company's headquarters, for example, might be divided among the company's divisions in proportion to the amount of space each of them occupies in the headquarters buildings.

Although this approach is promising, it can't succeed completely. Many indirect fixed costs just can't be identified clearly with determinants that can also be identified with individual segments. The salaries of the company's principal executive officers are a case in point. As a result, some or all of the indirect fixed costs are typically allocated arbitrarily, in proportion to some broad measure of segmental activity such as sales volume or the number of employees. Company income taxes are then allocated among the segments in proportion to the determinants of taxable income.

Darwin Books, for example, had $25,000 in headquarters fixed costs (indirect with respect to the activities of the individual divisions) in June 19x3. Darwin's accountants allocated $14,000 of this amount to the college division, against a budgeted allocation of $10,000. This left $3,000 ($17,000 − $14,000) income before taxes in June, against $2,000 in the original budget ($12,000 − $10,000). Darwin uses a 40 percent income tax rate in its monthly profit reports, leaving the divisional net income amounts shown on the bottom line of Exhibit 21–3.

Divisional net income is a better economic evaluation measure than profit contribution if the allocations of headquarters expenses fairly approximate the amount of headquarters expenses attributable to the division's activities. Unfortunately, most allocations of nontraceable fixed costs are arbitrary. How much of the president's salary should be charged to the college division is a question of metaphysics, not of scientific measurement. General percentage allocations are the worst because they make no pretense of measuring the amount of fixed cost the company could avoid by discarding the segment. The larger these allocations are, the less reliance management can place on net income. Even if the allocation problem could be solved, divisional net income alone wouldn't meet the needs of economic evaluation because it doesn't reflect the amount of investment attributable to each division's activities.

Divisional net income also fails the managerial evaluation test because it contains allocations of headquarters expenses the division manager can't control and because it doesn't reflect controllable investments. The controllability consideration can be met if headquarters allocations are entirely predetermined, yielding no differences from the budgeted amounts; reflecting divisional investments takes us away from the net income concept altogether, into return-on-investment or residual-income reporting.

Return on investment (ROI)

We've already said that the standard for economic evaluation is expressed as a rate of return on investment, linked to the cost of capital. We shouldn't be surprised, therefore, to find that return on investment (usually abbreviated ROI) is the most widely used measure of divisional profit performance.[2] The ratio is:

$$\text{Return on investment} = \frac{\text{Net income}}{\text{Investment}}$$

The rate of return should always be measured on an annual basis. Seasonal variations are difficult to allow for, and the effort seldom is worthwhile. Darwin Books' college division generated net income of $1,800 in June 19x3 (as shown in Exhibit 21–3) and $42,000 in the year as a whole. (The $42,000 was calculated by subtracting $287,000 in head-office charges and $28,000 in income taxes from the $357,000 divisional income reported in Exhibit 21–2.) The company's net investment in the college division (mainly in inventories

---

[2] See James S. Reece and William R. Cool, "Measuring Investment Center Performance," *Harvard Business Review*, June 1978, p. 29.

and receivables) averaged $800,000 in fiscal 19x3. The reported rate of return on investment in 19x3 therefore was:

$$\text{Return on investment} = \frac{\$42,000}{\$800,000} = 5.25 \text{ percent}$$

Measurement of a division's return on investment is intended to be used in two ways:

1. To direct top management's attention to segments that persistently earn less than the target return on investment.
2. To show how viable the segment is likely to be on a continuing basis—that is, are the revenues covering all the costs attributable to them? If not, the future is bleak, no matter how favorable the current cash-flow relationships.

A division with a persistently low return on investment is an obvious candidate for disposal. Conversely, as long as the reported return on investment is at a level management considers satisfactory, management probably won't find it necessary to consider disposing of the division. The measure is imperfect, however. The use of reported return on investment to measure divisional profit performance introduces all the measurement problems we identified in discussing net income, plus the additional problems of measuring divisional investment and annualizing both income and investment.

In any case, the disposal decision should be based, not on the amounts shown in the historical return-on-investment reports, but on estimates of cash flows, using the techniques outlined in Chapter 19. This analysis requires a comparison of the present value of the cash flows from continued operation with the cash flows to be generated by withdrawing from the segment immediately.

The cash flows from immediate withdrawal come from the after-tax liquidation value of the facilities and working capital attributable to the segment, less any liquidation costs (employee severance pay and so on), also adjusted for the tax effects. The cash flows from continued operation are the net receipts the company would lose if it were to drop out of the market now.

Before moving on, we should note one hidden danger in return-on-investment reporting. Faced with persistently low return-on-investment ratios in some of its operations, management may find it extremely difficult to remember that the failure of these segments to meet minimum profitability standards is a suitable topic for economic evaluation, not managerial appraisal. No manager should be rewarded for being placed in charge of a profitable operation or stigmatized for being assigned to activities that are inherently unprofitable.

Residual income

A variant of return on investment is residual income, defined as divisional net income less an investment carrying charge, determined by multiplying divisional investment by an interest rate based on the cost of capital. The interest rate should be an aftertax rate if income taxes have been deducted in calculating divisional income; for monthly reporting, it should be divided by 12.

For example, suppose Darwin Books has an aftertax cost of capital of 10 percent, which is approximately 0.8 percent a month. Budgeted investment for the month of June 19x3 was $750,000; actual investment was $800,000. Taking the divisional income amounts from Exhibit 21–3 and ignoring seasonal factors, we have the following:

	Actual	Budget	Over/(Under) Budget
Net income	$ 1,800	$ 1,200	$600
Investment carrying charge (0.8% of investment)	6,400	6,000	400
Residual income/(loss)	$(4,600)	$(4,800)	$200

Residual income's main advantage over return on investment is that it places budget-versus-actual differences (*variances*) on equivalent scales. For example, having $50,000 more inventory than the budget calls for can be said to cost the company $400 a month (0.8 percent × $50,000). If this much extra inventory increases divisional income by $1,000 a month after taxes, it certainly is worth having.

Even so, residual income shares most of the defects of return on investment. It reflects allocations of indirect fixed costs and centrally administered assets, allocations that may be partly arbitrary, and it includes noncontrollable variances in expenses and investments. Users should understand these limitations when interpreting residual income amounts.

ADJUSTING FOR INFLATION

The amounts reported for investments in assets, depreciation, and the cost of goods sold on most divisional profit-performance statements are based on measures of historical cost. Most depreciable assets in use today were acquired when prices were lower than they are now, however. A similar time lag affects some cost of goods sold amounts, particularly when inventories are measured on a FIFO basis. As a result, reported expenses are likely to understate the current cost of the resources used to obtain current revenues.

Similar problems surround the measurement of the inventory and plant asset components of the divisional investment base at their historical costs. Historical cost is likely to understate the investment currently required by the division's activities.

One solution to these problems is to measure assets, depreciation, and the cost of goods sold at their replacement costs. Most companies in the United States have shied away from doing this, perceiving the cost of measuring replacement prices to be far greater than the benefits to be derived. With income overstating the margin over current cost and with the investment base understating current investment requirements, however, historical-cost reporting may cover up deteriorating profit situations until price levels stabilize and asset replacement at higher prices begins to be felt in a lower return on investment. As inflation persists and large companies in the United States develop replacement-cost estimates for external financial reporting, the internal use of these estimates in divisional performance reporting is likely to increase.

ACHIEVING LONG-TERM GOALS

One danger of profit-based decentralization is that the managers of profit centers may sacrifice the company's long-term interests to increase their divisions' short-term profits. Two ways of counteracting this tendency can be tried: (1) establishing additional criteria for evaluating the performance of division managers, and (2) establishing centrally administered constraints and guidelines.

Multiple performance criteria

Current income reports can never capture the full effect of current actions. Decisions made now may pay off or have disastrous consequences a year, a decade, or a generation hence. Some decisions affect nonfinancial indexes before they have visible effects on reported income, however; market share, absenteeism, product defects, and productivity are among the many nonfinancial indexes head-office management may wish to monitor.

One way to insure that managers let these variables affect their decisions is to require them to set both profit and nonprofit objectives and include both in their proposed operating plans. These proposed objectives will be reviewed by top management or by the headquarters staff; after revision, they too will become standards against which future performance can be measured.

The development of multiple performance criteria may help division managers adopt the company's goals as their own—because more dimensions of their activities can be encompassed in the evaluation of managerial performance. Top management faces two problems in using multiple performance criteria, however. First, some goals are difficult to quantify. As a result, management is likely to measure performance by comparing actual inputs with planned inputs, rather than by measuring divisional outputs. Second, the goals may be inconsistent with each other: Expenditures designed to enhance management development may reduce the rate of growth; increases in market share may occur only at the expense of current profitability.

The presence of inconsistent goals forces division managers to determine the amount of effort to devote to the pursuit of each goal. Division managers are likely to learn to identify top management's implicit priorities by watching the responses to their successes and failures in meeting the various objectives. If top management wants the divisions to pursue nonprofit objectives, therefore, it must be prepared to react both when they are met and when they are missed.

Centrally administered constraints and guidelines

Many large decentralized companies attempt to protect their long-term interests by imposing centrally administered constraints and guidelines on their division managers. These may take the form of minimum-performance objectives, one in each performance dimension. These minima limit the managers' freedom to sacrifice progress toward one objective to achieve greater progress toward another.

Another possibility is to give central staff groups authority to review and reject portions of proposed divisional plans, and to audit compliance with centrally established standards. Internal control systems are subjected to this kind of review, for example. Similarly, a central maintenance staff might have the authority to make sure that divisional maintenance expenditures will be adequate to keep plant and equipment from accumulating "deferred maintenance" obligations.

These arrangements reduce the autonomy of the division managers, leading to some violation of the profit-center concept. The profit-center structure is only a means to an end, however, and top management is free to modify it if the benefits of these modifications seem likely to exceed the costs.

THE CONTROL PROCESS

Divisional income reports such as those illustrated in Exhibits 21–2 and 21–3 are only one feature of an overall management control system. The main elements are diagrammed in Exhibit 21–4. The control process begins at the upper left with the development of a plan. This plan includes a description of the actions management intends to take and a prediction of the results management expects these actions to produce.

The second control stage is the *action* stage—coordination, direction, and supervision—shown in the upper block at the center of the diagram. While planning is *control before the fact,* coordination, direction, and supervision are all designed to see that the plan is implemented as intended. If these functions aren't performed effectively, operations are likely to go out of control; no subsequent actions can recover the resulting loss of profits.

All the other blocks in Exhibit 21–4 are part of the control stage known as *control by feedback response* or *responsive control.* The rectangular blocks identify actions by line management; the ovals identify measurement or analytical functions in the responsive con-

EXHIBIT 21–4. Planning and Control Loops

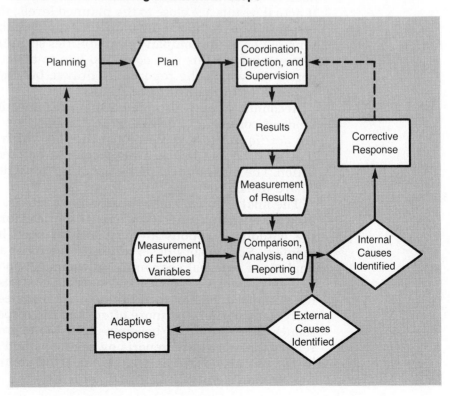

trol stage. Control by feedback response begins with the measurement of actual results, shown by the oval in the center of the diagram. These measurements are merged with data from the plan and with current external data to determine and, where feasible, to analyze the causes of deviations from the plan. The reports which are at the core of responsive control are often referred to as *scorecard controls.*

The differences from planned results are reported to management and interpreted to determine what responses are appropriate. A *corrective response,* consisting of a change in the way the plan is carried out, is appropriate when the departure from the plan is due to errors in the plan's execution. The linkage in the diagram is to the action stage of the control process, reflecting management's need to change the way it implements the plan.

An *adaptive response,* consisting of a revision in the planned actions or planned results for the next period, is suitable when the departure from the plan is due either to changes in external conditions or to errors in forecasting the state of the environment. The linkage here takes us back up the left side of the diagram to the planning stage of the control process, reflecting management's need to revise the plan to conform to the conditions now expected. If actual results are close to the planned levels, the proper adaptive response is to reconfirm the plan, unless major changes in the environment or in the company's capabilities seem imminent. Responsive controls of this sort come too late to affect the profits of the period for which the reports are drawn, but they are intended to improve performance in the future.

Accountants may also play a role in connection with two other kinds of controls not described in Exhibit 21–4. The first of these are *yes/no controls*—preestablished rules which list the conditions that must be met before a manager can proceed with a proposed action. The maximum capital-spending limits identified in Chapter 20 are yes/no controls.

The final group of controls, *steering controls,* consists of signals used to help management *anticipate* the need for action (or confirm the wisdom of actions already decided upon but not yet implemented). Supervisory observation is one form of steering control; analysis of external economic indicators is another.

Both responsive controls and steering controls use data on what has happened. The main differences are that steering controls typically come earlier and more often, and the response, if any, comes sooner. The similarity becomes even more pronounced once we realize that scorecard reports on segments and activities at lower levels can also serve as signals (steering controls) for action by higher management.

INTERDIVISIONAL TRANSFER PRICING

Profit centers and other organization units for which profit-performance measures must be prepared often buy from and sell to one another. The prices at which these interdivisional transactions are recorded are known as *transfer prices*. These prices can affect the amount of profit each division reports.

Criteria for transfer pricing

The first criterion to be observed in setting transfer prices is that *the transfer price should lead division management to make the same decisions headquarters management would make if it had the time to study the problems and apply all the data available to the managers of both divisions.* The second criterion is that *division managers should be able to regard the transfer prices as fair.* If managers doubt the fairness of the transfer prices, they may be less motivated to achieve profits for their divisions and the company as a whole.

Neither of these two criteria makes any reference to the effects of transfer prices on taxes or other fiscal variables. If fiscal considerations require the use of transfer prices which fail to meet the two managerially oriented criteria we've identified, management may try to find economical ways of maintaining two parallel transfer-pricing systems.

Transfer-pricing methods

Management has several transfer-pricing methods to choose from. We'll examine three of these:

1. Dictated prices equal to full cost.
2. Dictated prices equal to marginal cost.
3. Market-based negotiated prices.

Dictated prices equal to full cost. Under this pricing method, the pricing authority (higher management or one of the two divisions) establishes a price, which is then used to record transfers. The implicit assumption is that a transfer price set in this way measures the supplying division's long-run incremental cost of supplying the intermediate product on a continuing basis.

Even if a particular set of full-cost-based prices approximates long-run incremental cost, it will fail to provide a sound guide to current resource-utilization decisions, as required by our first design criterion. As long as a supplying division is operating below capacity—that is, in the portion of the volume range in which average cost exceeds the cost of a one-unit increase in volume—transfer prices based on full cost will overstate the supplying division's economic sacrifice and suboptimization may result.

The situation will be just the reverse if the supplying division is pressing its capacity limits. At full capacity, the market value of the intermediate product is likely to be higher than average full cost. If the transfer price is based on full cost, the buying division will receive a signal that understates the sacrifice the company makes in making the intermediate product available to the buying division. A forced transfer at this price may be suboptimal and will be perceived as unfair by the supplying division manager.

Dictated prices equal to marginal cost.   Under this pricing method, the division supplying the goods to be transferred quotes a schedule of prices equal to its estimated marginal costs of production. *Marginal cost* at any volume is the increase in total cost which is necessary to increase total volume by a single unit. The division wishing to use the goods decides how many units it wishes to buy, given the quoted price schedule.

When the supplying division is operating at capacity, marginal cost measures the sacrifice the supplying division (and therefore the company) makes by supplying the product. When the supplying division is operating at capacity, however, it is likely to be able to use its capacity to produce and sell products at prices exceeding marginal cost. The division's sacrifice therefore is measured by opportunity cost—the current market value of the amount of capacity the transferred product uses up. The buying division shouldn't be allowed to use the transferred product unless it can afford to pay this opportunity cost. Marginal cost understates opportunity cost in this situation and therefore fails to meet the first transfer-pricing criterion: congruence with top management's decision rules.

Marginal-cost transfer prices are also likely to seem unfair to one division manager or the other—or both. For one thing, the use of marginal cost implies that neither division can influence the price. Division managers therefore have no control over this variable. This abrogation of authority is likely to weaken the managers' perception of the fairness of the system. Furthermore, if volume is low enough so that marginal cost is lower than average full cost, most of the profit contribution of internally transferred goods will be lodged in the internal buying division. The supplying division manager therefore may find it more difficult to justify capital-expenditure proposals. If the system is seen to discriminate against the supplying division in this way, this may reduce its manager's commitment to the system's objectives.

Market-based negotiated prices.   In negotiated transfer pricing, the two divisions negotiate the amounts to be transferred and the prices

EXHIBIT 21–5. Market Influences on Transfer-Pricing Negotiations

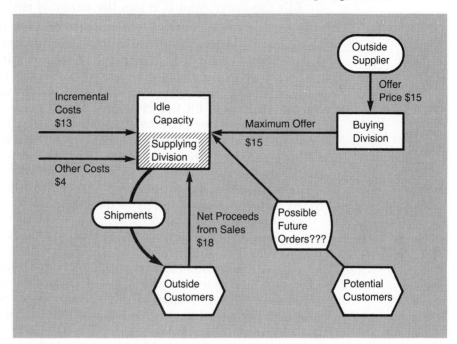

to be paid. Negotiated systems are based on the notion that the division managers, with intimate knowledge of their own markets and opportunities, are in the best position to decide whether internal transfers will take place. Part of the division manager's job is to be aware of market conditions affecting the division's operations. Each division manager is expected to make many decisions in which estimates of opportunity cost are crucial. The internal transfer decision is simply one of many.

A simple situation of this kind is illustrated in Exhibit 21–5. This shows a supplying division with average total costs of $17 and some outside customers paying enough to yield $18 a unit after marketing costs are deducted. The shaded area in the block representing the supplying division is the amount of capacity now devoted to filling outside customers' orders; the rest is idle.

The buying division has an opportunity to buy the product from an outside supplier for $15 and has offered to pay this amount to the supplying division. The situation can be summarized quickly:

1. The buying division won't buy at a higher price.
2. It appears that the company will be better off if the transfer takes place (cost will be $13, not $15).

3. The supplying division will be $2 better off ($15 − $13) if it fills the order than if it lets the capacity stand idle.

In these circumstances it would seem that the two division managers have a mutual interest in reaching agreement on a transfer price. They should fail to agree only if the supplying division's manager estimates that the potential customers in the lower right-hand corner of the diagram are likely to come in with higher-priced orders which will fill the division's capacity.

Division managers are paid to exercise their judgment in situations like this. They are expected to be right often enough to justify giving them the authority to make these decisions. The presumption is that the managers will negotiate an agreement if interdivisional transfers seem to be in the company's best interests, because both managers will benefit if this is the case.

Negotiation should also contribute to the participants' sense of the fairness of the system, if the conditions necessary to negotiation are present. Without negotiation, internal transfers are either take-it-or-leave-it decisions or command decisions made by higher management. In either case the division managers' freedom of action is reduced, and this reduces their accountability for profit. Negotiation restores the managers' freedom of action and thereby increases their accountability for profits.

Negotiation will work, however, only if four conditions are met:

1. There must be some form of outside market for the intermediate product.
2. Any available market information should be communicated to both parties to the negotiation.
3. Both parties must have freedom to deal outside.
4. Top management must indicate its support of the principle of negotiation.

Negotiation can be time-consuming and divisive, even when the four conditions are met. If these problems are serious enough, top management may decide to fall back on another transfer-pricing method, relying on other devices to offset the weaknesses of any such method.[3]

SUMMARY

Planning needs to be reinforced by control activities. Managerial accounting provides scorecard control information, primarily for use in managerial and economic evaluation of individual managers and activities. These control reports emphasize the differences be-

---

[3] For a more complete discussion of transfer pricing and a review of other methods, see Gordon Shillinglaw, *Managerial Cost Accounting*, 5th ed. (Homewood, Ill.: Richard D. Irwin, Inc., 1982), chap. 26.

tween actual results and appropriate performance standards for individual segments of the company's activities.

The major organization segments in decentralized companies are known as profit centers, designed to operate, within limits, much as independent businesses. The performance of a profit center is appraised primarily on the basis of comparisons of actual profit or return on investment with an appropriate performance standard. The appropriate performance standard for economic evaluation is the cost of capital; the relevant standard for managerial evaluation is the current profit plan, adjusted for any changes in economic conditions that were not anticipated in the plan.

The profit performance of a profit center may be measured by its profit contribution, its net income, its return on investment, or its residual income. Only return on investment and residual income encompass all the variables attributable to the profit center or controllable by its managers. Unfortunately, each of these measures also includes allocations of centrally administered assets and headquarters expenses, and these allocations may be neither attributable to the division's activities nor controllable by the division's management.

When a profit center transfers part of its output to or receives goods or services from another part of the company, the transfer is recorded by a transfer price. This price can be set by negotiation between the parties to the transfer if outside markets exist and other conditions are met; otherwise, some system abrogating a portion of the divisions' autonomy must be used.

Profit decentralization is designed to provide the motivation and flexibility to improve the company's profitability. A danger is that managers may sacrifice the company's long-term interests to increase the divisions' short-term profits. The use of multiple performance objectives and centrally administered constraints and guidelines should help counteract any such tendencies.

KEY TERMS

Adaptive response
Control
Corrective response
Decentralization
Divisional income
Economic evaluation
Feedback
Managerial evaluation
Marginal cost
Profit center

Profit contribution
Profit variance
Residual income
Responsive control
Return on investment (ROI)
Scorecard controls
Steering controls
Transfer price
Yes/no controls

INDEPENDENT STUDY PROBLEMS (Solutions in Appendix B)

1. Scorecard and steering controls. Prairie Airways, Inc., provides scheduled passenger airline service connecting Chicago with 14 other airports in the Midwest. It operates 18 flights each weekday and 10 flights each Saturday and Sunday. Each flight either originates or terminates in Chicago; some are nonstop but most take two or more stops on the way to or from Chicago.

Prairie Airways has a small staff of ground personnel at each airport it serves. Routine maintenance of its aircraft is performed on contract in Chicago by a major airline.

What kinds of steering control and scorecard control information do you think Prairie's management should have?

2. Managerial evaluation: residual income. The investment in division A consists of $200,000 in traceable working capital, $400,000 in traceable plant and equipment, and $100,000 in centrally administered assets, allocated to the division at a rate of one sixth of traceable investment. The budgeted amounts for these three totals were $150,000, $420,000, and $95,000.

Division A's net income for the year is $63,000, after deducting $30,000 in traceable depreciation, $40,000 in head-office charges (allocated to the division at the rate of 5 percent of sales), and income taxes at 50 percent. The budgeted amounts were $70,000, $32,000, $45,000, and 50 percent.

The company estimates that its minimum acceptable rate of return is 12 percent, after taxes.

a. Calculate budgeted and actual return on investment.
b. Calculate budgeted and actual residual income.
c. Discuss the division manager's performance. Explain why the information provided by your answer to part *a,* your answer to part *b,* or some other calculation is relevant to managerial evaluation.
d. What action should management take in response to your evaluation of this division's activities, based on the figures supplied here?

3. Transfer pricing; negotiation. Ballou Corporation, a diversified manufacturing company, has seven main product divisions, each with its own manufacturing facilities and selling most of its output to outside customers. One of these divisions, the Hull Division, manufactures and sells a broad range of industrial chemicals.

Hull Division supplies product X to outside customers and also to the Hingham Division, another of Ballou's seven product divisions. Hingham Division uses product X as a raw material in the manufacture of several products. Hull charges Hingham $1.80 a pound for product X, 10 percent less than it charges outside customers.

Hingham has been happy with this arrangement for several years, but an outside supplier has just offered to supply a perfectly satisfactory substitute for product X at a firm contract price of $1.60 a pound, delivered at the Hingham factory. The Hingham Division manager has proposed that the interdivisional transfer price of product X be reduced to $1.60 to meet the competing offer; otherwise, the contract will go outside.

You are the assistant controller in the Hingham Division. Your division manager has just given you a copy of Hull Division's estimated monthly income statement for product X (in $000):

Sales—outside (100,000 lbs. at $2)		$200
Sales—Hingham (50,000 lbs. at $1.80)		90
Total sales		290
Product-traceable costs:		
Variable manufacturing costs ($0.90 per lb.)	$135	
Sales commissions—outside sales	10	
Depreciation	20	
Other traceable fixed costs	40	205
Product profit contribution		85
Share of divisional fixed costs		60
Income before taxes		$ 25

The fixed costs traceable to product X wouldn't be reduced if the production volume were reduced by a third. The divisional fixed costs, allocated among the division's products at a flat 40 cents a pound, are even stickier. These costs would continue even if Hull Division stopped making product X entirely.

a. Draft a short memorandum, outlining the points Hingham's manager should make in trying to convince Hull's manager to reduce the transfer price.

b. Is negotiation the right way to determine a transfer price in this situation?

EXERCISES AND PROBLEMS

4. **Steering and scorecard controls.** The manager of a chain of motion-picture theaters relies on written reports to keep informed about the operations of the individual theaters. Films are booked for a week at a time, with an unlimited renewal option. Runs of six to eight weeks are not uncommon, but many films are replaced at the end of one week. The film shown at one theater may also be shown at one or more others in the chain, but a separate booking decision is made at each theater each week.

Each theater has a manager responsible for maintaining and operating the theater. Employees are hired by the local manager, but salaries must be approved by the chain manager. The chain manager selects the films to be shown, makes all the booking decisions, hires the theater managers, and controls all advertising and sales promotion activities.

a. What reports is the chain manager likely to find useful? Indicate how each of these reports would be used and whether you regard it as a steering control or a scorecard control.

b. What would you report to the individual theater managers, and how frequently would you report it? Indicate how the manager would use this information and whether it would be steering control or scorecard control information.

c. To what extent should the theater managers be held responsible for income from sale of refreshments? How would you evaluate their performance?

5. Planning and control information; role of accounting. Helen and Hilda Haldi, former Olympic downhill skiers, were hired by Haddon Hill Associates to manage the Haddon Hill ski area. Their facilities included restaurants, shops, ski lifts, snowmaking and grooming equipment, and five downhill ski runs. They also ran a full instruction program for children and adults.

The Haldi sisters were expected to decide when to open or close individual lifts, slopes, restaurants, and other customer service facilities. They hired and supervised the work of a controller and the heads of Haddon Hill's three operating departments: the restaurant manager, the chief ski instructor, and the maintenance manager. The chief instructor was in charge of all customer service activities except the restaurants, lifts, and ski runs. The maintenance manager was responsible for all maintenance of physical plant and equipment and for the operation of lifts and ski runs. The chief instructor also organized and supervised the ski patrol and first-aid operations.

The department heads determined how many employees they would need in their departments each day, following guidelines the Haldi sisters had established at the beginning of the season. Each department head was expected to control costs, maintain the quality of the services provided, hire and fire employees, and maintain effective employee relations. The restaurant manager and chief instructor were also expected to produce revenues in excess of the costs of operating their departments.

a. Outline the kinds of information the Haldi sisters probably received when they were planning for this year's skiing season and state how they probably used it. In what format (that is, what kinds of items and how much detail) did they probably express their financial plan for the year?

b. What kinds of financial information would management probably require during the skiing season? How often would this information be reported and to whom? What kinds of actions would you expect management to take in response to this information?

c. What part would you expect the controller (chief accounting officer) of the Haddon Hill ski area to play in the planning and control process?

6. Preparing a profit-contribution statement. Morgan Wicker Company markets three products. You have the following information (in $000):

	Product A	Product B	Product C
Contribution margin (percentage of sales)	40%	30%	45%
Sales revenues	$10,000	$8,000	$6,000
Fixed expenses*	2,000	2,300	3,100

*Includes allocations of nontraceable fixed costs at the rate of 10 percent of sales revenues.

a. Prepare a profit-contribution statement, with a separate column for each product and one column for the company as a whole.

b. Comment briefly on the profitability of each product.

7. Usefulness of profit-contribution reports. Epsom Company's plastics division is the company's largest division, both in sales volume and in profit contribution. The plastics division's marketing vice president received the following report on operations in the division's 10 sales districts in October (in $000):

District	Sales Amount	Sales Over/(Under) Budget	Profit Contribution Amount	Profit Contribution Over/(Under) Budget
Boston............	$ 220	$ (10)	$ 59	$ 4
New York	380	(20)	110	1
Pittsburgh	170	(30)	24	(16)
Atlanta............	340	20	91	6
Chicago...........	210	(40)	46	(9)
New Orleans	140	(10)	18	(6)
Denver	90	(30)	10	—
Dallas	120	—	21	11
Los Angeles	290	(10)	66	6
Seattle...........	130	(30)	25	(15)
Total	$2,090	$(160)	$470	$(18)

Each sales district is headed by a district manager who is responsible for selling the division's products to customers in the district. The district managers report to the marketing vice president, who also has a small central staff. All products are manufactured in the plastics division's factories under the general direction and supervision of the division's manufacturing vice president.

Divisional expenses (marketing, manufacturing, and administration) other than those reflected in the district profit contributions averaged 12 percent of sales in October. This percentage included both direct and indirect divisional expenses.

a. Give at least one example of a direct divisional expense and one example of an indirect divisional expense which isn't reflected in the district profit-contribution amounts, and explain why it isn't reflected there.

b. How would you expect the marketing vice president to use the sales district profit-contribution report? What significant facts does the October report reveal, and how would you expect the marketing vice president to respond to it?

c. How well does the $470,000 total of the district profit contributions measure managerial performance and economic performance in the plastics division? What additional amounts would you incorporate in the report if it is to be used for these purposes?

8. Calculating and interpreting residual income and return on investment. Thompson Enterprises regards 10 percent after taxes as the minimum acceptable rate of return on capital expenditures. You have the following data for the Digby division for the last three years:

	19x1 Actual	19x1 Budget	19x2 Actual	19x2 Budget	19x3 Actual	19x3 Budget
Net income	$ 500	$ 480	$ 700	$ 650	$1,000	$ 950
Net investment.....	2,500	2,500	4,000	3,800	6,400	6,300

a. Calculate budgeted and actual residual income and return on investment for each year.
b. Assuming that allocations haven't distorted the division's results materially, what do these data tell you about managerial performance and investment performance in this division?

9. Allocating indirect fixed costs. Localio Products Company has three divisions operating as profit centers and three central administrative departments operating as service centers. You have the following information on the three profit centers:

	Western Division	Central Division	Eastern Division	Total
Sales revenues	$2,000,000	$5,000,000	$3,000,000	$10,000,000
Profit contribution	300,000	1,200,000	1,100,000	2,600,000
Investment	1,500,000	4,000,000	3,500,000	9,000,000
Number of employees	1,250	2,500	1,250	5,000

The operating costs of the three administrative departments were:

Accounting	$300,000
Marketing	250,000
Executive offices	360,000

The income tax rate is 40 percent.

a. Calculate the return on investment in each division, allocating the costs of the three administrative departments on the following bases: accounting, number of employees; marketing, sales revenues; executive offices, investment.
b. Do these allocations give you a better basis for managerial evaluation or investment evaluation than you would have in their absence? As part of your answer, identify the criterion you believe should underlie allocations for each of these purposes.

10. Discussion question: identifying profit centers. Carnegie Improvements, Inc., buys parcels of land and builds condominium housing developments on them. Once a parcel of land has been bought, a manager is appointed to supervise construction and marketing operations at that development and to manage the commercial and recreational facilities in the development until it is completed and all facilities are sold.

Building plans for each development are drawn up by the headquarters design department. Most building materials are selected and bought by a central purchasing department, and the terms of sale of condominium units are established by Carnegie's central management. Central management also establishes the selling-price schedule, although the local manager is authorized to reduce individual offering prices by as much as 10 percent if this seems necessary to get condominium units sold.

a. What problems would have to be solved before income or return on investment could be calculated for a condominium development?
b. Should the individual developments be classified as profit centers? Indicate the elements in this situation affecting your answer.

11. Departmental evaluation. Lawrence & Company, an old-line investment banking firm, has hired three highly regarded recent business-school graduates to join its professional staff at annual salaries of $40,000 each. Each of the firm's seven operating departments is interested in having at least one of the new hires become a full-time member of its staff.

As a means of determining which departments will receive the new employees, the chairman of the board has proposed having three auctions, one for each new employee. In each auction, the department bidding the most money would win the auctioned employee. Although no money would change hands, the amount of each winning bid would become part of the victor's investment base in return-on-investment calculations. The new employee's salary would become an expense of the winning department. Each auction would occur after the winner of the previous auction was announced.

a. Would this system be consistent with the company's system of evaluating its departments and their managers on the basis of their reported return on investment? Explain.

b. What are the likely costs and benefits of this approach—to the firm, to the victorious departments, and to the new employees themselves?

12. Comparison of two divisions. BIG Industries, Inc., is a decentralized, multidivision company. The following data summarize the operations of two of BIG's divisions (Able and Baker) in 19x1:

	Able Division		Baker Division	
	Actual	Budget	Actual	Budget
Net sales	$110	$100	$280	$300
Cost of goods sold*	44	40	150	150
Selling and administrative expense	30	30	80	80
Income before taxes	$ 36	$ 30	$ 50	$ 70
* Including depreciation	10	10	12	12

The following amounts were taken from the two divisions' balance sheets of December 31, 19x1:

	Able Division		Baker Division	
	Actual	Budget	Actual	Budget
Current assets	$150	$140	$100	$105
Fixed assets (cost)	220	218	275	275
Accumulated depreciation	176	177	25	25
Current liabilities	50	45	50	55

During 19x1 the market conditions facing each division were about what had been expected when the 19x1 budgets were drawn up. The company estimated that its pretax cost of capital in 19x1 was about 20 percent.

a. Which division is in the more profitable business? Cite numbers to support your conclusions and defend the measures you have chosen.

b. Which division manager is doing the better job of running the division?

Again cite numbers to support your conclusions and defend the measures you have chosen.

(Prepared by Michael Ginzberg)

13. Evaluating managerial performance.   Harry Keeler was the president of Anorak, Inc., a manufacturer of consumer goods. The income statements for the company's two divisions indicated that division A was highly profitable, while division B was a break-even operation at best.

Keeler was due to retire soon, and the board of directors was examining the credentials of the two division managers. Both had been with the company for many years and had enviable performance records in other positions before being named to head their respective divisions.

Both division managers seemed to have organizational ability, and employee morale in both divisions was extremely good. Both were well liked by the board members and seemed capable of representing the company effectively in dealings with outsiders.

The main difference between the two seemed to be that the manager of division A was able to generate profits, while the manager of division B could not. The following divisional income statements were prepared for the month of September:

	Division A		Division B	
	Actual	Budget	Actual	Budget
Sales revenues	$1,000,000	$1,050,000	$500,000	$490,000
Cost of goods sold...............	600,000	630,000	400,000	395,000
Gross margin.....................	400,000	420,000	100,000	95,000
Operating expenses:				
Marketing and selling	100,000	95,000	50,000	50,000
Divisional administration	50,000	48,000	40,000	45,000
Head-office expense	42,000	41,000	21,000	19,000
Income taxes	85,000	94,000	(5,000)	(8,000)
Total operating expenses	277,000	278,000	106,000	106,000
Net income (loss)	$ 123,000	$ 142,000	$(6,000)	$(11,000)

The following assets and liabilities were traced or assigned to these divisions at the end of September:

	Division A		Division B	
	Actual	Budget	Actual	Budget
Directly traceable:				
Accounts receivable	$1,200,000	$1,200,000	$ 500,000	$ 520,000
Inventories	1,100,000	1,100,000	800,000	860,000
Plant and equipment	700,000	700,000	300,000	300,000
Accounts payable	(900,000)	(900,000)	(600,000)	(580,000)
Net traceable assets	2,100,000	2,100,000	1,000,000	1,100,000
Allocated (percentage of sales):				
Cash	400,000	389,000	200,000	181,000
Headquarters buildings, furniture, and equipment	300,000	307,000	150,000	143,000
Net assets	$2,800,000	$2,796,000	$1,350,000	$1,424,000

Additional information:

1. Each division is operated as a profit center. Each division manufactures all its products in its own factories and sells them through its own sales force.
2. The income statement comparisons for the year to date revealed similar relationships to those in the statements for September.
3. The company used a minimum aftertax rate of return on investment of 12 percent in evaluating new capital-expenditure proposals.
4. Head-office expenses were allocated to product lines in proportion to actual sales.
5. Market conditions for the products sold by both divisions were very close to those forecast at the beginning of the year.
6. The market for division B's products appeared unlikely to show any major improvement for some time. Barring a radical change in the market or the introduction of a major new product, industry sales were likely to remain at or near their current levels for some time.
7. The market for division A's products had been growing dramatically for several years, but the industry's growth had abated during this year, as anticipated.

Do these statements indicate that the manager of division A had a clearly superior profit performance in September? Prepare a summary report, showing, insofar as you can, the relative profit performance of the two managers, with your interpretation of the amounts you are assigning to each.

14. Supplementing divisional profit information. Monica Davis, a member of the board of directors of Anorak, Inc. (see problem 13) asked the company's controller for more information to help evaluate the qualifications of the two division managers. The controller provided the following data for the nine months in the year to date (19x4) and for the first nine months of 19x1, when both managers were fairly new to their present positions (no budget data were available for these items):

	Division A		Division B	
	19x1	19x4	19x1	19x4
Sales revenues	$7,200,000	$8,950,000	$3,950,000	$4,300,000
Research and development expense (included in divisional administration expense)	245,000	305,000	140,000	110,000
Product-warranty expense (included in marketing and selling expense)	210,000	195,000	45,000	90,000
Training and management development expenses (included in divisional administration expense) ..	36,000	42,000	26,000	27,000
Market share	10%	10%	8%	6%
Number of customers served	106	193	85	12
Employee turnover (percentage of work force)	8%	7%	5%	10%
Absenteeism (percentage of hours worked)	5%	4%	5%	8%

a. Use this information to throw additional light on the performance of Anorak's two division managers.
b. To what extent would comparisons of these statistics with budgeted amounts have helped you answer part *a*? Explain the role of budgeted data of this sort.
c. What conclusions can you draw from your analysis of the additional data in this problem as to the adequacy or relevance of divisional profit information to the evaluation of managerial performance?

15. Transfer pricing.   Caplow Company is a multidivision company, and its division managers have been given full profit responsibility and complete autonomy to accept or reject transfers to or from other divisions. Division A's factories manufacture a large number of products and most of these are sold to outside customers by division A's own sales force.

One of division A's products, accounting for about 10 percent of the division's sales, is a subassembly. Most of these subassemblies are sold at a price of $700 each to outside customers, in competition with roughly similar products marketed by other companies. Some of division A's subassemblies are now being sold to division B, however, for use in a final product (one subassembly per unit), which it sells outside at a price of $1,200 a unit. Division A charges division B $700 a unit for the subassembly, the same price it charges outside customers. Variable costs of the subassembly are $520 a unit in division A; division B's variable costs of the final product (excluding subassembly costs) are $600 a unit. Total fixed costs in the two divisions are unaffected by the volume of business represented by this subassembly or the final product made from it. Although other manufacturers make subassemblies of roughly similar design, they have features which prevent their use in division B's final product; that is, suitable subassemblies aren't available from any outside supplier.

Division B's manager feels that division A should transfer the subassembly at a price lower than market because division B is unable to make a profit if it has to pay the market price.

a. Calculate division B's profit contribution from the sale of a unit of the final product if transfers are made at the $700 price; also calculate the total profit contribution to the company of the sale of a unit of the final product.
b. Assume division A can sell all its production in the open market at a price of $700 a unit. Should division A transfer goods to division B? If so, at what price?
c. Assume division A can produce 1,000 units a month but can sell only 500 units in the open market at $700 each. A 20 percent price reduction would be necessary to sell full capacity. Division B could sell as many as 1,000 units of the final product at the $1,200 price. Should transfers be made? If so, how many units should be transferred and at what price? Submit a schedule showing comparisons of profit contribution under three different alternatives to support your decision.
d. Is negotiation between division A and division B likely to be an appro-

priate way to establish an economically sound transfer price in this situation? Explain why or why not.

(SMAC adapted)

16. Transfer pricing; selecting a source of supply. Gunnco Corporation has several divisions operating as profit centers. Two are the Ajax and Defco divisions. Each division sells most of its output to customers outside the Gunnco group.

Divisional residual income is used in the periodic evaluations of the performance of the divisions and of the division managers. Residual income for each division is calculated by deducting interest at a pretax annual rate of 18 percent on Gunnco's net investment in the division.

The Ajax division is now operating at capacity, meaning that it could expand its total production and sales volume in the near term only at a very high cost. Defco, on the other hand, is now operating at only 50 percent of its capacity, with many of its production employees either on unpaid furlough or on a short workweek. The division's administrative and clerical staffs have not been cut, with the result that a good deal of administrative capacity is idle.

Defco's manager is actively seeking profitable ways to utilize the division's idle capacity. A commercial airplane manufacturer has offered to buy 1,000 brake units from Defco, to be delivered during the next 12 months at a price of $52.50 each. Defco could meet this delivery schedule without difficulty. Defco's management sees this order as an opportunity to penetrate a new market which holds promise of substantial future growth, and is anxious to meet the price, if at all possible. Defco's estimated cost of the brake unit is as follows:

Purchased parts—outside vendors	$22.50
Ajax electrical fitting No. 1726	5.00
Other variable costs	14.00
Fixed overhead and administration	8.00
Total cost per unit	$49.50

Defco's total fixed overhead and administrative costs are unlikely to increase as a result of the brake unit order, but Defco's management believes any business it takes on should cover its fair share of the division's costs.

Defco's management estimates that $5,000 in additional working capital would be required to support the brake unit business.

The Ajax fitting required for this brake unit would be supplied by the Ajax division. This fitting is now being produced and sold to Ajax's outside customers at a price of $7.50 each, and approximately 10,000 of these fittings are likely to be sold this year at that price. Ajax's variable cost of producing fitting No. 1726 is $4.25 each. Estimated fixed cost is $1.25 a unit.

Other transfers to Defco now account for about 5 percent of Ajax's total volume; the transfer prices negotiated for these are generally the prices Ajax charges its outside customers for the same products. These prices aren't in dispute.

Defco could obtain roughly similar fittings from outside suppliers for about $7.50, the same price Ajax charges. If it had to pay this much, however, Defco's profit margin on the brake unit would virtually disappear.

Since Defco's marketing people see no possibility of getting a higher price for the brake units, Defco's manager has asked the Ajax manager to supply these fittings at a price of $5 each.

a. As the Ajax division controller, would you recommend that Ajax supply fitting No. 1726 to Defco at the $5 price? Cite figures and explain your reasoning in two or three well-chosen sentences. (Ignore income taxes.)

b. Suppose Ajax refuses to sell at any price less than $7.50. As the Defco division controller, would you recommend paying this price? Again cite figures and explain your reasoning.

c. As the Gunnco corporate controller, would you recommend that top management classify this item as one for which the transfer price should be set by top management? Give a brief explanation of your reasoning.

(CMA adapted)

17. Divisional performance, inflation impact. Argus Corporation is a diversified company operating four divisions, each competing in a different market: lumber, chemicals, rail equipment, and consumer retail stores. In each of the past five years (19x1–19x5) the consumer retail division has generated a higher ratio of contribution margin to sales, profit contribution to sales, and return on investment than any other division.

Argus isn't large enough to be required to prepare and disclose FASB-mandated information about the effects of changing prices (see Chapter 14). The corporate controller, however, believes that the consumer retail division may be the one Argus segment most directly and significantly affected by economy-wide inflation. The controller suggests that management take changes in the consumer price index (CPI) into consideration when it evaluates the profit performance of this one division.

The following data have been extracted from the consumer retail division's annual submissions for the past five years (in $ millions), together with the average consumer price index (1967 = 100.0):

	19x1	19x2	19x3	19x4	19x5
Sales revenue	$ 20	$ 25	$ 37	$ 49	$ 60
Identifiable net assets	6.0	6.6	7.5	8.2	8.5
Contribution margin	2.0	3.75	4.0	4.75	5.0
Profit contribution	1.5	1.8	2.3	2.2	2.7
Average CPI	181.5	195.4	217.4	246.8	272.3

a. Using the consumer price index, restate the historical amounts in constant dollars of 19x5 purchasing power. (See Chapter 14 for a brief description of this technique.)

b. What conclusions can you draw from these adjusted data about the impact of inflation on the consumer retail division's reported results? How meaningful are the adjustments you have made? What additional information would you find helpful?

18. Effect of return-on-investment measures on decisions.[4] Percy Jones, managing director of Orkney Biscuit Company, Ltd., is trying to decide

_____
[4] Copyright 1968 by l'Institut pour l'Etude des Méthodes de Direction de l'Entreprise (IMEDE), Lausanne, Switzerland. Published by permission.

EXHIBIT 1. Income Forecast for New Product Line

Year	(1) Forecasted Incremental Cash Flow from Operations	(2) Depreciation on New Equipment	(3) Forecasted Incremental Income before Tax (1) − (2)	(4) Income Tax at 40%*	(5) Forecasted Incremental Net Income after Tax (3) − (4)
1	−$ 350,000	$50,000	−$400,000	−$160,000	−$240,000
2	− 100,000	50,000	− 150,000	− 60,000	− 90,000
3	0	50,000	− 50,000	− 20,000	− 30,000
4	+ 200,000	50,000	+ 150,000	60,000	90,000
5	+ 500,000	50,000	+ 450,000	180,000	270,000
6	+ 1,000,000	50,000	+ 950,000	380,000	570,000
7	+ 900,000	50,000	+ 850,000	340,000	510,000
8	+ 650,000	50,000	+ 600,000	240,000	360,000

* When income before taxes is negative, the company is entitled to a tax rebate at 40 percent, either from taxes paid in previous years or from taxes currently due on other company operations.

whether to expand the company by adding an entirely new and different product line. The proposal seems likely to be profitable, and adequate funds can be obtained from outside investors to finance the new venture.

Orkney Biscuit has long been regarded as a well-managed company. It has succeeded in keeping its present product lines up to date and has maintained a small but profitable position in a highly competitive industry.

The amount of capital used by the company in support of its present operations is approximately $4 million, and it is expected to remain at this level whether the proposal for the new product line is accepted or rejected. Net income from these existing operations now amounts to about $400,000 a year, and Jones's best forecast of the future is that this will continue to be the income from present operations, regardless of whether the new product line is introduced or rejected.

Introduction of the new product line would require an immediate investment of $400,000 in equipment and $250,000 in additional working capital. A further $100,000 in working capital would be required a year later.

Sales of the new product line would be relatively low during the first year but would increase steadily until the sixth year. After that, changing tastes and increased competition would probably begin to reduce annual sales. After eight years, the product line would probably be withdrawn from the market. At that time, the company would sell the equipment for its scrap value and liquidate the working capital. The cash value of the equipment and working capital at that time would be about $350,000.

The low initial sales volume, combined with heavy promotional outlays, would lead to heavy losses in the first two years, and no net income would be reported until the fourth year. The profit forecasts for the new product line are summarized in Exhibit 1.

Using these figures, Jones has prepared the cash-flow analysis summarized in Exhibit 2. Investment cash flow, shown in the first column, is added to the operating cash flows in column (2) [from Exhibit 1, column (1)]. The total is then adjusted for income taxes and discounted to find

EXHIBIT 2. Orkney Biscuit Company, Ltd.*: Present Value of New Product Proposal (in $000)

Year	(1)† Investment Cash Flows	(2) Operating Cash Flows	(3) Total Cash Flow before Tax (1)+(2)	(4)‡ Tax Depreciation	(5)§ Taxable Income (2)−(4)	(6) Income Tax 40% of (5)	(7) Cash Flow after Tax (3)−(6)	(8)‖ Present Value Factor at 10%	(9) Present Value at 10% (7)×(8)
1	−650	− 350	−1,000	50	− 400	−160	− 840	0.9516	−799
2	−100	− 100	− 200	50	− 150	− 60	− 140	0.8611	−121
3	0	0	0	50	− 50	− 20	+ 20	0.7791	+ 16
4	0	+ 200	+ 200	50	+ 150	60	+ 140	0.7050	+ 99
5	0	+ 500	+ 500	50	+ 450	180	+ 320	0.6379	+204
6	0	+1,000	+1,000	50	+ 950	380	+ 620	0.5772	+358
7	0	+ 900	+ 900	50	+ 850	340	+ 560	0.5223	+292
8	+350	+ 650	+1,000	50	+ 600	240	+ 760	0.4726	+359
Total	−400	+2,800	+2,400	400	+2,400	960	+1,440		+408

* IMPORTANT NOTE: This exhibit is provided for later reference. It need not be reviewed prior to an analysis of the questions raised at the end of the problem.
† The first year's outlay consists of $400,000 for equipment and $250,000 for working capital. An additional working-capital outlay of $100,000 is required in the second year. Working-capital outlays are completely recovered in the eighth year.
‡ One eighth of the equipment costs are recorded each year as depreciation. Orkney Biscuit Company operates in a country which requires the use of straight-line depreciation for tax purposes.
§ When taxable income is negative, the company is entitled to a tax rebate at 40 percent, either from taxes paid in prior years or from taxes currently due on other company operations.
‖ These interest factors are based on the assumption that each year's cash flow is spread uniformly throughout the year. They differ slightly, therefore, from those in Appendix A.

its present value at a 10 percent rate. These present values are shown in the right-hand column of Exhibit 2.

As Exhibit 2 shows, the present value of the anticipated cash receipts from the new product line exceeds the present value of the anticipated cash outlays by $408,000.

Jones seldom has an opportunity to invest funds as profitably as this, and he would like to approve this investment proposal. He is concerned by its effect on Orkney Biscuit's reported rate of return on investment, however. His accountants have given him the following figures (in $000):

Year	Total Investment, Start of Year	Net Income after Tax	Reported Return on Investment
1	$4,000	$160	4.0%
2	4,600	310	6.7
3	4,650	370	8.0
4	4,600	490	10.7
5	4,550	670	14.7
6	4,500	970	21.6
7	4,450	910	20.4
8	4,400	760	17.3

The accountants explain that they have obtained the forecasted net income by adding the forecasted aftertax net income for the new product line [Exhibit 1, column (5)] to $400,000, the forecasted net income on the company's other product lines. They have obtained the total investment figures by adding $4 million to the investment outlays on equipment and working capital [Exhibit 2, column (1), cumulated] and subtracting depreciation on the new equipment [Exhibit 2, column (4), cumulated].

a. To what extent, if any, would the low anticipated rate of return on investment in the first three years be likely to affect the decision to launch the new product line if Orkney Biscuit is a private company, owned entirely by Jones?

b. How would your answer differ if you found that the Orkney Biscuit Company is a publicly owned company, with shares owned by a large number of small investors, and Jones is purely a salaried administrator?

c. How would your answer differ if the Orkney Biscuit Company were a wholly owned profit center of a much larger company and Jones expects to be a candidate to succeed one of the parent company's top executives who will retire from the company about two years from now?

22

Cost control with standard costing

Periodic profit reports are useful primarily to division managers and to members of top management with profit responsibility. By contrast, most control reports are more limited in scope, focusing on narrower sets of responsibilities in responsibility centers below the top-management level. Some control reports focus on *effectiveness*—that is, success in meeting output objectives. Reports on product deliveries or progress toward project completion are effectiveness reports. Other reports monitor *compliance*—success in observing rules and constraints on behavior. Reports on accident rates, employee absenteeism, and polluting emissions fall into this category. Finally, some reports focus on *efficiency*—success in minimizing the cost per unit of goods or services produced.

TERMINOLOGY

A *responsibility center* is an organization segment headed by a single manager, obligated to carry out a specified function or group of functions, and answerable to higher authority for its performance of these functions.

The purpose of this chapter is to examine some methods accountants use to measure and report on the efficiency of operations in certain kinds of responsibility centers and in project-oriented activities. We'll devote most of our attention to cost control reporting in factory production departments, ending with a short section on cost control reporting in product-development and other project-centered responsibilities. We'll begin, however, with a short review of the reasons for control reporting.

MANAGEMENT BY EXCEPTION

Managers need performance reports for either or both of two reasons. First, they may need reports to keep informed about what is going on; this is called *attention-directing* or *steering-control* information. Second, managers may need information to confirm or quantify the effects of events and actions they have observed or they themselves have taken; this is *scorecard* information, as we used that term in Chapter 21.

In both cases, management's interest focuses on the *deviations* of actual performance from the "standard" performance level. This emphasis on deviations is known as *management by exception,* which states that management should devote its scarce time only to operations in which results depart significantly from the performance standards. Operations in which results are close to the performance standard are presumed to be under control.

At any given level, the manager needs to divide the deviations from the performance standards into two groups:

1. Those arising from *external* conditions different from those implicit in the standard.
2. Those arising from *internal* causes.

As we pointed out in Chapter 21, deviations arising from external environmental sources call for adaptive responses—that is, planning anew. Deviations arising from internal causes, if large enough, call for corrective responses.

Causes and desirable responses are often readily apparent to the managers who are closest to the operations in question. In some cases, however, determining causes is costly and not always successful. Management has to estimate whether the benefit from any eventual response is likely to exceed both the costs of identifying the causes of deviations from performance standards and the costs of correcting or adapting to these causes. Although decision models are available to guide managers in making these comparisons of costs with benefits, in most cases the decisions will be based on management's judgment. This, too, is part of the practice of management by exception.

COST CONTROL REPORTING: PROCESS PRODUCTION

Responsibility centers may be classified in many ways, but the most useful distinction for cost control reporting is between those engaged in responsive activities and those engaged in programmed activities. *Responsive activities* are carried out to fill orders for goods or services or to provide goods intended for later delivery to customers. *Programmed activities* are carried out at management's discretion to achieve future benefits or to contribute to the achievement of goals other than business profit.

In this section and the next we'll see how reports on cost control performance in responsibility centers engaged in responsive activities can be developed and used. Our focus in this section will be on production centers engaged in homogeneous processing activities similar to those described in Chapter 17.

TERMINOLOGY REMINDER

A *production center* is a specific set of facilities in which end-product activities take place—the production of goods or services for inventory or delivery to customers.

Cost control standards

Cost control standards can be developed and applied to individual iterations of specified tasks—for example, assembling components to produce one unit of a consumer product. Control reporting on an individual-task basis is usually too fragmented to serve the needs of scorecard reporting, however. Of much more importance are the *cumulative* effects of the activities of the many people in individual responsibility centers *in a particular period*.

For any time period, the cost performance standards for a responsibility center should reflect the amounts of resources that should have been necessary to produce the amount of output the center produced in that period. Output-based cost-performance standards for a process production department are identified in that department's flexible budget. A *flexible budget* consists of a number of cost budgets, each for a particular operating volume. The applicable performance standard in any period is the specific budget for the level of output achieved in that period.

Since the number of possible volume levels is extremely large, a more practical approach usually is to establish a series of formulas, one for each cost element. Exhibit 22–1 shows the 19x1 flexible

EXHIBIT 22–1. Apex Company: Coatings Department Flexible Budget for the Year
19x1

	Fixed per Month	Variable per Gallon
Materials		$1.50
Processing labor		0.30
Support labor	$ 1,000	0.01
Supplies	2,000	0.04
Other controllable costs	15,000	0.10
Supervision	3,000	
Depreciation	4,000	
Factory management	25,000	0.05
Total	$50,000	$2.00

budget for Apex Company's factory coatings department.[1] Notice
how variations in output affect elements of cost in different ways.
For a cost such as materials or processing labor—each of which
is expected to be proportional to the volume of output—the cost
control performance standard in any period is ordinarily obtained
by multiplying the number of units of output by the *standard cost*
of a single unit:

Cost control performance standard	=	Quantity of output	×	Standard cost per unit of output

For each input element such as processing labor, the standard cost
of a unit of product is the *standard quantity* of input management
estimates should be necessary to manufacture a unit of that product,
multiplied by the standard price of a unit of that input—the price
the company expects to have to pay to obtain an input unit during
the current planning period.

Standard cost per unit of output	=	Standard quantity of input per unit of output	×	Standard price per unit of input

---

[1] The term *flexible budget* is ordinarily associated with department overhead
costs in job order production or with process production costs which aren't expected
to vary proportionally with volume. Because these are merely special cases of a
much broader set of relationships, we prefer to use the term pedagogically to describe
the cost standards in all responsibility centers engaged in responsive activities.

For example, the standard processing labor cost of a gallon of coatings in Apex Company's coatings department is 0.03 labor-hour at a standard wage rate of $10 an hour, or $0.30 a gallon. This is the amount shown in the second line of the right-hand column in Exhibit 22–1. The cost control performance standard for processing labor in any month during 19x1 is obtained by multiplying the number of gallons of output in that month by $0.30. If volume is 110,000 gallons, the cost control performance standard is $33,000 (110,000 × $0.30).

The flexible budget for support labor is slightly more complicated, because it contains both fixed and variable components. The budget for support labor is:

Budgeted support labor cost = $1,000 + $0.01 × Gallons

In a 110,000-gallon month, the cost control performance standard for this cost element is $2,100 ($1,000 + $0.01 × 110,000).

Finally, the flexible budget for costs that are entirely fixed is identical at all volumes.[2] Supervisory salaries in the coatings department, for example, are budgeted at $3,000 a month, no matter how much output is achieved. This constitutes the cost control performance standard for this cost element at *each* level of volume.

When costs are expected to vary in a linear fashion, the flexible budget for any month can be determined by (1) multiplying the budgeted variable cost per unit by the number of units produced, and (2) adding the budgeted fixed costs, if any. A straight-line formula isn't always right, however. Budgeted overtime premium, for example, could be zero for all volumes up to 90,000 gallons, 6 cents a gallon for the next 30,000 gallons, and 15 cents a gallon for all gallons in excess of 120,000. In such cases, the flexible budget should conform to the anticipated cost behavior; it shouldn't be distorted to conform to a straight-line formula.

Department cost control reports

The effectiveness of department managers in controlling costs is ordinarily reflected in cost reports which are prepared and issued at regular intervals. Some cost reports are issued daily, some weekly, and some at longer intervals. A month is the typical reporting interval for the main department cost summaries, although these are

---

[2] The flexible budget for some fixed costs increases in steps, each step in response to a large change in the volume of activity. These are the *stepped costs* identified in Chapter 16.

likely to be supplemented by daily or weekly reports on particular items, such as inspection rejects, scrap, and overtime.

The monthly cost summaries consist of *comparisons* of the actual costs incurred during the month with budget standards appropriate to the volume actually achieved during the month:

TERMINOLOGY

The differences between the costs actually charged to a responsibility center and the flexible budget standards at actual volume are the *spending variances* for that center.[3]

If the actual cost exceeds the flexible budget, the spending variance is called *unfavorable;* if cost is less than the budget, the spending variance is *favorable.*

Apex Company classifies each department's costs into two categories: costs which the department manager can influence or control directly (*controllable costs*), and costs which are controlled by decisions made by managers outside the department (*noncontrollable costs*). The monthly department cost reports list only the costs which are partly or completely controllable by department personnel. This is consistent with the *controllability criterion,* which states that managers should be held responsible only for those variances they are expected to influence or control.

For example, the report in Exhibit 22–2 was issued to the head of the coatings department, covering this department's operations in the month of June 19x1. During this month, the department produced 110,000 gallons of product. This volume, applied to the budget formulas of Exhibit 22–1, provides the flexible budget standards shown in the second column of Exhibit 22–2.[4]

Three of the costs Apex Company identifies with the coatings department—supervision, depreciation, and factory management—are excluded from the monthly cost report because they are controlled by decisions made outside the department. The amount and cost of supervision are the plant manager's responsibility, not the department manager's. Similarly, the amount of depreciation is

---

[3] The term *spending variance* is ordinarily associated with variances in factory overhead costs in job order production. We have found it more effective in the classroom to apply the term to all variances of actual costs from cost control performance standards.

[4]
$$110{,}000 \times \$1.50 \qquad\qquad = \$165{,}000$$
$$110{,}000 \times \$0.30 \qquad\qquad = \quad 33{,}000$$
$$110{,}000 \times \$0.01 + \$\ \ 1{,}000 = \quad\ \ 2{,}100$$
$$110{,}000 \times \$0.04 + \$\ \ 2{,}000 = \quad\ \ 6{,}400$$
$$110{,}000 \times \$0.10 + \$15{,}000 = \quad 26{,}000$$

EXHIBIT 22–2.   Apex Company: Coatings Department Cost-Performance Report for the Month of June 19x1

	Actual	Budget	(Under) or Over
Materials	$168,200	$165,000	$3,200
Processing labor	32,550	33,000	(450)
Support labor	2,450	2,100	350
Supplies	8,200	6,400	1,800
Other controllable costs	25,800	26,000	(200)
Total controllable costs	$237,200	$232,500	$4,700

determined by purchasing and disposal decisions made by top management. And the costs of factory management are controlled by the plant manager and by the company's vice president for manufacturing.

This being the case, the company could have simplified the flexible budget slightly by excluding these three cost elements from the schedule presented in Exhibit 22–1. Management's reason for providing flexible budget estimates for all department costs, not just controllable costs, is that management at higher responsibility levels does have responsibility for these costs and can make decisions affecting them. For example, the variability of the noncontrollable costs of a particular department is likely to be relevant to decisions on whether to take on work to be performed in that department.

None of the costs in Exhibit 22–2 was an allocation of a portion of the costs incurred in some other department. The reason is that no one in the coatings department had any power to influence the costs of service or support departments in Apex Company's factory. Allocations should be made and reported as controllable costs, however, whenever the department does have this kind of power. For example, if the department is a direct user of the factory's computer center and if the department head is the one who decides what kinds and how much computer services to use, the department should be charged for its actual use of these services. These charges should be made at prices agreed upon in advance, because coatings department personnel can control only the *amount* of service usage (e.g., the number of jobs it submits to the computer center), not the cost of performing them. If this is done, spending variances in the allocated amounts can be classified as controllable.

Management sometimes chooses to include some or all of a department's noncontrollable costs in the monthly cost reports. When this is done, these costs should be reported separately, "below the line," in a section clearly labeled *noncontrollable.*[5]

Price and usage variances

The structure of Exhibit 22–2 implies that the entire spending variance in each item is controllable. This may not be the case. Two kinds of events lead to spending variances. First are those that lead the company to use either more or fewer units of input than the performance standard calls for:

> The portion of a spending variance attributable to these events is the *usage variance,* defined as the difference between actual and budgeted input quantities for the input actually achieved.

Second are the events which affect the *prices* the company pays for the resources it uses (including the *wage rates* it pays its employees):

> The portion of a spending variance arising in this way is known as a *price variance* or a *rate variance,* defined as the difference between actual and standard prices for a specified quantity of resource inputs.

Usage variances. Usage variances are indexes of physical efficiency. They show the relationship between the quantities of resources used and the quantities of the outputs derived from them. Given enough data, we can always measure the usage variances in physical units.

For example, the production standards in the coatings department reflect the assumption that three hours of processing labor, when combined with other inputs, will yield 100 gallons of coatings. In other words, it is assumed that processing labor, if properly controlled, will vary in proportion to production volume.

In June 19x1, the department produced 110,000 gallons of coatings from 3,100 hours of processing labor and other inputs. Schematically:

---

[5] When this practice is followed, management may still prefer to exclude the department head's salary from the departmental cost reports (1) because he or she can't control it, and (2) because the department's other employees aren't entitled to know how much the department head earns.

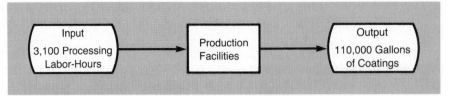

The output of 110,000 gallons of coatings can also be stated in terms of their *budgeted input* content of 3,300 hours of processing labor (110,000 × 3 ÷ 100). Substituting this amount in the schematic diagram, we have:

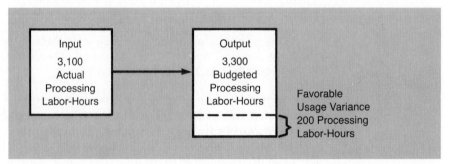

The usage variance is the difference between the actual input quantity (3,100 hours) and the budgeted input quantity for the work that has been done (3,300 hours). In this example, the department used 200 fewer hours of labor than the budget called for and the usage variance is *favorable*.

Although usage variances represent physical quantities, they are usually measured in monetary units (e.g., dollars). To get these dollar amounts, the accountant multiples the physical quantities by *standard* input prices. The standard wage rate in the coatings department in 19x1 was $10 an hour, and the usage variance in processing labor can be calculated in dollars as follows:

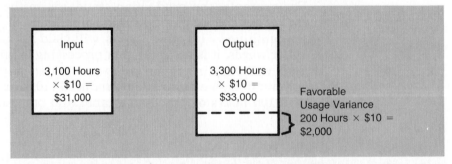

Usage variances are measured at standard prices rather than at actual prices, first, because standard prices are clerically simpler to use, and, second, because they make it easier to compare the usage variances from month to month. If the usage variance in processing labor in July 19x1 is $1,500—favorable—we know that the entire change is due to physical changes and is unaffected by changes in the average wage rate from one month to the next.

Price variances. Spending variances also arise because actual purchase prices or actual wage rates differ from standard prices or standard wage rates. Since the wage rate is the *price* of labor service per hour, the term *price variances* refers to variances in the prices of both materials and labor-hours.

We calculate price variances by multiplying the *actual* input quantity by the difference between the actual input price and the standard input price. For example, processing labor employees in the coatings department were paid $10.50 an hour in June 19x1, 50 cents more than the standard wage rate of $10. Since the department used 3,100 hours of this kind of labor, it paid $1,550 (3,100 × $0.50) more than the standard provided for. This is called a labor rate variance, and in this case it was *unfavorable*.

Reconciling the spending variance. Our analysis of the spending variance in processing labor costs in the coatings department is shown schematically in Exhibit 22–3. To isolate the price effect, we restate the actual input quantity at the standard input price, in this case the standard wage rate of $10 an hour. This amount is shown in the center block of the upper part of Exhibit 22–3. The difference between this amount and the actual processing labor cost—the amount in the block at the left—is identified as the labor rate variance, $1,550 in this case and unfavorable. The labor usage component is highly favorable, with actual usage being 200 fewer hours than the amount budgeted for the output volume actually achieved. At the standard wage rate of $10 an hour, the accountants would report a favorable usage variance in processing labor of $2,000. The algebraic sum of these two components is $450—favorable—which is the spending variance shown in Exhibit 22–2.

Since wage rates may not be controllable by a department, top management can keep the price component out of the reported spending variance by simply using standard prices in the charges to departments for their use of resources. In such cases the department head sees as the department's *actual* costs the product of actual input quantities and standard input prices. If this isn't done, any significant input price components of the spending variances should be separated in the performance-evaluation process.

Using cost-performance reports

Cost-performance reports patterned after Exhibit 22–3 are designed primarily to provide scorecard information. For example,

EXHIBIT 22–3.   Apex Company: Coatings Department Price and Usage Components of the Spending Variance in Processing Labor Costs

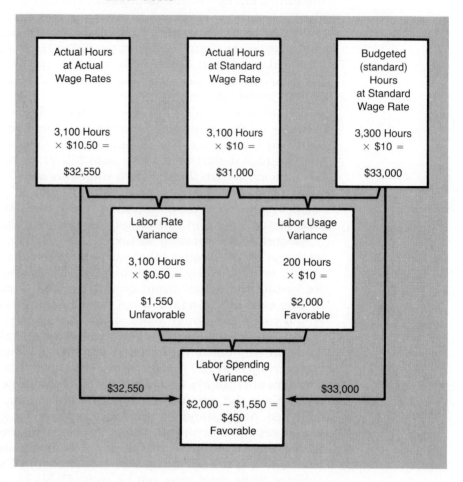

Apex's factory superintendent, Roger Blake, needs information on the operating costs of the two production centers in his factory (coatings and pesticides) for one purpose only—to measure how effectively the department heads have controlled these costs. If one department does well on this score, Blake offers praise and encouragement. If costs seem to have gone out of control, he asks for an explanation and a plan to bring them back into line.

For their part, the department heads in this factory don't need accounting reports to tell them when control efforts are needed; they are close enough to their own operations to identify problems as they arise and to respond to them. They need reports only as scorecards, to reinforce their motivation to control costs and to indicate how successful their efforts have been.

This means that this company doesn't need to accumulate and report usage variances in great detail. Instead, variances are calculated monthly, in total for each department. If management needs steering control information, usage variances should be developed in sufficient detail and promptly enough to enable management to pinpoint the sources of problems as they arise.

COST CONTROL REPORTING: JOB ORDER PRODUCTION

Few cost structures are as simple as in Apex's factory coatings department. Even in process production, most production centers identify many more cost elements than the eight we found in the coatings department. Rather than continue our illustration of cost control reporting in process production, however, we'll turn now to the more complex cost structures in production centers engaged in job order production.

The basic cost-reporting concepts in job order production centers are identical to those we applied to Apex Company's process production center, but the *costing structure* is more complex. Although job order production is characteristic of many service businesses—advertising agencies and consulting firms, for example—we'll illustrate cost control reporting in its most well-established setting, the batch processing or job order factory. For this purpose we've chosen a small factory in a company we'll call Lion Corporation. This factory has three production departments (A, B, and C) and three service and support centers (building services, equipment maintenance, and factory management). Most of its production is of products it has manufactured before or products made by methods it has used before.

Standard product cost

A typical production center in job order production performs a variety of operations on an even larger variety of products or production orders. In a complete cost control system, a standard cost is developed for each of these products—and these standard costs are assembled in a *standard cost file*.

For example, Lion Corporation's standard cost file contains the *standard cost sheet* shown in Exhibit 22–4. This lists the standard costs of a manufactured part identified as Door Front No. 6948. The columns in the center list the labor operations to be performed, the departments in which the work is done, the standard direct-labor times, the standard hourly wage rate, and the standard direct-

EXHIBIT 22–4. Lion Corporation: Standard Cost Sheet

LION CORPORATION
Standard Cost Sheet
Quantity 1,000

Description   Door Front No. 6948   Standard cost per unit $1.585

Operation	Department	Direct Labor			Overhead	
		Hours	Rate	Amount	Rate	Amount
Cut	A	4.5	$14.00	$ 63.00	$12.00	$ 54.00
Drill	A	16.0	13.00	208.00	12.00	192.00
Stamp	B	7.5	11.20	84.00	7.00	52.50
Finish	C	18.5	12.00	222.00	15.00	277.50
Total				$577.00		$576.00

Direct Materials				Summary	
Item	Quantity	Price	Amount		
Steel sheet	3,600	$0.12	$432.00	Direct materials	$ 432.00
				Direct labor	577.00
				Overhead	576.00
				Total	$1,585.00

labor cost. The two columns at the right show the department standard overhead rates (per direct labor-hour in each department) and the standard overhead cost (obtained by multiplying the rate times the number of standard direct labor-hours). Standard direct materials costs are calculated in the lower left, and all components of standard product cost are brought together in the summary at the lower right.

The standard unit cost shown in the upper right-hand corner of the standard cost sheet is obtained by dividing the $1,585 standard cost by 1,000, the number of units in a standard-sized batch of this product.

Total standard cost: Direct labor and materials

In a typical standard costing sytem, direct labor and direct materials costs are assumed to vary proportionally with volume. In other wo.ds, doubling the output will double the total standard cost of direct materials and direct labor—and total standard cost in a given time period ordinarily serves as the cost-performance standard for these cost elements. This means that department usage variances for direct labor and direct materials in job order production are calculated in the same way as the usage variances for proportionally variable costs in process costing—materials and processing labor in our Apex Company illustration.

The main difference from our earlier illustration is that department output in job order production in any period is likely to consist of many products, not just one. For example, suppose department C in Lion Corporation's factory produces the following products in July 19x1:

	Standard Direct Labor-Hours per Thousand Units	Thousands of Units Produced	Total Standard Direct Labor-Hours
Door Front No. 6848	18.5	10	185
Panel No. 8207	24.0	20	480
Base No. 1991	37.5	32	1,200
Total			1,865

The standard wage rate in department C is $12 an hour. Standard direct-labor cost for the period therefore is $22,380 (1,865 × $12). We can calculate the same total by multiplying the number of units of each product by its standard direct-labor cost per unit, in dollars, and adding the results, as in Exhibit 22–5.

EXHIBIT 22–5. Lion Corporation: Calculation of Total Standard Direct-Labor Cost of Units Completed by Department C

	Standard Direct Labor-Hours per Thousand Units	Standard Direct Cost per Thousand Units (at $12 an hour)	Thousands of Units Produced	Total Standard Direct-Labor Cost
Door Front No. 6948	18.5	$222	10	$ 2,220
Panel No. 8207	24.0	288	20	5,760
Base No. 1991	37.5	450	32	14,400
Total				$22,380

The output calculation is slightly more complicated if a department has work in process either at the beginning of the period or at the end. For example, suppose the amounts in Exhibit 22–5 referred to units *completed* by department C and transferred out of the department during the month. Upon further investigation, we find that the company had one batch of 2,000 door fronts in process at the start of operations on July 1, 19x1, and half of department C's work had been done on this batch in June. The standard cost of the work *already done* on these units was calculated as follows:

1. 2,000 half-processed units were equivalent to 1,000 fully processed units (2,000 × ½ = 1,000).
2. 1,000 fully processed units required 18.5 standard direct labor-hours.

3. At $12 a standard direct labor-hour, the July 1 inventory had a standard direct-labor cost of $222 (18.5 × $12).

In addition to the units completed in July, at the close of business on July 31, 19x1, the company had a batch of 4,000 door fronts in process; and three quarters of department C's work had been done on this batch in July. The standard cost of the work done on these units in July was calculated in the same way as the standard cost of the beginning inventory:

1. 4,000 partially processed units were equivalent to 3,000 fully processed units (4,000 × ¾ = 3,000).
2. 3,000 fully processed units required 55.5 standard direct labor-hours (18.5 × 3).
3. At $12 a standard direct labor-hour, the July 31 inventory had a standard direct-labor cost of $666 (55.5 × $12).

We can now see that department C actually accomplished *more* in July than we had given it credit for in Exhibit 22–5. It not only finished goods with a standard direct-labor cost of $22,380, but it also increased the standard direct-labor cost of the work in process by $444:

	Standard Hours	Standard Cost
Standard direct labor in process, July 31	55.5	$666
Standard direct labor in process, July 1	18.5	222
Increase in standard direct-labor cost in process	37.0	$444

This means that the standard direct-labor cost of all the work department C did in July 19x1 was as follows:

	Standard Hours	Standard Cost
Standard direct-labor cost of units completed (Exhibit 22–5)	1,865	$22,380
Increase in standard direct-labor cost in process	37	444
Total standard direct-labor cost, July 19x1	1,902	$22,824

These amounts are assembled in a different sequence in Exhibit 22–6. The blocks at the left of the equals sign represent the standard hours and standard costs to be accounted for in July, including some standard hours and standard costs of the work done last month (the July 1 work in process). The blocks at the right show how many standard hours and how much standard cost went out of the department in July and how much remained in process at the end of the month. In this diagram the ending work in process is larger than the beginning work in process; therefore the *total*

EXHIBIT 22–6. Lion Corporation: Output, Product Completion and Work in Process in Department C

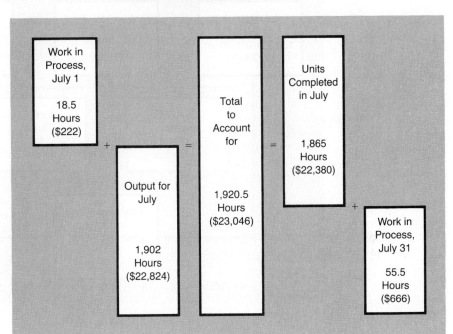

amount of work done (the output) was greater than the number of units completed during the period.

Analyzing spending variances in direct labor and direct materials

The spending variance for direct labor in job order production is calculated in exactly the same way as the spending variance for any proportionally variable cost element in process production. It is the difference between the performance standard (standard direct-labor cost of the actual output for the period) and the actual cost of direct labor.

Suppose department C in Lion Corporation's factory used 1,950 hours of direct labor in July 19x1 at an actual direct-labor cost of $23,985. Actual cost was determined by multiplying each worker's direct-labor time by that worker's straight-time wage rate (including a provision for fringe benefits but excluding overtime premiums). We now have all the information we need to calculate the spending variance and subdivide it into its price and usage components, using the same scheme as earlier:

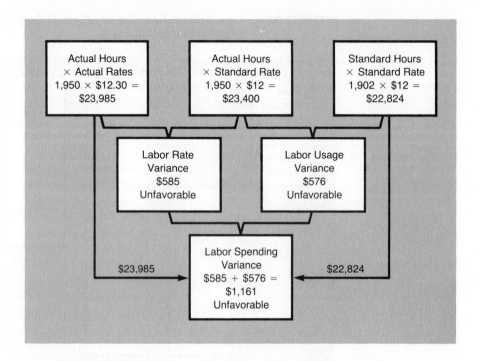

The calculation for direct materials is similar in concept, except that (1) the price variance is usually separated at the time of purchase, while the usage variance is determined at the time of use, and (2) the price variance therefore isn't departmentalized. For example, suppose Lion Corporation bought 100,000 pounds of steel sheet in July 19x1 at 13 cents a pound. The standard price was 12 cents a pound. Its only other purchase in July was 30,000 pounds of finishing material at 27 cents a pound (against a standard price of 25 cents). The $1,600 unfavorable price variance was calculated as follows:

	Actual Cost	Standard Cost	Price Variance
Steel sheet	100,000 × $0.13 = $13,000	100,000 × $0.12 = $12,000	$1,000 unf.
Finishing materials	30,000 × $0.27 = 8,100	30,000 × $0.25 = 7,500	600 unf.
Total	$21,100	$19,500	$1,600 unf.

The price variance was identified at the time of purchase, mainly because management wanted to know the effects of changing prices immediately, rather than at some future time when the materials were used in production.

The materials purchased in July were placed in the materials storeroom and were recorded in inventory at their standard prices.[6] During the month the company issued 90,000 pounds of steel sheet to department A and 25,000 pounds of finishing material to department C. Standard usage of steel sheet in department A in July (based on its output in that month) amounted to 85,000 pounds; standard usage of finishing material in department C amounted to 26,000 pounds. The materials usage variances for the month—$600 unfavorable in department A and $250 favorable in department C—were calculated as follows:

	Materials Issued	Standard Materials Cost	Usage Variance
Department A......	90,000 × $0.12 = $10,800	85,000 × $0.12 = $10,200	$600 unf.
Department C......	25,000 × $0.25 = 6,250	26,000 × $0.25 = 6,500	250 fav.

Both the quantities issued and the standard quantities for the amount of work done in July were multiplied by the *standard* prices in these usage variance calculations.

Flexible budgets for supportive overhead costs

In job order production, factory costs other than the direct labor and direct materials costs of specific job orders are called *overhead costs.* They are *supportive overheads,* incurred to enable management to service the sales or production orders it receives. Many supportive overheads aren't likely to vary proportionally with production, however. We therefore can't derive the performance standard by multiplying total output by standard overhead cost per unit.

The flexible budget for Lion Corporation's department C is shown in Exhibit 22–7. The first six lines in this table contain the flexible budget factors for overhead costs that are traceable to this department; the final three lines contain the flexible budget factors for the monthly allocations to department C of portions of the costs of operating Lion Corporation's three indirect service and support centers.

Measuring volume. The variable-cost components of the flexible budget formulas in Exhibit 22–7 are applied to *standard direct labor-hours* rather than to *physical units* of output. We usually can't use the number of units of output to measure volume in job order production because each production center is likely to work on a

---

[6] The journal entry to record purchases in July was:

Raw Materials Inventory	19,500	
Materials Price Variance	1,600	
Accounts Payable		21,100

EXHIBIT 22–7.   Lion Corporation: Department C Flexible
Budget for the Year 19x1

	Fixed per Month	Variable per Standard Direct Labor-Hour
Indirect labor	$ 1,000	$1.50
Overtime premium..................	—	—
Supplies	—	2.00
Other direct department overhead....	1,600	0.20
Equipment maintenance	300	1.35
Supervision.......................	3,000	—
Depreciation......................	5,000	—
Building services	4,000	—
Factory management	4,000	—
Total	$18,900	$5.05

variety of products, not just one. In addition, some units require a
great deal of work in department C and therefore are likely to require more overhead support from that department than units of
other products which pass through this department much more
quickly.

Although we can't measure overall output by the number of physical units, we do have a composite measure of output—standard
direct labor-hours in this case—in which each unit of output is
weighted in proportion to the number of standard direct labor-hours
it requires. Whether standard direct labor-hours is an appropriate
measure of volume for use in calculating overhead cost-performance standards depends on (1) whether the need for overhead
cost is generated by the amount of output or by the amount of one
or more direct inputs, and (2) whether total standard direct labor-
hours correlate better with the incidence of overhead cost than
with some other measure of output (e.g., standard machine-hours).

For example, suppose the overhead costs in department C vary
more closely with the *actual* number of standard direct labor-hours
than with the number of *standard* direct labor-hours. The flexible
budget for indirect labor costs in this case therefore might be derived from the following formula:

Indirect labor cost = $1,000 + $1.50 × Actual direct labor-hours

If the department uses 1,950 direct labor-hours in July, its flexible
budget standard for indirect labor costs is $3,925 ($1,000 + $1.50
× 1,950), no matter how many standard direct labor-hours are represented in its output that month.

EXHIBIT 22–8.   Lion Corporation: Department C Overhead Cost Report for the Month Ended July 31, 19x1

	Actual Overhead	Flexible Budget at 1,902 Standard Direct Labor- Hours	Over/ (Under) Budget
Controllable:			
Indirect labor	$ 4,210	$ 3,853	$ 357
Overtime premium	360	—	360
Supplies	3,792	3,804	(12)
Other direct overhead	2,635	1,980	655
Equipment maintenance......	2,700	2,868	(168)
Total controllable	13,697	12,505	1,192
Noncontrollable:			
Supervision	3,050	3,000	50
Depreciation	5,010	5,000	10
Building services	4,000	4,000	—
Factory management	4,000	4,000	—
Total	$29,757	$28,505*	$1,252

* Check figure based on column totals in Exhibit 22–7: $18,900 + $5.05 × 1,902 = $28,505.

Because Lion Corporation's management judges that the incidence of indirect labor and other overhead costs in department C is more closely related to *standard* direct labor-hours than to *actual* direct labor-hours, the flexible budget standards are calculated on the basis of standard direct labor-hours (1,902 in July), and the flexible budget for indirect labor in July is $3,853 ($1,000 + $1.50 × 1,902).

Analysis of spending variances.   A report summarizing department C's overhead costs for July 19x1 is shown in Exhibit 22–8. Variances in department direct labor and materials are reported separately; this report is restricted to the department's overhead costs. It differs from the report in Exhibit 22–2 because Lion Corporation, unlike Apex Company, does report noncontrollable costs to its department heads.

Notice that one of the allocated costs, the charge for equipment maintenance services, is shown "above the line" as a controllable cost. Although Lion Corporation's management recognizes that the amount of maintenance required depends to some extent on the quality of the services the equipment maintenance department provides, top management is convinced that the managers of the three production centers can have a great deal of influence over this quantity. The production center managers can exert their influence by supervising their employees properly, by insuring that routine maintenance is done on schedule, and by having department employees make simple repairs and adjustments on the spot (as part of indirect labor) rather than calling in the equipment maintenance department. Responsibility for maintenance control, in other words, is shared by the equipment maintenance department and the production center managers, and variances in this cost appear in both sets of performance reports.

The amounts in the right-hand column of Exhibit 22–8 are the spending variances in the department's overhead costs for July. Whether these spending variances contain both price and usage components, only a price component, or only a usage component, depends on the methods the company uses to determine the amounts to be charged to the department. If the department is charged for its actual use of indirect labor at the actual wage rates applicable to indirect labor time, then the spending variance is likely to contain both a wage rate component and a usage component. If charges for actual usage are based on predetermined (standard) wage rates, then the spending variance will include only a usage component.

COST CONTROL REPORTING: DISCRETIONARY OVERHEAD COSTS

Most overhead costs of factory production centers are of the kind we described as supportive overhead; that is, they are necessary to service the volume of orders that have entered the system. Another large group of overhead costs is *discretionary overhead,* incurred to secure some future benefit or to meet some independent objective set by management. In this category we have such costs as advertising, research, contributions to charitable organizations, and management consultants' fees. We'll devote the rest of this chapter to a brief examination of how management can use accounting information in (1) planning discretionary activities, and (2) responding to subsequent events.

Planning criteria

Discretionary costs are fixed costs—by definition, since only costs that vary in response to volume changes are variable costs. This being the case, most decisions that determine the level of discretionary costs are made when the budget is established. People are hired, commitments are made, and orders are placed on the strength of budget authorizations.

This means that the most crucial control process for discretionary overheads is budget review and approval. The basic criterion underlying these decisions is the cost-benefit criterion: Do the anticipated

EXHIBIT 22–9. Two-Stage Approval Process for Product-Development Projects

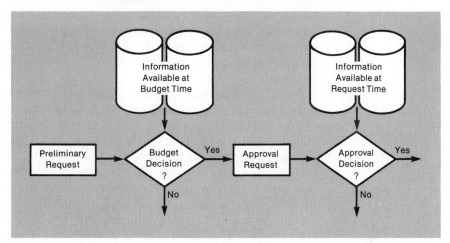

benefits justify the cost? For major self-standing activities, such as new-product-development projects, approval often comes in two stages, as diagrammed in Exhibit 22–9. The project is reviewed initially as part of the regular budgetary planning process. If it passes muster at that time, it is incorporated in the budget. Much can happen between the date the budget is approved and the date the first commitment of resources is made, however. Management is likely to take advantage of any additional information generated during this period before making the final decision to go ahead with the project or put it on the shelf.

Feedback reporting

Feedback reporting is no less important than budgetary planning in the control of discretionary overhead costs. First, although these are fixed costs, they do change in response to the decisions management makes about the activities they support. Reporting the costs and benefits from these activities calls management's attention to situations that may call for replanning. Second, even without any change in management's plans, actual expenditures may deviate from the fixed budgets. Feedback reports call such deviations to management's attention.

Marketing activities. Discretionary or programmed activities are of many types, each calling for its own reporting structure. Marketing expenditures are generally reviewed as part of profit-monitoring processes similar to those discussed in Chapter 21. Mere comparisons of actual expenses with budgeted expenses have little analytical value for marketing costs. What matters is whether revenues and contribution margins have responded to marketing expenditures as management anticipated they would when the profit plan was adopted. The analysis, therefore, focuses on deviations from planned profit performance—the profit variations—and on how they arose.

Product-development activities. Many discretionary activities consist of self-standing activities, such as company-initiated efforts to design and introduce new products which seem likely to be commercially successful—usually referred to as *product-development projects*. The usual focus of feedback reporting and control here is the individual project, clearly identifiable from start to completion and large enough to warrant specific management attention. The same techniques can be applied to individual job orders which are large enough and important enough to warrant this kind of attention—major construction projects are a case in point.

The key to feedback reporting in connection with product-development projects and other project-centered activities is to break the overall project objectives down into identifiable, timed subobjectives. Costs can then be accumulated on a subobjective basis, and the reports can compare these costs with the amounts management planned to incur to achieve each subobjective.

The breakdown of a simple project might take the form illustrated in Exhibit 22–10. This shows a project that was started on

EXHIBIT 22–10.   Project Milestones and Budget Allowances

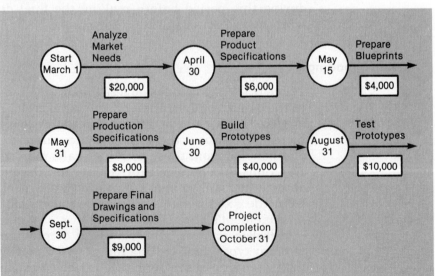

March 1 and scheduled for completion on October 31 of the same year. Each circle in this diagram represents a significant *milestone* along the road to the completion of the project. The arrows between milestones represent *activities,* each with its own budgeted cost. Most of the activities, in turn, can be further subdivided into subactivities and intermediate milestones if management wants this additional detail.

In this case, the analysis stage proceeded as planned and was completed on April 30 at a cost of $19,500. Snags were encountered in the development of product specifications, however, and this activity wasn't completed until May 31, at a cost of $12,000. A *cumulative* report for the months of March, April, and May should show the following comparison:

	Actual Cost	Budgeted Cost	Over/(Under) Budget
Analysis	$19,500	$20,000	$ (500)
Product specifications	12,000	6,000	6,000
Total to date	$31,500	$26,000	$5,500

This is an activity-centered report, showing clearly that the company has spent $5,500 more to do the work than it had planned, a signal of a serious cost overrun on this project.

To implement this approach, management has to divide the overall project into activities, each with its own budget estimate. Reports then can be issued either when key milestones are reached or periodically, at the end of each month or quarter. These reports require the following:

1. Accumulate costs by project, using some form of job order costing.
2. Record each milestone as it is passed, and estimate any progress that has been made toward the next milestone as of the date of the report.
3. Estimate the amount of cost budgeted for the amount of progress made during the period.
4. Compare actual costs with budgeted costs for the progress that has been achieved, explaining major variances whenever possible.

Reports of this kind focus exclusively on the past. Because discretionary activities can always be discontinued if the anticipated costs exceed the perceived benefits, a strong case can be made for incorporating revised forecasts of future costs and completion dates in the reports. Management can then decide whether to continue the project—based on a comparison of estimated *future* benefits with estimated *future* costs—and, if so, whether to increase or decrease the rate of spending to advance or defer the estimated completion date.

SUMMARY

Feedback reports to managers of responsibility centers may focus on effectiveness, efficiency, or compliance. Cost control reports are usually intended to monitor the efficiency of responsibility centers, mainly for scorecard purposes. They are used as an input to *management by exception,* helping management focus its attention on activities which seem to need it the most.

Cost control standards in responsibility centers engaged in response activities are reflected in flexible budgets, which adjust the performance standard to the actual volume of activity. For cost elements which are expected to vary proportionally with volume, the appropriate control standard is standard unit cost, multiplied by the number of units of output achieved in that period. Direct materials costs and direct labor costs in job order production usually fall into this category. For fixed costs and other costs that don't vary proportionally with volume, standard product cost isn't an appropriate standard. Instead, the flexible budget must provide separately for the fixed and variable components of cost.

Deviations of actual costs from the relevant cost control standards are known as spending variances. These spending variances can be subdivided into price variance and usage variance components. The amounts to be reported to the manager of a responsibility center should include price variances only if that manager has responsibility for decisions which affect resource prices. In any case, the periodic cost-performance reports to the managers of responsibility centers should focus on the controllable elements of cost, placing noncontrollable variances "below the line" or excluding them from the reports submitted at this level.

Costs allocated to a responsibility center may be classified as controllable if the manager is responsible for controlling the amount of service used and if the allocation rates are predetermined. Otherwise the allocation should be either classified as noncontrollable or omitted from the reports entirely.

Costs of discretionary activities require different kinds of control information. Marketing costs are monitored largely in the context of internal profit reporting. The costs of product-development projects and other project-oriented activities can be monitored, but the focus of control is the individual project rather than the individual responsibility center. Again, the comparison is between actual cost and the budgeted cost of the output or progress actually achieved by the project.

KEY TERMS

Controllability criterion	Spending variance
Cost control standard	Standard cost
Discretionary overhead	Standard cost sheet
Flexible budget	Standard price
Management by exception	Standard usage
Price (rate) variance	Supportive overhead
Responsive activity	Usage variance

INDEPENDENT STUDY PROBLEMS (Solutions in Appendix B)

1. **Calculating and analyzing labor cost variances.** You have the following information about the operations of department Y during the month of March:

	Product A	Product B
Units finished	5,000	10,000
Units in process:		
March 1	1,000	1,000
March 31	600	1,200
Standard direct-labor cost per unit	$2	$1

Products in process on any date are presumed to be half-processed by department Y's labor force.

Direct-labor cost in department Y amounted to $23,500 in March. The standard cost of this amount of labor totaled $22,000.

a. Calculate the total direct-labor cost variance (spending variance).
b. Analyze this variance in as much detail as you can and clearly label each component you have identified.
c. Calculate the standard direct-labor cost of the inventory in process at the end of the month.

2. **Calculating and analyzing materials cost variances.** The Hillman Company manufactures a single product known as Quik-Tite. Material A is the only raw material used in the manufacture of Quik-Tite. Transactions in material A for the month of June are as follows:

	Standard	Actual
Units of Quik-Tite produced		61,000
Pounds of material A required to produce one		
unit of Quik-Tite	1.6 lbs.	1.5 lbs.
Cost of material A purchases during June	$2.00 lb.	$2.05/lb.
Inventory of material A on June 1		4,000 lbs.
Material purchased during June		95,000 lbs.

Calculate and analyze the materials variances for the month.

3. **Cost-performance reporting: supportive overheads.** Riptide Company's factory manufactures on a job order basis, using department flexible

budgets for cost reporting. The fiscal year is divided into 13 "months" of four weeks each. Department T has a normal production volume of 4,000 direct labor-hours a month and the following flexible budget for department overhead costs. This budget is valid for volumes between 3,000 and 4,500 direct labor-hours a month:

	Fixed per Month	Variable per Direct Labor- Hour
Nonproductive time, machine operators	—	$0.25
Other indirect labor	$2,000	0.50
Operating supplies	—	0.15
Depreciation	2,000	—
Rent	700	—
Total	$4,700	$0.90

Actual costs and volumes in two successive months were as follows:

	Month 4	Month 5
Direct labor-hours	4,000	3,000
Nonproductive time	$ 800	$1,200
Other indirect labor	3,700	3,600
Operating supplies	650	430
Depreciation	2,100	2,150
Rent	770	730

a. Calculate the flexible budgets and prepare a cost-performance report for each of these months. This report should include each of the five overhead cost elements, arranged in any way you find appropriate.

b. Comment on the various items in these reports, indicating which items are likely to be of greatest significance in evaluating the cost control performance of the department supervisor.

c. Looking only at those items for which cost performance was poorer in month 5 than in month 4, what would be your reaction to the statement that the manager of this department had been lax in enforcing cost control during month 5? What remedial action would you suggest, if any?

4. Performance reporting: discretionary overheads. A research plan called for the expenditure of $48,000, to be spread evenly over a six-month period. At the end of two months, $16,200 had been spent, the project was one-quarter complete, and management estimated that the project would be completed successfully seven months after it was begun, at a total cost of $60,000.

a. Present a brief financial report to the project manager's immediate superior, highlighting the financial performance of the project team.

b. What responses might management take in this situation? What criteria might it use in choosing among these? What data might it reasonably ask for to aid in this choice?

EXERCISES AND PROBLEMS

5. Discussion question: application of flexible budgets. "I don't care what you say! Flexible budgets are used for overhead costs—for direct materials and direct labor you have to use standard costs for control reporting." Is this statement true? Does it make a difference whether it is applied to process production or to job order production?

6. Discussion question: communicating with managers. "What do you mean, I'm over my budget?" said Bob Dietz, shop supervisor. "It says right here in the annual budget that my monthly indirect labor allowance is $3,300. I didn't make up the budget; you did. I only spent $3,200, so where do you get off telling me I'm $200 over? Maybe it's those birds up in the accounting department, fouling me up again."

a. As Dietz's boss, how would you explain the situation to him? Was he right? Should he have had an allowance of $3,300?
b. If Dietz's attitude is typical of the shop supervisors, what do you think should be done to strengthen the factory's overhead cost control system?

7. Supplying missing information. You have the following data on Goodman Company's direct-labor costs:

Standard direct labor-hours	15,000
Actual direct labor-hours	14,500
Direct labor usage variance—favorable	$ 4,000
Direct labor rate variance—favorable	$ 5,800
Total direct labor payroll	$110,200

a. What was Goodman's actual direct-labor rate?
b. What was Goodman's standard direct-labor rate?

(AICPA adapted)

8. Calculating department output. Department X completed work on 4,300 units of product A and 2,700 units of product B in June. The standard direct material and standard direct labor costs of these two products were as follows:

	Product A	Product B
Standard direct materials cost per unit	$5	$ 2
Standard direct labor cost per unit	6	10

The standard costs of the amounts of these two products in process in department X at the beginning and end of June were as follows:

	Product A	Product B
June 1:		
Standard direct materials cost	$5,000	$1,000
Standard direct labor cost	3,000	2,500
June 30:		
Standard direct materials cost	4,000	1,200
Standard direct labor cost	3,200	3,500

Calculate department X's output for the month, as measured by its standard direct materials cost and by its standard direct labor cost.

9.   Sequential standard costing exercises.   Follow the instructions given for each of the following three exercises. Do these exercises in the sequence in which they are presented.

Exercise A.   Tapscott Enterprises, Inc., reports direct materials and direct labor usage variances to factory department heads each month. One department worked on only two products in January. Its standard inputs and actual outputs were as follows:

	Standard Direct Material Quantity per Unit (pounds)	Standard Direct Labor-Hours per Unit	Units of Product Manufactured during January
Product A	6	4	2,000
Product B	10	2	3,000

The following quantities of direct materials and direct labor were used in January: direct materials, 44,000 pounds; direct labor, 13,500 hours.

a.   Calculate direct materials and direct labor usage variances for the month in terms of pounds of materials and hours of labor. Indicate whether each variance is favorable or unfavorable.

b.   The standard materials price is $3 a pound. The standard wage rate is $10 an hour.

   1.   Calculate the standard unit cost for each product in dollars.

   2.   Restate your usage variances (from part *a*) in monetary terms.

Exercise B.   Preston Pans, Ltd., manufactures cookware. All its factory operations are performed in a single department. The department's facilities were used during February to manufacture the following three products:

	Standard Direct Materials Quantity (pounds per unit)		Standard Direct Labor-Hours per Unit	Units of Product Manufactured
	Material X	Material Y		
Product A	1	3	1	1,000
Product B	2	1	1	3,000
Product C	3	4	6	2,000

You have the following additional information:

1.   Standard materials prices: material X, $2 a pound; material Y, $5 a pound.
2.   Standard wage rate: $10 an hour.
3.   Direct materials purchased during February:
     Material X: 10,000 pounds, $21,000.
     Material Y: 15,000 pounds, $77,000.
4.   Direct material used during February:
     Material X: 12,600 pounds.
     Material Y: 15,000 pounds.

5. Direct labor used during February: 16,800 hours, $160,000.

a. Calculate direct labor and direct materials variances, in dollars.
b. Indicate to whom each of these variances should be reported.

Exercise C. Block Houses, Inc., manufactures prefabricated housing modules. The following information was collected for one department for the month of March.

1. Inventory of work in process, March 1 (at standard cost):
   Direct materials, $28,000.
   Direct labor, $16,000.
2. Direct materials with a standard cost of $22,000 were received in the department from the storeroom during the month.
3. Direct-labor cost for the month was $8,000 at actual wage rates and $7,500 at standard wage rates.
4. The standard cost of products finished and transferred out of the department during the month was as follows:
   Standard direct materials cost: $21,200.
   Standard direct labor cost: $7,800.
5. Inventory of work in process, March 31 (at standard cost):
   Direct materials, $24,000.
   Direct labor, $15,000.

a. Calculate the standard direct labor and standard direct materials costs of the work done during the month.
b. Calculate the direct labor and direct materials spending variances for the month, and subdivide them as you deem appropriate.
c. Comment on the department head's cost control performance during the month.

10. Calculating and analyzing labor variances. You have the following information for a factory department for the month of September:

1.

	Product X	Product Y
Units finished	2,000	1,500
Units in process:		
September 1	1,000	500
September 30	2,000	800
Standard direct-labor cost per unit (at $10 an hour)	$20	$30

2. Half the required department direct labor had been performed on each unit in process on the indicated dates.
3. Actual direct-labor cost, month of September: 9,500 hours, $100,000.

a. Calculate the standard direct-labor cost of the work done in this department during September.
b. Calculate and analyze the direct-labor spending variance.
c. Which portion of the spending variance is likely to be subject to the department head's control?

11. Supplying missing data.   You have the following information on direct labor and materials costs in two factory departments in the month of March.

	Department X	Department Y
Actual wage rate	$8.30 an hour	$9.00 an hour
Standard wage rate	A	$9.20 an hour
Actual labor quantity used	9,200 hours	E
Standard labor quantity required by work done	9,600 hours	4,600 hours
Labor rate variance	$2,760 unfav.	F
Labor usage variance	B	$1,840 unfav.
Actual materials quantity used	10,000 pounds	G
Standard materials quantity required by work done	C	31,000 gallons
Standard materials cost of work finished and transferred out of department	$17,500	H
Standard price of materials	$2 a pound	$5 a gallon
Historical cost of materials....................	$1.90 a pound	$4.90 a gallon
Materials usage variance	D	$5,000 fav.
Materials in process, March 1, at standard cost	$12,500	$25,000
Materials in process, March 31, at standard cost	$14,000	$23,200

Supply the information missing from this table.

12. Overhead performance report.   The monthly flexible budget standards for the assembly department of Boyce Furniture Company for various quantities of direct labor-hours are shown in the following table:

	Direct Labor-Hours				
	10,000	10,500	11,000	11,500	12,000
Supervision	$ 1,800	$ 1,800	$ 1,800	$ 1,800	$ 1,800
Indirect labor	7,000	7,350	7,700	8,050	8,400
Supplies	4,000	4,200	4,400	4,600	4,800
Power, fuel, and water	1,000	1,050	1,100	1,150	1,200
Depreciation	2,000	2,000	2,000	2,000	2,000
Space occupancy	3,000	3,000	3,000	3,000	3,000
General plant overhead	2,800	2,800	2,800	2,800	2,800
Total	$21,600	$22,200	$22,800	$23,400	$24,000

Actual charges to the department for the month of March were as follows:

Supervision	$ 1,900
Indirect labor	7,700
Supplies	4,020
Power, fuel, and water	930
Depreciation	1,950
Space occupancy	3,000
General plant overhead	3,000
Total	$22,500

The actual volume of production during March totaled 10,500 direct labor-hours.

a. How much of the budgeted overhead cost would you classify as fixed? What is the average budgeted variable cost per direct labor-hour?

b. Prepare a department overhead cost report for the month.

c. Comment on the possible causes of each of the variances shown on the report.

13. Validity of the flexible budgeting. Production in Balch Company's factory is on a job order basis. Each factory department has a monthly overhead cost budget, agreed upon at the beginning of the year, and a set of flexible budget formulas for overhead costs used for monthly performance reporting. The formulas for the finishing department are:

Supervision	$1,200 a month
Indirect labor	$800 a month + $1 per direct labor-hour
Overtime premium	$0.50 for each direct labor-hour in excess of 2,400 direct labor-hours a month
Supplies	$0.40 a direct labor-hour
Power	$200 a month + $0.15 a direct labor-hour
Depreciation	$500 a month
Other overhead	$0.10 a direct labor-hour

Normal volume in this department is 3,000 direct labor-hours a month, but this is a bad year and this year's budget anticipates volume to average only 2,700 hours a month. Volume in May was 2,500 direct labor-hours. The actual overhead costs for the month were as follows:

Supervision	$1,260
Indirect labor	3,340
Overtime premium	140
Supplies	860
Power	600
Depreciation	500
Other	300
Total	$7,000

a. Prepare an overhead cost-performance report for the month of May, using the flexible budget.

b. The company's president isn't sure that flexible budgeting is a good idea because it may make department heads look good even though their average overhead cost keeps going up. The president prefers to compare average actual overhead cost with average planned overhead cost at planned volume. Make the calculations necessary for a report on this basis and draft a reply to the president's argument.

14. Significance of spending variances. Some indirect labor in Balch Company (see problem 13) is performed by regular bench operators who normally perform direct labor operations. Management is reluctant to lay these operators off for short periods of time. Instead, some of the indirect labor work, such as cleaning and adjusting machines, is deferred until the production schedule is light.

The manager of the finishing department thinks this should be built into the flexible budget, with a larger indirect labor budget when volume is low, and vice versa. This would eliminate erratic fluctuations in the indirect labor spending variances. The plant controller disagrees, arguing that production creates the need for indirect labor services, even though these services may not be performed when production takes place.

Prepare a brief report on this issue, stating your position and indicating how management should interpret and use the spending variances arising under the solution you are recommending.

15. Process production: department performance report. Apex Company's coatings department operated at a volume of 80,000 gallons in August 19x1. The department's costs that month were as follows:

Materials	$127,400
Processing labor	26,250
Support labor	2,050
Supplies	4,200
Other controllable costs	24,800
Supervision	3,300
Depreciation	3,900
Factory management	29,000
Total	$220,900

a. Using the flexible budget set forth in Exhibit 22–1 at the beginning of this chapter, prepare a cost-performance report for the month of August. Unlike the cost-performance report in Exhibit 22–2, your report should include all costs charged to the department in August.

b. The flexible budget for materials in 19x1 reflected a standard materials price of $1.20 a pound, a standard wage rate of $10 an hour for processing labor, and a standard wage rate of $8 an hour for support labor. The coatings department used 98,000 pounds of materials, 2,500 hours of processing labor, and 250 hours of support labor in August. Use this additional information to help management evaluate cost control performance in the coatings department in August.

16. Preparing a control report. The Neptune Company operates a small factory which makes only one product. Four production operations are necessary, one in each of the factory's four departments. The company's engineers have determined that these operations should require the following labor-hour allowances under normal conditions:

	Labor-Hours per Unit of Product			
	Operation No. 1	Operation No. 2	Operation No. 3	Operation No. 4
Operators	1.0	3.0	1.5	0.5
Helpers	0.5	2.5	2.0	0.1
Handlers	0.2	0.5	1.0	0.3

Operators are paid $12 an hour, helpers $8 an hour, and handlers $6 an hour.

During August, the factory's operations were:

	Operation No. 1	Operation No. 2	Operation No. 3	Operation No. 4
Units produced	2,000	1,800	2,100	2,000
Labor-hours:				
Operators	1,100	5,200	3,400	980
Helpers	550	4,600	4,600	190
Handlers	210	1,000	2,200	610

a. Prepare a report for management, summarizing labor operations for the month in terms of both hours and dollars, and write a brief paragraph commenting on the effectiveness of labor control during the month.

b. What advantages, if any, do you see in including dollar figures on this report? Explain.

17. Physical unit comparisons. Art Dangerfield had been department supervisor for 30 years. "All I want are a few key figures," he said. "The rest of the accounting figures are rubbish. I want to know my scrap percentage [pounds of scrap, divided by pounds of materials] and the materials yield [pounds of product divided by pounds of materials]. If scrap is less than 5 percent and the materials yield is better than 80 percent, I've got it made."

The department processes a number of different materials, and a certain amount of waste is inherent in the process. Some materials are lost in the process itself; some take the form of recoverable scrap. Dangerfield retired last month and his longtime assistant, Dorothy Hellman, was promoted to take his place. The first report she saw contained the following statistics:

Scrap 3%
Materials yield 84%
Materials usage variance (percent of standard) ...... 10% unfavorable

"Art's formula doesn't seem to be working," she observed, "I'm well within his limits, but how did that usage variance get so big?" She asked the plant controller to look into the matter.

The controller analyzed the materials requisitions and production records and came up with the following data:

	Standard Price (per pound)	Standard Usage (in pounds)	Quantity Used (in pounds)
Material A	$ 0.10	4,000	3,700
Material B	1.00	600	630
Material C	10.00	400	450
Total		5,000	4,780

The percentage statistics were correct: the output weighed 4,015 pounds, 84 percent of the weight of the materials used, and 143 pounds of scrap were recovered.

a. Analyze the controller's figures and provide an explanation for Hellman.

b. Does your analysis indicate that the standards should be changed? What other suggestions would you make?

18. Department performance report. The Argus Company's research division has approximately 80 employees, organized as shown in the accompanying table:

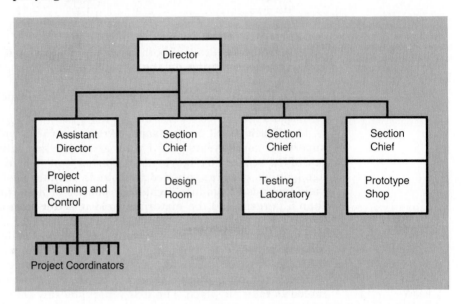

Research proposals are prepared initially in the project planning and control section (PPC). Once a project is approved, an engineer on the PPC staff is assigned to direct that project, evaluate progress, and attempt to keep it on schedule. Line authority over the research staff is vested in the three section chiefs, however.

The project coordinators receive cost and progress reports on their projects every month. In addition, each section chief receives a summary report on cost performance in that section. This is a two-page report, with an overall department summary on the first page and an element-by-element comparison on the second. The first-page summary for the testing laboratory for last October showed the following information:

	Actual	Budget	Variance
Project 246	$ 4,650	$ 4,700	$ 50
Project 289	3,300	1,300	(2,000)
Project 294	3,530	5,200	1,670
Total	$11,480	$11,200	$ (280)

a. What useful information, if any, would this report give to the section chief in charge of the testing laboratory?

b. What changes would you make in this report to make it more useful to management?

19. Discretionary overhead costs. The report shown here was prepared for Project No. 16321 at the end of the project's second month. It was issued on May 5, 19x1, to Gretchen Hill, project engineer in the research division, and to Hill's immediate superior.

RESEARCH DIVISION
PROJECT SPENDING REPORT

Project No.: 16321   Period: March–April 19x1

Project Title: Sandfly Attachment   Supervisor: G. Hill

Start Date: 3/6/x1   Scheduled Completion: 11/30/x1

	Actual	Budget	Under/(Over)
Professional salaries	$2,170	$1,000	$(1,170)
Technical salaries	1,130	450	(680)
Laboratory services	15	—	(15)
Drafting services	95	100	5
Purchased materials	350	—	(350)
Purchased equipment	3,100	3,000	(100)
Total	$6,860	$4,550	$(2,310)

Additional information:

1. The budget data in the report show the amounts the company had planned to spend to achieve the amount of progress it had planned to make during March and April.
2. The work done on this project in March and April consisted of synthesis and analysis (half the work on this phase was done in March and the remainder was finished in April) and preparation of design specifications (the first 20 percent of this work was done in April).
3. Budgeted costs of the first two project phases were as follows:

	Synthesis and Analysis	Design Specification
Professional salaries	$2,000	$ 300
Technical salaries	900	500
Laboratory services	—	100
Drafting services	200	50
Purchased materials	450	250
Purchased equipment	3,000	—
Total	$5,550	$1,200

4. Expenditures for all project inputs except purchased parts and equipment were budgeted to take place in steady flows while the phase was being carried out. The equipment purchase in the synthesis and analysis phase was scheduled to take place during the first half of that phase. Materials purchases were budgeted to take place in the second half of the synthesis and analysis phase and uniformly throughout the specifications design phase.

5. The original budget called for the completion of half the synthesis and analysis phase during the first two months (March and April). No work on any other phase was scheduled for that period.

6. Shortly after work started on the project, Hill found that staff technicians had enough unscheduled time in March and April to allow her to accelerate the work on the synthesis and analysis phase and complete it during April, with time left over to begin work on the design specification phase.

7. When asked for a projection, Hill said that early completion of the synthesis and analysis phase would probably enable her to complete the entire project one month ahead of schedule, but she saw no reason to revise the original cost budget for the portions of the project which still lay ahead on April 30.

a. Prepare a revised cost-performance report for Project No. 16321 for the months of March and April 19x1, reflecting performance standards appropriate to the work done in April.

b. What information would you add to the report to give it a useful "future orientation"?

20. Report format; interpreting variances. The following report on direct materials and direct labor costs was prepared for a factory for the month of July:

	Direct Materials		Direct Labor	
Materials inventory, July 1	$10,000		$ —	
Work in process inventory, July 1	4,000		4,500	
Materials purchased during July	24,000		—	
Labor used during July	—		45,000	
Total cost to be accounted for		$38,000		$49,500
Materials inventory, July 31	8,000		—	
Work in process inventory, July 31	3,000		3,750	
Goods completed during July	29,000		44,700	
Total cost accounted for		40,000		48,450
Variance		$ 2,000		$ (1,050)

Additional data were as follows:

Materials purchased during July:	
At actual cost	$24,000
At standard cost	26,400
Direct materials used during	
July (at standard cost)	28,400
Direct labor used during July:	
At actual cost	45,000
At standard cost	44,250
Indirect materials used	
during July	None

a. Calculate the price and usage variances for direct materials and for direct labor.

b. Suggest ways of improving the format of the report on direct labor and direct materials variances which the accounting staff presents to the factory manager each month. What purpose would this report serve?

21. Determining and reporting direct labor and direct materials variances. Tufwun Products Company manufactures a limited line of machined products in its Albany factory. You have the following information on direct labor and direct materials costs in the milling department in September:

1. Direct labor in the department is divided into three pay grades, as follows:

Grade	Standard Wage Rate per Hour
101	$ 7
102	8
105	10

2. Wages actually earned by employees differ from these standard rates due to seniority provisions. Actual hours worked and actual gross pay during the month were as follows:

Grade	Hours	Gross Wages
101	1,250	$ 9,050
102	1,500	12,150
105	1,520	15,100
Total	4,270	$36,300

3. Production and product cost standards for the month:

	Standard Direct Materials Cost per Unit	Standard Milling Department Direct Labor per Unit			Standard Direct Labor Cost	Units Produced, September
Product		101 Hours	102 Hours	105 Hours		
A	$ 6	0.5	1.0	—	$11.50	400
B	12	1.0	0.5	1.5	26.00	800
C	15	0.5	1.0	0.5	16.50	600

4. Direct materials costs charged to the department, at standard prices, $22,800.

5. The department had no unfinished work in process either at the beginning or at the end of the month.

a. Analyze the milling department's direct labor and direct materials cost variances in September and prepare a summary for the factory manager's use in evaluating the department head's effectiveness in controlling these costs.

b. If you identified any variance that wouldn't enter into the evaluation of the department head's performance, indicate who might be interested in it and for what purpose.

c. Under what circumstances would the department head need more information than this system provides? What kinds of additional information would be required, and what would have to be done to provide it?

22.   Analyzing, reporting, and interpreting overhead variances.   Tumbler Company uses a system of department flexible budgets to provide overhead cost control information for its factory department managers. The monthly flexible budget for overhead costs in the machining department is as follows:

	Volume (machine-hours)				
	10,000	12,000	14,000	16,000	18,000
Supervision	$ 1,900	$ 1,900	$ 1,900	$ 2,200	$ 2,200
Indirect labor	2,000	2,200	2,400	2,600	2,800
Supplies	500	600	700	800	900
Payroll taxes	1,210	1,430	1,660	1,930	2,210
Overtime premiums	50	70	220	400	1,000
Depreciation	800	800	800	800	800
Floor-space charges	3,000	3,000	3,000	3,000	3,000
Engineering services	600	650	700	750	800
Total	$10,060	$10,650	$11,380	$12,480	$13,710

During May, this department operated 16,000 machine-hours and was charged the following amounts:

Supervision	$ 2,500
Indirect labor	2,710
Supplies	720
Payroll taxes	2,000
Overtime premiums	900
Depreciation	850
Floor-space charges	2,700
Engineering services	820
Total	$13,200

The following additional information is available:

1.   The department supervision account is ordinarily charged for the straight-time wages earned by assistant supervisors. Although these assistant supervisors are paid on an hourly basis, they usually work a full workweek. When the department head deems it necessary, a senior machinist is given additional supervisory duties, and a proportional part of that person's wages is charged to the supervision account.

2.   The plant manager assigned a quality-control supervisor to this department for three days in May to assist the department manager in the production of a long run of parts with very tight specifications. The department supervision account was charged $330 for the supervisor's services during this period.

3. The indirect labor account is charged for the wages of department materials handlers and helpers and also for the nonproductive time of machine operators. During May, machine operators were idle for approximately 40 hours because of machine breakdowns and delays in receiving work from other departments. The account was charged $420 for this idle time. The indirect labor budget figure includes an allowance for such costs in the amount of 1 cent per machine-hour.

4. Departments are charged for payroll taxes on all department wages, both direct and indirect. Payroll taxes are charged to the departments at a predetermined rate per labor-dollar. This rate is not changed during the year.

5. Overtime work in each department is scheduled monthly by the production scheduling department on the basis of scheduled production for the month. The department manager's primary responsibility is to meet the production schedule, using whatever overtime is necessary to accomplish this objective.

6. The depreciation charge is computed monthly on the basis of the original cost of the equipment located in the department as of the first day of the month.

7. Floor-space charges are computed monthly by multiplying the number of square feet of floor space occupied by each department by the average cost of building depreciation, insurance, utilities, and janitorial and maintenance services for that month.

8. Engineering services are provided to production departments by the factory engineering department. These services consist primarily of methods studies prepared at the request of the plant manager or on the initiative of the chief engineer. The charge for these services is based on a predetermined rate per engineering-hour.

a. Calculate and list the overhead spending variances in May, *ignoring* the "additional information" provided.

b. Using all the information available to you, determine the amounts you would report to the department manager and indicate why you believe the manager would find these amounts relevant. State your reason(s) for excluding any portion of any overhead spending variance.

c. Do the spending variances in May seem to warrant any action by the department manager? By anyone else? Explain.

23

Standard costing: Overhead variances and behavioral issues

Accountants usually incorporate procedures to identify and subdivide manufacturing cost spending variances in the formal accounting records. They do this by installing and using a *standard costing system,* consisting of a set of accounts, procedures, files, and reports which measure inputs, outputs, and inventories at their standard costs. The purpose of this final chapter is to examine three aspects of standard costing sytems we haven't yet considered:

1. Matching system structure with system purpose.
2. Analyzing variances from standard overhead cost.
3. Reflecting behavioral factors in system design.

SYSTEM STRUCTURE AND SYSTEM PURPOSE

We saw in Chapter 21 that management needs both steering controls and scorecard controls. Standard costing systems differ, depending on which kind of control information management wants them to provide.

TERMINOLOGY REMINDER

Steering controls consist of signals which are used to help management anticipate the need for action. *Scorecard controls* consist of performance summaries which measure the progress activities and managers have achieved in pursuit of preestablished goals or objectives.

Scorecard control systems

The variance information we described in Chapter 22 is primarily scorecard information. It is generated by cost accounting systems which have the following main characteristics:

1. Materials price and labor rate variances are identified and isolated at the time the goods and services are acquired, and they are not reported to the managers of factory production centers.
2. Direct labor and direct materials costs are accumulated by production centers, not by individual job orders or products.
   a. Production centers are charged for the actual quantities of direct labor and direct materials they use, multiplied by their standard prices.
   b. The output of production centers is measured by the standard cost of the work done (standard input quantities multiplied by standard input prices).
   c. Usage variances in direct labor and direct materials are identified at the end of each period for the production center as a whole, not for individual job orders or products.
3. Flexible budgets are used to identify spending variances in costs which aren't expected to vary in proportion to variations in production volume.

The direct labor and direct materials usage variances generated by systems with these characteristics are scorecard controls because (1) they aren't measured until the end of the period, and (2) they measure the cumulative effect of many individual variance-causing events which have taken place during the period. They reflect an assumption that the production center managers are close to the operations they are responsible for and therefore can observe variance-causing events as they take place. These managers don't need variance information from the accounting system to signal the need for action or investigation.

Steering control systems

If management wants its system to provide steering control information, accountants can develop procedures to identify each usage variance in direct labor and direct materials as it occurs. Systems of this kind provide a great deal of useful detail, and variances can be reported promptly enough to be the basis for early remedial action.

Labor time tickets. If the system is to provide steering control information for direct-labor costs, it must incorporate a separate time ticket for each separate labor operation. A sample time ticket is

EXHIBIT 23–1.   Labor Time Ticket for Steering Control

Item: Base plate No. 423
Batch quantity: 1,000 pieces
 	
Operation: 472—Press
Department: A
Operator: P. Jones
Job No.: X4474
	Date 4/7/x1
	
	Actual Hours:
	  Finish _____ 11.1
	  Start _____ 8.1
	  Difference _____ 3.0
	Standard Hours 2.5
	Variance Hours 0.5

shown in Exhibit 23–1. Each ticket is a record of the work done and of the variance arising from it. Time is recorded in this case in 10ths of hours. All the data on this form can be written or punched in advance except the actual time and the variance time. Data from the file of standard wage rates can then be used to restate these figures in dollars and cents.

Materials requisitions.   When materials usage is recorded by flow meters, as in some chemical operations, the usage variances can be identified on materials usage forms similar to labor time tickets. When a requisition system is used, however, the usage variances and the standard costs of the work done may be recorded separately. At the time a production order is prepared, a standard requisition card is prepared for the standard quantity of each material shown on the standard cost sheet. When a department begins work on the job, the department head exchanges the cards for the standard quantities shown on them.

Whenever additional materials are issued to cover excessive spoilage as the job progresses, a supplemental requisition card of a different color and with a distinctive code number is prepared, showing the quantity and code number of each of the supplemental materials. Similarly, if a job is completed without consuming all the materials issued, the excess materials are returned to the stockroom, where a returned materials card is filled out with the quantity of each material returned.

The supplemental requisitions in this system measure the unfavorable materials usage variances; the returned materials cards measure the favorable variances, as we can see in Exhibit 23–2. Each standard requisition measures the amount of work done, the

EXHIBIT 23–2.   Use of Materials Requisitions for Steering Control Information

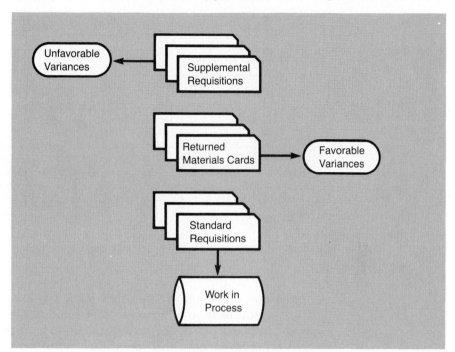

amount to be added to the work in process. The file of standard materials prices can be used to restate all these figures in monetary terms.

Reporting to management.   Systems of this sort allow the company's accountants to prepare variance reports in great detail. In many modern factories, computerized printouts of the previous day's labor performance are placed on each supervisor's desk at the start of each workday, with a separate line or lines for each operator. A truncated example of such a report is shown in Exhibit 23–3.

Reports of this kind are appropriate if they are to be used as steering controls. They may help the manager identify problems, trace them to their source, and do something about them before they have done much damage. Reporting too frequently may actually defeat its own purpose, however, by not making sufficient allowance for normal fluctuations in productive efficiency. Additional detail also makes reports difficult to read and obscures significant relationships. It also increases system cost. It is especially inappropriate when the manager's main need is for scorecard information rather than for steering control information.

For all these reasons, selective reporting is probably a better solu-

EXHIBIT 23–3.   Daily Labor Variance Report

Operator	Standard Hours	Actual Direct Hours (including personal time)	Variance	
			Hours	Percent of Standard
Department: Machining				Date: 3/6
Supervisor: P. B. Naum				
Brown, P.	8.2	8.0	0.2	2.4
Conrad, T. T.	8.6	8.0	0.6	7.0
Ennis, J.	3.3	4.0	(0.7)	(21.2)
Gordon, L.	8.4	9.5	(1.1)	(13.1)
King, M.	7.9	8.0	(0.1)	(1.3)

tion. At one extreme, the detailed variance data can be placed in a file, available to anyone who may need a special analysis for a specific purpose but not reported routinely to anyone. Alternatively, only variances larger than specified amounts or percentages might be reported, with all others remaining on file for later summarization and analysis.

System costs and benefits

Standard costing systems which are designed to provide steering control information tend to be more expensive than those intended to provide only scorecard information. Time tickets and requisitions may have roughly the same cost under either type of system, but steering control systems require more processing and prompter processing. Furthermore, as we pointed out earlier, they are capable of producing so much data that the managers may be overwhelmed.

For these reasons, management should call for greater system complexity only when it needs steering control information on a regular basis. If scorecard reports identify situations the department heads can't explain, detailed information can be obtained either by special processing of the time tickets and requisitions or by instituting detailed data-collection programs for short periods in the production center or centers in which the problem has occurred. These alternatives are likely to be less expensive and more flexible than routine generation of detailed usage variances on a daily basis.

OVERHEAD COST VARIANCES

In any costing system which uses predetermined overhead rates on a full-costing basis, the factory is given credit for the amounts assigned to individual products. These amounts are referred to as *absorbed overhead*. The difference between the actual overhead cost and the absorbed overhead is known as the *total overhead variance*.[1] Our objective in this section is to show how the overhead-cost spending variances identified in Chapter 22 can be reconciled with the total overhead variance.

Total overhead variance

In introducing job order costing in Chapter 18, we used a predetermined overhead rate with direct labor-hours as the denominator. The amount of overhead absorbed (charged to products) was determined by multiplying the rate by the number of direct labor-hours actually used. In a standard costing system, the procedure is the same but the amount of overhead absorbed is the predetermined overhead rate times the number of *standard* direct labor-hours, machine-hours, or other product characteristic which serves as the denominator of the overhead rate.

Morley Company, a small manufacturer in job order production, uses the number of standard direct labor-hours each product requires to measure the volume of output for purposes of overhead absorption in its machining department; that is, the amount of overhead required by any product is assumed to be proportional to the number of standard direct labor-hours it requires in machining. Total output therefore is measured by making the following calculation for each product, and adding across all products manufactured in the period:

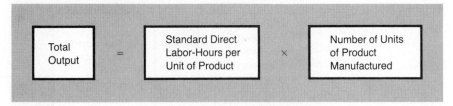

A product requiring two standard direct labor-hours in machining therefore causes twice as much machining department overhead

---

[1] When we encountered this distinction in Chapter 18, the total overhead variance was called the over- or underabsorbed overhead. Our concern there was limited to whether the entire variance should appear as an immediate determinant of income. Our present task is to identify the managerial significance of each component of the total overhead variance.

cost to be included in the cost of the total output as a product requiring one standard direct labor-hour.

The machining department's predetermined overhead rate in 19x1 was derived as follows:

The flexible budget for overhead costs was summarized in the following formula:

Budgeted overhead = $27,500 a month + $4 × Standard direct labor-hours

Normal volume was 2,500 standard direct labor-hours a month. The standard overhead rate therefore was ($27,500 + $4 × 2,500) divided by 2,500 hours = $15 a standard direct labor-hour.

In September 19x1:

1. The machining department was charged $35,910 in overhead costs.
2. The department's output required 2,300 standard direct labor hours, calculated as shown in Exhibit 23–4. In this case, 2,200 standard hours were required by the units finished, and 100 standard hours were required to increase the work in process from 400 standard hours on September 1 to 500 standard hours on September 30.
3. The total flexible budget for overhead costs for the month's actual output (2,300 standard direct labor-hours) was $27,500 + $4 × 2,300 = $36,700.
4. The amount of overhead absorbed was $34,500 (2,300 standard

EXHIBIT 23–4. Machining Department: Standard Direct Labor-Hours of Output in the Month of September 19x1

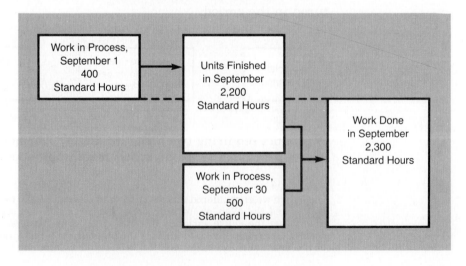

EXHIBIT 23–5. Machining Department: Derivation of Total Overhead Variance

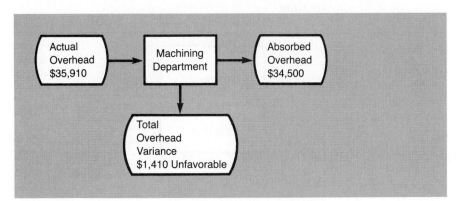

direct labor-hours × $15). The amount absorbed is called the standard overhead cost for the month. This amount was assigned to products manufactured in September and was placed in inventory accounts for later transfer to the cost of goods sold.

These numbers are assembled in Exhibit 23–5. This shows how the actual overhead for the period ($35,910) was split into two components. $34,500 of the total was spent to produce output with a standard overhead cost of $34,500—this was the amount of absorbed overhead in September 19x1. The rest of the overhead cost ($1,410) wasn't assigned to any of the department's output—instead, it was classified as an unfavorable cost variance, representing resources used without yielding any productive output.

Reasons for the overhead variance

The total overhead variance, also referred to as the amount of overhead over- or underabsorbed, arises mainly as a result of two forces:

1. *Spending* variations: Actual costs differ from the amounts that would normally be expected at the production volume actually achieved during the period.
2. *Volume* variations: Production volume during the period differs from the volume used in setting the overhead rate.

We know from Chapter 22 that a spending variance in overhead costs in job order production represents the difference between the actual overhead cost and the overhead-cost flexible budget for the actual volume of activity in the period. For Morley Company, we can calculate the September overhead spending variance as follows, using items 1 and 3 in the data supplied at the beginning of this section:

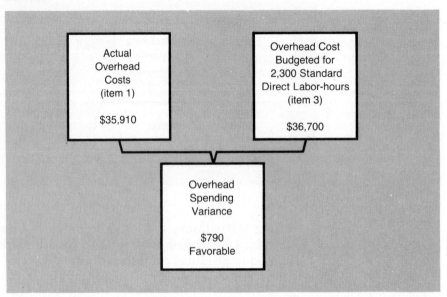

We also know that the *total* overhead cost variance this month was $1,410 and was *unfavorable.* This means that there was some other influence producing an unfavorable variance of $2,200:

Total variance	$1,410	unfavorable
Spending variance	790	favorable
Variance from other influences	$2,200	unfavorable

The other influence in this case was Morley's overall *production volume,* which amounted to 2,300 standard direct labor-hours in September instead of the 2,500-hour normal volume. Morley expected total fixed overhead cost to amount to $27,500 in an average month, and this fixed overhead cost accounted for $11 of the department's $15 predetermined overhead rate for 19x1:

$$\frac{\text{Total fixed cost}}{\text{Normal volume}} = \frac{\$27,500}{2,500 \text{ standard direct labor-hours}} = \$11 \text{ an hour}$$

If volume had reached 2,500 standard hours in September, then all the budgeted fixed costs would have been absorbed, as Exhibit 23–6 shows. Instead, actual volume was 200 standard direct labor-hours less than normal. This means that the fixed costs that would have been absorbed by these 200 hours had no place to go, no product

EXHIBIT 23–6. Overhead Volume Variance

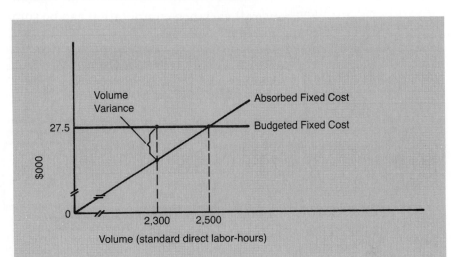

to absorb them. Low volume therefore accounted for 200 × $11 = $2,200 of the unabsorbed overhead. We call this the *overhead volume variance.*[2]

Interpreting the volume variance

The volume variance must be interpreted carefully. It doesn't mean that costs were $2,200 more than expected because volume was lower than normal. It merely says that no production was available to absorb $2,200 of the costs that were expected to occur. Expressed differently, $2,200 was spent to provide production capacity the company didn't use.

Department heads don't establish their own production schedules. The volume of activity is determined outside the factory, on the basis of the number of customer orders in hand or anticipated. This being so, volume variances aren't controllable by the department head or even by the plant manager. They should be reported to plant managers only to help them explain the total overhead variance to higher management, and they shouldn't be reported to the department managers at all.

---

[2] If the overhead rate had been recalculated at the actual volume (2,300 standard hours), the fixed-cost component would have been $11.956 an hour ($27,500/2,300). The $2,200 unfavorable volume variance therefore represents the additional $0.956 that each of the 2,300 standard hours would have absorbed because of the 200-hour shortfall (2,300 × $0.956 = $2,200).

Reconciling the variances

The overall variance computation can be summarized in the following manner:

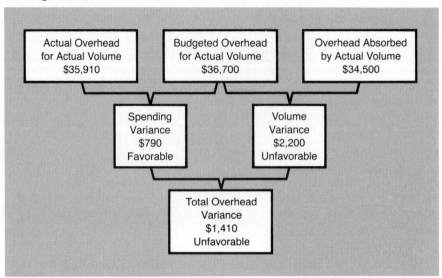

Exhibit 23–7 presents this same information in graphic form. This is similar to Exhibit 23–6 except that it includes the variable overhead costs as well as the fixed overhead. The amount of overhead absorbed is shown by the height of the straight line rising from the lower left-hand corner of the chart. The amount budgeted is shown by the height of the other line. Because some of the department's costs are fixed, this line has a gentler slope than the Absorbed Overhead line. Variable costs in this case are proportional to volume—$4 in budgeted variable costs for each standard direct labor-hour—and thus the flexible budget is shown as a straight line.

The amounts budgeted and absorbed at this month's volume of 2,300 standard hours are shown as large dots on these two lines. The actual amount spent is shown by another dot. By measuring the vertical distances between dots, we are able to identify the total variance and its two component parts.

Volume variances at volumes in excess of normal volume, such as *b* in Exhibit 23–7, represent *over*absorption and are classified as favorable. Volume variances at volumes lower than normal, such as *a* in the exhibit, represent underutilization of capacity and are referred to as unfavorable.

Three-variance analysis

The two-part division of the variance from standard overhead cost into spending and volume components is appropriate only if

EXHIBIT 23–7. Reconciliation of Overhead Cost Variances

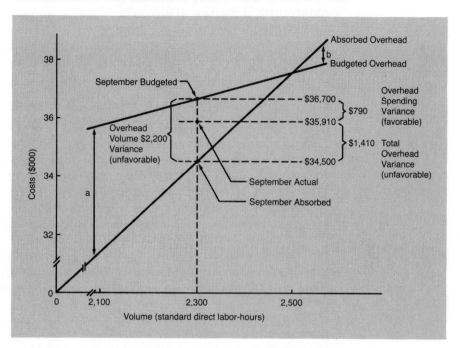

overhead costs are expected to vary with output, in this case measured by total standard direct labor-hours. If overhead costs vary with *actual inputs,* however, the two-variance approach is no longer appropriate. In those situations, three variances can be identified, and the spending variances are calculated by comparing actual costs with the flexible budget appropriate to the number of inputs actually used:

Spending Variances if Overhead Costs Vary with Actual Inputs: The Difference between Actual Costs and Budgeted Costs Appropriate for Actual Input Quantities	*Spending Variances if Overhead Costs Vary with Standard Inputs:* The Difference between Actual Costs and Budgeted Costs Appropriate for Standard Input Quantities

The difference between the total budget at the actual input level and the total budget at the standard input level then becomes a third variance, attributable to the company's efficiency in using these inputs.

For example, suppose management finds that variations in the machining department's overhead costs appear to be influenced by variations in the *actual* number of direct labor-hours used instead of by variations in output, as measured by the number of *standard* direct labor-hours. The flexible budget formula is:

$$\text{Total overhead cost} = \$27,500 + \$4 \times \text{Actual direct labor-hours}$$

This means that every time the department wastes (or saves) a direct labor-hour, it will be likely to waste (or ought to save) $4 in overhead costs. In September, the department wasted 20 direct labor-hours—it used 2,320 direct labor-hours instead of the 2,300 standard hours required by the work done during the month. Inefficiency in labor usage, in other words, increased the budgeted overhead cost by 20 × $4 = $80. We call this the labor efficiency component of the overhead cost variance or, more simply, the *labor efficiency variance*. It measures the estimated effect on the overhead cost of efficiency or inefficiency in the use of direct labor inputs.

This new variance fits into the total overhead variance in the manner shown in Exhibit 23–8. The volume variance is the same as in the two-variance system, but the spending variance is different. The difference lies in the new third variance, the labor efficiency variance. The sum of the spending and labor efficiency variances is equal to the spending variance in a two-variance system.

EXHIBIT 23–8.   Reconciling the Overhead Cost Variance: Three-Variance System

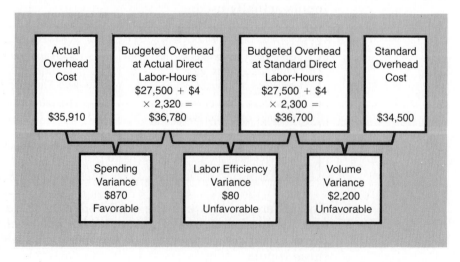

The significance of the three-variance system is that it sheds additional light on the $790 favorable spending variance we calculated earlier. It reveals that the spending variance was really $870, but that labor inefficiency deprived the department of $80 of that favorable variance. This additional disclosure enables the company to measure the full effect of using 20 more labor-hours than the 2,300 standard hours.

Overhead variance analysis in the absence of standard costing

Rather than use standard overhead costs for product costing, many companies use predetermined full-cost overhead rates, as we illustrated in Chapter 18. In these cases, the denominator of the overhead rate is likely to be the estimated number of *actual* input units that production in a normal period will require. When this is done, companies will be able to calculate only two variances— a spending variance and a volume variance. The spending variance will be the same as in the three-variance system (a favorable $870 in our example), but the volume variance will be different and the labor efficiency variance can't be calculated at all.

For example, if a direct-labor-hour denominator is used, the overhead rate will be as follows:

$$\text{Predetermined overhead rate} = \frac{\text{Estimated overhead cost}}{\text{Estimated actual direct labor-hours}}$$

The amount of overhead absorbed then becomes the predetermined rate multiplied by the number of direct input units (direct labor-hours in our illustration) actually used during the period. This amount is shown in the box in the upper right-hand corner of Exhibit 23–9.

The flexible budget under these conditions is also likely to use the number of actual direct inputs as the measure of overall volume. Morley Company's machining department, for example, might have the following flexible budget:

$$\text{Budgeted overhead} = \$27,500 + \$4 \times \text{Actual direct labor-hours}$$

Without standard costing, the amount of overhead absorbed by production in September would be $34,800 (2,320 actual hours × $15 predetermined rate). The flexible budget for the month would be

EXHIBIT 23–9.   Calculation of Overhead Variances without Standard Costing

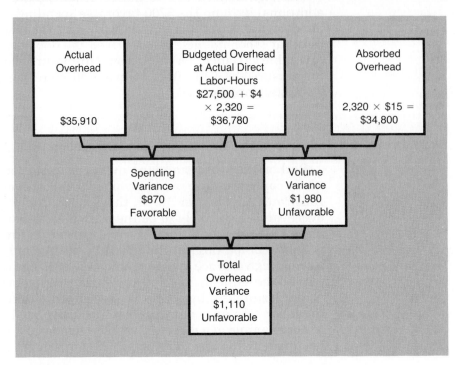

$36,780 ($27,500 + $4 × 2,320). The overhead variances would be those shown in the lower part of Exhibit 23–9.

Management's interest in overhead volume variances

Responsibility for factory overhead volume variances lies with those who are responsible for generating volume. In most cases, marketing management, not manufacturing management, has this responsibility. Information on volume variances can be useful as a partial determinant of the profit-generating ability of marketing managers and marketing activities. It also lets higher management know how much fixed overhead cost will be deducted directly from revenues because production is too low to absorb it.

Assigning manufacturing volume variances to marketing management is a simple process if all the factory's output goes to a single revenue segment. For example, Fortune Company produced and sold 100,000 units of its only product in June at a selling price of $20 each. Its factory has fixed costs of $320,000 a month and variable costs of $8 a unit. Normal production volume was 80,000 units a month, so that the standard product cost was $12 a unit

($320,000/80,000 + $8). The standard cost of goods sold in June therefore amounted to $1,200,000 (100,000 × $12). Since production volume in June was equal to sales volume (100,000 units), the overhead volume variance was as follows:

Factory costs absorbed by production: 100,000 × $12................. $1,200,000
Budgeted factory costs at actual volume: $320,000 + 100,000 × $8 1,120,000
Overhead volume variance (favorable) .... $ 80,000

Because total fixed cost is the same at normal volume as at actual volume, the $80,000 favorable volume variance is equal to the product of standard fixed cost ($4 a unit) and the difference between actual and budgeted volume, 20,000 units (100,000 − 80,000).

Fortune Company's gross margin can be calculated on both full-costing and variable-costing bases:

	Full Costing	Variable Costing
Sales revenues	$2,000,000	$2,000,000
Cost of goods sold:		
Standard cost	1,200,000	800,000
Overhead volume variance...................	(80,000)	—
Budgeted fixed cost........................	—	320,000
Total cost of goods sold	1,120,000	1,120,000
Gross margin	$ 880,000	$ 880,000

This indicates that by adjusting the cost of goods sold to reflect the favorable volume variance, the full-costing company allows management to reap the full credit for above-normal sales volume, as it would under variable costing.

Suppose, however, Fortunate Company had *two* marketing divisions, each selling 50,000 units of product manufactured in a single factory. Rather than split the volume variance equally between the two divisions (in proportion to unit sales), we need to determine how much of the variance each division was responsible for. In this case, we find that division A was budgeted to sell only 30,000 units, while division B was budgeted to sell the 50,000 units it actually sold. It is clear, therefore, that the entire volume variance should go to division A. In general, allocation of the volume variance becomes more and more difficult as the number of revenue segments served by a given factory increases.

In concluding our discussion of the overhead volume variance, we need to make only two final comments. First, overhead volume variances arise as a result of the volume of *production*. If production volume differs from sales volume, assigning the overhead volume variance to marketing management may distort the measure of the marketing group's profit performance in the current period. The overhead volume variance (from production) may even be favorable when *sales* volume is *below* its normal level, and vice versa.

Second, the argument for assigning volume variances to marketing management shouldn't be extended to factory spending variances. Marketing management is responsible for sales volume and sales mix, not for factory production costs. Only when marketing management's actions lead to changes in factory costs should it be charged or credited for portions of the factory spending variances. Design modifications or marketing-required changes in production schedules, for example, might justify distribution of some factory spending variances, but the controllability criterion will be violated unless the amounts to be distributed are established when the changes are authorized by marketing management.

BEHAVIORAL ISSUES IN COST CONTROL SYSTEMS

Cost standards designed for use in connection with a company's efforts to control its costs are only one element in a much broader system. Other elements include the leadership styles of managers at various levels and the structure of rewards and penalties for good and bad performance. In other words, the way standards are used may even be as important as the level at which they are set or the means by which they are derived. In this final section, we'll summarize very briefly some behavioral issues which must be resolved if standards are to be used effectively.

Identifying cost responsibility

Assigning costs to organizational units whose managers are responsible for controlling them is not as easy as we may have implied. A cardinal rule in management is that department heads can't be held responsible for personnel not under their supervision or for material or services they haven't requisitioned. For example, if workers and material under the supervision of Jones are used to provide a service used by Smith, Smith can't be held responsible for the cost of providing the service. Smith may be held responsible for the use of the service, but the primary point for control of cost is Jones.

One problem is that actual authority and responsibility relationships typically depart in significant respects from those embodied in the formal organization structure. This can't be blamed on management incompetence in establishing the organization structure. Organization charts are a gross oversimplification of reality. Even the plant manager has more than one boss, and to represent all the connections between a staff worker or a department manager and other personnel in a company, one would have to draw lines upward, laterally, and at various angles.

Given this, it is especially important for all levels of management

EXHIBIT 23–10.   Influences on Personal Aspiration Levels

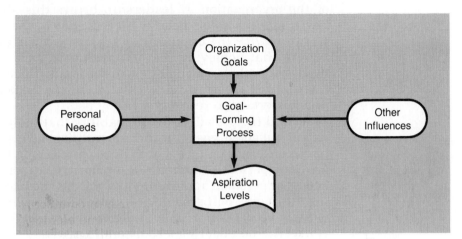

to recognize that (1) department managers aren't *solely* responsible for the costs assigned to them and (2) they aren't *without* responsibility for these costs. Once these points are recognized, it should be a simple matter to recognize that budgetary control systems should be used more to identify problem areas and effective actions than to assign absolute credit or absolute blame.

Budgets as operational objectives

The reporting systems we have been describing in these three final chapters are based on the assumption that management at all levels will strive to reach or surpass budgeted performance levels. In other words, it is assumed that other elements in the managerial system, not the budgets or standards themselves, will be effective in motivating managers. This doesn't happen automatically. Individual motivation is determined by the needs of the employees themselves and their perception that performance (e.g., achieving budgeted performance) will lead to the satisfaction of these needs.[3]

The diagram in Exhibit 23–10 attempts to show the relationships between the needs of the individuals in the organization and other factors influencing their behavior. Managerial leadership is one of the other influences—the right-hand oval in the diagram—which

---

[3] See Edward E. Lawler III, *Motivation in Work Organizations* (Monterey, Calif.: Brooks/Cole, 1973). The relationships between control systems and individual needs are summarized in an excellent book by Edward E. Lawler III and John Grant Rhode, *Information and Control in Organizations* (Pacific Palisades, Calif.: Goodyear Publishing Co., 1976), especially chap. 2.

determine whether the goals of the individual coincide with those of the organization. If leadership brings this about, we say that *goal congruence* has been achieved; that is, the managers accept or *internalize* the organization's goals as their own because they believe that achieving the organization's goals will satisfy their needs better than not achieving them. Goals which individuals have internalized are known as *aspiration levels,* the performance levels they undertake to reach.

Several factors affect the probability that individuals will internalize budgeted goals as their aspiration levels. One of these is past experience—success or failure in reaching budgeted goals in previous periods. Another is the priority they assign to their own needs for personal achievement. A third is the likelihood that meeting the budget will provide this sense of achievement. Still another is their perception of how difficult achieving the budgeted goals is likely to be under expected conditions.[4]

Goal congruence is the most critical behavioral problem management faces in the budgetary process. The prospect of promotion, incentive pay schemes, participation in setting the budget, and other means are used to bring about goal congruence. Aspiration levels differ among individuals, however. Some value the "good life" and the approval of their subordinates more than organizational success. Policies that achieve goal congruence for one individual may not succeed for another. Changes in operating conditions or in a person's thinking as time goes by may influence his or her aspiration level. This makes it difficult to use aspiration levels as the basis for performance standards.

Participation

One way to get subordinate managers to internalize performance standards is to have them participate in setting the standards. Participation means that decisions are, to some extent, joint decisions of managers and their superiors. It doesn't mean that both must be in full agreement on every decision, but the subordinates must be convinced that they are being given a fair shake.

Participation doesn't automatically insure the internalization of performance standards. The gap between the individual's goals and those of the organization may be too great to be bridged. Furthermore, conditions may be such that a more authoritarian managerial style will be more effective in raising the aspiration levels of subordinates. Even so, participation may be very useful. First, it can

---

[4] For a more extended discussion of the factors which influence performance, see L. W. Porter, E. E. Lawler, and J. R. Hackman, *Behavior in Organizations* (New York: McGraw-Hill, 1975).

be used to strengthen the bonds among members of the group by providing more effective communication. Second, it can increase the visibility of the progress that each member of the group is making toward internalization of organizational goals. The first of these increases the desire of individuals to share the goals of others in the group; the second increases their ability to do this.[5]

Attainability

One assumption underlying most responsibility accounting systems is that performance standards should be set at levels described as "tight but attainable" or "reasonably attainable." The argument for this assumption is that as long as performance standards don't exceed amounts that are reasonably attainable, managers will internalize them. If standards are set tighter than this, managers and their subordinates will regard them as unrealistic and will not be motivated by them.

The main issue isn't how to establish the performance level that is tight but attainable. The main problem is to design a package of techniques to motivate employees to perform better than they would in the absence of the standards. This shouldn't be confused with management by pressure. Some managers exert pressure on their subordinates to strive to meet standards which are difficult or even impossible to meet. This tactic is likely to backfire. Grievances mount and the relationships between managers and their subordinates deteriorate. Lower-level supervisors may unite with their subordinates against their superiors, creating problems which then serve as reasons for failure to meet standards. Alternatively, managers and supervisors may seek ways to beat the system—for example, by falsifying records or by performing in such a way that variances will arise elsewhere or in later periods.

In short, standards which are too tight to be internalized are unlikely to be effective motivators for long.

SUMMARY

Costing systems which incorporate standard product costs in the formal accounting records are known as standard costing systems. Simple standard costing systems identify direct labor and direct materials usage variances in total for each production center each period. Standard costing systems of this sort provide scorecard information only; if steering control information is needed, the system

---

[5] For a further examination of these and related issues, see Lawler and Rhode, *Information and Control in Organizations.*

can be refined to provide prompter, more detailed reporting of the usage variances—but at increased cost.

Standard overhead costs don't provide performance standards for cost control, but they facilitate inventory recordkeeping and they identify excess costs which will be likely to depress reported income. Variances between actual overhead cost and standard overhead cost in each period can be subdivided into components with the aid of data from the flexible budget. In most cases, there is (1) an overhead spending variance, which is the difference between actual overhead cost and the flexible budget for overhead cost in the current period, and (2) a volume variance, which reflects variations from the capacity utilization on which the overhead rates were predicated. Further subdivisions of the total overhead variance can be made to reflect other factors influencing the overhead cost.

In all cases, management should consider the behavioral consequences of its performance standards. Although standards are only part of the overall system designed to achieve goal congruence in the organization, they should be set in such a way and at such levels as to improve the chances of achieving goal congruence. Participation by subordinates in the standard-setting process is widely believed to be a useful means toward this end.

KEY TERMS

Aspiration level	Participation
Goal congruence	Scorecard control
Overhead labor efficiency variance	Standard costing system
Overhead spending variance	Steering control
Overhead volume variance	Total overhead variance

INDEPENDENT STUDY PROBLEMS (Solutions in Appendix B)

1. Calculating and analyzing factory overhead variances. Cotton Company uses a standard costing system and develops volume and spending variances in its overhead costs. You are given the following information for one of the company's factory departments for the month of May:

1. Overhead costs are expected to vary with output rather than with actual direct labor-hours. The overhead budget was $4,680 a month plus $1.15 per standard direct labor-hour.
2. The normal level of production was 9,000 standard direct labor-hours.
3. The standard overhead cost of the work in process inventory at the beginning of May was $6,680.

4. The standard direct labor content of the products completed and transferred out of the department during the month was 10,500 hours.
5. The standard direct labor content of the work in process was 4,000 hours at the start of the month and 3,600 hours at the end.
6. The department worked 10,800 direct labor-hours during the month.
7. The actual overhead cost for the month was $17,400.

a. Calculate the standard overhead cost of the work done in this department during the month.
b. What was the standard overhead cost of the work in process at the end of the month?
c. Develop the department's overhead spending and volume variances for the month.

2. Three-variance method. After further analysis, Cotton Company's management (see problem 1) has concluded that variable overhead costs in this department vary at the rate of $1.15 for each actual direct labor-hour. All other facts are as stated in problem 1.

a. Prepare an analysis of the total overhead variance in this department, using the three-variance method.
b. Why is the three-variance method appropriate here, whereas the two-variance method was appropriate under the conditions stated in problem 1?

EXERCISES AND PROBLEMS

3. Calculating department volume. A standard costing system is used. The department's overhead cost budget is based on standard direct labor-hours. Normal volume for the department is 20,000 standard direct labor-hours a month, and the overhead rate is $3 a standard direct labor-hour. Overhead cost fluctuations correlate more closely with product output than with direct labor input.

During the month, 21,300 actual direct labor-hours were used. The department finished and transferred to other departments products with a standard overhead cost of $69,000. The standard overhead cost of work in process in this department was $16,200 on the first of the month and $18,000 at the end of the month.

Calculate the number of hours on which the flexible budget allowances for the month should be based.

4. Variance calculation exercise. Overhead costs in one of Bastian Corporation's factory departments are expected to total $8,000 a month plus $1.40 per standard direct labor-hour. The normal level of output is 11,000 standard direct labor-hours a month.

During the month of June, the actual overhead costs were $22,100, and the actual level of activity was 9,300 standard direct labor-hours.

a. Calculate the standard overhead rate for this department.

b. Calculate the volume and spending variances for the month.

5. Variance calculation exercise; reporting to management. A standard costing system is in use, and standard factory overhead cost is $2 per standard direct labor-hour. Overhead costs vary with the number of standard direct labor-hours, according to the following formula:

Budgeted costs = $11,000 per month + $0.90 per standard direct labor-hour

Actual overhead costs for October totaled $22,140, and 11,200 direct labor-hours were recorded. Product standard costs and actual production volumes for October were:

Product	Standard Overhead Cost per Unit	Units Produced, October
A	$ 5	100
B	6	500
C	10	1,000
D	3	1,200
E	2	2,000

a. Compute the total overhead variance, an overhead spending variance, and an overhead volume variance for the month. Indicate in each case whether the variance is favorable or unfavorable.

b. How, if at all, should the volume variance be reported to management? To what management level would you report it?

6. System purpose and design. The voice of Gregory Fortesque, a department foreman in Artis Company's factory, got angrier and angrier as he complained to Chester van Allen, the factory controller. "How can I manage this department if you don't tell me where the variances come from?" he demanded. "Telling me at the end of the month that I had a 10 percent materials usage variance may make you feel better, but it doesn't do me any good, and that's for sure!"

Fortesque is responsible for the operations of a factory production department which uses 14 machines of three different types and functions, and he has 12 employees. He has been head of this department for six months; van Allen has been factory controller for three years and is likely to be promoted to a higher position in controllership later this year.

a. What is the basis of this argument? What message is Fortesque trying to convey?

b. As van Allen, how would you reply? Should the data-gathering and reporting system be changed?

7. Supplying missing information: two-variance analysis. Manchester Tool Works has a standard costing system. Variable factory overhead costs in each department vary with department output, measured by the number of standard direct labor-hours. You have the following data for two departments for the month of June:

	Department S	Department T
Standard overhead rate per standard direct labor-hour	A	$4.50
Actual direct labor-hours	1,900	4,500
Standard direct labor-hours (June)	1,800	F
Standard direct labor-hours at normal volume	B	4,000
Budgeted fixed cost	$5,000	G
Budgeted variable overhead cost for each standard direct labor-hour	$1	$2.50
Actual overhead cost................................	$6,700	$20,300
Standard overhead cost	C	$21,600
Overhead spending variance	D	H
Overhead volume variance	E	I
Total overhead variance	$400 unfavorable	J

Make the necessary calculations and supply the information missing from this table.

8. Supplying missing information: three-variance analysis. Dorset, Inc., has a factory with 15 production departments. A standard costing system is in use. The following data apply to two factory departments during the month of May:

	Department A	Department B
Standard overhead rate per standard direct labor-hour	A	$8
Actual direct labor-hours (May)	2,200	G
Standard direct labor-hours (May)	2,000	5,500
Normal volume (standard direct labor-hours)	2,500	H
Budgeted fixed overhead cost	$10,000	$25,000
Budgeted variable overhead cost for each actual direct labor-hour	$2	$3
Total overhead variance	$3,000 unfavorable	I
Overhead spending variance	B	J
Overhead labor efficiency variance	C	$900 favorable
Overhead volume variance	D	K
Actual overhead cost............................	E	$42,000
Standard overhead cost of actual work done	F	L

Make the necessary calculations and supply the information missing from this table.

9. Effect of variances on income. A company has made the following estimates of the percentages of expenses to sales revenues, based on a normal sales volume of $10 million:

Variable manufacturing	45%
Fixed manufacturing	30
Selling and administrative (all fixed)	15
Total expenses	90%

The cost of goods sold and the cost of units in inventory are measured at predetermined unit costs based on normal production volume. The company has units in inventory with a sale value of more than $1 million. The unit cost of manufacturing these units was identical to expected average manufacturing cost this year at normal volume. All factory cost variances are reported immediately in the income statement as they arise.

a. What effect would a $1 million increase in sales, unaccompanied by an increase in production, have on income before taxes?

b. What effect would increasing production by a quantity of goods with a sales value of $1 million have on income before taxes if that increase were unaccompanied by an increase in sales?

10. Interpreting changes in average overhead cost. The Dearborn Company manufactures product X in standard batches of 100 units. A standard cost system is in use. The standard costs for a batch are as follows:

Direct materials—60 pounds at $0.45 a pound	$ 27.00
Direct labor—12 hours at $8.60 an hour	103.20
Overhead—12 hours at $6.10 an hour	73.20
Total standard cost per batch	$203.40

Dearborn's normal monthly output is 2,400 batches (240,000 units). Factory fixed costs are budgeted at $89,280 a month.

Dearborn Company's management is worried by the size of factory overhead costs, which make up more than a third of the standard costs of product X. Accordingly, when the actual average overhead cost for April fell to $6.05 per actual direct labor-hour, management felt somewhat encouraged.

Actual production in April amounted to 2,100 batches. Actual overhead cost totaled $166,375. Variable overhead costs vary with the number of standard direct labor-hours.

a. Should Dearborn's management be encouraged by the reduction in average overhead cost? Prepare an analysis of the overhead variance that will help you come to a conclusion on this point.

b. List the departures from normal conditions which affected average cost per direct labor-hour in April, and indicate which of them probably increased average cost and which of them probably decreased average cost. You need not quantify the effects.

c. Would average overhead cost per direct labor-hour be a useful index of production efficiency for the factory manager? For the president? Comment.

11. Labor and overhead variance exercise. The data here relate to the month of April 19x1 for Marilyn, Inc., which uses a standard costing system:

Actual total direct-labor cost	$130,200
Actual direct labor-hours used	14,000
Standard direct labor-hours allowed for good output	15,000
Direct labor rate variance—unfavorable	$ 4,200
Actual total overhead cost	$ 32,000
Budgeted fixed overhead costs	$ 9,000
Normal volume in standard direct labor-hours	12,000
Total predetermined overhead rate per standard direct labor-hour	$2.25

Variable overhead costs are expected to vary with department output, measured by the number of standard direct labor-hours.

a. Calculate the direct labor usage variance for the month and indicate whether it was favorable or unfavorable.
b. Calculate the overhead spending variance for the month and indicate whether it was favorable or unfavorable.
c. Calculate the overhead volume variance and indicate whether it was favorable or unfavorable.

(AICPA adapted)

12. Standard costing: service organization. In an effort to control costs, Hilltop College has just established a "standard instructional cost per student" for each course in the college's catalog. A variance is then calculated each term for each course offered that term.

No standards have been developed for the costs of teaching materials and supplies, and the costs of these items are not assigned to individual courses.

The standard cost per student for Basket Weaving 476 is $90. In the spring term 30 students enrolled in this course. The actual cost assigned to the course that term was $5,500, representing one sixth of the annual salary and fringe benefits of the instructor, Professor J. B. Braithwaite, chairman pro tem of the Basket Weaving Department, plus the cost of 100 hours spent by a graduate student writing multiple-choice examination questions and grading student term papers.

The college's controller made the following analysis of the variance for this course:

Standard cost, actual enrollment: 30 × $90	$2,700	Enrollment variance = $1,800 unfavorable
Standard cost, planned enrollment: 50 × $90	4,500	
Actual cost	5,500	Salary variance = $1,000 unfavorable

Total variance = $2,800 unfavorable

The controller calculated that $800 of the salary variance arose because Braithwaite's salary per course was $800 more than the average salary of the members of the basket weaving faculty. The remainder arose because Braithwaite used more graduate-student time than was planned for this course.

a. How do the purposes of this system differ from the purposes ascribed in this chapter to factory standard costing systems? To what extent are they the same? In answering this, you should try to identify the actions management might take in response to information the system provides. Distinguish between the actions management might take in response to information contained in the standards themselves and actions it might take in response to variance information.
b. Does this system appear to be a good way to achieve the purposes you identified in part a? In answering this, try to identify any problems

that might arise in implementing this system and indicate whether they can be solved without great difficulty.

13.   Interpreting profit contribution. Georgia Ellis was the marketing manager for her company's cosmetic products. She reported to David Thompson, the company's marketing vice president. Ellis supervised a field sales force engaged exclusively in marketing the cosmetics line. Factory operations, however, were within the jurisdiction of the manufacturing vice president. Many steps in the production process for the cosmetics products were performed on a job order basis by the personnel of factory departments also engaged in the manufacture of other company products.

Ellis received the following income statement for the cosmetics line for the month of August (in $000):

	July Actual	August Actual	August Budget	August Variance
Sales	$1,000	$1,300	$1,200	$100
Standard cost of goods sold	600	800	720	(80)
Gross margin	400	500	480	20
Direct marketing expenses	150	155	150	(5)
Marketing margin	250	345	330	15
Favorable/(unfavorable) factory variances:				
Overhead volume variance	10	(50)	—	(50)
Overhead spending variance	5	(6)	—	(6)
Direct cost variances	(12)	(54)	—	(54)
Profit contribution	$ 253	$ 235	$ 330	$ (95)

Inventories of cosmetics products remained constant and at budgeted levels throughout July and August.

Thompson called Ellis into his office shortly after this report was issued and told her that in view of her poor performance in August, a scheduled promotion to the title of assistant vice president would be postponed. "We'll see how you do in September and October," she was told.

a.   You are a consultant on retainer for this company and you happened to overhear this conversation. Draft a statement, outlining your evaulation of Ellis's performance. If you would like to have additional information, say what you would like to have, but you must give a tentative answer to this question before the additional information becomes available.

b.   List changes, if any, that you would like to make in the company's reporting system and explain why you would make them.

14.   Setting a standard performance level. Alton Company is expanding its punch press department. It is about to purchase three new punch presses from Equipment Manufacturers, Inc. Equipment Manufacturers' engineers report that their mechanical studies indicate that for Alton's intended use, the output rate for one press should be 1,000 pieces an hour.

Alton has similar presses now in operation. Production from these presses averaged 600 pieces an hour last month, based on the following record of performance:

Worker	Hourly Output
L. Jones	750
J. Green	750
R. Smith	600
H. Brown	500
R. Alters	550
G. Hoag	450
Total	3,600
Average	600

Alton's management also plans to institute a standard cost accounting system in the near future. The company's engineers are supporting a standard based on 1,000 pieces an hour, the accounting department is arguing for 750 pieces an hour, and the production department supervisor is arguing for 600 pieces an hour.

a. What arguments would the various proponents be likely to use to support their recommendations?
b. Which alternative best reconciles the needs of cost control and the motivation of improved performance? Explain why you made that choice.

(CMA adapted)

15. Performance standards for motivation. Ray Carlson, president of Scientific Equipment Manufacturing Company, wants to introduce standard costing into his company's factory. As a result of his participation in a two-week management development course at a nearby university, Carlson is convinced that some kind of standard costing system is just what he needs to strengthen his control over factory cost. The factory now has a simple job order costing system, and no one has ever attempted to establish standard costs.

Scientific Equipment makes and sells a line of highly technical equipment for industrial users. The company is in a small midwestern city with a population of 80,000. Quality, or the supplier's ability to meet exacting technical specifications, is a major consideration for most of the company's customers when deciding where to place an order.

Production is organized on a job order basis, and orders are typically manufactured to customer specifications. Most orders can be filled by producing items of standard design and specifications, or items which require only minor modifications of the standard designs. Jobs requiring major redesign and nonstandardized production techniques amount to 30 percent of the total. The cost estimates Carlson uses in developing price bids for this kind of nonstandardized business have been close to the actual costs of filling the orders in most cases, or at least close enough to satisfy Carlson.

Scientific Equipment is a small company with about 75 employees. The two largest segments of the work force are 30 machine operators and 20 assemblers. The machine operators are all men. Their jobs require considerable skill and experience. The assemblers, on the other hand, are all women. Their jobs are relatively routine but require a good deal of concentration to avoid costly assembly defects. The employees generally lunch together in a nearby cafeteria. Many of the men socialize off the job, and so do several of the women.

Carlson is considering engaging a consulting firm to develop and install a standard costing system. A letter from the managing partner of the consulting firm contained the following key paragraphs:

> In order to motivate people to their maximum productivity, standards must be based upon the company's best workers and what they can achieve. If the standard were lower, the high performers could meet it too easily and it wouldn't offer sufficient motivation for the low performers. I'd set the standard at the level of performance of the top 10 to 15 percent of your employees. This would establish a high aspiration level for your people and, therefore, motivate their best efforts.
>
> I also suggest that superior performance be well rewarded. This means that employees who exceed standard should receive a substantial bonus, while those who do not exceed standard should receive no bonus.

Since Carlson doesn't feel qualified to evaluate this kind of statement, he has contacted the faculty member who conducted the sessions on standard costing at the local university (you), asking what you think of the philosophy underlying the proposed system.

a.	Prepare a reply to Carlson. Should he engage the consultant?

b.	If you agree with the consultant's basic approach, outline how you would implement it at Scientific Equipment Manufacturing Company. If you disagree with the consultant, state the basic principles underlying an alternative system and outline how you would go about developing a standard costing system for this compamy.

(Prepared by Eric Flamholtz)

16. Separate standards for motivation and for control. Harden Company was experiencing increased production costs. The primary area of concern identified by management was direct labor. The company was considering adopting a standard cost system to help control labor and other costs. Useful historical data were not available because detailed production records had not been maintained.

Harden Company retained Finch & Associates, an engineering consulting firm, to establish labor standards. After a complete study of the work process, the engineers recommended a labor standard of 1 unit of production every 30 minutes, or 16 units a day for each worker. Finch further advised that Harden's wage rates were below the prevailing rate of $12 an hour.

Harden's production vice president thought this labor standard was too tight and the employees would be unable to attain it. From his experience with the labor force, he believed a labor standard of 40 minutes a unit or 12 units a day for each worker would be more reasonable.

Nan Jones, Harden's president, believed the standard should be set at a high level to motivate the workers, but she also recognized the standard should be set at a level to provide adequate information for control and reasonable cost comparisons. After much discussion, management decided to use a dual standard. The labor standard recommended by the engineering firm—known as the *engineering standard,* 1 unit every 30 minutes—would be used in the plant as a motivation device, while a labor standard of 40 minutes a unit—the *reporting standard*—would be used in reporting. Management also concluded that the workers would not be informed of the cost standard used for reporting purposes. The production vice president conducted several sessions prior to implementation in the plant informing the workers of the new standard cost system and answering questions. The new standards were not related to incentive pay but were introduced at the time wages were increased to $12 an hour.

The new standard cost system was implemented on January 1. At the end of six months of operation, the following statistics on labor performance were presented to top management:

	Jan.	Feb.	Mar.	Apr.	May	June
Production (units) . . .	5,100	5,000	4,700	4,500	4,300	4,400
Direct labor hours . .	3,000	2,900	2,900	3,000	3,000	3,100
Labor usage variance from engineering standard	$5,400U	$4,800U	$6,600U	$9,000U	$10,200U	$10,800U
Labor usage variance from reporting standard	$4,800F	$5,200F	$2,800F	$ 0	$ 1,600U	$ 2,000U

Raw material quality, labor mix, and plant facilities and conditions did not change to any great extent during the six-month period.

a. Discuss the impact of different types of standards on motivation, and specifically discuss the effect on motivation in Harden Company's plant of adopting the labor standard recommended by the engineering firm.
b. Evaluate Harden Company's decision to use dual standards in its standard cost system.

(CMA adapted)

17. Reporting cost variances to management. Consolidated Industries operates several large factories in various parts of the world. Its factory in Rapperswil, Switzerland, manufactures industrial machinery and parts for customers in several countries. Most of the products are custom-designed, and all production is on a job order basis. Standard labor costs have been established for the most frequently performed operations in the factory, however.

Hans Hassenpfeffer is a department foreman in the Rapperswil factory. Each morning he receives a labor report listing the previous day's performance of each worker in his department. This report contains one line for each task performed by each worker during the day. Here is an excerpt from the report for January 23 listing all tasks performed on that day by Anna Buri and Jorg Staub, two workers in Hasenpfeffer's department:

| Employee Name | Job or Acct. No. | Rated Work | | | | Other Actual Hours | |
		Operation No.	Actual Hours	Standard Hours	Gain (Loss)	Nonrated Work	Nonpro- ductive
Buri, Anna	J75008	179–32	8.0	7.8	(0.2)		
Staub, Jorg	J75006	176–40	2.2	1.4	(0.8)		
Staub, Jorg	A1406						0.5
Staub, Jorg	J75012					2.4	
Staub, Jorg	J75023	179–32	2.9	2.0	(0.9)		

Nonrated work consists of all productive tasks for which no standards have been prepared. Nonproductive time is time spent waiting for materials, waiting for machine repair, etc. The twice-daily coffee breaks are not recorded as nonproductive time, however. Instead, standard labor-hours include a provision for this factor.

Hasenpfeffer has 12 workers in his department, and the typical daily report consists of approximately 40 lines. All workers in this department are paid a fixed hourly wage, which varies considerably from worker to worker.

a. This report is part of a much broader standard costing system this factory has used for a number of years. Would you guess that this system is designed primarily for use as a steering control or as a scorecard control? Why do you think so?

b. Would you recommend that this report be prepared and given to Hasenpfeffer each morning? State the assumptions or reasons behind your recommendation.

c. Assume that the company's management has answered part b in the negative. Would you recommend that the information necessary to prepare the daily report should continue to be collected and stored for possible future use? Give your reasons or, if you are not ready to make a recommendation without further data, describe how you would analyze this question.

d. Assume that the company's management has answered part b in the affirmative but that it wants a department labor performance summary report prepared each month. What information now likely to be available in this system would you recommend presenting on this monthly report? Give your reasons.

e. If you were Hasenpfeffer, what action, if any, would you probably take on the basis of the portion of the report dealing with Buri and Staub? Is Buri a better worker than Staub?

18. Preparing profit-contribution statement; sensitivity analysis. Lee Merritt is manager of a division which has its own production facilities and its own sales force. He received the following monthly income statement on one of his product lines:

Sales revenues		$700
Expenses:		
Cost of goods sold	$490	
Marketing and distribution	70	
Research and development	15	
Administration	35	610
Income before taxes		$ 90

Surprised by the size of the income figure, Merritt has asked you to prepare a statement in a format that will help him see the impact of volume and other factors more readily. You are given the following additional information:

1. All the products in this line are manufactured in a single factory, which is devoted exclusively to this product line.
2. The $490 cost of goods sold included the following:

Standard direct materials	$ 95
Standard direct labor	200
Standard overhead	160
Factory overhead volume variance	30
Factory overhead spending variance	(5)
Price and wage rate variances	(12)
Direct labor and materials usage variances	22
Total	$490

3. Budgeted factory overhead = $90 + $0.50 × Standard direct-labor cost.
4. Production volume was equal to sales volume during the month.
5. Marketing and distribution expenses were as follows:

Sales commissions	$14
Variable distribution costs	21
Product-traceable fixed marketing costs	18
Common marketing costs, allocated to product lines as a percentage of sales	17
Total	$70

6. Research and development costs consisted of $3 in general research costs, allocated among the product lines as a percentage of sales, and $12 in costs of projects for the development of new products for this line specifically.
7. Of the administrative expense, $5 was a fixed cost traceable to the product line, and the remainder consisted of allocated division and corporate headquarters fixed expenses.

a. Prepare a profit-contribution statement. The bottom line should be the same as on the report originally submitted to Merritt. Factory cost variances other than the overhead volume variance should be classified as variable costs.

b. How would the product line's income before taxes be affected by a 10 percent decrease in sales and production volume? Prepare a revised profit-contribution statement based on this assumption. Did the profit-contribution format help you in any way?

19. Adjusting the system to the need.   Dalton Products Company is a small but rapidly growing manufacturer of specialized electronic components. At the present time it manufactures only nine different component models, but that number should be multiplied many times as products now in development move into production.

Until recently, top management felt no need for detailed cost control information. Frank Baxter, one of the company's three founders, supervised factory operations directly. The factory accountant calculated average cost per direct labor-hour in each department each month, but this was done mainly for inventory costing purposes; Baxter seldom even looked at this report.

As the business grew, Baxter found it more and more difficult to oversee production as well as the company's product-development laboratories. About a year ago, he appointed his assistant, Marjorie Briscoe, to the newly created position of manufacturing vice president and began to devote his full time to product development. Briscoe had been with the company since shortly after its founding and was thoroughly familiar with all factory operations. A new wing of the factory opened shortly after she assumed her new post, however, and she soon found it necessary to play a less direct role in supervising factory operations. Instead, she began to bring the 10 factory department heads together each month for a meeting to discuss problems which had arisen and actions they had taken. Most department heads had been with the company for many years, some of them having started as line workers in production departments before moving into supervisory positions. None of them had ever expressed discontent with the monthly cost-reporting system.

Briscoe found her meetings with the department heads useful, but the department cost averages didn't seem to help her in these discussions. About six months ago she asked Zeno Snodgrass, the company's controller, to develop a system which would generate reports on cost control performance in each factory department. She told him she wanted a system he could develop and install quickly and one that would be relatively inexpensive to operate.

Snodgrass began by studying a sample of time tickets and materials requisitions to determine the direct labor and direct materials costs of several production orders for each of the company's nine products. For each product he prepared a listing similar to the following, which lists the standard direct labor and direct materials costs of 100 units of one product:

Department	Direct Labor	Direct Materials
A	$10	$23
B	3	2
C	8	1
E	12	4
J	6	16
Total	$39	$46

Working with each department head, he developed a flexible budget for department overhead costs, but he made no effort to establish a standard overhead cost for each product.

At Snodgrass's request, the company's purchasing agent established standard materials prices for each of the main materials used as direct materials in the factory. Snodgrass then instructed the factory accountant to record all purchases at those standard prices, placing any materials price variances in a separate account. Issues of materials were tabulated for each department, and at the end of each month the totals were multiplied by the standard prices to determine the cost each department was accountable for.

The labor-recording system was even simpler. Each worker's wages were assigned in their entirety to that worker's department. Time tickets were prepared only when a worker who normally performed direct labor operations was assigned to indirect labor duties in the department. As a result, Snodgrass was able to report actual direct labor cost and actual indirect labor cost for each department shortly after the end of each payroll period.

The standard cost of each department's output was determined by tabulating the number of units completed by each department each day. At the end of the month, the number of units completed was multiplied by the product's standard cost per unit. Work in process was small and didn't change much from month to month, and Snodgrass decided to ignore the fluctuations which did occur.

Snodgrass was proud of his new system. He prepared the first set of monthly department reports and gave them to Briscoe only three months after starting work on this project. He also gave each department head a copy of the report for his or her department at the same time. A portion of the first month's report for department A is as follows:

	Actual Costs	Standard or Budgeted Costs	Variance
Direct materials	$47,000	$43,000	$(4,000)
Direct labor	26,000	23,000	(3,000)
Indirect labor	7,200	7,500	300
Supplies	6,500	6,000	(500)

Department A received all its materials directly from the storeroom. Other departments received some materials from the storeroom and some from other departments. When a department damaged or lost units of partly processed products it had received from another department, the total standard cost of all operations in prior-processing departments was charged to an overhead account in the department in which the damage or loss occurred. Except for this, no cost transfers were made from department to department.

a. You are Briscoe's assistant and you have been attending the meeting at which Snodgrass presented the first set of reports and explained the basis on which they had been prepared. Prepare an overall assessment of Snodgrass's new system for Briscoe's use. How closely does it appear to match the criteria Briscoe established? What were those criteria? Did they call for steering-control or scorecard-control information?

b. Now that the new system is in operation, can you identify any aspects Snodgrass might consider changing? Why would these changes be desirable? Do you think of these as major changes or as minor adjustments? (In general, if your overall assessment in answer to part *a* was favorable, most changes you suggest are likely to be minor changes.)

Appendix A

Compound interest and bond tables

The tables in this appendix contain the *multipliers* or *conversion factors* necessary to convert cash flows of one or more periods into their equivalent values at some other time. The basic explanation of the reasons for conversion is given in Chapter 6; only the mechanical details of how the numbers in the tables should be used are explained here. If more extensive tables or specialized tables are needed, they can be found in readily available financial handbooks or derived from simple computer programs.

TABLE 1: FUTURE VALUE OF $1

Each number in Table 1 is the future value to which $1 will grow by the end of n periods at an interest rate r, compounded once per period. To obtain the future value of any sum:

1. Select a future date to serve as a *reference date*.
2. Determine the number of periods (n) between the receipt or payment of cash and the reference date.
3. Determine the interest rate (r) at which amounts are to be compounded.
4. Find the multiplier in Table 1 corresponding to these values of n and r.
5. Multiply the cash sum by this multiplier.

For example, suppose we have $10,000 now and expect to receive another $10,000 two years from now. We want to find the future values of these sums at a reference date five years from now, compounded annually at 10 percent.

The first of these sums will grow for five years, and the multiplier is found by using the appropriate row and column in Table 1. The factor that appears at the intersection of the five-year row and the 10 percent column of Table 1 is 1.6105. This indicates that $1 now will grow to $1.6105 in five years. The future value of $10,000 therefore is $1.6105 \times \$10,000 = \$16,105$.

The second sum will have only three years to grow. The multiplier from the three-year row of the 10 percent column is 1.3310, and the future value at the reference date is $1.3310 \times \$10,000 = \$13,310$.

These calculations can be summarized in a timetable of cash flows and futures values:

Years before Reference Date	Cash Flow	Future Value Multiplier at 10% (Table 1)	Future Value Amount
5	+$10,000	1.6105	$16,105
3	+ 10,000	1.3310	13,310
Total			$29,415

In using this table, care must be taken to insure that the *interest rate* is appropriate to the *period*. Thus, if an amount is compounded *semiannually* at *r* percent *per annum* for *n* years, the number of interest periods is 2*n,* and the interest rate per period is $r/2$. To illustrate, if interest is compounded *annually* at 10 percent, $10,000 now will grow to $67,275 by the end of 20 years. If interest is compounded semiannually at 5 percent every six months, however, the value 20 years from now is $70,400, reflecting interest at 5 percent per six-month period for 40 periods.[1]

Extending Table 1

Table 1 can be extended easily to provide multipliers for any number of periods. For example, suppose we want to find the future value of $10,000 compounded annually at 10 percent for 31 periods. No 31-period row is in the table. By consulting Table 1, however,

---

[1] Interest of 5 percent each six months is equivalent to an annual interest rate of $(1.05)^2 - 1 = 10.25$ percent, because interest earned in the first six months will earn interest in the second six months of the year. The semiannual compounding rate equivalent to a 10 percent annual rate is $\sqrt{1.10} - 1 = 4.8809$ percent. Table 1 can be used only if the interest rate *per period* is equal to the rate in one of the column headings. Since no column is provided for future values at 10.25 percent, Table 1 can't be used to calculate these amounts.

FIGURE A–1. Future Values of $10,000 at 10 Percent

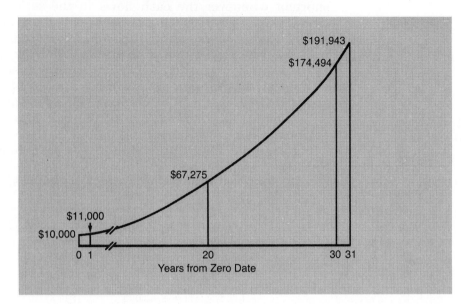

we find that the future value of $1 30 years from now, compounded annually at 10 percent, is $17.4494 (20-year row and 10 percent column). The future value of $10,000 30 years ahead therefore is $174,494. If it is reinvested for one more year at 10 percent, this sum will amount to 1.10 × $174,494 = $191,943. This is the future value of $10,000 31 periods hence at 10 percent per period.

Alternatively, $10,000 will grow to $67,275 in 20 years (from the 20-year row in Table 1). To find the future value of this amount 11 years later (31 years from now), we can multiply it by the future-value factor in the 11-year row, 2.8531. The future value is $67,275 × 2.8531 = $191,943. These relationships are diagrammed in Figure A–1.

In other words, the future value of a $1 at any time in the future can be obtained by multiplying together any two or more multipliers for which the number of periods adds up to the desired number. Thus, the multiplier for 31 periods can be obtained by multiplying the factors for 1 and 30 periods, or 3 and 28 periods, or any other combination of periods totaling 31. The resulting figures will be identical except for the insignificant effects of rounding errors.

TABLE 2: FUTURE VALUE OF AN ANNUITY OF $1

The future value of a series of cash flows can always be determined with the aid of the multipliers in Table 1. Because this is time-consuming, Table 2 has been developed as a computational shortcut whenever the cash flows in the series are identical in amount each period; such a series is called an *annuity*.

The key to understanding this table is to recognize that an annuity is really a combination of several cash flows, identical in amount and separated from each other by identical time intervals. Thus, a two-year, $10,000 annuity is simply a series of two annual cash flows of $10,000 each. The future value of an annuity, therefore, is the sum of the future values of the individual cash receipts or payments.

For example, the future value in two years of $10,000 now and $10,000 a year from now, compounded annually at 10 percent, can be calculated with the aid of Table 1, as follows:

| Years before Reference Date | Cash Flow | Future Value | |
		Multiplier at 10% (Table 1)	Amount
2	+$10,000	1.2100	$12,100
1	+ 10,000	1.1000	11,000
Total			$23,100

The same answer can be found by multiplying the $10,000 annual cash flow by the *sum* of the annual multipliers, 2.3100.

This is an example of an annuity *in advance;* that is, the cash flow took place at the *beginning* of each period. Suppose, instead, that the payments were made *in arrears*—that is, at the *end* of each period.[2] The first payment would be made a year from now and would thus have only one year to grow before the two-year period ended. Thus, its future value would be only $11,000. The second payment, made at the end of the second year, would have no time at all to grow, and thus its future value would be $10,000.

The future value of a two-year, $10,000 annuity in arrears, compounded annually at 10 percent, therefore, is $11,000 + $10,000 = $21,000.

The multipliers in Table 2 are for annuities *in arrears.* The factor for a two-year, 10 percent annuity in arrears is 2.1000. Multiplying this by the $10,000 annual cash flow produces a future value of $21,000, the amount we derived in the preceding paragraph.

---

[2] An annuity *in advance* is sometimes called an *annuity due,* and an annuity *in arrears* is sometimes called an *ordinary annuity.*

Converting Table 2 to distant future equivalents

Table 2 consists of multipliers that can be used to calculate the future value of an annuity—on the date the last payment is due to be made. Any multiplier in this table can also be translated into the multiplier that will determine future value as of any number of periods after the date of the final payment.

The procedure is to multiply the multiplier in Table 2 by the multiplier in Table 1 for the appropriate number of periods after the date of the last payment. For example, at 10 percent, the future value 15 years from now of a series of 10 annual payments of $10,000 each, with the first payment to be made one year from now, is calculated as follows:

$$\begin{array}{ccccc} \$10,000 & \times & 15.9374 & \times & 1.6105 & = & \$25,667 \\ \text{(annual} & & \text{(Table 2,} & & \text{(Table 1,} & & \text{(future value,} \\ \text{cash flow)} & & \text{10 years)} & & \text{5 years)} & & \text{15 years)} \end{array}$$

The first multiplier determines the sum that $10,000 a year will build up to by the end of 10 years, and the second multiplier determines the amount this sum will grow to in another five years.

An even simpler way to perform this particular calculation is to recognize that this annuity consists of the first 10 payments in a 15-year annuity. The multiplier for the five "missing" payments is the multiplier for a five-year annuity, 6.1051. We can obtain the appropriate multiplier for the other 10 payments by subtracting this multiplier from the multiplier for a full 15-year annuity, 31.7725, leaving the 25.6674 factor we had before.

Converting Table 2 for annuities in advance

The multipliers in Table 2 can also be used to calculate the future values of annuities in advance. To do this, we need to recognize that the interval between each payment and the future date is one year longer than in an annuity in arrears. The first payment in a three-year annuity in advance is made just three years before the future reference date. Since the first payment in a four-year annuity in arrears is also made exactly three years before the reference date, a three-year annuity in advance can be seen to be exactly the same as a four-year annuity in arrears without the final payment.

This relationship is diagrammed in Figure A-2. Future value is to be calculated as of the end of year 3. From a vantage point at the end of year 3, the only difference between a four-year annuity in arrears and a three-year annuity in advance is a single payment

FIGURE A–2. Annuities in Arrears and in Advance

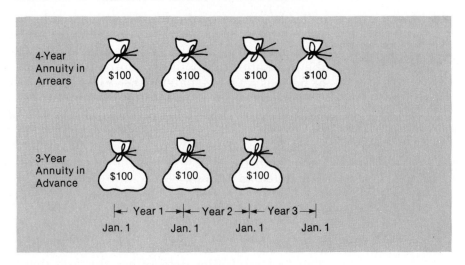

at the end of the third year. The calculation of the future value of a three-year, $10,000 annuity in advance, compounded at 10 percent to a reference date three years in the future, is as follows:

$10,000 × 4.6410 − $10,000 = $36,410
(annual (Table 2, (omitted (future value
cash flow, 4 years) final 3 years hence)
4 years) payment)

An identical result would be obtained by subtracting 1.0000 from the multiplier in Table 2:

$$(4.6410 - 1.0000) \times \$10{,}000 = 3.6410 \times \$10{,}000 = \$36{,}410$$

The general rule is: To obtain the multiplier for the future value of an n-period annuity in advance, *take the multiplier from Table 2 for an annuity of $(n + 1)$ periods, and subtract 1.0000.*

TABLE 3:   PRESENT VALUE OF $1

Each number in Table 3 is a multiplier—depicting the present value on a given reference date of $1 to be paid or received n periods later. To obtain the present value of any sum:

1.   Select a date to serve as a reference date.
2.   Determine the number of periods (n) between the reference date and the date on which the cash is to be paid or received.
3.   Determine the interest rate (r) at which amounts are to be discounted.

4. Find the multiplier in Table 3 corresponding to these values of n and r.
5. Multiply the cash sum by this multiplier.

For example, to find the present value of $10,000 to be received five years from now, discounted at a compound annual rate of 10 percent, multiply $10,000 by the number 0.6209 from the five-year row in the 10 percent column of Table 3. This says that $6,209 invested now at 10 percent will grow to $10,000 in five years if the interest is left on deposit and reinvested each year at 10 percent interest.

Once again, if compounding is to be semiannual, the factor should be taken from the column for a semiannual interest rate equal to $r/2$ and the row for a number of periods equal to $2n$. If quarterly compounding is used, use $r/4$ and $4n$ (for example, 2½ percent for 40 periods to show present value compounded quarterly at 2½ percent a quarter for 10 years.[3]

Extending Table 3

Table 3 can be extended easily to provide multipliers for any number of periods. The procedure consists of three steps:

1. Select the column for the desired interest rate.
2. From this column select any two or more multipliers for which the number of periods adds up to the number of periods (n) for which a multiplier is needed.
3. Multiply these multipliers.

For example, the present value of $1 35 years in the future at 10 percent compounded annually can be calculated in many ways. Three of these are:

Multiplier for (n = 5) × multiplier for (n = 30) = 0.6209 × 0.0573 = 0.0356
Multiplier for (n = 10) × multiplier for (n = 25) = 0.3855 × 0.0923 = 0.0356
Multiplier for (n = 15) × multiplier for (n = 20) = 0.2394 × 0.1486 = 0.0356

Why does this work? Suppose the company expects to receive $1 35 years from now. Multiplying it by the discount factor for n = 30 brings it to its present value *at a point five years from now,* $0.0573. That amount is not the present value today, however. It is the future value five years from now. The present value today

---

[3] Quarterly compounding at 2½ percent a quarter is equivalent to an annual rate of $(1.025)^4 - 1 = 10.3813$ percent. The quarterly compounding rate equivalent to a 10 percent annual compounding rate is ($\sqrt[4]{1.10} - 1$), or approximately 2.41 percent each quarter. If this amount of precision is important, specially constructed quarterly tables, calculators, or computer programs should be used.

of any sum five years in the future can be calculated by discounting it for five years—in other words, by multiplying $0.0573 by 0.6209.

TABLE 4: PRESENT VALUE OF AN ANNUITY OF $1 PER PERIOD

The present value of a series of cash flows can be determined by using the multipliers in Table 3. For example, a series of three payments of $10,000 each, the first one a year from now, the second a year later, and the third a year after that, has a present value at 10 percent, compounded annually, as follows:

Years after Reference Date	Cash Flow	Multiplier at 10% (Table 3)	Present Value at 10%
1	$10,000	0.9091	$ 9,091
2	10,000	0.8264	8,264
3	10,000	0.7513	7,513
Total			$24,868

Doing this for a large number of periods would be time-consuming. Table 4, therefore, is used whenever the cash flows in a series are identicial each period (an *annuity*). The multiplier in Table 4 for a three-year annuity at 10 percent is 2.4869. Multiplying this by the annual cash flow, $10,000, produces a present value of $24,869, identical to the amount we derived above except for an insignificant rounding error. *Each multiplier in Table 4 is merely the sum of the multipliers in Table 3* for periods 1 through *n*.

Converting Table 4 to earlier equivalents

The multipliers in Table 4 are used to calculate the present value of a series of cash payments on a reference date that is exactly one period prior to the date of the first payment. To find the present value at a still earlier reference date, the present value of the annuity is multiplied by the multiplier from Table 3 for the number of additional years desired.

For example, the present value at 10 percent of a 10-year, $10,000 annuity in arrears is:

$$\$10,000 \times 6.1446 = \$61,446$$

Suppose, however, that the first payment in this annuity is five years from now and that we want to know its present value as of today. The $61,446 figure is the present value *one year before the first payment is made,* or four years from now:

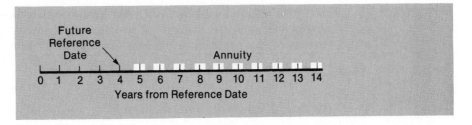

The present value today, therefore, can be obtained by multiplying $61,446 by the four-year multiplier from Table 3:

$$\$61,446 \times 0.6830 = \$41,968$$

The same present value can be derived in a different way. A 10-year annuity starting five years from now is the same as a 14-year annuity in arrears minus the first four payments. The multiplier in Table 4 for 14 years at 10 percent is 7.3667, and the multiplier for four years is 3.1699. The appropriate multiplier, therefore, is:

$$7.3667 - 3.1699 = 4.1968$$

Multiplying this by the $10,000 annual cash flow produces a present value of $41,968, the same present value amount we derived earlier.

Converting Table 4 for annuities in advance

A somewhat similar procedure can be used to find the present value of an annuity in advance—that is, one in which the first payment is made on the date at which present value is to be calculated. A 10-year annuity in advance is simply a nine-year annuity in arrears plus one payment immediately. For $10,000 a year at 10 percent, the calculation is:

$$\begin{array}{cccc} \$10,000 & + & (\$10,000 \times 5.7590) & = & \$67,590 \\ \text{(immediate} & & \text{(annual} \quad \text{(Table 4,} & & \text{(present value,} \\ \text{payment)} & & \text{cash flow,} \quad \text{9 years)} & & \text{10-year annuity)} \\ & & \text{9 years)} & & \end{array}$$

The general rule is: To convert a multiplier for the present value of an annuity in arrears to a multiplier for an annuity in advance, *take the multiplier for an interval one period shorter and add 1.0000.*

Finding equivalent annuities

It is sometimes useful to calculate an annuity that is equivalent to a given present sum. For example, how large a 10-year annuity could be bought with a $100,000 investment today in a 10 percent market? Since the present sum *and* the interest rate are known, this becomes a basic arithmetic operation. The formula for the present value of an annuity can be expressed as:

$$\text{Present value} = \text{Table 4 multiplier} \times \text{Annual cash flow}$$

Restating this equation, we find:

$$\text{Annual cash flow} = \frac{\text{Present value}}{\text{Table 4 multiplier}}$$

The 10-year annuity in arrears that is equivalent at 10 percent interest to a present sum of $100,000 is:

$$\text{Annual cash flow} = \frac{\$100,000}{6.1446} = \$16,274$$

In other words, someone who is willing to pay $100,000 to buy a 10-year annuity in a 10 percent market can expect to receive $16,274 at the end of each year for 10 years.

TABLES 5–11: PRESENT VALUE OF A $100 BOND

Tables 5–11 give the present values—at various yield rates—of bonds bearing coupon rates ranging from 6 percent to 18 percent, for terms that vary from six months to 30 years. These tables are applicable to bonds on which interest is paid semiannually.[4]

To find the present value of a bond when the yield to maturity is known, turn to the table with the appropriate coupon rate (for example, Table 6 for an 8 percent coupon) and find the column corresponding to the number of years to maturity (for example, 10 years). Finally, find the row identified by the known yield to maturity at the left (say, 9.5 percent) and read the present value from the appropriate column in that row (90.45). This indicates that an 8 percent coupon bond with a face value of $100 has a present value of $90.45 in a 9.5 percent market. To find the present value of any other face amount, multiply the face value by 1/100 of the factor shown in the table. For example, if 10-year bonds with an 8 percent coupon rate and $3,500,000 total face amount are issued in a 9.5 percent market, the proceeds will be $3,165,750 ($3,500,000 × 0.9045).

These tables can also be used to find the yield to maturity when the market value and number of years to maturity are known. To find the yield to maturity of a fixed-payment bond, turn to the table

---

[4] The concepts and accounting measurement standards relating to bond interest are discussed in detail in Chapter 10.

for the bond's coupon rate, find the column for the number of years until the bond matures, and go down to the row on which the quoted market price is located. The yield is the number at the left end of this row. To pursue our example, let's assume that when five years remain until maturity, the market value of each $100, 8 percent bond is $86.97. Reference to the same 8 percent coupon table indicates that the yield to maturity is now 11.5 percent.

TABLE 1. Future Value of $1 (compounded once each period)

$$F_n = P(1+r)^n$$

Periods	5%	6%	7%	8%	9%	10%	11%	12%
1	1.0500	1.0600	1.0700	1.0800	1.0900	1.1000	1.1100	1.1200
2	1.1025	1.1236	1.1449	1.1664	1.1881	1.2100	1.2321	1.2544
3	1.1576	1.1910	1.2250	1.2597	1.2950	1.3310	1.3676	1.4049
4	1.2155	1.2625	1.3108	1.3605	1.4116	1.4641	1.5181	1.5735
5	1.2763	1.3382	1.4026	1.4693	1.5386	1.6105	1.6851	1.7623
6	1.3401	1.4185	1.5007	1.5869	1.6771	1.7716	1.8704	1.9738
7	1.4071	1.5036	1.6058	1.7138	1.8280	1.9487	2.0762	2.2107
8	1.4775	1.5938	1.7182	1.8509	1.9926	2.1436	2.3045	2.4760
9	1.5513	1.6895	1.8385	1.9990	2.1719	2.3579	2.5580	2.7731
10	1.6289	1.7908	1.9672	2.1589	2.3674	2.5937	2.8394	3.1058
11	1.7103	1.8983	2.1049	2.3316	2.5804	2.8531	3.1518	3.4785
12	1.7959	2.0122	2.2522	2.5182	2.8127	3.1384	3.4985	3.8960
13	1.8856	2.1329	2.4098	2.7196	3.0658	3.4523	3.8833	4.3635
14	1.9799	2.2609	2.5785	2.9372	3.3417	3.7975	4.3104	4.8871
15	2.0789	2.3966	2.7590	3.1722	3.6425	4.1772	4.7846	5.4736
16	2.1829	2.5404	2.9522	3.4259	3.9703	4.5950	5.3109	6.1304
17	2.2920	2.6928	3.1588	3.7000	4.3276	5.0545	5.8951	6.8660
18	2.4066	2.8543	3.3799	3.9960	4.7171	5.5599	6.5436	7.6900
19	2.5270	3.0256	3.6165	4.3157	5.1417	6.1159	7.2633	8.6128
20	2.6533	3.2071	3.8697	4.6610	5.6044	6.7275	8.0623	9.6463
21	2.7860	3.3996	4.1406	5.0338	6.1088	7.4002	8.9492	10.8038
22	2.9253	3.6035	4.4304	5.4365	6.6586	8.1403	9.9336	12.1003
23	3.0715	3.8197	4.7405	5.8715	7.2579	8.9543	11.0263	13.5523
24	3.2251	4.0489	5.0724	6.3412	7.9111	9.8497	12.2392	15.1786
25	3.3864	4.2919	5.4274	6.8485	8.6231	10.8347	13.5855	17.0001
30	4.3219	5.7435	7.6123	10.0627	13.2677	17.4494	22.8923	29.9599
40	7.0400	10.2857	14.9745	21.7245	31.4094	45.2593	65.0009	93.0510
50	11.4674	18.4202	29.4570	46.9016	74.3575	117.3908	184.5648	289.0022

Periods	13%	14%	15%	16%	17%	18%	19%	20%	25%
1	1.1300	1.1400	1.1500	1.1600	1.1700	1.1800	1.1900	1.2000	1.2500
2	1.2769	1.2996	1.3225	1.3456	1.3689	1.3924	1.4161	1.4400	1.5625
3	1.4429	1.4815	1.5209	1.5609	1.6016	1.6430	1.6852	1.7280	1.9531
4	1.6305	1.6890	1.7490	1.8106	1.8739	1.9388	2.0053	2.0736	2.4414
5	1.8424	1.9254	2.0114	2.1003	2.1924	2.2878	2.3864	2.4883	3.0518
6	2.0820	2.1950	2.3131	2.4364	2.5652	2.6996	2.8398	2.9860	3.8147
7	2.3526	2.5023	2.6600	2.8262	3.0012	3.1855	3.3793	3.5832	4.7684
8	2.6584	2.8526	3.0590	3.2784	3.5115	3.7589	4.0214	4.2998	5.9605
9	3.0040	3.2519	3.5179	3.8030	4.1084	4.4355	4.7854	5.1598	7.4506
10	3.3946	3.7072	4.0456	4.4114	4.8068	5.2338	5.6947	6.1917	9.3132
11	3.8359	4.2262	4.6524	5.1173	5.6240	5.1759	6.7767	7.4301	11.6415
12	4.3345	4.8179	5.3503	5.9360	6.5801	7.2876	8.0642	8.9161	14.5519
13	4.8980	5.4924	6.1528	6.8858	7.6987	8.5994	9.5964	10.6993	18.1899
14	5.5348	6.2613	7.0757	7.9875	9.0075	10.1472	11.4198	12.8392	22.7374
15	6.2543	7.1379	8.1371	9.2655	10.5387	11.9737	13.5895	15.4070	28.4217
16	7.0673	8.1372	9.3576	10.7480	12.3303	14.1290	16.1715	18.4884	35.5271
17	7.9861	9.2765	10.7613	12.4677	14.4265	16.6722	19.2441	22.1861	44.4089
18	9.0243	10.5752	12.3755	14.4625	16.8790	19.6733	22.9005	26.6233	55.5112
19	10.1974	12.0557	14.2318	16.7765	19.7484	23.2144	27.2516	31.9480	69.3889
20	11.5231	13.7435	16.3665	19.4608	23.1056	27.3930	32.4294	38.3376	86.7362
21	13.0211	15.6676	18.8215	22.5745	27.0336	32.3238	38.5910	46.0051	108.4202
22	14.7138	17.8610	21.6447	26.1864	31.6293	38.1421	45.9233	55.2061	135.5253
23	16.6266	20.3616	24.8915	30.3762	37.0062	45.0076	54.6487	66.2474	169.4066
24	18.7881	23.2122	28.6252	35.2364	43.2973	53.1090	65.0320	79.4968	211.7582
25	21.2305	26.4619	32.9190	40.8742	50.6578	62.6686	77.3881	95.3962	264.6978
30	39.1159	50.9502	66.2118	85.8499	111.0646	143.3706	184.6753	237.3763	807.7936
40	132.7816	188.8835	267.8636	378.7212	533.8687	750.3783	1051.6675	1469.7716	7523.1641
50	450.7359	700.2330	1083.6575	1670.7039	2566.2154	3927.3568	5988.9138	9100.4382	70064.9260

TABLE 2.   Future Value of Annuity of $1 in Arrears

$$F = A \left[\frac{(1+r)^n - 1}{r} \right]$$

Periods	5%	6%	7%	8%	9%	10%	11%	12%
1	1.0000	1.0000	1.0000	1.0000	1.0000	1.0000	1.0000	1.0000
2	2.0500	2.0600	2.0700	2.0800	2.0900	2.1000	2.1100	2.1200
3	3.1525	3.1836	3.2149	3.2464	3.2781	3.3100	3.3421	3.3744
4	4.3101	4.3746	4.4399	4.5061	4.5731	4.6410	4.7097	4.7793
5	5.5256	5.6371	5.7507	5.8666	5.9847	6.1051	6.2278	6.3528
6	6.8019	6.9753	7.1533	7.3359	7.5233	7.7156	7.9129	8.1152
7	8.1420	8.3938	8.6540	8.9228	9.2004	9.4872	9.7833	10.0890
8	9.5491	9.8975	10.2598	10.6366	11.0285	11.4359	11.8594	12.2997
9	11.0266	11.4913	11.9780	12.4876	13.0210	13.5795	14.1640	14.7757
10	12.5779	13.1808	13.8164	14.4866	15.1929	15.9374	16.7220	17.5487
11	14.2068	14.9716	15.7836	16.6455	17.5603	18.5312	19.5614	20.6546
12	15.9171	16.8699	17.8885	18.9771	20.1407	21.3843	22.7132	24.1331
13	17.7130	18.8821	20.1406	21.4953	22.9534	24.5227	26.2116	28.0291
14	19.5986	21.0151	22.5505	24.2149	26.0192	27.9750	30.0949	32.3926
15	21.5786	23.2760	25.1290	27.1521	29.3609	31.7725	34.4054	37.2797
16	23.6575	25.6725	27.8881	30.3243	33.0034	35.9497	39.1899	42.7533
17	25.8404	28.2129	30.8402	33.7502	36.9737	40.5447	44.5008	48.8837
18	28.1324	30.9057	33.9990	37.4502	41.3013	45.5992	50.3959	55.7497
19	30.5390	33.7600	37.3790	41.4463	46.0185	51.1591	56.9395	63.4397
20	33.0660	36.7856	40.9955	45.7620	51.1601	57.2750	64.2028	72.0524
21	35.7193	39.9927	44.8652	50.4229	56.7645	64.0025	72.2651	81.6987
22	38.5052	43.3923	49.0057	55.4568	62.8733	71.4027	81.2143	92.5026
23	41.4305	46.9958	53.4361	60.8933	69.5319	79.5430	91.1479	104.6029
24	44.5020	50.8156	58.1767	66.7648	76.7898	88.4973	102.1742	118.1552
25	47.7271	54.8645	63.2490	73.1059	84.7009	98.3471	114.4133	133.3339
30	66.4388	79.0582	94.4608	113.2832	136.3075	164.4940	199.0209	241.3327
40	120.7998	154.7620	199.6351	259.0565	337.8825	442.5926	581.8261	767.0914
50	209.3480	290.3359	406.5289	573.7702	815.0836	1163.9085	1668.7712	2400.0183

Note: To convert this table to values of an annuity in advance, take one more period and subtract 1.0000.

Periods	13%	14%	15%	16%	17%	18%	19%	20%	25%
1	1.0000	1.0000	1.0000	1.0000	1.0000	1.0000	1.0000	1.0000	1.0000
2	2.1300	2.1400	2.1500	2.1600	2.1700	2.1800	2.1900	2.2000	2.2500
3	3.4069	3.4396	3.4725	3.5056	3.5389	3.5724	3.6061	3.6400	3.8125
4	4.8498	4.9211	4.9934	5.0665	5.1405	5.2154	5.2913	5.3680	5.7656
5	6.4803	6.6101	6.7424	6.8771	7.0144	7.1542	7.2966	7.4416	8.2070
6	8.3227	8.5355	8.7537	8.9775	9.2068	9.4420	9.6830	9.9299	11.2588
7	10.4047	10.7305	11.0668	11.4139	11.7720	12.1415	12.5227	12.9159	15.0735
8	12.7573	13.2328	13.7268	14.2401	14.7733	15.3270	15.9020	16.4991	19.8419
9	15.4157	16.0853	16.7858	17.5185	18.2847	19.0859	19.9234	20.7989	25.8023
10	18.4197	19.3373	20.3037	21.3215	22.3931	23.5213	24.7089	25.9587	33.2529
11	21.8143	23.0445	24.3493	25.7329	27.1999	28.7551	30.4035	32.1504	42.5661
12	25.6502	27.2707	29.0017	30.8502	32.8239	34.9311	37.1802	39.5805	54.2077
13	29.9847	32.0887	34.3519	36.7862	39.4040	42.2187	45.2445	48.4966	68.7596
14	34.8827	37.5811	40.5047	43.6720	47.1027	50.8180	54.8409	59.1959	86.9495
15	40.4175	43.8424	47.5804	51.6595	56.1101	60.9653	66.2607	72.0351	109.6868
16	46.6717	50.9804	55.7175	60.9250	66.6488	72.9390	79.8502	87.4421	138.1086
17	53.7391	59.1176	65.0751	71.6730	78.9792	87.0680	96.0218	105.9306	173.6357
18	61.7251	68.3941	75.8364	84.1407	93.4056	103.7403	115.2659	128.1167	218.0446
19	70.7494	78.9692	88.2118	98.6032	110.2846	123.4135	138.1664	154.7400	273.5558
20	80.9468	91.0249	102.4436	115.3797	130.0329	146.6280	165.4180	186.6880	342.9447
21	92.4699	104.7684	118.8101	134.8405	153.1385	174.0210	197.8474	225.0256	429.6809
22	105.4910	120.4360	137.6316	157.4150	180.1721	206.3448	236.4385	271.0307	538.1011
23	120.2048	138.2970	159.2764	183.6014	211.8013	244.4868	282.3618	326.2369	673.6264
24	136.8315	158.6586	184.1678	213.9776	248.8076	289.4945	337.0105	392.4842	847.0330
25	155.6196	181.8708	212.7930	249.2140	292.1049	342.6035	402.0425	471.9811	1054.7912
30	293.1992	356.7868	434.7451	530.3117	647.4391	790.9480	966.7122	1181.8816	3227.1743
40	1013.7043	1342.0251	1779.0903	2360.7572	3134.5218	4163.2130	5529.8290	7343.8579	30088.656
50	3459.5072	4994.5214	7217.7163	10435.6488	15089.5017	21813.0937	31515.3363	45497.191	280255.7

TABLE 3. Present Value of $1

$$P = F_n (1 + r)^{-n}$$

Periods	5%	6%	7%	8%	9%	10%	11%	12%
1	0.9524	0.9434	0.9346	0.9259	0.9174	0.9091	0.9009	0.8929
2	0.9070	0.8900	0.8734	0.8573	0.8417	0.8264	0.8116	0.7972
3	0.8638	0.8396	0.8163	0.7938	0.7722	0.7513	0.7312	0.7118
4	0.8227	0.7921	0.7629	0.7350	0.7084	0.6830	0.6587	0.6355
5	0.7835	0.7473	0.7130	0.6806	0.6499	0.6209	0.5935	0.5674
6	0.7462	0.7050	0.6663	0.6302	0.5963	0.5645	0.5346	0.5066
7	0.7107	0.6651	0.6227	0.5835	0.5470	0.5132	0.4817	0.4524
8	0.6768	0.6274	0.5820	0.5403	0.5019	0.4665	0.4339	0.4039
9	0.6446	0.5919	0.5439	0.5002	0.4604	0.4241	0.3909	0.3606
10	0.6139	0.5584	0.5083	0.4632	0.4224	0.3855	0.3522	0.3220
11	0.5847	0.5268	0.4751	0.4289	0.3875	0.3505	0.3173	0.2875
12	0.5568	0.4970	0.4440	0.3971	0.3555	0.3186	0.2858	0.2567
13	0.5303	0.4688	0.4150	0.3677	0.3262	0.2897	0.2575	0.2292
14	0.5051	0.4423	0.3878	0.3405	0.2992	0.2633	0.2320	0.2046
15	0.4810	0.4173	0.3624	0.3153	0.2745	0.2394	0.2090	0.1827
16	0.4581	0.3936	0.3387	0.2919	0.2519	0.2176	0.1883	0.1631
17	0.4363	0.3714	0.3166	0.2703	0.2311	0.1978	0.1696	0.1456
18	0.4155	0.3503	0.2959	0.2502	0.2120	0.1799	0.1528	0.1300
19	0.3957	0.3305	0.2765	0.2317	0.1945	0.1635	0.1377	0.1161
20	0.3769	0.3118	0.2584	0.2145	0.1784	0.1486	0.1240	0.1037
21	0.3589	0.2942	0.2415	0.1987	0.1637	0.1351	0.1117	0.0926
22	0.3418	0.2775	0.2257	0.1839	0.1502	0.1228	0.1007	0.0826
23	0.3256	0.2618	0.2109	0.1703	0.1378	0.1117	0.0907	0.0738
24	0.3101	0.2470	0.1971	0.1577	0.1264	0.1015	0.0817	0.0659
25	0.2935	0.2330	0.1842	0.1460	0.1160	0.0923	0.0736	0.0588
30	0.2314	0.1741	0.1314	0.0994	0.0754	0.0573	0.0437	0.0334
40	0.1420	0.0972	0.0668	0.0460	0.0318	0.0221	0.0154	0.0108
50	0.0872	0.0543	0.0339	0.0213	0.0134	0.0085	0.0054	0.0035

Periods	13%	14%	15%	16%	17%	18%	19%	20%	25%
1	0.8850	0.8772	0.8696	0.8621	0.8547	0.8475	0.8403	0.8333	0.8000
2	0.7831	0.7695	0.7561	0.7432	0.7305	0.7182	0.7062	0.6944	0.6400
3	0.6931	0.6750	0.6575	0.6407	0.6244	0.6086	0.5934	0.5787	0.5120
4	0.6133	0.5921	0.5718	0.5523	0.5337	0.5158	0.4987	0.4823	0.4096
5	0.5428	0.5194	0.4972	0.4761	0.4561	0.4371	0.4190	0.4019	0.3277
6	0.4803	0.4556	0.4323	0.4104	0.3898	0.3704	0.3521	0.3349	0.2621
7	0.4251	0.3996	0.3759	0.3538	0.3332	0.3139	0.2959	0.2791	0.2097
8	0.3762	0.3506	0.3269	0.3050	0.2848	0.2660	0.2487	0.2326	0.1678
9	0.3329	0.3075	0.2843	0.2630	0.2434	0.2255	0.2090	0.1938	0.1342
10	0.2946	0.2697	0.2472	0.2267	0.2080	0.1911	0.1756	0.1615	0.1074
11	0.2607	0.2366	0.2149	0.1954	0.1778	0.1619	0.1476	0.1346	0.0859
12	0.2307	0.2076	0.1869	0.1685	0.1520	0.1372	0.1240	0.1122	0.0678
13	0.2042	0.1821	0.1625	0.1452	0.1299	0.1163	0.1042	0.0935	0.0550
14	0.1807	0.1597	0.1413	0.1252	0.1110	0.0985	0.0876	0.0779	0.0440
15	0.1599	0.1401	0.1229	0.1079	0.0949	0.0835	0.0736	0.0649	0.0352
16	0.1415	0.1229	0.1069	0.0930	0.0811	0.0708	0.0618	0.0541	0.0281
17	0.1252	0.1078	0.0929	0.0802	0.0693	0.0600	0.0520	0.0451	0.0225
18	0.1108	0.0946	0.0808	0.0691	0.0592	0.0508	0.0437	0.0376	0.0180
19	0.0981	0.0829	0.0703	0.0596	0.0506	0.0431	0.0367	0.0313	0.0144
20	0.0868	0.0728	0.0611	0.0514	0.0433	0.0365	0.0308	0.0261	0.0115
21	0.0768	0.0638	0.0531	0.0443	0.0370	0.0309	0.0259	0.0217	0.0092
22	0.0680	0.0560	0.0462	0.0382	0.0316	0.0262	0.0218	0.0181	0.0074
23	0.0601	0.0491	0.0402	0.0329	0.0270	0.0222	0.0183	0.0151	0.0059
24	0.0532	0.0431	0.0349	0.0284	0.0231	0.0188	0.0154	0.0126	0.0047
25	0.0471	0.0378	0.0304	0.0245	0.0197	0.0160	0.0129	0.0105	0.0038
30	0.0256	0.0196	0.0151	0.0116	0.0090	0.0070	0.0054	0.0042	0.0012
40	0.0075	0.0053	0.0037	0.0026	0.0019	0.0013	0.0010	0.0007	0.0001
50	0.0022	0.0014	0.0009	0.0006	0.0004	0.0003	0.0002	0.0001	—

TABLE 4.   Present Value of Annuity of $1 in Arrears

$$P_A = A \left[\frac{1 - (1+r)^{-n}}{r} \right]$$

Periods	5%	6%	7%	8%	9%	10%	11%	12%
1	0.9524	0.9434	0.9346	0.9259	0.9174	0.9091	0.9009	0.8929
2	1.8594	1.8334	1.8080	1.7833	1.7591	1.7355	1.7125	1.6901
3	2.7232	2.6730	2.6243	2.5771	2.5313	2.4869	2.4437	2.4018
4	3.5460	3.4651	3.3872	3.3121	3.2397	3.1699	3.1024	3.0373
5	4.3295	4.2124	4.1002	3.9927	3.8897	3.7908	3.6959	3.6048
6	5.0757	4.9173	4.7665	4.6229	4.4859	4.3553	4.2305	4.1114
7	5.7864	5.5824	5.3893	5.2064	5.0330	4.8684	4.7122	4.5638
8	6.4632	6.2098	5.9713	5.7466	5.5348	5.3349	5.1461	4.9676
9	7.1078	6.8017	6.5152	6.2469	5.9952	5.7590	5.5370	5.3282
10	7.7217	7.3601	7.0236	6.7101	6.4177	6.1446	5.8892	5.6502
11	8.3064	7.8869	7.4987	7.1390	6.8052	6.4951	6.2065	5.9377
12	8.8633	8.3838	7.9427	7.5361	7.1607	6.8137	6.4924	6.1944
13	9.3936	8.8527	8.3577	7.9038	7.4869	7.1034	6.7439	6.4236
14	9.8986	9.2950	8.7455	8.2442	7.7861	7.3667	6.9819	6.6282
15	10.3797	9.7122	9.1079	8.5595	8.0607	7.6061	7.1909	6.8109
16	10.8378	10.1059	9.4466	8.8514	8.3126	7.8237	7.3792	6.9740
17	11.2741	10.4773	9.7632	9.1216	8.5436	8.0216	7.5488	7.1196
18	11.6896	10.8276	10.0591	9.3719	8.7556	8.2014	7.7016	7.2497
19	12.0853	11.1581	10.3356	9.6036	8.9501	8.3649	7.8393	7.3658
20	12.4622	11.4699	10.5940	9.8181	9.1285	8.5136	7.9633	7.4694
21	12.8212	11.7640	10.8355	10.0168	9.2922	8.6487	8.0751	7.5620
22	13.1630	12.0416	11.0612	10.2007	9.4424	8.7715	8.1757	7.6446
23	13.4886	12.3034	11.2722	10.3711	9.5802	8.8832	8.2664	7.7184
24	13.7986	12.5504	11.4693	10.5288	9.7066	8.9847	8.3481	7.7843
25	14.0939	12.7834	11.6536	10.6748	9.8226	9.0770	8.4217	7.8431
30	15.3725	13.7648	12.4090	11.2578	10.2737	9.4269	8.6938	8.0552
40	17.1591	15.0463	13.3317	11.9246	10.7570	9.7791	8.9511	8.2438
50	18.2559	15.7619	13.8007	12.2335	10.9617	9.9148	9.0417	8.3045

Note: To convert this table to values of an annuity in advance, take one less period and add 1.0000.

Periods	13%	14%	15%	16%	17%	18%	19%	20%	25%
1	0.8850	0.8772	0.8696	0.8621	0.8547	0.8475	0.8403	0.8333	0.8000
2	1.6681	1.6467	1.6257	1.6052	1.5852	1.5656	1.5465	1.5278	1.4400
3	2.3612	2.3216	2.2832	2.2459	2.2096	2.1743	2.1399	2.1065	1.9520
4	2.9745	2.9137	2.8550	2.7982	2.7432	2.6901	2.6386	2.5887	2.3616
5	3.5172	3.4331	3.3522	3.2743	3.1993	3.1272	3.0576	2.9906	2.6893
6	3.9975	3.8887	3.7845	3.6847	3.5892	3.4976	3.4098	3.3255	2.9514
7	4.4226	4.2883	4.1604	4.0386	3.9224	3.8115	3.7057	3.6046	3.1611
8	4.7988	4.6389	4.4873	4.3436	4.2072	4.0776	3.9544	3.8372	3.3289
9	5.1317	4.9464	4.7716	4.6065	4.4506	4.3030	4.1633	4.0310	3.4631
10	5.4262	5.2161	5.0188	4.8332	4.6586	4.4941	4.3389	4.1925	3.5705
11	5.6869	5.4527	5.2337	5.0286	4.8364	4.6560	4.4865	4.3271	3.6564
12	5.9176	5.6603	5.4206	5.1971	4.9884	4.7932	4.6105	4.4392	3.7251
13	6.1218	5.8424	5.5831	5.3423	5.1183	4.9095	4.7147	4.5327	3.7801
14	6.3025	6.0021	5.7245	5.4675	5.2293	5.0081	4.8023	4.6106	3.8241
15	6.4624	6.1422	5.8474	5.5755	5.3242	5.0916	4.8759	4.6755	3.8593
16	6.6039	6.2651	5.9542	5.6685	5.4053	5.1624	4.9377	4.7296	3.8874
17	6.7291	6.3729	6.0472	5.7487	5.4746	5.2223	4.9897	4.7746	3.9099
18	6.8399	6.4674	6.1280	5.8178	5.5339	5.2732	5.0333	4.8122	3.9279
19	6.9380	6.5504	6.1982	5.8775	5.5845	5.3162	5.0700	4.8435	3.9424
20	7.0248	6.6231	6.2593	5.9288	5.6278	5.3527	5.1009	4.8696	3.9539
21	7.1016	6.6870	6.3125	5.9731	5.6648	5.3837	5.1268	4.8913	3.9631
22	7.1695	6.7429	6.3587	6.0113	5.6964	5.4099	5.1486	4.9094	3.9705
23	7.2297	6.7921	6.3988	6.0442	5.7234	5.4321	5.1668	4.9245	3.9764
24	7.2829	6.8351	6.4338	6.0726	5.7465	5.4509	5.1822	4.9371	3.9811
25	7.3300	6.8729	6.4641	6.0971	5.7662	5.4669	5.1951	4.9476	3.9849
30	7.4957	7.0027	6.5660	6.1772	5.8294	5.5168	5.2347	4.9789	3.9950
40	7.6344	7.1050	6.6418	6.2335	5.8713	5.5482	5.2582	4.9966	3.9995
50	7.6752	7.1327	6.6605	6.2463	5.8801	5.5541	5.2623	4.9995	3.9999

TABLE 5. Bond Values: Coupon Rate of 6 Percent (semiannual interest payments; semiannual compounding)

Annual Yield (%)	Years to Maturity							
	½	1	5	10	15	19½	20	30
5.0	100.49	100.96	104.38	107.79	110.47	112.37	112.55	115.45
5.5	100.24	100.48	102.16	103.81	105.06	105.94	106.02	107.31
6.0	100.00	100.00	100.00	100.00	100.00	100.00	100.00	100.00
6.5	99.76	99.52	97.89	96.37	95.25	94.52	94.45	93.44
7.0	99.52	99.05	95.84	92.89	90.80	89.45	89.32	87.53
7.5	99.28	98.58	93.84	89.58	86.63	84.76	84.59	82.20
8.0	99.04	98.11	91.89	86.41	82.71	80.42	80.21	77.38
8.5	98.80	97.65	89.99	83.38	79.03	76.39	76.15	73.01
9.0	98.56	97.19	88.13	80.49	75.57	72.66	72.40	69.04
9.5	98.33	96.73	86.32	77.72	72.31	69.19	68.91	65.43
10.0	98.10	96.28	84.56	75.08	69.26	65.97	65.68	62.14
10.5	97.86	95.83	82.84	72.54	66.38	62.97	62.68	59.13
11.0	97.63	95.38	81.16	70.12	63.67	60.18	59.88	56.38
11.5	97.40	94.94	79.52	67.81	61.11	57.58	57.28	53.84
12.0	97.17	94.50	77.92	65.59	58.71	55.15	54.86	51.52
12.5	96.94	94.06	76.36	63.47	56.44	52.89	52.60	49.37
13.0	96.71	93.63	74.84	61.44	54.29	50.77	50.49	47.38
13.5	96.49	93.20	73.35	59.49	52.27	48.79	48.52	45.55
14.0	96.26	92.77	71.91	57.62	50.36	46.94	46.67	43.84
14.5	96.04	92.34	70.49	55.84	48.56	45.20	44.95	42.26
15.0	95.81	91.92	69.11	54.12	46.85	43.57	43.33	40.78
15.5	95.59	91.50	67.76	52.48	45.24	42.04	41.80	39.41
16.0	95.37	91.08	66.45	50.91	43.71	40.61	40.38	38.12
16.5	95.15	90.67	65.17	49.40	42.26	39.28	39.03	36.91
17.0	94.93	90.26	63.91	47.95	40.89	37.98	37.77	35.78
17.5	94.71	89.85	62.69	46.56	39.59	36.78	36.58	34.71
18.0	94.50	89.45	61.49	45.23	38.36	35.65	35.46	33.71
18.5	94.28	89.04	60.33	43.95	37.19	34.58	34.40	32.77
19.0	94.06	88.64	59.19	42.72	36.07	33.57	33.39	31.87
19.5	93.85	88.25	58.07	41.54	35.02	32.61	32.44	31.03
20.0	93.64	87.85	56.99	40.41	34.01	31.70	31.55	30.23

TABLE 6. Bond Values: Coupon Rate of 8 Percent (semiannual interest payments; semiannual compounding)

Annual Yield (%)	½	1	5	10	15	19½	20	30
5.0	101.46	102.89	113.13	123.38	131.40	137.10	137.65	146.36
5.5	101.22	102.40	110.80	119.03	125.31	129.68	130.10	136.53
6.0	100.97	101.91	108.53	114.88	119.60	122.81	123.11	127.68
6.5	100.73	101.43	106.32	110.90	114.24	116.45	116.66	119.69
7.0	100.48	100.95	104.16	107.11	109.10	110.55	110.68	112.47
7.5	100.24	100.47	102.05	103.47	104.46	105.08	105.14	105.93
8.0	100.00	100.00	100.00	100.00	100.00	100.00	100.00	100.00
8.5	99.76	99.53	98.00	96.68	95.81	95.28	95.23	94.60
9.0	99.52	99.06	96.04	93.50	91.86	90.89	90.80	89.68
9.5	99.28	98.60	94.14	90.45	88.13	86.79	86.68	85.19
10.0	99.05	98.14	92.28	87.54	84.63	82.98	82.84	81.07
10.5	98.81	97.68	90.46	84.75	81.32	79.43	79.27	77.30
11.0	98.58	97.23	88.69	82.07	78.20	76.11	75.93	73.83
11.5	98.35	96.78	86.97	79.51	75.25	73.00	72.82	70.63
12.0	98.11	96.33	85.28	77.06	72.47	70.10	69.91	67.68
12.5	97.88	95.89	83.63	74.71	69.84	67.38	67.19	64.95
13.0	97.65	95.45	82.03	72.45	67.35	64.84	64.64	62.42
13.5	97.42	95.01	80.46	70.29	65.00	62.45	62.25	60.07
14.0	97.20	94.58	78.93	68.22	62.77	60.21	60.00	57.88
14.5	96.97	94.14	77.43	66.23	60.66	58.10	57.90	55.84
15.0	96.74	93.72	75.98	64.32	58.66	56.11	55.92	53.94
15.5	96.52	93.29	74.55	62.49	56.77	54.25	54.06	52.16
16.0	96.30	92.87	76.16	60.73	54.97	52.49	52.30	50.49
16.5	96.07	92.45	71.80	59.04	53.26	50.83	50.65	48.93
17.0	95.85	92.03	70.47	57.41	51.64	49.26	49.08	47.46
17.5	95.63	91.62	69.18	55.86	50.10	47.77	47.61	46.07
18.0	95.41	91.20	67.91	54.36	48.63	46.37	46.21	44.76
18.5	95.19	90.80	66.67	52.92	47.24	45.04	44.89	43.52
19.0	94.98	90.39	65.47	51.53	45.91	43.79	43.64	42.36
19.5	94.76	89.99	64.29	50.20	44.64	42.59	42.45	41.25
20.0	94.55	89.59	63.13	48.92	43.44	41.46	41.33	40.20

TABLE 7. Bond Values: Coupon Rate of 10 Percent (semiannual interest payments; semiannual compounding)

Annual Yield (%)	Years to Maturity							
	½	1	5	10	15	19½	20	30
5.0	102.44	104.82	121.88	138.97	152.33	161.83	162.76	177.27
5.5	102.19	104.32	119.44	134.26	145.56	153.42	154.18	165.75
6.0	101.94	103.83	117.06	129.75	139.20	145.62	146.23	155.35
6.5	101.69	103.34	114.74	125.44	133.22	138.38	138.86	145.94
7.0	101.45	102.85	112.47	121.32	127.59	131.65	132.03	137.42
7.5	101.20	102.37	110.27	117.37	122.29	125.40	125.69	129.67
8.0	100.96	101.89	108.11	113.59	117.29	119.58	119.79	122.62
8.5	100.72	101.41	106.01	109.97	112.58	114.17	114.31	116.19
9.0	100.48	100.94	103.96	106.50	108.14	109.11	109.20	110.32
9.5	100.24	100.47	101.95	103.18	103.96	104.40	104.44	104.94
10.0	100.00	100.00	100.00	100.00	100.00	100.00	100.00	100.00
10.5	99.76	99.54	98.09	96.95	96.26	95.89	95.85	95.46
11.0	99.53	99.08	96.23	94.02	92.73	92.04	91.98	91.28
11.5	99.29	98.62	94.41	91.22	89.39	88.43	88.35	87.41
12.0	99.06	98.17	92.64	88.53	86.24	85.05	84.95	83.84
12.5	98.82	97.72	90.91	85.95	83.24	81.88	81.77	80.53
13.0	98.59	97.27	89.22	83.47	80.41	78.90	78.78	77.45
13.5	98.36	96.82	87.57	81.09	77.73	76.10	75.98	74.59
14.0	98.13	96.38	85.95	78.81	75.18	73.47	73.34	71.92
14.5	97.90	95.95	84.38	76.62	72.77	70.99	70.85	69.43
15.0	97.67	95.51	82.84	74.51	70.47	68.65	68.51	67.10
15.5	97.45	95.08	81.34	72.49	68.30	66.45	66.31	64.92
16.0	97.22	94.65	79.87	70.55	66.23	64.36	64.23	62.87
16.5	97.00	94.22	78.44	68.68	64.26	62.40	62.26	60.94
17.0	96.77	93.80	77.04	66.88	62.39	60.53	60.40	59.13
17.5	96.55	93.38	75.67	65.15	60.60	58.77	58.64	57.42
18.0	96.33	92.96	74.33	63.49	58.91	57.10	56.97	55.81
18.5	96.11	92.55	73.02	61.89	57.29	55.51	55.39	54.28
19.0	95.89	92.14	71.75	60.34	55.74	54.01	53.89	52.84
19.5	95.67	91.73	70.50	58.86	54.27	52.58	52.46	51.47
20.0	95.45	91.32	69.28	57.43	52.87	51.21	51.10	50.16

TABLE 8. Bond Values: Coupon Rate of 12 Percent (semiannual interest payments; semiannual compounding)

Annual Yield (%)	Years to Maturity							
	½	1	5	10	15	19½	20	30
5.0	103.41	106.75	130.63	154.56	173.26	186.56	187.86	208.18
5.5	103.16	106.24	128.08	149.49	165.81	177.16	178.25	194.97
6.0	102.91	105.74	125.59	144.63	158.80	168.42	169.34	183.03
6.5	102.66	105.24	123.16	139.98	152.20	160.31	161.07	172.20
7.0	102.42	104.75	120.79	135.53	145.98	152.76	153.39	162.36
7.5	102.17	104.26	118.48	131.27	140.12	145.72	146.24	153.41
8.0	101.92	103.77	116.22	127.18	134.58	139.17	139.59	145.25
8.5	101.68	103.29	114.02	123.27	129.36	133.05	133.39	137.79
9.0	101.44	102.81	111.87	119.51	124.43	127.34	127.60	130.96
9.5	101.19	102.33	109.77	115.91	119.78	122.01	122.20	124.69
10.0	100.95	101.86	107.72	112.46	115.37	117.02	117.16	118.93
10.5	100.71	101.39	105.72	109.15	111.21	112.34	112.44	113.62
11.0	100.47	100.92	103.77	105.98	107.27	107.96	108.02	108.72
11.5	100.24	100.46	101.86	102.93	103.54	103.86	103.88	104.20
12.0	100.00	100.00	100.00	100.00	100.00	100.00	100.00	100.00
12.5	99.76	99.54	98.18	97.19	96.65	96.38	96.35	96.11
13.0	99.53	99.09	96.41	94.49	93.47	92.97	92.93	92.48
13.5	99.30	98.64	94.67	91.90	90.45	89.76	89.70	89.11
14.0	99.07	98.19	92.98	89.41	87.59	86.74	86.67	85.96
14.5	98.83	97.75	91.32	87.01	84.87	83.88	83.81	83.02
15.0	98.60	97.31	89.70	84.71	82.28	81.19	81.11	80.26
15.5	98.38	96.87	88.12	82.49	79.82	78.65	78.56	77.68
16.0	98.15	96.43	86.58	80.36	77.48	76.24	76.15	75.25
16.5	97.92	96.00	85.07	78.31	75.26	73.97	73.87	72.96
17.0	97.70	95.57	83.60	76.34	73.13	71.81	71.71	70.81
17.5	97.47	95.15	82.16	74.44	71.11	69.76	69.67	68.78
18.0	97.25	94.72	80.75	72.61	69.18	67.82	67.73	66.86
18.5	97.03	94.30	79.37	70.85	67.34	65.98	65.89	65.04
19.0	96.80	93.88	78.02	69.16	65.58	64.23	64.13	63.32
19.5	96.58	93.47	76.71	67.52	63.90	62.56	62.47	61.68
20.0	96.36	93.06	75.42	65.95	62.29	60.97	60.88	60.13

TABLE 9.   Bond Values: Coupon Rate of 14 Percent (semiannual interest payments; semiannual compounding)

Annual Yield (%)	Years to Maturity							
	½	1	5	10	15	19½	20	30
5.0	104.39	108.67	139.38	170.15	194.19	211.29	212.96	239.09
5.5	104.14	108.16	136.72	164.72	186.06	200.90	202.33	224.20
6.0	103.88	107.65	134.12	159.51	178.40	191.23	192.46	210.70
6.5	103.63	107.15	131.58	154.52	171.18	182.24	183.28	198.45
7.0	103.38	106.65	129.11	149.74	164.37	173.86	174.74	187.31
7.5	103.13	106.15	126.69	145.16	157.95	166.05	166.79	177.15
8.0	102.88	105.66	124.33	140.77	151.88	158.75	159.38	167.87
8.5	102.64	105.17	122.03	136.56	146.14	151.94	152.46	159.38
9.0	102.39	104.68	119.78	132.52	140.72	145.57	146.00	151.60
9.5	102.15	104.20	117.59	128.64	135.60	139.62	139.97	144.44
10.0	101.90	103.72	115.44	124.92	130.74	134.03	134.32	137.86
10.5	101.66	103.24	113.35	121.35	126.15	128.80	129.03	131.79
11.0	101.42	102.77	111.31	117.93	121.80	123.89	124.07	126.17
11.5	101.18	102.30	109.31	114.63	117.68	119.28	119.42	120.98
12.0	100.94	101.83	107.37	111.47	113.76	114.95	115.05	116.16
12.5	100.71	101.37	105.46	108.43	110.05	110.87	110.94	111.68
13.0	100.47	100.91	103.59	105.51	106.53	107.03	107.07	107.52
13.5	100.23	100.45	101.78	102.70	103.18	103.41	103.43	103.63
14.0	100.00	100.00	100.00	100.00	100.00	100.00	100.00	100.00
14.5	99.77	99.55	98.26	97.40	96.97	96.78	96.76	96.60
15.0	99.53	99.10	96.57	94.90	94.09	93.73	93.70	93.42
15.5	99.30	98.66	94.91	92.50	91.35	90.85	90.81	90.43
16.0	99.07	98.22	93.29	90.18	88.74	88.12	88.08	87.62
16.5	98.85	97.78	91.71	87.95	86.25	85.54	85.48	84.98
17.0	98.62	97.34	90.16	85.80	83.88	83.09	83.03	82.49
17.5	98.39	96.91	88.64	83.74	81.61	80.76	80.70	80.13
18.0	98.17	96.48	87.16	81.74	79.45	78.55	78.49	77.90
18.5	97.94	96.06	85.72	79.82	77.39	76.45	76.38	75.80
19.0	97.72	95.63	84.30	77.97	75.41	74.45	74.38	73.80
19.5	97.49	95.21	82.92	76.18	73.53	72.54	72.48	71.90
20.0	97.27	94.79	81.57	74.46	71.72	70.73	70.66	70.10

TABLE 10. Bond Values: Coupon Rate of 16 Percent (semiannual interest payments; semiannual compounding)

Annual Yield (%)	Years to Maturity							
	½	1	5	10	15	19½	20	30
5.0	105.37	110.60	148.14	185.74	215.12	236.02	238.07	270.00
5.5	105.11	110.08	145.36	179.94	206.31	224.64	226.41	253.42
6.0	104.85	109.57	142.65	174.39	198.00	214.04	215.57	238.38
6.5	104.60	109.06	140.01	169.06	190.16	204.17	205.49	224.70
7.0	104.35	108.55	137.42	163.96	182.76	194.96	196.10	212.25
7.5	104.10	108.04	134.90	159.06	175.77	186.37	187.34	200.89
8.0	103.85	107.54	132.44	154.36	169.17	178.34	179.17	190.49
8.5	103.60	107.05	130.04	149.85	162.92	170.83	171.54	180.97
9.0	103.35	106.55	127.69	145.53	157.01	163.80	164.41	172.23
9.5	103.10	106.06	125.40	141.37	151.42	157.22	157.73	164.19
10.0	102.86	105.58	123.17	137.39	146.12	151.05	151.48	156.79
10.5	102.61	105.10	120.98	133.56	141.10	145.26	145.62	149.95
11.0	102.37	104.62	118.84	129.88	136.33	139.82	140.12	143.62
11.5	102.13	104.14	116.76	126.34	131.82	134.71	134.95	137.76
12.0	101.89	103.67	114.72	122.94	127.53	129.90	130.09	132.32
12.5	101.65	103.20	112.73	119.67	123.46	125.37	125.52	127.26
13.0	101.41	102.73	110.78	116.53	119.59	121.10	121.22	122.55
13.5	101.17	102.27	108.88	113.50	115.91	117.07	117.16	118.15
14.0	100.93	101.81	107.02	110.59	112.41	113.26	113.33	114.04
14.5	100.70	101.35	105.21	107.79	109.08	109.67	109.72	110.19
15.0	100.47	100.90	103.43	105.10	105.91	106.27	106.30	106.58
15.5	100.23	100.45	101.70	102.50	102.88	103.05	103.06	103.19
16.0	100.00	100.00	100.00	100.00	100.00	100.00	100.00	100.00
16.5	99.77	99.56	98.34	97.59	97.25	97.11	97.10	97.00
17.0	99.54	99.11	96.72	95.27	94.63	94.36	94.34	94.16
17.5	99.31	98.68	95.13	93.03	92.12	91.75	91.73	91.48
18.0	99.08	98.24	93.58	90.87	89.73	89.27	89.24	88.95
18.5	98.86	97.81	92.07	88.79	87.44	86.92	86.88	86.55
19.0	98.63	97.38	90.58	86.78	85.25	84.67	84.63	84.28
19.5	98.41	96.95	89.13	84.84	83.15	82.53	82.49	82.12
20.0	98.18	96.53	87.71	82.97	81.15	80.49	80.44	80.07

TABLE 11.   Bond Values: Coupon Rate of 18 Percent (semiannual interest payments; semiannual compounding)

Annual Yield (%)	½	1	5	10	15	19½	20	30
5.0	106.34	112.53	156.89	201.33	236.05	260.75	263.17	300.91
5.5	106.08	112.00	154.00	195.17	226.56	248.38	250.49	282.64
6.0	105.83	111.48	151.18	189.26	217.60	236.85	238.69	266.05
6.5	105.57	110.96	148.48	183.60	209.15	226.10	227.70	250.96
7.0	105.31	110.45	145.74	178.17	201.16	216.06	217.45	237.20
7.5	105.06	109.94	143.12	172.96	193.60	206.69	207.89	224.62
8.0	104.81	109.43	140.55	167.95	186.46	197.92	198.96	213.12
8.5	104.56	108.93	138.05	163.15	179.70	189.72	190.62	202.57
9.0	104.31	108.43	135.61	158.54	173.30	182.03	182.81	192.87
9.5	104.06	107.93	133.22	154.11	167.24	174.83	175.49	183.95
10.0	103.81	107.44	130.89	149.85	161.49	168.07	168.64	175.72
10.5	103.56	106.95	128.61	145.76	156.04	161.72	162.20	168.11
11.0	103.32	106.46	126.38	141.83	150.87	155.75	156.16	161.07
11.5	103.07	105.98	124.21	138.05	145.96	150.13	150.48	154.55
12.0	102.83	105.50	122.08	134.41	141.29	144.85	145.14	148.48
12.5	102.59	105.02	120.00	130.91	136.86	139.86	140.11	142.84
13.0	102.35	104.55	117.97	127.55	132.65	135.16	135.36	137.58
13.5	102.11	104.08	115.99	124.31	128.64	130.72	130.89	132.67
14.0	101.87	103.62	114.05	121.19	124.82	126.53	126.66	128.08
14.5	101.63	103.15	112.15	118.18	121.18	122.56	122.67	123.78
15.0	101.40	102.69	110.30	115.29	117.72	118.81	118.89	119.74
15.5	101.16	102.24	108.48	112.50	114.41	115.25	115.31	115.95
16.0	100.93	101.78	106.71	109.82	111.26	111.88	111.92	112.38
16.5	100.69	101.33	104.98	107.23	108.25	108.68	108.71	109.01
17.0	100.46	100.89	103.28	104.73	105.37	105.64	105.66	105.84
17.5	100.23	100.44	101.62	102.32	102.63	102.75	102.76	102.84
18.0	100.00	100.00	100.00	100.00	100.00	100.00	100.00	100.00
18.5	99.77	99.56	98.41	97.76	97.49	97.38	97.38	97.31
19.0	99.54	99.13	96.86	95.59	95.08	94.89	94.88	94.76
19.5	99.32	98.69	95.34	93.50	92.78	92.51	92.49	92.34
20.0	99.09	98.26	93.86	91.49	90.57	90.24	90.22	90.03

Appendix B

Solutions to independent study problems

Chapter 2

1. *a.* The $14,860 retained earnings is the amount entered in the balance sheet in part *b* to achieve equality between *total assets* and *total liabilities and owners' equity.*

b.

BOLTER COMPANY
Balance Sheet
December 31, 19x1

Assets

Current assets:

Cash	$ 6,600	
Accounts receivable	8,120	
Inventory	11,200	
Total current assets		$ 25,920

Plant assets:

Land	18,000	
Buildings	65,760	
Equipment	4,450	
Total plant assets		88,210
Total assets		$114,130

Liabilities and Owners' Equity

Current liabilities:

Accounts payable	$13,300	
Notes payable	9,000	
Wages payable	1,770	
Total current liabilities		$ 24,070

Long-term liability:

Bonds payable		40,200
Total liabilities		64,270

Owners' equity:
Capital stock 35,000
Retained earnings 14,860
Total owners' equity 49,860
Total liabilities and owners' equity $114,130

2. *a.* The way to solve this problem is to calculate the owners' equity at the beginning of the year, adjust it for the year's transactions other than income transactions, and then subtract this adjusted balance from the owners' equity at the end of the year, calculated by subtracting the year-end liabilities from the year-end assets:

	Assets	− Liabilities	=	Capital Stock	+	Retained Earnings
January 1	$120,000	$64,000		$20,000		$36,000
New stock				+ 6,000		
Dividends						− 24,000
Adj. balance						12,000
December 31	140,000	68,000		26,000		46,000
Income						$34,000

b. Capital stock: 2,100 shares $26,000
Retained earnings... 46,000
Total owners' equity $72,000

3. 1. Collections from customers = $100 + $500 − $80 = $520.
2. Purchases on account = $250 + $40 − $50 = $240.
3. Ending balance = $20 + $300 − $295 = $25.
4. Beginning balance = $90 + $265 − $240 = $115.
5. Rent expense = $45 + $130 − $60 = $115.

4. *a.* 1. Asset, Merchandise, increased by $1 million; Liability, Accounts Payable, increased by $1 million.
2. Asset, Accounts Receivable, increased by $1.5 million; Owners' Equity increased by this amount. (Note: We know that the owners' equity didn't increase by this amount once all expenses were taken into consideration. This figure is a first approximation, to be corrected by additional information.)
3. Liability, Wages Payable, increased by $300,000; Owners' Equity decreased by this amount. (Note: This is one of the expenses offsetting the gross increase in owners' equity identified in item 2.)
4. Liability, Accounts Payable, increased by $100,000; Owners' Equity decreased by this amount. (This is another expense, offsetting the gross increase in owners' equity identified in item 2.)
5. Asset, Cash, decreased by $1,050,000; Liability, Accounts Payable, decreased by the same amount.
6. Asset, Cash, decreased by $280,000; Liability, Wages Payable, decreased by this amount.
7. Asset, Cash, increased by $1.6 million; Asset, Accounts Receivable, decreased by this amount.

8. Asset, Equipment, increased by $40,000; Asset, Cash, decreased by $25,000; Liability, Accounts Payable, increased by $15,000.
9. Asset, Merchandise, decreased by $940,000; Owners' Equity decreased by this same amount, the cost of the goods that were sold.
10. Asset, Equipment, decreased by $18,000; Owners' Equity decreased by the same amount.
11. Liability, Dividends Payable, increased by $10,000; Owners' Equity decreased by this amount.
12. Asset, Cash, decreased by $7,500; Liability, Dividends Payable, decreased by this amount.

b.

A STORE
Income Statement
For the Year Ended December 31, 19x1

Sales revenue		$1,500,000
Expenses:		
Cost of goods sold	$940,000	
Wages	300,000	
Depreciation	18,000	
Other	100,000	1,358,000
Net income		$ 142,000

5. *a.* 1. *July 1:* Asset, Furniture, increased by $4,200; Liability, Accounts Payable, increased by the same amount. *October 1:* Liability, Accounts Payable, decreased by $4,200; Asset, Cash, decreased by the same amount.
2. *October 1:* No effect. *November 15:* Asset, Cash, decreased by $1,500; Owners' Equity decreased by the same amount. *December 15:* Same as November 15.
3. Asset, Accounts Receivable, increased by $300,000; Asset, Inventory, decreased by $220,000; Owners' Equity increased by $80,000.
4. Asset, Cash, decreased by $24,000; Liability, Accounts Payable, decreased by the same amount.
5. Asset, Cash, decreased by $22,500; Asset, Prepaid Rent, increased by $18,750 ($\frac{5}{6} \times$ $22,500); Owners' Equity decreased by $3,750 ($\frac{1}{6} \times$ $22,500).

b. 1. Assuming that the equipment is equally useful in each of the 12 years, the annual depreciation should be $4,200/12 = $350. Since the furniture was purchased on July 1, only one-half year's depreciation, or $175, should be taken in 19x3.
2. The timing of the payments is irrelevant. The sales representative worked three months in 19x3, and expense is 3 × $1,500 = $4,500.
3. The cost of goods sold is $220,000, and this is an expense, deductible from the revenues recognized in 19x3.
4. No expense. The payment merely canceled a liability that was assumed in 19x2.
5. Rent expense = three months' rentals = $\frac{3}{6} \times$ $22,500 = $11,250.

6. *a and b.*

Assets:

Cash

Bal. 1/1	12,510
(2)	+296,000
(7b)	− 44,400
(8)	−248,850
(10)	+ 60,000
Bal. 12/31	75,260

Accounts Receivable

Bal. 1/1	23,060
(1)	+301,000
(2)	−296,000
Bal. 12/31	28,060

Merchandise Inventory

Bal. 1/1	67,200
(1)	−181,000
(3)	+246,300
Bal. 12/31	132,500

Equipment

Bal. 1/1	19,020
(4)	+ 3,800
(9)	− 4,800
Bal. 12/31	18,020

Liabilities:

Accounts Payable

Bal. 1/1	35,180
(3)	+246,300
(4)	+ 3,800
(5)	+ 15,000
(6)	+ 21,000
(8)	−248,850
Bal. 12/31	72,430

Salaries Payable

Bal. 1/1	1,400
(7a)	+ 43,000
(7b)	− 44,400
Bal. 12/31	0

Dividends Payable

(1)	+25,000

Owners' equity:

Capital Stock

Bal. 1/1	50,000
(10)	+60,000
Bal. 12/31	110,000

Retained Earnings

Bal. 1/1	35,210
(11)	−25,000
Bal. 12/31	10,210

Income

Bal. 1/1	—
(1)	+301,000
(1)	−181,000
(5)	− 15,000
(6)	− 21,000
(7)	− 43,000
(9)	− 4,800
Bal. 12/31	36,200

c.

HANDYMAN TOOL SHOP, INC.
Income Statement
For the Year Ended December 31, 19x2

Sales revenues		$301,000
Cost of goods sold		181,000
Gross margin		120,000
Operating expenses:		
Salaries	$43,000	
Rent	15,000	
Depreciation	4,800	
Other	21,000	83,800
Net income		$ 36,200

HANDYMAN TOOL SHOP, INC.
Balance Sheet
December 31, 19x2

Assets		*Liabilities and Owners' Equity*		
Current assets:		Current liabilities:		
Cash	$ 75,260	Accounts payable .		$ 72,430
Accounts receivable . .	28,060	Dividends payable .		25,000
Merchandise		Total current		
inventory	132,500	liabilities		97,430
Total current		Owners equity:		
assets	235,820	Capital stock	$110,000	
Plant assets:		Retained earnings .	46,410	156,410
Equipment	18,020	Total liabilities and		
Total assets	$253,840	owners' equity		$253,840

Chapter 3

1. *a and c.*

Cash					Accounts Payable			
Bal. 3/1	13,200	(4)	61,300	(4)	61,300	Bal. 3/1	65,000	
(3)	60,000	(6)	7,500			(1)	46,500	
Bal. 3/31	4,400					Bal. 3/31	50,200	

Accounts Receivable					Sales Revenue		
Bal. 3/1	72,000	(3)	60,000			Bal. 3/1	130,000
(2a)	57,000					(2a)	57,000
Bal. 3/31	69,000					Bal. 3/31	187,000

Merchandise Inventory				Cost of Goods Sold		
Bal. 3/1	92,000	(2b)	36,000	Bal. 3/1	79,000	
(1)	46,500			(2b)	36,000	
Bal. 3/31	102,500			Bal. 3/31	115,000	

Salaries and Wages Payable				Salaries and Wages Expense		
(6)	7,500	Bal. 3/1	450	Bal. 3/1	14,500	
		(5)	7,200	(5)	7,200	
		Bal. 3/31	150	Bal. 3/31	21,700	

b.

1.	Merchandise Inventory	46,500	
	Accounts Payable		46,500
2.	Accounts Receivable	57,000	
	Sales Revenues		57,000

Cost of Goods Sold	36,000
Merchandise Inventory	36,000

3. Cash.................................... 60,000
   Accounts Receivable 60,000

4. Accounts Payable 61,300
   Cash................................. 61,300

5. Salaries and Wages Expense 7,200
   Salaries and Wages Payable.......... 7,200

6. Salaries and Wages Payable 7,500
   Cash................................. 7,500

d. Each account balance was determined by adding its debits, adding its credits, and determining the amount by which the larger sum exceeded the smaller.

    Cash on hand was $4,400.

    Accounts Receivable of $69,000 signifies the amount owed to Kelly by its customers.

    Merchandise Inventory of $102,500 identifies the cost of goods on hand and available for sale.

    Salaries and Wages Payable of $150 represents the amount Kelly owed its employees for services already performed.

    Accounts Payable of $50,200 is the amount Kelly owed suppliers and other providers of goods and services.

    Sales Revenues of $187,000 is the cumulative sales value of merchandise sold since the beginning of the year.

    Cost of Goods Sold of $115,000 is the cost to Kelly of the merchandise it sold (for $187,000) since the beginning of the year.

    Salaries and Wages Expense contains the $21,700 in salaries and wages earned by Kelly's employees since the beginning of the year.

2. a. Truck 10,000
   Cash 10,000

  Depreciation Expense 2,000
   Accumulated Depreciation 2,000

b.

Truck			Accumulated Depreciation		
1/1/x6	10,000			12/31/x6	2,000
				12/31/x7	2,000
				12/31/x8	2,000
Bal.	10,000			Bal.	6,000

c. Cash 2,500
  Accumulated Depreciation 6,000
  Loss on Sale of Truck 1,500
   Truck 10,000

3. 1. Merchandise Inventory .... (+A) 5,000
   Notes Payable .... (+L) 5,000

2. Cash .... (+A) 4,000
    Accounts Receivable .... (−A)   4,000

3. Accounts Payable .... (−L) 6,000
    Cash .... (−A)   6,000

4. Salaries Expense .... (−OE) 1,000
    Salaries Payable .... (+L)   1,000

5. Salaries Payable .... (−L) 900
    Cash .... (−A)   900

6. Cash .... (+A) 50,000
    Note Payable .... (+L)   50,000

7. Accounts Receivable .... (+A) 8,000
    Sales Revenue.................. (+OE)   8,000

    Cost of Goods Sold .... (−OE) 6,000
    Merchandise Inventory .... (−A)   6,000

8. Land.............................. (+A) 7,000
    Cash .... (−A)   7,000

9. Dividends Declared .... (−OE) 3,000
    Dividends Payable .... (+L)   3,000

10. Office Supplies Expense .... (−OE) 60
    Accounts Payable .... (+L)   60

11. Accounts Receivable .... (+A) 100
    Cash .... (−A)   100

4. *a* and *c.* To save space, the journal entries (part *b*) are not listed here. They can be identified easily from the numerals in parentheses in the T-accounts that follow.

Cash

Bal.	12,510	(7b)	44,400
(2)	296,000	(8)	248,850
(10)	60,000		
Bal.	75,260		

Capital Stock

		Bal.	50,000
		(10)	60,000
		Bal.	110,000

Accounts Receivable

Bal.	23,060	(2)	296,000
(1)	301,000		
Bal.	28,060		

Retained Earnings

		Bal.	35,210

Merchandise Inventory

Bal.	67,200	(1)	181,000
(3)	246,300		
Bal.	132,500		

Sales Revenues

		(1)	301,000

Equipment			
Bal.	36,140		
(4)	3,800		
Bal.	39,940		

Cost of Goods Sold			
(1)	181,000		

Accumulated Depreciation			
		Bal.	17,120
		(9)	4,800
		Bal.	21,920

Salaries Expense			
(7)	43,000		

Rental Expense			
(5)	15,000		

Accounts Payable			
(8)	248,850	Bal.	35,180
		(3)	246,300
		(4)	3,800
		(5)	15,000
		(6)	21,000
		Bal.	72,430

Depreciation Expense			
(9)	4,800		

Salaries Payable			
(7b)	44,400	Bal.	1,400
		(7a)	43,000
		Bal.	0

Miscellaneous Expenses			
(6)	21,000		

Dividends Payable			
		(11)	25,000

Dividends Declared			
(11)	25,000		

d.

Sales Revenues		301,000	
Income Summary			301,000
Income Summary		264,800	
Cost of Goods Sold			181,000
Salaries Expense			43,000
Rental Expense			15,000
Depreciation Expense			4,800
Miscellaneous Expense			21,000
Income Summary		36,200	
Retained Earnings			36,200
Retained Earnings		25,000	
Dividends Declared			25,000

Chapter 4

1. *a.* 2. Asset, Accounts Receivable, +$500,000; Owners' Equity, +$500,000. These amounts overstate the actual effects; these overstatements are corrected in item 5.
   3. Asset, Cash, +$510,000; Asset, Accounts Receivable, −$510,000.
   4. No change in assets, liabilities, or owners' equity.
   5. Asset, Accounts Receivable, −$11,200; Owners' Equity, −$11,200 [$11,200 = $28,200 − ($25,000 − $8,000)].

b. 2. Accounts Receivable 500,000
      Sales Revenues 500,000

   3. Cash 510,000
      Accounts Receivable 510,000

   4. Allowance for Uncollectibles 8,000
      Accounts Receivable 8,000

   5. Estimated Customer Defaults 11,200
      Allowance for Uncollectibles 11,200

c. Accounts receivable, gross $932,000
   Less: Allowance for uncollectibles 28,200
   Accounts Receivable, Net $903,800

d. $11,200.

2. *a.* 11/14 Interest paid, two months at 14 percent of $6,000 .... $140.00
   12/14 Interest accrued, one month at 14 percent of $6,000 .... 70.00
   12/31 Interest accrued for 17 days:
          17/360 × 14% × ($6,000 + $70 − $4,000) 13.69
          Total interest expense $223.69

b. Interest Expense 13.69
      Interest Payable 13.69

c. Interest Expense 10.46
      Interest Payable 13.69
      Note Payable 2,070.00
      Cash 2,094.15

3. *a.* $83,500 − ($55,000 − $40,000) = $68,500.

b. Liability for Service Warranty 40,000
      Cash 10,000
      Inventory 30,000

   Warranty Expense 68,500
      Liability for Service Warranty 68,500

4. *a.* 1. Allowance for Uncollectibles 165
         Accounts Receivable 165

   2. Estimated Customer Defaults 785
      Allowance for Uncollectibles 785
      [$91,600 − $165 − $89,315 − ($1,500 − $165)]

3. Cost of Goods Sold 347,060
        Purchases   344,500
        Inventory   2,560
        [$89,000 − $86,440 = $2,560]

4. Inventory   975
        Accounts Payable   975

5. Insurance Expense   700
        Prepaid Insurance   700

6. Depreciation Expense 1,240
        Accumulated Depreciation   1,240

7. Interest Expense   400
        Interest Payable......................   400

8. Salaries and Wages Expense   240
        Salaries and Wages Payable   240

b.

THE GUYTON COMPANY
Adjusted Trial Balance
December 31, 19x3

	Debits	Credits
Cash	$ 30,900	
Notes receivable	17,700	
Accounts receivable................................	91,435	
Allowance for uncollectibles		$ 2,120
Inventory of merchandise	87,415	
Prepaid insurance...................................	1,725	
Other prepayments	1,340	
Land	16,000	
Building and equipment.............................	45,800	
Accumulated depreciation..........................		9,340
Accounts payable...................................		19,775
Salaries and wages payable		240
Interest payable		400
Mortgage payable..................................		45,000
Capital stock		150,000
Retained earnings		53,720
Sales revenues		400,000
Estimated customer defaults	785	
Interest revenue		480
Cost of goods sold.................................	347,060	
Advertising expense................................	1,200	
Salaries and wages expense	16,640	
Depreciation expense	1,240	
Insurance expense	700	
Miscellaneous selling expense	5,800	
Property tax expense...............................	3,300	
Miscellaneous general expense......................	8,435	
Interest expense	3,600	
Totals	$681,075	$681,075

c.

THE GUYTON COMPANY
Income Statement
For the Year Ended December 31, 19x3

Sales revenue		$400,000
Less: Estimated customer defaults		785
Net sales revenue		399,215
Interest revenue		480
Total revenue		399,695
Expenses:		
Cost of goods sold	$347,060	
Salaries and wages expense	16,640	
Depreciation expense	1,240	
Insurance expense	700	
Advertising expense	1,200	
Miscellaneous selling expenses	5,800	
Property tax expense	3,300	
Miscellaneous general expense	8,435	
Interest expense	3,600	
Total expenses		387,975
Net Income		$ 11,720

THE GUYTON COMPANY
Balance Sheet
December 31, 19x3

Assets

Current assets:		
Cash		$ 30,900
Notes receivable		17,700
Accounts receivable	$91,435	
Less: Allowance for uncollectibles	2,120	89,315
Inventory of merchandise		87,415
Prepaid insurance		1,725
Other prepayments		1,340
Total current assets		$228,395
Plant assets:		
Land		16,000
Building and equipment	45,800	
Less: Accumulated depreciation	9,340	36,460
Total plant assets		52,460
Total assets		$280,855

Liabilities and Owners' Equity

Current liabilities:		
Accounts payable	$ 19,775	
Salaries and wages payable	240	
Interest payable	400	
Total current liabilities	20,415	
Long-term liability:		
Mortgage payable	45,000	
Total liabilities		$65,415
Owners' equity:		
Capital stock	150,000	
Retained earnings	65,440	
Total owners' equity		215,440
Total liabilities and owners' equity		$280,855

Chapter 5

1.

STRONG CABINETS, INC.
Schedule of Manufacturing Costs and Cost of Goods Sold
For the Year Ended December 31, 19x2

Materials costs:			
Materials on hand, Jan. 1, 19x2		$ 80,000	
Materials purchased		400,000	
Cost of materials available for use		480,000	
Less: Materials on hand, Dec. 31, 19x2		90,000	
Cost of materials used			$ 390,000
Factory labor cost			450,000
Other factory costs:			
Depreciation		16,000	
Rent		84,000	
Miscellaneous		130,000	230,000
Total factory cost			1,070,000
Add: Work in process, Jan. 1, 19x2			110,000
Total cost in production			1,180,000
Less: Work in process, Dec. 31, 19x2			80,000
Cost of goods finished			1,100,000
Add: Finished goods inventory, Jan. 1, 19x2			70,000
Cost of goods available for sale			1,170,000
Less: Finished goods inventory, Dec. 31, 19x2			120,000
Cost of goods sold			$1,050,000

2.

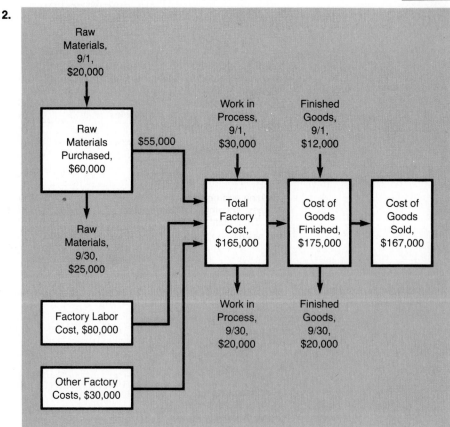

3. *a* and *c.*

Raw Materials Inventory		
Bal. 9/1	20,000	55,000
	60,000	
Bal. 9/30	25,000	

Work in Process Inventory		
Bal. 9/1	30,000	175,000
	55,000	
	80,000	
	30,000	
Bal. 9/30	20,000	

Finished Goods Inventory		
Bal. 9/1	12,000	167,000
	175,000	
Bal. 9/30	20,000	

Cost of Goods Sold	
167,000	

b.

Raw Materials Inventory	60,000	
Accounts Payable		60,000
Work in Process Inventory	55,000	
Raw Materials Inventory		55,000
Work in Process Inventory	80,000	
Wages and Salaries Payable..............		80,000
Work in Process Inventory	30,000	
Accounts Payable, etc.		30,000
Finished Goods Inventory	175,000	
Work in Process Inventory		175,000
Cost of Goods Sold	167,000	
Finished Goods Inventory		167,000

4. *a.*

Materials Inventory		
Bal.	11,650	(2) 7,250
(1)	4,500	
Bal.	8,900	

Work in Process		
Bal.	8,320	(6) 12,650
(2)	7,250	
(3)	5,100	
(4)	400	
(5)	1,820	
Bal.	10,240	

Finished Goods		
Bal.	11,100	(7) 14,500
(6)	12,650	
Bal.	9,250	

Accounts Receivable		
Bal.	xxx	
(8)	19,350	

Accumulated Depreciation		
		Bal. xxx
		(4) 500

Salaries and Wages Payable		
		Bal. xxx
		(3) 7,700

Accounts Payable			Cost of Goods Sold	
	Bal.	xxx	(7)	14,500
	(1)	4,500		
	(5)	3,555		

Sales Revenues			Selling and Admin. Expenses	
	(8)	19,350	(3)	2,600
			(4)	100
			(5)	1,735

b.

KING APPLIANCE COMPANY
Income Statement
For the Month of October 19xx

Sales revenues			$19,350
Less: Cost of goods sold		$14,500	
Selling and administrative expenses		4,435	18,935
Net income			$ 415

Chapter 6

1. *a.*

Present value of outlay...	−$ 35,000
Present value of receipts: 0.3220 × $100,000 =	+ 32,200
Net present value	−$ 2,800

b.

Present value of 1/1/85 outlay.................................	−$ 80,000
Present value of 1/1/90 outlay: 0.5674 × $20,000	− 11,348
Present value of receipt of $10,000 per period for six periods: 4.1114 × $10,000......................................	+ 41,114
Present value of receipt of $20,000 per period for 10 periods starting six periods hence: (6.9740 − 4.1114) × $20,000	+ 57,252
Net present value	+$ 7,018

c.

Present value of 1/1/85 outlay: 1.0000 × $20,000	−$ 20,000
Present value of next 10 outlays: 5.6502 × $20,000	− 113,004
Present value of receipt: 0.2567 × $250,000......................	+ 64,175
Net present value	−$ 68,829

2. *a.*

Future value of outlay: 3.1058 × $35,000	−$108,703
Future value of receipt: 1.0000 × $100,000	+ 100,000
Net future value	−$ 8,703

Verification: Present value of $8,703 = 0.3220 × $8,703 = $2,802, which differs from the answer to 1*a* by a rounding error only.

b.

Future value of 1/1/85 outlay: 6.1304 × $80,000	−$490,432
Future value of 1/1/90 outlay: 3.4785 × $20,000	− 69,570
Future value of receipt of $10,000 per period for six periods: (42.7533 − 17.5487) × $10,000	+ 252,046
Future value of receipt of $20,000 per period for 10 periods: 17.5487 × $20,000	+ 350,974
Net future value	+$ 43,018

Verification: 0.1631 × $43,018 = $7,016, which differs from the answer to 1*b* by a rounding error only.

   c. Future value of outlays: 20.6546 × $20,000 .... −$518,182
      Future value of receipt: 1.0000 × $250,000 .... + 250,000
      Net future value .... −$268,182

      Verification: 0.2567 × $268,182 = $68,842, virtually identical to answer to 1c.

3. *a.* The annuity formula is: $F = \text{multiplier} \times A$

$$A = F/\text{multiplier}$$
$$= \$1,000,000/14.4866 = \$69,029.31$$

   b. $A = \$1,000,000/17.5487 = \$56,984.28$
   c. $A = \$1,000,000/36.7856 = \$27,184.55$

4. The key here is to find a seven-year annuity in advance that will have the same present value as a five-year annuity in arrears which starts in year 4:

   Present value of five-year annuity
$$= (5.7466 - 2.5771) \times \$4,000 = \$12,678$$

   Present value of seven-year annuity $= (4.6229 + 1.0000) \times \text{Annuity}$
$$\text{Annuity} = \$12,678/5.6229 = \$2,255$$

This can be checked by calculating the amount of interest accrued on the amount invested, and deducting the amounts repaid:

Year	Cash Flow before Interest	Amount Invested after Cash Flow	Interest @ 8%	Amount Invested One Year Later
0	−2,255	2,255	180	2,435
1	−2,255	4,690	375	5,065
2	−2,255	7,320	586	7,906
3	−2,255	10,161	813	10,974
4	$\begin{cases} -2{,}255 + 4{,}000 \\ = \ +1{,}745 \end{cases}$	9,229	738	9,967
5	+1,745	8,222	658	8,880
6	+1,745	7,135	571	7,706
7	+4,000	3,706	296	4,002
8	+4,000	2*	0	0

   * Rounding error.

The amounts invested, with interest, are just adequate to cover the five payments of $4,000 each.

5. *a.*

Year	Cash Flow	Multiplier (Table 3)	Present Value
1............................	$150,000	0.8929	$133,935
2............................	230,000	0.7972	183,356
Total			$317,291

   b.

0............................	$150,000	1.0000	$150,000
1............................	230,000	0.8929	205,367
Total			$355,367

   c. Income = $355,367 − $317,291 = $38,076.
      (This can also be obtained, with a $1 rounding error, by taking 12 percent of $317,291 = $38,075.)

d. Present value, end of year 2 .... $230,000
    Present value, beginning of year 2 205,367
    Income, year 2 .... $ 24,633

e. The richer opportunity elsewhere reduces the value of this asset
    slightly without changing the future cash flows. These cash flows
    then provide a greater annual income because they start from a
    smaller present value base.

Year	Cash Flow	Beginning of Year 1		Beginning of Year 2	
		Multiplier (Table 3)	Present Value	Multiplier (Table 3)	Present Value
1	$150,000	0.8696	$130,440	1.0000	$150,000
2	230,000	0.7561	173,903	0.8696	200,008
Total			$304,343		$350,008

Income = $350,008 − $304,343 = $45,665 in year 1.
Income = $230,000 − $200,008 = $29,992 in year 2.

Chapter 7

1. *a.* We start with two basic calculations:
1. The profit on a unit is $25 − $12 − $6 = $7.
2. The inventory should be listed at sale price less future selling
    costs, $25 − $6 = $19.

Effect of producing one unit:
  Cash decreased by $12.
  Inventory increased by $19.
  Owners' equity increased by $7.
Effect of shipping one unit:
  Cash decreased by $6.
  Inventory decreased by $19.
  Receivables increased by $25.
Effect of collecting $25:
  Cash increased by $25.
  Receivables decreased by $25.

b.

	First Year	Second Year
Revenue	$1,500,000	$1,875,000
Cost of goods sold	720,000	900,000
Selling expense	360,000	450,000
Administrative expense	200,000	200,000
Net income	$ 220,000	$ 325,000

2. *a.*

Gross revenues..		$500,000
Customer defaults		10,000
Net revenue...		490,000
Manufacturing costs		350,000
Gross margin		140,000
Other expenses:		
Selling	$80,000	
Administrative	50,000	130,000
Income before taxes		$ 10,000

    b. Inventory would be reported at $4.90 a unit, a total of $49,000.

    c. Gross margin on a delivery basis would be 90,000 units × ($5.00 −
$0.10 − $3.50) = $126,000. The company, therefore, would report a
$4,000 *loss* before income taxes.

    d. Inventory would be reported at $3.50 a unit (average manufacturing
cost), or $35,000 total. This is $14,000 less than the amount reported
under the production basis.

Note: Information on depreciation and production payments would be
relevant if you had been asked to calculate the cash flow; it has no
bearing on the measurement of income in an accrual-basis accounting
system.

Chapter 8

1.   *a.*

Year	LIFO Cost of Goods Sold	LIFO Ending Inventory
19x1	55,000 × $3.10 = $170,500	10,000 × $3.00 = $ 30,000 5,000 × 3.10 = 15,500 $ 45,500
19x2	68,000 × $3.50 = $238,000	10,000 × $3.00 = $ 30,000 5,000 × 3.10 = 15,500 2,000 × 3.50 = 7,000 $ 52,500
19x3	80,000 × $3.75 = $300,000	10,000 × $3.00 = $ 30,000 5,000 × 3.10 = 15,500 2,000 × 3.50 = 7,000 10,000 × 3.75 = 37,500 $ 90,000
19x4	70,000 × $3.80 = $266,000 2,000 × $3.75 = 7,500 $273,500	10,000 × $3.00 = $ 30,000 5,000 × 3.10 = 15,500 2,000 × 3.50 = 7,000 8,000 × 3.75 = 30,000 $ 82,500
19x5	75,000 × $4.00 = $300,000	10,000 × $3.00 = $ 30,000 5,000 × 3.10 = 15,500 2,000 × 3.50 = 7,000 8,000 × 3.75 = 30,000 5,000 × 4.00 = 20,000 $102,500
19x6	70,000 × $4.25 = $297,500 5,000 × 4.00 = 20,000 5,000 × 3.75 = 18,750 $336,250	10,000 × $3.00 = $ 30,000 5,000 × 3.10 = 15,500 2,000 × 3.50 = 7,000 3,000 × 3.75 = 11,250 $ 63,750
19x7	85,000 × $4.40 = $374,000	10,000 × $3.00 = $ 30,000 5,000 × 3.10 = 15,500 2,000 × 3.50 = 7,000 3,000 × 3.75 = 11,250 15,000 × 4.40 = 66,000 $129,750
19x8	95,000 × $4.50 = $427,500	(Same as 19x7) = $129,750

b.

Year	FIFO Cost of Goods Sold	FIFO Ending Inventory
19x1	10,000 × $3.00 = $ 30,000 45,000 × 3.10 = 139,500 $169,500	15,000 × $3.10 = $ 46,500
19x2	15,000 × $3.10 = $ 46,500 53,000 × 3.50 = 185,500 $232,000	17,000 × $3.50 = $ 59,500
19x3	17,000 × $3.50 = $ 59,500 63,000 × 3.75 = 236,250 $295,750	27,000 × $3.75 = $101,250
19x4	27,000 × $3.75 = $101,250 45,000 × 3.80 = 171,000 $272,250	25,000 × $3.80 = $ 95,000
19x5	25,000 × $3.80 = $ 95,000 50,000 × 4.00 = 200,000 $295,000	30,000 × $4.00 = $120,000
19x6	30,000 × $4.00 = $120,000 50,000 × 4.25 = 212,500 $332,500	20,000 × $4.25 = $ 85,000
19x7	20,000 × $4.25 = $ 85,000 65,000 × 4.40 = 286,000 $371,000	35,000 × $4.40 = $154,000
19x8	35,000 × $4.40 = $154,000 60,000 × 4.50 = 270,000 $424,000	35,000 × $4.50 = $157,500

2. *a* and *b.*

Inventory, January 1	0
Purchases	8,500 units, $29,840
Sales	6,000 units
Inventory, December 31	2,500 units

	FIFO	LIFO
Inventory, December 31:		
(1,800 × $4.05) + (700 × $4)	$10,090	
(1,000 × $3.00) + (1,500 × $3.25)		$ 7,875
Cost of goods sold:		
Purchases ($29,840) − 12/31 inventory	19,750	21,965
Gross margin:		
Sales ($30,000) − Cost of goods sold	10,250	8,035

   c. LIFO would reduce income before taxes by $2,215 ($10,250 − $8,035) and net income by $1,661.25 [$2,215 × (1 − 0.25)]; it would increase cash flow by $553.75 ($2,215 × 0.25).

3. *a.* Item by item:

	Lower of Cost or Market	
Product	Per Unit	Total
A	$ 8	$ 80,000
B	15	300,000
C	20	600,000
D	8	320,000
Total		$1,300,000

Pooled inventory:

Product	Total Cost	Total Market
A	$ 100,000	$ 80,000
B	300,000	320,000
C	600,000	690,000
D	400,000	320,000
Total	$1,400,000	$1,410,000

Lower of cost or market is $1,400,000.

b. The pooled-inventory approach increases the net income by $100,000 ($1,400,000 − $1,300,000).

c. The answer depends on what the financial statements are intended to convey. The item-by-item method is the most "conservative" and should be used if the objective is to have the balance sheet show the smallest inventory total consistent with the accrual basis of accounting. The pooled-inventory method should be used if the objective of the lower-of-cost-or-market rule is simply to protect investors against an overstatement of the amount recoverable from inventories as a whole. Finally, if the objective is to produce an inventory figure that best predicts future cash flows, the answer will depend on which amount is more likely to be related to this quantity.

4. *a.*

	Inventory			Cost of Goods Sold	
Date	FIFO	LIFO	Year	FIFO	LIFO
January 1, 19x2 ...	$1,875,000	$1,875,000			
			19x2	$12,175,000	$12,350,000
December 31, 19x2	2,700,000	2,525,000			
			19x3	14,600,000	14,500,000
December 31, 19x3	700,000	625,000			

b. The involuntary liquidation increased reported income before taxes by $125,000. The liquidation amounted to 15,000 tons, but the first 5,000 of these were liquidated voluntarily. The involuntary part of the liquidation caused the transfer from the LIFO inventory of 10,000 tons at $125. The effect on reported income was:

10,000 tons at current prices of $140	$1,400,000
10,000 tons at inventory price of $125	1,250,000
Net effect on reported income	$ 150,000

c. The effect is to increase the cost of the inventory by $200,000 over the level that would have prevailed if there had been no involuntary liquidation:

Base quantity, 5,000 tons	$ 625,000
19x4 layer, 10,000 tons	1,450,000
Total	2,075,000
LIFO cost of 15,000 tons, 12/31/x2	1,875,000
Net effect on inventory	$ 200,000

d.

	Pretax Income Difference	Tax Effect at 50%	
19x2	$175,000	$87,500	FIFO pays more tax
19x3	(100,000)	(50,000)	LIFO pays more tax
19x4	25,000*	12,500	FIFO pays more tax

* Calculation:

	FIFO	LIFO
Beginning inventory	$ 700,000	$ 625,000
Purchases	14,500,000	14,500,000
Goods available	15,200,000	15,125,000
Ending inventory	2,175,000	2,075,000
Cost of goods sold	$13,025,000	$13,050,000

Chapter 9

1. *a.* Straight-line depreciation:
Depreciable cost = $30,000 − $1,500 = $28,500.
Rate = 1/5 = 20%.
Depreciation = 20% × $28,500 = $5,700 a year.

b and *c.*

	DDB Depreciation		SYD Depreciation	
Year	Beginning Balance	Depreciation at 40%	Fraction of Depreciable Cost	Depreciation
1	$30,000	$12,000	5/15	$9,500
2	18,000	7,200	4/15	7,600
3	10,800	4,320	3/15	5,700
4	6,480	2,592	2/15	3,800
5	3,888	1,555	1/15	1,900

d. Implicit-interest depreciation:

Year	Beginning Book Value	Cash Flow	Imputed Interest @ 10%	Depreciation
1	$30,000	$7,668	$3,000	$4,668
2	25,332	7,668	2,533	5,135
3	20,197	7,668	2,020	5,648
4	14,549	7,668	1,455	6,213
5	8,336	7,668	834	6,834

2.

	Each Machine	All Machines
Asset cost:		
Purchase price	$16,250	$ 97,500
Freight..	700	4,200
Handling	200	1,200
Installation:		
Labor.......................................	800	4,800
Materials	100	600
Total	$18,050	$108,300

If the bookkeeping system is loosely designed, the installation materials and perhaps even some of the installation labor might be expensed. In theory, though, they should be capitalized.

3. *a.*

Original cost	$50,000
Accumulated depreciation 4 × $2,500	10,000
Book value	$40,000

b.

Equipment	6,000	
Cash		6,000

c.

Depreciation Expense	2,875	
Accumulated Depreciation		2,875

The life of the machine wasn't extended, and the $40,000 + $6,000 = $46,000 book value had to be depreciated during the remaining 16 years of life.

d.

Original cost: $50,000 + $6,000		$56,000
Accumulated depreciation:		
4 × $2,500	$10,000	
12 × $2,875	34,500	
Overhaul	(12,000)	32,500
Book value		$23,500

Depreciation = $23,500/9 = $2,611 a year.

4. *a.* The conventional answer here is an accelerated depreciation formula should be used, because cash flows are likely to decline rapidly as the textbook ages. If the time value of money is considered, an argument can be made for implicit-interest depreciation, but with sharply declining cash flows, this could be approximated by a diminishing-charge method or possibly by straight-line.

b. If we look at textbook A only, the accelerated methods will lead to lower reported income in the first two years and higher reported income in the last two years than straight-line depreciation would show. If we look at all the company's textbooks as a group, however, the effect of the choice depends on the rate of growth. If the company is growing, accelerated depreciation would reduce reported income in all years, unless the company stopped bringing out new textbooks in any quantity for a year or two. The assets' book value would be greater under straight-line depreciation than under any accelerated method.

Chapter 10

1. *a.* The face value is $1 million, the payments each year will be $120,000, and the amount paid equals the present value of the future payments when the latter are discounted at 14 percent, or 7 percent compounded semiannually.

b. $866,700, because the price must be less than the maturity value to produce a yield in excess of the coupon rate.

c. The term is 20 years (the factor of 86.67 is found in the 20-year column, 14.0 percent row of Table 8).

d. Interest expense = 14%/2 × $866,700 = $60,669.

Interest Expense	60,669	
Cash		60,000
Discount on Bonds.......................		669

e. Principal = $866,700 + $669 = $867,369.
Interest expense = 14%/2 × $867,369 = $60,716.

Interest Expense	60,716	
Cash		60,000
Discount on Bonds.......................		716

f.

Bonds payable, maturity value	$1,000,000
Less: Unamortized bond discount	131,915
Bonds payable, net...	$ 868,085

2. a.

Income before depreciation and taxes		$6,000,000
Depreciation		850,000
Income after depreciation		5,150,000
Income tax: Current ($4,750,000* × 50%)	$2,375,000	
Deferred ($5,150,000 × 50% − $2,375,000)	200,000	2,575,000
Net income		$2,575,000

* Current taxable income = $6,000,000 − $1,250,000 = $4,750,000.

b.

Depreciation	850,000	
Accumulated Depreciation		850,000
Income Tax Expense	2,575,000	
Income Taxes Payable		2,375,000
Deferred Income Taxes		200,000

3. a. Annuity factor in advance at 12% = 3.0373 + 1.0000 = 4.0373. Capitalized amount = 4.0373 × $2,000 = $8,075 (to the nearest dollar).

Asset: Rights to leased property	$8,075
Liability: Liability for future lease	
payments = $8,075 − $2,000	6,075

b.

Depreciation = 1/5 × $8,075	$1,615
Interest = 12% × $6,075	729
Total	$2,344

c. Book value of asset = $8,075 − $1,615 = $6,460.
Book value of liability = $6,075 − ($2,000 − $729) = $4,804.

Note: In practice, this method would not be used unless the lease payments entitled the lessee to virtually all the lifetime service values of the leased equipment.

Chapter 11

1. *a.* Shares issued: par value $160,000.
   Additional paid-in capital $480,000.
   Added to retained earnings: $441,600 − $0.20 × 960,000 = $249,600.
   The shareowners' equity at December 31, 19x1:

Common stock, 960,000 shares	$ 960,000
Additional paid-in capital	780,000
Retained earnings	749,600
Total	$2,489,600

   b. The book value of the common equity wasn't diluted because the new shares were issued at $4, whereas the book value of the earlier shares was only $2. The market value *may* have been diluted, if investors estimated that the company's return on the $4 was likely to be less than the return each previous share had been expected to earn before the new issue was offered for sale.

2. Retained earnings would decrease by $30,000, the total par value of the common stock would increase by $10,000, and additional paid-in capital would increase by $20,000.

3. *Purchase of treasury stock:* decreased cash by $3,000 and decreased shareowners' equity by $3,000. It is classified temporarily as a negative component of the shareowners' equity.
   Dividend declaration: decreased retained earnings by $0.30 × 99,900 = $29,970; increased the liability, dividends payable, by this same amount.
   Dividend payment: decreased the asset, cash, and the liability, dividends payable, by $29,970.
   Sale of treasury stock: increased cash by $4,000 and increased shareowners' equity by this amount, canceling the $3,000 negative component and adding $1,000 to additional paid-in capital.

4. *a.* Income available for common stock = $312,000 − $50,000 = $262,000.
   Primary earnings per share = $262,000/100,000 = $2.62.
   b. Equivalent common shares = 100,000 + 2 × 10,000 = 120,000.
   Fully diluted earnings per share = $312,000/120,000 = $2.60.

Chapter 12

1. *a.* Cantara's ownership interest in Denby was large enough to require the use of the equity method. Cantara therefore should include 25 percent of $30,000 = $7,500 in its reported income for 19x1.
   b. Cantara's investment can be calculated as follows:

Purchase price (2,500 × $30) $75,000
Equity in 19x1 retained earnings* (2,500 × $1.40) 3,500
Total $78,500

> * Equity in net income: ¼ × $30,000 .... $7,500
> Less: Dividends received: 2,500 shares × $1.60 4,000
> Equity in retained earnings $3,500

2. *a.* Purchase price .... $ 92,000
Essex's owners' equity $110,000
Pilot's percentage .... × 80%
Book value acquired 88,000
Goodwill .... $ 4,000

b. Essex's owners' equity $110,000
Minority percentage .... × 20%
Minority interest .... $ 22,000

3. *a.* The problem is to find the yield rate which a market price of $87,590 would provide on bonds with $100,000 face value—which translates into $87.59 for a bond with $100 face value. The yield rate is found by consulting Table 8 of Appendix A, which shows the yield rates of 12 percent bonds at various prices and maturities. Durant's bonds had 15 years to maturity at the time of purchase, so the answer is in the 15-year column of Table 8. The $87.59 price is found in the 14.0 percent row of the 15-year column. The anticipated yield to maturity therefore was 14 percent.

b. Investments 87,590
    Cash 87,590

c. Carrying the calculations to the nearest dollar produces the following amounts:

June 30: 14%/2 × $87,590 .... $ 6,131
December 31: 14%/2 × $87,721* 6,140
Total interest revenue $12,271

> * $87,590 + $131 amortization of bond discount ($6,131 − 12%/2 × $100,000).

d. Table 8 in Appendix A indicates that the market value of a 12 percent, $100 bond 10 years from maturity when the yield rate is 15 percent is $84.71, and $89.41 when the yield is 14 percent. The proceeds therefore were $84,710, and the loss was $4,700 ($89,410 − $84,710).

e. Cash 84,710
Loss on Sale of Investment 4,700
    Investments 89,410

4. *a.* The amount payable by Alcon has no effect on consolidated net income. The eliminating entry is:

Accounts Payable 35,000
    Accounts Receivable 35,000

The investment income represents dividends paid by Nonon during the year. Since this will be replaced on the consolidated income statement by Nonon's revenues and expenses, and since the dividends weren't paid to outsiders and therefore don't belong on a consolidated statement, the following elimination is appropriate:

Investment Income 50,000
    Dividends Declared 50,000

Sales revenue is overstated by $250,000, inventory is overstated by $30,000, and the cost of goods sold is overstated by $220,000. (The actual cost of goods sold was $180,000 − $70,000 = $110,000. Alcon showed a cost of goods sold of $250,000 − $100,000 = $150,000, and Nonon showed a cost of goods sold of $180,000, a total of $330,000. The difference between these two totals is $220,000.) The entry is:

Sales Revenues 250,000
    Inventory 30,000
    Cost of Goods Sold 220,000

b.

ALCON CORPORATION AND SUBSIDIARY
Consolidated Income Statement
For the Year Ended December 31, 19x1

Sales revenues	$5,750,000
Cost of goods sold	3,480,000
Gross margin	2,270,000
Other expenses	1,700,000
Net income	$ 570,000

5. *a.*

Company X income as reported		$55,000
Less: Dividends received (0.8 × $10,000)		8,000
Operating income		47,000
Add: Equity in Company Y's income:		
Company Y dividends	$10,000	
Increase in Y's retained earnings	5,000	
Company Y's income	15,000	
Company's X's interest	× 80%	12,000
Net income		$59,000

b. $80,000 + $12,000 − $8,000 = $84,000.

c.

Company X	$ 47,000
Company Y	15,000
Combined income	62,000
Minority interest (0.2 × $15,000)	3,000
Consolidated net income	$ 59,000

d.

Company Y owners' equity	$105,000
Minority percentage	× 20%
Minority interest..	$ 21,000

Chapter 13

1. *a.* Transactions were:
        Purchases of plant and equipment for $1,700.
        Sale of plant and equipment for $300.
        Depreciation of $900.

    b. To be added back to net income to derive funds provided by operations:
        Depreciation, $900.
        Loss on retirements, $400.
    To be listed with other sources of funds:
        Sale of plant and equipment, $300.
    To be listed as a use of funds:
        Purchase of plant and equipment, $1,700.

2.

ANDERSON COMPANY
Statement of Changes in Financial Position
For the Year Ended December 31, 19x1
(in $000)

Sources of working capital:
  From operations:

Net income	$ 8,243
Add: Depreciation	5,501
Deferred income tax	537
Total from operations	14,281
From issue of common stock	12,047
From sale of long-term bonds	7,000
From sale of property, plant, and equipment	83
Total sources of working capital	$33,411

Uses of working capital:

To buy property, plant, and equipment	$18,082
To buy long-term marketable securities	1,005
To retire preferred stock	261
To pay preferred dividends	80
To increase working capital	13,983
Total uses of working capital	$33,411

An alternative layout would disclose four sources ($14,281 + $12,047 + $7,000 + $83), four uses ($18,082 + $1,005 + $261 + $80) and a bottom line consisting of the $13,983 increase in working capital.

3.

Net income		$28,100
Add: Depreciation expense	$14,900	
Patent amortization expense	1,800	
Deferred taxes	3,100	19,800
		47,900
Less: Equity in Wilson earnings	12,000	
Premium amortization	2,700	14,700
Working capital provided by operations		$33,200

4.

	Income Statement	Noncash Elements	Cash Flow
Revenues/collections:			
Cash sales (0.3 × $325,400)	$ 97,620		$ 97,620
Credit sales/collections:			
Credit sales (0.7 × $325,400)	227,780		227,780
Less: Estimated customer defaults	(4,100)*	$ (3,800)*	(300)
Add: Decrease in accounts receivable		14,300	14,300
Net collections from credit sales			241,780
Net sales/collections	321,300		339,400
Equity in Wilson Corporation's earnings	12,000	12,000	—
Net revenues/collections	333,300		339,400
Expenses/payments:			
Cost of goods sold	178,600		
Add: Increase in inventory		5,400†	
Less: Increase in accounts payable		(11,300)	
Payments to suppliers			172,700
Salaries expense	68,800		
Add: Decrease in salaries payable		4,100	
Payments to employees			72,900
Depreciation expense	14,900	14,900	—
Insurance expense	1,000		
Add: Increase in prepaid insurance		1,400	
Payments for insurance			2,400
Research and development	2,500		2,500
Patent amortization	1,800	1,800	—
Interest expense	21,300		
Add: Bond premium amortization		2,700	
Interest payments			24,000
Income tax expense	16,300		
Less: Deferred portion		3,100	
Change in current taxes payable		0	
Income tax payments			13,200
Total expenses/operating cash payments	305,200		287,700
Net income/cash provided by operations	$ 28,100		$ 51,700

* With no write-offs, collections would have been equal to credit sales plus the decrease in gross receivables. Part of the $14,300 decrease in gross receivables, however, was due to write-offs of specific accounts. The company provided $4,100 for estimated customer defaults, but the increase in the allowance for uncollectibles (representing a decrease in working capital) was only $3,800. The write-off of gross receivables therefore was the remaining $300 ($4,100 − $3,800).
† Purchases = Cost of goods sold + Increase in inventory = $178,600 + $5,400 = $184,000.

Chapter 14

1. *a.* Current cost of goods sold:

January 1–May 15, 55,000 × $2	$110,000
May 16–December 31, 35,000 × $2.20	77,000
Total	$187,000
Current-cost, ending inventory, 60,000 × $2.20	$132,000

b. Holding gain:
  Inventory on May 16: 50,000 − 15,000 = 35,000 units.
  Price increase: 20 cents a unit.
  Holding gain = 35,000 × $0.20 = $7,000.

c. Current-cost margin:

Revenues:
January 1–May 15, 55,000 × $3	$165,000
May 16–December 31, 35,000 × $3.10	108,500
Total	273,500
Cost of goods sold (from part *a*)	187,000
Current-cost margin	$ 86,500

2. *a.*
Current cost of goods sold (as in problem 1)	$187,000
Inventory holding gain	0
Current-cost margin (as in 1)	86,500

b. The conclusion is that Company A benefitted by having an inventory position when prices went up. Company B had to rely entirely on its merchandising operations to generate income. The purpose of this question is to emphasize a very simple point which is often overlooked: Companies without inventories have no inventory holding gains and losses, no matter what inventory-costing method is used.

3. *a.*

	Units	Cost
Beginning inventory	50,000	$ 97,500
Purchases:		
January 1–May 15	40,000	80,000
May 16–December 31	60,000	132,000
Goods available	150,000	309,500
Ending inventory	60,000	132,000
Cost of goods sold	90,000	$177,500

b.

	January 1	December 31
Current cost of inventory (from problem 1)	$100,000	$132,000
FIFO cost of inventory (from part *a*)	97,500	132,000
Unrealized holding gain	$ 2,500	$ —

c. Inventory holding gain included in net income:

Current cost of goods sold (from problem 1)	$187,000
FIFO cost of goods sold (from part *a*)	177,500
Inventory profit	$ 9,500

This $9,500 is the sum of the $7,000 holding gain for the year (problem 1, part *b*) and the $2,500 change in the unrealized holding gain between the beginning and end of the year (problem 3, part *b*). It is included in gross margin and is not identified separately in the income statement.

4. *a.*

Year of Purchase	Historical Book Value	Multiplier	Replacement Cost
19x0	$ 60,000	180/100	$108,000
19x2	24,000	180/110	39,273
19x5	44,000	180/150	52,800
Total	$128,000		200,073
Subtract historical cost			128,000
Unrealized holding gain			$ 72,073

b.

Year of Purchase	Historical Cost Depreciation	Multiplier	Replacement-Cost Depreciation
19x0	$10,000	190/100	$19,000
19x2	3,000	190/110	5,182
19x5	4,000	190/150	5,067
Total	$17,000		$29,249

c. Realized holding gain = $29,249 − $17,000 = $12,249. The historical-cost income statement classifies the $12,249 realized holding gain as an *undisclosed* component of operating income. The current-cost income statement excludes this amount (because it actually arose in previous years), but reports the entire 19x9 holding gain (part *e*'s $20,691) on a separate line.

d.

Year of Purchase	Historical Book Value	Multiplier	Replacement Cost
19x0	$ 50,000	200/100	$100,000
19x2	21,000	200/110	38,182
19x5	40,000	200/150	53,333
Total	$111,000		191,515
Subtract historical cost			111,000
Unrealized holding gain			$ 80,515

e.

Realized holding gain (part *c*)		$12,249
Increase in unrealized holding gain:		
December 31 (part *d*)	$80,515	
January 1 (part *a*)	72,073	8,442
Total holding gain		$20,691

5. *a.*

	January 1	December 31
Cash	$10	$15
Accounts receivable	20	40
Total monetary assets	30	55
Accounts payable	5	7
Notes payable	10	30
Bonds payable	10	10
Total monetary liabilities	25	47
Net monetary position	$ 5	$ 8

b.

	Amount	Effect on Monetary Position
1. Sales	$320	+ $320
2. Merchandise purchases	170	− 170
3. Equipment purchases	40	− 40
4. Payments to suppliers	208	no effect
5. Collections	300	no effect
6. Payments to employees, etc.	100	− 100
7. Sale of equipment	3	+ 3
8. Borrowings	20	no effect
9. Dividends	10	− 10
Net effect		+ $ 3

c.

	Nominal Dollars	Relative Index	Constant Dollars
Net monetary position, January 1	$5	200/180	$5.56
Net monetary transactions	+3	200/190	3.16
Total			8.72
Net monetary position, December 31	$8	200/200	8.00
Purchasing-power loss			$0.72

Chapter 15

			19x3	19x4	19x5	19x6
1.	*a.*	Number of shares (000)	50,000	50,000	52,000	52,000
		Earnings available for common stock (000)		$96,000	$101,300	$99,100
		Earnings per share		$1.92	$1.95	$1.91
	b.	Book value per share	$16.60	$17.52	$18.60	$19.51
	c.	Average common equity (000)		$853,000	$921,650	$990,850
		Return on common equity		11.3%	11.0%	10.0%

2. *a.* 1. Debt decreases while equity remains unchanged; the debt/equity ratio therefore will fall.

2. Cash increases and then decreases by the same amount; current liabilities also remain unchanged. The current ratio will not be affected.

3. Since total assets have decreased, the ratio of sales to total assets (asset turnover) will increase.

b. 1. If the capitalized amount is equal to the book value of the building before the sale-leaseback, total debt will remain unchanged and the debt/equity ratio will be unaffected. If the capitalized amount is less than the former book value, the debt/equity ratio will fall.

2. If the first lease payment falls within the next 12 months or the next operating cycle, the present value of that payment will appear as a current liability. The current ratio therefore will fall.

3. Again, the effect depends on the amount capitalized. If this amount is equal to the book value of the building before the sale-leaseback, total assets will remain unchanged and the asset-turnover ratio will be unaffected. If a smaller amount is capitalized, asset turnover will increase.

3. *a.*
$$\text{Return on assets} = \frac{\text{Earnings before interest and taxes (EBIT)}}{\text{Total assets}}$$

Because this equation contains two unknowns, we must start by deriving one of them.

$$\text{Return on common equity} = \frac{(\text{EBIT} - \text{Interest}) \times (1 - \text{Tax rate})}{\text{Common equity}}$$

Again we have two unknowns, but we know that the common equity equals total assets minus total liabilities and that liabilities are 25 percent of the common equity. Putting these together, we find that:

$$\text{Common equity} = \$100,000 / 1.25 = \$80,000$$

This permits the calculation of EBIT:

$$7.2\% = \frac{\text{EBIT} - \$2,000}{\$80,000} \times 0.55$$

$$\text{EBIT} = \$10,473 + \$2,000 = \$12,473$$

Return on assets (before taxes) = \$12,473/\$100,000 = 12.47%.
Return on assets (after taxes) = 12.47% × (1 − 0.45) = 6.86%.

b. Since the aftertax return on assets is less than the return on common equity, the use of leverage succeeded in increasing the rate of return on the common equity.

Chapter 16

1. *a and b.* The first step is to calculate total cost at each volume. The second step is to extrapolate this schedule backward, to estimate total cost at zero volume. This is the estimated total fixed cost. The third step is to subtract this amount from estimated total cost at each volume—the difference is total variable cost. The final step is to divide this total by the number of units to get average variable cost. Average fixed cost is calculated in the same manner, by dividing total fixed cost by the number of units:

Volume (units)	Total Cost	Total Variable Cost	Average Variable Cost	Average Fixed Cost
0	$10 (est.)	$ 0	—	—
1	11	1	$1.00	$10.00
2	12	2	1.00	5.00
3	13	3	1.00	3.33
4	14	4	1.00	2.50
5	15	5	1.00	2.00
6	16	6	1.00	1.67
7	17	7	1.00	1.43
8	18	8	1.00	1.25
9	20	10	1.11	1.11
10	23	13	1.30	1.00

   c. This calls for an estimate of incremental cost: total cost at 10 units ($23) less total cost at 9 units ($20), or $3.

2. The only relevant number is opportunity cost, reflecting the cash flows Smith will receive in the future. None of the past prices is relevant to this decision because Smith can do nothing now to change them. The $6 price was an opportunity cost in 19x5. Her decision not to sell then was the same as a decision to buy 200 shares at that price at that time. It no longer has any more relevance, however, than the $15 and $20 historical purchase prices. Even the $8 price has no relevance because the $10 tender offer makes that the effective floor under the market price; it can't go lower as long as the tender offer is in effect, and it will go higher only if enough shareholders believe that the stock is worth more than $10.

3. *a.* The first step is to identify the alternatives. One alternative is to operate trucks A and B; the other is to operate truck A and use the independent trucker. The second step is to decide which costs will be totally unaffected by the choice (sunk costs). In this case, all the fixed costs are irrelevant to the decision because they will be unaffected by it. (Both trucks will be in service during the whole period under either alternative.)

	Trucks A and B	Truck A and Independent
Truck A:		
Driver	$15 × 40 = $ 600	$15 × 40 = $ 600
Gas and oil	$0.20 × 400 = 80	$0.20 × 600 = 120
Maintenance	$0.08 × 400 = 32	$0.08 × 600 = 48
Truck B:		
Driver	$15 × 40 = 600	—
Gas and oil	$0.22 × 600 = 132	—
Maintenance	$0.10 × 600 = 60	—
Independent	—	780
Total	$1,504	$1,548

Since the use of both company trucks will reduce total cash outflows by $44 ($1,548 − $1,504), this alternative should be selected.

b. By disposing of truck B, the company could save the following annual cash outflows:

Fixed:
Garage space .... $ 800
Registration and insurance 1,500
Maintenance 500
Variable:
Driver: $15 × 650 9,750
Gas and oil: $0.22 × 650 × 15 2,145
Maintenance: $0.10 × 650 × 15 975
Total $15,670

If the independent trucker's charges would exceed $15,670, the company would find it profitable to keep truck B in service. At any lower price, the company should use the independent. (Depreciation was ignored in this calculation because it didn't represent a cash flow to be affected by the decision. If keeping the truck would affect its salvage or resale value, this effect would have to be considered, as we'll see in Chapter 19.)

4.   Revenue at lower prices (90 percent × $15,000) $13,500
Cost of doing the work:
Labor: 600 hours × $8 .... $4,800
Additional labor: 80 hours × $8   640
Materials 6,000
Other processing costs: 600 hours × $2 .... 1,200*
    Total   12,640
Incremental profit .... $ 860

* If costs vary with labor input rather than with service output, this cost should be $1,360; the decision remains the same.

The incremental cost of doing the work is less than the incremental revenue. Therefore, the shop should reduce its prices and improve its service, and thereby keep the business.

Chapter 17

1. a. This company has two separate—and very different—products, each of which is likely to be the focus of pricing and other managerial decisions. This would require adding a "product" dimension to the cost account structure, at least in manufacturing.

An organizational classification probably would be useful as well. The company's activities are classified into three major functions: manufacturing, marketing, and administration. Each probably has two or more organizational subdivisions (the factory has vacuum assembly, two or more duct work production centers, a maintenance shop, a parts department, and a manager's office, at a minimum). Management probably would find an organization breakdown useful, both for reporting on department performance (which we haven't discussed yet) and for increasing the accuracy of product-costing data.

Finally, some object-of-expenditure accounts probably should be further subdivided. Wages costs, for example, even if departmentalized, cover different kinds of employee services, and management may need to know how much each kind of service costs. Freight costs, too, should be divided between inbound and outbound freight. Furthermore, the "miscellaneous" category may be too large, covering up differences in the behavior of the various cost elements in this category.

b. One plausible explanation is that Zebra has been growing rapidly and has been managed by a small group of managers who have participated in its growth and know its secrets. When the company was small, direct observation substituted for detailed reporting. And for managers who know the operations well, less formal information is necessary than for the new managers a growing company will have to add.

2. *a* and *b*.

| | Average Cost | |
Department	Variable	Full
A.............	$0.60	$0.80
B.............	1.60	2.00
C	0.64	1.04
D	0.40	0.72

Product	Full Cost		Variable Cost	
PDX ..	$0.80 + $2.00	= $2.80	$0.60 + $1.60	= $2.20
QYK ..	$0.80 + $1.04 + $0.72 =	2.56	$0.60 + $0.64 + $0.40 =	1.64

c. Relative costs (PDX/QYK):
   Full cost: $2.80/$2.56 = 1.09.
   Variable cost: $2.20/$1.64 = 1.34.

The reason for the difference in these ratios is that QYK is processed in departments which have a heavier mix of fixed costs than department B, where PDX is processed.

3. *a.*

	Labor Ratio			Apportionment
PDX	12,500	12,500	18.18%	$ 5,000
QYK	37,500 × 1.5	56,250	81.82	22,500
Total......		68,750	100.00%	$27,500

	Unit Service Cost	Direct Full Cost	Total Cost
PDX......	$ 5,000/12,500 = $0.40	$2.80	$3.20
QYK	$22,500/37,500 = 0.60	2.56	3.16

b. Average service cost per unit = $27,500/50,000 = $0.55 a unit.
   Allocation:
   To PDX = $0.55 × 12,500 = $ 6,875.
   To QYK = $0.55 × 37,500 = 20,625.

Allocated unit cost:
  PDX: $2.80 + $0.55 = $3.35.
  QYK: $2.56 + $0.55 = $3.11.

c. The sales manager's proposal increases the apparent profitability of QYK by $0.05 a unit ($3.16 − $3.11), or $1,875 a month. This increase is spurious, however, because the problem states that a unit of QYK is responsible for more costs of the service centers than a unit of PDX. The proposal to change the allocation method should be rejected. "Fairness" has no meaning in this context. It ought to describe a causal relationship, but the sales manager probably has in mind obtaining a cost result which will enable sales of QYK to appear to be profitable. Good managerial accounting can't be built on this kind of unstable foundation.

Chapter 18

1. a. Overhead rate = $900,000/100,000 = $9 a direct labor-hour. Cost of Job No. 423:

Materials	$ 800
Labor	400
Overhead ($9 × 60)	540
Total	$1,740

b.

Actual overhead	$106,000
Absorbed overhead (10,000 × $9)	90,000
Underabsorbed overhead	$ 16,000

2. a.

Materials:

Beginning inventory	$10,000
Purchases	16,000
	26,000
Issues	18,000
Ending inventory	$ 8,000

Work in process:

Beginning inventory	$ 15,000
Additions:	
Direct materials	18,000
Direct labor	48,000
Overhead: 5,000 × $4	20,000
	101,000
Completions	80,000
Ending inventory	$ 21,000

b.

Beginning finished goods inventory	$ 20,000
Completions	80,000
	100,000
Ending finished goods inventory	23,000
Cost of goods sold	$ 77,000

c.

Actual overhead	$ 17,000
Absorbed overhead: 5,000 × $4	20,000
Overabsorbed overhead	$ 3,000

3. First calculate plantwide and departmental overhead rates:

			Hours		
Product	Output	Dept. 1	Dept. 2	Dept. 3	All Depts
A	40,000	80,000	40,000	40,000	
B	40,000		80,000	80,000	
C	10,000	20,000	30,000	30,000	
Total hours		100,000	150,000	150,000	400,000
Overhead		$400,000	$300,000	$100,000	$800,000
Overhead rate....		$4.00	$2.00	$0.67	$2.00

Then calculate unit overhead cost for each product:

	Product A		Product B		Product C	
	Hours	Cost	Hours	Cost	Hours	Cost
Department rates:						
Department 1	2	$ 8.00	—		2	$ 8.00
Department 2	1	2.00	2	$4.00	3	6.00
Department 3	1	0.67	2	1.34	3	2.01
Total unit cost		$10.67		$5.34		$16.01
Plantwide rate	4	$ 8.00	4	$8.00	8	$16.00

As this shows, the effect on the unit costs of product A and B is substantial, and the department overhead rates presumably indicate more accurately the amount of resources used to support production of the product. If production and sales are not equal, the difference will also affect reported income.

4.   *a.*   *Step 1:*   Allocate building costs ($5,000):

Office	Storeroom	Maintenance	Able	Baker
750	500	250	2,000	1,500

Step 2: Allocate office costs, including share of building costs ($6,370 + $750). Hours spent in building and office departments should not be included in the allocation base because the building department's costs have already been allocated and the office department can't allocate costs to itself. The allocation base therefore is 8,900 labor-hours, and the allocation is:

Storeroom	Maintenance	Able	Baker
240	400	4,480	2,000

Step 3: Allocate storeroom costs ($2,260 + $500 + $240):

Maintenance	Able	Baker
150	1,050	1,800

Step 4: Allocate maintenance costs ($6,000 + $250 + $400 + $150). Only 400 maintenance hours enter into the calculation. The 10 hours used in the office must be ignored because that department's costs have already been allocated. The allocation is:

Able	Baker
2,550	4,250

The cost allocation schedule now shows the following:

	Building	Office	Store-room	Mainte-nance	Able	Baker
Direct overhead	$5,000	$6,370	$2,260	$6,000	$ 2,770	$ 3,100
Allocations:						
Building	(5,000)	750	500	250	2,000	1,500
Office		(7,120)	240	400	4,480	2,000
Storeroom			(3,000)	150	1,050	1,800
Maintenance				(6,800)	2,550	4,250
Total					$12,850	$12,650
Normal volume (direct labor-hours)...............					5,000	2,000
Overhead rate					$2.57	$6.325

b.

	Job 123	Job 321
Able at $2.57 an hour	$12.85	$ 5.14
Baker at $6.325 an hour	12.65	31.62
Total	$25.50	$36.76

5. a. Full-costing overhead rates:
   Department A: $25,000/5,000 = $5 a direct labor-hour
   Department B: $60,000/10,000 = $6 a pound
   Job order costs:

	Job 1	Job 2
Direct materials	$2,400	$ 4,800
Direct labor:		
Department A	1,620	900
Department B	420	280
Overhead:		
Department A at $5	900	500
Department B at $6	2,880	9,000
Total	$8,220	$15,480
Unit cost	$13.70	$15.48

b. Variable costing overhead rates:
   Department A: $15,000/5,000 = $3 a direct labor-hour
   Department B: $20,000/10,000 = $2 a pound
   Job order costs:

	Job 1	Job 2
Direct materials	$2,400	$4,800
Direct labor:		
Department A	1,620	900
Department B	420	280
Overhead:		
Department A at $3	540	300
Department B at $2	960	3,000
Total	$5,940	$9,280
Unit cost	$9.90	$9.28

c. Variable unit cost of job 2 is less than that of job 1; full cost was greater for job 2 than for job 1. The main reason is that job 2 used much more of department B's capacity than job 1, and department B has a much higher proportion of fixed costs than department A. Total profit is thus much more sensitive to variations in sales of product Y (job 2) than to variations in sales of product X.

Chapter 19

1. Each of these proposals has the same average annual cash flow after the initial outlay is made ($1,750), but present value ranges from a small negative sum to +$3,311 and the internal rate of return varies from 9.7 percent to 15.5 percent:

a.

Time	Cash Flow	10 Per- cent Factor	Present Value at 10 Percent	Present Value at X Percent	Internal Rate of Return
				12%	
0..........	−$10,000	1.0000	−$10,000	−$10,000	
1–10	+ 1,750/yr.	6.1446	+ 10,753	+ 9,888	
Net pres. value			+$ 753	−$ 112	11.7%

b.

Time	Cash Flow	10 Per- cent Factor	Present Value at 10 Percent	Present Value at X Percent	Internal Rate of Return
				13%	
0..........	−$10,000	1.0000	−$10,000	−$10,000	
1–10	+ 1,500/yr.	6.1446	+ 9,217	+ 8,139	
1–5........	+ 500/yr.	3.7908	+ 1,895	+ 1,759	
Net pres. value			+$ 1,112	−$ 102	12.7%

c.

Time	Cash Flow	10 Per- cent Factor	Present Value at 10 Percent	Present Value at X Percent	Internal Rate of Return
				11%	
0..........	−$10,000	1.0000	−$10,000	−$10,000	
1–5........	+ 1,500/yr.	3.7908	+ 5,686	+ 5,544	
6–10	+ 2,000/yr.	2.3538	+ 4,708	+ 4,387	
Net pres. value			+$ 394	−$ 69	10.9%

d.

Time	Cash Flow	10 Per- cent Factor	Present Value at 10 Percent	Present Value at X Percent	Internal Rate of Return
				9%	
0..........	−$10,000	1.0000	−$10,000	−$10,000	
1–10	+ 1,350/yr.	6.1446	+ 8,295	+ 8,664	
10.........	+ 4,000	0.3855	+ 1,542	+ 1,690	
Net pres. value			−$ 163	+$ 354	9.7%

e.

Time	Cash Flow	10 Per- cent Factor	Present Value at 10 Percent	Present Value at X Percent	Internal Rate of Return
				15%	
0..........	−$10,000	1.0000	−$10,000	−$10,000	
1–15	+ 1,750/yr.	7.6061	+ 13,311	+ 10,233	
Net pres. value			+$ 3,311	+$ 233	
				16%	
0..........	−$10,000			−$10,000	
1–15	+ 1,750/yr.			+ 9,757	
Net pres. value				−$ 243	15.5%

2. Payback period:

   a. $10,000/$1,750 = 5.7 years (6 years if payments come in annually).
   b. $10,000/$2,000 = 5 years.
   c. Unpaid after five years: $10,000 − 5 × $1,500 = $2,500.
      Number of years to pay back this amount: $2,500/$2,000 = 1.25 years.
      Total payback period: 5 + 1.25 = 6.25 years (7 years with annual payments).
   d. $10,000/$1,350 = 7.4 years (8 years with annual payments).
   e. $10,000/$1,750 = 5.7 years (6 years with annual payments).

   Average return on investment:

	Average Cash Flow	Average Depreciation	Average Income	Average Investment*	Average Return (percent)
a.	$1,750	$1,000	$ 750	$5,000	15%
b.	1,750	1,000	750	5,000	15
c.	1,750	1,000	750	5,000	15
d.	1,350	600	750	7,000	10.7
e.	1,750	667	1,083	5,000	21.7

   * These averages are halfway between the initial investment and the end-of-life salvage value.

3. a. Pretax analysis: *Cash Flow*

   Immediate cash flow (time = 0):
   To make: cost of new machine .... −$7,000
   To buy: proceeds from sale of old machine .... + 1,500
       Difference (incremental cash flow) .... −$8,500

   Annual cash flow (time = 1–7):
   To make: out-of-pocket production
               costs, at $0.20 .... −$1,200
   To buy: purchase costs, at $0.50 .... − 3,000
       Difference (incremental cash flow) .... +$1,800 a year

   b. Aftertax analysis:

   Investment outlay (time = 0):
   To buy: proceeds from sale of old machine .... +$1,500
           Tax [40% of ($1,500 − $2,000)] .... + 200*
      Net proceeds from sale .... + 1,700
   To make: cost of new machine .... − 7,000
       Difference (incremental cash flow) .... −$8,700

   * A tax credit is equivalent to a cash inflow.

Annual cash flow (years 1 through 7):

Year	Pretax Cash Flow	Tax Depreciation Old Machine	Tax Depreciation New Machine	Total	Taxable Income	Tax	Aftertax Cash Flow
1	+$ 1,800	$ 500	$1,050	$1,550	$ 250	$ 100	$ 1,700
2	+ 1,800	500	1,540	2,040	(240)	(96)	1,896
3	+ 1,800	500	1,470	1,970	(170)	(68)	1,868
4	+ 1,800	500	1,470	1,970	(170)	(68)	1,868
5	+ 1,800	—	1,470	1,470	330	132	1,668
6	+ 1,800	—	—		1,800	720	1,080
7	+ 1,800	—	—		1,800	720	1,080
Total	+$12,600	$2,000	$7,000	$9,000	$3,600	$1,440	$11,160

4. *a.*

Cost of machine	$100,000
Less: Tax reduction on portion expensed (0.4 × $50,000)	(20,000)
10% tax credit on portion capitalized	(5,000)
Plus: Working capital required	10,000
Total	$ 85,000

b.

	Year 1	Year 2
1. Before-tax reduction in operating costs.................	$20,000	$20,000
2. Tax depreciation: ($50,000 − $2,500) × ACRS % (15% and 22%)	7,125	10,450
3. Taxable saving (line 1 − line 2)	12,875	9,550
4. Tax (line 3 × 0.4)	5,150	3,820
5. Aftertax cash flow (line 1 − line 4)	$14,850	$16,180

5. *a.* Initial cash flow:

New facility:		
Installed cost		$65,000
Less tax effect, expensed portion (40% × $15,000)		6,000
Net cash outlay, new facility		59,000
Replaced facilities:		
Market value	$10,000	
Tax basis	32,000	
Taxable loss	22,000	
Tax credit at 40%	8,800	
Net proceeds, old facilities ($10,000 + $8,800)		18,800
Incremental initial cash outlay		$40,200

Annual cash flows:

The pretax incremental cash inflow is $19,800 a year ($17,775 + $2,500 − $475). The $2,500 incremental depreciation shown in the table of savings isn't a difference in cash inflows and should be ignored. The $475 indicated saving in general factory management costs is illusory; these costs are fixed in total and are unlikely to change in response to changes in the amount of labor used.

Calculation of aftertax cash flows:

		Tax Depreciation					
Years from Now	(1) Pretax Cash Flow	(2) Present Facility	(3) New Facility*	(4) Difference	(5) Taxable Income (1) − (4)	(6) Income Tax (5) × 40%	(7) Aftertax Cash Flow (1) − (6)
0	[as calculated above]						−$40,200
1	+$19,800	$ 4,000	$ 7,500	$ 3,500	$ 16,300	$ 6,520	+ 13,280
2	+ 19,800	4,000	11,000	7,000	12,800	5,120	+ 14,680
3	+ 19,800	4,000	10,500	6,500	13,300	5,320	+ 14,480
4	+ 19,800	4,000	10,500	6,500	13,300	5,320	+ 14,480
5	+ 19,800	4,000	10,500	6,500	13,300	5,320	+ 14,480
6	+ 19,800	4,000	—	(4,000)	23,800	9,520	+ 10,280
7	+ 19,800	4,000	—	(4,000)	23,800	9,520	+ 10,280
8	+ 19,800	4,000	—	(4,000)	23,800	9,520	+ 10,280
9	+ 19,800	—	—	—	19,800	7,920	+ 11,880
10	+ 19,800	—	—	—	19,800	7,920	+ 11,880
Total	+$198,000	$32,000	$50,000	$18,000	$180,000	$72,000	+$85,800

* ACRS-based 15%, 22%, 21%, 21% and 21%.

b. Calculation of present value:

Years from Now	Aftertax Cash Flow	12% Multiplier	Present Value
0	−$40,200	1.0000	−$40,200
1	+ 13,280	0.8929	+ 11,858
2	+ 14,680	0.7972	+ 11,703
3	+ 14,480	0.7118	+ 10,307
4	+ 14,480	0.6355	+ 9,202
5	+ 14,480	0.5674	+ 8,216
6	+ 10,280	0.5066	+ 5,208
7	+ 10,280	0.4524	+ 4,651
8	+ 10,280	0.4039	+ 4,152
9	+ 11,880	0.3606	+ 4,284
10	+ 11,880	0.3220	+ 3,825
Net present value			+$33,206

The proposal should be accepted.

Chapter 20

1. *a.*

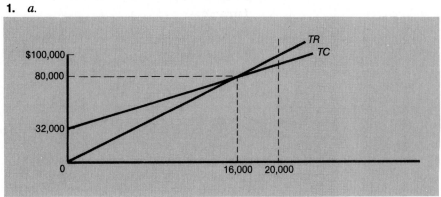

b.   Break-even point: $32,000/($5 − $3) = 16,000 units.

Margin of safety: 20,000 − 16,000 = 4,000 units.

Anticipated profit:

Revenues at $5	$100,000
Variable costs at $3	60,000
Fixed costs	32,000
Income before taxes	$ 8,000

c.   1.   Break-even point: $32,000/($5.50 − $3) = 12,800 units.

Margin of safety: 18,000 − 12,800 = 5,200 units.

Anticipated profit:

Revenues at $5.50	$ 99,000
Variable costs at $3	54,000
Fixed costs	32,000
Income before taxes	$ 13,000

2.   The effect of the price increase is to increase the spread between total cost and total revenue at any given volume. When volume is measured in physical units, as it is in this case, this increased spread is reflected in the profit-volume chart as a steeper slope for the total revenue line. The revised chart is shown here:

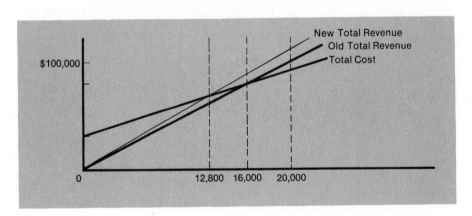

3. Profit target: 1.1 × $8,000 .... $ 8,800
Total fixed costs 32,000
Needed contribution margin $40,800

Crossover volume = $40,800/$2.50 = 16,320 units.

d. 1. Break-even point: $36,000/($4.60 − $3) = 22,500 units.

2. Profit target: 1.1 × $8,000 .... $ 8,800
Total fixed cost 36,000
Needed contribution margin $44,800

Crossover volume = $44,800/$1.60 = 28,000 units.

2. *a.*

			Present Program		Proposed Program
Product	Contribution Margin per Unit	Volume	Profit Contribution	Volume	Profit Contribution
A	$2.00	30,000	$60,000	40,000	$ 80,000
B	0.75	40,000	30,000	32,000	24,000
Total contribution margin			90,000		104,000
Fixed costs			72,000		81,700
Income before taxes			$18,000		$ 22,300

The proposal looks desirable.

b.

Product	Contribution Margin per Unit	Units Sold	Profit Contribution
A	$1.90	35,000	$66,500
B	0.65	45,000	29,250
Total contribution margin			95,750
Fixed costs			72,000
Income before taxes			$23,750

This alternative is even better than the one in part *a*. A good question to ask now, however, is what would happen if more selling effort (as in part *a*) were devoted to the redesigned and repriced products; this might produce even better results.

3. *a.*

Profit Plan	Division A	Division B	Division C	Total
Sales revenues	$1,000	$3,000	$2,100	$6,100
Divisional expenses:				
Cost of goods sold	650	1,650	1,260	3,560
Marketing	150	500	300	950
Administrative	150	300	200	650
Total	950	2,450	1,760	5,160
Division margin	$ 50	$ 550	$ 340	940
Headquarters expenses				400
Net income				$ 540

Cash Budget				
Revenues	$1,000	$3,000	$2,100	$6,100
Less: Increase in receivables	10	200	50	260
Collections	990	2,800	2,050	5,840
Cost of goods sold	650	1,650	1,260	3,560
Add: Inventory increase	50	100	50	200
Purchases	700	1,750	1,310	3,760
Less: Increases in payables	15	50	80	145
Payments to suppliers	685	1,700	1,230	3,615
Division marketing costs	150	500	300	950
Division administration (expense less deprec.)	145	285	180	610
Total divisional disbursements	980	2,485	1,710	5,175
Division cash flow	$ 10	$ 315	$ 340	665
Head-office disbursements:				
Central administration				390
Equipment purchases				130
Dividends				350
Total head-office disbursements				870
Net decrease in cash				$ (205)

b.

Anticipated cash balance: $290 − $205	$ 85
Minimum cash balance: 5% × $6,100	305
Cash shortage	$220

Since the company has only a $100 line of credit, the proposed plan is not financially feasible.

Chapter 21

1. Steering control information might consist of advance booking data on individual flights and on individual origin/destination pairs. These data, combined with similar historical information, might be used to signal the need to expand or curtail individual portions of the service, to discontinue service at some airports altogether, or to expand the size of ground crews in some locations.

Other information that might serve steering control purposes would be data on the costs and revenues of individual flights, individual origin/destination pairs, and individual origin or destination points; and data on operating statistics such as fuel consumption, maintenance cost, on-ground costs in comparison to plan, and maintenance turnaround time in Chicago.

Scorecard information would consist largely of comparisons, by responsibility, of actual costs and revenues with the amounts budgeted, perhaps adjusted for variations in external conditions.

2. *a.*

	Actual	Budgeted
Income	$ 63,000	$ 70,000
Investment	700,000	665,000
Return on investment	9.0%	10.5%
b. Income	$ 63,000	$ 70,000
Investment charge at 12%	84,000	79,800
Residual income (loss)	$ (21,000)	$ (9,800)

c. Neither the ROI figures nor the residual income figures are relevant to managerial evaluation because of the changes in the allocated amounts and the changes in traceable investments and depreciation, none of which is controllable in any meaningful sense. Using budgeted amounts to replace the actual amounts reported for these elements, we can calculate a revised residual income figure as follows:

Working capital (actual)		$200,000
Traceable plant and equipment (budgeted)		420,000
Allocated investments (budgeted)		95,000
Adjusted investment		$715,000
Income as reported		$ 63,000
Less: Change in depreciation	$2,000	
Change in allocations	5,000	(7,000)
Add: Tax on the changes		3,500
Adjusted income		59,500
Carrying charge (12% × $715,000)		(85,800)
Adjusted residual income (loss)		$ (26,300)

This indicates that the division manager's performance was actually a good deal worse than the initial comparisons indicated. One problem is that investment in working capital exceeded the plan by $50,000. Sales volume was $100,000 more than the budgeted amount (evidenced by the increase in the allocation of head-office costs), but this alone wouldn't account for the increase in working capital. Furthermore, the increase in sales volume was accompanied by a $10,500 aftertax decrease in divisional income (from $70,000 to $59,500). The sources of this decrease should be investigated to see how much of it was within the division manager's control.

d. The ratio of profit contribution to traceable investment is 13.8 percent ($63,000 income plus 50 percent of $40,000 in head-office charges, divided by $600,000 traceable investment). This indicates that the division may be paying its way. It is close enough to the minimum, however, to justify asking how many costs in the head office and how many investments administered by the head office are attributable to this division. If a study finds that attributable costs and investments in the head office are large enough to push the division's attributable return on investment substantially below 12 percent, then top management should analyze the division's incremental cash flows, both now and in the future when major capital investments are being considered. The purpose: to find out whether withdrawal would be desirable.

3. *a.* The memorandum should stress the following points:

(1) If the alternative is idleness, the only incremental costs may be the variable costs of 90 cents a pound, and this is far less than the proposed transfer price. Hull's profit will be 70 cents more for every pound of X it processes for the Hingham Division. Without these 50,000 pounds, product X would show a loss of $20,000 after deducting its share of division fixed costs; with this production, the net profit figure would be $15,000. This can be summarized in the following schedules for the Hull Division:

	If Hingham Buys from Hull @ $1.60	If Hingham Buys Outside
Sales—outside (100,000 lbs.)	$200,000	$200,000
Sales—Hingham (50,000 lbs.)	80,000	—
Total sales	280,000	200,000
Product-traceable costs:		
Variable manufacturing costs	135,000	90,000
Sales commissions	10,000	10,000
Depreciation	20,000	20,000
Other traceable costs	40,000	40,000
Total traceable costs	205,000	160,000
Product profit contribution	75,000	40,000
Share of division fixed costs	60,000	60,000
Income before taxes	$ 15,000	$ (20,000)

(2) If the Hull division will retain idle workers on the payroll to avoid losing a skilled work force, the incremental cost could be even less than 90 cents a pound because some labor costs would be sunk.

(3) Even if the traceable fixed costs increase in steps, it is unlikely that these could be high enough to make an incremental loss. At the present volume they average only 27 cents a pound.

(4) The Hull Division manager should recognize a longer-term problem—if cheaper substitutes are available, this may indicate a serious competitive weakness for the long run.

b. Some economists establish such a strict set of necessary conditions for the use of negotiation that they are almost never met. If you are willing to use the criteria established in this chapter, however, negotiation should be appropriate here. Hull has access to outside customer markets; Hingham has access to outside suppliers. If Hull were busy, the company might even be better off to have Hingham buy outside. If profit decentralization is to mean anything, we must rely on the division managers to identify situations of this type.

Chapter 22

1. *a.*

	Product A	Product B	Total
Equivalent units:			
Finished units	5,000	10,000	
Ending inventory	300	600	
	5,300	10,600	
Beginning inventory	500	500	
Total	4,800	10,100	
Standard direct-labor cost per unit .	× $2	× $1	
Total standard direct-labor cost	$9,600	$10,100	$19,700
Actual direct-labor cost			23,500
Direct labor spending variance			$ 3,800 unfavorable

b.

Standard direct-labor cost		$ 19,700
Actual hours × standard rates		22,000
Labor usage variance		$ 2,300 unfavorable
Actual hours × actual rates		23,500
Labor rate variance		1,500 unfavorable

c. Ending inventory:

Product A: 600 × ½ × $2		$ 600
Product B: 1,200 × ½ × $1		600
Total		$ 1,200

2.

Actual cost of materials purchased:		
95,000 × $2.05	$194,750	
Standard cost of materials purchased:		
95,000 × $2.00	190,000	
Materials price variance		$ 4,750 unfavorable
Actual quantity of materials used:		
61,000 × 1.5 × $2	183,000	
Standard quantity of materials used:		
61,000 × 1.6 × $2	195,200	
Materials usage variance		12,200 favorable
Materials spending variance		$ 7,450 favorable

3. *a.*

	Month 4			Month 5		
	Actual	Budget	Variance	Actual	Budget	Variance
Controllable:						
Nonproductive time	$ 800	$1,000	$ 200	$1,200	$ 750	$(450)
Other indirect labor	3,700	4,000	300	3,600	3,500	(100)
Operating supplies	650	600	(50)	430	450	20
Total controllable	5,150	5,600	450	5,230	4,700	(530)
Noncontrollable:						
Depreciation	2,100	2,000	(100)	2,150	2,000	(150)
Building service charges	770	700	(70)	730	700	(30)
Total	$8,020	$8,300	$ 280	$8,110	$7,400	$(710)

b. Only the first three overhead cost items listed are likely to be of any significance in evaluating the cost control performance of the department supervisor, and, of these, nonproductive time and other indirect labor have the greatest impact. Depreciation and building service charges are noncontrollable and have no bearing on managerial evaluation in this department.

c. Labor costs did not go down with decreasing volume. There are many possible reasons for this. This may merely be a time lag—management may have decided not to cut the labor force to meet the volume reduction in the hope that volume would recover quickly. This should be examined more critically if volume continues at these newer lower levels. We cannot ignore any one month's reports, but we need to examine them in the context of a longer period of time. Even two months is likely to be too short a period for random forces to have averaged themselves out.

The other item in which the variance has increased is depreciation, and this should be labeled as noncontrollable.

4. *a.*

Historical evaluation:

Overexpenditure = $16,200 − $16,000		$ 200

Cost overrun:

Actual cost of progress achieved	$16,200	
Budgeted cost of progress achieved	12,000	
Overrun to date		$4,200

Slippage:

Actual time	2 months	
Budgeted time for progress achieved	1½ months	
Slippage to date		½ month

Projection
Cost overrun:

Revised budget	$60,000
Original budget...........................	48,000
Projected cost overrun	12,000
Overrun to date	4,200
Projected additional overrun	$ 7,800

Slippage:

Revised time table	7 months
Original time table	6 months
Projected slippage.......................	1 month
Slippage to date	½ month
Projected additional slippage..............	½ month

Rate of expenditure:

Original budget...........................		$8,000 a month
Revised budget:		
Estimated total cost	$60,000	
Costs to date	16,200	
Estimated remaining costs.......	$43,800	
Projected rate: $43,800/5		8,760 a month
Projected increase in rate of expenditure		$ 760 a month

b. Possible responses:

1. Abandon the project.
2. Increase the rate of expenditure to try to complete the project at the originally scheduled time.
3. Stretch out the project, possibly to reduce future costs and possibly to spread out the drain on the company's cash resources.
4. Appoint a new project manager.

The main criterion for choosing among the first three of these is the anticipated net benefit (benefit minus research costs, stated at present value). For this purpose, management should ask for new estimates of benefit from the marketing or economic research staff, together with estimates of the costs of different research configurations.

The criterion for evaluating the manager's performance is *effectiveness.* The variances to date should be studied to see why progress has been slow and estimated future costs have been increased. If this analysis seems to indicate incompetence, then a new manager should be found.

Chapter 23

1. *a.* Overhead rate:
Fixed costs: $4,680/9,000 = $0.52 per standard direct labor-hour
+ $1.15 = $1.67 per standard direct labor-hour. Total: $0.52.
Standard overhead cost:
(10,500 hrs. + 3,600 hrs. − 4,000 hrs.) × $1.67 = $16,867.

b. Month-end balance: 3,600 hrs. × $1.67 = $6,012.

c.

Actual overhead	$17,400	
Budgeted at standard hours (10,100)	16,295	
Spending variance		$1,105 unfavorable
Standard overhead	16,867	
Volume variance		572 favorable
Total overhead variance		$ 533 unfavorable

2. *a.*

Actual overhead	$17,400	
Budgeted overhead at 10,800 actual hours	17,100	
Spending variance		$ 300 unfavorable
Budgeted overhead at 10,100 standard hours	16,295	
Labor efficiency variance (700 hours × $1.15)		805 unfavorable
Standard overhead	16,867	
Volume overhead		572 favorable
Total overhead variance		$ 533 unfavorable

b. The three-variance method is appropriate here because the need for overhead costs is determined by the number of *actual* direct labor-hours. The spending variances therefore should measure departures of actual costs from the budget based on actual hours, and this is the hallmark of the three-variance method.

The two-variance method was appropriate in problem 1, part *c.*, because the need for overhead costs there was determined by the number of *standard* direct labor-hours. The spending variance therefore was correctly measured as the departure of actual overhead cost from the budget based on standard hours.

Index

*This book has been set VideoComp, in 10 and
9 point Primer, leaded 2 points. Part numbers
are 18 point Spectra Black. Part titles and chapter numbers are 36 point Spectra Black. Chapter
titles are 24 point Spectra Black. The overall
type area is 36 by 47 picas.*